GUIDE TO ILLUSTRATIONS

	Source of Book Illustration	Artistic Style	Visual Elements	Elements of Fiction
1.	Hopkinson, Deborah. *Under the Quilt of Night.* Illustrated by James Ransome. Atheneum, 2001.	Realistic	Composition, color, mood	Setting, theme, character, plot, author's style
2.	Zolotow, Charlotte. *Mr. Rabbit and the Lovely Present.* Illustrated by Maurice Sendak. HarperCollins, 1962.	Impressionistic	Composition, line, texture	Setting, theme
3.	Raschka, Chris. *Yo! Yes?* Orchard, 1993.	Expressionistic	Shape/space	Plot, character, theme
4.	McDermott, Gerald. *Anansi the Spider: A Tale from the Ashanti.* Holt, 1972.	Abstract	Color, composition	Setting, character

Essentials of

CHILDREN'S LITERATURE

Essentials of

CHILDREN'S LITERATURE

Fifth Edition

CAROL LYNCH-BROWN
Florida State University

CARL M. TOMLINSON
Northern Illinois University

Boston   New York   San Francisco

Mexico City   Montreal   Toronto   London   Madrid   Munich   Paris

Hong Kong   Singapore   Tokyo   Cape Town   Sydney

Senior Editor: *Aurora Martínez Ramos*
Editorial Assistant: *Erin Beatty*
Senior Marketing Manager: *Krista Groshong*
Manufacturing Buyer: *Andrew Turso*
Editorial–Production Services: *P. M. Gordon Associates, Inc.*
Production Supervisor: *Joe Sweeney*
Cover Administrator: *Linda Knowles*
Electronic Composition: *Omegatype Typography, Inc.*

Between the time Web site information is gathered and published, some sites may have closed. Also, the transcription of URLs can result in typographical errors. The publisher would appreciate notification where these occur so that they may be corrected in subsequent editions.

LIBRARY OF CONGRESS CATALOGING-IN-PUBLICATION DATA

Lynch-Brown, Carol
    Essentials of children's literature / Carl M. Tomlinson, Carol Lynch-Brown.—5th ed.
      p. cm.
    Rev. ed. of: Essentials of children's literature / Carl M. Tomlinson, Carol Lynch-Brown.
4th ed. 2002.
    Includes bibliographical references and index.
    ISBN 0-205-42015-X
    1. Children's literature—Study and teaching (Higher) 2. Children's literature—History and criticism. 3. Children and literature. 4. Children's literature—Bibliography. I. Tomlinson, Carl M. II. Tomlinson, Carl M. Essentials of children's literature. III. Title.
PN1009.A1 L96 2005
809'.89282'0711—dc21

                    2004055061

Printed in the United States of America
10 9 8 7 6 5 4 3   08 07 06

The cover illustration by Eric Velasquez, from the *Read Around America* poster, part of the "Read Around America Poster Set," was reprinted by permission of the artist and The Children's Book Council, a nonprofit trade association encouraging the use and enjoyment of books and related literacy materials for young people. Information on the CBC and its programs, including National Children's Book Week materials, can be obtained from its web site: www.cbcbooks.org or through its headquarters: CBC, 12 West 37th Street, 2nd Floor, New York, NY 10018-7480, 212-966-1990.

Additional credits are listed on pages 333 and 334, which constitute a continuation of the copyright page.

To my nieces, Diane Bick, Mary Manion Bick, Amie DeHarpporte,
Jean Lynch, Mary Lynch, and Marti Markley, who are carrying
on a family tradition of teaching (C.L.-B.)

To my brother, Harry Mires Tomlinson (C.M.T.)

Contents

2 Learning about Books   24

3 Poetry and Plays   43

PART III   LITERATURE IN THE SCHOOL   217

11 Planning the Curriculum   218

FEATURES

EXCELLENT BOOKS TO READ ALOUD

MILESTONES

NOTABLE AUTHORS AND ILLUSTRATORS

USING LITERATURE ACROSS THE CURRICULUM

P REFACE

E *ssentials of Children's Literature* is a brief, affordable, comprehensive textbook with rich resources—a true compendium of information about children's literature. It is tailored to a survey course in children's literature, but by virtue of its brevity and affordability, is also suitable as a companion text in an integrated language arts course.

The primary focus of a survey course in children's literature should be reading children's trade books, not reading an exhaustive textbook about children's books. Students need direct experience with these trade books—reading them, reading them aloud to others, discussing them, writing about them, comparing them, criticizing them, evaluating them, applying them to their own lives, and thinking about sharing them with children.

One of our goals is to awaken or reawaken college-level students to the joy of reading. This reawakening can only happen if they experience the pleasure and excitement of reading excellent trade books. At the same time, the body of knowledge about literature and about teaching literature to children can be conveyed most efficiently through a textbook. *Essentials of Children's Literature* presents this body of knowledge in a clear, concise, direct narrative using brief lists, examples, figures, and tables in combination with prose, thus freeing class time for involvement with literature.

Notable Features of the Fifth Edition

- Full-color illustrations from notable children's picture books as examples of visual elements, artistic styles, and the contributions to story made by illustrations
- Illustrations conveniently located on inside covers with facing chart detailing visual elements and artistic styles
- Expanded treatment of literature across the curriculum
- New feature pages demonstrating literature across the curriculum in social studies, language arts, and science
- Expanded treatment of literature's role in reading programs in response to federal mandates
- New section on graphic novels
- Inclusion of the important but often neglected genre of plays
- Author–title index of children's books (including award books in Appendix A)
- Suggested read-aloud list for each genre

- Updated and streamlined end-of-chapter book lists include more than 2,000 recommended book titles for students, categorized by genres and subgenres with age levels noted
- Extensive coverage of children's book awards from the United States, Canada, Great Britain, and Australia
- Caldecott and Newbery books annotated for genre and age level to help students in selection
- A thorough integration of multicultural and international children's literature as well as a separate chapter on these topics
- Extensive list of recommended bilingual literature in Chapter 10
- Expanded treatment of informational literature to include elements of nonfiction, guides to reading and understanding, and related research
- Updated treatment of censorship, selection, and First Amendment rights
- New tables summarizing research in reading, writing, and literature across the curriculum and its significance to students and teachers
- Notable author and illustrator lists for each genre
- Introductory poems for each chapter to highlight the importance of introducing and sharing poetry throughout the school year

ACKNOWLEDGMENTS

For their generous help, good advice, and valued opinions concerning this revision of *Essentials of Children's Literature,* we wish to express our appreciation to the following people:

Colleagues Brenda Del Maramo, Thiel College; Janice M. Del Negro, University of Illinois at Urbana–Champaign; Marsha Gontarski, Florida State University; Priscilla L. Griffith, University of Oklahoma; Ann M. Trousdale, Louisiana State University; and Sylvia Vardell, Texas Woman's University, for their opinions, advice, and factual information.

The librarians who helped us to locate information and books and were always willing to discuss books with us: Michael Furlong, Claudia E. Montague, and Aimee Reist, Goldstein Library of Florida State University; Carole Fiore, State of Florida Library; Kathy Burnsed, Gary Crew, Annette Goldsmith, Maria Mena, and Bart Pisapia, Leon County Public Library, Tallahassee, Florida; and Roberta Mann, Killearn Lakes Elementary School, Tallahassee, Florida.

The reviewers of the fifth edition: Gail A. Bauman, Florida A&M University; Carol L. Butterfield, Central Washington University; Michael Cadden, Missouri Western State College; Thomas A. Caron, Marshall University Graduate College; Janice DeLong, Liberty University; Lori Elliot, Georgia State University; and Dorothy L. Kulesza, University of Nevada, Las Vegas.

We are indebted to Eric Velasquez for the splendid cover for this edition of *Essentials of Children's Literature.* In his picture storybooks, Velasquez imbues his characters with all of the best traits we want to associate with children the world over—curiosity, joy, and the capacity to love and learn. The cover captures these traits and projects the overall message that reading and sharing good books is a joyous, rewarding enterprise.

I

CHILDREN
AND
LITERATURE

The two chapters in Part I introduce material you will need in order to begin selecting, reading, and evaluating children's books. Chapter 1 defines children's literature, discusses its values for children, and provides research evidence supporting its use with children. Concepts about literature, elements of fiction, visual elements, and aspects of book format are treated extensively in Chapter 2. On the inside covers of the book you will find illustrations from well-known picture books with a guide on the facing page to assist you in looking at picture books, judging their merits, and appreciating them.

Throughout this text, examples of notable books are given as needed, but we include no lengthy plot summaries or reviews. We believe that more is gained from your reading and discussing the books themselves than reading *about* the books in a lengthy text.

1

LEARNING *about* CHILDREN *and* THEIR LITERATURE

*A story is a doorway
That opens on a wider place.
A story is a mirror
To reflect the reader's face.*

*A story is a question
You hadn't thought to ponder,
A story is a pathway,
Inviting you to wander.*

*A story is a window,
A story is a key,
A story is a lighthouse,
Beaming out to sea.*

*A story's a beginning,
A story is an end,
And in the story's middle,
You just might find a friend.*

—RICHARD PECK

A child leans forward, head cupped in hands, eyes wide with anticipation, listening to a story: This is an image for all time. Whether that child is seated beside an open fire in the Stone Ages, on a rough bench in a medieval fairground, or in a modern-day classroom, the message of the image is the same: Children love a good story.

DEFINITION OF CHILDREN'S LITERATURE

This book is written about literature for children from infancy to adolescence, for you who will be meeting and working with these children as teachers, librarians, and parents. In these roles, your opportunities to lead children to literature will be unparalleled, if you have the prerequisite knowledge.

Children's literature is good-quality trade books for children from birth to adolescence, covering topics of relevance and interest to children of those ages, through prose and poetry, fiction and nonfiction. This definition contains several key concepts that will be explained in the following sections. Understanding these concepts will help you find your way around the more than 250,000 children's titles currently in print (*Children's Books in Print,* 2003), the more than 8,000 new children's titles being published annually in the United States (*Bowker Annual: Library and Book Trade Almanac,* [Bogart, 2004]), as well as the additional thousands of children's books published worldwide each year in English.

Content

Children's books are about the experiences of childhood, both good and bad. Whether these experiences are set in the past, present, or future, they should still be relevant to the child of today. Enjoying birthday parties, losing a tooth for the first time, anticipating adulthood, camping out and telling ghost stories, getting a new pet, enduring siblings, and dealing with family situations are experiences common to children today. The content of children's books also includes the amazingly diverse topics that are of interest to children, such as dinosaurs, Egyptian mummies, world records, and fighter planes.

The manner in which content is treated also helps to define children's books. Childhood stories told in a forthright, humorous, or suspenseful manner are appropriate for young readers; stories *about* childhood told in nostalgic or overly sentimental terms are inappropriate. Likewise, when stories show children as victims of natural and human-made disasters, the stories should emphasize the hope for a better future rather than the hopelessness and utter despair of the moment.

The subject matter of children's literature can be expressed in prose or poetry. If the literary work is prose, it must be presented as fiction (a product of the imagination, an invented story), nonfiction (factual), or a combination of the two.

Teachers and librarians distinguish between the terms *textbook* and *trade book.* A *textbook,* by design and content, is for the purpose of instruction. The basal reader used in many classrooms for reading instruction is an example of a textbook. In contrast, a *trade book,* by design and content, is primarily for the purposes of entertainment and information. Trade books are often referred to as *library books* and *storybooks.* The books that we will be discussing in this text will be trade books, not textbooks.

Quality

Not all trade books aimed at young readers are worth attention. Books ranging in quality from excellent to poor are now readily available to parents, teachers, and children through bookstores and libraries. Look around and you will see racks of children's books in department stores, drugstores, and even grocery stores. But the question is: Are they *good* children's books?

Quality in writing is never easy to define, but it has to do with originality and importance of ideas, imaginative use of language, and beauty of literary and artistic style that enable a work to remain fresh, interesting, and meaningful for years and years. These books have permanent value.

This is not to say that books of good-but-not-great quality have no value. Children have enjoyed fast-moving, adventure-filled, easily predictable stories from the so-called chapbooks of the seventeenth and eighteenth centuries to the serial adventures of the *Hardy Boys, Nancy Drew,* the *Babysitters Club,* and the *Animorphs* of more recent times. These works have won no literary prizes, but many young readers enjoy them; and because books such as these encourage newly independent readers to read more, they have worth. However, you will probably not want to select books of this calibre to read aloud to your students. Why deprive them of the pleasure of reading such easy and enjoyable books independently? If children's entire literary experience were limited to serial adventures and other books of trendy but passing interest, they would miss much of the wonder of the natural world and the human experience. The best children's books offer readers enjoyment as well as memorable characters and situations and valuable insights into the human condition.

Many so-called children's books today are actually nothing more than advertisements for film and television characters and associated products, such as candy, clothing, and toys. These books represent the low end of the quality spectrum.

THE PERSONAL VALUE OF LITERATURE TO CHILDREN

Literature for children leads to personal fulfillment and academic gains. Separating the values into personal and academic is an intellectual distinction, since both types benefit the child and are all proper parts of a child's schooling. The distinction is useful, however, since teachers and librarians must often justify the benefits of literature in the classroom and find the academic benefits the most convincing ones for administrators and parents.

Enjoyment

The most important personal gain that good books offer to children is the most obvious one—enjoyment. Those of you who read widely as children will never forget the stories that were so funny that you laughed out loud, the poem that was so lilting that you never forgot it, or the mystery that was so scary that your heart thumped with apprehension. Such positive early experiences often lead to a lifetime of reading enjoyment.

Imagination and Inspiration

By seeing the world around them in new ways and by considering ways of living other than their own, children increase their ability to think divergently. Stories often map the divergent paths that our ancestors might have taken or that our descendants might someday take. Through the vicarious experience of entering a different world from the present one, children develop their imaginations. In addition, stories about people, both real and imaginary, can inspire children to overcome obstacles, accept different perspectives, and formulate personal goals.

Vicarious Experience

When a story is so convincingly written that readers feel as though they have lived through an experience or have actually been in the place and time where the story is set, the book has given them a *vicarious* experience. Experiences such as these are broadening for children because they, as readers, are taken to places and times that they could never actually visit—and might not want to! A vicarious experience can also be a good mental exercise for children, since they are asked to view situations from perspectives other than their own.

Understanding and Empathy

Literature helps young people to gain an appreciation of the universality of human needs across history, which makes it possible for them to understand that all humans are, to some degree, alike. By introducing children to stories from many lands and cultures, teachers and librarians are building a solid foundation for multicultural and international understanding. Walking in someone else's shoes often helps children to develop a greater capacity to empathize with others. Children around the world can benefit from stories that explain what life is like for people who are restricted by disabilities, politics, or circumstance or whose lives are different from theirs because of culture or geography. Likewise, young readers of today can relate on a more personal level with the events and people of history.

Heritage

Stories that are handed down from one generation to the next connect us to our past, to the roots of our specific cultures, national heritage, and general human condition. Stories are the repositories of culture. Knowing the tales, characters, expressions, and adages that are part of our cultural heritage is part of being culturally literate. In addition, stories based on actual events in the past help young people to gain a greater appreciation for what history is and for the people, both ordinary and extraordinary, who made history.

Moral Reasoning

Often, story characters are placed in situations that require them to make moral decisions. Young readers naturally consider what they themselves would do in such a situation. As the story unfolds and the character's decision and the consequences of that choice are disclosed, readers discover whether their own decisions would have had positive outcomes. Regular experience with these types of stories can help young people to formulate their own concepts of right and wrong.

Literary and Artistic Preferences

Another valuable result of children interacting with literature is that they quickly come to recognize the literary and artistic styles of many authors and illustrators. This is an important first step to literary awareness—that is, to recognize that the style of one writer or illustrator differs from another and that a piece of writing or an illustration has personal appeal. Children who read regularly from a wide variety of children's books soon develop their own personal preferences for types of books and select favorite authors and illustrators. Good teachers and librarians have long recognized that personal preference and interest as expressed through self-selection of reading materials are powerful reading motivators. They also know that the more children read and the greater the variety of literature they read, the more discerning readers they become.

The more children know about their world, the more they discover about themselves—who they are, what they value, and what they stand for. These personal insights alone are sufficient to warrant making good books an essential part of any child's home and school experiences. But literature is also valuable for its academic benefits, as will be discussed in the following section.

THE ACADEMIC VALUE OF LITERATURE TO CHILDREN

In addition to the personal benefits of literature for young readers, there are several important academic benefits.

Reading

Many of you already may have reached the commonsense deduction that reading ability, like any other skill, improves with practice. Many teachers and librarians believe that regular involvement with excellent and appropriate literature can foster language development in young children and can help them to learn to read and to value reading. This belief was supported in the landmark study *Becoming a Nation of Readers* (Anderson, Hiebert, Scott, & Wilkinson, 1985), which concludes, "The single most important activity for building the knowledge required for eventual success in reading is reading aloud to children" (p. 23).

In 1997 the *National Reading Panel* (NRP) was formed, at the request of Congress, to assess the status of research-based knowledge about reading, including the effectiveness of various approaches to teaching children to read. The *Report of the National Reading Panel* (National Institutes of Health, 2000) was met with great controversy and skepticism because of its narrow definition of scientific research studies. In this report, the NRP identified four components of instruction considered to be essential to the teaching of reading: phonemic awareness, phonics, vocabulary, and comprehension, including oral reading fluency. Literature-based research studies that support reading aloud to students and independent silent reading by students were not included because they did not meet the NRP's narrow definition of scientific research.

Based on our personal and professional experience with children, we contend that reading aloud to children by parents and caregivers and sharing literature with students in the classroom greatly benefit children's acquisition of reading skills and their attitude toward reading. In addition, we contend that literature-based studies support not only the reading instruction strategies endorsed by the NRP, but also the important instructional practices that the NRP report ignores.

As educators, you should be aware of research findings about the worth of literature for children. Research studies summarized in Table 1.1 show that in teaching children to read, two procedures seem especially important: reading excellent literature aloud to children and silent independent reading of free-choice material by children, both on a daily basis, if possible. To discover another truth, you must read between the lines of the table. The truth is that there must first be someone, more than likely an adult, who has the knowledge, willingness, and patience to guide children to books. Who will this be? For some children, it will be their parents; for many others, it will be you—their teacher or librarian. For a more thorough discussion of literature and the teaching of reading, see the section *Know the Reading Process* on pages 12–13 and the section *Basal Reading Program Supplemented by Children's Literature* on pages 231–232.

TABLE 1.1   Important Studies on Literature and Reading

Researcher(s)	Subjects	Findings
Butler (1975)	Cushla, from ages 4 months to 3 years	Reading aloud from children's picture books to a severely disabled child from age 4 months enabled the child to learn to read.
Durkin (1966)	Children who learned to read before attending school	Children who learned to read before attending school were read to regularly from the age of 3. Early reading and early writing are often linked.
Dowhauer (1987)	Second-graders	Reading the same books multiple times significantly improves students' oral reading rate (fluency), accuracy, and comprehension.
Eldredge and Butterfield (1986)	1,149 beginning readers in 50 classrooms	Use of children's literature to teach reading has a much greater positive effect on students' achievement and attitudes toward reading than does use of basals with traditional homogeneous grouping.
Anderson (1996)	Elementary-grade children	Even slight increases (10 minutes a day) in time spent reading independently lead to gains in reading achievement. Amount of free reading in early grades helps determine reading ability in grades 5 and 6.
Carlsen and Sherrill (1988)	College students who were committed readers	Conditions that promote a love of reading include: Freedom of choice in reading material Availability of books and magazines Family members who read aloud Adults and peers who model reading Role models who value reading Sharing and discussing books Owning books Availability of libraries and librarians

Writing

Since people tend to assimilate or adopt what they like of what they read and hear, children may, by listening to and reading literature, begin to develop their own writing "voice," or unique, personal writing style. By listening to and reading excellent literature, children are exposed to rich vocabulary and excellent writing styles, which serve as good models for their own speaking and writing voices. The acquisition of a larger vocabulary through reading offers young writers a better word choice for their own stories. Devices found in books such as the use of dialect, dialogue, and precise description are often assimilated into students' own writing. Research studies summarized in Table 1.2 show that skill in reading and skill in writing go hand in hand.

TABLE 1.2   Important Studies on Literature and Writing

Researcher(s)	Subjects	Findings
McConaghy (1990)	First-graders in a literature-based reading and writing program	Children use in their own writing the literary conventions and forms they encounter in literature.
DeFord (1981)	First-graders in phonics-, skills-, and literature-based reading classes	Children in literature-based reading classrooms tend to produce a wider variety of written forms and better written stories than children in phonics or skills-based reading classes.
Eckhoff (1983)	Second-graders who used basal readers	Children adopt writing styles from their reading texts. Some inappropriate writing structures may be learned from oversimplified reading texts.
Lancia (1997)	Second-graders	Good books are effective models for children's writing. Students "borrowed" plots, plot elements, characters, stylistic devices, and information from books to use in their own writing.
Dressel (1990)	Fifth-graders	Student writing was directly affected by the characteristics of the stories they heard and discussed, regardless of the students' reading abilities. The better the quality of the read-aloud, the better the quality of the student writing. *Which* stories teachers read aloud is important.

Content Area Subjects

In reading about and discussing children's literature, you will often hear the phrase *literature across the curriculum.* This means using works of literature as teaching materials in the content areas of social studies and history, science, health, and, possibly, math. Good teachers have always used literature across the curriculum. The logic for this practice is sound. Many trade books contain information that is relevant to the topics studied in school. Moreover, this information is presented through captivating, sometimes beautifully illustrated, narratives. Information thus presented is interesting to students and, therefore, is more comprehensible and memorable. When using literature across the curriculum, teachers and students are not confined to the textbook as the sole resource. Using resource books such as those that are listed in Appendix B, you can find several trade books on almost any topic. Using several sources of information has always been considered prudent both in and out of school, since doing so usually provides fuller factual coverage of topics and leads to wiser, more informed decisions on issues. Few resources are available to the teacher that will help as much to make learning interesting and memorable to children as good trade fiction and nonfiction. Using literature across the curriculum is particularly appropriate today, given the abundance of masterfully written, information-relevant children's trade books available to teachers and librarians.

Art Appreciation

Illustration in children's picture books can be appreciated both for its ability to help tell the story (cognitive value) and for its value as art (aesthetic value). The cognitive value of illustration in picture books will be dealt with in more detail in Chapter 4, but the point to be emphasized here is that if you appreciate art for its own sake, there is much that you can do in your classroom to instill in your students a similar appreciation. It takes only a moment to call to your students' attention particularly striking and unusual illustrations. By doing so, you show them that you value art. You can also discuss the artist's style, the medium used (watercolor, oils, pastels, etc.), the palette (range of colors), and how the artist's style compares to the style of other artists. In addition, picture book art serves well as a model for applied art lessons. By suggesting to your students that they use media, techniques, and topics suggested by picture book illustrations in their own artwork, you make good use of a handy, valuable resource and in yet another way show that you value this art.

Research studies summarized in Table 1.3 suggest some of the benefits of using literature across the curriculum.

TABLE 1.3   Important Studies on Literature Across the Curriculum

Researcher(s)	Subjects	Findings
Morrow, Pressley, Smith, and Smith (1997)	Third-graders from diverse backgrounds divided into three groups: 1. Those who received literature-based reading and literature-based science instruction 2. Those who received literature-based reading and textbook-based science instruction 3. Those who received basal reading and textbook-based science instruction	Students who received yearlong literature-based reading and literature-based science instruction scored higher than control groups in reading and total language score on the California Test of Basic Skills and on two measures of science content.
VanSledright and Kelley (1996)	Fifth-grade history students	Students' interest in history and their ability to retain information increased significantly when their history instruction included literature.
Levstik (1986)	Sixth-grade class that used narrative literature to learn history	Children use "human behavior" schemata to make sense of historical information. Personal narrative descriptions of historical fiction have a greater impact on young students than textbooks' depersonalized explanations.
Kiefer (1994)	Children in grades 1–5	Exposure to picture books can increase children's awareness of art and aesthetics. Children's awareness of stylistic factors in picture books grows developmentally.

From the foregoing discussion, it should be clear that students are not the only ones in schools who can benefit from children's literature. As a teacher or librarian, you will find that excellent literature is rich in social, historical, and scientific information about the world and its people and that it has great potential for developing the entire elementary and middle school curriculum.

APPROACHES TO STUDYING AND INTERPRETING LITERATURE

The scholarly study of literature generally focuses on the meaning to be found in a work. Some people seek insights into the work by studying the author's life. Some interpret the work by associating it with the social and political milieu within which it was written, while others analyze works from the past in light of today's prevailing attitudes. Deep analysis of a work through exact and careful reading is referred to as *structural criticism* or *New Criticism*. In this approach, the analysis of the words and structure of a work is the focus; the goal is to find the "correct" interpretation.

Until the 1960s, structural criticism held sway in most literature classrooms. Most teachers who used literature in their classes took the view that there is only one correct interpretation of any work of literature. According to this view, reading is a process of taking from the text only what was put there by the author. Young readers' success with any work of literature was determined by how closely their interpretations matched the "authorized" interpretation. Students' responses to literature were thus limited to naming (or guessing) the "right" answers to teachers' questions.

In 1938, Louise Rosenblatt introduced the *transactional view of reading*. She asserted that what the reader brings to the reading act—his or her world of experience, personality, and current frame of mind—is just as important in interpreting the text as is what the author writes. According to this view, reading is a fusion of text and reader. Consequently, any text's meaning will vary from reader to reader and, indeed, from reading to reading of the same text by the same reader. Almost everyone has experienced reading a book only to discover that a friend has reacted to or interpreted the same book quite differently. Although Rosenblatt (1978) points out that the text of any book guides and constrains the interpretation that is made, an important corollary to her view of reading is that personal interpretations, within reason, are valid, permissible, and, in fact, desirable.

Another interesting aspect of Rosenblatt's theory is that reading is done for two distinct purposes: to take knowledge from the text (efferent reading) and to live through a literary experience, in the sense of assuming the identity of a book character (aesthetic reading). Whether we read efferently or aesthetically depends on what we are reading (e.g., a want ad versus a mystery novel) and why we are reading it (e.g., for information versus for pleasure). Rosenblatt's view of reading has important implications for the way you will encourage your students to respond to the literature you share with them.

CHOOSING BOOKS FOR CHILDREN

If given a choice in housing, child care, education, food, or clothing, parents usually choose what they consider to be the best for their children. Why should it be any different with the literature adults choose to share with children? The points made about quality and content of literature at the beginning of this chapter definitely play a part in any book selection for children. In addition, you will also want to consider the following suggestions.

Know the Child

The best teachers tend to know their students well. For instance, you will find it helpful to know your students' long-term and short-term interests, their home environment (family makeup, siblings, pets), their friends and social activities, their hobbies, their skills (athletic, academic, artistic), and their hopes or plans for the future. Children's interests have been shown to be one of the most powerful motivating forces available to teachers. Since there are now books on almost every topic conceivable and written at varying degrees of difficulty, you should be able to assemble a collection of books from which your students will be able to make satisfying selections. In addition, you will want to have a general grasp of your students' reading and listening levels. Often, a child's ability to read and ability to listen are on different levels. Young children, in particular, are able to listen to and comprehend more difficult material than they are able to read and comprehend. This difference is one that teachers accommodate by reading aloud more challenging books and providing a choice of easier reading material for students' independent reading.

Know the Books

Teachers and librarians who read children's books regularly, who are familiar with a wide variety of genres, and who are informed about recently published books are likely to be able to interest children in books. Of course, it is advantageous to have read widely and to be able to share and compare your reactions to a book with the children. However, it is not necessary to read every book that your students read to be well versed in children's literature or to be an effective promoter of good books. Aside from reading the books, there are a number of other ways to become familiar with them. You can ask librarians for information about the most current titles, share information about books with your colleagues, and read book reviews (see the *Reliable Sources* section for specific review journals). Your own reading program can be made more effective if you focus on award-winning and notable books, as well as on those selected for their appeal to individual children under your care. Knowledge of children's *classics* (works whose excellent quality and enduring appeal to children through several generations are generally recognized) is also an advantage. After you have read a number of books from a genre, particularly classic examples, you will develop a framework for thinking about books of that kind, whether or not you have read an individual title. You will, of course, want to have read any book you plan to read aloud to a class.

Two other features for teachers and librarians to consider are the readability and conceptual difficulty of books. *Readability* is defined as "the ease of comprehension because of style of writing" (Harris & Hodges, 1995, p. 203). Generally, texts with shorter sentences and a predominance of common, high-frequency words, such as *go* and *because* and *little,* are rated as easier to comprehend. Readability can be estimated using one of a number of *readability formulas.* One of the best-known of these, Fry's Readability Graph, is based on the average number of sentences and the average number of syllables in randomly selected 100-word passages. The graphs and directions for using them are available at http://school.discovery.com/schrockguide/fry.

Readability is expressed as either grade level (2.3 = second grade, third month) or age level (7.5 = seven years, five months) and refers to the average grade or age at which a child should be able to read the text. For example, using Fry's Readability Graph, we estimate that the well-known classic *Charlotte's Web* (White, 1952) is written at a 5.3 grade level and a 10.4 age level. Using the same formula, we estimate that the Caldecott Award–winning picture book *The Stray Dog* (Simont, 2001) is written at a 2.1 grade level and an 8.0 age level.

Readability formulas can be helpful to teachers, librarians, and parents in selecting books for children, but they are not without their limitations and drawbacks. Different readability formulas will give different estimates for the same text. Also, readability formulas do not factor in students' background knowledge of, or interest in, a text's topic. These important variables can significantly influence a student's ability to read a text with good comprehension. Moreover, some applications of readability formulas are misguided. Computerized management supplementary reading programs such as *Accelerated Reader,* for example, require students to read a narrow range of materials in which they often have no interest, simply because they are assessed (by readability formulas) to be at the child's readability level. And then the student has to take a computerized, multiple-choice comprehension test on the passage! Such practices may be responsible for the finding that, by sixth grade, many students find reading a chore and do not read voluntarily.

Conceptual difficulty pertains to the complexity of ideas treated in the work and to how these ideas are presented. Symbolism, abstraction, and lengthy description contribute to the complexity of ideas, just as the use of flashbacks or shifting points of view contributes to the complexity of plot presentation. Consider the work of modern fantasy, *Skellig* (Almond, 1999), in which two children become involved with an otherworldly "being" who has hidden in a garage. The text, having easy vocabulary and short sentences, has a readability of about 3.7. But the story concepts of spirituality, faith, and prejudice elevate the conceptual difficulty of this book to between fifth- and ninth-grade level.

Know the Reading Process

Children learn to read at different ages and in different ways, depending on their early experiences with books, their innate abilities, and the quality of their early reading instruction. There is no absolute, lockstep method for learning to read, though some would claim otherwise and subscribe to one of the two prevailing approaches, "phonics based" and "meaning based." Advocates of phonics-based reading instruction believe that children learn to read by progressing from letter names to letter sounds to words and, finally, to meaning. Emphasis is placed on decoding more than comprehension. Advocates of meaning-based reading instruction believe that children primarily use their oral language skills and knowledge of grammar and the world to make meaning of written text, and resort to phonetic decoding when other meaning-making strategies fail.

We subscribe to an interactive model of reading that synthesizes aspects of both approaches. Generally, whether they are consciously taught or learn on their own, children come to know that stories can be found in books, that certain formalities, known as concepts of print, apply in reading (front-to-back, left-to-right, top-to-bottom), that letters represent sounds (sound-symbol relationships), that letters can be used to code spoken language (writing), that words convey meaning, and that finding meaning in the text (comprehension) is the goal of reading. In addition, we agree with Rosenblatt that reading is a *transaction* between the reader and the text, and that what the reader brings to the reading act—his or her world of experience, personality, and current frame of mind—is important in interpreting the text.

Using good, carefully selected literature in the classroom can support many of the findings of the NRP report. For example, use of nursery rhymes, pattern books, and poems can help children develop phonemic awareness. *Reading aloud by the teacher, paired reading, readers' theatre,* and *choral reading* can increase children's reading fluency by giving them models of fluent reading. *Shared reading* with its emphasis on repeated oral reading can teach children sound-symbol relationships and increase their reading fluency. Independent *silent reading* of good literature, especially if followed up with some reflection on what was read, can increase children's meaning vocabulary and conceptual knowledge, as well as develop their reading comprehension. For full descriptions and explanations of these strategies, see Chapter 12.

Overemphasis of any one component of reading instruction, such as phonics, to the exclusion of the others in beginning reading instruction would be detrimental to some, if not all, students who are learning to read. Programs advocating heavy emphasis on phonics but no daily teacher read-aloud or daily independent silent reading of excellent books of the student's own choosing should be viewed with suspicion. We strongly advocate daily read-alouds by the teacher and independent silent reading, because they give students models of fluency, build meaning vocabulary and conceptual knowledge, give reading practice, and improve students' attitudes toward reading. As students' reading ability grows, logic would suggest (despite the dictates of any scripted-reading-program teacher's manual) that teachers shift their emphasis from letter and word decoding toward strategies that involve reading actual stories, poems, and plays. It is important to note that reading aloud and independent silent reading are *not* substitutes for direct reading instruction, however. Primary- and intermediate-grade schedules should include all three every day.

Consider the Mode of Delivery

Whether the book is intended for independent reading by children or for reading aloud by an adult is another important consideration in choosing a book for children. Children can listen with good comprehension to a book that is too difficult for them to read independently. In fact, good teachers often select books that challenge their students intellectually and guide them forward an appreciation of deeper works of literature.

RELIABLE SOURCES FOR BOOK TITLES

Several awards were established in the twentieth century for the purposes of elevating and maintaining the literary standards of children's books and for honoring the authors and illustrators whose work is judged by experts in the field to be the best. These awards lists provide the teacher with one means for selecting excellent works to share with children.

Tables 1.4 and 1.5 itemize what are considered to be the major awards for children's books in the United States, Canada, and Great Britain. Complete lists of the books that won these awards can be found in Appendix A. See page 323 for helpful web sites.

Many states have their own awards for children's books, often generated from school children who nominate and vote on books based on appeal or popularity. Teachers and librarians across the country report that children enjoy participating in the selection process and give these award programs high

TABLE 1.4   Major U.S., Canadian, and British Children's Book Awards

Award/Country	Period	For/Year Established
Newbery Medal/ United States	Annual	The most distinguished contribution to children's literature published in the previous year. Given to a U.S. author. Established 1922.
Caldecott Medal/ United States	Annual	The most distinguished picture book for children published in the previous year. Given to a U.S. illustrator. Established 1938.
Coretta Scott King Award for writing	Annual	Outstanding inspirational and educational contribution to literature for children and young people by an African-American author published in the previous year. Established 1970.
Coretta Scott King Award for illustration	Annual	Outstanding inspirational and educational contribution to literature for children and young people by an African-American illustrator published in the previous year. Established 1974.
Mildred L. Batchelder Award/United States	Annual	The most distinguished translated work for children published in the previous year. Given to a U.S. publisher. Established 1968.
Pura Belpré Awards for writing and illustration	Biennial (every 2 years)	Writing and illustration in a work of literature for youth published in the previous year by a Latino writer and illustrator whose work best portrays, affirms, and celebrates the Latino cultural experience. Established 1996.
Governor General's Literature for Children Award for Writing/Canada	Annual	Best book for children published in the previous year. Separate prizes for works in English and French. Established 1987.
Governor General's Literature for Children Award for Illustration/Canada	Annual	Best illustration in a children's work published in the previous year. Separate prizes for works in English and French. Established 1987.
Carnegie Medal/ Great Britain	Annual	The most distinguished contribution to children's literature first published in the United Kingdom in the previous year. Given to an author. Established 1936.
Kate Greenaway Medal/ Great Britain	Annual	The most distinguished picture book for children first published in the United Kingdom in the previous year. Given to an illustrator. Established 1956.

marks for reading motivation. Your state library association is the most reliable source for information about your state's children's choice award program.

Because journals are published several times yearly, they are helpful for keeping current with children's book publishing. *The Horn Book Magazine, School Library Journal, Booklist,* and *Bulletin of the Center for Children's Books* are review journals that evaluate, annotate, and discuss the most recently published trade books on a monthly or semimonthly basis. Two language-related teacher jour-

TABLE 1.5   Major Genre-Specific U.S. Children's Book Awards

Award	Period	For/Year Established
NCTE Excellence in Poetry for Children Award	Every 3 years	A living poet whose poetry has contributed substantially to the lives of children. Established 1977.
NCTE Orbis Pictus Award	Annual	Excellence in writing of nonfiction for children published in the United States in the preceding year. Established 1990.
ALA Robert F. Sibert Informational Book Award	Annual	The most distinguished informational book published during the preceding year. Established 2001.
Scott O'Dell Award	Annual	The most distinguished work of historical fiction set in the New World and published in English by a U.S. publisher. Established 1982.
Edgar Allen Poe Award: Juvenile	Annual	The best mystery written for young readers published during the preceding year. Established 1961.

nals to which elementary teachers often subscribe, *Language Arts* and *The Reading Teacher,* have columns devoted to reviewing new children's books in each monthly issue. *The New Advocate* and *The Journal of Children's Literature,* journals dedicated entirely to children's literature and those involved in it, also have extensive reviews of newly published children's books. *Book Links,* an American Library Association bimonthly publication, helps teachers and librarians to integrate the best children's books into their curricula by presenting annotated lists of books selected around themes and topics. These journals are readily available in school libraries and the children's section of most public libraries.

In cooperation with various national teaching associations, the Children's Book Council (www.cbcbooks.org) publishes annual, annotated lists of the best trade books to supplement content area subjects in grades K–8. Two excellent lists of this kind are Outstanding Science Trade Books for Students K–12 (published in cooperation with the National Science Teachers Association) and Notable Social Studies Trade Books for Young People (published in cooperation with the National Council for the Social Studies).

Extensive lists or bibliographies, often annotated, of both older and newer books are valuable aids in book selection. These are usually organized around subject headings and can be remarkably helpful and efficient when you are developing units of study and topical reading lists for students or when you are seeking read-aloud literature about a specific subject. Some of the most helpful bibliographic sources are the following:

> *A to Zoo: Subject Access to Children's Picture Books,* 6th ed. (Lima & Lima, 2001)
> *Adventuring with Books: A Booklist for Pre-K–Grade 6,* 13th ed. (McClure & Kristo, 2002)
> *Children's Catalog,* 18th ed. (2001). Includes annual paperback supplements through 2005.
> *Selecting Books for the Elementary School Library Media Center: A Complete Guide* (Van Orden, 2000)

LITERATURE FOR THE DEVELOPING CHILD

In this section we will discuss types of books and general topics most likely to be appreciated by children of different age levels. Children's physical, cognitive, language, and moral development are important considerations in book selection, as is their developing concept of story. By overlaying this general information with the specific interests of any child, you can recognize and make available literature that the children in your care will read with interest and enjoyment.

Ages 0 to 2

Infants can enjoy and benefit from good literature. In choosing books for them, we must consider such practical aspects of physical development as how well they can see the illustrations and how long they will sit still for a book experience. For instance, books chosen for babies to hold and look at by themselves should feature clearly defined, brightly colored pictures, usually placed on a plain background. Most often, these books will be brief, plotless, idea books called *concept books,* and they will concern the everyday routines and familiar objects that fill the infants' lives. These books are often constructed of heavy, nontoxic cardboard and are called *board books.* Helen Oxenbury has many classics in this field, including her set of Baby Beginning Board Books, *I Can, I See, I Hear, I Touch* (1986/1995), and the trilogy *Clap Hands, All Fall Over,* and *Say Goodnight* (1999). A word of warning: many picture storybooks and concept books appropriate for 4- to 8-year-olds are being reissued in board book format and marketed for babies. These are not baby books.

Since babies have a strong, positive reaction to any exaggerated patterns in sound or movement, the natural music created by strong rhymes and rhythms in *nursery rhymes,* as well as the brevity and humor of these verses, make them appropriate read-aloud material for children at this age level. For example, see *Here Comes Mother Goose* edited by Iona Opie and illustrated by Rosemary Wells (1999).

To take advantage of the primacy of the senses and muscular coordination in early learning, you will want to use *interactive books* with children from birth to age 2. In these books, participation (clapping, moving) or manipulation of the book (touching, opening little doors) is encouraged. A classic example is *Pat the Bunny* by Dorothy Kunhardt (1962/2001). Another good example is *Who Said Moo?* by Harriet Ziefert (2002), illustrated by Simms Taback.

All of the best baby books, whether wordless or with brief text, invite the reader or readers to "talk the book through." In this way the books promote oral language development, which is the child's first step toward literacy.

Ages 2 to 4

Many aspects of the recommended books for babies apply as well to books for toddlers. Daily routines and objects familiar to the child remain good topics. For this audience, such topics can be incorporated into *picture storybooks* that feature simple plots, beautiful illustrations that tell part of the story, and interesting, humorous characters and situations. Story characters often exhibit the physical skills, such as running, buttoning and unbuttoning clothes, and locking and unlocking doors, that 2- to 4-year-olds take pride in having accomplished. These books are meant to be read aloud to the child. Peter Sís's *Madlenka* (2000) is a good example.

Concept books are excellent for children who are beginning to make sense of their world, and these concepts can now include numbers (*counting books*), letters (*ABC books*), and more complex concepts like opposites. The *illustrated dictionary* or *word book* is a type of concept book that promotes the naming and labeling of objects, actions, and people. Examples are *Toddler Two* by Anastasia Suen (2002), illustrated by Winnie Cheon, and *My First Word Book* by Angela Wilkes (1999).

Children aged 2 to 4 will enjoy nursery rhymes even more than they did as infants and will easily commit these verses to memory. *Folktales,* an important part of our literary heritage, work well with children at this age level, particularly the repetitive stories such as *Henny Penny* and *The Gingerbread Boy.* These stories and verses are also appropriate because their "good" and "bad" characters fit the 2- to 4-year-old's simplistic "right or wrong" sense of morality.

Ages 4 to 7

Picture storybooks will still be the heart of the literature experience for children during these years. Most of these books are meant to be read aloud to children by a fluent reader, but it is common for children at this stage to choose a favorite picture storybook, memorize the text over repeated hearings, and enjoy the book on their own through "play-reading." Folktales are still a favorite for storytelling and read-aloud experiences, as are humorous poems with strong rhyme and rhythm.

During these years many children will acquire the fundamentals of reading: the notion that stories and the words within them carry meaning, the letter-sound relationship, left-to-right and top-to-bottom progression of print on the page, and a sight vocabulary (certain words that children can recognize and say on sight). *Easy-to-read books* (sometimes referred to as *books for beginning readers*) support children's enthusiasm for learning to read; these books make use of familiar words, word patterns, informative illustrations, and, in some cases, rhyme to make the text predictable. Examples are *No, David!* (1998) by David Shannon and *There Was an Old Lady Who Swallowed a Fly* by Simms Taback (1997). Physical growth and increasing independence are prominent topics in stories in which children interact with other children more than with adults, spend time away from home, and begin school. Kevin Henkes's *Lily's Purple Plastic Purse* (1996) is a good example.

Children at this age level exhibit great enthusiasm for finding out about the world and how it works. This interest can be fed and stimulated through *informational books* for the beginning reader. Examples include *A. Lincoln and Me,* written by Louise Borden and illustrated by Ted Lewin (1999), and *What Do You Do with a Tail like This?* by Steve Jenkins and Robin Page (2003).

Easy-to-read books are all heavily illustrated but vary widely in readability and level of conceptual difficulty. At the lower end are wordless picture books that tell straightforward stories and word or naming books in which the text is limited to brief captions. At the higher end are brief chapter books of about 250–300 words with illustrations on about every other page. It is especially important that books selected for beginning readers precisely match their interests and reading abilities, so as not to bore or dishearten them. Two helpful guides to books of this type are *Beyond Picture Books: A Guide to First Readers* (Barstow & Riggle, 1995) and *Best Books for Beginning Readers* (Gunning, 1998).

Ages 7 to 9

During these years most children who have had the benefit of a rich literature experience will become fluent and willing readers. This skill, combined with their increased flexibility in thinking, makes many new story types appropriate for these children. Now that they can understand and accept others' perspectives, they can enjoy reading about the lives of other children of the past, present, or future in *transitional readers* and later in *novels.*

Transitional readers are chapter books with simple, straightforward plots and writing styles for children who are ready to read slightly longer picture books and short chapter books, but not full-fledged novels. A helpful guide to transitional books is *Best Books for Building Literacy for Elementary School Children* (Gunning, 2000). Examples include the *Ike and Mem* series by Patrick Jennings and Anne Fine's *The Jamie and Angus Stories* (2002), illustrated by Penny Dale. At 8 or 9, children begin to assert their growing abilities to meet their own needs by doing such things as camping out in the backyard or biking to school alone. Fittingly, books for these children often center on the adventures of young characters within their neighborhoods and communities.

Chapter books with more sophisticated writing styles or more complicated plots can be greatly enjoyed as read-alouds in the classroom and as independent reading by the better readers. Also, many picture storybooks are appropriate for independent reading by children at this age level. For example, see *Don't Let the Pigeon Drive the Bus* by Mo Willems (2003), and *The Gardener,* written by Sarah Stewart and illustrated by David Small (1997). Story characters having both good and bad qualities and realistic problems mirror the 7- to 9-year-olds' maturing sense of morality as they begin to recognize that life and people do not fit into neat "good" and "bad" categories and that opinions different from their own may have validity. Lois Lowry's books about Sam, such as *See You Around, Sam!* (1996), are good examples.

A common phenomenon among children who are learning to read is the penchant for rereading the same book many times. Often misconstrued by adults as somehow wrong, the act of rereading the same text many times is, in fact, good reading practice made palatable to the child by the security of a familiar, or "friendly," text.

Although folktales continue to be popular with many 7-year-olds, studies have shown that interest in this genre generally peaks and falls off by age 8. Children then begin to show more interest in the here and now and begin to shift toward a preference for realism in their stories and poems.

Ages 9 to 12

With their rapidly developing physical and mental skills and abilities, 9- to 12-year-olds are ready for the great variety of literature that awaits them. Plots in novels can now be more complicated, including such devices as flashback and symbolism. Language devices such as speech patterns and dialects of earlier or different cultures can be managed. Both historical fiction and science fiction, which are set in the distant past and distant future, respectively, can be understood and enjoyed. Examples are *Esperanza Rising* by Pam Muñoz Ryan (2001) and *The City of Ember* by Jeanne Duprau (2003).

These children are particularly interested in reading about young people who, like themselves, are growing up, asserting and using their new-found skills, moving toward independence, and experiencing growth through meeting challenges. Survival stories, peer stories, and realistic animal stories intrigue these children. Moreover, stories that present alternative points of view, nontraditional characters, and moral dilemmas are well suited to young people whose moral development allows them to recognize the legitimacy of opinions, mores, and lifestyles different from their own. Examples include *Colibrí* by Ann Cameron (2003) and *Wringer* by Jerry Spinelli (1997).

An interesting parallel to the 7- to 9-year-old's tendency to reread books occurs at this age level. Many 9- to 12-year-olds discover *series books,* such as the *Nancy Drew* and *Hardy Boys* mysteries of the twentieth century, the more recent *Animorphs* science fantasy series by K. A. Applegate, and the sports-oriented stories of Matt Christopher, of which there are more than a hundred. Books in a series share the same genre or topic, and in most series books there is a recurring character or characters. Usually, a child reads each book in the series, one after the other. This is rereading of a sort, since all books within a series vary only slightly one from the other. Reading these books is beneficial to young readers, simply because of the hours of reading practice they willingly gain. A recent, highly successful newcomer to this genre is the *Series of Unfortunate Events* books by Lemony Snicket, a pseudonym for the elusive author who writes these melodramatic adventures about three orphaned siblings.

In some cases, the stated author of a series is actually a pseudonym for several writers who are hired to write stories according to a prescribed formula. In these cases, the books are referred to as *formula fiction.* They appear as mysteries, fantasy and science fantasy adventures, historical fiction, and romances. Of note here is the *American Girl* Collection, works of historical fiction focusing on the lives of eight girls growing up in various periods of American history from 1764 to 1944, each girl being the heroine of a separate series of books. This collection is at the high end of series-fiction quality, with more emphasis placed on historical accuracy than on formulaic sameness. (See the *Trends in Children's Literature* section at the end of this chapter for other aspects of this collection.)

Although most 9- to 12-year-olds are competent readers, there is no valid reason for librarians or teachers to discontinue their read-aloud programs for these children. More challenging novels as well as sophisticated picture books for older children sometimes can be more fully appreciated by children when read aloud by an excellent reader. Examples include *Holes* by Louis Sachar (1998) and *Ug: Boy Genius of the Stone Age* by Raymond Briggs (2002).

Teachers and librarians who are consistently successful in helping children find books they like rapidly narrow the field of choices by first considering general factors such as age level and types of books appropriate for children of that general age level. Then they consider more personal factors such as the child's current reading interests and reading ability to select specific titles. Knowing children's general reading preferences provides some guidance in book selection, but there is no substitute for knowing the child.

CHILDREN'S READING PREFERENCES

A *reading preference* is a stated or implied choice among several reading options. For example, if in response to the question: Which would you rather read: a romance, a mystery, or a science fiction adventure? you choose the mystery option, you are stating a reading preference for mystery.

Many studies of children's reading preferences have been conducted. Differences in the choices offered to children and in the ways data were gathered from study to study make extensive generalization difficult, but a few patterns have emerged from these studies (Haynes, 1988):

- There are no significant differences between the preferences of boys and girls before age 9.
- The greatest differences in reading preferences of boys and girls occur between ages 10 and 13.
- Boys and girls in the middle grades (ages 10 to 13) share a pronounced preference for mystery and, to a lesser degree, humor, adventure, and animals.

- Preferences of boys in the middle grades include action and adventure stories and sports stories.
- Preferences of girls in the middle grades include fantasy stories, animal stories, and stories about people.

A teacher or librarian might use this information to make general predictions about what types of books boys or girls of a certain age might enjoy.

Reading preferences should not be the sole guide in making specific book recommendations to individuals. The reason for this should be clear when you consider the hypothetical question involving romance, mystery, and science fiction books posed earlier. Even though you had to choose one or the other of the options offered to you, it is quite possible that you rarely, if ever, read any of these types of books; mystery may have been just the least uninteresting to you of the three. Knowing this so-called preference would not benefit, and could possibly hinder, a teacher or librarian who was seeking to help you find a book that you would enjoy.

CHILDREN'S READING INTERESTS

Reading interests and reading preferences are not the same. A *preference,* as noted above, implies a forced choice between options selected by someone other than oneself. An *interest,* on the other hand, comes from within oneself, can encompass whatever can be imagined, and implies freedom of choice. Knowledge of children's reading preferences provides information about children in general, but knowledge of children's reading interests is personal and individual. Since most teachers and school librarians work with particular groups of children over an extended time, they can learn the interests of each child within the group. In so doing, they gain powerful, effective knowledge to use in successfully matching children and books.

Common sense tells us that children will apply themselves more vigorously to read or learn something that they are interested in than they will to read or learn something that they find uninteresting or boring. Interest generates motivation, and good teachers and librarians put that motivation to work by guiding students to good books on topics that satisfy individual interests.

Learning your students' interests can be accomplished in several ways. The best way is to get to know your students by talking to them in whole-class sharing and in one-to-one conferences. All people like to talk about themselves and their interests; children are no different. One or more of the following questions might start a productive dialogue between you and a student:

1. What are your favorite things to do?
2. Are you very good at doing something? Tell me about it.
3. What would you like to learn more about?
4. What kinds of books do you like to read?
5. Who is in your family? Tell me a little about each family member.

You can also learn about children's interests through their free-choice writing. Journal writing is particularly helpful in this regard. A perfectly valid and more direct approach is to ask children to list their interests. Many teachers keep such lists in their students' writing folders to use during individual conferences. Because children's interests change often, data of this sort must be updated regularly.

WOULD YOU LIKE TO READ THIS BOOK?
As you look at each book, answer this question by circling either YES or NO next to the appropriate book number. Be sure to match the book number and the item number before circling your answer.

1.	YES	NO		18.	YES	NO
2.	YES	NO		19.	YES	NO
3.	YES	NO		20.	YES	NO

Etc.

FIGURE 1.1   Sample Student Response Form for Interest Inventory

Yet another way for teachers and librarians to keep current on students' interests is to conduct their own *interest inventories* several times a year to assure that the reading selections available in their classrooms or school libraries reflect the general interests of their students. The following steps show one way to conduct a classroom interest inventory:

1. Collect appropriate books that represent a wide variety of genres and topics.
2. Number the books with Post-it notes and record the title, number, and genre of each book.
3. Design a response form for students, such as the one shown in Figure 1.1.
4. Encourage students to examine the books and mark their response forms.
5. Collect and tally students' responses to find types and titles of books that currently interest your students.

Classroom interest inventories not only provide teachers and librarians with helpful information about their students' current interests but also introduce children to new genres, topics, and titles. In this way, teachers and librarians can help accomplish their fundamental task of expanding students' fields of interest and knowledge bases.

TRENDS IN CHILDREN'S LITERATURE

Looking at publishing and usage trends in the field of children's books over time helps to forecast future developments. Some of the following trends are heartening and deserve our support. Others are more questionable.

- Increased numbers of adults reading children's books, primarily because of the *Harry Potter* phenomenon.
- More small press publishers assuming the task of publishing more challenging, original, "risky" books, as established independent book publishers fall to corporate takeovers.
- More novels being written in verse, such as Hesse's (1997) *Out of the Dust* and Woodson's (2003) *Locomotion.*
- Increasing dominance of illustration in children's books. Readers are becoming more visually oriented as they spend more time watching television and playing video games and spend less time reading.
- Fewer full-length novels and more short, high-interest, low-reading-level novels being written for 10- to 14-year-olds.

- Rapid growth of technology in all areas of publishing. As schools adopt computerized management reading programs such as Accelerated Reader, reading and books become less a means to enjoyment and discovering new information and more a matter of gaining points.
- Rapid increases in home schooling and charter schools that have created a need for more children's librarians in public libraries who can select good literature for purchase, advise readers effectively, and offer interesting programs for children of all ages.
- An increase in the publication of bilingual books, primarily English-Spanish, and Spanish-only books to accommodate the rapid increase in second language learner (SLL) students.
- Increased merchandising of book-related paraphernalia, such as games, craft kits, cookbooks, dolls, and doll accessories (e.g., the *American Girl Collection* book series with its character dolls and their expensive period outfits for both dolls and doll owners, hats, jewelry, furniture)
- More picture storybooks and books for beginning readers being reformatted as board books and incorrectly marketed as baby books.

REFERENCES

Almond, D. (1999). *Skellig.* New York: Delacorte.

Anderson, R. C. (1996). Research foundations to support wide reading. In V. Greaney (Ed.), *Promoting reading: Views on making reading materials accessible to increase literacy levels* (pp. 55–77). Newark, DE: International Reading Association.

———, Hiebert, E. H., Scott, J. A., & Wilkinson, I. A. G. (1985). *Becoming a nation of readers: The report of the commission on reading.* Washington, DC: National Institute of Education.

Barstow, B., & Riggle, J. (1995). *Beyond picture books: A guide to first readers* (2nd ed.). New York: R. R. Bowker.

Bogart, D. (Ed.) (2004). *Bowker annual: Library and book trade almanac.* New Providence, NJ: R. R. Bowker.

Borden, L. (1999). *A. Lincoln and me.* Illustrated by T. Lewin. New York: Scholastic.

Briggs, R. (2002). *Ug: Boy genius of the Stone Age.* New York: Knopf.

Butler, D. (1975). *Cushla and her books.* Boston: Horn Book.

Cameron, A. (2003). *Colibrí.* New York: Farrar.

Carlsen, G. R., & Sherrill, A. (1988). *Voices of readers: How we come to love books.* Urbana, IL: National Council of Teachers of English.

Children's books in print. (2003). New Providence, NJ: R. R. Bowker.

Children's catalog (18th ed.). (2001). New York: H. W. Wilson.

DeFord, D. (1981). Literacy, reading, writing, and other essentials. *Language Arts, 58*(6), 652–658.

Dowhauer, S. L. (1987). Effects of repeated reading on second-grade transitional readers' fluency and comprehension. *Reading Research Quarterly, 22,* 389–406.

Dressel, J. H. (1990). The effects of listening to and discussing different qualities of children's literature on the narrative writing of fifth graders. *Research in the Teaching of English, 24*(4), 397–414.

Duprau, J. (2003) *The city of Ember.* New York: Random.

Durkin, D. (1966). *Children who read early.* New York: Columbia Teachers College Press.

Eckhoff, B. (1983). How reading affects children's writing. *Language Arts, 60*(5), 607–616.

Eldredge, J. L., & Butterfield, D. (1986). Alternatives to traditional reading instruction. *The Reading Teacher, 40,* 32–37.

Fine, A. (2002). *The Jamie and Angus stories.* Illustrated by P. Dale. New York: Candlewick.

Gunning, T. G. (1998). *Best books for beginning readers.* Needham Heights, MA: Allyn and Bacon.

———. (2000). *Best books for building literacy for elementary school children.* Needham Heights, MA: Allyn and Bacon.

Harris, T. L., & Hodges, R. E. (1995). *The literacy dictionary: The vocabulary of reading and writing.* Newark, DE: International Reading Association.

Haynes, C. (1988). Explanatory power of content for identifying children's literature preferences. *Dissertation Abstracts International, 49–12A,* p. 3617 (University Microfilms No. DEW8900468).

Henkes, K. (1996). *Lily's purple plastic purse.* New York: Greenwillow.

Hesse, K. (1997). *Out of the dust.* New York: Scholastic.

Jenkins, S., & Page, R. (2003). *What do you do with a tail like this?* New York: Houghton.

Jennings, P. (2001). *The bird shadow: An Ike and Mem story.* Illustrated by A. Alter. New York: Holiday. Others in the *Ike and Mem* series: *The ears of corn* (2003); *The lightning bugs* (2003); *The tornado watches* (2002); *The weeping willow* (2002).

Kiefer, B. Z. (1994). *The potential of picturebooks: From visual literacy to aesthetic understanding.* Englewood Cliffs, NJ: Prentice Hall.

Kunhardt, D. (1962/2001). *Pat the bunny.* New York: Golden.

Lancia, P. J. (1997). Literary borrowing: The effects of literature on children's writing. *The Reading Teacher, 50*(6), 470–475.

Levstik, L. (1986). The relationship between historical response and narrative in a sixth-grade classroom. *Theory and Research in Social Education, 14,* 1–15.

Lima, C. W., & Lima, J. A. (2001). *A to zoo: Subject access to children's picture books* (6th ed.). New York: R. R. Bowker.

Lowry, L. (1996). *See you around, Sam!* Illustrated by D. de Groat. New York: Houghton.

McClure, A. A., & Kristo, J. V. (Eds.). (2002). *Adventuring with books: A booklist for pre-K–grade 6* (13th ed.). Urbana, IL: National Council of Teachers of English.

McConaghy, J. (1990). *Children learning through literature: A teacher researcher study.* Portsmouth, NH: Heinemann.

Morrow, L. M., Pressley, M., Smith, J. K., & Smith, M. (1997). The effect of a literature-based program integrated into literacy and science instruction with children from diverse backgrounds. *Reading Research Quarterly, 32*(1), 54–76.

National Institutes of Health. (2000). *Report of the National Reading Panel: Teaching children to read: An evidence-based assessment of the scientific research literature on reading and its implications for reading instruction.* NIH Publication No. 00-4769. Washington, DC: U.S. Government Printing Office.

Opie, I. (Ed.). (1999). *Here comes Mother Goose.* Illustrated by R. Wells. New York: Candlewick.

Oxenbury, H. (1995). *Baby Beginner Board Books (I can, I hear, I see, I touch).* New York: Candlewick.

———. (1999). *Clap hands; All fall over; Say good night.* New York: Little Simon.

Peck, R. A story is a doorway. Unpublished.

Rosenblatt, L. (1978). *The reader, the text, the poem.* Carbondale, IL: Southern Illinois University.

Ryan, P. M. (2001). *Esperanza rising.* New York: Scholastic.

Sachar, L. (1998). *Holes.* New York: Farrar.

Shannon, D. (1998). *No, David!* New York: Scholastic.

Simont, M. (2001). *The stray dog.* New York: HarperCollins.

Sís, P. (2000). *Madlenka.* New York: Farrar.

Spinelli, J. (1997). *Wringer.* New York: HarperCollins.

Stewart, S. (1997). *The gardener.* Illustrated by D. Small. New York: Farrar.

Suen, A. (2002). *Toddler two.* Illustrated by W. Cheon. New York: Lee & Low.

Taback, S. (1997). *There was an old lady who swallowed a fly.* New York: Viking.

Van Orden, P. (2000). *Selecting books for the elementary school library media center: A complete guide.* New York: Neal-Schuman.

VanSledright, B. A., & Kelley, C. A. (1996). *Reading American history: How do multiple text sources influence historical learning in fifth grade?* Reading Research Report 68 (ERIC Document Reproduction Service No. ED 400 525).

White, E. B. (1952). *Charlotte's web.* Illustrated by G. Williams. New York: Harper.

Wilkes, A. (1999). *My first word book.* New York: DK.

Willems, M. (2003). *Don't let the pigeon drive the bus.* New York: Hyperion.

Woodson, J. (2003). *Locomotion.* New York: Putnam.

Ziefert, H. (2002). *Who said moo?* Illustrated by S. Taback. Brooklyn, NY: Handprint Books.

2

LEARNING *about* BOOKS

A BOOK

I'm a strange contradiction; I'm new and I'm old,
I'm often in tatters, and oft deck'd in gold;
Though I never could read, yet letter'd I'm found;
Though blind, I enlighten; though loose, I am bound—
I am always in black, and I'm always in white;
I am grave and I'm gay, I am heavy and light.
In form too I differ—I'm thick and I'm thin,
I've no flesh, and no bones, yet I'm covered with skin;
I've more points than the compass, more stops than the flute—
I sing without voice, without speaking confute;
I'm English, I'm German, I'm French and I'm Dutch;
Some love me too fondly; some slight me too much;
I often die soon, though I sometimes live ages,
And no monarch alive has so many pages.

—HANNAH MORE

In Chapter 1 we stated that reading is a fusion of text and reader and that each reading of a particular literary work results in a different transaction. Even rereadings by the same reader will result in a different experience. But if the transaction is different each time a book is read, how can general assessments of literary merit be made? Rosenblatt answers that although the notion of a single, correct reading of a literary work is rejected, "*given agreed-upon criteria,* it is possible to decide that some readings are more defensible than others" (1985, p. 36). Although each reading of a given literary work will be different, there are certain generally agreed-upon interpretations of that work by a community of educated readers. In this chapter, traditional literary elements are reviewed in order to heighten your awareness of literary criticism and to provide a more precise vocabulary for you to express your responses to children's books. Literary terms may also be considered as tools that your students can use to initiate and sustain conversations about literature. In using these terms in the classroom you can help children to acquire a literary vocabulary.

ELEMENTS OF FICTION

Learning to evaluate children's books can best be accomplished by reading as many excellent books as possible. Gradually, your judgment on the merits of individual books will improve. Discussing your responses to these books with children, teachers, and other students and listening to their responses will also assist you in becoming a more appreciative critic. Understanding the different parts, or elements, of a piece of fiction and how they work together can help you to become more analytical about literary works; and this, too, can improve your judgment of literature. The elements of fiction are discussed separately in the following sections, but it is the unity of all these elements that produces the story.

Plot

The events of the story and the sequence in which they are told constitute the plot of the story. In other words, the plot is what happens in the story. Plot is the most important element of fiction to the child reader. Often, adults believe that a story for children needs only to present familiar, everyday activities—the daily routines of life. Perhaps 2- and 3-year-olds will enjoy hearing narratives such as this, but by age 4, children want to find more excitement in books. A good plot produces conflict to build the excitement and suspense that are needed to keep the reader involved.

The nature of the *conflict* within the plot can arise from different sources. The basic conflict may be one that occurs within the main character, called *person-against-self.* In this type of story, the main character struggles against inner drives and personal tendencies to achieve some goal. Stories about adolescence will frequently have this conflict as the basis of the story problem. For example, in *Ghost Boy* (2000) by Iain Lawrence, 14-year-old Harold struggles to find himself and to accept himself and others. A conflict usually found in survival stories is the struggle the character has with the forces of nature. This conflict is called *person-against-nature.* Worthy examples are *Island of the Blue Dolphins* (1960) by Scott O'Dell and *Hatchet* (1987) by Gary Paulsen. In other children's stories, the source of the conflict is found between two characters. Conflicts with peers, problems with sibling rivalries, and stories of children rebelling against an adult are *person-against-person* conflicts. For example, the young badger, Frances, in *A Bargain for Frances* (1970) by Russell Hoban, struggles to get a fair deal from her friend, Thelma, who sells Frances a tea set.

Occasionally, a story for children presents the main character in conflict with society. This conflict in children's stories is most often either about the environment being destroyed by new technology or changing times or about children caught up in a political upheaval such as war. The conflict is then called *person-against-society. Shades of Gray* (1989) by Carolyn Reeder and *Across Five Aprils* (1964) by Irene

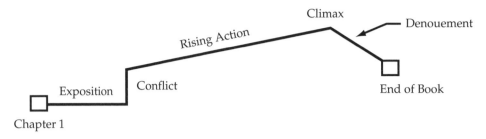

FIGURE 2.1   Diagram of a Progressive Plot

Hunt, both war stories, pose this type of conflict. In Jean Craighead George's *Julie of the Wolves* (1972), protagonist Julie/Miyax struggles with the societal changes occurring in her native Alaskan community.

Plots are constructed in many different ways. The most usual plot structures found in children's stories are *chronological plots,* which cover a particular period of time and relate the events in order within the time period. For example, if a book relates the events of one week, then Monday's events will precede Tuesday's, and so on. An example of a story with a chronological plot is *Charlotte's Web* (1952) by E. B. White. There are two distinct types of chronological plots, progressive and episodic. In books with *progressive plots,* the first few chapters are the exposition, in which the characters, setting, and basic conflict are established. Following the expository chapters, the story builds through rising action to a climax. The climax occurs, a satisfactory conclusion (or denouement) is reached, and the story ends. Figure 2.1 suggests how a progressive, chronological, plot might be visualized.

An *episodic plot* ties together separate short stories or episodes, each an entity in itself with its own conflict and resolution. These episodes are typically unified by the same cast of characters and the same setting. Often, each episode comprises a chapter. Although the episodes are usually chronological, time relationships among the episodes may be nonexistent or loosely connected by "during that same year" or "later that month." An example of a short chapter book with an episodic plot structure is *Ramona Quimby, Age 8* (1981) by Beverly Cleary. Because episodic plots are less complex, they tend to be easier to read. Thus, the reader who is just making the transition from picture books to chapter books may find these plots particularly appealing. Many easy-to-read books for the beginning reader are also structured in this way. *Frog and Toad Are Friends* (1970) by Arnold Lobel is a good example of an episodic plot in an easy-to-read book. Figure 2.2 suggests how a chronological, episodic plot might be visualized.

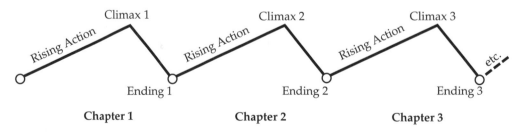

FIGURE 2.2   Diagram of an Episodic Plot

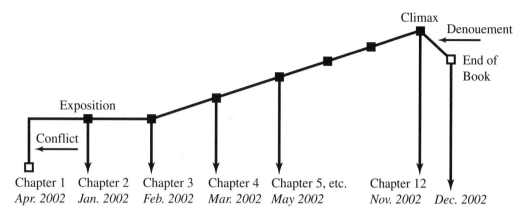

FIGURE 2.3   Diagram of a Flashback

Authors use a *flashback* to convey information about events that occurred earlier—for example, before the beginning of the first chapter. In this case, the chronology of events is disrupted, and the reader is taken back to an earlier time. Flashbacks can occur more than once and in different parts of a story. The use of a flashback permits authors to begin the story in the midst of the action but later fill in the background for full understanding of the present events. Flashbacks in children's books are mostly found in chapter books for older readers, since such plots can confuse children younger than age 8 or 9. Teachers can help students understand this plot structure by reading aloud good examples of this type of story, such as Jean Craighead George's *My Side of the Mountain* (1959). Class discussion can then focus on the sequence of events and why the author may have chosen to relate the events in this manner. Figure 2.3 illustrates the structure of a flashback in a book in which some events occurred before the beginning of the book.

A stylistic plot device that prepares readers for coming events in a story is *foreshadowing.* This device gives clues to a later event, possibly even the climax of the story. For example, in *Tuck Everlasting* (1975) by Natalie Babbitt the detailed description of the long yellow road in the first chapter foreshadows the long journey the Tuck family members must travel in their lives. You can alert young readers to one of the subtle ways authors prepare them for the outcomes of stories by discussing foreshadowing.

Plot is an important element to all readers, but especially to young readers, who enjoy fast-moving, exciting stories. A well-constructed plot contributes substantially to children's acceptance and enjoyment of stories.

Characters

Memorable characters populate the world of children's literature. Ferdinand the bull, Charlotte the spider, Frances the badger, Little Toot the young tugboat, Karana the Native American girl, and Peter, the African-American child with his dog Willie are all remembered fondly by generations of readers.

Characters, the "actors" in a story, are another element of fiction vital to the enjoyment of a story. A well-portrayed character can become a friend, a role model, or a temporary parent to a child reader.

Although young readers enjoy exciting events, the characters involved in those events must matter to the reader or the events no longer seem important. How characters are depicted and how they develop in the course of the story are important to the reader. Two aspects to consider in studying a character are characterization and character development.

Characterization refers to the way an author helps the reader to know a character. The most obvious way an author can do this is to describe the character's physical appearance and personality. Portraying the character's emotional and moral traits or revealing her relationships with other characters are more subtle and effective techniques. In the most convincing characterizations, we see the character through a combination of her own actions and dialogue, the responses of other characters to her, and the narrator's descriptions.

Character development refers to the changes, good or bad, the character undergoes during the course of events in the story. If a character experiences significant, life-altering events, we, as readers, expect that the character will somehow be different as a result of those events. For example, Matt, a boy of 11, who was left alone for months in the Maine territory to take care of his family's new cabin, becomes a stronger, more independent young man by the end of *The Sign of the Beaver* (1973) by Elizabeth George Speare.

In a work of fiction for children there are usually one or two main characters and some minor characters. Ideally, each main character, sometimes called the *protagonist*, will be a fully described, complex individual who possesses both good and bad traits, like a real person. Such a character is called a *round character*. For example, in the historical fiction novel *Catherine, Called Birdy* (1994) by Karen Cushman, Birdy, the protagonist whose father is seeking a suitable husband for her, is presented as a complex character with many strengths and weaknesses.

Minor, or *secondary, characters* may be described in a less complete or partial manner. The extent of description depends on what the reader needs to know about the character for a full understanding of the story. Some of the minor character's traits are described fully, whereas other facets of the character's personality may remain obscure. Because the purpose is to build the story and make it comprehensible, fragmentary knowledge of a minor character may suffice. In the novel *Under the Red-Blood Sun* (1994) by Graham Salisbury, Billy Wilson is portrayed as a loyal friend to Tomi, the protagonist, in this story about the treatment of Tomi's Japanese family in Hawaii during World War II. Occasionally, an author will insert a *flat character*—that is, a character described in a one-sided or underdeveloped manner. Although such people do not exist in real life, they may be justified within the story to propel the plot. Sometimes the character is shown as an all-evil or all-frivolous person; for instance, folktales present flat characters as symbols of good and evil. In some stories, a flat character plays the role of *character foil,* a person who is in direct juxtaposition to another character (usually the protagonist) and who serves to highlight the characteristics of the other individual. A character foil may occur as a flat or as a round character. For example, the neighborhood bully, Beans, who was pushing 10-year-old Palmer to participate in wringing the necks of pigeons as part of the town's annual Family Fest is portrayed as a flat character in *Wringer* (1997) by Jerry Spinelli. The character or force that is in direct opposition to the main character is called the *antagonist.* In Avi's *The True Confessions of Charlotte Doyle* (1990) , the ship's captain is a frightening antagonist to Charlotte.

The main characters in an excellent work of fiction for children are rounded, fully developed characters who undergo change in response to life-altering events. Because children generally prefer personified animals or children of their own age, or slightly older, as the main characters of their stories, authors of children's books often face a dilemma. Although in real life, children usually have restricted freedom of action and decision making within the confines of a family, the author can develop a more vivid and exciting story if the main characters are "on their own." Thus, in many children's stories, parents are absent, no longer living, or no longer functioning. Furthermore, by making up situations, authors are able to focus on just one aspect of life, thereby enabling young readers to see and understand this one facet of life more clearly.

Setting

The time when the story occurs and the place(s) where it occurs constitute the setting of a story. The setting has a more or less important function depending on the story. For example, in historical fiction the authentic recreation of the period is essential to the comprehension of the story's events. In this situation, the setting, fully described in both time and place, is called an *integral setting*. The story could not be the same if placed in another setting. For example, in the historical novel *Bull Run* (1993) by Paul Fleischman, battle maps are included, and many of the sixteen characters whose points of view are presented discuss the battlegrounds.

By contrast, the setting in folktales is often vague and general. For example, "long ago in a cottage in the deep woods" is meant to convey a universal, timeless tale, one that could have happened anywhere and almost anytime except the present or very recent past. This type of setting is called a *backdrop setting*. It simply sets the stage and the mood.

Theme

The literary theme of a story is its underlying meaning or significance. The term *theme* should not be confused with topic or theme as used in the sense of a thematic unit. Although we sometimes think of the literary *theme* as the message or moral of the story, it can just as likely be an aesthetic understanding, such as an appreciation for nature, or a viewpoint on a current societal issue. To identify the theme, you may ask yourself what the author's purpose was in writing the story or what the author is saying through this story.

A theme is better expressed by means of a complete sentence than by a single word. For example, students often suggest that a theme found in *Charlotte's Web* (1952) by E. B. White is friendship. A better statement of the theme is "Friendship is one of the most satisfying things in the world," as Wilbur the pig tells us in the story. The single word *friendship* may be a topic found in the story, but it is not an expression of the theme.

Themes in children's books should be worthy of children's attention and should convey truth to them. Furthermore, the themes should be based on high moral and ethical standards. A theme must not overpower the plot and characters of the story, however; children read fiction for enjoyment, not for enlightenment. If the theme is expressed in a heavy-handed, obvious fashion, then the pleasure of the reading experience is diminished. Likewise, overly "teachy" or didactic themes detract from a reader's enjoyment of a story. Certainly a well-written book may convey a moral message, but it should also tell a good story from which the message evolves. In this way the theme is subtly conveyed to the reader. For example, in the picture book *Heroes* (1995), written by Ken Mochizuki and illustrated by Dom Lee, Donnie's dad and uncle help Donnie and his friends discover that peaceful alternatives to war exist.

Often, adults write stories not for children's pleasure but to teach morality lessons. Although we think of stories of this sort as the thinly disguised religious tracts found in the early history of children's literature, we must be alert to a tendency for some current authors to use children's literature as a platform to preach about drug abuse, animal rights, and other issues of contemporary interest. If the literary quality of these so-called problem novels is weakened, then the story and characters become secondary to the issue or problem. However, when moral values are embedded within the fabric of a powerful story, children can be led to develop a sense of right and wrong without feeling as if they are being indoctrinated.

Style

Style is the way an author tells the story; it can be viewed as the writing itself, as opposed to the content of the book. However, the style must suit the content of the particular book; the two are intertwined.

Different aspects of style are considered in evaluating a work of fiction. Most obviously, you can look at the *words* chosen to tell the story. Are they long or short, common or uncommon, rhyming or melodic, boring and hackneyed or rich and challenging, unemotional or emotional, standard dialect or regional/minority dialect? The words should be appropriate to the story being told. As an evaluator of books for children, you will want to ask the following questions as you read: Why did the author choose these words? What effect was the author trying to achieve?

The *sentences* may also be considered. Do they read easily? Do they flow without the reader needing to reread to gain the meaning of the text? Sometimes an author chooses to limit the word choices to write a book that can be read by a beginning reader. Yet in the hands of a gifted writer, the sentences will remain no less melodic, varied in length and structure, and enjoyable to read and hear than sentences in the best books for the more advanced reader. A good example of a well-written book for beginning readers is Arnold Lobel's *Frog and Toad Are Friends* (1970).

The *organization* of the book may be considered by noting the paragraphs and transitions, length of chapters, headings and chapter titles, preface, endnotes, prologue, epilogue, and length of the book. For the beginning reader it is important whether a story is divided into chapters. After years of looking at, listening to, and reading books without chapters, it is quite an accomplishment for a 6-year-old to move up to so-called chapter books, even if each chapter is only three pages long.

Chapter titles can provoke interest in what will follow, as well as provide the reader with clues to predict story events. Some books provide the readers with a prologue, an introductory statement telling events that precede the start of the story. Some authors include an epilogue, a concluding statement telling events that occur after the story has ended. Adeline Yen Mah, author of *Chinese Cinderella: The True Story of an Unwanted Daughter* (1999), speaks directly to the reader in an informative prologue about the Chinese language. She invites the reader to become interested in a Chinese girl's language, history, and culture.

In the epilogue of *Tuck Everlasting* (1975), Natalie Babbitt allows the readers to revisit the scene of the story some years later and resolve at least one of the questions they inevitably have at the story's end. Occasionally, an author presents information on the sources or historical facts used in the story. In *Friedrich* (1970), for example, Hans Peter Richter adds a chronology of historical events in the endnotes.

Point of view is another aspect of an author's style. If the story is told through the eyes and voice of a *third-person narrator* (the use of *he, she, it*), then the reader can know whatever the narrator knows about the events of the story. In many stories, the narrator is *omniscient* and can see into the minds of all characters and be at many places at the same time. The reader of E. B. White's *Charlotte's Web* (1952) can understand and interpret the story from many different perspectives because of White's use of the omniscient point of view.

Other stories are narrated from the perspective of only one character in the story. In this case, the story is still told in the third person, but the reader knows only what that particular character can see and understand. This latter technique is called *limited omniscient* point of view. In Mildred Taylor's *Roll of Thunder, Hear My Cry* (1976), the story is told by Cassie, the very astute 9-year-old protagonist.

Other times authors choose to tell the story through a *first-person narrator* (the use of *I*), generally the main character of the story. In such cases the reader gains a sense of closeness to the main character but is not privy to any information unavailable to this character. As you read, you will note that some authors have accomplished a first-person point of view by writing as though their main character were writing a diary or letters, as in *Flight to Freedom* (2002) by Ana Veciana-Suarez. Occasionally, a story is told in first person through the eyes of a minor character. For example, *Faith and the Electric Dogs* (1996) by Patrick Jennings is a humorous fantasy novel about 10-year-old Faith told through the first-person narration of Eddie, a stray dog. A *shifting point of view* permits the reader to see events from different characters' points of view. This technique is demanding on young readers' skill. When the point of view shifts, the author must carefully cue readers to the changing point of view, as Avi does in *Nothing but the Truth* (1991) by identifying sender, receiver, or discussants at the beginning of each letter, memorandum, telephone call, or face-to-face conversation.

Symbolism is an artistic invention that authors use to suggest invisible or intangible meanings by analogy to something else through association, resemblance, or convention. Often a symbol—a person, object, or situation—represents an abstract or figurative meaning in the story in addition to its literal meaning. Some symbols are universal and can be found repeatedly in literary works; others may be particular to the story. For example, a farm often stands for love and security in works of literature. Children often read only on a literal level, but they can be helped by teachers to note more obvious symbols existing in the books they are reading. If the symbolic feature recurs in the story, it is referred to as a *motif*. The number 3 is a common motif in folktales, for example.

A story for children must be more than a plot and a character study; a story integrates all the elements of fiction into a pleasing whole. In drawing together these elements, authors create new worlds for young readers.

VISUAL ELEMENTS

In many children's books the story is told through both text and pictures. This is particularly true of picture books but is also true of other books for children in which pictures serve an important function. Many different purposes can be accomplished through book illustrations. They convey meaning and feeling by helping the reader to visualize the physical settings and the characters' appearance and actions. They also provide an aesthetic dimension to books by offering the readers additional pleasure and insights beyond the message within the text. Thus, the role of pictures in children's books is both to reflect the text and to extend and enrich it without contradicting its message.

When you read many illustrated books and carefully observe the illustrations and their relationships to the texts, you begin to increase your appreciation of this aspect of children's literature. You may consider the different parts of illustrations as one aspect of your evaluation of illustrations. In the picture book *The Picture That Mom Drew* (1997) by Kathy Mallat and Bruce McMillan, a visual and textual demonstration of the visual elements is presented. This book can be used to help students to become more observant of illustrations and their roles in books. These *visual elements* are line, color, shape, texture, and composition. They can help you to become more observant of illustrations so that you will learn to select well-illustrated books.

Line

The stroke marks that form part of a picture and often define its outline are the lines. The line of a picture generally defines the objects within the picture. Artists may choose to use lines that are dark or pale, heavy or light, solid or broken, wide or thin, straight or curved, or have combinations of these elements. The lines may be mostly vertical, horizontal, or on a diagonal. In pictures of the ocean and open prairies, the lines are predominantly horizontal; the impression is one of calm and tranquility. If the ocean is stormy, then the lines are more likely diagonal and upward moving, suggesting action or emotion or both. Each of these choices results in a different visual effect and can help to set a different mood. In evaluating the element of line within a picture, you may ask yourself whether the lines of the picture help to create and convey both the meaning and the feeling of the story. John Steptoe's use of thick black outlines for the children in *Stevie* (1969) is successful in showing the resistance to friendship between the characters. Also see Illustrations 7 and 8, inside back cover.

Color

Color, another visual element of a book, may be observed for its hue, lightness, and saturation. Colors may be considered for the actual part of the color spectrum they represent or for their hue. The predominant colors may be from the cool end of the spectrum (the blues, greens, and gray-violets) or from the warm end of the color chart (the reds, oranges, and yellows). The colors may be intense or pale (that is, more or less saturated). The lightness of the colors may range from diaphanous to opaque. The colors used must first complement the text. For example, if the mood of the story is that of calm and contentment, the illustrator may choose soft, warm tones that strengthen the emotional warmth of the story. If the events and mood of the text change during the course of the story, then the colors will change to reflect and signal the shift occurring in the story. In Margaret Wise Brown's *Goodnight Moon* (1947), the colors gradually darken from page to page, as the sun sets and night falls. Sometimes an illustrated book will be noteworthy for its lack of color, which can be very appropriate and effective, as in *A Day, A Dog* (1999) by Gabrielle Vincent. Also see Illustrations 1 and 4, inside front cover.

Shape

Shape, or the spatial forms of a picture, is produced by areas of color and by lines joining and intersecting to suggest outlines of forms. Shapes can be evaluated for their simplicity or complexity, their definition or lack of definition, their rigidity (as in geometric shapes) or suppleness (as in organic shapes), and their size. It is easy to see how this visual element can help to create a mood or carry a message. In looking at shapes in a picture, the proportion of one object to another and the spaces surrounding the shapes are noteworthy for the nonverbal messages they carry (the bigger, the more important). The use of negative space or blank space may also be observed for its ability to highlight an object or to show isolation or loneliness. Chris Raschka effectively uses space on successive double-spreads to demonstrate a developing friendship between two boys in the Caldecott Honor book, *Yo! Yes?* (1993), as can be seen in Illustration 3, inside front cover.

Texture

The tactile surface characteristics of pictured objects comprise the texture of a picture. More simply, the impression of how a pictured object feels is its texture. Textures may be rough or slick, firm or spongy, hard or soft, jagged or smooth. Textural effects generally offer a greater sense of reality to a picture, as happens in Leo Lionni's *Frederick* (1967), in which the torn edges of paper collage lend a convincing furriness to the little mice's bodies. Texture also permits the artist to provide contrasts within the picture. See Illustrations 5 and 7, inside back cover.

Composition

Composition includes the arrangement of the visual elements within a picture and the way in which these visual elements relate one to the other and combine to make the picture. Many artists arrange each illustration around a single focal point, which is often a key to understanding composition. The artist decides on proportion, balance, harmony, and disharmony within the various elements to produce the desired visual impact. The total effect should not overpower the story but rather extend and enrich the meaning and mood of the text. See also Illustrations 1 and 2, inside front cover, and Illustrations 6 and 8, inside back cover.

Obviously, the details in the illustrations must not conflict with those in the text. Surprisingly, many examples can be cited in which the illustrator was not true to the text in all details. Children are keenly observant of these contradictions and find them distracting. Although children accept illustrations that are varied in all visual elements and artistic styles, they have little tolerance for inaccuracies.

A R T I S T I C   S T Y L E S

Children come to note the distinctive features that identify the work of their favorite illustrators. Although the style of a picture is individual to each artist, artwork in general can be grouped by style similarities. Five broad categories of artistic styles are realistic, impressionistic, expressionistic, abstract, and surrealistic. Although an artist's works seldom fit neatly into one single art style, facets of these styles may be merged into the artist's personal expression of the world.

Realistic art represents natural forms and provides accurate representations without idealization. Wendell Minor's illustrations in *Heartland* (1989) by Diane Siebert are examples of realistic art, as is Henri Silberman's photographic rendering of the haiku collection *Stone Bench in an Empty Park* (2000), selected by Paul B. Janeczko. Also see Illustration 1, inside front cover.

Impressionistic art depicts natural appearances of objects by rendering fleeting visual impressions with an emphasis on light. The watercolor illustrations in *The Stray Dog* (2001) by Marc Simont emphasize the play of light in nature. Also see Illustration 2, inside front cover.

Expressionistic art communicates an inner feeling or vision by distorting external reality. An example can be found in *A Chair for My Mother* (1982) by Vera B. Williams. Graphic art, used heavily in advertising and billboards, can be considered a form of expressionistic art. The intent of the artist is to draw attention to the central message by eliminating competing details. Donald Crews has successfully developed this art style into concept books for the very young child in *Truck* (1980) and *Freight Train* (1978). Also see Illustration 3, inside front cover.

Abstract art emphasizes intrinsic form and surface qualities with little or no direct representation of objects but rather an emphasis on mood and feeling. The illustrations by Leo and Diane Dillon in *Why Mosquitoes Buzz in People's Ears* (1975) by Verna Aardema distort reality and thus convey the feelings evoked by the African tale. Also see Illustration 4, inside front cover.

In emphasizing the unconscious, *surrealistic art* often presents incongruous dream and fantasy images, sometimes juxtaposing unlikely objects. David Wiesner's illustrations in *Tuesday* (1991), a nearly wordless book, present a humorous and fantastic nighttime adventure. The unusual use of color and unlikely happenings reassure the reader that this wordless book is an imaginary story. Also see Illustration 5, inside back cover.

In addition, *primitive art* and *folk art* styles are seen in books about a particular era or culture. The style of art is reminiscent of the style prevalent at the time the story events occurred. In illustrating *Ox-Cart Man* (1979) by Donald Hall, Barbara Cooney uses features of Early American art in order to express the culture of early nineteenth-century New England. Folktales from tribal societies also present occasions for artists to choose a folk art style reminiscent of the art from earlier cultures. Also see Illustrations 6 and 7, inside back cover.

Because *cartoons* are popular with children, some artists select this style for their children's books. In this type of art, exaggerated, rounded figures with little or no background are the focal point of the illustrations. Dr. Seuss's many books, such as *Horton Hatches the Egg* (1940) and *The Cat in the Hat* (1957) as well as many of William Steig's popular stories, including *The Amazing Bone* (1976) and *Sylvester and the Magic Pebble* (1969), have illustrations representative of the cartoon style. Also see Illustration 8, inside back cover.

A R T I S T I C   M E D I A

The artistic media refer to the materials and technical means used by artists to create pictures. Although the variety of techniques and materials used by book illustrators is virtually unlimited, some of the more common media found in children's books are listed here.

Drawing: Pen and ink, colored pencils, pastels (colored chalk), charcoal pencils

The use of pastels combined with pen-and-ink drawings is found in the humorous illustrations of *Helen Oxenbury's ABC of Things* (1993).

Collage: Real objects of assorted textures and designs such as lace, birchbark, buttons, torn paper, and cotton used to construct an illustration

Ezra Jack Keats used collage to illustrate his landmark picture book *The Snowy Day* (1962), in which Peter, an African-American child, is first introduced.

Print making: Woodcuts, linoleum prints, block prints, lithography

Marcia Brown captures the flavor of an old folktale by using linocuts in *Dick Whittington and His Cat* (1950).

Photography: Black and white, color

Tana Hoban draws on photography to illustrate her many concept books. She uses black-and-white photos, as in *Push Pull, Empty Full* (1972) as well as color photos, as in *Color Everywhere* (1995).

Painting: Oils, acrylics, watercolors, gouache, tempera

In *The Rough-Face Girl* (1992) by Rafe Martin, illustrator David Shannon makes dramatic use of acrylics. Of course, the tools with which the artist applies the paint will affect its look. Tools as varied as brushes, air brushes, and sponges are used for applying paint.

Artists will generally design a picture in one predominant medium, drawing from other media for special effects. Occasionally, an artist will choose to combine media more liberally to achieve the desired effect. Brief explanations of the artist's techniques and materials have recently begun to be included on the publishing history page of children's picture books; at other times they appear at the end of illustrated books.

BOOK FORMAT

Children's books are more than text or text and pictures combined. Other parts of a book contribute to the final product we call a book. The *dust jacket* is a removable paper cover wrapped around the book; it serves as protection against soiling. It also attracts purchasers and readers as well as informs them about the book, its author, and its illustrator. The *covers* of a book are usually made of two boards, which make the book more durable and allow it to stand on a shelf. When no dust jacket is on a book, the front cover provides the reader with a first impression of the story. The *title,* an important part of the text—usually first seen by the reader on the dust jacket or front cover—combines with the illustrations of the dust jacket or cover to communicate the nature of the story to young readers who choose books primarily by title and cover. Many titles suggest the topic of the story and can assist readers in deciding whether to read the book. Other titles and covers may not offer as much information about the story. In such cases, some explanation by a teacher or librarian in the form of a booktalk may prove invaluable to young readers seeking just such a book.

The *endpapers* are the pages glued to the inside front and back boards of the cover, and the *flyleaf* is the page facing each endpaper. In many fine, well-illustrated books, the endpaper and flyleaf are used to provoke curiosity in the reader for what follows, to set a mood, or to evoke an affective response in preparation for the story. Often, those first colors and first decorative touches are the visual introduction to the story. When readers turn the flyleaf, they are further prepared by the artist for the story by viewing the title page. The *title page* tells the book's full title and subtitle, if there is one; the names of the author(s) and illustrator(s); and the name and location of the publisher. Occasionally, a book will include a *frontispiece,* an illustration facing the title page, which is intended to establish the tone and to entice the reader to begin the story.

On the reverse side of the title page, often referred to as the *verso* of the title page, is the *publishing history* of the book. On this page is the copyright notice, a legal right giving only the holder permission to produce and sell the work. Others who wish to reproduce the work in any way must request permission of the copyright holder. The copyright is indicated by the international symbol ©. This symbol is followed by the name of the person(s) holding the copyright and the date it takes effect, which is the year the book is first published. Later publications are also listed. The country in which the book was printed, the number assigned to the book by the Library of Congress, the International Standard Book Number (ISBN), and the edition of the book are also included on this page. Many publishers now include on this page cataloguing information for libraries, a very brief annotation of the story, and a statement on the media and techniques used in the illustrations.

The title page typically presents the *typeface,* the style of print to be used throughout the book. The size and legibility of the typeface must be suited to the book's intended audience. In children's books this can be extremely important. Books for the young child who is just learning to read should have large, well-spaced print for easy eye scanning. The print style for an easy-to-read book should be a somewhat larger-than-average standard block print with easily distinguishable and recognizable uppercase and lowercase letters. Many children's trade books are now being produced in "big book" size for beginning reading activities with a whole class or group of children. In this case, the print needs to be large enough to be readily seen from a distance of 10 to 12 feet minimum. Legibility is diminished when background colors are used behind the text, leaving insufficient contrast for easy reading.

The size, shape, and darkness of the print type may vary from book to book. The lines may be heavy and strong or light and willowy. The choice of print type should enhance the overall visual message of the illustrations and fit with the illustrations in style and mood. Note also that the placement of the print on the pages in relation to the illustrations can subtly guide the reader and become a functional part of the story.

Unusual print styles are sometimes selected for a children's book. In a book with a diary format, the use of script print gives the impression of handwriting. In this case, the amount of script print is usually brief, and standard block print is used throughout most of the book for greater ease of reading. In place of print some illustrators choose to hand-letter the text. Classic examples of lettering as part of the illustrative component of a book are found in *Millions of Cats* (1928) by Wanda Gág and *The Story of Babar* by Jean de Brunhoff (1933).

The *page layout* is also worth observing. You will notice that illustrations are variously placed one on a page, on facing pages, on alternating pages, or on parts of pages. When the picture extends across the two facing pages, it is called a *doublespread.* A doublespread gives the effect of motion, since the eye is drawn to the next page. It can also give a feeling of grandeur, openness, and expansiveness. Sometimes, a picture will begin on a right-hand page and spill over to the following page, the reverse side. This offers a strong sense of continuity from one part of the story to the next. Some pictures have a *frame.* Framing of a picture can work to distance the reader from the action, lend a sense of order to the story, or make the mood more formal. The frame itself may be anything from a simple line to a broad, ornately decorated ribbon of information. Decorations on a frame may repeat certain images or symbols to reinforce the meaning of the story.

Pages are another part of the book makeup. In evaluating the pages, you should ask yourself, What is the quality of the paper? Is it thick, high quality? Is it glossy or textured, white or colored? Are the pages square, rectangular, or shaped in the form of a concrete object? Are they in keeping with the rest of the book? Are unique or unusual page formats, such as half-pages, see-through pages, engineered pages, or partial pages, appropriate and logical?

The *size* of the book is also worth noting. Large picture books are well suited for reading aloud to a class. Smaller picture books are usually not satisfactory choices for read-alouds, unless, of course, you are reading to only one child or to a small group of children.

Next, consider the *book binding*. Books may be bound in hard cover, paperback, or in some special-purpose material. For example, books for babies are frequently bound in sturdy cardboard or vinyl to withstand the dual role of toy and book. When buying a hardcover book, determine whether the binding is glued or sewn. Look for the stitching. Sewn bindings last much longer than glued ones. Durability relative to cost is the usual trade-off you must weigh in selecting paper or hardcover bindings for classroom or school libraries. Generally speaking, the cost of hardcover books is justified when you expect fairly heavy use.

BALANCE AND VARIETY IN BOOK SELECTIONS

In addition to evaluating the various textual and visual elements that are central to the issue of quality, the child's age and development and the balance and variety among books are also important considerations. Because children in any elementary-grade class have a wide range of reading abilities and reading interests, you need to provide many different types of books, including picture books, easy-to-read books, short chapter books, longer books, and books of prose, poetry, fiction, and nonfiction. Selecting outstanding biographies for an entire year of reading aloud to a class would hardly offer students a range of literary experiences. Thus, balance among the *genres of literature* as well as *variety in topic* are essential. An overview of the genres, their relationships to one another, and topics found within the genres is displayed in Table 2.1. These genres can be used in making balanced choices for library and classroom reading collections and for choosing books to read aloud. The number of the chapter in which each genre of literature is discussed is noted next to the genre.

In sharing books with students the *mood* of the books must also be varied to include stories that are sad, humorous, silly, serious, reflective, boisterous, suspenseful, or even a little scary. A steady diet of light, humorous books might appeal to students at first, but eventually, the sameness will become boring. For a teacher to read aloud over many months works of literature with the same predominant emotion is to ignore the rapid change and growth in personal lives and choices that are the hallmark of youth.

Which stories teachers choose to read aloud to students is important, as Dressel (1990) found in her study on the effects of students' listening to literature of higher and lesser *quality*. Students were affected by the characteristics of the stories they heard and discussed. Varying choices for read-alouds will challenge students and enhance the resulting academic benefits for their language and cognitive development, as discussed in Chapter 1.

A balance between *male and female main characters* over the course of a year is necessary if you are to meet the needs of children of both sexes and to help members of each sex understand more fully the perspectives, problems, and feelings of members of the opposite sex. Classroom and school library collections need to have a wide range of topics with a balance of male and female main characters.

TABLE 2.1   Genres and Topics of Children's Literature

POETRY (3)	PLAYS (3)	PROSE					Nonfiction (9)
		Fiction					
		Fantasy		Realism			
		Traditional Literature (5)	Modern Fantasy (6)	Realistic Fiction (7)	Historical Fiction (8)		
Nursery rhymes Lyric poems Narrative poems	Original plays Adaptations	Myths Epics Legends and tall tales Folktales Fables Religious stories	Modern folktales Animal fantasy Personified toys and objects Unusual characters and situations Worlds of little people Supernatural events and mystery fantasy Historical fantasy Quest stories Science fiction and science fantasy	Families Peers Special challenges Cultural diversity Animals Sports Mysteries Romance and sexuality Rites of passage Adventure and survival	Era: Beginnings of civilization Era: Civilizations of the ancient world Era: Civilizations of the medieval world Era: Emergence of modern nations Era: Development of industrial society Era: World wars in the twentieth century Era: Post–World War II		Biographies Biological science Physical science Social science Applied science Humanities

In addition, understanding and empathy for people with disabilities can be gained through portrayals in books of children and adults with impairments. A positive image of people with disabilities needs to be conveyed in these books. Furthermore, children with disabilities need to see characters like themselves in books.

The representation of minorities as main characters is also essential if you are to present a realistic view of society and the world. Through well-written *multicultural literature,* children can see that someone from a different race, ethnic group, or religion has many of the same basic needs and feelings that they themselves have. Literature by and about people different from oneself can help to develop an understanding and appreciation for all peoples. Minority children will enjoy reading books in which children from backgrounds similar to their own play the leading, and sometimes, heroic roles. Characters with whom one can identify permit a deeper involvement in literature and at the same time help children to understand situations in their own lives.

International literature, literature from other nations and regions of the world, needs to be included in read-aloud choices and in classroom and library collections in order to guide students toward global understanding. Through reading or listening to the favorite books of children from other nations, your children will experience cultural literacy on a worldwide basis.

Classroom libraries are usually limited in scope; therefore, school libraries are necessary to provide adequate balance and variety of books for students' research needs and independent reading. Frequent visits to the library by the class and by individual students need to be arranged by the teacher and librarian.

REFERENCES

Aardema, V. (1975). *Why mosquitoes buzz in people's ears.* Illustrated by L. & D. Dillon. New York: Dial.

Avi. (1990). *The true confessions of Charlotte Doyle.* New York: Orchard.

———. (1991). *Nothing but the truth.* New York: Orchard.

Babbitt, N. (1975). *Tuck everlasting.* New York: Farrar.

Brown, M. (1950). *Dick Whittington and his cat.* New York: Scribner's.

Brown, M. W. (1947). *Goodnight moon.* Illustrated by C. Hurd. New York: Harper.

Brunhoff, J. de. (1933). *The story of Babar, the little elephant.* New York: Random House.

Cleary, B. (1981). *Ramona Quimby, age 8.* Illustrated by A. Tiegreen. New York: Morrow.

Crews, D. (1978). *Freight train.* New York: Greenwillow.

———. (1980). *Truck.* New York: Greenwillow.

Cushman, K. (1994). *Catherine, called Birdy.* New York: Clarion.

Dressel, J. H. (1990). The effects of listening to and discussing different qualities of children's literature on the narrative writing of fifth graders. *Research in the Teaching of English, 24*(4), 397–414.

Fleischman, P. (1993). *Bull Run.* New York: Harper-Collins.

Gág, W. (1928). *Millions of cats.* New York: Coward-McCann.

George, J. C. (1959). *My side of the mountain.* New York: Dutton.

———. (1972). *Julie of the wolves.* Illustrated by J. Schoenherr. New York: Harper.

Hall, D. (1979). *Ox-cart man.* Illustrated by B. Cooney. New York: Viking.

Hoban, R. (1970). *A bargain for Frances.* Illustrated by L. Hoban. New York: Harper.

Hoban, T. (1972). *Push pull, empty full.* New York: Macmillan.

———. (1995). *Color everywhere.* New York: Morrow.

Hunt, I. (1964). *Across five Aprils.* New York: Follett.

Janeczko, P. B. (Ed.). (2000). *Stone bench in an empty park.* Photos, H. Silberman. New York: Orchard.

Jennings, P. (1996). *Faith and the electric dogs.* New York: Scholastic.

Keats, E. J. (1962). *The snowy day.* New York: Viking.

Lawrence, I. (2000). *Ghost boy.* New York: Delacorte.

Lionni, L. (1967). *Frederick.* New York: Pantheon.

Lobel, A. (1970). *Frog and toad are friends.* New York: Harper.

Mah, A. Y. (1999). *Chinese Cinderella: The true story of an unwanted daughter.* New York: Delacorte.

Mallat, K., & McMillan, B. (1997). *The picture that Mom drew.* New York: Walker.

Martin, R. (1992). *The rough-face girl.* Illustrated by D. Shannon. New York: Putnam.

Mochizuki, K. (1995). *Heroes.* Illustrated by D. Lee. New York: Lee & Low.

More, H. (1961). A book. In W. Cole (Ed.), *Poems for seasons and celebrations.* Cleveland: World Publishing.

O'Dell, S. (1960). *Island of the blue dolphins.* Boston: Houghton.

Oxenbury, H. (1993). *ABC of things.* New York: Macmillan.

Paulsen, G. (1987). *Hatchet.* New York: Bradbury.

Raschka, C. (1993). *Yo? Yes!* New York: Orchard.

Reeder, C. (1989). *Shades of gray.* New York: Macmillan.

Richter, H. P. (1970). *Friedrich.* Translated by E. Kroll. New York: Holt.

Rosenblatt, L. M. (1985). The transactional theory of the literary work: Implications for research. In C. R. Cooper (Ed.), *Researching response to literature and the teaching of literature: Points of departure* (pp. 33–53). Norwood, NJ: Ablex.

Salisbury, G. (1994). *Under the red-blood sun.* New York: Delacorte.

Seuss, Dr. (1940). *Horton hatches the egg.* New York: Random.

———. (1957). *The cat in the hat.* New York: Random.

Siebert, D. (1989). *Heartland.* Illustrated by W. Minor. New York: Crowell.

Simont, M. (2001). *The stray dog.* New York: Harper-Collins.

Speare, E. G. (1973). *The sign of the beaver.* Boston: Houghton.

Spinelli, J. (1997). *Wringer.* New York: HarperCollins.

Steig, W. (1969). *Sylvester and the magic pebble.* New York: Simon & Schuster.

———. (1976). *The amazing bone.* New York: Farrar.

Steptoe, J. (1969). *Stevie.* New York: Harper.

Taylor, M. (1976). *Roll of thunder, hear my cry.* New York: Dial.

Veciana-Suarez, A. (2002). *Flight to freedom.* New York: Orchard.

Vincent, G. (1999). *A day, a dog.* Asheville, NC: Front Street.

White, E. B. (1952). *Charlotte's web.* Illustrated by G. Williams. New York: Harper.

Wiesner, D. (1991). *Tuesday.* New York: Clarion.

Williams, V. B. (1982). *A chair for my mother.* New York: Greenwillow.

II

CATEGORIES OF LITERATURE

In Part II we present a broad spectrum of the genres of literature for children as outlined in Table 2.1. From the outset we acknowledge that literary genres defy absolute definitions and that some find them oversimplified. Most books can be sorted in more than one way because the stories address more than one topic. For example, stories about peers are often about families, too. However, we believe that the organization by types and topics as found in Chapters 3–10 will prove to be convenient and helpful in locating books on many different topics for you and your students.

Special features in Part II deserve your attention. The Milestones features in Chapters 3–10 give you the history of the development of each genre at a glance. Excellent Books to Read Aloud lists found in Chapters 4–9 will help make your read-aloud experiences successful. The lists of Notable Authors and Illustrators found at the end of Chapters 3–10 will familiarize you with well-known creators of literature and will help you make good choices for author studies. The suggestions for ways to use literature across the curriculum found in the Using Literature across the Curriculum boxes in Chapters 5, 8, and 9 can be a springboard for many other original ideas of your own.

In this edition, as in past editions, we have updated the important Recommended Books section at the end of each genre chapter. Our overall goal has been to include the best books for children from the recent past as well as a number of classics and modern classics. Inevitably, some titles must be dropped from edition to edition, just as libraries periodically remove books from their shelves to make room for newer books. Please note that titles in the Recommended Books lists are organized by type, just as they are presented in the body of the chapter to make finding specific types of books easier for you. Even more good children's titles can be found in Appendices A, D, and E. Please note that we have integrated multicultural and international titles throughout this book, in addition to focusing on these books in Chapter 10.

3

POETRY
and
PLAYS

POETRY

What is Poetry? Who knows?
Not a rose, but the scent of the rose;
Not the sky, but the light in the sky;
Not the fly, but the gleam of the fly;
Not the sea, but the sound of the sea;
Not myself, but what makes me
See, hear, and feel something that prose
Cannot: and what it is, who knows?

—ELEANOR FARJEON

This chapter is presented in two sections. The first section focuses on poetry, information about poetry, and its uses in the classroom. The second section focuses on plays, information about plays, and their importance in a good language arts curriculum.

Poetry and plays represent two of the three major components of literature: prose, poetry, and plays. While poetry is an accepted, albeit underused, genre in the elementary classroom, the genre of plays is truly neglected. Because of their underuse and neglect we have chosen to discuss poetry and plays before other types of literature. We hope you will read and reread favorite poems to your students each day and bring plays and the theatre into your classroom on a regular basis.

SECTION ONE: *Poetry*

Poetry, in the form of nursery rhymes, is a natural beginning to literature for young children and an enjoyable literary form for all ages. In their earliest years, children acquire language and knowledge of the world around them through listening and observing. Poetry, primarily an oral form of literature that draws heavily on the auditory perceptions of the listeners, is ideally suited to children at this stage. Then, throughout the elementary and middle school years, poetry that relates to any and every subject can be found and shared orally during the school day, providing a flash of humor or a new perspective on the subject.

DEFINITION AND DESCRIPTION

Poetry is the expression of ideas and feelings through a rhythmical composition of imaginative and beautiful words selected for their sonorous effects. Originally, poetry was oral, and as various minstrels traversed the countryside, they recited poetry and sang songs to groups of listeners of all ages. The musicality of poetry makes it an especially suitable literary form for teachers to read aloud and, at times, to put to music.

Children often believe that rhyme is an essential ingredient of poetry; yet some types of poetry do not rhyme. What, then, distinguishes poetry from prose? The concentration of thought and feeling expressed in succinct, exact, and beautiful language, as well as an underlying pulse or rhythm are the traits that most strongly set poetry apart from prose.

Not all rhyming, rhythmical language merits the label of poetry. *Verse* is a language form in which simple thoughts or stories are told in rhyme with a distinct beat or meter. Mother Goose and nursery rhymes are good examples of well-known, simple verses for children. And, of course, we are all too aware of the *jingle,* a catchy repetition of sounds heard so often in commercials. The most important feature of verses and jingles is their strong rhyme and rhythm. Content is light or even silly. Although verses and jingles can be enjoyable and have a place in the classroom, poetry can enrich children's lives by giving them new insights and fresh views on life's experiences and by bringing forth strong emotional responses.

The term *poetry* is used in this chapter both to refer to a higher quality of language—a form of language that can evoke great depth of feeling and provoke new insights through imaginative and beautiful language—and to refer to favorite verses of childhood.

TYPES OF POETRY BOOKS

Poetry touches our minds and hearts through drawing on our five senses. Children, too, are reached by poetry, even though the subjects that move them may differ from those that move adults. A wide variety of poetry books is available today for use by students and teachers. Selecting books of poetry for use in the classroom as bridges between classroom activities, as materials for reading, and as literature for enjoyment will require teachers to review and evaluate the many types of poetry books: anthologies, Mother Goose and nursery rhyme books, nursery and folk songbooks, books of poems on special topics and by favorite poets, and single illustrated poems in picture book formats.

Mother Goose and Nursery Rhyme Books

Mother Goose and nursery rhyme books are heavily illustrated collections of traditional verse. *Tomie dePaola's Mother Goose,* collected and illustrated by Tomie dePaola, is a good example. Often, a familiar illustration is all a child needs to get her or him to recite one of these well-loved verses. Collected nursery rhymes first appeared in editions of Charles Perrault's *Tales of Mother Goose* in France in the early eighteenth century. These verses are now part of our children's literary heritage. Also, they have proven to be a wonderful introduction to the world of literature for young children. In societies in which countless allusions are made every day to the characters and situations found in nursery rhymes, knowledge of this literature is a mark of being culturally literate.

Because so many of these verses exist, the better collections include large numbers of them thoughtfully organized around themes or topics; they are indexed by titles or first lines. A favorite book of this kind is *The Book of Nursery and Mother Goose Rhymes,* collected and illustrated by Marguerite de Angeli. Some lesser-known traditional verses were collected and illustrated by Arnold Lobel in *The Random House Book of Mother Goose.*

Nursery and Folk Songbooks

Nursery and folk songbooks are heavily illustrated collections of both traditional and modern verses and their musical notation. *Songs from Mother Goose,* compiled by Nancy Larrick and illustrated by Robin Spowart, is a good example. Melody further emphasizes the innate musicality of these verses and turns some verses into games ("Ring around the Roses") and others into lullabies ("Rock-a-bye Baby"). In choosing a songbook, teachers, librarians, and parents should ascertain that there is a good selection of songs and that the music is well arranged for young voices and playable. Those who plan to work with preschoolers and first- and second-graders will be wise to make these songs part of their repertoire.

Anthologies of Poetry

A large, comprehensive *anthology* of poetry for children is a must in every classroom. Anthologies should be organized by subject for easy retrieval of poems appropriate for almost any occasion. In addition, indices of poets and titles, or first lines, are usually provided in these texts. Works by contemporary and traditional poets can be found in most of these anthologies; they appeal to a wide age range, providing nursery rhymes for toddlers as well as longer, narrative poems for the middle-grade student. An example is *A New Treasury of Children's Poetry: Old Favorites and New Discoveries,* selected by Joanna Cole.

Specialized Poetry Books

Specialized poetry books are also readily available in which the poems are all by one poet, on one topic, for one age group, or of one poetic form. These specialized collections become necessary adjuncts for a teacher and class who come to love certain kinds of poetry or specific poets. Beautifully illustrated collections are also available and seem to be especially enjoyed by children for independent reading of poetry. Examples include *Mathematickles* by Betsy Franco and *Doodle Soup* by John Ciardi.

Single Illustrated Poems

Single narrative poems of medium length are presented more frequently in picture book formats. These editions make poetry more appealing and accessible to many children, but in some cases the illustrations may remove the opportunity for children to form their own mental images from the language created by poets. The poetry section of your school library is worth perusing for interesting poetry books to use in the classroom.

E L E M E N T S   O F   P O E T R Y

Just as with a work of fiction, the elements of a poem should be considered if the reader is to understand and evaluate the poem. Each of these parts—meaning, rhythm, sound patterns, figurative language, and sense imagery—is discussed in the following list.

- *Meaning.* Meaning is the underlying idea, feeling, or mood expressed through the poem. As with other literary forms, poetry is a form of communication; it is the way a poet chooses to express emotions and thoughts. Thus, the meaning of the poem is the expressed or implied message the poet conveys.
- *Rhythm.* Rhythm is the beat or regular cadence of the poem. Poetry, usually an oral form of literature, relies on rhythm to help communicate meaning. A fast rhythm is effected through short lines, clipped syllables, sharp, high vowel sounds, such as the sounds represented by the letters *a, e,* and *i,* and abrupt consonant sounds, such as the sounds represented by the letters *k, t, w,* and *p.* A fast rhythm can provide the listener with a feeling of happiness, excitement, drama, and even tension and suspense. A slow rhythm is effected by longer lines, multisyllabic words, full or low vowel sounds such as the sounds represented by the letters *o* and *u,* and resonating consonant sounds such as the sounds represented by the letters *m, n,* and *r.* A slow rhythm can evoke languor, tranquility, inevitability, and harmony, among other feelings. A change in rhythm during a poem signals the listener to a change in meaning.

In the poems that follow, "Song for a Blue Roadster" exhibits a fast rhythm that evokes the rapid speed of an automobile; "Slowly" proceeds more slowly in communicating the calm and quiet of summer.

S O N G   F O R   A   B L U E   R O A D S T E R

Fly, roadster, fly!
The sun is high,
Gold are the fields
We hurry by,
Green are the woods
As we slide through
Past harbor and headland,
Blue on blue.

Fly, Roadster, fly!
The hay smells sweet,
And the flowers are fringing
Each village street,

Where carts are blue
And barns are red,
And the road unwinds
Like a twist of thread.

Fly, Roadster, fly!
Leave Time behind;
Out of sight
Shall be out of mind.
Shine and shadow
Blue sea, green bough,
Nothing is real
But Here and Now.

—RACHEL FIELD

S L O W L Y

Slowly the tide creeps up the sand,
Slowly the shadows cross the land.
Slowly the cart-horse pulls his mile,
Slowly the old man mounts the stile.

Slowly the hands move round the clock,
Slowly the dew dries on the dock.
Slow is the snail—but slowest of all
The green moss spreads on the old brick wall.

—JAMES REEVES

- *Sound Patterns.* Sound patterns are made by repeated sounds and combinations of sounds in the words. Words, phrases, or lines are sometimes repeated in their entirety. Also, parts of words may be repeated, as with rhyme, the sound device that children most recognize and enjoy. *Rhyme* occurs when the ends of words (the last vowel sound and any consonant sound that may follow it) have the same sounds. Examples of rhyming words are *vat, rat, that, brat,* and *flat,* as well as *hay, they, flay, stray,* and *obey. Assonance* is another pattern poets use for effect. In this case, the same vowel sound is heard repeatedly within a line or a few lines of poetry. Assonance is exemplified in these words: *hoop, gloom, moon, moot,* and *boots. Alliteration* is a pattern in which initial consonant sounds are heard frequently within a few lines of poetry. Examples are *ship, shy,* and *shape. Consonance* is similar to alliteration but usually refers to a close juxtaposition of similar final consonant sounds, as in fla*k*e, chu*ck,* and stro*k*e. *Onomatopoeia* is the device in which the sound of the word imitates the real-world sound. Examples are *buzz* for the sound of a bee and *hiss* for the sound a snake makes.
- *Figurative Language.* Figurative language takes many different forms, but it involves comparing or contrasting one object, idea, or feeling with another one. A *simile* is a direct comparison, typically using *like* or *as* to point out the similarities. A *metaphor* is an implied comparison without a signal word to evoke the similarities. *Personification* is the attribution of human qualities to animate, nonhuman beings or to inanimate objects for the purpose of drawing a comparison between

the animal or object and human beings. *Hyperbole* is an exaggeration to highlight reality or to point out ridiculousness. Children often delight in hyperbole because it appeals to their strong sense of the absurd.

- *Sense Imagery.* A poet will play on one or more of the five senses in descriptive and narrative language. *Sight* may be awakened through the depiction of beauty; *hearing* may be evoked by the sounds of a city street; *smell* and *taste* may be recalled through the description of a fish left too long in the sun; and finally, *touch* can be sensitized through describing the gritty discomfort of a wet swimsuit caked with sand from the beach. After listening to a poem, children can be asked to think about which of the senses the poet is appealing to.

These elements of poetry may be considered to select varied types of poems and to group them for presentation. However, little is gained by teaching each of these elements as a separate item to be memorized and/or analyzed. Poetic analysis has caused many students to dislike poetry. On the other hand, students whose teachers love poetry, select it wisely, read it aloud well, and share it often and in many enjoyable ways will come to appreciate poetry.

EVALUATION AND SELECTION OF POETRY

The criteria to keep in mind in evaluating a poem for use with children are as follows:

- The ideas and feelings expressed are worthy, fresh, and imaginative.
- The expression of the ideas and feelings is unique, often causing the reader to perceive ordinary things in new ways.
- The poem is appropriate to the experiences of children and does not preach to them.
- The poem presents the world through a child's perspective and focuses on children's lives and activities as well as on activities to which people of all ages can relate.
- A poem that panders to children's base instincts is probably best avoided and replaced by other enjoyable, worthy choices.
- Poetry collections should be judged on the quality of the poetry choices first and illustrations and the appearance of the book second. Beautiful illustrations do not ensure a good collection of poems within the covers.
- Children report a preference for narrative poems. You will want to share narrative poems regularly.
- Although certain poets may be favored by your students, they will also enjoy the poetry of many other writers. Thus, be sure to share with your students poems by a variety of authors.

In selecting poems to read to students, the list of notable poets at the end of this chapter, the Golden Age poets listed on page 51, and the list of poets who have won the National Council of Teachers of English (NCTE) Award are good starting points. The NCTE Award was established in 1977 in the United States to honor living U.S. poets whose poetry has contributed substantially to the lives of children. This award is given to a poet for the entire body of writing for children ages 3 through 13 and is now given every three years. In addition, a recent reference book, *Young Adult Poetry: A Survey and Theme Guide* (Schwedt & DeLong, 2002), can be a useful tool for students and teachers in upper elementary and middle grades for locating poems to support the curriculum and to address student interests. This bibliography annotates 198 poetry books and identifies themes in more than 6,000 poems.

NCTE EXCELLENCE IN POETRY FOR CHILDREN AWARD WINNERS

1977	David McCord	1988	Arnold Adoff
1978	Aileen Fisher	1991	Valerie Worth
1979	Karla Kuskin	1994	Barbara Juster Esbensen
1980	Myra Cohn Livingston	1997	Eloise Greenfield
1981	Eve Merriam	2000	X. J. Kennedy
1982	John Ciardi	2003	Mary Ann Hoberman
1985	Lilian Moore		

Although more poetry for children is being written and published and many teachers and their students are enjoying this genre of literature, some teachers report that they do not share poetry because of their uncertainty about selecting poems for their students. By learning about students' preferences in poetry and some of the best-loved poems and most respected poets, a teacher can become more skillful at selecting good and enjoyable poems for students. The next section will review research on children's preferences in poetry.

Children's Poetry Preferences

The findings from two surveys of children's poetry preferences can be helpful to teachers in selecting poems for a new group of students. Fisher and Natarella (1982) surveyed primary-grade children and their teachers, and Terry (1974) studied intermediate-grade children. The two age groups were similar, although not identical, in their preferences.

- Both age groups preferred narrative poems over lyric poems.
- Limericks were the favored poetic form of both age groups; free verse and haiku were not well liked by either age group.
- Children of both age groups preferred poems that had pronounced sound patterns of all kinds, but especially enjoyed poems that rhymed.
- Rhythm was also an important element to students of both age groups; they preferred poems with regular, distinctive rhythm.
- Children of both age groups liked humorous poems, poems about animals, and poems about enjoyable familiar experiences.
- The subjects most preferred by primary-grade children were strange and fantastic events, animals, and other children; the older children preferred the realistic contents of humor, enjoyable familiar experiences, and animals.
- Children in both age groups often found figurative language in poetry confusing.

A study by Kutiper and Wilson (1993) was conducted to determine whether an examination of school library circulation records would confirm the findings of the earlier poetry preference studies. The findings of this library circulation study indicated that the humorous contemporary poetry of Shel Silverstein and Jack Prelutsky dominated the students' choices. The collections of poetry written by the

NCTE award winners did not circulate widely; nor were they widely available in the school libraries studied, even though these poets reflect a higher quality of language and usage than is found in the light verse so popular with students. Kutiper and Wilson stated that real interest in poetry must go beyond Prelutsky and Silverstein. This interest needs to be developed by teachers who provide an array of poetry that builds on students' natural interests.

Children's appreciation of poetry can be broadened and deepened by a good teacher, but you may be wise to proceed with caution on less-liked aspects of poetry until your students become fans of poetry. Thus, a good selection of rhyming, narrative poems with distinct rhythms about humorous events, well-liked familiar experiences, and animals is a good starting point for students who have little experience with poetry.

HISTORICAL OVERVIEW OF POETRY

Poetry for children began centuries ago in the form of nursery rhymes that were recited to babies and toddlers by caregivers. These verses were passed along via the oral tradition. The earliest published collection of nursery rhymes that survives today is *Tommy Thumb's Pretty Song Book* (1744), which is housed in the British Museum (Gillespie, 1970). This songbook contains familiar rhymes such as "Hickory Dickory Dock" and "Mary Mary Quite Contrary." These rhymes and others like them came to be called *Mother Goose rhymes,* but the term *Mother Goose* was first used in France by Charles Perrault in his *Stories and Tales of Past Times with Morals; or, Tales of Mother Goose* (1697) to refer to his collection of fairy tales. Later editions contained nursery rhymes, which became so popular that Mother Goose became a general name for nursery rhymes. For many, nursery rhymes and other poems were the first forms of literature experienced; these poems symbolize the reassuring sounds of childhood.

Poems of a moral and religious bent were shared with obvious didactic intent, reflecting the strict attitude toward the rearing of children that held sway in the Western world from the Middle Ages to the late nineteenth century. Fear of death and punishment was instilled as a means of gaining obedience to authority. Ann and Jane Taylor's *Original Poems, for Infant Minds, by Several Young Persons* (1804) provided verse of this kind. Some titles of poems from this early collection are "The Idle Boy," "Greedy Richard," "Meddlesome Matty," and "The Church-Yard."

Poetry for children flourished from the middle of the nineteenth century through the 1920s, a period that can be considered the Golden Age of Poetry for Children. Page 51 lists the poets, countries, landmark works and dates, and characteristics. The Golden Age of Poetry moved away from moralistic poetry and instead provided children with poems describing the beauty of life and nature, with poems of humor, nonsense, and word fun, and with imaginative poems that interpreted life from the child's perspective. Much of the Golden Age poetry retains its appeal for today's children; for example, *A Child's Garden of Verses* (1885) by Robert Louis Stevenson remains a favorite collection of poems among parents and children. This positive shift in poetry for children set the standard for poetry for the remainder of the twentieth century.

In the 1960s and 1970s, the general trend toward realism in children's literature was also reflected in poetry. More topics considered suitable for the child audience resulted in protest poetry, poems about girls in nontraditional roles, and irreverent poems. For example, parents, teachers, and other adults became fair game for ridicule and mockery. Minority poets were more frequently published, and their poetry gained in popularity.

M I L E S T O N E S

in POETRY during the GOLDEN AGE

DATE	POET	LANDMARK WORK	COUNTRY	CHARACTERISTIC
1846	Edward Lear	*A Book of Nonsense*	England	Father of nonsense poetry, limericks
1864	Lewis Carroll	"Jabberwocky"	England	Nonsense verses, such as those in *Alice's Adventures in Wonderland*
1872	Christina Rossetti	*Sing Song*	England	Poems on children and the small things around them
1885	Robert Louis Stevenson	*A Child's Garden of Verses*	England	Descriptive poems of childhood memories
1888	Ernest Thayer	"Casey at the Bat"	U.S.A.	Famous ballad on baseball
1890	Laura E. Richards	*In My Nursery*	U.S.A.	Poems with hilarious situations, wordplay, and strong rhythm
1896	Eugene Field	*Poems of Childhood*	U.S.A.	Poems reflecting on children and child life
1902	Walter de la Mare	*Songs of Childhood*	England	Musical and imaginative poetry
1920	Rose Fyleman	*Fairies and Chimneys*	England	Imaginative poems about fairies
1922	A. A. Milne	*When We Were Very Young*	England	Poems of fun in which the child's world is observed
1926	Rachel Field	*Taxis and Toadstools*	U.S.A.	Poems about city and country through the child's eyes

Popularity of poetry in the classroom began in the 1980s and continues to the present day. Developments in the publishing industry attest to this popularity. For example, Boyds Mills Press has a division devoted to children's poetry, called Windsong. Publishers continue to present both single poems and collections of poems in beautifully illustrated book formats. In the 1980s, Nancy Willard's *A Visit to William Blake's Inn: Poems for Innocent and Experienced Travelers* and Paul Fleischman's *Joyful Noise: Poems for Two Voices* received Newbery Medals, indicating greater recognition of poetry for young people in the United States. In 1994, the Japanese poet Michio Mado was awarded the international Hans Christian Andersen Medal, an honor seldom bestowed on a poet. An increase in the publication of anthologies of poems by and about minorities, such as *Pass It On,* edited by Wade Hudson, has also been noted in the 1990s. This increased publication has also resulted in greater attention to earlier African American poets, such as Paul Laurence Dunbar, Countee Cullen, and Langston Hughes.

POETRY TYPES AND FORMS

Poetry can be classified in many ways; one way is to consider two main types that generally differ in purpose: lyric and narrative poetry. *Lyric poetry* captures a moment, a feeling, or a scene, and is descriptive in nature, whereas *narrative poetry* tells a story or includes a sequence of events. From this definition, you will recognize the following selection to be a lyric poem.

GIRAFFES

Stilted creatures,
Features fashioned as a joke,
Boned and buckled,
Finger painted,
They stand in the field
On long-pronged legs
As if thrust there.
They airily feed,
Slightly swaying,
Like hammer-headed flowers.

Bizarre they are,
Built silent and high,
Ornaments against the sky.
Ears like leaves
To hear the silken
Brushing of the clouds.

— S y   K a h n

The next selection is an example of a narrative poem:

THE BROKEN-LEGG'D MAN

I saw the other day when I went shopping in the store
A man I hadn't ever ever seen in there before,
A man whose leg was broken and who leaned upon a crutch—
I asked him very kindly if it hurt him very much.
"Not at all!" said the broken-legg'd man.

I ran around behind him for I thought that I would see
The broken leg all bandaged up and bent back at the knee;
But I didn't see the leg at all, there wasn't any there,
So I asked him very kindly if he had it hid somewhere.
"Not at all!" said the broken-legg'd man.

"Then where," I asked him, "is it? Did a tiger bite it off?
Or did you get your foot wet when you had a nasty cough?
Did someone jump down on your leg when it was very new?
Or did you simply cut it off because you wanted to?"
"Not at all!" said the broken-legg'd man.

"What was it then?" I asked the man, and this is what he said:
"I crossed a busy crossing when the traffic light was red;
A big black car came whizzing by and knocked me off my feet."
"Of course you looked both ways," I said, "before you crossed the street."
"Not at all!" said the broken-legg'd man.

"They rushed me to a hospital right quickly," he went on,
"And when I woke in nice white sheets I saw my leg was gone;
That's why you see me walking now on nothing but a crutch."
"I'm glad," said I, "you told me, and I thank you very much!"
"Not at all!" said the broken-legg'd man.

— J O H N   M A C K E Y   S H A W

Poetry can also be categorized by its *poetic form,* which refers to the way the poem is structured or put together. *Couplets, tercets, quatrains,* and *cinquains* refer to the number (two, three, four, and five) of lines of poetry in a stanza—a set of lines of poetry grouped together. Couplets, tercets, quatrains, and cinquains usually rhyme, though the rhyme scheme may vary; these poetic forms may constitute an entire poem, or a poem may be comprised of a few stanzas of couplets, tercets, and so on. "Higglety, Pigglety, Pop!" is an example of the cinquain poetic form found in a traditional nursery rhyme.

H I G G L E T Y ,   P I G G L E T Y ,   P O P

Higglety, pigglety, pop!
The dog has eaten the mop.
The pig's in a hurry,
The cat's in a flurry,
Higglety, pigglety, pop!

— T R A D I T I O N A L

Other specific poetic forms frequently found in children's poetry are limericks, ballads, haiku, free verse, and concrete poetry.

A limerick is a humorous, one-stanza, five-line verse form (usually a narrative), in which lines 1, 2, and 5 rhyme and are of the same length and lines 3 and 4 rhyme and are of the same length but shorter than the other lines. The following is an example of a limerick by Edward Lear, the poet who popularized this poetic form in the nineteenth century.

T H E R E   W A S   A N   O L D   P E R S O N   W H O S E   H A B I T S

There was an old person whose habits
Induced him to feed upon rabbits;
When he'd eaten eighteen,
He turned perfectly green,
Upon which he relinquished those habits.

— E D W A R D   L E A R

A *ballad* is a fairly long narrative poem of popular origin, usually adapted to singing. These traditional story poems are often romantic or heroic. "The Outlandish Knight," a thirteen-stanza ballad, tells the tale of the clever young woman who tricks the man who deceived her.

THE OUTLANDISH KNIGHT

An outlandish knight came out of the North,
  To woo a maiden fair;
He promised to take her to the North lands,
  Her father's only heir.

"Come, fetch me some of your father's gold,
  And some of your mother's fee;
And two of the best nags out of the stable,
  Where they stand thirty and three."

She fetched him some of her father's gold
  And some of her mother's fee;
And two of the best nags out of the stable,
  Where they stood thirty and three.

He mounted her on her milk-white steed,
  He on the dapple grey;
They rode till they came unto the sea-side,
  Three hours before it was day.

"Light off, light off thy milk-white steed,
  And deliver it unto me;
Six pretty maids have I drowned here,
  And thou the seventh shall be."

"Pull off, pull off thy silken gown,
  And deliver it unto me;
Methinks it looks too rich and too gay
  To rot in the salt sea."

"Pull off, pull off thy silken stays,
  And deliver them unto me;
Methinks they are too fine and gay
  To rot in the salt sea."

"Pull off, pull off the Holland smock
  And deliver it unto me;
Methinks it looks too rich and gay
  To rot in the salt sea."

"If I must pull off my Holland smock,
  Pray turn thy back unto me,
For it is not fitting that such a ruffian
  A woman unclad should see."

He turned his back towards her,
  And viewed the leaves so green;
She catch'd him round the middle so small,
  And tumbled him into the stream.

He dropped high, and he dropped low,
  Until he came to the tide—
"Catch hold of my hand, my pretty maiden,
  And I will make you my bride."

"Lie there, lie there, you false-hearted man,
  Lie there instead of me;
Six pretty maidens have you drowned here,
  And the seventh has drowned thee."

She mounted on her milk-white steed,
  And led the dapple grey.
She rode til she came to her father's hall,
  Three hours before it was day.

— T R A D I T I O N A L

Haiku is a lyric, unrhymed poem of Japanese origin with seventeen syllables, arranged on three lines with a syllable count of five, seven, and five. Haiku is highly evocative poetry that frequently espouses harmony with and appreciation of nature. Here is an example.

Small bird, forgive me.
I'll hear the end of your song
in some other world.

— A N O N Y M O U S   (T R A N S L A T E D   B Y   H A R R Y   B E H N)

Free verse is unrhymed poetry with little or light rhythm. Sometimes words within a line will rhyme. The subjects of free verse are often abstract and philosophical; they are always reflective.

A U T U M N   L E A V E S

gather in gutters,
pile on walks,
tumble
        from the tips
of toes,
crunching
fall hellos
to back-to-school feet.

— R E B E C C A   K A I   D O T L I C H

Concrete poetry is written and printed in a shape that signifies the subject of the poem. Concrete poems are a form of poetry that must be seen as well as heard to be fully appreciated. These poems do not usually have rhyme or definite rhythm; they rely mostly on the words, their meanings and shapes, and the way the words are arranged on the page to evoke images. In "Concrete Cat" you will note through the position of the word that the mouse appears to have met with an accident.

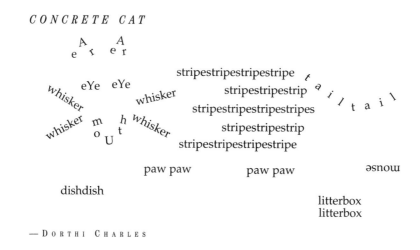

— D O R T H I   C H A R L E S

POETRY IN THE CLASSROOM

Poetry is enjoyable for students of all ages. It enhances students' development of literacy. Teachers and librarians can entice students into a lifelong love for poetry through making available a well-balanced collection of poetry books and through providing many experiences with poetry.

Students' Listening to and Saying Poems

Teachers and librarians can begin by providing even very young students with many opportunities to hear and say poems. Later, when students have developed a love of poetry and an affinity for the language play in poems, students can read poetry by fine poets and poems by their classmates and can begin to write poems themselves. In other words, poetry needs to be shared in both oral and written forms.

Poetry should be introduced first and often to children in an oral form. As discussed earlier, poetry was in its origins an oral form of literature; it still relies heavily on the auditory perceptions of listeners. Moreover, children's oral language is the basis for their later acquisition of literacy. These two facts combine nicely to make listening to poems and saying poems a natural early introduction to literature for children. Some teachers report that they do not share poetry with their students because of their uncertainty about how to read it aloud. By practicing the poems ahead of time and by reading poetry frequently, a teacher can overcome this reluctance. The rewards to both students and teachers are worth the effort. The next section offers suggestions to help you become an effective reader of poetry.

READING POETRY ALOUD TO CHILDREN   Poetry should be read aloud to students on a daily basis. Brief, positive encounters with one to three poems at a time are best. Too many poems in one sitting may overwhelm students or make the reading tedious. Introduce the poem to the class before reading it aloud, either by tying the poem in with something else or by briefly telling why you chose to read this poem aloud. Then state the title of the poem and begin to read. After reading the poem, be sure to announce the name of the poet so that students discover the writers they especially enjoy. In addition, the following points will help you to read poetry well:

- Keep in mind that poetry should be read for its meaning. Stress the meaning elements of the poem just as you do when reading prose. The pauses must be determined by the meaning units of the poem, not by the end of the lines.

- A reader should not overemphasize the beat of the poem. Doing so results in an annoying singsong effect. Let the poetic language provide the rhythm.

- Poetry should be enunciated clearly. Each sound and each syllable of a poem are important and must be heard to be appreciated. You may need to slow down your normal reading pace to give full value to each sound.

- Poetry needs to be performed and dramatized. Take some chances and try out different effects (using different voices, elongating words, singing, shouting, whispering, pausing dramatically, and so on) as you read poems aloud. Your voice is a powerful tool: You may change it from louder to softer to only a whisper; you may start at a deep, low pitch and rise to a medium and eventually high pitch; you may speak very quickly in a clipped fashion and then slow down and drawl out the words. Sara Holbrook's *Wham! It's a Poetry Jam: Discovering Performance Poetry* (2002) offers good suggestions for performing poetry and even for running a poetry contest.

- Some poems may need to be read aloud a number of times for the meaning to be fully understood by listeners. Also, favorite poems can be enjoyed again and again, as teachers and students savor one more reading.

- Consider recording audiotapes of poems for the listening center and making them available along with the poem in print, on a chart or in a book, for the student to listen to and read. Commercially made tapes with popular poets reading their works, accompanied by music, are available and are quite popular with children. Some teachers have asked parents to peruse a poetry anthology, select a favorite poem, and then read the poem on tape for use in the listening center.

- After reading a poem aloud, some form of response is usually enjoyed. Some poems warrant discussion, and students can take the opportunity to tell how the poem made them feel or what it made them think about.

CHORAL POETRY   A time-honored technique for providing opportunities to say and hear poems over and over again is given by choral poetry. *Choral poetry* consists of interpreting and saying a poem together as a group activity. These poems may either be practiced and recited aloud or rehearsed and read aloud. Students enjoy this way of experiencing poetry because they have a participatory role in the activity. Most poetry, intended to be listened to, is suitable for choral presentation. The following sections explain how to select choral poems and teach them to students.

1. *Selection*

   At first, select a short poem (from one to four stanzas) until your students develop some skill in memorizing, reciting, and performing poems. Humorous narrative poems are good first choices. Later, you will want to experiment with longer poems.

2. *Memorization*

   For most choral presentations, the first step is for the teacher to select and read aloud a poem that is well liked by the students. Then each line or pair of lines is said by the teacher and repeated by the students until they know them. It is preferable for the students to repeat the lines after the teacher and for the teacher to avoid reciting with the class, so that the students will commit the poem to memory instead of waiting for the teacher's voice. Once the entire poem is learned in this way, variations can be added for performing the poem. Although students need to rehearse a poem to intone it similarly, some longer poems with older students who read well will not be memorized but will be practiced and read together as a group.

3. *Arrangements*

Options for reading a poem chorally include unison, two- or three-part, solo voices, cumulative buildup, and simultaneous voices, as is now explained.

- In unison choral speaking, the students learn the poem and recite it together as a group. Two-part or three-part choral poetry is usually based on arranging students into voice types (for example, high, medium, and low) to achieve different effects and by selecting lines of the poem for each group to recite or read.

- Solo voices can be added to either of these presentations and are sometimes used for asking a question or making an exclamation.

- Some poems lend themselves to cumulative buildup presentations. A cumulative buildup is effected by having, for example, only two voices say the first line, then two more join in on the second, and then two more, gradually building to a crescendo until the entire class says the last line or stanza.

- Poems can be presented by simultaneous recitation, which forms a presentation similar to a musical round. In this case, group one begins the poem and recites it all the way through. When group one begins the third line, for example, then group two starts the first line, and the two groups recite simultaneously until the end. Other groups can, of course, be added.

- Poetry selected and arranged for dramatic choral readings on a particular theme infuses an interesting variation into choral poetry. Paul Fleischman's *Joyful Noise: Poems for Two Voices* and *I Am Phoenix: Poems for Two Voices* are collections of poetry written in a manner that is already suitable for choral reading. These collections were written to be read aloud by two readers at once, one reading the left half of the page and one reading the right half, as well as certain lines simultaneously. Pairs of students may each take a different poem from the collection for presentation.

Many other variations can be developed for use in choral presentations. Let imagination be your guide. Words and lines can be spun into ghostly moans, or barked, or sung, or repeated. Choreography adds visual impact, as do simple props. As soon as children learn that poems do not have to be read sedately through exactly as written, they will begin to find excitement and deeper meaning in poetry.

4. *Performance*

Incorporating action, gestures, body movements, and finger plays can produce more interesting and enjoyable presentations. Occasionally performing a well-honed choral poem for an audience can bring pride to young performers. Remember, the best audiences are close by—the class next door, the principal, the librarian, the custodian, or a visiting parent.

In addition to the group activity of performing choral poetry, teachers can encourage an individual student to learn a poem by heart, voluntarily, and then to recite the poem in a small group or as part of a group performance, perhaps around a theme. For example, a small group of interested students might each select a poem about weather as part of their study about weather in science. Jane Yolen's collection of weather poems, *Weather Report,* could be a resource for this activity.

Students' Reading and Writing Poems

LEARNING TO READ POETRY   Children enjoy reading poetry silently and aloud to others. The classroom library corner should have one or two comprehensive poetry anthologies for students to browse through for general purposes. In addition, two or three specialized collections by a single poet, such as *A Pocketful of Poems* by Nikki Grimes, and another two or three books of poems on a single topic, such as *Around the World in Eighty Poems,* edited by James Berry, are needed as well. Students can be encouraged to make copies of their favorite poems from these various collections to develop personal, individual anthologies. Many students choose to illustrate these and arrange the poems in new and inventive ways. Rotating the poetry books occasionally over the course of the school year will spark renewed interest in reading poetry.

Other activities to encourage the reading of poetry by students follow:

- Place students in pairs to take turns reading favorite poems to one another. Make videotapes or audiotapes of these readings and permit students to listen to or watch their own and other students' readings of poetry.
- Ask each student to select three poems by one poet (for example, a Golden Age poet or an NCTE poet) and find something out about the poet; then place students in small groups of five or six to tell briefly about the poet and read the three poems aloud. Paul B. Janeczko's *The Place My Words Are Looking For: What Poets Say about and through Their Work* (1990) is an excellent resource for this purpose.
- Have students find three poems on the same topic, such as trees, mice, or friendship; then read them aloud in small groups.
- Encourage students to find poems that are of the same poetic form—cinquains, limericks, and so forth; or that exhibit similar poetic elements—rhyme, alliteration, or onomatopoeia; or that have fast or slow rhythms. These poems can then comprise the poems for reading aloud that day or week.

LEARNING TO WRITE POETRY   A rich poetry environment stimulates children's interest in writing their own poems. Children need to be very familiar with poetry of many kinds and by many poets before they should be expected to compose poems. The collection of poems *Inner Chimes: Poems on Poetry* (1992) may be a natural starting place for helping students to think about poetry and what it is. Poems by various renowned children's poets writing about creating poetry have been selected by Bobbye S. Goldstein for this volume. Other books that provide suggestions on how to include poetry in the classroom are *Sunrises and Songs: Reading and Writing Poetry in an Elementary Classroom* (1990) by Amy McClure, Peggy Harrison, and Sheryl Reed and *How to Write a Poem* (1996) by Margaret Ryan.

Teachers often start the writing of poetry as a collaborative effort. The class brainstorms for ideas, then composes the poem orally as the teacher writes it on the board or on chart paper. As students become comfortable with writing group poetry, they can branch off and begin composing poems in pairs or their own individual poems.

Children should be reminded that poetry is a form of communication and that they should think of an idea, feeling, or event to write about in their poems. They should be reminded that poetry does not have to rhyme and that they may write about something of interest to them. Children's poetry follows no absolute rules; perfection of form should not be a goal. Other suggestions to foster poetry writing include the following:

- Have students compile personal and class anthologies of their own poems or their favorite poems.
- Design bulletin boards with poetry displays of students' own poems as well as copies of poems by favorite poets. Students may also design posters, individually or in groups, to illustrate a favorite poem. Posters are then displayed around the school for a few weeks.
- Encourage students to model the works of professional poets by attempting imitation of a whole poem or of specific techniques.
- Read aloud many poems of one poetic form; then analyze the form with the students to reveal the characteristics of its structure. Quatrains, cinquains, haiku, concrete poems, and limericks can all be used as models with students once they have an appreciation for poetry and for the specific poetic form.

Some poets have suggested other models and patterns for students to follow in writing poetry. Kenneth Koch's *Rose, Where Did You Get That Red?* (1990) and *Wishes, Lies, and Dreams* (1999); M. K. Glover's *A Garden of Poets: Poetry Writing in the Elementary Classroom* (1999); Lee Bennett Hopkins's *Pass the Poetry, Please!* (1987); Myra Cohn Livingston's *Poem Making: Ways to Begin Writing Poetry* (1991); Paul Janeczko's *How to Write Poetry* (1999); and Paul Janeczko's *Poetry from A to Z: A Guide for Young Writers* (1994) are useful resources for teachers who want to encourage students to compose poems.

Do	Don't
Read poetry aloud every day	Limit poetry choices to one or two poets or types of poems
Practice reading a poem before reading it aloud for the first time to students	Read poems in a singsong style
Choose poetry the students will like	Choose all poems from one anthology
Make a variety of excellent poetry anthologies and specialized poetry books available in the classroom	Have poetry marathon days or weeks to make up for not sharing poetry regularly
Encourage students to recite and write poems	Force students to memorize and recite poems
Direct choral poetry presentations	Make the analysis of poetry the focus of poetry study
Feature a notable poet each month	Have students copy poems for handwriting practice
Begin and end each day with a poem	Make the main emphasis of poetry be the writing of formula poems

SECTION TWO: *Plays*

Plays should be included in a well-balanced literary curriculum for children. Children, when allowed to play freely, often dramatize their daily lives and fantasies. In playacting, children can act out in ways not normally allowed, giving expression to hidden feelings. Children's linguistic abilities can improve if they become actively engaged in the literature of the theatre by reading plays, performing plays, and watching others perform plays. And, of course, children delight in plays and playacting.

The use of the same word, *play,* for the main, natural activity of childhood is not a coincidence. The development and use of the imagination in the child's creation of play and in the creation of theatre are similar. The same human needs are met. In a play and in a child's own play, imagination transforms reality and endows ordinary objects with fantastic qualities. Imagination also helps the actor create a character for the enjoyment of the audience (Davis, 1981). The persons who long ago performed plays for the enjoyment of audiences were called players long before they were called actors.

Plays provide many of the same personal benefits to young readers as prose. Students enjoy reading plays and are able to experience a story vicariously quite readily through the play form. Plays can also help students develop their imaginations and ability to empathize with others (Smolkin, 1995). In addition, reading plays aloud and performing plays are natural ways to develop and demonstrate a child's oral reading fluency—the ability to read smoothly without hesitation and with good comprehension—a reading goal many teachers have for their students. McKean (2000–2001) offers practical acting tips for teachers and students to develop excellent oral reading interpretations. Plays provide a natural reason to develop these traits and put oral reading to use in a purposeful way.

DEFINITION AND DESCRIPTION

*P*lays, as a literary genre, refers to written, dramatic compositions or scripts intended to be acted. A play may be divided into parts called *acts;* in turn, each act may be divided into *scenes.* The script usually has set, costume, and stage directions noted, as well as dialogue provided for each actor.

Plays are usually published in *playbooks* or *acting editions,* 4 × 8 paperback books, by publishers who specialize in plays. These playbooks are quite inexpensive and can be purchased directly from the publishers or ordered through bookstores. A teacher or school may purchase a set of playbooks for children's use in group reading situations. Generally, if the plays are for classroom use, no royalty need be paid. If they are being used in a school but for an audience beyond the classroom, there is usually a moderate royalty fee as indicated in the publisher's catalog.

Some other terms are worth clarifying:

- *Readers' theatre* is the oral presentation of literature by actors, and usually a narrator, reading from a script; it is a form of play reading, a dramatic reading that depends largely on voice and gestures to convey additional meaning. Generally no stage sets, costumes, or stage movements are involved in readers' theatre.
- *Creative drama* is informal drama that lends itself to the reenactment of story experiences. This form of drama is spontaneously generated by the participants who compose and act out their parts as the drama progresses. Generally no scripts are developed or lines read or memorized. Creative drama is a process-centered form of drama performed for the benefit of the participants.

- *Recreational drama* is a formal theatrical presentation where the development and experience of the performers is as important as the enjoyment by the audience. School and camp plays are examples of recreational drama.
- *Children's theatre,* sometimes referred to as theatre for young audiences, is a formal theatrical experience in which a play is presented for an audience of children. Usually the performers are skilled actors, and the production is overseen by trained directors (Goldberg, 1974).

In this chapter we address published plays found in books and magazines as a literary genre—that is, as material to be read by children, either independently or in small groups. Some of these same plays also may be performed in children's theatres. We recommend that teachers and librarians emphasize the informal reading of plays by children during the elementary school years. Recreational plays and formal play productions are better left to middle school or older students. The dramatic processes of creative drama and readers' theatre, discussed in Chapter 12, are also suitable for elementary grade students.

E V A L U A T I O N   A N D   S E L E C T I O N   O F   P L A Y S

A good play has a subject that appeals to children, an interesting character or two, and a problem that thickens or worsens, but gets resolved satisfactorily in the end. Humor always appeals to children, and conflict between characters is needed for interest and drama. Dialogue must be natural and reflect the personality of the character speaking. One or more of the characters in the play must have child appeal; typically such a character is a child or a childlike figure; a personified animal, doll, or other creature; or an adult with magical traits. Many published plays are planned for more elaborate productions than time will permit in the classroom. Such details can be interesting for children to read about, even if they are not likely to be able to produce the play as suggested.

Children's plays in the United States have been viewed as the stepchild both in the field of theatre and in the field of children's literature. Although some writers have given substantial attention to the development of play scripts for children, their work has not always been as highly valued by theatre producers and critics as that of playwrights who write for adults. Locating and selecting plays can be a challenge.

Children's Book and Play Review, a professional journal that appears five times a year, provides reviews of ten or twelve children's plays in each issue and has feature articles occasionally about the publication status of children's plays. (See Appendix B for subscription information.) Other review journals, such as *School Library Journal, Booklist,* and *Horn Book* Magazine, occasionally review published plays as well. The International Association of Theatre for Children and Young People periodically publishes international bibliographies of plays organized by country and provides a synopsis of each play, as well as its length, type, number of characters, languages in which it is available, and source for ordering (Oaks, 1996).

Anthologies are a good source of plays for children's reading enjoyment. One publisher, Smith and Kraus, Inc., has many play anthologies available on a variety of topics, such as holidays, cultural diversity, and mythology. Some recent anthologies from Smith and Kraus have been included in the Recommended Books of Plays at the end of this chapter.

At the present time eighteen to twenty publishing houses handle children's plays. Eleven publishers have specialized in plays for children and deserve special mention here:

Anchorage Press Plays, P.O. Box 2901, Louisville, KY 40201–2901, formerly Children's Theatre Press, one of the oldest publishing houses for children's plays, remains a major publisher of children's plays with a backlist of approximately 290 plays for children.

Baker's Plays, P.O. Box 699222, Quincy, MA 02269, is a general play publisher with a specialization in children's plays with both a backlist and recent titles. The current list has approximately 110 plays.

Contemporary Drama Service, 885 Elkton Drive, Colorado Springs, CO 80907, publishes plays for middle school and high school students, has approximately 500 plays, and publishes 25 new plays each year.

Dramatic Publishing Company, 311 Washington Street, Woodstock, IL 60098, has a large list of approximately 180 children's and young adults' plays.

Eldredge Publishing, P.O. Box 1595, Venice, FL 34284, is one of the oldest children's play publishers with a large list of approximately 600 plays and publishes 30 or more new plays each year.

I. E. Clark, Inc., Box 246, Schulenberg, TX 78956, is a general publisher with over 60 children's plays including some bilingual plays.

New Plays, Inc., New Plays for Children, P.O. Box 5074, Charlottesville, VA 22905, is a publisher that specializes in children's plays with 100 titles available, many for the middle school level.

Pioneer Drama Service, P.O. Box 4267, Englewood, CO 80155, is a general publisher of plays with more than 130 plays for children.

Samuel French, Inc., 45 W. 25th St., New York, NY 10010, is a large general publisher of plays with a large backlist of children's plays, but is publishing few new children's plays currently.

Smith and Kraus, Inc. c/o IDS, 300 Bedford Street, Building B, Suite 213, Manchester, NH 03101, is a publisher of plays and play anthologies for children.

Sterling Partners, P. O. Box 600160, Newton, MA 02460, is a general publisher that publishes 50–60 royalty-free new plays for children each year in the moderately priced magazine, *Plays, the Drama Magazine for Young People.* Anthologies drawn from these plays are also available.

The American Alliance for Theatre and Education (AATE) gives two awards that are useful in identifying notable children's plays and playwrights. The Distinguished Play Award, established in 1983, is given annually to honor the playwright and publisher of the works voted as the best original plays for young people published during the preceding year in category A, for upper and secondary school age audiences, and category B, for elementary and middle school age audiences. Beginning in 1997 category C was added for the best adaptation. (See Appendix A for the complete list of winners.) The Charlotte B. Chorpenning Playwright Award, first conferred in 1967, honors a body of work by a children's playwright. The award is given annually, if merited.

CHARLOTTE B. CHORPENNING PLAYWRIGHT AWARD WINNERS

1967	Aurand Harris	1981–1984	No award
1968	Martha Bennett King	1985	Aurand Harris
1969	Marian Johnson	1986	Virginia Glasgow Koste
1970	Madge Miller	1987–1988	No award
1971	Joanna Halpert Kraus	1989	Brian Kral
1972	Ed Graczxk	1990–1993	No award
1973	Alan Cullen	1994	James Still
1974	Rosemary Musil	1995	Max Bush
1975	Helen P. Avery	1996–1998	No award
1976	Joseph Robinette	1999	Sandra Fenichel Asher
1977	Flora B. Atkin	2000–2001	No award
1978	Suzan L. Zeder	2002	Y York
1979	Jonathan Levy	2003	Laurie Brooks
1980	Moses Goldberg		

HISTORICAL OVERVIEW OF PLAYS

Plays were seldom written exclusively for children prior to the twentieth century, yet for centuries plays were written and performed for a general audience that included children. Church dramas also have a long tradition that can be traced back to the Middle Ages when the Catholic Church used such plays as a means of educating. Examples of plays appealing to children but intended for a general audience are *Gulliver's Travels, Huckleberry Finn,* and Shaw's *Androcles and the Lion,* among others. J. M. Barrie's *Peter Pan,* the most widely acknowledged classic of the genre of plays for children, has had great appeal to children during its long history of production beginning in 1904.

The main stimulus for writing plays has been the development and existence of children's theatres and theatre groups that have a need for material. Children's theatre in the United States has generally been independent of the adult professional theatre, is community based with substantial contributions by amateurs, has suffered from limited budgets, and yet has tenaciously survived. Programs by theatres specializing in productions for young people began in the early twentieth century when the influential, though short-lived, Children's Educational Theatre was founded in 1903 in New York.

Following the establishment of theatres for children, a small number of plays and collections of plays for children began to be written and published. Small children's theatres gradually arose in many communities.

With the spread of children's theatre groups there was an increase in the number of published scripts; for example, as early as 1921, *A Treasury of Plays for Children* by Montrose J. Moses appeared. An early children's playwright of exceptional note was Charlotte B. Chorpenning (1872–1955), who published with Anchorage Press Plays. She was artistic director of the Goodman Children's Theatre of the Art Institute of Chicago from 1931 until her death and wrote many plays for its use. Her contributions to juvenile dramatic literature were outstanding for both the quality and quantity of her work. Her observations of children's interests at each age level are still useful to playwrights (McCaslin, 1971).

During the 1960s and 1970s professional theatre companies for young audiences began to appear. They encountered an extremely limited body of children's plays suitable to their needs. This lack was the major stimulus for a rapid increase in children's play publishing (Oaks, 1997). An outstanding children's playwright who wrote during this period was Aurand Harris, a playwright of children's plays from 1945 to the time of his death in 1996. He left behind a rich legacy of published plays that include original works as well as adaptations of folktales and modern literature. He is particularly noted for exploring different styles for children's theatre, including a vaudevillian show (*The Toby Show*), a melodrama (*Rags to Riches*), and even a serious drama that treats the topic of death (*The Arkansaw Bear*). He remained for many years the most produced children's playwright in the United States. He was the first winner of the Charlotte B. Chorpenning Award and the only playwright to win it twice, in 1967 and in 1985. Other children's playwrights who have been honored for a number of their children's plays include James Still, Edward Mast, and Suzan L. Zeder.

TYPES OF PLAYS

Traditionally, plays are categorized within types such as drama, comedy, farce, melodrama, and tragedy. Dramas and comedies are the most common play types found in children's plays. Some children's theatres produce *participation plays*, sometimes referred to as interactive theatre. A participation play is the presentation of a drama with an established story line constructed to involve structured opportunities for active involvement by the audience.

In children's plays the distinction between adaptations and original plays is important. Many adaptations of traditional literature, generally folktales, fables, and Bible stories, have been made and are readily available from most of the children's play publishers. Adaptations of modern children's literature, such as Mary Hoffman's *Amazing Grace* and Maurice Sendak's *Where the Wild Things Are,* are being published with increasing frequency.

Original plays, that is, stories originating in play form, represent fewer than one third of the new plays published annually. According to Sather (1976), children indicate a preference for plays with stories never heard before. Perhaps in response to this, the publication of children's plays is growing rapidly. It has increased substantially from ten or twelve a year in the early 1960s to more than 200 a year at the beginning of the twenty-first century.

The natural play of children and the theatre are "manifestations of the same human need to make concrete the intangible, to make explicable the inexplicable, to make accessible the incomprehensible, and to make memorable the significant" (Davis, 1981, p. 14). Plays help children come to terms with the unknown and the threatening and help to heighten their appreciation of the actual and the enjoyment of the human comedy. Make plays a vital part of your literary curriculum.

REFERENCES

Charles, D. (1982). Concrete cat. In X. J. Kennedy & D. M. Kennedy (Eds.), *Knock at a star.* Illustrated by K. A. Weinhaus. Boston: Little, Brown.

Davis, D. (1981). *Theater for young people.* New York: Beaufort.

Dotlich, R. K. (2003). Autumn leaves. In R. K. Dotlich (Ed.), *In the spin of things: Poetry of motion.* Illustrated by Karen Dugan. Honesdale, PA: Boyds Mills.

Farjeon, Eleanor. (1983). Poetry. In J. Prelutsky (Ed.), *The Random House Book of Poetry for Children.* Illustrated by Arnold Lobel. New York: Random House.

Field, Rachel. (1957). Song for a Blue Roadster. In H. Ferris (Ed.), *Favorite Poems, Old and New.* Illustrated by Leonard Weisgard. New York: Doubleday.

Fisher, C. J., & Natarella, M. A. (1982). Young children's preferences in poetry: A national survey of first, second and third graders. *Research in the Teaching of English, 16*(4), 339–354.

Gillespie, M. C. (1970). *Literature for children: History and trends.* Dubuque, IA: Wm. C. Brown.

Glover, M. K. (1999). *A garden of poets: Poetry writing in the elementary classroom.* Urbana, IL: National Council of Teachers of English.

Goldberg, M. (1974). *Children's theatre: A philosophy and a method.* Englewood Cliffs, NJ: Prentice-Hall.

Holbrook, S. (2002). *Wham! It's a poetry jam: Discovering performance poetry.* Honesdale, PA: Boyds Mills.

Hopkins, L. B. (1987). *Pass the poetry please!* New York: Harper & Row.

Janeczko, P. B., Selector. (1990) *The place my words are looking for: What poets say about and through their work.* New York: Bradbury.

———. (1994). *Poetry from A to Z: A guide for young writers.* New York: Bradbury.

———. (1999). *How to write poetry.* New York: Scholastic.

Kahn, S. (1967). Giraffes. In S. Dunning, E. Lueders, & H. Smith (Eds.), *Reflections on a gift of watermelon pickle.* New York: Lothrop, Lee and Shepard.

Koch, K. (1990). *Rose, where did you get that red?* New York: Random.

———. (1999). (1970). *Wishes, lies and dreams: Teaching children to write poetry.* New York: Random.

Kutiper, K., and P. Wilson. (1993). Updating poetry preferences: A look at the poetry children really like. *The Reading Teacher, 47*(1), 28–35.

Lear, E. (1946). *The complete nonsense book.* New York: Dodd, Mead.

Livingston, M. C. (1991). *Poem making: Ways to begin writing poetry.* New York: HarperCollins.

McCaslin, N. (1971). *Theatre for children in the United States.* Norman: University of Oklahoma Press.

McClure, A., P. Harrison, & S. Reed. (1990). *Sunrises and songs: Reading and writing poetry in an elementary classroom.* Portsmouth, NH: Heinemann.

McKean, B. (2000–2001). Speak the speech, I pray you! Preparing to read aloud dramatically. *The Reading Teacher, 54*(4), 358–360.

Moses, M. J. (Ed.). (1921). *A treasury of plays for children.* Boston: Little, Brown.

Oaks, H. (Ed.). (1996). *Outstanding plays for young audiences: International bibliography,* vol. 5. Seattle, WA: United States Center for the International Association of Theatre for Children and Young People.

———. (1997). Collections of plays for young audiences. *Children's Book and Play Review, 17*(4), 1–3.

Reeves, J. (1963). Slowly. In E. Blishen (Ed.), *Oxford book of poetry for children.* Illustrated by B. Wildsmith. Oxford: Oxford University Press.

Ryan, M. (1996). *How to write a poem.* New York: Watts.

Sather, S. P. (1976). A critical assessment of children's plays. *Children's Theatre Review, 25*(1), 2–5.

Schwedt, R., and J. DeLong. (2002). *Young adult poetry: A survey and theme guide.* Westport, CT: Greenwood.

Shaw, J. M. (1967). The broken-legg'd man. In J. M. Shaw (Ed.), *The things I want: Poems for two children.* Tallahassee, FL: Florida State University Library.

Small bird. (1971). In H. Behn (Ed. and Trans.), *More cricket songs.* San Diego: Harcourt.

Smolkin, L. B. (1995). The literature of the theatre and aesthetic response: Welcoming plays into the world of children's literature. *The New Advocate, 8*(2), 109–123.

Terry, A. C. (1974). *Children's poetry preferences: A national survey of upper elementary grades.* Urbana, IL: National Council of Teachers of English.

NOTABLE *POETS AND PLAYWRIGHTS*

Arnold Adoff, recipient of the National Council of Teachers of English (NCTE) Award for Excellence in Poetry for Children. Many poems about relating to people across racial groups. *All the Colors of the Race.*

Sandra Fenichel Asher, a playwright whose plays focus on the real life struggles of young adults. *Things Are Seldom What They Seem; A Woman Called Truth.*

Max Fatchen, Australian poet noted for his poems about children's thoughts and activities. *The Country Mail Is Coming: Poems from Down Under.*

Aileen Fisher, an NCTE award-winning poet whose poems express a closeness to nature and all its inhabitants. *Going Barefoot.*

Paul Fleischman, winner of the Newbery Medal for his *Joyful Noise: Poems for Two Voices* in which the poems are composed and printed for two readers to read lines in unison and solo.

Moses Goldberg, playwright noted for his participation plays for very young audiences. *Puss in Boots: A Participation Play; Aladdin: A Participation Play.*

Eloise Greenfield, recipient of the NCTE Award for Excellence in Poetry and an African-American poet noted for poems of courage and love. *Under the Sunday Tree.*

Nikki Grimes, African-American award-winning poet whose poetry celebrates children, their friendships and families. *Meet Danitra Brown; A Pocketful of Poems.*

Aurand Harris, prolific children's playwright and author of *Androcles and the Lion,* a play performed more than 9,000 times. *The Arkansaw Bear; The Prince and the Pauper; Rags to Riches.*

Mary Ann Hoberman, 2003 recipient of the NCTE Award for Excellence in Poetry, is known for her humorous, colorful poetry. *Fathers, Mothers, Sisters, Brothers: A Collection of Family Poems.*

Paul B. Janeczko, contemporary poet and anthologist of poetry that especially appeals to young adults. *Dirty Laundry Pile: Poems in Different Voices; A Poke in the I: A Collection of Concrete Poems.*

X. J. Kennedy, a favorite creator of nonsense and humorous verse about contemporary themes. *Fresh Brats.*

Dennis Lee, popular Canadian poet known for humorous poetry. *Alligator Pie.*

Naomi Shihab Nye, a poet and anthologist whose meditative poems offer global perspectives and whose edited collections include Mexican, Native American, and Middle Eastern poetry. *This Same Sky: A Collection of Poems from Around the World; 19 Varieties of Gazelle: Poems of the Middle East.*

Shel Silverstein, popular contemporary children's poet who creates nonsense and humorous poetry. *Where the Sidewalk Ends.*

James Still, award-winning playwright noted for his highly original fantasy play, *In the Suicide Mountains,* and for cross-generational plays. *And Then They Came for Me: Remembering the World of Anne Frank; Amber Waves.*

David Wood, noted British playwright for children who has developed screenplays and musical plays from children's literature. *Babe, the Sheep-Pig; The Gingerbread Man.*

Suzan L. Zeder, experimental playwright who has written contemporary plays and musicals for a multigenerational audience. *Step on a Crack; Mother Hicks; The Taste of Sunrise.*

RECOMMENDED POETRY BOOKS

Because poetry is usually of interest to a broad age group, entries of poetry books indicate age only for books mainly suitable for young adults. These books are marked YA.

Mother Goose and Nursery Rhyme Books

Arenson, Roberta. *One, Two, Skip a Few! First Number Rhymes.* Illustrated. Barefoot, 1998.

Cook, Scott. *Mother Goose.* Knopf, 1994.

Crews, Nina. *The Neighborhood Mother Goose.* Greenwillow, 2004. Illustrated with photographs in a city setting.

de Angeli, Marguerite. *Marguerite de Angeli's Book of Nursery and Mother Goose Rhymes.* Doubleday, 1954.

dePaola, Tomie, compiler. *Tomie dePaola's Mother Goose.* Putnam, 1985.

Engelbreit, Mary. *Mary Engelbreit's Mother Goose.* HarperCollins, 2004. Illustrated.

Foreman, Michael. *Michael Foreman's Mother Goose.* Candlewick, 1991.

————. *Michael Foreman's Playtime Rhymes.* Candlewick, 2002. Includes activities and motions to accompany rhymes.

Lobel, Arnold, selector. *The Random House Book of Mother Goose.* Random, 1986.

Moses, Will. *Will Moses' Mother Goose.* Philomel, 2003.

Opie, Iona, editor. *Here Comes Mother Goose.* Illustrated by Rosemary Wells. Candlewick, 1999.

Petersham, Maud, and Miska Petersham. *The Rooster Crows: A Book of American Rhymes and Jingles.* Macmillan, 1945.

Rojankovsky, Feodor. *The Tall Book of Mother Goose.* Harper, 1942.

Sutherland, Zena. *The Orchard Book of Nursery Rhymes.* Illustrated by Faith Jaques. Orchard, 1990.

Zemach, Margot, compiler. *Some from the Moon, Some from the Sun: Poems and Songs for Everyone.* Farrar, 2001.

Nursery and Folk Songbooks

Eddleman, David, editor. *The Great Children's Songbook.* Illustrated by Andrew J. Dowty. Carl Fischer, 1998.

Fox, Dan, editor. *Go In and Out the Window: An Illustrated Songbook for Young People.* Holt/Metropolitan Museum of Art, 1987.

Guthrie, Woody. *This Land Is Your Land.* Illustrated by Kathy Jakobsen. Little, 1998.

Higgensen, Vy, selector. *This Is My Song!: A Collection of Gospel Music for the Family.* Illustrated by Brenda Joysmith. Crown, 1995.

Hinojosa, Tish. *Cada Niño/Every Child: A Bilingual Songbook for Kids.* Illustrated by Lucia Angela Perez. Cinco Puntos, 2002.

Krull, Kathleen, editor. *Gonna Sing My Head Off! American Folk Songs for Children.* Illustrated by Allen Garns. Knopf, 1992.

Larrick, Nancy, compiler. *Songs from Mother Goose: With the Traditional Melody for Each.* Illustrated by Robin Spowart. Harper, 1989.

Orozco, José-Luis. *De Colores and Other Latin-American Folk Songs for Children.* Illustrated by Elisa Kleven. Dutton, 1994.

Anthologies of Poetry

Cole, Joanna, compiler. *A New Treasury of Children's Poetry: Old Favorites and New Discoveries.* Illustrated by Judith Gwyn Brown. Doubleday, 1984.

de Regniers, Beatrice Schenk, Eva Moore, Mary Michaels White, and Jean Carr. *Sing a Song of Popcorn: Every Child's Book of Poems.* Scholastic, 1988.

Ferris, Helen, compiler. *Favorite Poems Old and New.* Illustrated by Leonard Weisgard. Doubleday, 1957.

Hall, Donald, editor. *The Oxford Illustrated Book of American Children's Poems.* Oxford University, 1999.

Harrison, Michael, and Christopher Stuart-Clark, editors. *The Oxford Treasury of Classic Poems.* Oxford, 1996. Ages 11–YA.

Hopkins, Lee Bennett, editor. *Climb into My Lap: First Poems to Read Together.* Illustrated by Kathryn Brown. Simon & Schuster, 2000.

————. *My America: A Poetry Atlas of the United States.* Simon & Schuster, 2000.

Kennedy, X. J., and Dorothy Kennedy, editors. *Knock at a Star: A Child's Introduction to Poetry,* Rev. Ed. Illustrated by Karen Lee Baher. Little, Brown, 1999.

Nye, Naomi Shihab, editor. *What Have You Lost?* Illustrated. Greenwillow, 1999.

Prelutsky, Jack, editor. *The Random House Book of Poetry for Children.* Illustrated by Arnold Lobel. Random House, 1983.

————, editor. *The 20th Century Children's Poetry Treasury.* Illustrated by Meilo So. Knopf, 1999.

Rosenberg, Liz, editor. *The Invisible Ladder: An Anthology of Contemporary American Poems for Young Readers.* Holt, 1996. Ages 11–YA.

————. *Earth-Shattering Poems.* Holt, 1997. Both books with commentary by poets and ideas for writing.

Specialized Poetry Books

Adoff, Arnold. *All the Colors of the Race.* Illustrated by John Steptoe. Lothrop, 1982.

————. *Touch the Poem.* Illustrated by Lisa Desimini. Scholastic, 2000.

Alarcon, Francisco X. *From the Bellybutton of the Moon and Other Summer Poems: Del ombligo de la luna y otros poemas de verano.* Illustrated by Maya Christina Gonzalez. Children's Book Press, 1998.

————. *Laughing Tomatoes: And Other Spring Poems.* Illustrated by Maya Christina Gonzalez. Children's Book Press, 1997. Bilingual, Spanish-English.

Appelt, Kathi. *Poems from Homeroom: A Writer's Place to Start.* Holt, 2002. Ages 12–YA. Includes a bibliography of adult books on writing poems and stories.

Ashman, Linda. *The Essential Worldwide Monster Guide.* Illustrated by David Small. Simon & Schuster, 2003.

Berry, James, editor. *Around the World in Eighty Poems.* Illustrated by Katherine Lucas. Chronicle, 2002. Fifty countries represented and many narrative poems.

Carlson, Lori M., editor. *Cool Salsa: Bilingual Poems on Growing Up Latino in the United States.* Holt, 1994. Age: YA.

Ciardi, John. *Doodle Soup.* Illustrated by Merle Nacht. Houghton, 1985.

————. *You Read to Me, I'll Read to You.* Illustrated by Edward Gorey. Lippincott, 1962.

Clinton, Catherine, *I, Too, Sing America: Three Centuries of African-American Poetry.* Illustrated by Stephen Alcorn. Houghton, 1998.

————, editor. *A Poem of Her Own: Voices of American Women Yesterday and Today.* Illustrated by Stephen Alcorn. Abrams, 2003. Ages 10–YA.

Cullen, Countee. *The Lost Zoo.* Illustrated by Brian Pinkney. Silver Burdett, 1991 (1969).

Cullinan, Bernice E., editor. *A Jar of Tiny Stars: Poems by NCTE Award–Winning Poets.* Boyds Mills, 1995.

Dunbar, Paul Laurence. *Jump Back, Honey: The Poems of Paul Laurence Dunbar.* Hyperion, 1999.

Fatchen, Max. *The Country Mail Is Coming: Poems from Down Under.* Little, Brown, 1990.

Fisher, Aileen. *Out in the Dark and the Daylight.* Harper, 1980.

Fleischman, Paul. *Big Talk: Poems for Four Voices.* Illustrated by Beppe Giacobbe. Candlewick, 2000. Ages 9–14.

————. *I Am Phoenix: Poems for Two Voices.* Illustrated by Eric Beddows. Harper, 1985.

————. *Joyful Noise: Poems for Two Voices.* Illustrated by Eric Beddows. Harper, 1988.

Florian, Douglas. *Lizards, Frogs, and Polliwogs: Poems and Paintings.* Harcourt, 2001.

————. *Mammalabilia.* Illustrated. Harcourt, 2000.

————. *Winter Eyes.* Illustrated. Greenwillow, 1999.

Franco, Betsy. *Mathematickles.* Illustrated by Steven Salerno. Simon & Schuster, 2003.

George, Kristine O'Connell. *The Great Frog Race and Other Poems.* Illustrated by Kate Kiesler. Clarion, 1997.

————. *Little Dog Poems.* Illustrated by June Otani. Clarion, 1999.

————. *Old Elm Speaks: Tree Poems.* Illustrated by Kate Kiesler. Clarion, 1998.

————. *Toasting Marshmallows: Camping Poems.* Illustrated by Kate Kiesler. Clarion, 2001.

Glaser, Isabel Joshlin, editor. *Dreams of Glory: Poems Starring Girls.* Simon & Schuster, 1995.

Goldstein, Bobbye S., editor. *Inner Chimes: Poems on Poetry.* Illustrated by Jane Breskin Zalben. Wordsong/Boyds Mills, 1992.

Gordon, Ruth, editor. *Pierced by a Ray of Sun: Poems about the Times We Feel Alone.* HarperCollins, 1995. Ages 12–YA.

Greenberg, Jan. *Heart to Heart: New Poems Inspired by Twentieth Century American Art.* Abrams, 2001. Ages 11–YA.

Greenfield, Eloise. *Honey, I Love, and Other Love Poems.* Illustrated by Diane and Leo Dillon. Crowell, 1978.

Grimes, Nikki. *It's Raining Laughter.* Photos by Myles C. Pinkney. Dial, 1997.

———. *Meet Danitra Brown.* Illustrated by Floyd Cooper. Morrow, 1994.

———. *My Man Blue.* Illustrated by Jerome Lagarrigue. Dial, 1999.

———. *A Pocketful of Poems.* Illustrated by Javaka Steptoe. Clarion, 2001.

———. *Stepping Out with Grandma Mac.* Orchard, 2001.

Harrison, David L. *Somebody Catch My Homework.* Illustrated by Betsy Lewin. Boyds Mills, 1993.

Hoberman, Mary Ann. *Fathers, Mothers, Sisters, Brothers: A Collection of Family Poems.* Illustrated by Marylin Hafner. Little, 1991.

———, editor. *My Song Is Beautiful: Poems and Pictures in Many Voices.* Little, 1994.

Holbrook, Sara. *By Definition: Poems of Feelings.* Illustrated by Scott Mattern. Boyds Mills, 2003.

Holman, Felice, compiler. *Side by Side: Poems to Read Together.* Illustrated by Hilary Knight. Simon & Schuster, 1988.

Hopkins, Lee Bennett, editor. *April Bubbles Chocolate: An ABC of Poetry.* Illustrated by Barry Root. Simon & Schuster, 1994.

———, compiler. *Hand in Hand: An American History through Poetry.* Illustrated by Peter M. Fiore. Simon & Schuster, 1994.

———, selector. *Opening Days: Sports Poems.* Illustrated by Scott Medlock. Harcourt, 1996.

Hudson, Wade, editor. *Pass It On: African American Poetry for Children.* Illustrated by Floyd Cooper. Scholastic, 1993.

Hughes, Langston. *The Dream Keeper and Other Poems.* Illustrated by Brian Pinkney. Knopf, 1994 (1932).

In Daddy's Arms I Am Tall: African Americans Celebrating Fathers. Illustrated by Javaka Steptoe. Lee & Low, 1997.

James, Simon, editor. *Days Like This: A Collection of Small Poems.* Illustrated. Candlewick, 2000.

Janeczko, Paul B., editor. *Dirty Laundry Pile: Poems in Different Voices.* Illustrated by Melissa Sweet. HarperCollins, 2001.

———, editor. *Looking for Your Name: A Collection of Contemporary Poems.* Orchard, 1993. Ages: YA.

———. *Poetry from A to Z: A Guide for Young Writers.* Bradbury, 1994.

———, editor. *A Poke in the I: A Collection of Concrete Poems.* Illustrated by Chris Raschka. Candlewick, 2000.

———. *A Rumpus of Rhymes: A Book of Noisy Poems.* Illustrated by Susan Estelle Kwas. Dutton, 2001.

———, editor. *Stone Bench in an Empty Park.* Photographs by Henri Silberman. Orchard, 2000. Haiku poetry.

———. *We, the People.* Illustrated by Nina Crews. Greenwillow, 2000. First-person poems focused on U.S. history; could be used as dramatic monologues.

Katz, Susan. *Mrs. Brown on Exhibit: And Other Museum Poems.* Illustrated by R. W. Alley. Simon & Schuster, 2002. Includes a list of "amazing museums" around the United States.

Kennedy, X. J. *Brats.* Illustrated by James Watts. Atheneum, 1986.

———. *Fresh Brats.* Illustrated by James Watts. Macmillan, 1990.

Kurtz, Jane. *River Friendly, River Wild.* Illustrated by Neil Brennan. Simon & Schuster, 2000.

Kuskin, Karla. *Dogs & Dragons, Trees & Dreams: A Collection of Poems.* Harper, 1980.

Larrick, Nancy, compiler. *Cats Are Cats.* Illustrated by Ed Young. Philomel, 1988.

Lear, Edward. *The Complete Nonsense Book.* Dodd, 1946.

Lee, Dennis. *Garbage Delight.* Illustrated by Frank Newfeld. Houghton, 1978.

Lewis, J. Patrick. *Doodle Dandies: Poems That Take Shape.* Illustrated by Lisa Desimini. Simon & Schuster, 1998.

———. *Freedom Like Sunlight: Praisesongs for Black Americans.* Creative Editions, 2000.

Lillegard, Dee. *Wake up House! Rooms Full of Poems.* Illustrated by Don Carter. Knopf, 2000.

Liu, Siyu, and Orel Protopopescu. *A Thousand Poems: Poems from China.* Illustrated by Siyu Liu. Pacific View Press, 2001. Ages 10–YA.

Mado, Michio. *The Magic Pocket.* Illustrated by Mitsumasa Anno. Translated from Japanese by The Empress Michiko of Japan. Simon & Schuster, 1998.

Mak, Kam. *My Chinatown.* Illustrated by Kam Mak. HarperCollins, 2002.

McCord, David. *One at a Time: Collected Poems for the Young.* Illustrated by Henry B. Kane. Little, 1977.

Merriam, Eve. *The Inner City Mother Goose.* Illustrated by David Diaz. Simon & Schuster, 1996 (1969). Ages 14–YA.

Myers, Walter Dean. *Harlem.* Illustrated by Christopher Myers. Scholastic, 1997. Ages 11–YA.

Nye, Naomi Shihab. *Come with Me: Poems for a Journey.* Illustrated by Dan Yaccarino. Greenwillow, 2000.

———, editor *19 Varieties of Gazelle: Poems of the Middle East.* HarperCollins, 2002. Ages 11–YA.

———, editor. *The Space Between Our Footsteps: Poems and Paintings from the Middle East.* Simon & Schuster, 1998.

———, editor. *This Same Sky: A Collection of Poems from around the World.* Four Winds, 1992. Ages: YA.

Nye, Naomi, and Paul B. Janeczko, editors. *I Feel a Little Jumpy around You: A Book of Her Poems and His Poems Collected in Pairs.* Simon & Schuster, 1996. Ages 12–YA.

O'Neill, Mary. *Hailstones and Halibut Bones: Adventures in Color.* Illustrated by Leonard Weisgard. Doubleday, 1989 (1961).

Orozco, José-Luis. *Fiestas: A Year of Latin American Songs of Celebration.* Illustrated by Elisa Kleven. Dutton, 2002. Bilingual.

Otten, Charlotte F. *January Rides the Wind: A Book of Months.* Illustrated by Todd L. W. Doney. Lothrop, 1997.

Pearson, Susan. *The Drowsy Hours: Poems for Bedtime.* Illustrated by Peter Malone. HarperCollins, 2002.

Peters, Lisa Westberg. *Earthshake: Poems from the Ground Up.* Illustrated by Cathie Felstead. Greenwillow, 2003. Poems about geology.

Prelutsky, Jack. *The New Kid on the Block.* Illustrated by James Stevenson. Greenwillow, 1984.

———. *A Pizza the Size of the Sun.* Illustrated by James Stevenson. Greenwillow, 1996.

Rochelle, Belinda. *Words with Wings: A Treasury of African-American Poetry and Art.* HarperCollins/Amistad, 2001.

Rylant, Cynthia. *God Went to Beauty School.* Harper/Tempest, 2003. Ages 11–YA.

Silverstein, Shel. *A Light in the Attic.* Illustrated by author. Harper, 1981.

———. *Where the Sidewalk Ends: The Poems and Drawings of Shel Silverstein.* Harper, 1974.

Singer, Marilyn. *Turtle in July.* Illustrated by Jerry Pinkney. Macmillan, 1989.

Stevenson, James. *Popcorn.* Greenwillow, 1998.

———. *Sweet Corn: Poems.* Greenwillow, 1995.

Stevenson, Robert Louis. *A Child's Garden of Verses.* Chronicle, 1989 (1885).

Strickland, Dorothy S., and Michael R., editors. *Families: Poems Celebrating the African American Experience.* Illustrated by John Ward. Wordsong/Boyds Mills, 1994.

Thomas, Joyce Carol. *Crowning Glory: Poems.* Illustrated by Brenda Joysmith. Joanna Cotler, 2002.

Updike, John. *A Child's Calendar.* Illustrated by Trina Schart Hyman. Holiday, 1999.

Viorst, Judith. *If I Were in Charge of the World and Other Worries: Poems for Children and Their Parents.* Illustrated by Lynne Cherry. Atheneum, 1982.

Whipple, Laura, editor. *Celebrating America: A Collection of Poems and Images of the American Spirit.* Putnam/Philomel, 1994. Age: YA.

———, compiler. *Eric Carle's Animals Animals.* Illustrated by Eric Carle. Philomel, 1989.

Wilbur, Richard. *The Disappearing Alphabet.* Illustrated by David Diaz. Harcourt, 1998.

Willard, Nancy. *A Visit to William Blake's Inn: Poems for Innocent and Experienced Travelers.* Illustrated by Alice and Martin Provensen. Harcourt, 1981.

Zolotow, Charlotte. *Seasons: A Book of Poems.* Illustrated by Erik Blegvad. HarperCollins, 2002. Easy to read book.

Single Illustrated Poems

Note the distinction between poems *and* stories told in verse. *Heavily illustrated poems are listed here. Illustrated stories told in verse are included under the heading of Picture Storybooks in Chapter 4.*

Browning, Robert. *The Pied Piper of Hamelin.* Illustrated by Kate Greenaway. Warne, 1888.

Bryan, Ashley. *Turtle Knows Your Name.* Atheneum, 1989.

Burleigh, Robert. *Hoops.* Illustrated by Stephen T. Johnson. Harcourt, 1997.

cummings, e.e. *hist whist.* Illustrated by Deborah Kogan Ray. Crown, 1989.

———. *little tree.* Illustrated by Deborah Kogan Ray. Crown, 1987.

Fisher, Aileen. *Listen Rabbit.* Illustrated by Symeon Shimin. Crowell, 1964.

Frost, Robert. *Stopping by Woods on a Snowy Evening.* Illustrated by Susan Jeffers. Dutton, 1978.

Johnson, James Weldon. *The Creation.* Illustrated by James Ransome. Holiday, 1994.

Lear, Edward. *The Jumblies.* Illustrated by Ted Rand. Putnam, 1989.

———. *The Owl and the Pussycat.* Illustrated by Jan Brett. Putnam, 1991.

———. *The Scroobious Pip.* Completed by Ogden Nash. Illustrated by Nancy Ekholm Burkert. Harper, 1968.

Lewis, J. Patrick. *A Hippopotamusn't and Other Animal Verses.* Illustrated by Victoria Chess. Dial, 1990.

Little, Lessie Jones. *Children of Long Ago.* Illustrated by Jan Spivey Gilchrist. Putnam, 1988.

Longfellow, Henry Wadsworth. *Paul Revere's Ride.* Illustrated by Ted Rand. Dutton, 1990.

Moore, Clement Clarke. *The Night before Christmas.* Illustrated by Tomie dePaola. Holiday House, 1980.

Ryder, Joanne. *Earthdance.* Illustrated by Norman Gorbaty. Holt, 1996.

Rylant, Cynthia. *Waiting to Waltz: A Childhood.* Illustrated by Stephen Gammell. Bradbury, 1984.

Service, Robert W. *The Cremation of Sam McGee.* Illustrated by Ted Harrison. Greenwillow, 1987.

———. *The Shooting of Dan McGrew.* Illustrated by Ted Harrison. Godine, 1988.

Siebert, Diane. *Heartland.* Illustrated by Wendell Minor. HarperCollins, 1989.

———. *Sierra.* Illustrated by Wendell Minor. HarperCollins, 1991.

Steig, Jeanne. *Consider the Lemming.* Illustrated by William Steig. Farrar, 1988.

Taylor, Jane. *Twinkle, Twinkle, Little Star.* Illustrated by Michael Hague. Morrow, 1992.

Thayer, Ernest L. *Casey at the Bat.* Illustrated by Patricia Polacco. Putnam, 1992 (1888).

———. *Casey at the Bat: A Ballad of the Republic Sung in the Year 1888.* Illustrated by C. F. Payne. Simon & Schuster, 2003.

Thomas, Joyce Carol. *Cherish Me!* Illustrated by Nneka Bennett. HarperFestival, 1998.

Treece, Henry. *The Magic Wood.* Illustrated by Barry Moser. HarperCollins, 1992 (1945).

Willard, Nancy. *The Tale I Told Sasha.* Illustrated by David Christiana. Little, Brown, 1999.

Young, Ruth. *Golden Bear.* Illustrated by Rachel Isadora. Viking, 1992.

RECOMMENDED BOOKS OF PLAYS

Anthologies of Plays

Bruchac, Joseph. *Pushing Up the Sky: Seven Native American Plays for Children.* Dial, 2000. Ages 7–11.

Bush, Max. *Plays for Young Audiences.* Edited by Roger Ellis. Meriwether, 1995. Ages 9–YA. Ten full-length plays by award-winning playwrights.

Carlson, Lori Marie, selector. *You're On! Seven Plays in English and Spanish.* Morrow, 1999. Ages 9–15.

Ellis, Roger, editor. *Audition Monologues for Student Actors: Selections from Contemporary Plays.* Meriwether, 1999. Ages 13–YA.

———, editor. *International Plays for Young Audiences: Contemporary Works from Leading Playwrights.* Meriwether, 2000. Ages 12–YA.

———. *New International Plays for Young Audiences: Plays of Cultural Conflict.* Meriwether, 2002. Ages 12–YA.

Ellis, Roger, and Ted Zapel, editors. *Multicultural Theatre II: Contemporary Hispanic, Asian, and African American Plays.* Meriwether, 1998. Ages 12–YA.

Espinosa, Resurrección. *Don Quixote in America: Plays in English and Spanish, Grades 1–6.* Libraries Unlimited, 2002. Ages 6–12.

Gerke, Pamela. *Multicultural Plays for Children, vol. 1: Grades K–3.* Smith and Kraus, 1996. Ages 5–8.

———. *Multicultural Plays for Children, vol. 2: Grades 4–6.* Smith and Kraus, 1996. Ages 9–12.

Halligan, Terry. *Funny Skits and Sketches.* Illustrated by Joyce Behr. Players Press, 1999. Ages 6–12. (Primarily related to holidays and appropriate for schools and community functions.)

Harris, Aurand, editor. *Short Plays of Theatre Classics.* Anchorage, 1991. Ages 9–YA. An international selection.

Jennings, Coleman A., editor. *Theatre for Young Audiences.* St. Martin's Press, 1998. Ages 9–12. Mostly recent short plays.

Jennings, Coleman A., and Aurand Harris, editors. *Plays Children Love, vol. 2: A Treasury of Contemporary and Classic Plays for Children.* St. Martin's Press, 1988. Ages 7–12. Contains 20 plays.

Kamerman, Sylvia E. *Thirty Plays from Favorite Stories.* Plays, Inc., 1998. Ages 7–12.

McCaslin, Nellie. *Legends in Action: Ten Plays of Ten Lands.* Players Press, 2001. Ages 8–12.

McCullough, L. E. *"Now I Get It!": 12 Ten-Minute Classroom Drama Skits for Science, Math, Language, and Social Studies.* Smith and Kraus, 2000. Vol. 1 for ages 5–8; Vol. 2 for ages 9–12.

———. *Plays from Fairy Tales: Grades K–3.* Also, *Plays from Mythology: Grades 4–6.* Smith and Kraus, 1998. Ages 5–8.

———. *Plays of Exploration and Discovery, Grades 4–6.* Smith and Kraus, 1999. Ages 9–12. (The 12 plays depict moments of discovery in science and geography.)

Slaight, C., and J. Sharrar. *Multicultural Monologues for Young Actors.* Smith and Kraus, 1995. Ages 11–14.

Stevens, Chambers. *Magnificent Monologues for Kids.* Sandcastle, 1999. Ages 6–11. Includes 51 brief monologues.

Surface, Mary Hall. *Most Valuable Player: And Four Other All-Star Plays for Young Audiences.* Smith and Kraus, 1999. Ages 13–YA.

———. *Short Scenes and Monologues for Middle School Actors.* Smith and Kraus, 2000. Ages 11–14. Includes monologues and scenes for two actors.

Swortzell, Lowell, editor. *Theatre for Young Audiences: Around the World in 21 Plays.* Applause Theatre Book Publishers, 1997. Ages 13–YA.

Thistle, Louise. *Dramatizing Aesop's Fables: Grades K–6.* Smith and Kraus, 1997. Ages 5–12.

———. *Dramatizing Mother Goose: Introducing Students to Classic Literature through Drama.* Smith and Kraus, 1998. Ages 5–12.

Williams, Marcia, adapter. *Tales from Shakespeare: Seven Plays.* Illustrated. Candlewick, 1998. Ages 7–11.

Winther, Barbara. *Plays from Hispanic Tales: One Act, Royalty-Free Dramatizations for Young People from Hispanic Stories and Folktales.* Plays, Inc., 1998. Ages 10–YA.

Single Plays

Asher, Sandra Fenichel. *The Wolf and Its Shadow.* Anchorage, 2000. Ages 6–9.

Brooks, Laurie. *The Wrestling Season.* Dramatic Publishing, 2000. Ages 12–YA. Unique approach, play performed on an arena wrestling mat with actors answering audience questions at the end.

Burdett, Lois. *Hamlet for Kids.* Firefly, 2000. Ages 8–12. (Also, *The Tempest for Kids,* Firefly, 1999. Ages 6–10.)

Bush, Max. *Ghost of the Riverhouse.* Anchorage, 1997. Ages 9–12.

———. *Sarah.* Dramatic Publishing, 2000. Ages 12–YA.

Butterfield, Moira. *Hansel and Gretel.* Playtales Series. Heinemann, 1997. Also, *Sleeping Beauty.* Ages 7–10.

DeVita, James. *Bambi, a Life in the Woods.* Anchorage, 1995. Ages 9–12.

———. *Excavating Mom.* Dramatic Publishing, 1998. Ages 12–14.

Goldberg, Moses. *Puss in Boots* (a participation play). Anchorage, 1992. His plays are especially appealing for children in early childhood, ages 3–8.

Harris, Aurand. *Androcles and the Lion* (a musical). Anchorage, 1964. Ages 4–8.

———. *The Arkansaw Bear.* Anchorage,1980. Ages 4–8.

Hezlip, William. *Kokopelli's Cave.* Players, 2002. Ages 10–YA. (Part of a series of time travel plays including *Trouble in the Mountains.* Players Press, 2003.)

Ledoux, Paul. *Anne.* Playwrights Canada Press, 1999. Ages 8–12.

Mast, Edward. *Wolf Child: The Correction of Joseph.* Anchorage, 1999. Ages 6–10.

Myers, Walter Dean. *Monster.* HarperCollins, 1998. Ages 13–YA. A novel written as a television script.

Shapiro, Jacqui. *Joshua's Egg: A Play for Children.* Samuel French, 1999. Ages 5–9.

Soto, Gary. *Nerdlandia: A Play.* Penguin, 1999. Ages 13–YA. Some Spanish dialogue.

Still, James. *And Then They Came for Me: Remembering the World of Anne Frank.* Dramatic Publishing, 1999. Ages 12–YA.

Wing, Paula. *Naomi's Road.* PUC Play Service, 1999. (Based on a novel by Joy Kogawa with the same name.) Ages 11–YA.

Wood, David, adapter. *Babe, the Sheep-Pig: A Play.* Samuel French, 1997. Ages 6–10.

York, Y, adapter. *Afternoon of the Elves.* Dramatic Publishing, 2000. Ages 9–12.

———, adapter. *The Garden of Rikki Tikki Tavi.* Dramatic Publishing, 1999. Ages 8–12.

Zeder, Suzan L. *Mother Hicks, Playscript.* Anchorage, 1986. Ages 5–8.

———. *Step on a Crack.* Anchorage, 1976. Ages 6–12.

———. *The Taste of Sunrise* (prequel to *Mother Hicks*). Anchorage, 1999. Ages 5–9.

PICTURE BOOKS

MY BOOK!

I did it!
I did it!
Come and look
At what I've done!
I read a book!
When someone wrote it
Long ago
For me to read,
How did he know
That this was the book
I'd take from the shelf
And lie on the floor
And read by myself?
I really read it!
Just like that!
Word by word,
From first to last!
I'm sleeping with
This book in bed,
This is the FIRST book
I've ever read!

— DAVID L. HARRISON

In an era when picture books abound and provide many children with a delightful introduction to the world of books, it is difficult to imagine a time when books had no illustrations. Nonetheless, the picture book as we know it is a product of the twentieth century. The development of different types of picture books over the last three quarters of a century can be seen as a response to our developing awareness of the importance of early learning.

DEFINITION AND DESCRIPTION

Picture books are profusely illustrated books in which both words and illustrations contribute to the story's meaning. In a true picture book, the story would be diminished, and in some cases confusing, without the illustrations, and so we say that illustrations in picture books are integral, or essential, to the story. Picture books are written in all genres; they have illustrations on every page or, at least, every other page; and, as a general rule, they are thirty-two pages long. A good example of a picture book is *Officer Buckle and Gloria* by Peggy Rathmann. See Illustration 8, inside back cover.

Books with occasional illustrations that serve to break up or decorate the text, add interest, or depict isolated incidents are called *illustrated books.* Illustrations in these books are said to be incidental, or nonessential, to the content. Illustrated books are not picture books. A good example of an illustrated book is Russell Freedman's biography, *Out of Darkness: The Story of Louis Braille,* illustrated by Kate Kiesler.

EVALUATION AND SELECTION
OF PICTURE BOOKS

Children's first experiences with books must be enjoyable or they will soon not want to be involved with books. Negative experiences could mean that they may never learn to read or to enjoy reading. Over a period of time, evaluation and selection of picture books become a matter of achieving a good balance between what children naturally enjoy and what you want to lead them to enjoy.

The following criteria will help you to identify the best of the picture books:

- The ideas in picture books should be original or presented in an original way. Picture books on topics that children enjoy and find interesting are preferable to books about childhood, in the sense of nostalgia for or reminiscence of childhood. Books of the latter sort are for adults, not children.
- Picture books should avoid racial, ethnic, or sexual stereotyping in text and illustrations.
- Language and writing style should be rich and varied but not so complicated as to be incomprehensible to the child. It is desirable to feature new or unusual vocabulary within the context of interesting situations and complementary illustrations. Avoid books with overly sentimental and trite language, as well as writing characterized by short, choppy sentences and lifeless vocabulary.
- Illustrations should be appropriate in complexity to the age of the intended audience. In picture books for infants, look for relatively uncomplicated pages showing outlined figures against a plain background. Elements of perspective or unusual page design in which only parts of a figure are shown may not be readily understood or appreciated by very young children.
- Children prefer color in illustrations, but color is not essential if illustrations are to work well in picture books. The more important point to consider is whether color or black and white is right for the story.
- When a book is to be shared with a large group, the illustrations must be large enough to be seen from a distance.
- Picture books selected for reading aloud to children by adults, especially parents and preschool and kindergarten teachers, should offer something to both listener and reader and promote interactive discussion between them (Brabham & Lynch-Brown, 2002). Multiple layers of meaning,

---

Excellent P I C T U R E   B O O K S   t o   R e a d   A l o u d

Alborough, Jez. *Where's My Teddy?* Ages 5–8. Humorous story in verse.
Baker, Olaf. *Where the Buffaloes Begin.* Illustrated by Stephen Gammell. Ages 8–11.
Collington, Peter. *The Coming of the Surfman.* Ages 11–14.
Dorros, Arthur. *Abuela.* Illustrated by Elisa Kleven. Ages 8–11.
Hoffman, Mary. *Amazing Grace.* Illustrated by Caroline Binch, Ages 5–8.
Rathman, Peggy. *Officer Buckle and Gloria.* Ages 5–8.
Steig, William. *The Amazing Bone.* Ages 7–10.
Van Allsburg, Chris. *The Wretched Stone.* Ages 8–11.
Waddell, Martin. *Farmer Duck.* Illustrated by Helen Oxenbury. Ages 5–8.
Yorinks, Arthur. *Hey, Al.* Illustrated by Richard Egielski. Ages 8–11.

---

child and adult perspectives, and humor are sources of enjoyment found in books that adults willingly read and reread to children.

- The amount of text on the pages of a picture book determines how long it will take to read the book aloud or for a child to read the book to herself or himself. Generally, the longer the text, the older the intended audience. Note that children's willingness to listen to stories grows with experience, which may result in a younger child who has been read to regularly having a much longer attention span than an older child with no story experience.

Teachers and librarians often rely on the professional judgment of committees that choose what they consider to be the most outstanding picture books published each year in this country and abroad. The most prestigious picture book award in the United States is the Caldecott Medal, sponsored by the Association for Library Service to Children division of the American Library Association. (See page 323 for web site information.) The equivalent award in Great Britain is the Kate Greenaway Medal, and in Canada the Governor General's Award for Illustration. (See Appendix A for lists of award winners.) Another reliable source of information about good quality picture books is "The New York Times Best Illustrated Children's Books of the Year," published in early November as a part of *The New York Times Book Review Supplement.*

O B S E R V I N G   T H E   R O L E   O F   I L L U S T R A T I O N S   I N   P I C T U R E   B O O K S

Adults sometimes have difficulty perceiving the contributions that illustrations make to picture books. In terms of the literary elements of a story, as described in Chapter 2, illustrations in picture storybooks can help tell what happens (plot) or give clues to character traits, settings, themes, and moods. The following general guidelines may improve your ability to "read" illustrations:

- Note characters and actions that are *not* mentioned in the text. Illustrations can contribute to plot. See Illustration 7, inside back cover: note the baby crawling in the upper left corner, an action that is never mentioned in the text.

- Note how characters' physical characteristics are conveyed through the illustrations. Illustrations can contribute to characterization. See Illustrations 5, 6, 7, and 8, inside back cover: in each example, the reader is wholly dependent on the illustrations for the physical description of the characters.
- Note how details such as clothing, architecture, and modes of transportation establish and depict place and era of the story. Illustrations can contribute to setting. See Illustration 1, inside front cover: the woman's clothing helps to set this story in the past.
- Note whether and how the story's message and mood are conveyed by or underscored in the illustrations. Illustrations can contribute to theme and mood. See Illustration 1, inside front cover, and Illustration 6, inside back cover: In Illustration 1, the danger and seriousness associated with the underground railroad are reflected in the dark colors, the anxious expression on the woman's face, and the diagonal position of her body; in Illustration 6, the story's theme of family unity and caring is projected by the characters' calm expressions, the many horizontal lines, and details such as the father's hand resting on his son's shoulder.

HISTORICAL OVERVIEW OF PICTURE BOOKS

Orbis Pictus (The World in Pictures), an ABC book written and illustrated by John Amos Comenius in Moravia and published in 1657, is considered to be the first children's picture book. Comenius's emphasis on using pictures to explain and expand the meaning of the text in books for young people was an important first. But since early books were rare and prohibitively expensive, they were seen by very few children. Moreover, until well into the nineteenth century, Europeans and Americans believed that books were for the serious business of educating and soul saving, not for enjoyment! Today's full-color, extravagantly illustrated, highly amusing picture book is the product of the following important developments.

- Technological advances in color printing. Improved four-color printing presses and printing techniques made high-quality illustrations in books more affordable. These advances were a direct result of the Industrial Revolution.
- A more understanding attitude toward childhood. As late as the eighteenth century, the Western world thought of children as miniature adults and expected them to behave and work accordingly. During the nineteenth century, society began to accept the notion of childhood as a time for playing and learning. At the same time, the general economy began to be able to afford the average child the leisure time these activities require.
- Higher standards of excellence in picture book illustrations. The first great children's book illustrators lived in the 1800s. The beauty, charm, and humor of the illustrations of Randolph Caldecott, Kate Greenaway, and Walter Crane brought children's book art to the attention of the general public. The establishment of national awards for excellence in children's book illustration in the twentieth century had the same effect and encouraged more artists to enter the children's book field.
- A greater demand for books. Growth of public school systems and public and school library systems accounted for much of this increase in the number of books for children. In addition, reading came to be recognized as one of the child's best tools for learning and for gaining a worthy source of entertainment.

MILESTONES

in the Development of the PICTURE BOOK

DATE	EVENT	SIGNIFICANCE
1484	Publication of *Aesop's Fables,* illustrated by William Caxton.	One of the first known illustrated books enjoyed by children.
1657	Publication of *Orbis Pictus,* written and illustrated by John Amos Comenius.	Considered to be the first picture book for children.
1860–1900	Golden Age of children's book illustration in Great Britain, led by Randolph Caldecott, Walter Crane, and Kate Greenaway.	Increased awareness, stature, popularity, and appreciation of children's picture books.
1902	Publication of *The Tale of Peter Rabbit* by Beatrix Potter.	Early important modern picture storybook in English.
1928	Publication of *Millions of Cats* by Wanda Gág.	Early important modern American picture storybook.
1938	Establishment of the Caldecott Award for illustration in children's books in the United States.	Promoted excellence in illustrating for children and encouraged talented artists to illustrate children's books.
1940	Publication of *Pat the Bunny* by Dorothy Kunhardt.	One of the first books for babies. Began the move to supply different types of picture books for different child audiences.
1957	Publication of *The Cat in the Hat,* written and illustrated by Dr. Seuss, and *Little Bear,* written by Else Minarik and illustrated by Maurice Sendak.	Introduced the easy-to-read genre of picture books.
1962	Publication of *A Snowy Day,* written and illustrated by Ezra Jack Keats.	One of the first picture books with a minority character as the protagonist to win the Caldecott Medal.
1967	Publication of *A Boy, a Dog, and a Frog,* illustrated by Mercer Mayer.	Popularized the wordless book genre.
1972	Publication of *Push Pull, Empty Full* by Tana Hoban.	Signaled the growing popularity of the concept picture book.
1974	Publication of *Arrow to the Sun: A Pueblo Indian Tale* by Gerald McDermott.	Signaled the emergence of picture books for older readers as a distinct type of picture book.
1981	Publication of "The Baby Board Books" by Helen Oxenbury.	Baby books were established as a distinct and important type of picture book.
1990	*Color Zoo* by Lois Ehlert wins a Caldecott Honor Award.	Recognition of the engineered book genre.
1991	*Black and White* by David Macaulay wins Caldecott Medal.	Denoted acceptance of nontraditional picture book formats.

As a result of these developments, an economic, social, and political infrastructure that would support the widespread publishing of children's books was in place in most of the Western world by the early twentieth century. With its superb children's book illustrators and color printers of the time, England led the world in publishing picture books from the 1860s until the 1930s. Milestones in the development of picture books are highlighted on page 79.

Today, the picture book genre is well established. Current trends in the field are toward an ever-widening audience, more multicultural themes, and realistic themes, such as the effects of war, poverty, immigration, and disabilities on the lives of children. Other current trends include greater diversity in formats and more illustrated retellings of folktales. An interesting trend of the 1990s is to publish picture books with high levels of conceptual difficulty and artistic sophistication, intended for middle grade and junior high school students. (See p. 84 for more on this type of picture book.) Other trends are toward more bilingual (especially English-Spanish) picture books and toward greater and more effective use of illustration in informational books. Microchip technology has made it possible to produce books that emit sounds or talk when certain pages are opened. More and more books are available on CD-ROM and are reader-interactive.

TYPES OF PICTURE BOOKS

The first picture books were meant to be read aloud to children. The latter half of the twentieth century, in response to new educational theories and new markets, saw the development of new types of picture books to be read and enjoyed independently by a wider range of children than just kindergartners and first-graders. Thus, today's picture books differ in intended audience, purpose, format, and relative amount of text and illustration. These differences are not absolute, however; quite often, one will find a picture book having characteristics of several specific types. With the understanding that overlap between types is inevitable, you will want to learn to recognize the following kinds of picture books (organized by the intended age of the primary audience from youngest to oldest). Informational picture books are covered in Chapter 9.

Baby Books

Baby books are simply designed, brightly illustrated, durable picture books that are intended for use with children aged 0 to 2. Safety is ensured by rounded corners, nontoxic materials, washable pages, and no loose attachments. An example is *Baby Radar* by Naomi Shihab Nye. Baby books gained popularity in the 1980s in response to the growing evidence of the remarkable learning capacity of very young children. The types of baby books actually denote the material used in their construction. *Board books* are constructed of heavy, laminated cardboard and are either bound as a book with pages or made to fold out in an accordion fashion. *Vinyl books* and *cloth books* are also types of baby books. These books have little or no text. Their content, which deals with the objects and routines that are familiar to the infant and toddler, is presented mainly by the illustrations. The best baby books, such as those produced by Helen Oxenbury, are intelligently designed to emphasize patterns and associations to promote dialogue between the caregiver and the young child, who will often look at these books together.

Interactive Books

Interactive books are picture books that stimulate a child's verbal or physical participation as the book is read. These books ask the child direct questions, invite unison recitation of chants or repeated lines, encourage clapping or moving to the rhythm of the words, or require the child to touch or manipulate the book or find objects in the illustrations. Amy Schwartz's *What James Likes Best* is a good example. The intended audience is usually children aged 2 to 6, and the books are seen as an extension of their world of play. One classic example of this type of book that is still greatly enjoyed by toddlers today is Dorothy Kunhardt's *Pat the Bunny.*

Toy Books

Sometimes called *engineered* or *mechanical books,* toy books use paper that has been engineered (i.e., cut, folded, constructed) to provide pop-up, see-through, movable, changeable, or three-dimensional illustrations. Toy books can be found for all ages, but only those that have the simpler types of engineering, such as pages of varying widths or drilled holes for see-through effects (as in Eric Carle's *The Very Hungry Caterpillar*), would be appropriate for most young children. Toy books with fragile or elaborate pop-up features, such as Robert Sabuda's amazing pop-up version of *Alice in Wonderland,* would not last in the hands of a very young child, but would delight older children (and adults).

Wordless Books

The wordless book depends entirely on carefully sequenced illustrations to present the story. There is no text, or the text is limited to one or two pages in the book, so the illustrations must be highly narrative. *A Small Miracle* by Peter Collington is a good example of this category. Wordless books are generally intended for prereaders, usually children aged 4 to 6. When children "read" these illustrations in their own words, they benefit from the book's visual story structure in several ways:

- They develop a concept of story as a cohesive narrative with a beginning and an end.
- They use language inventively, which promotes language development.
- They learn the front-to-back, left-to-right page progression in reading.
- They begin to understand that stories can be found not only in books but in themselves.

Publishers began to produce wordless picture books in noticeable quantities in the 1960s. Mercer Mayer, with his wordless book series about a boy, a dog, and a frog, helped to popularize this type of picture book. More sophisticated wordless books for older readers, such as David Weisner's *Sector 7,* are also available.

Alphabet Books

The alphabet, or ABC, book presents the alphabet letter by letter to acquaint young children with the shapes, names, and, in some cases, the sounds of the twenty-six letters. For example, see *ABC: A Child's First Alphabet Book* by Alison Jay. Almost all ABC book authors and illustrators choose a theme (animals, elves, fruit, etc.) or device (finding the many objects in the accompanying illustration beginning with the featured letter) to give their books cohesion. In choosing an ABC book, consider the appropriateness of the theme or device for students, whether both uppercase and lowercase letters are displayed, and the use of a simple, easy-to-read style of print.

Most ABC books are intended for the nonreader or beginning reader. Some authors and illustrators use the alphabet itself as a device for presenting information or wordplay. In these cases, the intended audience already knows the alphabet. In *Tomorrow's Alphabet,* written by George Shannon and illustrated by Donald Crews, each letter is presented as a puzzle to solve on two pages.

Counting Books

The counting book presents numbers, usually 1 through 10, to acquaint young children with the numerals and their shapes (1, 2, 3, . . .), the number names (one, two, three, . . .), the sense of what quantity each numeral represents, and the counting sequence. *Let's Count* by Tana Hoban is a good example of this type of book. As with alphabet books, authors and illustrators of counting books employ themes or devices to make them more cohesive and interesting. Specific considerations in evaluating a counting book include the appeal to children of the theme and objects chosen to illustrate the number concepts, and the clarity with which the illustrator presents the concept of number.

Illustrators often fill their alphabet and counting books with unusual and intriguing objects for children to name and count, such as aardvarks, barracudas, and chameleons. Children pick up a great deal of interesting information and vocabulary in this way. You will be in the best position to decide whether the novelty of these objects will be motivating or confusing to your students.

Concept Books

A concept book is a picture book that explores or explains an idea or concept (e.g., opposites), an object (e.g., a train), or an activity (e.g., working) rather than telling a story. Many concept books have no plot but use repeated elements in the illustrations and text to tie the book together. A good example is *Trucks, Trucks, Trucks* by Peter Sís. Limited text and clearly understood illustrations in the best concept books stimulate children's exploratory talk about the concepts, objects, and activities presented.

Alphabet and counting books are considered types of concept books. Another variety of the concept book that is popular with 2- to 4-year-olds is the naming book, which presents simple, labeled pictures of people, animals, and objects for young children to identify. *My First Word Book* by Angela Wilkes is an example of a naming book.

Pattern Books

Picture books that strongly emphasize word patterns are called *pattern books.* They are also called *decodable books* because of their language regularities in which certain phonological features are repeated, as is the line, "Is this the bus for us, Gus?" in Suzanne Bloom's *The Bus for Us.* In addition, *predictable books,* such as Bill Martin, Jr., and Eric Carle's *Brown Bear, Brown Bear, What Do You See?* and its companion books, *Polar Bear. . . .* and *Panda Bear. . . .* , are sometimes included in this category because of meaning and illustration clues.

Picture Storybooks

The picture storybook is a book in which a story is told through both the words and pictures. Text and illustration occur with equal frequency in these books, and on most double spreads, both are in view. A good example is *Officer Buckle and Gloria* by Peggy Rathmann. The picture storybook is the most common type of picture book.

The text of most picture storybooks is meant to be read aloud to the intended audience of 4- to 7-year-olds, at least for the first time or two, and often includes challenging vocabulary. Many of the best picture storybooks are also read and enjoyed independently by children 8 years old and up.

Easy-to-Read Books

Easy-to-read books are created to help the beginning reader read independently with success. These books have limited text on each page, large print, double spacing, and short sentences. There is usually an illustration on about every other page. Language is often, but not always, controlled, and words are short and familiar. For example, see *Good Night, Good Knight* by Shelley M. Thomas, illustrated by Jennifer Plecas. Easy-to-read picture books were first developed in the 1950s by such authors as Dr. Seuss (*The Cat in the Hat, Fox in Sox*) and Else Holmelund Minarik, who, along with illustrator Maurice Sendak, created the *Little Bear* series. Easy-to-read books can be used with children whenever they want to learn to read, but the audience for this type of book is usually the 5- to 7-year-old.

The easy-to-read book differs in appearance from the picture storybook in several obvious ways. Because they are intended for independent reading, they do not have to be seen from a distance and may be smaller; the text takes up a greater proportion of each page; and the text is often divided into short chapters.

Picture Books for Older Readers

Picture books for older readers are generally more sophisticated, abstract, or complex in themes, stories, and illustrations and are suitable for children aged 10 and older. This type of picture book began to appear in the 1970s, perhaps in response to our increasingly visual modes of communication, and now artists such as Anthony Browne, D. B. Johnson, David Macaulay, and the team of Jörg Müller and Jörg Steiner are known for their work in this area.

Picture books for older readers lend themselves well to use across the middle school curriculum, including social studies, science, language arts, math, art, music, and physical education. Consider the advantages of using picture books for older readers in middle and secondary schools:

- They can be used as teacher read-alouds for introductions and supplements to textbook-based units of instruction.
- They can be used in text sets (several books on the same topic) for small group in-class reading, analysis, and discussion.
- They can be used by individual students as models of excellent writing. (Each year NCTE's Children's Literature Assembly publishes a list of books, including many picture books, that are notable for their use of language. Go to http://archive.ncte.org/elem/notable/index.shtml for these lists.)

- They can inject humor and stimulate interest in a topic, and possibly provoke discussion, which would result in a deeper understanding of the content (Albright, 2000, 2002), as Jorge Diaz's *The Rebellious Alphabet* does for the topic of First Amendment rights.
- They can demonstrate practical applications of concepts (Alvermann & Phelps, 1998), as D. B. Johnson's *Henry Climbs a Mountain* does for the concept of civil disobedience.
- They often have factual content that reinforces or adds to that found in textbooks, as Brett Harvey's *Cassie's Journey: Going West in the 1860s,* illustrated by Deborah Kogan Ray, does for a unit of instruction about pioneer life in the mid-nineteenth century by adding a wealth of detail about daily life in a wagon train.
- They offer different perspectives on issues, such as the African-American perspective on the Civil War in Patricia Polacco's *Pink and Say.*

The traditional notion that picture books are only for younger children no longer applies. Although some adults may persist in guiding older children away from picture books, as Gontarski (1994) found, today's teachers and librarians would be wise to make picture books for older readers an option in any learning situation.

Graphic Novels

The last decade has seen the emergence of *graphic novels* as a book format related to picture books. These novel-length books feature text written in speech bubbles or as captions in comic book–like illustrations. Graphic novels are popular with middle and high school students, and are beginning to be written for elementary-grade students. Reluctant readers especially enjoy having these books as a reading option. Art Spiegelman's two-volume Jewish holocaust biography, *Maus: A Survivor's Tale,* brought attention to this genre in 1992 by winning a Pulitzer Prize. *Pedro and Me: Friendship, Loss, and What I Learned* by Judd Winick, a biography, is an example of a graphic novel appropriate for middle and high school students. Although few graphic novels have been written for 9- to 12-year-olds in the United States, translations of the French author Hergé's *Tintin* boy detective series, as well as the Japanese author Rumiko Takahashi's *Inu Yasha* science fantasy series, are popular.

Transitional Books

Transitional books are a special type of book for the child who can read but has not yet become a fluent reader. These books, which are less profusely illustrated and have lengthier text than the other types of books discussed in this chapter, are not picture books. They lie somewhere between picture books and full-length novels. A good example of a transitional book is *Not My Dog* by Colby Rodowsky, illustrated by Thomas Yezerski.

Characteristics of transitional books are an uncomplicated writing style and vocabulary, an illustration on about every third page, division of text into chapters, slightly enlarged print, and a length of approximately 50–100 pages. Children who read these books are typically between the ages of 8 and 11. Often, books for the transitional reader occur in series, such as Donald Sobol's Encyclopedia Brown books, Ann Cameron's Julian books, and Robert Newton Peck's Soup books. See Appendix E for a list of good transitional books.

To write well for the beginning reader is a real challenge, since these stories must treat interesting topics in vivid language while remaining relatively easy to read. Finding the best of these books for the beginning and transitional readers in your charge will be time well spent.

The Center for Children's Books and the Graduate School of Library and Information Science of the University of Illinois at Urbana–Champaign established the Gryphon Award for transitional books in 2004. The $1,000 prize is given annually to the author of the English-language work of fiction or non-fiction published in the preceding year that best exemplifies qualities that successfully bridge the gap in difficulty between picture books and full-length books. The first winner of the Gryphon Award was Douglas Florian for *bow wow meow meow: it's rhyming cats and dogs.*

During the twentieth century the picture book was begun and developed as a genre, diversified to meet the demands of an ever-expanding audience and market, and improved as a result of new and refined printing technology. As researchers came to realize the connections between positive early experiences with good literature, early learning, and future school success, new types of picture books were developed to serve both younger and older audiences. Today, high-quality picture books on nearly every imaginable topic can enrich the lives and imaginations of young children and the classrooms and libraries where they learn.

REFERENCES

Albright, L. K. (2000). "The effects on attitudes and achievement of reading aloud picture books in seventh-grade social studies classes." Unpublished doctoral dissertation, Ohio University, Athens.

———. (2002). Bringing the Ice Maiden to life: Engaging adolescents in learning through picture book read-alouds in content areas. *Journal of Adolescent and Adult Literacy, 45*(5), 418–428.

Alvermann, D. E., & Phelps, S. F. (1998). *Content reading and literacy: Succeeding in today's diverse classrooms* (2nd ed.). Boston: Allyn and Bacon.

Brabham, E. G., and Lynch-Brown, C. (2002). Effects of teachers' reading aloud styles on vocabulary acquisition and comprehension of students in the early elementary grades. *Journal of Educational Psychology, 94*(3), 465–474.

Gontarski, M. (1994). "Visual literacy as it relates to picture book use by selected fifth grade students." Unpublished doctoral dissertation, The Florida State University, Tallahassee, FL.

Harrison, David L. (1993). My book! In D. L. Harrison (Ed.), *Somebody catch my homework.* Illustrated by Betsy Lewin. Honesdale, PA: Boyds Mills.

Molly Bang, author/illustrator. Wordless and concept books illustrated in a variety of styles and media. *The Grey Lady and the Strawberry Snatcher; Ten, Nine, Eight.*

Marcia Brown, author/illustrator. Reteller and illustrator of folktales from foreign lands. Three Caldecott Medals, six Caldecott Honor Book Awards. *Once a Mouse . . . ; Stone Soup.*

Eric Carle, author/illustrator. Unusually formatted picture storybooks and concept books about insects and animals. *The Grouchy Ladybug; The Very Busy Spider.*

Barbara Cooney, author/illustrator. Picture storybooks reflect values of New England. *Miss Rumphius.*

Floyd Cooper, illustrator. Uses watercolor and erasers to create characters from many cultures. *The Girl Who Loved Caterpillars.*

Tomie dePaola, author/illustrator. Droll characters like Strega Nona and Big Anthony; uses formal, balanced artistic style. *The Legend of the Bluebonnet; Strega Nona: An Old Tale.*

Denise Fleming, author/illustrator. Creates pattern books of handmade paper. *In the Small, Small Pond; Mama Cat Has Three Kittens.*

Stephen Gammell, illustrator. Uses colored pencil in an informal, airy style. *The Relatives Came* (by Cynthia Rylant).

Kevin Henkes, author/illustrator. Creator of family situation animal fantasies featuring mice. *Chrysanthemum; Julius, the Baby of the World; Owen.*

Tana Hoban, author/illustrator. Using photographs, created some of the first and best concept books. *Push Pull, Empty Full; Is It Rough? Is It Smooth? Is It Shiny?*

Ezra Jack Keats, author/illustrator. One of the first to portray ethnic minorities in the United States as major characters in picture books. *A Snowy Day; Peter's Chair.*

Steven Kellogg, author/illustrator. Uses animals as characters in picture storybooks. *Island of the Skog.*

Leo Lionni, author/illustrator. Uses collage technique to illustrate modern fables. *Swimmy; Frederick.*

Bill Martin, Jr., author. Pattern and rhyming stories for the beginning reader. *Brown Bear, Brown Bear, What Do You See?* (illustrated by Eric Carle).

Patricia McKissack, author. Picture storybooks with African-American characters and themes. *Nettie Jo's Friends* (illustrated by Scott Cook).

Helen Oxenbury, author/illustrator. British. Board books for babies. *Dressing; Say Goodnight.*

Brian Pinkney, illustrator. Uses distinctive scratch-board technique in folktales and biographies featuring African Americans. *Duke Ellington: The Piano Prince and His Orchestra* (by Andrea Davis Pinkney).

Chris Raschka, illustrator. Spare, expressionist watercolors and brief texts elegantly capture mood. *Yo! Yes?; Mysterious Thelonious.*

Jon Scieszka, author. Fractured folktales and books for reluctant readers. *The Stinky Cheese Man and Other Fairly Stupid Tales.*

Maurice Sendak, author/illustrator. Explores the dreams and imagination of children in complex picture storybooks. *Where the Wild Things Are; Outside Over There.*

Peter Sís, author/illustrator. Noted for abstract style and complex subjects in picture books for older readers. *Starry Messenger.*

David Small, illustrator. Two-time Caldecott medalist known for his loose style and narrative-rich watercolors. *The Gardener; So You Want to Be President?*

Simms Taback, author/illustrator. Noted for folk art style and effective use of paper engineering in engaging interpretations of poems. *Joseph Had a Little Overcoat.*

Chris Van Allsburg, author/illustrator. Uses shadow and unusual perspectives to create mysterious moods in picture storybooks for intermediate-grade readers. *Jumanji; The Garden of Abdul Gasazi.*

Eric Velasquez, illustrator. Exuberant realistic style enlivens novels for intermediate grades. *Journey to Jo'burg* (Naidoo); Sobol's *Encyclopedia Brown* mysteries; The *Skirt* (Soto).

David Wiesner, author/illustrator. Creator of wordless fantasy stories. *Tuesday; Free Fall.*

Vera B. Williams, author/illustrator. Expressive artistic style used to depict nontraditional families in picture storybooks. *A Chair for My Mother; Three Days on a River in a Red Canoe.*

David Wisniewski, author/illustrator. Uses intricate cut paper and layering technique to illustrate ancient stories and legends. *Golem; Rain Player.*

Charlotte Zolotow, editor, publisher, author. Revered figure responsible for numerous modern classic picture books. *Mr. Rabbit and the Lovely Present; William's Doll.*

RECOMMENDED PICTURE BOOKS

Ages refer to approximate interest levels.
YA = young adult.

Baby Books

These books are generally suitable for ages 0 to 2.

Ashman, Linda. *Babies on the Go.* Illustrated by Jane Dyer. Harcourt, 2003. Ages 2–4.

Burningham, John. *Hushabye.* Knopf, 2001. Ages 1–3.

Henkes, Kevin. *Owen's Marshmallow Chick.* Harper-Collins, 2002. Ages 2–5. (Board book.)

Nye, Naomi Shihab. *Baby Radar.* Illustrated by Nancy Carpenter. Greenwillow, 2003. Ages 2–4.

Ormerod, Jan. *To Baby with Love.* Lothrop, 1994.

Oxenbury, Helen. "The Baby Board Books." *Dressing.* Simon & Schuster, 1981. (Others in this series: *Family; Friends; Playing; Working.*)

Ricklen, Neil. *Baby's Clothes.* Simon & Schuster, 1994. (Others in this series of 24: *Baby's Friends; Baby's Home; Baby's Toys.*)

———. *My Clothes/Mi Ropa.* Macmillan, 1994. (Others in this bilingual English/Spanish series: *My Numbers/Mis Números.*)

Suen, Anastasia. *Toddler Two.* Illustrated by Winnie Cheon. Lee & Low, 2002. Ages 1–3. Also available in Spanish (*Dos años*) and English/Spanish editions. (Board book.)

Uff, Caroline. *Lulu's Busy Day.* Walker, 2000. (See also *Happy Birthday, Lulu.*)

Wells, Rosemary. "Very First Books." *Max's Bath.* Dial, 1985.

Ziefert, Harriet. *Who Said Moo?* Illustrated by Simms Taback. Handprint Books, 2002. Ages 1–3. (Board book.)

Interactive Books

Ahlberg, Janet, and Allen Ahlberg. *Each Peach Pear Plum: An I-Spy Story.* Viking, 1978. Ages 2–4.

Hill, Eric. *Where's Spot?* Putnam, 1980. (Others in this series: *Spot's First Walk; Spot's Birthday Party; Spot's First Christmas.*) Ages 3–5.

Knight, Hilary. *Where's Wallace?* Simon & Schuster, 2000 (1964). Ages 4–7.

Kunhardt, Dorothy. *Pat the Bunny.* Golden, 2001 (1940). Ages 2–4.

Marzollo, Jean. *I Spy Fantasy: A Book of Picture Riddles.* Illustrated by Walter Wick. Scholastic, 1994. Ages 5–9. (Others in this series: *I Spy Mystery.*)

Schwartz, Amy. *What James Likes Best.* Simon & Schuster, 2003. Ages 3–5.

Spires, Elizabeth. *With One White Wing: Puzzles in Poems and Pictures.* Illustrated by Eric Blegvad. Simon & Schuster, 1995. Ages 7–10.

Tafuri, Nancy. *Have You Seen My Duckling?* Greenwillow, 1984. Ages 3–5.

Williams, Vera B. *"More More More," Said the Baby.* Greenwillow, 1990. Ages 2–4.

Toy Books

Baum, L. Frank. *The Wonderful World of Oz: A Commemorative Pop-Up.* Illustrated by Robert Sabuda. Simon & Schuster, 2000. Ages 6–9.

Carle, Eric. *The Honeybee and the Robber: A Moving/Picture Book.* Philomel, 1995 (1981). Ages 5–7.

———. *The Very Hungry Caterpillar.* World, 1968. Ages 4–6.

———. *The Very Quiet Cricket.* Putnam, 1990. Ages 2–6.

Gomi, Taro. *I Lost My Dad.* Kane/Miller, 2001. Ages 4–7.

Hill, Eric. *Where's Spot?* Putnam, 1980. Ages 3–5.

Jonas, Ann. *Where Can It Be?* Greenwillow, 1986. Ages 5–7.

Sabuda, Robert. *Alice's Adventures in Wonderland.* Simon & Schuster, 2003. Ages 8–12.

Taback, Simms. *There Was an Old Lady Who Swallowed a Fly.* Viking, 1997. Ages 5–7. (See also Pattern Books.)

Zelinsky, Paul O., adapter. *Knick-Knack Paddywhack! A Moving Parts Book.* Dutton, 2002. Ages 5–8.

Wordless Books

These books are generally suitable for ages 3 to 6. Ages will be provided only for those books intended for an older audience.

Baker, Jeannie. *Window.* Greenwillow, 1991. Ages 7–12.

Collington, Peter. *A Small Miracle.* Knopf, 1997. Ages 4–7.

Day, Alexandra. *Carl Goes Shopping.* Farrar, 1989. (See others in the series.)

Feelings, Tom. *The Middle Passage: White Ships/ Black Cargo.* Dial, 1995. Ages 9–14.

Hutchins, Pat. *Changes, Changes.* Macmillan, 1971.

Mayer, Mercer. *A Boy, a Dog, and a Frog.* Dial, 1967. (Others in this series: *Frog, Where Are You?; A Boy, a Dog, and a Friend; Frog on His Own; Frog Goes to Dinner; One Frog Too Many,* with Marianna Mayer.)

McCully, Emily Arnold. *Four Hungry Kittens.* Dial, 2001. Ages 4–7.

Popov, Nikolai. *Why?* North-South, 1996. Ages 8–12. (See also Picture Books for Older Readers.)

Rohmann, Eric. *Time Flies.* Crown, 1994. Ages 7–12.

Spier, Peter. *Oh, Were They Ever Happy!* Doubleday, 1978. Ages 6–8.

———. *Peter Spier's Rain.* Doubleday, 1982.

Vincent, Gabrielle. *A day, a dog.* Front Street, 1999. Ages 6–8.

Weitzman, Jacqueline Preiss. *You Can't Take a Balloon into the Museum of Fine Arts.* Illustrated by Robin Preiss Glasser. Dial, 2002. Ages 5–8.

Wiesner, David. *Free Fall.* Lothrop, 1988. Ages 6–10.

———. *Sector 7.* Clarion, 1999. Ages 6–10.

———. *Tuesday.* Clarion, 1991. Ages 6–10.

Alphabet Books

These books are generally suitable for ages 3 to 6. Ages will be provided only for those books intended for an older audience.

Aylesworth, Jim. *Old Black Fly.* Illustrated by Stephen Gammell. Holt, 1992.

Bunting, J. *My First ABC Book.* Dorling Kindersley, 1993.

Dodson, Peter. *An Alphabet of Dinosaurs.* Illustrated by Wayne D. Barlowe. Scholastic, 1995. Ages 4–9.

Ehlert, Lois. *Eating the Alphabet: Fruits and Vegetables from A to Z.* Harcourt, 1989.

Feelings, Muriel. *Jambo Means Hello: Swahili Alphabet Book.* Illustrated by Tom Feelings. Dial, 1974. Ages 6–8.

Fleming, Denise. *Alphabet under Construction.* Holt, 2002. Ages 4–7.

Greenaway, Kate. *A—Apple Pie.* Warne, 1886.

Holtz, Lara Tankel. *DK Alphabet Book.* Illustrated by Dave King. DK, 1997. Ages 5–8.

Inkpen, Mick. *Kipper's A to Z: An Alphabet Adventure.* Harcourt, 2001. Ages 5–7.

Jay, Alison. *ABC: A Child's First Alphabet Book.* Dutton, 2003. Ages 4–7.

Johnson, Stephen T. *Alphabet City.* Viking, 1995. Ages 6–9.

Kalman, Maira. *What Pete Ate from A to Z: (Really!).* Putnam, 2001, Ages 5–8.

Martin, Bill, Jr., and John Archambault. *Chicka Chicka Boom Boom.* Illustrated by Lois Ehlert. Simon & Schuster, 1989.

Mullins, Patricia. *V for Vanishing: An Alphabet of Endangered Animals.* HarperCollins, 1993. Ages 6–8.

Musgrove, Margaret. *Ashanti to Zulu: African Traditions.* Illustrated by Leo and Diane Dillon. Dial, 1976. Ages 8–12.

Nathan, Cheryl. *Bugs and Beasties ABC.* Cool Kids Press, 1995. Ages 4–6.

Pelletier, David. *The Graphic Alphabet.* Orchard, 1996. Ages 9–12.

Pomeroy, Diana. *Wildflower ABC: An Alphabet of Potato Prints.* Harcourt, 1997. Ages 3–6.

Seeger, Laura Vaccaro. *The Hidden Alphabet.* Roaring Brook, 2003. Ages 4–7.

Shannon, George. *Tomorrow's Alphabet.* Illustrated by Donald Crews. Greenwillow, 1996. Ages 6–8.

Shaw, Eve. *Grandmother's Alphabet.* Pfeifer-Hamilton, 1997. Ages 5–8.

Tapahonso, Luci, and Eleanor Schick. *Navajo ABC: A Dine Alphabet Book.* Illustrated by Eleanor Schick. Simon & Schuster, 1995. Ages 5–8.

Wood, Audrey. *Alphabet Mystery.* Illustrated by Bruce Wood. Scholastic, 2003. Ages 3–6.

Counting Books

These books are generally suitable for ages 4 to 7. Ages will be provided only for those books intended for an older audience.

Alda, Arlene. *Arlene Alda's 1 2 3: What Do You See?* Tricycle, 1998. Ages 3–7.

Falwell, Cathryn. *Turtle Splash! Countdown at the Pond.* Greenwillow, 2001. Ages 3–6.

Hoban, Tana. *26 Letters and 99 Cents.* Greenwillow, 1987.

———. *Let's Count.* Greenwillow, 1999.

Jonas, Ann. *Splash!* Morrow, 1995.

Lifesize Animal Counting Book, The. Dorling Kindersley, 1994.

Moss, Lloyd. *Zin! Zin! Zin! A Violin.* Illustrated by Marjorie Priceman. Simon & Schuster, 1995. Ages 4–7.

Shea, Pegi Deitz, and Cynthia Weill. *Ten Mice for Tet!* Illustrated by Tô Ngoc Trang and Pham Viét Đinh. Chronicle, 2003. Ages 5–8.

Sturges, Philemon. *Ten Flashing Fireflies.* Illustrated by Anna Vojtech. North-South, 1995. Ages 4–6.

Tafuri, Nancy. *Who's Counting?* Greenwillow, 1986.

Concept Books

These books are generally suitable for ages 3 to 5. Ages will be provided only for those books intended for an older audience.

Bang, Molly. *When Sophie Gets Angry—Really, Really Angry . . . .* Scholastic, 1999. Ages 3–6.

Barton, Byron. *My Car.* Greenwillow, 2001. Ages 2–4.

Brown, Craig. *Tractor.* Greenwillow, 1995. Ages 4–6.

Cabrera, Jane. *Cat's Colors.* Dial, 1997. Ages 1–4.

Crews, Donald. *Freight Train.* Greenwillow, 1978.

Ehlert, Lois. *Growing Vegetable Soup.* Harcourt, 1987.

Hoban, Tana. *Color Everywhere.* Morrow, 1995.

———. *Push Pull, Empty Full: A Book of Opposites.* Macmillan, 1972.

Hughes, Shirley. *Alfie Gets in First.* Lothrop, 1982.

———. *Alfie Gives a Hand.* Lothrop, 1984.

Jenkins, Emily. *Five Creatures.* Illustrated by Tomek Bogacki. Farrar, 2001. Ages 4–7.

Krauss, Ruth. *A Hole Is to Dig.* Illustrated by Maurice Sendak. Harper, 1952.

Lesser, Carolyn. *What a Wonderful Day to Be a Cow.* Illustrated by Melissa B. Mathis. Knopf, 1995. Ages 5–7.

London, Jonathon. *Like Butter on Pancakes.* Illustrated by G. Brian Karas. Viking, 1995. Ages 4–6.

McCloskey, Robert. *Time of Wonder.* Viking, 1957.

McDonald, Golden. (pseudonym of Margaret Wise Brown). *The Little Island.* Illustrated by Leonard Weisgard. Doubleday, 1946.

Meyers, Susan. *Everywhere Babies.* Illustrated by Marla Frazee. Harcourt, 2001. Ages 3–5.

Miller, Margaret. *Now I'm Big.* Greenwillow, 1996. Ages 4–6.

———. *Whose Shoe?* Greenwillow, 1991.

Rogers, Fred. *Making Friends.* Photographs by Jim Judkis. Putnam, 1987.

Rotner, Shelley. *Wheels Around.* Houghton, 1995. Ages 4–7.

Scarry, Richard. *My First Word Book.* Random House, 1986.

———. *Richard Scarry's Biggest Word Book Ever!* Random House, 1985.

Serfozo, Mary. *What's What: A Guessing Game.* Illustrated by Keiko Narahashi. McElderry, 1996. Ages 2–5.

Sís, Peter. *Fire Truck.* Greenwillow, 1998. Ages 1–3. (Also a counting book.)

———. *Trucks, Trucks, Trucks.* Greenwillow, 1999. Ages 1–3.

Wilkes, Angela. *My First Word Book.* DK, 1999.

Pattern Books

Bloom, Suzanne. *The Bus for Us.* Boyds Mills, 2001. Ages 3–6.

Chodos-Irvine, Margaret. *Ella Sarah Gets Dressed.* Harcourt, 2003. Ages 2–5.

Fleming, Denise. *In the Small, Small Pond.* Holt, 1993. Ages 4–6.

———. *Mama Cat Has Three Kittens.* Holt, 1998. Ages 2–5.

Guarino, Deborah. *Is Your Mama a Llama?* Illustrated by Stephen Kellogg. Scholastic, 1989.

Hogrogian, Nonny. *One Fine Day.* Macmillan, 1971.

Martin, Bill, Jr. *Brown Bear, Brown Bear, What Do You See?* Illustrated by Eric Carle. Holt, 1983.

———. *Panda Bear, Panda Bear, What Do You See?* Illustrated by Eric Carle. Holt, 2003. Ages 3–6.

———. *Polar Bear, Polar Bear, What Do You Hear?* Illustrated by Eric Carle. Holt, 1991.

Rosen, Michael, reteller. *We're Going on a Bear Hunt.* Illustrated by Helen Oxenbury. Macmillan, 1989.

Shannon, David. *No, David!* Scholastic, 1998. Ages 2–5.

Taback, Simms. *Joseph Had a Little Overcoat.* Viking, 1999. Ages 3–6.

———. *There Was an Old Lady Who Swallowed a Fly.* Viking, 1997. Ages 5–7. (See also Toy Books.)

Williams, Sue. *I Went Walking.* Illustrated by Julie Vivas. Harcourt, 1990.

Picture Storybooks

Agee, Jon. *Milo's Hat Trick.* Hyperion, 2001. Ages 5–8.

Alarcón, Karen B. *Louella Mae, She's Run Away.* Illustrated by Roseann Litzinger. Holt, 1997. Ages 3–5.

Allard, Harry. *Miss Nelson Is Missing.* Illustrated by James Marshall. Houghton, 1977. Ages 6–8.

Baker, Jeannie. *Where the Forest Meets the Sea.* Greenwillow, 1988. Ages 8–10.

Baker, Olaf. *Where the Buffaloes Begin.* Illustrated by Stephen Gammell. Warne, 1981. Ages 8–10.

Banks, Kate. *And If the Moon Could Talk.* Illustrated by George Hallensleben. Farrar, 1998.

———. *Baboon.* Illustrated by George Hallensleben. Farrar, 1997. Ages 3–5.

Bemelmans, Ludwig. *Madeline.* Viking, 1939. Ages 5–7.

Best, Cari. *Goose's Story.* Illustrated by Holly Meade. Farrar, 2002. Ages 4–8.

———. *Three Cheers for Catherine the Great!* Illustrated by Giselle Potter. DK Ink, 1999. Ages 6–9.

Blos, Joan W. *Old Henry.* Illustrated by Stephen Gammell. Morrow, 1987. Ages 7–9.

Bradby, Marie. *More Than Anything Else.* Illustrated by Chris K. Soentpiet. Orchard, 1995. Ages 4–8.

Brown, Marc. *D. W. the Picky Eater.* Little, Brown, 1995. Ages 5–8.

Brown, Margaret Wise. *Goodnight Moon.* Illustrated by Clement Hurd. Harper, 1947. Ages 4–6.

Browne, Anthony. *Gorilla.* Knopf, 1985. Ages 7–9.

———. *The Shape Game.* Farrar, 2003. Ages 5–8.

———. *Voices in the Park.* DK Ink, 1998. Ages 6–10.

Bunting, Eve. *Train to Somewhere.* Illustrated by Ronald Himler. Clarion, 1996. Ages 7–10.

———. *The Wall.* Illustrated by Ronald Himler. Clarion, 1990. Ages 7–9.

———. *The Wednesday Surprise.* Illustrated by Donald Carrick. Clarion, 1989. Ages 6–10.

Burningham, John. *Grandpa.* Crown, 1985. Ages 5–7.

———. *Mr. Gumpy's Motor Car.* Harper, 1976.

Burton, Virginia Lee. *The Little House.* Houghton, 1942. Ages 5–7.

———. *Mike Mulligan and His Steam Shovel.* Houghton, 1939. Ages 5–7.

Carle, Eric. *The Grouchy Ladybug.* Crowell, 1971. Ages 5–7.

———. *The Very Busy Spider.* Philomel, 1984. Ages 5–7.

Carrick, Carol. *What Happened to Patrick's Dinosaurs?* Illustrated by Donald Carrick. Clarion, 1986. Ages 6–8.

Catalanotto, Peter. *The Painter.* Orchard, 1995. Ages 4–7.

Caudill, Rebecca. *A Pocketful of Cricket.* Illustrated by Evaline Ness. Holt, 1964. Ages 6–8.

Cole, Brock. *Buttons.* Farrar, 2000. Ages 6–8.

———. *Larky Mavis.* Farrar, 2001. Ages 5–7.

Cooney, Barbara. *Island Boy.* Viking, 1988. Ages 6–10.

———. *Miss Rumphius.* Viking, 1982. Ages 6–10.

Coy, John. *Night Driving.* Illustrated by Peter McCarty. Holt, 1996. Ages 4–6.

Crews, Donald. *Bigmama's.* Greenwillow, 1991. Ages 4–7.

Cronin, Doreen. *Click, Clack, Moo: Cows That Type.* Illustrated by Betsy Lewin. Simon & Schuster, 2000. Ages 4–7.

Deacon, Alexis. *Beegu.* Farrar, 2003. Ages 3–6.

de Brunhoff, Jean. *The Story of Babar.* Random House, 1933. Ages 6–8.

dePaola, Tomie. *The Art Lesson.* Putnam, 1989. Ages 6–8.

———. *Nana Upstairs, Nana Downstairs.* Putnam, 1973. Ages 6–8.

———. *Strega Nona.* Prentice Hall, 1975. Ages 5–7.

Dorros, Arthur. *Abuela.* Illustrated by Elisa Kleven. Dutton, 1991. Ages 5–7.

Duvoisin, Roger. *Petunia.* Knopf, 1950. Ages 6–8.

Egan, Tim. *Metropolitan Cow.* Houghton, 1996. Ages 4–7.

Erdrich, Louise. *Grandmother's Pigeon.* Illustrated by Jim LaMarche. Hyperion, 1996. Ages 5–8.

Ets, Marie Hall, and Aurora Labastida. *Nine Days to Christmas.* Illustrated by Marie Hall Ets. Viking, 1959. Ages 7–9.

Falconer, Ian. *Olivia..* Atheneum, 2000. Ages 4–7.

———. *Olivia Saves the Circus.* Atheneum, 2001. Ages 3–7.

Feiffer, Jules. *Bark, George.* HarperCollins, 1999. Ages 3–5.

————. *I Lost My Bear.* Morrow, 1998. Ages 3–7.

Flack, Marjorie. *The Story about Ping.* Illustrated by Kurt Wiese. Viking, 1933. Ages 7–9.

Fleming, Candace. *Muncha! Muncha! Muncha!* Illustrated by Brian Karas. Simon & Schuster, 2002. Ages 3–7.

Fox, Mem. *Hattie and the Fox.* Illustrated by Patricia Mullins. Bradbury, 1987. Ages 6–8.

————. *Wilfrid Gordon McDonald Partridge.* Illustrated by Julie Vivas. Kane/Miller, 1985. Ages 6–8.

Frazee, Marla. *Roller Coaster.* Harcourt, 2003. Ages 4–7.

Freeman, Don. *Corduroy.* Viking, 1968. Ages 3–5.

————. *A Pocket for Corduroy.* Viking, 1978. Ages 3–5.

Gág, Wanda. *Millions of Cats.* Coward-McCann, 1928. Ages 4–6.

Gerstein, Mordecai. *The Man Who Walked Between the Towers.* Millbrook, 2003. Ages 5–8.

————. *The Mountains of Tibet.* Harper, 1987. Ages 7–9. (Modern folktale.)

Graham, Bob. *Benny, An Adventure Story.* Candlewick, 1999. Ages 5–8.

————. *"Let's Get a Pup!" Said Kate.* Candlewick, 2001. Ages 3–6.

————. *Max.* Candlewick, 2000. Ages 4–7.

Greenfield, Eloise. *Nathaniel Talking.* Illustrated by Jan Spivey Gilchrist. Writers and Readers, 1989. Ages 6–8.

Grifalconi, Ann. *The Village of Round and Square Houses.* Little, Brown, 1986. Ages 6–8.

Griffith, Helen. *Grandaddy's Stars.* Illustrated by James Stevenson. Morrow, 1995. Ages 6–8.

Hader, Berta, and Elmer Hader. *The Big Snow.* Macmillan, 1948. Ages 6–8.

Hall, Donald. *Ox-Cart Man.* Illustrated by Barbara Cooney. Viking, 1979. Ages 7–9.

Heide, Florence Parry, and Judith Heide Gilliland. *The Day of Ahmed's Secret.* Illustrated by Ted Lewin. Lothrop, 1990. Ages 6–10.

Henkes, Kevin. *Chrysanthemum.* Greenwillow, 1991. Ages 5–7.

————. *Julius, the Baby of the World.* Greenwillow, 1990. Ages 5–7.

————. *Lily's Purple Plastic Purse.* Greenwillow, 1996. Ages 5–7.

————. *Owen.* Greenwillow, 1993. Ages 2–4.

————. *Sheila Rae the Brave.* Greenwillow, 1987. Ages 5–7.

————. *Sheila Rae's Peppermint Stick.* Greenwillow, 2001. Ages 3–5.

————. *Wemberley Worried.* Greenwillow, 2000. Ages 5–8.

Hest, Amy. *In the Rain with Baby Duck.* Candlewick, 1995. Ages 3–6.

Ho, Minfong. *Hush!: A Thai Lullaby.* Illustrated by Holly Meade. Orchard, 1996. Ages 4–6.

Hoban, Russell. *A Baby Sister for Frances.* Illustrated by Lillian Hoban. Harper, 1964. (Others in this series: *Bedtime for Frances,* illustrated by Garth Williams, 1969; *Best Friends for Frances,* illustrated by Lillian Hoban, 1969; *A Bargain for Frances,* illustrated by Lillian Hoban. Harper, 1970.) Ages 4–6.

Hoberman, Mary Ann. *One of Each.* Illustrated by Marjorie Priceman. Little, Brown, 1997. Ages 3–7.

Hoffman, Mary. *Amazing Grace.* Illustrated by Caroline Binch. Dial, 1991. Ages 5–7.

Hort, Lenny. *The Seals on the Bus.* Illustrated by G. Brian Karas. Holt, 2000. Ages 4–7.

Isaacs, Anne. *Swamp Angel.* Illustrated by Paul O. Zelinsky. Dutton, 1994.

Johnson, Angela. *Tell Me a Story, Mama.* Illustrated by David Soman. Orchard, 1989. Ages 6–8.

Johnson, Crockett. *Harold and the Purple Crayon.* Harper, 1955. Ages 5–7.

Jonas, Ann. *The Quilt.* Greenwillow, 1984. Agest 7–9.

Jonell, Lynne. *Mommy Go Away!* Illustrated by Petra Mathers. Putnam, 1997. Ages 4–6.

Joose, Barbara M. *Snow Day!* Illustrated by Jennifer Plecas. Clarion, 1995. Ages 5–7.

Joyce, William. *Bently and Egg.* HarperCollins, 1992. Ages 4–8.

Jukes, Mavis. *Like Jake and Me.* Illustrated by Lloyd Bloom. Knopf, 1984. Ages 6–8.

Keats, Ezra Jack. *Goggles.* Macmillan, 1969. Ages 5–7.

————. *Peter's Chair.* Harper, 1967. Ages 4–6.

————. *The Snowy Day.* Viking, 1962. Ages 4–6.

————. *Whistle for Willie.* Viking, 1964. Ages 5–7.

Kellogg, Steven. *Pinkerton, Behave!* Dial, 1979. Ages 6–8.

Kesey, Ken. *Little Tricker the Squirrel Meets Big Double the Bear.* Illustrated by Barry Moser. Viking, 1990. Ages 8–11.

Kleven, Elisa. *The Puddle Pail.* Dutton, 1997. Ages 5–8.

Krensky, Stephen. *How Santa Got His Job.* Illustrated by S. D. Schindler. Simon & Schuster, 1998. Ages 5–8.

Krudop, Walter L. *Something Is Growing.* Atheneum, 1995. Ages 5–7.

Kvasnosky, Laura McGee. *Zelda and Ivy.* Candlewick, 1998. Ages 6–8.

———. *Zelda and Ivy One Christmas.* Candlewick, 2000. Ages 6–8.

Leaf, Munro. *The Story of Ferdinand.* Illustrated by Robert Lawson. Viking, 1936. Ages 7–9.

Lee, Ho Baek. *While We Were Out.* Kane/Miller, 2003. Ages 4–7.

Lester, Helen. *Hooway for Wodney Wat.* Illustrated by Lynn Munsinger. Houghton, 1999. Ages 4–7.

Lester, Julius. *Sam and the Tigers: A New Telling of Little Black Sambo.* Illustrated by Jerry Pinkney. Dial, 1996. Ages 3–8.

Lewis, Kim. *My Friend Harry.* Candlewick, 1995. Ages 3–5.

Lincoln, Abraham. *The Gettysburg Address.* Illustrated by Michael McCurdy. Houghton, 1995. Ages 5–YA.

Lionni, Leo. *Alexander and the Wind-up Mouse.* Pantheon 1967. Ages 6–8.

———. *The Biggest House in the World.* Pantheon, 1968. Ages 5–7.

———. *Inch by Inch.* Astor-Honor, 1960. Ages 5–7.

———. *Swimmy.* Pantheon, 1963. Ages 6–8.

Long, Melinda. *How I Became a Pirate.* Illustrated by David Shannon. Harcourt, 2003. Ages 5–8.

Loomis, Christine. *Astro Bunnies.* Illustrated by Ora Eitan. Putnam, 2001. Ages 4–7.

Lum, Kate. *What? Cried Granny: An Almost Bedtime Story.* Illustrated by Adrian Johnson. Dial, 1999. Ages 5–8.

MacLachlan, Patricia. *Mama One, Mama Two.* Illustrated by Ruth Lercher Bornstein. Harper, 1982. Ages 8–10.

Mahy, Margaret. *17 Kings and 42 Elephants.* Illustrated by Patricia McCarthy. Dial, 1987. Ages 6–10.

Marshall, James. *George and Martha.* Houghton, 1972. Ages 6–8.

———. *George and Martha Round and Round.* Houghton, 1988. Ages 6–8.

Mayer, Mercer. *There's a Nightmare in My Closet.* Dial, 1968. Ages 5–7.

McClintock, Barbara. *Dahlia.* Farrar, 2002. Ages 5–7.

McCloskey, Robert. *Blueberries for Sal.* Viking, 1948. Ages 5–7.

———. *Make Way for Ducklings.* Viking, 1941. Ages 5–7.

———. *One Morning in Maine.* Viking, 1952. Ages 7–9.

McCully, Emily A. *The Pirate Queen.* Putnam, 1995. Ages 7–10.

McDonald, Megan. *Insects Are My Life.* Illustrated by Paul B. Johnson. Orchard, 1995. Ages 5–8.

McFarland, Lyn Rossiter. *Widget.* Illustrated by Jim McFarland. Farrar, 2001. Ages 4–6.

McKissack, Patricia C., and Fredrick L. *Christmas in the Big House, Christmas in the Quarters.* Illustrated by John Thompson. Scholastic, 1994. Ages 8–12.

———. *Flossie and the Fox.* Illustrated by Rachel Isadora. Dial, 1986. Ages 7–9.

McMullan, Kate. *I Stink!* Illustrated by Jim McMullan. HarperCollins, 2002. Ages 4–7.

McNaughton, Colin. *Suddenly!* Harcourt, 1995. Ages 4–6.

Meddaugh, Susan. *Martha Blah Blah.* Houghton, 1996. Ages 5–7.

———. *Martha Speaks.* Houghton, 1992. Ages 4–8.

Melmed, Laura K. *The Rainbabies.* Illustrated by Jim LaMarche. Lothrop, 1992. Ages 7–9.

Mochizuki, Ken. *Baseball Saved Us.* Illustrated by Dom Lee. Lee & Low, 1993. Ages 7–9.

———. *Heroes.* Illustrated by Dom Lee. Lee & Low, 1995. Ages 7–9.

Mollel, Tololwa. *The Orphan Boy.* Illustrated by Paul Morin. Clarion, 1991. Ages 7–9.

Mosel, Arlene, adapter. *The Funny Little Woman.* Illustrated by Blair Lent. Dutton, 1972. Ages 6–8.

Napoli, Donna Jo. *Albert.* Illustrated by Jim LaMarche. Harcourt, 2001. Ages 5–8.

Peet, Bill. *Cyrus the Unsinkable Sea Serpent.* Houghton, 1975. Ages 5–7.

Peters, Lisa Westberg. *Cold Little Duck, Duck, Duck.* Illustrated by Sam Williams. Greenwillow, 2000. Ages 1–4.

Pilkey, Dav. *The Hallo-Weiner.* Scholastic, 1995. Ages 5–8.

———. *The Paperboy.* Orchard, 1996. Ages 6–9.

Polacco, Patricia. *Chicken Sunday.* Putnam, 1992. Ages 4–9.

———. *The Keeping Quilt.* Simon & Schuster, 1988. Ages 6–8.

———. *Thunder Cake.* Putnam, 1990. Ages 6–8.

Pomerantz, Charlotte. *The Chalk Doll.* Illustrated by Frané Lessac. Harper, 1989. Ages 7–9.

Potter, Beatrix. *The Tale of Peter Rabbit.* Warne, 1902. (See 20 other titles in the series.) Ages 5–7.

Priceman, Marjorie. *How to Make an Apple Pie and See the World.* Knopf, 1994. Ages 6–8.

Provensen, Alice, and Martin Provensen. *The Glorious Flight: Across the Channel with Louis Blériot.* Viking: 1983. Ages 8–10.

Ransome, Arthur. *The Fool of the World and the Flying Ship.* Illustrated by Uri Shulevitz. Farrar, 1968. Ages 6–8.

Raschka, Chris. *Can't Sleep.* Orchard, 1995. Ages 3–5.

———. *Mysterious Thelonious.* Orchard, 1997. Ages 5–8.

Rathmann, Peggy. *The Day the Babies Crawled Away.* Putnam, 2003. Ages 4–7.

———. *Officer Buckle and Gloria.* Putnam, 1995. Ages 6–8.

———. *10 Minutes till Bedtime.* Putnam, 1998. Ages 3–6.

Rey, Hans A. *Curious George.* Houghton, 1941. (See others in the Curious George series.) Ages 5–7.

Riley, Linnea. *Mouse Mess.* Scholastic, 1997. Ages 4–6.

Ringgold, Faith. *Aunt Harriet's Underground Railroad in the Sky.* Crown, 1992. Ages 6–9.

———. *Tar Beach.* Crown, 1991. Ages 8–10.

Rounds, Glen. *Once We Had a Horse.* Holiday, 1996. Ages 5–8.

Rylant, Cynthia. *The Relatives Came.* Illustrated by Stephen Gammell. Bradbury, 1985. Ages 6–10.

———. *When I Was Young in the Mountains.* Illustrated by Diane Goode. Dutton, 1982. Ages 7–9.

Sanfield, Steve. *Bit by Bit.* Illustrated by Susan Gaber. Philomel, 1995. Ages 5–8.

Say, Allen. *Tree of Cranes.* Houghton, 1991. Ages 7–9.

Schwartz, Amy. *Annabelle Swift, Kindergartner.* Orchard, 1988. Ages 5–7.

Scieszka, Jon. *Math Curse.* Illustrated by Lane Smith. Viking, 1995. Ages 8–10.

———. *The Stinky Cheese Man and Other Fairly Stupid Tales.* Illustrated by Lane Smith. Viking, 1992. Ages 7–10.

Sendak, Maurice. *In the Night Kitchen.* Harper, 1970. Ages 7–9.

———. *Where the Wild Things Are.* Harper, 1963. Ages 5–7.

Seuss, Dr. (pseudonym of Theodor S. Geisel). *And to Think That I Saw It on Mulberry Street.* Vanguard, 1937. Ages 5–7.

———. *The 500 Hats of Bartholomew Cubbins.* Vanguard, 1938. Ages 5–7.

———. *Horton Hatches the Egg.* Random, 1940. Ages 6–8.

———. *Oh, the Places You'll Go!* Random, 1990. Ages 6–8.

———. *Thidwick the Big-Hearted Moose.* Random, 1948. Ages 6–8.

Shannon, David. *David Gets in Trouble.* Scholastic, 2002. Ages 4–6.

———. *Duck on a Bike.* Scholastic, 2002. Ages 3–6.

Shannon, George. *Tippy-Toe Chick, Go!* Illustrated by Laura Dronzek. Greenwillow, 2003. Ages 4–6.

Shelby, Anne. *Homeplace.* Illustrated by Wendy A. Halperin. Orchard, 1995. Ages 4–7.

Shulevitz, Uri. *Snow.* Farrar, 1998. Ages 3–6.

Simont, Marc. *The Goose That Almost Got Cooked.* Scholastic, 1997. Ages 4–7.

———. *The Stray Dog: From a True Story by Reiko Sassa.* HarperCollins, 2001. Ages 4–7.

Sís, Peter. *Madlenka.* Farrar, 2000. Ages 5–8.

———. *Madlenka's Dog.* Farrar, 2002. Ages 3–7.

Slobodkina, Esphyr, *Caps for Sale.* Addison-Wesley, 1947. Ages 4–6.

Soto, Gary. *Chato's Kitchen.* Illustrated by Susan Guevara. Putnam, 1995.

———. *Too Many Tamales.* Illustrated by Ed Martinez. Putnam, 1993.

Stanley, Diane. *Saving Sweetness.* Illustrated by G. Brian Karas. Putnam, 1996. Ages 4–7.

Steen, Sandra and Susan. *Car Wash.* Illustrated by Brian Karas. Putnam, 2001. Ages 3–7.

Steig, William. *The Amazing Bone.* Farrar, 1976. Ages 7–9.

———. *Doctor De Soto.* Farrar, 1982. Ages 7–9.

———. *Pete's a Pizza.* HarperCollins, 1998. Ages 2–5.

———. *Sylvester and the Magic Pebble.* Simon & Schuster, 1969. Ages 7–9.

———. *The Toy Brother.* HarperCollins, 1996. Ages 6–9.

Steptoe, John. *Stevie.* Harper, 1969. Ages 5–7.

Stevens, Janet. *From Pictures to Words: A Book about Making a Book.* Holiday, 1995. Ages 5–8.

Stevenson, James. *All Aboard!* Greenwillow, 1995. Ages 6–8.

Stewart, Sarah. *The Gardener.* Illustrated by David Small. Farrar, 1997. Ages 4–7.

Stock, Catherine. *Where Are You Going, Manyoni?* Morrow, 1993.

Stuve-Bodeen, Stephanie. *Elizabeti's Doll.* Illustrated by Christy Hale. Lee & Low, 1998. Ages 3–7.

Udry, Janice May. *The Moon Jumpers.* Illustrated by Maurice Sendak. Harper, 1959. Ages 5–7.

Van Allsburg, Chris. *Jumanji.* Houghton, 1981. Ages 6–10.

———. *The Sweetest Fig.* Houghton, 1993. Ages 8–11.

———. *Two Bad Ants.* Houghton, 1988.

———. *The Wretched Stone.* Houghton, 1991. Ages 8–11.

Van Laan, Nancy. *Possum Come a-Knockin'.* Illustrated by George Booth. Knopf, 1990. Ages 7–9.

Vincent, Gabrielle. *Where Are You, Ernest and Celestine?* Greenwillow, 1986. Ages 6–8.

Viorst, Judith. *Alexander and the Terrible, Horrible, No Good, Very Bad Day.* Illustrated by Ray Cruz. Atheneum, 1972. Ages 5–7.

———. *Alexander, Who's Not (Do You Hear Me? I Mean It!) Going to Move.* Illustrated by Robin Glasser. Atheneum, 1995. Ages 4–8.

———. *Alexander Who Used to Be Rich Last Sunday.* Illustrated by Ray Cruz. Atheneum, 1978. Ages 6–8.

———. *I'll Fix Anthony.* Illustrated by Arnold Lobel. Harper, 1969. Ages 4–6.

Waber, Bernard. *Do You See a Mouse?* Houghton, 1995. Ages 5–9.

———. *Ira Says Goodbye.* Houghton, 1988. Ages 6–8.

———. *Ira Sleeps Over.* Houghton, 1972. Ages 6–8.

Waddell, Martin. *Can't You Sleep, Little Bear?* Illustrated by Barbara Firth. Candlewick, 1992. Ages 2–4.

———. *Farmer Duck.* Illustrated by Helen Oxenbury. Candlewick, 1992. Ages 4–6.

———. *Hi, Harry! The Moving Story of How One Slow Tortoise Slowly Made a Friend.* Illustrated by Barbara Firth. Candlewick, 2003. Ages 3–5.

———. *When the Teddy Bears Came.* Illustrated by Penny Dale. Candlewick, 1995. Ages 3–5.

Wells, Rosemary. *Bunny Cakes.* Dial, 1997. Ages 2–6.

Wiesner, David. *June 29, 1999.* Clarion, 1992. Ages 6–9.

Wild, Margaret. *The Very Best of Friends.* Illustrated by Julie Vivas. Harcourt, 1990. Ages 6–8.

Willems, Mo. *Don't Let the Pigeon Drive the Bus.* Hyperion, 2003. Ages 4–7.

Williams, Margery. *The Velveteen Rabbit.* Illustrated by William Nicholson. Doubleday, 1922. Ages 6–8.

Williams, Sherley Anne. *Working Cotton.* Illustrated by Carole Byard. Harcourt, 1992. Ages 5–7.

Williams, Vera B. *A Chair for My Mother.* Greenwillow, 1982. Ages 6–8.

———. *Stringbean's Trip to the Shining Sea.* Illustrated by author and Jennifer Williams. Greenwillow, 1988. Ages 7–9.

Wong, Janet S. *Buzz.* Harcourt, 2000. Ages 3–5.

Wood, Audrey. *Hookedy Peg.* Illustrated by Don Wood. Harcourt, 1987. Ages 6–8.

Yaccarino, Dan. *Deep in the Jungle.* Atheneum, 2000. Ages 5–9.

Yashima, Taro (pseudonym of Jun Iwamatsu). *Crow Boy.* Viking, 1955. Ages 7–9.

Yolen, Jane. *Owl Moon.* Illustrated by John Schoenherr. Putnam, 1987. Ages 6–8.

Yorinks, Arthur. *Company's Coming.* Illustrated by David Small. Crown, 1988. Ages 7–9.

———. *Hey, Al.* Illustrated by Richard Egielski. Farrar, 1986. Ages 7–9.

Young, Ed. *Seven Blind Mice.* Philomel, 1992. Ages 6–10. (Modern folktale)

Zion, Gene. *Harry, the Dirty Dog.* Illustrated by Margaret B. Graham. HarperTrophy, 1976 (1956). Ages 4–6.

Zolotow, Charlotte. *If It Weren't for You.* Illustrated by Ben Shecter. Harper, 1966. Ages 6–8.

———. *Mr. Rabbit and the Lovely Present.* Illustrated by Maurice Sendak. Harper, 1962. Ages 5–7.

———. *William's Doll.* Illustrated by William Pène du Bois. Harper, 1972. Ages 6–8.

Easy-to-Read Books

These books are generally suitable for ages 4 to 8.

Adler, David A. *Young Cam Jansen and the Double Beach Mystery.* Illustrated by Susanna Natti. Viking, 2002. Ages 5–7.

Barrett, Judi. *Animals Should Definitely Not Wear Clothing.* Atheneum, 1977.

Barton, Byron. *The Wee Little Woman.* HarperCollins, 1995. Ages 4–6.

Brown, Margaret Wise. *Four Fur Feet.* Illustrated by Woodleigh M. Hubbard. Hyperion, 1994. Ages 3–6.

———. *Goodnight Moon.* Harper, 1947.

———. *The Runaway Bunny.* Illustrated by Clement Hurd. Harper, 1991 (1942). Ages 2–5.

Byars, Betsy, *Ant Plays Bear.* Illustrated by Marc Simont. Viking, 1997. Ages 6–8.

———. *My Brother, Ant.* Illustrated by Marc Simont. Viking, 1996. Ages 6–8.

Coerr, Eleanor. *The Josefina Story Quilt.* Illustrated by Bruce Degen. Harper, 1986.

Cole, Joanna, and Stephanie Calmenson. *The Gator Girls.* Illustrated by Lynn Munsinger. Morrow, 1995. Ages 7–8.

———, compilers. *Ready ... Set ... Read!: The Beginning Reader's Treasury.* Illustrated by Anne Burgess and Chris Demarest. Doubleday, 1990.

Danziger, Paula. *Get Ready for Second Grade, Amber Brown.* Illustrated by Tony Ross. Putnam, 2002. Ages 5–7.

———. *It's a Fair Day, Amber Brown.* Illustrated by Tony Ross. Putnam, 2002. Ages 5–7.

dePaola, Tomie. *Hide-and-Seek All Week.* Grosset and Dunlap, 2001. Ages 5–7.

de Regniers, Beatrice Schenk. *May I Bring a Friend?* Illustrated by Beni Montresor. Atheneum, 1964.

Dunrea, Olivier. *Gossie.* Houghton, 2002. Ages 3–5. Also *Gossie and Gertie.*

Fleming, Denise. *Buster.* Holt, 2003. Ages 5–7.

Gág, Wanda. *Millions of Cats.* Coward-McCann, 1928.

Guest, Elissa Haden. *Iris and Walter.* Illustrated by Christine Davenier. Harcourt/Gulliver, 2000. Ages 6–8.

———. *Iris and Walter: The Sleepover.* Illustrated by Christine Davenier. Harcourt, 2002. Ages 5–7.

Haskins, Lori. *Ducks in Muck.* Illustrated by Valeria Petrone. Random, 2000. Ages 5–7.

Hoberman, Mary Ann. *You Read to Me, I'll Read to You. Very Short Stories to Read Together.* Illustrated by Michael Emberley. Little, Brown, 2001. Ages 5–7.

Holub, Joan. *The Garden That We Grew.* Illustrated by Hiroe Nakata. Viking, 2001. Ages 5–7.

Horowitz, Ruth. *Breakout at the Bug Lab.* Illustrated by Joan Holub. Dial, 2001. Ages 5–8.

Howe, James. *Pinky and Rex and the Just-Right Pet.* Illustrated by Melissa Sweet. Simon & Schuster, 2001. Ages 6–8.

Hutchins, Pat. *The Doorbell Rang.* Greenwillow, 1986.

———. *Rosie's Walk.* Macmillan, 1968.

———. *Titch.* Macmillan, 1971.

Johnson, Crockett. *A Picture for Harold's Room.* Harper, 1960.

Koss, Amy Goldman. *Where Fish Go in Winter and Other Great Mysteries.* Illustrated by Laura J. Bryant. Dial, 2000. Ages 5–7.

Kraus, Robert. *Leo the Late Bloomer.* Illustrated by José Aruego. Dutton, 1971.

Little, Jean. *Emma's Magic Winter.* Illustrated by Jennifer Plecas. HarperCollins, 1998. Ages 6–8.

Livingstone, Star. *Harley.* Illustrated by Molly Bang. North-South, 2001. Ages 5–7.

Lobel, Arnold. "Frog and Toad Series." *Frog and Toad Are Friends.* Harper, 1970. (Others in this series: *Frog and Toad Together,* 1972; *Frog and Toad All Year,* 1976; *Days with Frog and Toad,* 1979.)

———. *Mouse Soup.* Harper, 1977.

Minarik, Else Holmelund. *Little Bear.* Illustrated by Maurice Sendak. Harper, 1957. (Others in the Little Bear series: *Father Bear Comes Home,* 1959; *Little Bear's Friend,* 1960; *Little Bear's Visit,* 1961; *A Kiss for Little Bear,* 1968.)

Numeroff, Laura Joffe. *If You Give a Mouse a Cookie.* Harper, 1985.

Paterson, Katherine. *Marvin One Too Many.* Illustrated by Jane Clark Brown. HarperCollins, 2001. Ages 5–7.

Raschka, Chris. *Yo! Yes?* Orchard, 1993. (See also *Ring! Yo?*)

Rodda, Emily. *Power and Glory.* Illustrated by Geoff Kelly. Greenwillow, 1996. Ages 5–7.

Root, Phyllis. *Mouse Goes Out.* Illustrated by James Croft. Candlewick, 2002. Ages 4–6.

Rylant, Cynthia. *Henry and Mudge.* Illustrated by Suçie Stevenson. Bradbury, 1987. (See others in this series.)

———. *Henry and Mudge and the Snowman Plan.* Illustrated by Suçie Stevenson. Simon & Schuster, 1999. Ages 5–7.

———. *Mr. Putter & Tabby Feed the Fish.* Illustrated by Arthur Howard. Harcourt, 2001. Ages 5–7.

Seuss, Dr. (pseudonym of Theodor S. Geisel). *The Cat in the Hat.* Random, 1957.

———. *The Cat in the Hat Comes Back.* Random, 1958.

———. *Fox in Sox.* Random, 1965.

Thomas, Shelley Moore. *Good Night, Good Knight.* Illustrated by Jennifer Plecas. Dutton, 2000. Ages 5–8.

Van Leeuwen, Jean. *Amanda Pig, Schoolgirl.* Illustrated by Ann Schweninger. Dial, 1997. Ages 5–6.

Waber, Bernard. *Bearsie Bear and the Surprise Sleepover Party.* Houghton, 1997. Ages 4–7.

Wallace, Karen. *Wild Baby Animals.* Dorling Kindersley, 2000. Ages 5–8.

Welch, Willy. *Playing Right Field.* Illustrated by Marc Simont. Scholastic, 1995. Ages 5–8.

Wells, Rosemary. *Noisy Nora.* Dial, 1973.

Winter, Jeanette. *Follow the Drinking Gourd.* Knopf, 1988.

Wood, Audrey. *The Napping House.* Illustrated by Don Wood. Harcourt, 1984.

Zolotow, Charlotte. *Do You Know What I'll Do?* Illustrated by Garth Williams. Harper, 1958.

———. *If It Weren't for You.* Harper, 1966.

Picture Books for Older Readers

Avi. *Silent Movie.* Illustrated by C. B. Mordan. Atheneum, 2003. Ages 8–12.

Bang, Molly. *Goose.* Scholastic, 1996. Ages 8–10.

———. *The Paper Crane.* Greenwillow, 1985. Ages 8–10.

Briggs, Raymond. *The Man.* Random House, 1995. Ages 9–14.

———. *Ug: Boy Genius of the Stone Age.* Knopf, 2002. Ages 8–12.

Browne, Anthony. *Piggybook.* Knopf, 1986. Ages 9–YA.

———. *The Tunnel.* Knopf, 1990. Ages 8–12.

———. *Zoo.* Knopf, 1993. Ages 8–YA.

Bunting, Eve. *Riding the Tiger.* Illustrated by David Frampton. Clarion, 2001. Ages 8–11.

Cendrars, Blaise. *Shadow.* Illustrated by Marcia Brown. Scribner's, 1982. Ages 8–10.

Collington, Peter. *The Coming of the Surfman.* Knopf, 1994. Ages 8–14.

Crew, Gary. *The Watertower.* Illustrated by Steven Woolman. Kane/Miller, 1995. Ages 10–14.

Diaz, Jorge. *The Rebellious Alphabet.* Illustrated by Øivind S. Jorfald. Translated by Geoffrey Fox. Holt, 1993. Ages 9–12.

Gallaz, Christophe, and Roberto Innocenti. *Rose Blanche.* Illustrated by Roberto Innocenti. Creative Education, 1985. Ages 9–YA.

Harvey, Brett. *Cassie's Journey: Going West in the 1860s.* Illustrated by Deborah Kogan Ray. Holiday, 1988. Ages 8–10.

Heide, Florence P. *The Shrinking of Treehorn.* Illustrated by Edward Gorey. Holiday, 1971. See also *Treehorn Times Three* (Dell, 1992), a collection which includes *The Shrinking of Treehorn.* Ages 8–11.

Hodges, Margaret. *Saint George and the Dragon.* Illustrated by Trina Schart Hyman. Little, Brown, 1984. Ages 8–10.

Hooks, William H. *The Ballad of Belle Dorcas.* Illustrated by Brian Pinkney. Knopf, 1990. Ages 10–12.

Johnson, D. B. *Henry Builds a Cabin.* Houghton, 2002. Ages 9–13.

———. *Henry Climbs a Mountain.* Houghton, 2003. Ages 9–13.

———. *Henry Hikes to Fitchburg.* Houghton, 2000. Ages 9–13.

Kerley, Barbara. *The Dinosaurs of Waterhouse Hawkins.* Illustrated by Brian Selznick. Scholastic, 2001. Ages 8–12.

Macaulay, David. *Motel of the Mysteries.* Houghton, 1979. Ages 11–14.

Martin, Jacqueline, M. *Grandmother Bryant's Pocket.* Illustrated by Petra Mathers. Houghton, 1996. Ages 8–11.

Maruki, Toshi. *Hiroshima No Pika.* Lothrop, 1980. Ages 9–YA.

McDermott, Gerald. *Arrow to the Sun: A Pueblo Indian Tale.* Viking, 1974. Ages 8–10.

Moss, Marissa. *Brave Harriet: The First Woman to Fly the English Channel.* Illustrated by C. F. Payne. Harcourt, 2001. Ages 8–10.

Myers, Walter Dean. *Blues Journey.* Illustrated by Christopher Myers. Holiday, 2003. Ages 10–14.

Palatini, Margie. *The Web Files.* Illustrated by Richard Egielski. Hyperion, 2001. Ages 8–12.

Paterson, Katherine. *The Tale of the Mandarin Ducks.* Illustrated by Leo and Diane Dillon. Dutton, 1990. Ages 8–10.

Polacco, Patricia. *Pink and Say.* Philomel, 1994. Ages 8–11.

Popov, Nikolai. *Why?* North-South, 1996. Ages 8–12. (Wordless.)

Schwartz, David M. *G Is for Googol: A Math Alphabet Book.* Illustrated by Marissa Moss. Tricycle, 1998. Ages 10–YA.

Scieszka, Jon. *The True Story of the 3 Little Pigs By A. Wolf.* Illustrated by Lane Smith. Viking, 1989. Ages 8–11.

Sís, Peter. *Starry Messenger.* Farrar, 1996.

———. *Tibet through the Red Box.* Farrar, 1998.

Steiner, Jörg. *The Bear Who Wanted to Be a Bear.* Illustrated by Jörg Müller. Atheneum, 1977. Ages 8–12.

———. *Rabbit Island.* Illustrated by Jörg Müller. Harcourt, 1978. Ages 8–12.

Van Allsburg, Chris. *The Mysteries of Harris Burdick.* Houghton, 1984. Ages 8–10.

———. *The Wreck of the Zephyr.* Houghton, 1983. Ages 8–10.

Ward, Lynd. *The Biggest Bear.* Houghton, 1952. Ages 7–9.

Wick, Walter. *Walter Wick's Optical Tricks.* Scholastic, 1998. Ages 9–YA.

Wisniewski, David. *Elfwyn's Saga.* Lothrop, 1990. Ages 8–10.

———. *Rain Player.* Houghton, 1991. Ages 8–10.

Graphic Novels

Chase, John C. *Louisiana Purchase: An American Story.* Pelican, 2002 (revised edition). Ages 10–14.

Crilley, Mark. *Akiko on the Planet Smoo.* Random, 2000. Ages 9–14.

Eisner, Will. *Sundiata: A Legend of Africa.* NBM, 2003. Ages 10–14.

Gaiman, Neil. *The Wolves in the Walls.* Illustrated by Dave McKean. HarperCollins, 2003. Ages 9–12.

Gownley, Jimmy. *Amelia Rules! The Whole World's Crazy.* ibooks, 2003. Ages 8–11.

Hartman, Rachel. *Amy Unbounded: Belondweg Blossoming.* Pug House, 2002. Ages 9–14.

Hosler, Jay. *Clan Apis.* Active Synapse, 2000. Ages 10–14.

Irwin, Jane, and Jeff Verndt. *Vögelein: A Clockwork Faerie.* Fiery Studio, 2003. Ages 12–YA.

Medley, Linda. *Castle Waiting: The Curse of the Brambly Hedge.* Olio, 1991. Ages 9–14.

Rodi, Rob. *Crossovers.* CrossGeneration, 2003. Ages 11–YA.

Roman, Dave, and John Green. *Jax Epoch and the Quicken Forbidden.* Ait/Planet Lar, 2002. Ages 9–14.

Sfar, Joann. *Little Vampire Does Kung Fu!* Simon & Schuster, 2003. Ages 9–14.

Spiegelman, Art. *Little Lit: Folklore & Fairy Tale Funnies.* HarperCollins, 2000. Ages 9–YA.

———. *Maus: A Survivor's Tale* (Vol. 1). Pantheon, 1973. Age YA.

———. *Maus: A Survivor's Tale* (Vol. 2). Pantheon, 1986. Age YA.

Sturm, James. *The Golem's Mighty Swing.* Drawn & Quarterly, 2001. Ages 13–YA.

Winick, Judd. *Pedro and Me: Friendship, Loss, and What I Learned.* Holt, 2000. Age YA.

Illustrated Books of Poetry

See Chapter 3 recommended books list.

Illustrated Nursery Rhymes and Folk Songbooks

See Chapter 3 recommended books list.

Illustrated Traditional Folktales

See Chapter 5 recommended books list.

Illustrated Modern Folktales

See Chapter 6 recommended books list.

5

Traditional Literature

Visual narratives told by ancient cave paintings in Europe, Asia, and Australia show us that prehistoric humans had stories to tell long before they had a written language. For thousands of years before writing was discovered, the best of these stories were preserved through the art of storytelling from one generation to the next. Surely these stories survived because people enjoyed hearing them. Even today, their entertainment value cannot be denied. In folk literature we have our most ancient stories and a priceless literary heritage that links us to our beginnings as thinking beings.

DEFINITION AND DESCRIPTION

Traditional literature is the body of ancient stories and poems that grew out of the oral tradition of storytelling before being eventually written down. Having no known or identifiable authors, these stories and poems are attributed to entire groups of people or cultures. Although in ancient times some traditional stories may have been told as truths or may have been thought to contain elements of truth, today we consider them to be mostly or wholly fantasy.

Traditional literature includes several different types of stories, but because they were all shared orally for so long, they have many features in common. For example, plots are generally shorter than in other genres of literature because all but the essential details were omitted during countless retellings. Action is concentrated, which keeps audiences alert and interested. Characters tend to have only one outstanding quality, and are easily identified as good or bad. Settings are unimportant and are described and referred to in the vaguest of terms, such as "In the beginning . . ." or "Long ago in a land far away. . . ." Language, though full of rhythm and melody, is sparse, since lengthy explanations and descriptions were also pared down or eliminated by countless retellings. Style is characterized by stock beginnings and endings ("Once upon a time" and "They lived happily ever after"), motifs or recurring features (use of the number 3, as in three sisters, three wishes), and repetition of refrains or chants ("Mirror, mirror, on the wall . . ."). Themes are largely limited to good versus evil, the power of perseverance, and explanations for the ways of the world. One feature that makes these stories particular favorites of young children is that they almost always have a happy ending.

Folklore is still being created, particularly in some of the developing countries where the oral tradition remains the chief means of communication. In the United States, urban legends, jokes, and jump-rope rhymes are all part of the constantly evolving body of folklore. These stories and rhymes are of unknown origin, but because they are certainly not ancient, they will not be treated in this chapter.

EVALUATION AND SELECTION OF TRADITIONAL LITERATURE

For thousands of years, people of all ages were the intended audience for traditional stories. In our scientifically enlightened times, these stories have come to be seen as childlike in their use of the supernatural and magic but nonetheless charming and entertaining. The following list of evaluation criteria was developed with a general child audience in mind:

- A traditional tale, even though written down, should preserve the narrative, or storytelling, style and should sound as though it is being told.
- A traditional tale should preserve the flavor of the culture or country of its origin through the use of colloquialisms, unusual speech patterns, a few easily understood foreign terms, or proper names that are common to the culture.
- In illustrated versions of traditional literature, text and illustrations must be of high quality, and illustrations must match the tone of the text and help to capture the essence of the culture of origin.
- Though simple in other respects, traditional tales employ a rich literary style. Even very young children are fascinated by the chants, stylistic flourishes, and colorful vocabulary that are characteristic of masterful storytelling.

- In evaluating collections of traditional literature, consider the number and variety of tales in the collection and the quality of reference aids, such as tables of contents and indexes.

Some adults raise concerns that the gruesome violence that is sometimes found in traditional stories harms or traumatizes children. In recent times, many traditional stories have been rewritten to omit the violence, as in the Disney versions of folktales. In a "softened" version of "Snow White," the evil stepmother is either forgiven by the heroine or banished from the kingdom. Earlier versions of the tale end like this:

> Then she [the stepmother] railed and cursed, and was beside herself with disappointment and anger. First she thought she would not go to the wedding; but then she felt she should have no peace until she went and saw the bride. And when she saw her she knew her for Snow-white, and could not stir from the place for anger and terror. For they had ready red-hot iron shoes, in which she had to dance until she fell down dead. (From Jakob Grimm and Wilhelm Grimm, *Household Stories,* translated by Lucy Crane [Macmillan, 1886].)

Critics of the softened versions of traditional tales claim that altering the stories robs them of their power, their appeal, and their psychological benefit to children, who are reassured that the evil force is gone forever and cannot come back to hurt them. We believe that young children who have heard "softened" versions of folktales have a right to know the earlier, unaltered versions when they are old enough to cope with the violence or harsh justice they contain. Likewise, as children enter the upper intermediate and middle grades, they should be made aware of the male chauvinism and poor feminine role models, from ever-sinister stepmothers to ever-helpless princesses, rampant in folktales.

HISTORICAL OVERVIEW OF TRADITIONAL LITERATURE

Perhaps the world's first stories grew out of the dreams, wishes, ritual chants, or retellings of the notable exploits of our earliest ancestors. No one knows. Little can be said about the early history of this genre except that these stories existed only in oral form for thousands of years.

Folklorists are intrigued by the startling similarity of traditional tales around the world. Cinderella-like tales, for example, can be found in every culture. One explanation for this is that the first humans created these stories and took them along as they populated the globe. We call this theory *monogenesis,* or "single origin." Another theory credits the fundamental psychological similarity of humans for the similarity of their stories. *Polygenesis,* or "many origins," holds that early humans had similar urges and motives; asked similar, fundamental questions about themselves and the world around them; and, logically, created similar stories in response. Both theories have merit; and since the answer lies hidden in ancient prehistory, neither theory has prevailed over the other.

The popularity of traditional literature with children has continued to grow in the twenty-first century, owing in part to a renewed interest in storytelling. Other trends contributing to the popularity of this genre are the publication of single illustrated retellings of works of traditional literature, publication of cultural variants of traditional tales from around the world, and publication of newly discovered ethnic folk literature of many Canadian and U.S. minorities in collections and single illustrated works.

TYPES OF TRADITIONAL LITERATURE

For the beginning student of traditional literature, classification of stories can be confusing. For instance, not everyone uses the same terms when referring to certain types of traditional stories. Also, we have a large body of modern stories that were written by known authors in the style of the traditional ones but are not of ancient and unknown origin and therefore are not "traditional" in the strict sense.

We have chosen the term *traditional literature* to refer to the entire body of stories passed down from ancient times by the oral tradition. The term *folktale* is sometimes used in the same way. The term *retold tale* refers to a version of a tale that is obviously based upon an earlier, well-known tale but in which the language and bits of the plot have been altered to modernize or further dramatize the story. Nowadays, retold tales are often accompanied by completely new and original illustrations that sometimes give remarkable insights into the deeper meaning or relevance of these tales. *Variant,* a term often used in reference to folktales, refers to a story that shares fundamental elements of plot or character with other stories, and therefore is said to be in the same story family. There are hundreds of variants of "Cinderella," for example, from all over the world. All of the following types of traditional literature occur in variant and retold tale versions.

Myths

Myths are stories that recount and explain the origins of the world and the phenomena of nature. They are sometimes referred to as *creation stories*. The characters in these stories are mainly gods and goddesses, with occasional mention of humans, and the setting is high above earth in the home of the gods. Though often violent, myths nonetheless mirror human nature and the essence of our sometimes primitive emotions, instincts, and desires. Some folklorists believe that myths are the foundation of all other ancient stories. The best-known mythologies are of Greek, Roman, and Norse origin.

The complexity and symbolism often found in myths make them appropriate for an older audience (9 years and up) than is usual with traditional literature. Some myths have been simplified for a younger audience, but oversimplification robs these stories of their power and appeal.

M I L E S T O N E S

in the Development of TRADITIONAL LITERATURE

DATE	EVENT	SIGNIFICANCE
Prehistory–1500s	Oral storytelling	Kept ancient stories alive and provided literature to common people
500 B.C.	Aesop, a supposed Greek slave, wrote classic fables	Established the fable as a type of traditional literature
1484	*Aesop's Fables* published by William Caxton in England	First known publication of traditional literature
1500–1700	Puritan Movement	Prevented the publication of traditional literature by the legitimate press
	Chapbooks emerge	Helped keep interest in traditional heroes alive during Puritan Movement
Late 1600s	Jean de La Fontaine of France adapted earlier fables in verse form	Popularized the fable
1697	*Tales of Mother Goose* published by Charles Perrault in France	First written version of folktales
1700s	Romantic Movement	Traditional fantasy promoted and embraced in Europe
1812	Wilhelm and Jakob Grimm collected and published *Nursery and Household Tales* in Germany	Helped to popularize folk literature
1851	Asbjörnsen and Moe collected and published *The Norwegian Folktales* in Norway	Helped to popularize folk literature
1894	Joseph Jacobs collected and published *English Fairy Tales* in England; adapted many tales for a child audience	Helped to popularize folk literature
1889–1894	Andrew Lang collected and published four volumes of folktales from around the world	Growing popularity and knowledge of folktales worldwide helped to popularize folk literature

Epics

Epics are long stories of human adventure and heroism recounted in many episodes, sometimes in verse. Epics are grounded in mythology, and their characters can be both human and divine. However, the hero is always human or, in some cases, superhuman, as was Ulysses in the *Odyssey,* Beowulf in the epic of that name, and Roland in *The Song of Roland.* The setting is earthly but not always realistic. Because of their length and complexity, epics are perhaps more suitable for students in high school or college, but on the strength of their compelling characters and events, some epics have been successfully adapted and shortened for younger audiences. *Dragonslayer,* an adaptation of *Beowulf* by Rosemary Sutcliff, is a good example.

Legends and Tall Tales

Legends are stories based on either real or supposedly real individuals and their marvelous deeds. Legendary characters such as King Arthur and Robin Hood and legendary settings such as Camelot are a tantalizing mix of realism and fantasy. Although the feats of the heroes of legend defy belief today, in ancient times these stories were considered factual.

Tall tales are highly exaggerated accounts of the exploits of persons, both real and imagined, so they may be considered a subcategory of legends, albeit of much more recent origin. In the evolution of the tall tale, however, as each teller embroidered upon the hero's abilities or deeds, the tales became outlandishly exaggerated and were valued more for their humor and braggadocio than for their factual content. Legends, in contrast, are more austere in tone. Well-known North American tall-tale heroes are Pecos Bill, Paul Bunyan, John Henry, and Johnny Appleseed. Lesser known but equally amazing are such tall-tale heroines as Annie Christmas and Sally Ann Thunder Ann Whirlwind Crockett. Legends, because of their length, seriousness, and complexity, are often suitable for middle-graders; the shorter and more humorous tall tales can be enjoyed by children aged 7 and up.

Folktales

Folktales are stories that grew out of the lives and imaginations of the people, or folk. Folktales have always been children's favorite type of traditional literature and are enjoyed by children from about age 3 and up.

Folktales vary in content as to their original intended audiences. Long ago, the nobility and their courtiers heard stories of the heroism, valor, and benevolence of people like themselves—the ruling classes. In contrast, the stories heard by the common people portrayed the ruling classes as unjust or hard taskmasters whose riches were fair game for those common folk who were quick-witted or strong enough to acquire them. These class-conscious tales are sometimes referred to as *castle* and *cottage* tales, respectively.

Some people use the terms *folktale* and *fairy tale* interchangeably. In fact, the majority of these stories have no fairies or magic characters in them, so to use one term in place of the other can be confusing and erroneous. We categorize fairy tales under *magic tales,* a kind of folktale having magic characters such as fairies.

The following is a list of the most prevalent kinds of folktales. Note that some folktales have characteristics of two or more folktale categories.

CUMULATIVE   The cumulative tale uses repetition, accumulation, and rhythm to make an entertaining story out of the barest of plots. Because of its simplicity, rhythm, and humor, the cumulative tale has special appeal to 3- to 5-year-olds. "The Gingerbread Man," with its runaway cookie and his growing host of pursuers, is a good example of this kind of tale.

HUMOROUS   The humorous tale revolves around a character's incredibly stupid and funny mistakes. These tales are also known as noodleheads, sillies, drolls, and numbskulls. They have endured, no doubt, for their comic appeal and the guaranteed laughter they evoke. Some famous noodleheads are the Norwegian husband who kept house (and nearly demolished it) and Clever Elsie, who was so addle-brained that she got herself confused with someone else and was never heard from again.

BEAST   Beast tales feature talking animals and overstated action. Human characters sometimes occur. Young children accept and enjoy these talking animals, and older children can appreciate the fact that the animals symbolize humans. "Goldilocks and the Three Bears," perhaps the best-loved folktale of all, is a good example of a beast tale.

MAGIC   Magic tales, also known as wonder tales or fairy tales, contain elements of magic or enchantment in characters, plots, or settings. Fairies, elves, pixies, brownies, witches, magicians, genies, and fairy godparents are pivotal characters in these stories, and they use magic objects or words to weave their enchantments. Talking mirrors, hundred-year naps, glass palaces, enchanted forests, thumb-sized heroines, and magic kisses are the stuff of magic tales. "Aladdin and the Wonderful Lamp" is a well-loved magic tale.

POURQUOI   Pourquoi tales explain phenomena of nature. The word *pourquoi* is French for *why,* and these tales can be understood as primitive explanations for the many "why" questions early humans asked. The strong connection between these tales and myths is obvious, which is why some folklorists identify pourquoi tales as the simplest myths. Note, however, that deities play no role in pourquoi tales as they do in myths. Moreover, the setting in pourquoi tales is earthly, while the setting in myths is the realm of the gods. An example of a pourquoi tale is "Why the Sun and the Moon Live in the Sky."

REALISTIC   Realistic tales are those whose characters, plot, and setting could conceivably have occurred. There is no magic in these tales, and any exaggeration is limited to the possible. Only a few realistic tales exist. "The Hero of Bremen" is a good example.

Fables

The fable is a simple story that incorporates characters—typically animals—whose actions teach a moral lesson or universal truth. Often, the moral is stated at the end of the story. Throughout history, fables have appealed to adults as well as to children, for the best of these stories are both simple and wise. Moreover, their use of animals as symbols for human behavior have made them safe, yet effective, political tools. Perhaps because of their adult appeal, fables were put into print far earlier than other forms of traditional literature.

Aesop's fables compose the best-known collection of fables in the Western world, but other collections deserve our notice. From Persia, there are the *Panchatantra Tales;* from India, the *Jataka Tales;* and from France, the collected fables of Jean de La Fontaine.

Religious Stories

Stories based on religious writings or taken intact from religious manuscripts are considered to be religious stories. These stories may recount milestones in the development of a religion and its leadership, or they may present a piece of religious doctrine in narrative form. Stories of the latter sort are usually called *parables.*

USING TRADITIONAL LITERATURE
ACROSS THE CURRICULUM:
Language Arts

ACTIVITY	GRADE LEVEL	SUGGESTED STORIES, BOOKS, CHARACTERS
Compare three or four variants of a single folktale for similarities and differences of such features as plots, characters, and settings. Rank these variants in terms of their interest for other readers.	1–3	"Cinderella" Variants: *Cinderella* by Ruth Sanderson *Moss Gown* by William Hooks *Princess Furball* by Charlotte Huck *Cendrillon: A Caribbean Cinderella* by Robert San Souci *Yeh-Shen* by Ai-Ling Louie
Select a specific type of folktale (such as a pourquoi tale) and read several good examples. Analyze the selections for their shared features. Write an original story having these features. This activity would work with fables, also.	4–8	Pourquoi Tales: *How Chipmunk Got His Stripes: A Tale of Bragging and Teasing* by Joseph and James Bruchac *How the Manx Cat Lost Its Tail* by Janet Stevens *Why Mosquitoes Buzz in People's Ears* by Verna Aardema
Choose a folktale and write a modernized variant.		"Sleeping Beauty"
Select a folktale character in a favorite folktale. List all of this character's good and bad traits. Write a more realistic character sketch of this character, giving him or her traits that you think he or she lacks.		Snow White's stepmother Snow White's Prince Charming
Look at several picture book retellings of the same folktale, then list or tell how the illustrations changed the story in each version. Tell which you preferred and explain why.	1–8	"Jack and the Beanstalk" *Jack and the Beanstalk* by Ann Beneduce *Jack and the Beanstalk* by Steven Kellogg *Jack and the Beanstalk and the Beanstalk Incident* by Timothy Paulson

Scholars of religion, language, and mythology have found a definite thread of continuity from myth and folk narrative to early religious thinking and writing. Many of the stories, figures, and rituals described in the sacred scriptures of Christianity, Hinduism, and Buddhism, among other religions, have their roots in ancient mythology.

Regardless of whether one considers the religious stories to be fact or fiction, the important point is that these wonderful stories should be shared with children. Because religion in the classroom is potentially controversial, however, many teachers and librarians do not feel comfortable sharing stories with any religious connection. This is unfortunate, since many wonderful stories and some superlative

USING TRADITIONAL LITERATURE ACROSS THE CURRICULUM:
Social Studies

ACTIVITY	GRADE LEVEL	SUGGESTED STORIES AND BOOKS
Discuss or debate issues such as right and wrong, fairness, and good versus bad in various folktales.	K–3	"Stone Soup": the soldiers' honesty "Jack and the Beanstalk": Jack's stealing the goose "The Gingerbread Man": rightness or wrongness of the fox's eating the gingerbread man
Analyze multicultural folklore for its social messages, such as triumph over oppression, social injustice, and power versus powerlessness.	4–8	*Flossie and the Fox* by Patricia McKissack *Big Jabe* by Jerdine Nolen *Jump! The Adventures of Brer Rabbit* by Van Dyke Parks and Malcolm Jones
Look for the social messages found in an illustrated folktale. Discuss the relevance of this story to today's world.		*Hansel and Gretel* by Jakob and Wilhelm Grimm, illlustrated by Anthony Browne
Look at various illustrated versions of "Little Red Riding Hood" and analyze the story in terms of its message for girls and women today.		*Little Red Riding Hood* by Beni Montresor *Little Red Riding Hood* by Charles Perrault, illustrated by Sarah Moon
Compare "unsoftened" and "softened" versions of folktales. Discuss what differences you find and your reactions to them.		*Snow-White and the Seven Dwarfs* translated by Randall Jarrell, illustrated by Nancy E. Burkert *Walt Disney's Snow White and the Seven Dwarfs* retold by Walt Disney
Compare heroes or heroines in folktales from different cultures for similarities and differences.		*Boots and His Brothers* retold by Eric Kimmel (Norway) *The Three Princes* retold by Eric Kimmel (Middle East) *Three Sacks of Truth* retold by Eric Kimmel (France)
Compare the character traits of traditional female heroines and modern folktale heroines.		*Sleeping Beauty* retold and illustrated by Trina Schart Hyman *Sleeping Ugly* by Jane Yolen

literature, as well as characters, sayings, and situations essential to the culturally literate person, are therefore missed.

Traditional literature, the wealth of ancient stories accumulated over the course of human existence, is one of the treasures of our species. We listen to these endlessly fascinating stories, we reflect on them, and they help to tell us who we are. Good companions of our childhood, they easily become part of us and stay with us throughout our lives. Every child deserves access to this wonderful literary heritage.

NOTABLE

NOTABLE RETELLERS AND ILLUSTRATORS OF TRADITIONAL LITERATURE

Verna Aardema, reteller of African folktales. *When the Rains Came to Kapiti Plain; Why Mosquitoes Buzz in People's Ears.*

Marcia Brown, author and illustrator; seven of her nine Caldecott Medals or Honor Book Awards are for illustrating folktales. *Cinderella; Once a Mouse.*

Paul Goble, author and illustrator. Reteller and illustrator of folktales and legends of the North American Indian. *Beyond the Ridge.*

Trina Schart Hyman, reteller and illustrator of classic folktales. *Little Red Riding Hood; The Sleeping Beauty.*

Julius Lester, reteller of African-American folktales and creation stories. *When the Beginning Began: Stories about God, the Creatures, and Us; John Henry.*

James Marshall, reteller and illustrator of humorously irreverent versions of classic folktales. *Goldilocks and the Three Bears.*

Gerald McDermott, reteller and illustrator of Native American myths and folktales. *Raven: A Trickster Tale from the Pacific Northwest.*

Jerry Pinkney, Caldecott medalist whose realistic watercolors invigorate folktales, many from the African-American tradition. *Noah's Ark; John Henry; The Ugly Duckling.*

Robert D. San Souci, adaptor of obscure or almost-forgotten stories from many different places and ethnic groups. *The Faithful Friend; The Talking Eggs.*

Janet Stevens, reteller and illustrator of humorous beast tales from around the world. *Tops & Bottoms;* various *Anansi* tales from Africa.

Paul O. Zelinsky, illustrator whose realistic oil paintings provide insights into the meaning of folktales. *Hansel and Gretel; Rumpelstiltskin.*

REFERENCES

de la Mare, Walter. (1930). Listen! In W. de la Mare (Ed.), *Poems for children.* New York: Holt.

Grimm, J., & Grimm, W. (1886). *Household stories.* Translated by L. Crane. New York: Macmillan.

RECOMMENDED TRADITIONAL LITERATURE

Ages refer to approximate interest levels.
YA = young adult.

Myths

Aliki, reteller. *The Gods and Goddesses of Olympus.* HarperCollins, 1994. Ages 8–12.

Bierhorst, John. *The Woman Who Fell from the Sky: The Iroquois Story of Creation.* Illustrated by Robert A. Parker. Morrow, 1993. Ages 7–10.

Climo, Shirley, reteller. *Atalanta's Race: A Greek Myth.* Illustrated by Alexander Koshkin. Clarion, 1995. Ages 8–13.

d'Aulaire, Ingri, and Edgar Parin d'Aulaire. *Book of Greek Myths.* Doubleday, 1962. Ages 8–10.

———. *Norse Gods and Giants.* Doubleday, 1967. Ages 8–10.

Fisher, Leonard Everett. *Cyclops.* Holiday, 1991. Ages 8–10.

————. *Jason and the Golden Fleece.* Holiday, 1990. Ages 9–12.

————. *Theseus and the Minotaur.* Holiday, 1988. Ages 8–10.

Hamilton, Virginia, reteller. *In the Beginning: Creation Stories from Around the World.* Illustrated by Barry Moser. Harcourt, 1988. Ages 9–12.

Heaney, Marie. *The Names Upon the Harp: Irish Myth and Legend.* Illustrated by P. J. Lynch. Scholastic, 2000. Ages 10–13.

Hofmeyr, Diane. *The Star-Bearer: A Creation Myth from Ancient Egypt.* Illustrated by Judy Daly. Farrar, 2001. Ages 8–12.

Hutton, Warwick, reteller. *Theseus and the Minotaur.* Macmillan, 1989. Ages 8–10.

McCaughrean, Geraldine. *The Golden Hoard: Myths and Legends of the World.* Illustrated by Bee Willey. McElderry, 1996. Ages 8–12.

McDermott, Gerald. *Creation.* Dutton, 2003. Ages 8–12.

Zeitlain, Steve. *The Four Corners of the Sky: Creation Stories and Cosmologies from Around the World.* Illustrated by Chris Raschka. Holt, 2000. Ages 12–YA.

Epics

McCaughrean, Geraldine. *Gilgamesh the Hero.* Illustrated by David Parkins. Eerdmans, 2003. Ages 10–14.

Sutcliff, Rosemary. *Black Ships before Troy: The Story of the Iliad.* Illustrated by Alan Lee. Delacorte, 1993. Ages 11–14.

————. *Dragonslayer: The Story of Beowulf.* Puffin, 1986 (1966).

————. *The Wanderings of Odysseus: The Story of the Odyssey.* Illustrated by Alan Lee. Delacorte, 1996. Ages 10–13.

Verma, Jatinder, reteller. *Rama, Sita, and the Story of Divaali.* Illustrated by Nilesh Mistry. Barefoot Books, 2002. Ages 8–14.

Legends and Tall Tales

dePaola, Tomie. *The Legend of the Poinsettia.* Putnam, 1994. Ages 6–8.

Dixon, Ann, reteller. *The Sleeping Lady.* Illustrated by Elizabeth Johns. Alaska Northwest Books, 1994. Ages 8–14.

Goble, Paul. *The Girl Who Loved Wild Horses.* Bradbury, 1978. Ages 7–9.

Hodges, Margaret. *Saint George and the Dragon.* Illustrated by Trina Schart Hyman. Little, Brown, 1984. Ages 8–10.

Kellogg, Steven, reteller. *Johnny Appleseed.* Morrow, 1988. Ages 6–8.

————, reteller. *Paul Bunyan.* Morrow, 1984. Ages 6–8.

————, reteller. *Pecos Bill.* Morrow, 1986. Ages 6–8.

Kimmel, Eric A., reteller. *Gershon's Monster: A Story for the Jewish New Year.* Illustrated by Jon J. Muth. Scholastic, 2000. Ages 6–11.

Lester, Julius. *John Henry.* Illustrated by Jerry Pinkney. Dial, 1994. Ages 8–10.

Lindbergh, Reeve. *Johnny Appleseed.* Illustrated by Kathy Jacobsen. Little, Brown, 1990. Ages 6–8.

Lister, Robin. *The Legend of King Arthur.* Illustrated by Alan Baker. Doubleday, 1990.

Lunge-Larsen, Lise. *The Race of the Birkebeiners.* Illustrated by Mary Azarian. Houghton, 2001. Ages 5–9. (Norway)

Maggi, María Elena, reteller. *The Great Canoe: A Kariña Legend.* Translated by Elisa Amado. Illustrated by Gloria Calderón. Groundwood, 2001. Ages 6–11.

Martin, Rafe. *The World Before This One: A Novel Told in Legend.* Illustrated by Calvin Nicholls. Scholastic, 2002. Ages 12–14. (Seneca Indian)

McCully, Emily Arnold. *Beautiful Warrior: The Legend of the Nun's Kung Fu.* Scholastic, 1998. Ages 5–9.

Nolen, Jerdine. *Big Jabe.* Illustrated by Kadir Nelson. HarperCollins, 2000. Ages 6–10. (African-American; American South)

Osborne, Mary Pope. *American Tall Tales.* Illustrated by Michael McCurdy. Knopf, 1991. Ages 8–11.

————. *New York's Bravest.* Illustrated by Steve Johnson and Lou Fancher. Knopf, 2002. Ages 5–8.

Pyle, Howard. *The Merry Adventures of Robin Hood.* Scribner's, 1946 (1883). Ages 9–12.

————. *The Story of King Arthur and His Knights.* Scribner's, 1984 (1883). Ages 9–12.

Rounds, Glen. *Washday on Noah's Ark: A Story of Noah's Ark According to Glen Rounds.* Holiday, 1985. Ages 6–8.

San Souci, Robert D. *Cut from the Same Cloth: American Women of Myth, Legend, and Tall Tale.* Illustrated by Brian Pinkney. Philomel, 1993. Ages 8–12.

———. *Young Merlin.* Illustrated by Daniel Horne. Doubleday, 1990. Ages 9–12.

Shepard, Aaron, reteller. *Master Man: A Tall Tale of Nigeria.* Illustrated by David Wisniewski. HarperCollins, 2001. Ages 5–10.

Stamm, Claus. *Three Strong Women: A Tall Tale from Japan.* Illustrated by Jean and Mou-sien Tseng. Viking, 1990 (1962). Ages 6–8.

Thomassie, Tynia. *Feliciana Feydra LeRoux: A Cajun Tall Tale.* Illustrated by Cat Bowman Smith. Little, Brown, 1995. Ages 6–9.

Willey, Margaret. *Clever Beatrice: An Upper Peninsula Conte.* Illustrated by Heather Solomon. Atheneum, 2001. Ages 5–9. (Michigan)

Folktales

(Note country, continent, or culture of origin after each entry.)

Aardema, Verna, reteller. *Why Mosquitoes Buzz in People's Ears.* Illustrated by Leo and Diane Dillon. Dial, 1975. Ages 5–7. (Kenya)

Aylesworth, Jim, reteller. *The Tale of Tricky Fox: A New England Trickster Tale.* Illustrated by Barbara McClintock. Scholastic, 2001. Ages 5–8. (United States, New England)

Babbitt, Natalie. *Ouch! A Tale from Grimm.* Illustrated by Fred Marcellino. HarperCollins, 1998. Ages 4–7. (Germany)

Beneduce, Ann K., reteller. *Jack and the Beanstalk.* Illustrated by Gennady Spirin. Philomel, 1999. Ages 6–9. (England)

Bierhorst, John, editor. *The Dancing Fox: Arctic Folktales.* Illustrated by Mary K. Okheena. Morrow, 1997. Ages 9–13. (Inuit)

Brown, Marcia. *Stone Soup.* Scribner's, 1975 (1947). Ages 6–8. (France)

Bruchac, Joseph. *The First Strawberries: A Cherokee Story.* Illustrated by Anna Vojtech. Dial, 1993. Ages 7–9. (Native American)

Bruchac, Joseph, & James Bruchac, retellers. *How Chipmunk Got His Stripes: A Tale of Bragging and Teasing.* Illustrated by Jose Aruego and Ariane Dewey. Dial, 2001. Ages 5–8. (Native American: Abenaki, Cherokee, Mohawk)

Bryan, Ashley, adapter. *Beautiful Blackbird.* Atheneum, 2003. Ages 5–7. (Zambia)

Casanova, Mary. *The Hunter: A Chinese Folktale.* Illustrated by Ed Young. Atheneum, 2000. Ages 5–8. (China)

Cecil, Laura, reteller. *The Frog Princess.* Illustrated by Emma C. Clark. Greenwillow, 1995. Ages 4–8. (United Kingdom)

Climo, Shirley. *The Egyptian Cinderella.* Illustrated by Ruth Heller. Crowell, 1989. Ages 7–9. (Egypt)

———. *The Korean Cinderella.* Illustrated by Ruth Heller. HarperCollins, 1993. Ages 7–9. (Korea)

Cohn, Amy L., editor. *From Sea to Shining Sea: A Treasury of American Folklore and Folk Songs.* Scholastic, 1993. Ages 4–10. (United States)

Cooper, Susan. *Tam Lin.* Illustrated by Warwick Hutton. McElderry, 1991. Ages 8–10. (Scotland)

Corrin, Sara and Stephen, retellers. *The Pied Piper of Hamelin.* Illustrated by Errol Le Cain. Harcourt, 1989. Ages 7–9. (Germany)

Cummings, Pat. *Ananse and the Lizard: A West African Tale.* Holt, 2002. Ages 4–8. (Ghana)

Day, Nancy R. *The Lion's Whiskers: An Ethiopian Folktale.* Illustrated by Ann Grifalconi. Scholastic, 1995. Ages 8–14. (Ethiopia)

Demi. *One Grain of Rice.* Scholastic, 1997. Ages 8–11. (India)

dePaola, Tomie. *Strega Nona.* Prentice Hall, 1975. Ages 5–8. (Italy)

Disney, Walt. *Walt Disney's Snow White and the Seven Dwarfs.* Western, 1984. Ages 5–8. (Germany)

Ehlert, Lois. *Cuckoo/Cucu.* Harcourt, 1997. Ages 4–7. (Hispanic)

Emberley, Rebecca, reteller. *Three Cool Kids.* Little, Brown, 1995. Ages 4–7. (Norway)

Esbensen, Barbara Juster, reteller. *The Star Maiden: An Ojibway Tale.* Illustrated by Helen K. Davie. Little, Brown, 1988. Ages 7–9. (Native American)

Galdone, Paul. *The Gingerbread Man.* Clarion, 1975. Ages 4–6. (England)

———. *The Little Red Hen.* Seabury, 1973. Ages 5–7. (England)

———. *Old Mother Hubbard and Her Dog.* McGraw-Hill, 1960. Ages 5–7. (England)

————. *The Three Billy Goats Gruff.* Seabury, 1973. Ages 5–7. (Norway)

Galloway, Priscilla. *Truly Grim Tales.* Delacorte, 1995. Ages 9–12.

Garland, Sherry. *Children of the Dragon; Selected Tales from Vietnam.* Illustrated by Trina Schart Hyman. Harcourt, 2001. Ages 8–12. (Vietnam)

Geringer, Laura, adapter. *The Seven Ravens.* Illustrated by E. S. Gazsi. HarperCollins, 1994. Ages 7–10. (Germany)

Gerson, Mary-Joan. *Fiesta Femenina: Celebrating Women in Mexican Folktales.* Barefoot, 2001. Ages 10–13. (Mexico)

Glass, Andrew, reteller. *Folks Call Me Appleseed John.* Doubleday, 1995. Ages 7–10. (United States)

Gobel, Paul. *Beyond the Ridge.* Bradbury, 1989. Ages 8–10. (Native American)

————. *Buffalo Woman.* Bradbury, 1984. Ages 7–9. (Native American)

————, reteller. *Iktomi and the Berries: A Plains Indian Story.* Orchard, 1989. Ages 7–9. (Native American)

————. *Storm Maker's Tipi.* Atheneum, 2001. Ages 7–12. (Native American: Siksika)

Grimm, Jakob, and Wilhelm Grimm. *The Bremen Town Musicians.* Illustrated by Joseph Palecek. Translated by Anthea Bell. Picture Book Studio, 1988. Ages 6–8. (Germany)

————. *Favorite Tales from Grimm.* Retold by Nancy Garden. Illustrated by Mercer Mayer. Four Winds, 1982. Ages 6–8. (Germany)

————. *Hansel and Gretel.* Illustrated by Anthony Browne. Knopf, 1998 (1981). Ages 8–14. (Germany)

————. *Little Red Riding Hood.* Illustrated by Trina Schart Hyman. Holiday, 1982. Ages 6–8. (Germany)

————. *Rumpelstiltskin.* Retold and illustrated by Paul O. Zelinsky. Dutton, 1986. Ages 7–9. (Germany)

————. *Snow-White and the Seven Dwarfs.* Translated by Randall Jarrell. Illustrated by Nancy Ekholm Burkert. Farrar, 1972. Ages 8–10. (Germany)

Hadithi, Mwenye. *Crafty Chameleon.* Illustrated by Adrienne Kennaway. Little, Brown, 1987. Ages 6–8. (Africa)

————. *Hot Hippo.* Illustrated by Adrienne Kennaway. Little, Brown, 1986. Ages 6–8. (Africa)

————. *Lazy Lion.* Illustrated by Adrienne Kennaway. Little, Brown, 1990. Ages 6–8. (Africa)

Hamilton, Virginia. *Bruh Rabbit and the Tar Baby Girl.* Illustrated by James Ransome. Scholastic, 2003. Ages 5–7. (Gullah, South Carolina)

————. *The Girl Who Spun Gold.* Illustrated by Leo and Diane Dillon. Blue Sky, 2000. Ages 5–8. (West Indian)

————. *Her Stories: African American Folktales, Fairy Tales, and True Tales.* Illustrated by Leo and Diane Dillon. Scholastic, 1995. Ages 9–YA. (United States)

————. *The People Could Fly: American Black Folktales.* Illustrated by Leo and Diane Dillon. Knopf, 1985. Ages 8–10. (African-American)

————. *When Birds Could Talk and Bats Could Sing: The Adventures of Bruh Sparrow, Sis Wren, and Their Friends.* Scholastic, 1996. Illustrated by Barry Moser. Ages 9–12. (United States, South)

Han, Suzanne C. *The Rabbit's Escape.* Illustrated by Yumi Heo. Holt, 1995. Ages 5–8. (Korea)

Haviland, Virginia. *Favorite Fairy Tales Told in India.* Illustrated by Blair Lent. Little, Brown, 1973. Ages 7–9. (India)

Heo, Yumi, reteller. *The Green Frogs: A Korean Folktale.* Houghton, 1996. Ages 4–7. (Korea)

Hodges, Margaret. *The Hero of Bremen.* Illustrated by Charles Mikolaycak. Holiday, 1993. Ages 8–11. (Germany)

Hong, Lily Toy, reteller. *Two of Everything: A Chinese Folktale.* Albert Whitman, 1993. Ages 5–8. (China)

Hooks, William H. *The Ballad of Belle Dorcas.* Illustrated by Brian Pinkney. Knopf, 1990. Ages 8–10. (United States)

————. *Freedom's Fruit.* Illustrated by James Ransome. Random House, 1995. Ages 8–11. (United States, Carolinas)

————, reteller. *Moss Gown.* Illustrated by Donald Carrick. Clarion, 1987. Ages 7–9. (United States; a Cinderella variant)

Huck, Charlotte. *The Black Bull of Norroway: A Scottish Tale.* Illustrated by Anita Lobel. Greenwillow, 2001. Ages 7–12. (Scotland)

————. *Princess Furball.* Illustrated by Anita Lobel. Greenwillow, 1989. Ages 6–8. (Germany; a Cinderella variant)

Hutton, Warwick. *Beauty and the Beast.* Atheneum, 1975. Ages 7–9. (France)

———, reteller. *The Trojan Horse.* Macmillan/McElderry, 1992. Ages 6–10. (Greece)

Hyman, Trina Schart. *The Sleeping Beauty.* Little, Brown, 1977. Ages 5–8. (Germany)

Joseph, Lynn. *A Wave in Her Pocket: Stories from Trinidad.* Illustrated by Brian Pinkney. Clarion, 1991. Ages 7–9. (Trinidad)

Kajikawa, Kimiko, adaptor. *Yoshi's Feast.* Illustrated by Yumi Heo. DK Ink, 2000. Ages 5–9. (Japan)

Karlin, Barbara, reteller. *Cinderella.* Illustrated by James Marshall. Little, Brown, 1989. Ages 6–8. (France)

Kellogg, Steven. *Jack and the Beanstalk.* Morrow, 1991. Ages 5–8. (England)

Kimmel, Eric A. *Anansi and the Talking Melon.* Illustrated by Janet Stevens. Holiday, 1994. Ages 5–7. (Africa)

———. *Boots and His Brothers: A Norwegian Tale.* Illustrated by Kimberly Bulcken Root. Holiday, 1992. Ages 5–9.

———. *Coyote Steals the Blanket: A Ute Tale.* Illustrated by Janet Stevens. Holiday, 1993. Ages 5–7. (Native American: Ute)

———. *Iron John.* Illustrated by Trina Schart Hyman. Holiday, 1994. Ages 8–10. (Germany)

———. *The Three Princes.* Illustrated by Leonard Everett Fisher. Holiday, 1995. Ages 5–9. (Middle East)

———. *Three Sacks of Truth: A Story from France.* Illustrated by Robert Rayevsky. Holiday, 1993. Ages 5–8.

Lester, Julius. *How Many Spots Does a Leopard Have? and Other Tales.* Illustrated by David Shannon. Scholastic, 1989. Ages 7–9. (African-American)

———, reteller. *The Tales of Uncle Remus: The Adventures of Brer Rabbit.* Illustrated by Jerry Pinkney. Dial, 1987. (See also: *More Tales of Uncle Remus: Further Adventures of Brer Rabbit, His Friends, Enemies, and Others.* Dial, 1988.) Ages 7–9. (African-American)

Louie, Ai-Ling. *Yeh-Shen: A Cinderella Story from China.* Illustrated by Ed Young. Philomel, 1982. Ages 7–9. (China)

Lunge-Larsen, Lise, reteller. *The Troll with No Heart in His Body: And Other Tales of Trolls from Norway.* Illustrated by Betsy Bowen. Houghton, 1999. Ages 7–11. (Norway)

Mahy, Margaret. *The Seven Chinese Brothers.* Illustrated by Jean and Mou-sien Tseng. Scholastic, 1990. Ages 6–8. (China)

Marshall, James. *Goldilocks and the Three Bears.* Dial, 1988. Ages 5–7. (England)

———. *Red Riding Hood.* Dial, 1987. Ages 6–8. (Germany)

———. *The Three Little Pigs.* Dial, 1989. Ages 5–7. (England)

Martin, Rafe, reteller. *Foolish Rabbit's Big Mistake.* Illustrated by Ed Young. Putnam, 1985. Ages 6–8. (India)

———. *Mysterious Tales of Japan.* Illustrated by Tatsuro Kiuchi. Putnam, 1996. Ages 8–13. (Japan)

———. *The Rough-Face Girl.* Illustrated by David Shannon. Putnam, 1992. Ages 8–10. (Native American)

Mayer, Mercer. *East of the Sun and West of the Moon.* Four Winds, 1980. Ages 7–9. (Norway)

McDermott, Gerald. *Anansi the Spider.* Holt, 1972. Ages 6–8. (Africa)

———. *Arrow to the Sun.* Viking, 1974. Ages 8–10. (Native American)

———. *Raven: A Trickster Tale from the Pacific Northwest.* Harcourt, 1993. Ages 5–9. (Native American)

McKissack, Patricia C. *Flossie and the Fox.* Illustrated by Rachel Isadora. Dial, 1986. Ages 7–9. (American South)

McVitty, Walter, reteller. *Ali Baba and the Forty Thieves.* Illustrated by Margaret Early. Abrams, 1989. Ages 6–8. (Middle East)

Milligan, Bryce. *The Prince of Ireland and the Three Magic Stallions.* Illustrated by Preston McDaniels. Holiday, 2003. Ages 6–8. (Ireland)

Mollel, Tololwa. *Subira Subira.* Illustrated by Linda Saport. Clarion, 2000. Ages 5–10. (Tanzania)

Montresor, Beni, adapter. *Little Red Riding Hood.* Doubleday, 1991. Ages 10–14. (Germany)

Morimoto, Junko. *The Two Bullies.* Translated from Japanese by Isao Morimoto. Crown, 1999. Ages 5–7. (Japan)

Mosel, Arlene. *The Funny Little Woman.* Illustrated by Blair Lent. Dutton, 1972. Ages 6–8. (Japan)

Newton, Pam. *The Stonecutter: An Indian Folktale.* Putnam, 1990. Ages 7–9. (India)

Parks, Van Dyke, and Malcolm Jones, adaptors and retellers. (Original story by Joel Chandler Harris.) *Jump!: The Adventures of Brer Rabbit.* Illustrated by Barry Moser. Harcourt, 1986. Ages 7–9. (African-American)

Paterson, Katherine. *The Tale of the Mandarin Ducks.* Illustrated by Leo and Diane Dillon. Lodestar, 1990. Ages 7–9. (Japan)

Paulson, Timothy. *Jack and the Beanstalk and the Beanstalk Incident.* Illustrated by Mark Corcoran. Birch Lane, 1990. Ages 7–9. (England) (Note: second half of this flip book is a modern folktale.)

Perrault, Charles. *Cinderella.* Illustrated by Marcia Brown. Scribner's, 1954. Ages 6–8. (France)

———. *Little Red Riding Hood.* Illustrated by Sarah Moon. Creative Education, 1983. Ages 10–14. (France)

———. *Puss in Boots.* Illustrated by Fred Marcellino. Farrar, 1990. Ages 6–8. (France)

Polacco, Patricia. *Babushka Baba Yaga.* Philomel, 1993. Ages 7–9. (Russia)

Reneaux, J. J. *How Animals Saved the People: Animal Tales from the South.* Illustrated by James Ransome. Morrow, 2001. Ages 9–14. (Rural Southern United States: African-American, Appalachian, Native American)

Rounds, Glen, reteller. *Old MacDonald Had a Farm.* Holiday, 1989. Ages 4–6. (England)

San Souci, Robert D., reteller. *Cendrillon: A Caribbean Cinderella.* Illustrated by Brian Pinkney. Simon & Schuster, 1998. Ages 5–7. (The Caribbean)

———. *The Faithful Friend.* Illustrated by Brian Pinkney. Simon & Schuster, 1995. Ages 11–14. (Martinique)

———. *Sootface: An Ojibwa Cinderella Story.* Illustrated by Daniel San Souci. Doubleday, 1994. Ages 5–8. (Native American)

———. *The Talking Eggs: A Folktale from the American South.* Illustrated by Jerry Pinkney. Dial, 1989. Ages 7–9. (African-American)

Sanderson, Ruth, reteller. *Cinderella.* Little, Brown, 2002. Ages 4–8. (Germany)

———. *The Golden Mare, the Firebird, and the Magic Ring.* Little, Brown, 2001. Ages 8–12. (Russia)

Shannon, George. *More Stories to Solve: Fifteen Folktales from Around the World.* Illustrated by Peter Sís. Greenwillow, 1990. Ages 7–10.

Sierra, Judy, selector and reteller. *Can You Guess My Name? Traditional Tales Around the World.* Illustrated by Stefano Vitale. Clarion, 2002. Ages 8–10.

———. *The Gift of the Crocodile: A Cinderella Story.* Illustrated by Reynold Ruffins. Simon & Schuster, 2000. Ages 5–9. (Indonesia/Spice Islands)

———, reteller. *Nursery Tales around the World.* Illustrated by Stefano Vitale. Clarion, 1996. Ages 3–7.

———. *Tasty Baby Belly Buttons: A Japanese Folktale.* Illustrated by Meilo So. Knopf, 1999. Ages 4–7. (Japan)

———, reteller. *Wiley and the Hairy Man.* Illustrated by Brian Pinkney. Lodestar, 1996. Ages 5–8. (United States, Alabama)

Simonds, Nina, Leslie Swartz, and the Children's Museum, Boston. *Moonbeams, Dumplings and Dragon Boats: A Treasury of Chinese Holiday Tales, Activities and Recipes.* Illustrated by Meilo So. Harcourt, 2002. Ages 9–12. (China)

Singer, Isaac Bashevis. *When Shlemiel Went to Warsaw and Other Stories.* Translated by the author and Elizabeth Shub. Illustrated by Margot Zemach. Farrar, 1968. Ages 8–10. (Jewish)

Snyder, Diane. *The Boy of the Three-Year Nap.* Illustrated by Allen Say. Houghton, 1988. Ages 7–9. (Japan)

Souhami, Jessica. *The Leopard's Drum. An Asante Tale from West Africa.* Little, Brown, 1996. Ages 4–8. (Africa)

Steptoe, John. *Mufaro's Beautiful Daughters: An African Tale.* Lothrop, 1987. Ages 6–8. (Africa)

———. *The Story of Jumping Mouse.* Lothrop, 1984. Ages 7–9. (Native American)

Stevens, Janet, adaptor. *How the Manx Cat Lost Its Tail.* Harcourt, 1990. Ages 6–8. (England; Isle of Man)

———. *Tops and Bottoms.* Harcourt, 1995. Ages 5–8. (Europe and American South)

Taback, Simms. *This Is the House That Jack Built.* Putnam, 2002. Ages 5–7. (Hebrew)

Tchana, Katrin. *The Serpent Slayer and Other Stories of Strong Women.* Illustrated by Trina Schart Hyman. Little, Brown, 2000. Ages 7–12. (World)

Tejima. *Ho-Limlim: A Rabbit Tale from Japan.* Philomel, 1990. Ages 6–8. (Japan)

Van Laan, Nancy. *So Say the Little Monkeys.* Illustrated by Yumi Heo. Atheneum, 1998. Ages 2–5. (Brazil)

———. *With a Whoop and a Holler: A Bushel of Lore from Way Down South.* Illustrated by Scott Cook. Atheneum, 1998. Ages 9–12. (American South)

Wattenberg, Jane. *Henny-Penny.* Scholastic, 2000. Ages 7–12. (England)

Wells, Ruth, reteller. *The Farmer and the Poor God: A Folktale from Japan.* Illustrated by Yoshi. Simon & Schuster, 1996. Ages 5–11. (Japan)

Wiesner, David. *The Three Pigs.* Clarion, 2001. Ages 6–9. (Fractured folktale)

Winthrop, Elizabeth. *Vasilissa the Beautiful.* Illustrated by Alexander Koshkin. HarperCollins, 1991. Ages 7–9. (Russia)

Wisniewski, David. *Elfwyn's Saga.* Lothrop, 1990. Ages 8–10. (Iceland)

Yolen, Jane. *Not One Damsel in Distress: World Folktales for Strong Girls.* Illustrated by Susan Guevara. Silver Whistle, 2000. Ages 8–13. (World)

Young, Ed. *Lon Po Po: A Red Riding-Hood Story from China.* Philomel, 1989. Ages 7–9. (China)

———. *What About Me?* Putnam, 2002. Ages 5–8. (Sufi)

Zelinsky, Paul O., reteller. *Rapunzel.* Dutton, 1997. Ages 5–8. (Germany)

———, reteller. *Rumpelstiltskin.* Dutton, 1986. Ages 6–8. (Germany)

Zemach, Harve. *Duffy and the Devil.* Illustrated by Margot Zemach. Farrar, 1973. Ages 6–8. (England)

Zemach, Margot. *It Could Always Be Worse.* Farrar, 1977. Ages 6–8. (Jewish)

Fables

Aesop's Fables. Illustrated by Jerry Pinkney. North-South/Sea Star, 2000. Ages 5–9.

Brett, Jan. *Town Mouse, Country Mouse.* Putnam, 1994. Ages 6–8.

Brown, Marcia. *Once a Mouse.* Scribner's, 1961. Ages 6–8.

De Roin, Nancy. *Jataka Tales: Fables from the Buddha.* Illustrated by Ellen Lanyon. Houghton, 1975. Ages 7–9.

Goodall, Jane. *The Eagle and the Wren.* Illustrated by Alexander Reichstein. North-South, 2000. Ages 5–8.

Oberman, Sheldon. *The Wisdom Bird: A Tale of Solomon and Sheba.* Illustrated by Neil Waldman. Boyds Mills, 2000. Ages 5–9. (Also religious story)

Rumford, James. *Nine Animals and the Well.* Houghton, 2003. Ages 5–10. (Modern)

Stevens, Janet. *The Town Mouse and the Country Mouse: An Aesop Fable.* Holiday, 1987. Ages 6–8.

Ward, Helen, adapter. *The Hare and the Tortoise: A Fable from Aesop.* Millbrook, 1999. Ages 4–8.

Religious Stories

Bible, New Testament. *Christmas: The King James Version.* Illustrated by Jan Pieńkowski. Knopf, 1984. Ages 6–10.

———. *Easter: The King James Version.* Illustrated by Jan Pieńkowski. Knopf, 1989. Ages 6–8.

Bierhorst, John, translator. *Spirit Child: A Story of the Nativity.* Illustrated by Barbara Cooney. Morrow, 1984. Ages 7–9.

Chaikin, Miriam, adaptor. *Exodus.* Illustrated by Charles Mikolaycak. Holiday, 1987. Ages 6–8.

Demi. *Buddha.* Holt, 1996. Ages 8–12.

———. *Buddha Stories* (Jataka tales). Holt, 1997. Ages 7–10.

Goldin, Barbara Diamond. *Journeys with Elijah: Eight Tales of the Prophet.* Illustrated by Jerry Pinkney. Harcourt, 1999. Ages 7–YA.

Goodhart, Pippa. *Noah Makes a Boat.* Illustrated by Bernard Lodge. Houghton, 1997. Ages 4–6.

Hutton, Warwick. *Jonah and the Great Fish.* Atheneum, 1983. Ages 6–8.

———, adaptor. *Adam and Eve: The Bible Story.* Macmillan, 1987. Ages 6–8.

Johnson, James Weldon. *The Creation.* Illustrated by James E. Ransome. Holiday, 1994.

Kimmel, Eric A., reteller. *The Spotted Pony: A Collection of Hanukkah Stories.* Illustrated by Leonard Everett Fisher. Holiday, 1992.

Lester, Julius. *When the Beginning Began: Stories about God, the Creatures, and Us.* Illustrated by Emily Lisker. Harcourt, 1999. Ages 11–14.

Pinkney, Jerry. *Noah's Ark.* North-South, 2002. Ages 5–8.

Root, Phyllis. *Big Momma Makes the World.* Illustrated by Helen Oxenbury. Candlewick, 2003. Ages 4–7.

Schwartz, Howard. *Invisible Kingdoms: Jewish Tales of Angels, Spirits, and Demons.* Illustrated by Stephen Feiser. HarperCollins, 2002. Ages 8–12. (World)

Vivas, Julie. *The Nativity.* Harcourt, 1988. Ages 6–10.

Wisniewski, David. *Golem.* Clarion, 1996. Ages 6–12.

Young, Ed. *Monkey King.* HarperCollins, 2001. Ages 5–8. (Buddhist)

6

Modern Fantasy

Do you know
If you try
You really can
Touch the sky?

Lean a ladder
Against the moon
And climb, climb high
Talk to the stars
And leave your handprints
All across the sky

Jump on a cloud
And spend the day
Trampoline-jumping
Through the air
Climb a rainbow
And watch the world
From way up there
Then ride that rainbow slide

Back home.

— SHEREE FITCH

Modern fantasy has its roots in traditional fantasy from which motifs, characters, stylistic elements, and, at times, themes have been drawn. Many of the most revered works of children's literature fall into the genre of modern fantasy. *The Adventures of Pinocchio, Alice's Adventures in Wonderland, The Wizard of Oz, The Wind in the Willows, Winnie-the-Pooh, Pippi Longstocking,* and *Charlotte's Web* immediately come to mind. The creation of stories that are highly imaginative—yet believable—is the hallmark of this genre.

DEFINITION AND DESCRIPTION

Modern fantasy refers to the body of literature in which the events, the settings, or the characters are outside the realm of possibility. A fantasy is a story that cannot happen in the real world, and for this reason this genre has been called the literature of the fanciful impossible. In these stories, animals talk, inanimate objects come to life, people are giants or thumb-sized, imaginary worlds are inhabited, and future worlds are explored, just to name a few of the possibilities. Modern fantasies are written by known authors, and this distinguishes the genre from traditional literature, in which the tales are handed down through the oral tradition and have no known author. Although the events could not happen in real life, modern fantasies often contain truths that help the reader to understand today's world.

The *cycle format,* in which one book is linked to another through characters, settings, or both, is especially prevalent in modern fantasy. Elleman (1987) states, "Events in [fantasy] cycle books are often strung out over three or four volumes. Authors attempt to make each novel self-contained, with varying degrees of success, but usually readers need the entire series for full impact" (p. 418). The cycle format appeals to readers who become attached to certain characters and then delight in reading the next book in the series. An example of the cycle format can be found in the chronicles of the creatures of Redwall Abbey, a series of animal fantasies by Brian Jacques.

EVALUATION AND SELECTION OF MODERN FANTASY

The usual standards for fine fiction must also be met by authors of modern fantasy. Believable and well-rounded characters who develop and change, well-constructed plots, well-described settings with internal consistency, a style appropriate to the story, and worthy themes are elements to be expected in all fiction. In addition, the following criteria apply specifically to modern fantasy:

- Authors of modern fantasy have the challenge of persuading readers to open themselves up to believing that which is contrary to reality, strange, whimsical, or magical, yet has an internal logic and consistency. Sometimes, authors will accomplish this through beginning the story in a familiar and ordinary setting with typical, contemporary human beings as characters. A transition is then made from this realistic world to the fantasy world. An example of this literary device is found in C. S. Lewis's *The Lion, the Witch, and the Wardrobe,* in which the children in the story enter a wardrobe in an old house only to discover that the back of the wardrobe leads into the land of Narnia, a fantasy world with unusual characters. Other fantasies begin in the imagined world but manage, through well-described settings and consistent well-rounded characters, to make this new reality believable. Either way, the plot, characters, and setting must be so well developed that the child reader is able to suspend disbelief and to accept the impossible as real.
- For a modern fantasy to be truly imaginative, the author must provide a unique setting. In some stories, the setting may move beyond the realistic in both time (moving to the past, future, or holding time still) and place (imagined worlds); in other stories only one of these elements (place or time) will go beyond reality. Moreover, a modern fantasy author's creation must be original.

Excellent M O D E R N   F A N T A S Y   t o   R e a d   A l o u d

Almond, David. *Skellig.* Ages 9–12.
Andersen, Hans Christian. *The Ugly Duckling.* Illustrated by Jerry Pinkney. Ages 6–9.
Avi. *Poppy.* Ages 8–11.
Bunting, Eve. *Riding the Tiger.* Illustrated by David Frampton. Ages 8–11.
Burgess, Thornton W. *Old Mother West Wind.* Illustrated by Thea Kliros. Ages 5–8. Collection of animal fantasies.
Clements, Andrew. *Things Not Seen.* Ages 12–YA.
Dahl, Roald. *James and the Giant Peach.* Ages 8–11.
Jennings, Richard W. *Orwell's Luck.* Ages 9–12.
Levine, Gail Carson. *Ella Enchanted.* Ages 10–13.
Martin, Ann M., and Laura Godwin. *The Meanest Doll in the World.* Illustrated by Brian Selznick. Ages 7–11.
McGraw, Eloise. *Moorchild.* Ages 11–14.
Rodda, Emily. *Rowan of Rin.* Ages 8–11.
Waugh, Sylvia. *Space Race.* Ages 9–12.

HISTORICAL OVERVIEW OF MODERN FANTASY

Imaginative literature did not appear until the eighteenth century. These stories were not intended primarily for children but were political satires that came to be enjoyed by children as well as adults. *Gulliver's Travels* (1726) by the Irish clergyman Jonathan Swift is the most noteworthy of such books. In this adult satire ridiculing the antics of the English court and its politics, the hero, Gulliver, travels to strange, imaginary places—one inhabited by six-inch Lilliputians, another inhabited by giants. These imaginary worlds are described in fascinating detail and with sufficient humor to appeal to a child audience.

In England in 1865, Charles Lutwidge Dodgson, an Oxford don who used the pen name Lewis Carroll, wrote *Alice's Adventures in Wonderland,* which tells of a fantastic journey Alice takes to an imaginary world. The total absence of didacticism—replaced by humor and fantasy—resulted in the book's lasting appeal and world fame. Other fantasies that originated in England shortly after the appearance of *Alice* include *The Light Princess* (1867) and *At the Back of the North Wind* (1871) by George MacDonald, and *Just So Stories* (1902) by Rudyard Kipling. This early development of modern fantasy for children in England was unrivaled by any other country and established the standard for the genre worldwide.

Modern fantasy has continued to thrive in England. Noteworthy contributions from England include *The Tale of Peter Rabbit* (1902) by Beatrix Potter, *The Wind in the Willows* (1908) by Kenneth Grahame, *The Velveteen Rabbit* (1922) by Margery Williams, *Winnie-the-Pooh* (1926) by A. A. Milne, *Mary Poppins* (1934) by Pamela Travers, *The Hobbit* (1937) by J. R. R. Tolkien, *The Lion, the Witch, and the Wardrobe* (1950) by C. S. Lewis, *The Borrowers* (1953) by Mary Norton, and *The Children of Green Knowe* (1955) by Lucy M. Boston.

Early books of modern fantasy from other countries include *The Adventures of Pinocchio* (1881) by Carlo Collodi (Carlo Lorenzini) from Italy and *Journey to the Center of the Earth* (1864), *Twenty Thousand Leagues under the Sea* (1869), and *Around the World in Eighty Days* (1872) by the Frenchman

Jules Verne. Verne's works are considered the first science fiction novels and remain popular today with adults and children. Later in France, Jean de Brunhoff wrote an internationally popular series of animal fantasies about a family of elephants. The first of these was *The Story of Babar* (1937).

Some works of fantasy from Scandinavia also deserve recognition. Hans Christian Andersen, a Dane, published many modern folktales, stories that were very similar in literary elements to the traditional tales. However, Andersen was the originator of most of his tales, for which his own life experiences were the inspiration. "The Ugly Duckling," "The Emperor's New Clothes," and "Thumbelina" are three of the most loved of Andersen's stories. His tales were published in 1835 and are considered the first modern fairy tales. A century later, Swedish author Astrid Lindgren produced *Pippi Longstocking* (1945). Pippi, a lively, rambunctious, and very strong heroine who throws caution to the wind, lives an independent life of escapades that are envied by children the world over.

The United States also produced some outstanding early modern fantasies, beginning with *The Wonderful Wizard of Oz* (1900) by L. Frank Baum, which is considered to be the first classic U.S. modern fantasy for children. Other landmark U.S. works of modern fantasy are the memorable animal fantasy *Rabbit Hill* (1944) by Robert Lawson; *Charlotte's Web* (1952) by E. B. White, the best-known and best-loved U.S. work of fantasy; *The Book of Three* (1964), the first of the Prydain Chronicles by Lloyd Alexander; and *A Wrinkle in Time* (1962) by Madeleine L'Engle, which is considered a modern classic in science fiction for children.

Science fiction, the most recent development in modern fantasy, is said to owe its birth to the aforementioned nineteenth-century novels of Jules Verne and H. G. Wells (*Time Machine*, 1895). Adults, not children, were the primary audience for these novels, however. It was not until the twentieth century that science fiction began to be aimed specifically at children. The Tom Swift series by Victor Appleton (collective pseudonym for the Stratemeyer Syndicate), although stilted in style and devoid of female characters, can be considered the first science fiction for children. The first Tom Swift book appeared in 1910 (*Tom Swift and His Airship*), with additional titles of the series appearing in rapid succession. The success of the science fiction magazine *Amazing Stories*, launched in 1926, brought formal recognition to the genre of science fiction.

In 1963, Madeleine L'Engle's novel *A Wrinkle in Time* was awarded the Newbery Medal. From this point forward, many science fiction novels for children began to appear. In the late 1960s and 1970s, the theme of mind control was popular. John Christopher's Tripods trilogy and William Sleator's *House of Stairs* (1974) are good examples. Space travel and future worlds were frequent science fiction topics in the 1980s. Milestones in the development of modern fantasy are highlighted on page 119.

Modern fantasy for children remains strong, especially in Great Britain and other English-speaking countries. Although personified toys and animals remain popular and prevalent in children's books, growth in this genre appears to be in stories in which fantasy is interwoven into other genres—science fiction, science fantasy, and historical fantasy. Fractured folktales, traditional tales with a contemporary twist or a tale told from a new perspective, took on new popularity with the publication of Jon Scieszka's *The True Story of the 3 Little Pigs by A. Wolf*, illustrated by Lane Smith and published in 1989. This blurring of traditional genres can also be seen in the interesting mixture of the logic of realistic mystery stories with supernatural elements, as in the popular mysteries of John Bellairs and Mary Downing Hahn. Modern fantasy is likely to continue to be a popular genre with children and authors, as evidenced by the extraordinary popularity of the best-selling Harry Potter quest series by J. K. Rowling, whose first novel in the series was published in 1998.

M I L E S T O N E S

in the Development of MODERN FANTASY

DATE	EVENT	SIGNIFICANCE
1726	*Gulliver's Travels* by Jonathan Swift (England)	An adult novel prototype for children's fantasy adventures
1835	*Fairy Tales* by Hans Christian Andersen (Denmark)	First modern folktales
1864	*Journey to the Center of the Earth* by Jules Verne (France)	First science fiction novel (for adults)
1865	*Alice's Adventures in Wonderland* by Lewis Carroll (England)	First children's masterpiece of modern fantasy
1881	*The Adventures of Pinocchio* by Carlo Collodi (Italy)	Early classic personified toy story
1900	*The Wonderful Wizard of Oz* by L. Frank Baum (United States)	First classic U.S. modern fantasy for children
1908	*The Wind in the Willows* by Kenneth Grahame (England)	Early classic animal fantasy
1910	*Tom Swift and His Airship* by Victor Appleton (United States)	First science fiction novel for children
1926	*Winnie-the-Pooh* by A. A. Milne (England)	Early classic personified toy story
1937	*The Hobbit* by J. R. R. Tolkien (England)	Early quest adventure with a cult following
1950	*The Lion, the Witch, and the Wardrobe* by C. S. Lewis (England)	Early classic quest adventure for children; first of the Narnia series
1952	*Charlotte's Web* by E. B. White (United States)	Classic U.S. animal fantasy
1953	*The Borrowers* by Mary Norton (England)	Classic little people fantasy
1962	*A Wrinkle in Time* by Madeleine L'Engle (United States)	Classic U.S. science fiction novel for children
1993	*The Giver* by Lois Lowry (United States)	Popular futuristic fiction novel; Newbery Medal winner
1998	*Harry Potter and the Sorcerer's Stone* by J. K. Rowling (England)	First book in the best-selling quest fantasy series

TYPES OF MODERN FANTASY

In modern fantasy, as in other genres, the distinctions between types are not totally discrete. The types of modern fantasy in the sections that follow are a starting point for thinking about the variety of fantastic stories, motifs, themes, and characters that gifted authors have created. Additional categories could be listed, and you will find that some stories may fit appropriately in more than one category. For example, Terry Pratchett's *The Wee Free Men*, categorized as a "little people" story, could also be considered a *quest fantasy.*

Modern Folktales

Modern folktales, or *literary folktales* as they are also called, are tales told in a form similar to that of a traditional tale with the accompanying typical elements: little character description; strong conflict; fast-moving plot with a sudden resolution; vague setting; and, in some cases, magical elements. But these modern tales have a known, identifiable author who has written the tale in this form. In other words, the tales do not spring from the cultural heritage of a group of people through the oral tradition but rather from the mind of one creator. However, this distinction does not matter at all to children, who delight in these tales as much as they do in the old folktales. Fractured folktales are a recent addition to the modern folktale genre.

The tales of Hans Christian Andersen are the earliest and best known of these modern tales. More recently, other authors, including Robin McKinley (*Beauty* and *Spindle's End*) and Jane Yolen (*Sword of the Rightful King: A Novel of King Arthur*) have become known for their modern folktales.

Modern folktales are an important counterbalance to traditional tales. As was noted in Chapter 5, many of the traditional tales present an old-fashioned, stereotypic view of male and female characters. Many of the modern tales present more assertive female characters who are clearly in charge of their own destinies. An example is *Swamp Angel* by Anne Isaacs.

Animal Fantasy

Animal fantasies are stories in which animals behave as human beings in that they experience emotions, talk, and have the ability to reason. Usually, the animals in fantasies will (and should) retain many of their animal characteristics. In the best of these animal fantasies, the author will interpret the animal for the reader in human terms without destroying the animal's integrity or removing it from membership in the animal world. For example, a rabbit character in an animal fantasy will retain her natural abilities of speed and camouflage to outsmart her adversaries. At the same time, however, the author will permit the reader to see human qualities such as caring and love by having the rabbit carry on conversations with family members.

Animal fantasies can be read to very young children who enjoy the exciting but reassuring adventures in books. Examples are *The Tale of Peter Rabbit* by Beatrix Potter and *The Runaway Bunny* by Margaret Wise Brown. Books for children in primary grades include somewhat longer stories, often in a humorous vein, such as Beverly Cleary's mouse stories, *Runaway Ralph* and *The Mouse and the Motorcycle,* and Deborah and James Howe's humor-filled books, *Bunnicula* and *Howliday Inn.* Enjoyable animal fantasies for the young reader often have easy-to-follow, episodic plots.

Fully developed novels of modern fantasy with subtle and complex characterizations and a progressive plot are especially suitable for reading aloud to children in their elementary school years. *Charlotte's Web* by E. B. White remains a favorite read-aloud book; *Poppy* by Avi is also popular. A beautifully written book with richly drawn characterizations is *The Wind in the Willows* by Kenneth Grahame, who describes in artistic detail the life of animal friends along a riverbank. This book features an episodic plot structure but has a challenging style that is appropriate to intermediate-grade students. *Orwell's Luck* by Richard W. Jennings, a novel with a progressive plot, is also appreciated by intermediate-grade students who enjoy reflecting on what separates reality from fantasy.

Although the interest in animal fantasy peaks at age 8 or 9, many children and adults continue to enjoy well-written animal fantasies. In animal fantasies for older readers, an entire animal world is usually created, with all of the relationships among its members that might be found in a novel portraying human behavior. *Redwall* by Brian Jacques and *The Amazing Maurice and His Educated Rodents* by Terry Pratchett are examples of complex, fully developed animal fantasy novels for readers in fifth grade through adulthood.

Personified Toys and Objects

Stories in which admired objects or beloved toys are brought to life and believed in by a child or adult character in the story are the focus of this type of fantasy. An early classic example of these stories is *The Adventures of Pinocchio* by Carlo Collodi (Carlo Lorenzini), in which a mischievous puppet comes to life, runs away from his maker, and has many exciting and dangerous escapades. In these stories, the object, toy, or doll becomes real to the human protagonist and, in turn, becomes real to the child reader (who has perhaps also imagined a toy coming to life). Close family relationships are also demonstrated in *The Mennyms* by Sylvia Waugh. This motif of family is also found in *The Doll People* and *The Meanest Doll in the World* by Ann M. Martin and Laura Godwin. Personified toy and object stories appeal to children from preschool through upper elementary grades.

Unusual Characters and Strange Situations

Some authors approach fantasy through reality but take it beyond reality to the ridiculous or exaggerated. Generally, those stories can be best described as having unusual characters or strange situations. Without doubt, *Alice's Adventures in Wonderland* by Lewis Carroll is the best known of this type of modern fantasy. Writers of modern fantasy have described such strange situations as a boy sailing across the Atlantic Ocean in a giant peach (*James and the Giant Peach* by Roald Dahl) and such unusual characters as a perfect, factory-made boy (*Konrad* by Christine Nöstlinger).

Modern fantasy appeals to readers of all ages. Florence Parry Heide's *The Shrinking of Treehorn* portrays a young boy who, one day, starts to shrink, but no one notices. The story is fascinating to middle-school students. Andrew Clements' *Things Not Seen* also is enjoyed by students from ages 11 to 15. This story features a boy who steps out of the shower, looks in the mirror, and discovers he has become invisible. In *Tuck Everlasting,* Natalie Babbitt explores the theme of immortality and its consequences, a provocative theme for children and adults.

Worlds of Little People

Some authors have written about worlds inhabited by miniature people who have developed a culture of their own in this world or who live in another world. In Mary Norton's *The Borrowers,* small people live in our world but take our discards to create their own world. It is, of course, eventually human beings who threaten their existence and cause them to seek safety elsewhere. Carol Kendall described the Land Between the Mountains where the Minnipins live in *The Gammage Cup,* a story about little people struggling against the pressure to conform. A version of *Gulliver's Travels* can be found in *The Minpins* (1991) by Roald Dahl. Stories of little people delight children because they can identify with the indignities foisted upon little and powerless people and because the big people in these stories are invariably out-done by the more ingenious little people.

Supernatural Events and Mystery Fantasy

Many recent fantasies evoke the supernatural. One common form of supernatural literature found in children's books is the ghost story. Some ghost stories intrigue younger children, especially when the topic is treated humorously and reassuringly, as in *The Ghosts of Hungryhouse Lane* by Sam McBratney. In this story, children find out about three ghosts in their new home but unearth ways to satisfy the needs of the ghosts. In a similar vein the goblins of Hilari Bell's *The Goblin Wood* eventually become allies of the protagonist. Ghosts in children's books can be fearful threats or helpful protectors. The ghost of the priest in John Bellairs' *The Curse of the Blue Figurine* is the very soul of evil, whereas the ghost of Cynthia DeFelice's *The Ghost of Fossil Glen* is seeking revenge for a murder. Many authors write mysteries for children in which the solution is partially supernatural or arrived at with supernatural assistance.

Witchcraft and other aspects of the occult sometimes play a role in children's fantasy books. Witches are often portrayed as the broom-wielding villains of both traditional and modern tales, such as the Russian stories of Baba Yaga. Halloween and its traditions are also frequently presented in children's stories. Witchcraft has recently been the focus of criticism because of an upsurge of sects whose members refer to themselves as witches. Also, some parents' groups have attempted to censor children's books featuring witches, Halloween, and other elements of the occult. Chapter 11 has a full discussion on censorship and schools' responsibilities in these situations.

Historical Fantasy

Historical fantasy, sometimes called *time-warp fantasy,* is a story in which a present-day protagonist goes back in time to a different era. A contrast between the two time periods is shown to readers through the modern-day protagonist's discoveries of and astonishment with earlier customs. Historical fantasies must fully and authentically develop the historical setting, both time and place, just as in a book of historical fiction. Mary Hoffman, in *Stravaganza: City of Masks,* succeeds in producing this type of mixed-genre story. Thea Beckman, in *Crusade in Jeans,* also presents an interesting historical fantasy that will appeal to middle-grade students and older.

Quest Stories

Quest stories are adventure stories with a search motif. The quest may be pursuit for a lofty purpose, such as justice or love, or for a rich reward, such as a magical power or a hidden treasure. Quest stories that are serious in tone are called *high fantasy.* Many of these novels are set in medieval times and are reminiscent of the search for the holy grail. In these high fantasies, an imaginary otherworld fully portrays the society, its history, family trees, geographic location, population, religion, customs, and traditions. The conflict in these tales usually centers on the struggle between good and evil. Often, characters are drawn from myth and legend. The protagonist is engaged in a struggle against external forces of evil and internal temptations of weakness. Thus, the quest usually represents a journey of self-discovery and personal growth for the protagonist, in addition to the search for the reward. *The Hobbit,* written by J. R. R. Tolkien in 1937, is one of the first of these high fantasies; it retains a cult of followers even today, especially since the movie trilogy of Tolkien's *Lord of the Rings* became quite popular. Because of the greater complexity of these novels, their allure is for children in fifth grade and higher, including adults, of course. Good examples are C. S. Lewis's Narnia series starting with *The Lion, the Witch, and the Wardrobe,* Philip Pullman's *His Dark Materials* trilogy, and J. K. Rowling's *Harry Potter* series.

Science Fiction and Science Fantasy

Science fiction is a form of imaginative literature that provides a picture of something that could happen based on real scientific facts and principles. Therefore, story elements in science fiction must have the appearance of scientific plausibility or technical possibility. Hypotheses about the future of humankind and the universe presented in science fiction appear plausible and possible to the reader because settings and events are built on extensions of known technologies and scientific concepts.

In novels of science fiction, such topics as mind control, genetic engineering, space technologies and travel, visitors from outer space, and future political and social systems all seem possible to the readers. These novels especially fascinate many young people because they feature characters who must learn to adjust to change and to become new people, two aspects of living that adolescents also experience. In addition, science fiction stories may portray the world, or one very much like it, that young people will one day inhabit; for this reason, science fiction has sometimes been called *futuristic fiction.*

Science fiction is a type of fiction that you will want to know about because of its growing popularity among children and adolescents. If you are reluctant to read science fiction or have never read it, you may want to start with some books by Nancy Farmer (*The House of the Scorpion*), H. M. Hoover (*Children of Morrow; This Time of Darkness*), or John Christopher (*The White Mountains*).

The distinction between science fiction and science fantasy is not clearly defined or universally accepted. *Science fantasy* is a popularized type of science fiction in which a scientific explanation, though not necessarily plausible, is offered for imaginative leaps into the unknown. Science fantasy presents a world that often mixes elements of mythology and traditional fantasy with scientific or technological concepts, resulting in a setting that has some scientific basis but never has existed or never could exist. A worthy example is Sylvia Waugh's *Earthborn,* in which the protagonist discovers her parents are space aliens. Science fantasy novels, which usually appear in series, appeal to adolescents and young adults and, like many series, are sometimes formulaic and of mixed quality.

Modern fantasy has appeal for persons with nonliteral minds, for people who go beyond the letter of a story to its spirit. Children, with their lively imaginations, are especially open to reading fantasies. The many types and topics within this genre—animal fantasies, little people stories, tales of personified toys, mystery fantasies, stories of unusual people and situations, quest tales, science fiction, and so on—offer children a breadth of inspiring and delightful entertainment. Since the level of conceptual difficulty varies considerably in this genre, modern fantasy offers many excellent stories for children, from the youngest to the oldest.

REFERENCES

Elleman, B. (1987). Current trends in literature for children. *Library Trends, 35*(3): 413–426.

Fitch, S. (1998). Ladder to the sky. In J. Prelutsky (Ed.), *Imagine that!* Illustrated by Kevin Hawkes. New York: Knopf.

NOTABLE   *A U T H O R S   O F   M O D E R N   F A N T A S Y*

David Almond, British writer noted for magical realism novels for young adults. *Skellig,* Carnegie Medal winner, and *Kit's Wilderness.*

John Bellairs, author of mysteries containing supernatural elements. The *House with a Clock in Its Walls* is the first book of a trilogy.

John Christopher, British science fiction author who created the Tripods series set in the twenty-first century. *The White Mountains; The City of Gold and Lead.*

Susan Cooper, author of high fantasies based on Arthurian legends. *Over Sea, under Stone* is the first in a five-book series.

Roald Dahl, British author of many popular fantasies known for humor and exaggerated characters. *James and the Giant Peach; Charlie and the Chocolate Factory.*

Peter Dickinson, British author of modern fantasies including science fiction novels. *Eva.*

Nancy Farmer, author of young adult novels including *The House of the Scorpion,* National Book Award winner for young people's literature. Also, *The Ear, the Eye, and the Arm,* Newbery Honor Book.

Brian Jacques, author of the Redwall Abbey animal fantasy series. *The Bellmaker; Mossflower.*

Dick King-Smith, British author of animal fantasies. *Pigs Might Fly; Babe: The Gallant Pig.*

C. S. Lewis, British creator of the Chronicles of Narnia, a series of adventure quest stories. *The Lion, the Witch, and the Wardrobe.*

Lois Lowry, winner of the 1994 Newbery Medal for *The Giver,* a popular work of science fiction.

Robin McKinley, author of quest tales and modern folktales with female protagonists. *The Hero and the Crown; Beauty; Spindle's End.*

Terry Pratchett, British author of the Discworld series that includes *The Wee Free Men.* Winner of the Carnegie Medal for *The Amazing Maurice and His Educated Rodents,* a work of humorous fantasy.

Philip Pullman, British creator of His Dark Materials fantasies, a trilogy comprised of *The Golden Compass, The Subtle Knife,* and *The Amber Spyglass.*

J. K. Rowling, British author of the popular, bestselling series about Harry Potter, a child wizard. *Harry Potter and the Sorcerer's Stone.*

Sylvia Waugh, British author of the Mennyms series about a family of life-sized rag dolls. Also, author of a science fantasy series that includes *Space Race.*

E. B. White, author of the classic animal fantasy *Charlotte's Web.*

RECOMMENDED MODERN FANTASY BOOKS

*Ages refer to approximate interest levels
YA = young adult readers.*

Modern Folktales

Andersen, Hans Christian. *The Emperor's New Clothes.* Illustrated by Angela Barrett. Translated by Naomi Lewis. Candlewick, 1997. Ages 7–9.

———. *The Ugly Duckling.* Illustrated by Jerry Pinkney. Morrow, 1989. Ages 6–9.

Brooke, William J. *Teller of Tales.* Illustrated by Eric Beddows. HarperCollins, 1994. Ages 10–YA.

Crossley-Holland, Kevin. *At the Crossing Places.* Scholastic, 2002. Ages 10–YA.

———. *The Seeing Stone.* Arthur Trilogy, Book One. Scholastic, 2001. Ages 10–YA.

Hale, Shannon. *Goose Girl.* Bloomsbury, 2003. Ages 11–YA.

Isaacs, Anne. *Swamp Angel.* Illustrated by Paul Zelinsky. Dutton, 1994. Ages 7–10.

Levine, Gail Carson. *Ella Enchanted.* HarperCollins, 1997. Ages 10–13.

Lobel, Arnold. *Fables.* Harper, 1980. Ages 8–10.

McKinley, Robin. *Beauty: A Retelling of the Beauty and the Beast.* Harper, 1978. Ages 10–YA.

———. *Rose Daughter.* Greenwillow, 1997. Ages 11–YA.

———. *Spindle's End.* Putnam, 2000. Ages 12–YA.

Napoli, Donna Jo. *Crazy Jack.* Delacorte, 1999. Ages 11–YA.

———. *Zel.* Dutton, 1996. Ages 13–YA.

Osborne, Mary Pope. *Kate and the Beanstalk.* Illustrated by Giselle Potter. Schwartz/Atheneum, 2000. Ages 5–8.

Pattou, Edith. *East.* Harcourt, 2003. Ages 12–YA.

Pyle, Howard. *Bearskin.* Illustrated by Trina Schart Hyman. Morrow, 1997. Ages 7–9.

Sandburg, Carl. *The Huckabuck Family: And How They Raised Popcorn in Nebraska and Quit and Came Back.* Illustrated by David Small. Farrar, 1999. Ages 5–8.

Scieszka, Jon. *The True Story of the 3 Little Pigs by A. Wolf.* Illustrated by Lane Smith. Viking, 1989. Ages 7–12.

Stanley, Diane. *Rumpelstiltskin's Daughter.* Morrow, 1997. Ages 5–9.

Yolen, Jane. *Sleeping Ugly.* Illustrated by Diane Stanley. Coward, 1981. Ages 7–10.

———. *Sword of the Rightful King: A Novel of King Arthur.* Harcourt, 2003. Ages 11–YA.

Animal Fantasies

Arkin, Alan. *Cassie Loves Beethoven.* Hyperion, 2000. Ages 9–12. Humorous.

Atwater, Richard, and Florence Atwater. *Mr. Popper's Penguins.* Illustrated by Robert Lawson. Little, 1938. Ages 8–11.

Avi. *Poppy.* Illustrated by Brian Floca. Orchard, 1995. Ages 8–11.

Burgess, Thornton W. *Old Mother West Wind.* Illustrated by Thea Kliros. Dover, 1995 (1910). Ages 5–8.

Cleary, Beverly. *The Mouse and the Motorcycle.* Illustrated by Louis Darling. Morrow, 1965. Ages 7–11.

———. *Runaway Ralph.* Illustrated by Louis Darling. Morrow, 1970. Ages 7–11.

Clement-Davies, David. *Fire Bringer.* Dutton, 2000. Ages 12–YA.

DiCamillo, Kate. *The Tale of Despereaux.* Illustrated by Timothy B. Ering. Candlewick, 2003. Ages 7–10.

Dickinson, Peter. *Chuck and Danielle.* Delacorte, 1996. Ages 8–11.

Grahame, Kenneth. *The Wind in the Willows.* Illustrated by E. H. Shepard. Scribner's, 1908. Ages 8–12.

Howe, Deborah, and James Howe. *Bunnicula: A Rabbit-Tale of Mystery.* Illustrated by Alan Daniel. Atheneum, 1979. Ages 8–11.

Howe, James. *Howliday Inn.* Atheneum, 1982. Ages 8–11.

Jacques, Brian. *Lord Brocktree.* (Redwall series.) Philomel, 2000. Ages 9–12.

————. *Redwall.* Illustrated by Gary Chalk. Philomel, 1987. Ages 11–YA. Others in the Redwall series are *Mossflower, Mattimeo, Mariel of Redwall, Salamandastron, The Bellmaker.*

Jennings, Patrick. *Faith and the Electric Dogs.* Scholastic, 1996. Ages 8–11.

Jennings, Richard W. *Orwell's Luck.* Houghton, 2000. Ages 9–12.

King-Smith, Dick. *Babe: The Gallant Pig.* Illustrated by Mary Rayner. Crown, 1985. Ages 7–11.

————. *Pigs Might Fly.* Illustrated by Mary Rayner. Viking, 1982. Ages 8–11.

Kipling, Rudyard. *Just So Stories.* Doubleday, 1902. Ages 6–10.

Labatt, Mary. *Aliens in Woodford.* Kids Can Press, 2000. Ages 7–10. Humorous.

Lawson, Robert. *Rabbit Hill.* Viking, 1944. Ages 8–11.

Pinkwater, Daniel. *Mush, A Dog from Space.* Simon & Schuster, 1995. Ages 7–9.

Pratchett, Terry. *The Amazing Maurice and His Educated Rodents.* HarperCollins, 2001. Ages 12–YA.

Said, S. F. *Varjak Paw.* Illustrated by Dave McKean. Knopf, 2003. Ages 9–12.

Seidler, Tor. *Mean Margaret.* Illustrated by Jon Agee. HarperCollins, 1997. Ages 8–11.

Selden, George. *The Cricket in Times Square.* Illustrated by Garth Williams. Farrar, 1960. Ages 8–11.

Steig, William. *Abel's Island.* Farrar, 1976. Ages 8–11.

White, E. B. *Charlotte's Web.* Illustrated by Garth Williams. Harper, 1952. Ages 8–11.

————. *Stuart Little.* Illustrated by Garth Williams. Harper, 1945. Ages 8–11.

Personified Toys and Objects

Clarke, Pauline. *The Twelve and the Genii.* Jane Nissan Books, 2001 (1962). Ages 9–12. Great Britain. Toy soldiers fantasy. Reissue.

Collodi, Carlo (pseudonym of Carlo Lorenzini). *The Adventures of Pinocchio.* Illustrated by Attilio Mussino. Translated by Carol Della Chiesa. Macmillan, 1881. Ages 8–10.

Martin, Ann M., and Laura Godwin,. *The Doll People.* Illustrated by Brian Selznick. Hyperion, 2000. Ages 8–12.

————. *The Meanest Doll in the World.* Illustrated by Brian Selznick. Hyperion, 2003. Ages 7–11. Sequel to *The Doll People.*

Milne, A. A. *The House at Pooh Corner.* Illustrated by Ernest Shepard. Dutton, 1928. Ages 6–9.

————. *Winnie-the-Pooh.* Illustrated by Ernest Shepard. Dutton, 1926. Ages 6–9.

Waugh, Sylvia. *The Mennyms.* Morrow, 1994. Ages 8–12.

————. *Mennyms in the Wilderness.* Greenwillow, 1995. Ages 8–11.

Winthrop, Elizabeth. *The Battle for the Castle.* Holiday, 1993. Ages 8–12.

Unusual Characters and Strange Situations

Ahlberg, Allan. *The Giant Baby.* Illustrated by Fritz Wegner. Viking, 1995. Ages 7–11.

Aiken, Joan. *Cold Shoulder Road.* Delacorte, 1996. Ages 10–13.

Babbitt, Natalie. *Tuck Everlasting.* Farrar, 1975. Ages 10–YA.

Barrie, Sir James. *Peter Pan.* Illustrated by Nora Unwin. Scribner's, 1911. Ages 8–11.

Baum, L. Frank. *The Wonderful Wizard of Oz.* Illustrated by Lisbeth Zwerger. North-South, 1996 (1900). Ages 8–11.

Billingsley, Franny. *The Folk Keeper.* Simon & Schuster, 1999. Ages 10–13.

————. *Well Wished.* Simon & Schuster, 1997. Ages 10–12.

Boston, Lucy M. *The Children of Green Knowe.* Illustrated by Peter Boston. Harcourt, 1955. Ages 8–11. The first of a series of fantasies set in an English manor house.

Carroll, Lewis (pseud. for Charles Lutwidge Dodgson). *Alice's Adventures in Wonderland* and *Through the Looking Glass.* First published in 1865. A recent edition is illustrated by Anthony Browne. Knopf, 1988. Ages 9–13.

Clements, Andrew. *Things Not Seen.* Putnam/Philomel, 2002. Ages 12–YA.

Dahl, Roald. *Charlie and the Chocolate Factory.* Illustrated by Joseph Schindelman. Knopf, 1964. Ages 8–11.

———. *James and the Giant Peach.* Illustrated by Nancy E. Burkert. Knopf, 1961. Ages 8–11.

———. *Matilda.* Illustrated by Quentin Blake. Viking, 1988. Ages 8–11.

Farmer, Nancy. *The Ear, the Eye, and the Arm.* Orchard, 1994. Ages 11–14. Humorous.

Heide, Florence Parry. *The Shrinking of Treehorn.* Illustrated by Edward Gorey. Holiday, 1971. Ages 7–10.

Lindgren, Astrid. *Pippi Longstocking.* Translated by Florence Lamborn. Viking, 1950. Ages 8–11.

McGraw, Eloise. *The Moorchild.* Simon & Schuster, 1996. Ages 9–12.

Nöstlinger, Christine. *Konrad.* Watts, 1977. Ages 8–11.

Pullman, Philip. *I Was a Rat!* Illustrated by Kevin Hawkes. Knopf, 2000. Ages 8–12.

Sachar, Louis. *Wayside School Gets a Little Stranger.* Morrow, 1995. Ages 8–12. Humorous.

Travers, P. L. *Mary Poppins.* Illustrated by Mary Shepard. Harcourt, 1934. Ages 9–12.

Worlds of Little People

Dahl, Roald. *The Minpins.* Illustrated by Patrick Benson. Viking, 1991. Ages 5–8.

Kendall, Carol. *The Gammage Cup.* Illustrated by Erik Blegvad. Harcourt, 1959. Ages 8–12.

Norton, Mary. *The Borrowers.* Illustrated by Beth and Joe Krush. Harcourt, 2003 (1953). Ages 8–11. This is the first of a series of little people fantasies.

———. *The Borrowers.* Illustrated by Diane Stanley. Harcourt, 2003 (1953).

Pratchett, Terry. *The Wee Free Men.* HarperCollins, 2003. Ages 10–13.

Swift, Jonathan. *Gulliver in Lilliput.* Retold by Margaret Hodges. Illustrated by Kimberly Bulcken Root. Holiday, 1995. Ages 8–11. Nine-chapter, illustrated retelling.

Supernatural Events and Mystery Fantasy

Almond, David. *Heaven Eyes.* Delacorte, 2001. Ages 10–13.

———. *Kit's Wilderness.* Delacorte, 2000. Ages 12–YA.

———. *Skellig.* Delacorte, 1999. Ages 9–12.

Bell, Hilari. *Flame.* Simon & Schuster, 2003. Ages 11–YA.

———. *The Goblin Wood.* HarperCollins, 2003. Ages 11–YA.

Bellairs, John. *The Curse of the Blue Figurine.* Dial, 1983. Ages 10–YA.

———. *The House with a Clock in Its Walls.* Puffin, 1993 (1973). Ages 10–12.

Bunting, Eve. *The Presence: A Ghost Story.* Clarion, 2003. Ages 12–YA.

Coville, Bruce. *The Skull of Truth.* Illustrated by Gary A. Lippincott. Harcourt, 1997. Ages 9–12.

DeFelice, Cynthia. *The Ghost of Fossil Glen.* Farrar, 1998. Ages 9–12.

Dickinson, Peter. *The Ropemaker.* Delacorte, 2001. Ages 11–YA.

———. *The Tears of the Salamander.* Random, 2003. Ages 11–14.

Fleischman, Sid. *The Midnight Horse.* Illustrated by Peter Sís. Greenwillow, 1990. Ages 8–11.

Funke, Cornelia. *The Thief Lord.* Translated from the German by Oliver Latsch. Scholastic, 2002. Ages 10–14.

Ibbotson, Eva. *Island of the Aunts.* Illustrated by Kevin Hawkes. Dutton, 2000. Ages 9–12.

Jones, Diana Wynne. *Dark Lord of Derkholm.* Greenwillow, 1998. (Also its sequel, *Year of the Griffin.* Greenwillow, 2000.) Ages 12–YA.

Key, Alexander. *Escape to Witch Mountain.* Illustrated by Leon B. Wisdom, Jr. Westminster, 1968. Ages 10–12.

Lively, Penelope. *The Ghost of Thomas Kempe.* Illustrated by Anthony Maitland. Dutton, 1973. Ages 9–12.

McBratney, Sam. *The Ghosts of Hungryhouse Lane.* Holt, 1989. Ages 7–10.

McKissack, Patricia C. *The Dark-Thirty: Southern Tales of the Supernatural.* Illustrated by Brian Pinkney. Knopf, 1992. Ages 9–12.

Pearce, Philippa. *Tom's Midnight Garden.* Lippincott, 1959. Ages 9–12.

Prue, Sally. *Cold Tom.* Scholastic, 2003. Ages 10–13.

Pullman, Philip. *Clockwork.* Illustrated by Leonid Gore. Scholastic, 1998. Ages 9–13.

Rodda, Emily. *Rowan of Rin.* Greenwillow, 2001. Ages 8–11.

———. *Rowan and the Zebak.* HarperCollins, 2002. Ages 8–11.

Historical Fantasy

Beckman, Thea. *Crusade in Jeans.* Front Street, 2003. Ages 11–YA. Time travel to Middle Ages.

Branford, Henrietta. *Fire, Bed, and Bone.* Candlewick, 1998. Ages 10–13. Set in late fourteenth-century England; told from a hunting hound's point of view.

Chetwin, Grace. *Friends in Time.* Bradbury, 1992. Ages 9–12.

Cooney, Caroline B. *Both Sides of Time.* Delacorte, 1995. Ages 12–YA.

Cooper, Susan. *King of Shadows.* Simon & Schuster, 1999. Ages 10–13.

Dickinson, Peter. *A Bone from a Dry Sea.* Delacorte, 1993. Ages 12–YA.

Hoffman, Mary. *Stravaganza: City of Masks.* Bloomsbury, 2002. Ages 12–YA. Sixteenth-century Venice. (Also a sequel, *Stravaganza II: City of Stars.* Bloomsbury, 2003. Ages 12–YA. Sixteenth-century Italy.)

Lawson, Robert. *Ben and Me.* Little, 1939. Ages 9–12.

McKay, Hillary. *The Amber Cat.* Simon & Schuster, 1997. Ages 9–12.

Myers, Laurie. *Lewis and Clark and Me.* Illustrated by Michael Dooling. Holt, 2002. Ages 8–12. The 1803 exploration of Lewis and Clark told by Seaman, a Newfoundland dog.

Yolen, Jane. *The Devil's Arithmetic.* Viking, 1988. Ages 10–13.

Quest Stories

Alexander, Lloyd. *The Book of Three.* Holt, 1964. Ages 10–YA. The first of the Prydain Chronicles, a series of five quest fantasies, including *The Black Cauldron, The Castle of Llyr, The High King,* and *Taran Wanderer.*

Collins, Suzanne. *Gregor the Overlander.* Scholastic, 2003. Ages 9–YA.

Cooper, Susan. *Over Sea, under Stone.* Illustrated by Margery Gill. Harcourt, 1965. Ages 10–YA. This is the first of a five-book Arthurian quest series, including *The Dark Is Rising, Greenwitch, The Grey King,* and *Silver on the Tree.*

Divakaruni, Chitra Banerjee. *The Conch Bearer.* Millbrook, 2003. Ages 10–14.

Ibbotson, Eva. *The Secret of Platform 13.* Dutton, 1998. Ages 9–13.

———. *Which Witch?* Dutton, 1999. Ages 10–14.

Le Guin, Ursula K. *A Wizard of Earthsea.* Parnassus, 1968. Ages 11–YA. Other books in this series are *The Farthest Shore, The Tombs of Atuan,* and *Tehanu: The Last Book of Earthsea.*

Lewis, Clive Staples. *The Lion, the Witch, and the Wardrobe.* Illustrated by Pauline Baynes. Macmillan, 1950. Ages 9–12. The first in a series of quest fantasies, including *The Horse and His Boy, The Last Battle, The Magician's Nephew, Prince Caspian, The Silver Chair,* and *The Voyage of the Dawn Treader.*

McKinley, Robin. *The Hero and the Crown.* Greenwillow, 1984. Ages 11–YA.

Paterson, Katherine. *Parzival: The Quest of the Grail Knight.* Lodestar, 1998. Ages 10–YA.

Pierce, Meredith Ann. *Treasure at the Heart of the Tanglewood.* Viking, 2001. Ages 12–YA.

Pullman, Philip. *The Golden Compass.* Knopf, 1996. Ages 12–YA. First of His Dark Materials trilogy. Also *The Subtle Knife,* Knopf, 1998, and *The Amber Spyglass,* Knopf, 1999.

Rowling, J. K. *Harry Potter and the Sorcerer's Stone.* Scholastic, 1998. Ages 9–13. The first in a series of quest fantasies, including *Harry Potter and the Chamber of Secrets,* 1999; *Harry Potter and the Prisoner of Azkaban,* 1999; *Harry Potter and the Goblet of Fire,* 2000; and *Harry Potter and the Order of the Phoenix.* 2003.

Tolkien, J. R. R. *The Hobbit.* Houghton, 1938. Ages 10–YA.

Turner, Megan Whelan. *The Thief.* Greenwillow, 1996. Ages 11–YA.

Science Fiction and Science Fantasy

Alcock, Vivien. *The Monster Garden.* Delacorte, 1988. Ages 10–14.

Atwater-Rhodes, Amelia. *Hawksong.* Delacorte, 2003. Ages 12–YA.

Bechard, Margaret. *Star Hatchling.* Viking, 1995. Ages 9–12.

Bell, Hilari. *A Matter of Profit.* HarperCollins, 2001. Ages 11–YA.

Brittain, Bill. *Shape-Changer.* HarperCollins, 1994. Ages 8–12.

Cameron, Eleanor. *The Wonderful Flight to the Mushroom Planet.* Illustrated by Robert Henneberger. Little, 1954. Ages 7–9.

Christopher, John. *The White Mountains.* Macmillan, 1967. Ages 11–YA. (Also included in the Tripods series: *The City of Gold and Lead,* 1967, and *The Pool of Fire,* 1968.)

Conly, Jane Leslie. *Racso and Rats of NIMH.* Illustrated by Leonard Lubin. Harper, 1986. Ages 9–12.

———. *R. T., Margaret, and the Rats of NIMH.* HarperCollins, 1990. Ages 9–12.

Dickinson, Peter. *Eva.* Delacorte, 1989. Ages 12–YA.

du Bois, William Pène. *The Twenty-One Balloons.* Viking, 1947. Ages 8–12.

Engdahl, Sylvia. *Enchantress from the Stars.* Atheneum, 1970. Ages 11–YA.

Etchemendy, Nancy. *The Power of Un.* Front Street, 2000. Ages 10–13.

Farmer, Nancy. *The House of the Scorpion.* Simon & Schuster, 2002. Ages 12–YA.

Hoover, H. M. *Children of Morrow.* Four Winds, 1973. Ages 11–YA.

———. *This Time of Darkness.* Viking, 1980. Ages 11–YA.

Hughes, Monica. *Invitation to the Game.* Simon & Schuster, 1990. Ages 12–YA.

Key, Alexander. *The Forgotten Door.* Westminster, 1965. Ages 10–12.

Klause, Annette Curtis. *Alien Secrets.* Delacorte, 1993. Ages 10–13.

L'Engle, Madeleine. *A Wrinkle in Time.* Farrar, 1962. Ages 11–YA.

Lowry, Lois. *Gathering Blue.* Houghton, 2000. Ages 10–YA.

———. *The Giver.* Houghton, 1993. Ages 11–YA.

McCaffrey, Anne. *Dragonsinger.* Atheneum, 1977. Ages 11–YA.

Nix, Garth. *Shade's Children.* HarperCollins, 1997. Ages 12–YA.

O'Brien, Robert C. *Mrs. Frisby and the Rats of NIMH.* Illustrated by Zena Bernstein. Atheneum, 1971. Ages 9–12. (See sequels by Conly.)

Sleator, William. *The Boy Who Reversed Himself.* Dutton, 1986. Ages 10–YA.

———. *The Duplicate.* Dutton, 1988. Ages 11–YA.

———. *House of Stairs.* Dutton, 1974. Ages 11–YA.

Waugh, Sylvia. *Earthborn.* Delacorte, 2002. Ages 9–13.

———. *Space Race.* Delacorte, 2000. Ages 9–12.

Realistic Fiction

LISTENING
TO GROWNUPS
QUARRELING,

*standing in the hall against the
wall with my little brother, blown
like leaves against the wall by their
voices, my head like a pingpong ball
between the paddles of their anger:
I knew what it meant
to tremble like a leaf.*

*Cold with their wrath, I heard
the claws of the rain
pounce. Floods
poured through the city,
skies clapped over me,
and I was shaken, shaken
like a mouse
between their jaws.*

— RUTH WHITMAN

Children's lives are sometimes sad and harsh. Realistic stories of today openly address these situations as well as the happy and humorous situations of life. Children of all ages appreciate stories about people who seem like themselves or who are involved in familiar activities. These realistic fiction stories have appealed to children for many years and continue to do so today.

DEFINITION AND DESCRIPTION

Realistic fiction refers to stories that could indeed happen to people and animals; that is, it is within the realm of possibility that such events could occur or could have occurred. The protagonists of these stories are fictitious characters created by the author, but their actions and reactions are quite like those of real people or real animals. Sometimes, events in these stories are exaggerated or outlandish—hardly probable but definitely possible. These stories, too, fit under the definition of realistic fiction.

Realism in literature is a complex, multifaceted concept. Marshall (1988) considers various components of realism in literature, including factual, situational, emotional, and social. *Factual realism* is provided by the description of actual people, places, and events in a book. When this occurs, the facts need to be recorded accurately. For example, usually in historical fiction and occasionally in realistic fiction, the names and locations of actual places are included in the story, with accurate and complete descriptions. *Situational realism* is provided by a situation that is not only possible but also quite likely, often in an identifiable location with characters of an identifiable age and social class, making the whole treatment believable. Family stories are often examples of stories built on situational realism. *Emotional realism* is provided by the appearance of believable feelings and relationships among characters. Rite-of-passage or growing-up stories often employ emotional realism. *Social realism* is provided by an honest portrayal of society and its conditions of the moment. In almost all good realistic stories, several of these components of realism occur, with varying degrees of emphasis.

Contemporary realism is a term used to describe stories that take place in the present time and portray attitudes and mores of the present culture. Unlike realistic books of several decades ago that depicted only happy families and were never controversial, today's contemporary realism often focuses on current societal issues, such as alcoholism, racism, poverty, and homelessness. Contemporary books still tell of the happy, funny times in children's lives, but they also include the harsh, unpleasant times that are, sadly, a part of many children's lives.

Authors of contemporary realistic fiction set their stories in the present or recent past. But, in time, features of these stories, such as dialogue and allusions to popular culture, customs, and dress become dated and the stories are therefore no longer contemporary, though they may still be realistic. Older stories that obviously no longer describe today's world, though they may have once been contemporary realistic fiction, are now simply realistic fiction. Older realistic fiction stories that are considered modern classics are included in this chapter.

EVALUATION AND SELECTION OF REALISTIC FICTION

The criteria for evaluating realistic fiction are the same as those for any work of fiction. Well-developed characters who manifest change as a result of significant life events, a well-structured plot with sufficient conflict and suspense to hold the reader's interest, a time and place suitable to the storyline, and a worthy theme are basic literary elements expected of any work of fiction, including works of realistic fiction.

- Even stories that portray adverse and discouraging social situations should permit some cause for optimism. Children need to trust that problems can be overcome or ameliorated and that the world can be a good place in which to live.
- Themes in realistic stories often convey moral values, such as the rewards of kindness and generosity to others. However, these moral values must not be the main reason for the story. At times, adults write books for children with the sole intent of teaching or preaching, and the story itself is nothing more than a thin disguise for a heavy-handed moral lesson. The moral must not overwhelm the story but may be its logical outcome.
- A novel of realistic fiction must be believable, and the events must be possible, even though all aspects may not be probable. Sometimes, an author goes closer to the edge of the believable range to produce a more exciting, suspense-filled story.
- Controversy involving children's books often centers on topics that are found in realistic fiction novels, such as premarital sex, pregnancy, homosexuality, and the use of profanity. Many of these controversial books fall within the types of realism labeled "Moral Choices" and "Romance and Sexuality" in the recommended reading list at the end of this chapter. Chapter 11 provides a full discussion of issues surrounding censorship and selection.
- An aspect of writing style that students greatly appreciate is humor. Although humor may be found in stories of any genre, it is more often found in realistic fiction. Humorous stories feature characters caught up in silly situations or involved in funny escapades. *Anastasia Krupnik* by Lois Lowry is a good example of a humorous story.

Selection of realistic fiction for classroom and library collections and for read-alouds should be balanced among the different types of realistic stories. A steady diet of humorous read-alouds does not offer the richness of experience to children that they deserve, nor does it provide for the varied reading interests of a group of children. The Edgar Allan Poe Award for Juvenile Mystery Novels can be helpful to you in selecting good mysteries. This award was established in 1961 by the Mystery Writers of America and is awarded annually in order to honor U.S. authors of mysteries for children. The list of winners is included in Appendix A. Intermediate-grade children report on reading interest surveys that realistic fiction is their favorite genre. Of course, some children may prefer other categories, but realistic fiction does hold high appeal for many children at all grade levels.

HISTORICAL OVERVIEW OF REALISTIC FICTION

The earliest realistic stories were didactic ones that were intended to teach morality and manners to young readers. The characters of the children's stories of the 1700s were usually wooden, lifeless boys and girls whose lives were spent in good works; however, in England during this period, two significant events affecting the future of children's literature occurred. *Robinson Crusoe* by Daniel Defoe, an exciting survival story, was published in 1719 for adults but became a popular book among children. Then in 1744, John Newbery began to publish, expressly for a child audience, books of realistic fiction intended to entertain as well as to educate. These two events laid the groundwork for establishing children's literature as a separate branch of literature. Milestones in the development of realistic fiction are highlighted on page 134.

┌───┐

Excellent R E A L I S T I C   F I C T I O N   to Read Aloud

Cameron, Ann. *Colibrí.* Ages 10–YA. Set in Guatemala.

Creech, Sharon. *Ruby Holler.* Ages 8–11.

DiCamillo, Kate. *Because of Winn-Dixie.* Ages 8–11.

Ellis, Sarah. *The Several Lives of Orphan Jack.* Illustrated by Bruno St.-Aubin. Ages 7–11.

Fogelin, Adrian. *Crossing Jordan.* Ages 11–14.

Gantos, Jack. *Joey Pigza Swallowed the Key.* Ages 9–12.

Horvath, Polly. *Everything on a Waffle.* Ages 9–12.

Lowry, Lois. *Anastasia Krupnik.* Illustrated by Diane De Groat. Ages 8–11. Humorous.

Myers, Walter Dean. *Scorpions.* Ages 10–YA.

O'Connor, Barbara. *Moonpie and Ivy.* Ages 10–13.

Ritter, John H. *The Boy Who Saved Baseball.* Ages 10–13.

Stauffacher, Sue. *Donuthead.* Ages 9–12. Humorous.

Woodson, Jacqueline. *Locomotion.* Ages 9–12. Told through a series of poems.

└───┘

The first type of realistic fiction for children that avoided the heavy didactic persuasion was the adventure story. Imitators of *Robinson Crusoe* were many, including the very popular *Swiss Family Robinson* by Johann Wyss of Switzerland in 1812. Later adventure stories of renown from England were *Treasure Island* (1883) and *Kidnapped* (1886) by Robert Louis Stevenson; and from the United States, *The Adventures of Tom Sawyer* (1876) and *The Adventures of Huckleberry Finn* (1884) by Mark Twain (pseudonym of Samuel Clemens).

Realistic family stories also came on the scene during the 1800s with *Little Women* (1868) by Louisa May Alcott. The family story remains a favorite in the twentieth century, with early memorable books such as the series *Anne of Green Gables* (1908) by Canadian Lucy Maud Montgomery and *The Secret Garden* (1911) by Frances Hodgson Burnett. Since Anne of *Anne of Green Gables* and Mary of *The Secret Garden* were orphans, the books by Burnett and Montgomery can be considered precursors of adjustment stories that addressed the special needs of children with problems. Stories of happy and often large families continued to thrive and peaked in the 1940s and 1950s in family story series about the Moffat family by Eleanor Estes and about the Melendy family by Elizabeth Enright. These *happy family* stories compared with much of today's contemporary realism for children seem almost lighthearted.

Children from other lands is another theme that can be found in many realistic stories for children. *Hans Brinker, or The Silver Skates* (1865) by Mary Mapes Dodge and *Heidi* (1880) by Johanna Spyri of Switzerland are set in Holland and Switzerland, respectively, and were two of the earliest *other lands* books.

Realistic animal stories for children began to appear in the latter half of the nineteenth century. *Black Beauty* (1877) by Anna Sewell was a plea for humane treatment of animals and, though quite sentimental in places and completely personified (i.e., the animal is given human qualities), is still appreciated by some readers. Animal stories showing the maturing of the young human protagonist who assists the animal in the story remained popular throughout the twentieth century.

M I L E S T O N E S

in the Development of REALISTIC FICTION

DATE	EVENT	SIGNIFICANCE
1719	*Robinson Crusoe* by Daniel Defoe (England)	Early survival/adventure on a desert island; many imitators
1812	*Swiss Family Robinson* by Johann Wyss (Switzerland)	Most successful imitation of *Robinson Crusoe*
1868	*Little Women* by Louisa May Alcott (United States)	An early family story of great popularity
1876	*The Adventures of Tom Sawyer* by Mark Twain (United States)	Classic adventure story set along the Mississippi
1877	*Black Beauty* by Anna Sewell (England)	Early horse story deploring inhumane treatment of animals
1880	*Heidi* by Johanna Spyri (Switzerland)	An early international story popular in the United States
1883	*Treasure Island* by Robert Louis Stevenson (England)	Classic adventure story with pirates
1908	*Anne of Green Gables* by Lucy Maud Montgomery (Canada)	Early family story about an orphan and her new family
1911	*The Secret Garden* by Frances Hodgson Burnett (United States)	A classic sentimental novel of two children adjusting to life
1938	*The Yearling* by Marjorie Kinnan Rawlings (United States)	Classic animal story and coming-of-age story
1945	*Strawberry Girl* by Lois Lenski (United States)	Regional story set in Florida
1964	*Harriet the Spy* by Louise Fitzhugh (United States)	The beginning of the new realism movement
1970	*Are You There, God? It's Me, Margaret* by Judy Blume (United States)	Early book with frank treatment of sex
2000	*Monster* by Walter Dean Myers (United States)	First winner of the Michael L. Printz Award for Excellence in Literature for Young Adults

Regional stories and stories about children of minority groups began to appear with more frequency in the 1940s. *Strawberry Girl* (1945), by Lois Lenski, featured rural Florida and was one of the first regional stories. It was only in the 1960s and 1970s that books written by minorities began to achieve national recognition. *Zeely* (1967) by Virginia Hamilton and *Stevie* (1969) by John Steptoe portray African-American childhood experiences and are two of the earliest and most noteworthy books representing this trend toward increased minority authorship—a trend that continues today.

A new era in realistic fiction for children was ushered in with the publication of *Harriet the Spy* by Louise Fitzhugh in 1964. This story of an unhappy and, at times, unpleasant girl depicted Harriet, her parents, and her classmates as anything but ideal or sympathetic human beings. This trend toward a more graphic and explicitly truthful portrayal of life and the inclusion of many topics that were previously considered taboo continued in children's books in the 1970s and 1980s and still prevails today. Controversial topics such as death, divorce, drugs, alcoholism, and disabilities, which have always been a part of childhood, became permissible topics in children's books. Parents and other adults began to be portrayed as they truly are, not as one might believe they should be. This newer, franker brand of realism, sometimes referred to as the *new realism,* changed the world of children's books. The *new realism* books may be less lighthearted than their predecessors, but they are also more truthful and more real. At the present time, censorship of materials for children, including children's trade books, is rampant, in part, because of this trend toward more graphic and explicit writing in children's books.

TYPES OF REALISTIC FICTION

The subject matter of realistic fiction includes the child's whole world of relationships with self and others: the joys, sorrows, challenges, adjustments, anxieties, and satisfactions of human life. Realistic books will often treat more than one aspect of human life; thus, some realistic fiction books can be categorized by more than one of the following topics.

Families

Stories about the *nuclear family*—children and their relationships with parents and siblings—are a natural subject of books for children. Childhood for most children is spent in close contact with family members. Family stories for younger children often portray a happy child with loving parents. In these stories the everyday activities are shown—from brushing teeth to cooking dinner. Easy chapter books appealing to newly independent readers can be found within this type. These stories often show the child at play and sometimes explore sibling relationships as well. *Anastasia Krupnik* by Lois Lowry and *Ramona Quimby, Age 8* by Beverly Cleary are good examples of this type of book.

Extended families can also be found in children's books. Aunts, uncles, grandparents, and cousins are important in the real lives of many children and may also be enjoyed in stories written for children. See *The Same Stuff as Stars* by Katherine Paterson and *Dillon Dillon* by Kate Banks.

The *alternative family* of today's world is also depicted in family stories. Not all family stories present the safe and secure world of healthy, intact families. Separation, divorce, single-parent families, adoptive families, foster families, and reconstructed families of stepparents and stepchildren are often the backdrop of stories today. For example, see *Pictures of Hollis Woods* by Patricia Reilly Giff and *Ruby Holler* by Sharon Creech. The difficulty children and adults encounter in adjusting to these new family situations becomes the primary conflict in some stories. It is important for children to see families other than the typical mother, father, and two children portrayed positively in books.

Peers

In addition to adapting to one's family situation, children must also learn to cope with their peers. Many realistic stories show children struggling for *acceptance by peers* in a group situation. School settings are common in these stories. Examples include *Donuthead* by Sue Stauffacher and *Fame and Glory in Freedom, Georgia* by Barbara O'Connor.

Developing *close friendships* is another focus of stories about peer relationships. Friends may be of the same sex or the opposite sex, of the same age or a very different age, or of the same culture or a different culture. A concern for friendship and how to be a good friend to someone are shared traits of these stories. *The Misfits* by James Howe and *Granny Torrelli Makes Soup* by Sharon Creech are good examples of this type of book.

Special Challenges

Many children must deal with difficult challenges in their lives. Some children have disabilities; others have a family member or a friend with a disability. These disabilities may be physical, such as scoliosis; emotional, such as bipolar disorder; mental, such as mental retardation or learning disabilities; behavioral, such as hyperactivity; or multiple. Yet children do not like to appear different or strange to others. Authors of children's books are becoming increasingly sensitive to the need for positive portrayals of individuals with special challenges. Well-written, honest stories of such individuals in children's books can help other children to gain an understanding of disabilities and to empathize with people who have disabilities. As inclusion of special education students into regular classrooms becomes a more common practice, this trend in children's literature can be an important educational resource. As examples, Jane Leslie Conly's Newbery Honor Book winner, *Crazy Lady!*, deals with physical disabilities and mental retardation, and June Rae Wood's *The Man Who Loved Clowns* addresses Down syndrome.

Cultural Diversity

Part of growing up involves the discovery that not all people are the same; part of becoming a healthy and humane adult is accepting the differences in oneself and in others. Today's children are growing up in a multicultural society in which an understanding and appreciation of cultural and linguistic differences among peoples are essential for societal harmony and cooperation. *Multicultural books* are those in which the main characters are from a racial, language, religious, or ethnic microculture such as African Americans, Asian Americans, Hispanic Americans, Jewish Americans, or Native Americans. These books can be instrumental in developing in all children new understanding and appreciation for others as well as providing characters with whom minority children themselves may more readily identify. *Locomotion* by Jacqueline Woodson is a good example.

As our earth hastens toward becoming an international community, children will be members of an international community. Books set in *foreign countries* may be written by U.S. authors about life in another culture or by a foreign author about his own country. These books can help children develop an awareness of people from other countries and an appreciation for children whose lives differ from their own. Examples include *Colibrí* by Ann Cameron and *Shabanu: Daughter of the Wind* by Suzanne Fisher Staples. For further discussion of multicultural and international children's literature of a variety of genres, see Chapter 10.

Animals

Animal stories remain an ever-popular genre with children, dog and horse stories being the most popular. In realistic animal stories the animal protagonist behaves like an animal and is not personified. Usually, a child is also a protagonist in these stories. Examples are *Because of Winn-Dixie* by Kate DiCamillo and *Shiloh* by Phyllis Reynolds Naylor.

Sports

Sports stories often present a story in which a child protagonist struggles to become accepted as a member of a team and does eventually succeed through determination and hard work. *The Boy Who Saved Baseball* by John H. Ritter is a good example of a sports story. Although traditionally written with boys as the main characters, some sports stories are now available that feature girls as protagonists.

Mysteries

Mysteries, popular with boys and girls, range from simple "whodunits" to complex character stories. The element of suspense is a strong part of the appeal of these stories. Mysteries have won more state children's choice awards than any other type of story, a fact that suggests that mysteries are truly favorites of many children. See *Mystery in Mt. Mole* by Richard W. Jennings and *Sammy Keyes and the Search for Snake Eyes* by Wendelin Van Draanen.

Moral Choices

Characters in many realistic fiction novels face moments of crisis, situations of great difficulty, or events in which a decision may change someone's life. These situations are often similar to those that children will face in their lives. Through these stories children can understand the difficult decisions the character is faced with and can discuss the consequences that may result from the choice made. Teachers often select these books for class study with intermediate- and middle-grade students. Using a book in which a character is faced with a difficult moral choice can stimulate lively discussions. An example is Paul Fleischman's *Whirligig,* in which the main character must face the devastating consequences of his choice.

Romance and Sexuality

Romance stories are popular with preteens and teens, especially girls. Some stories depict boy-girl friendships, as in *Flipped* by Wendelin Van Draanen. Other novels portray physical attraction as in Iain Lawrence's *Ghost Boy.* Since the 1990s more stories of characters dealing with pregnancy and teenage parenting have appeared; some realistic examples are Virginia Euwer Wolff's *Make Lemonade* and *True Believer.*

Children become aware of their *growing sexuality* during preteen and teen years as they begin to mature. Some stories for older teens show attraction between members of the opposite sex as well as members of the same sex, with the beginning of sexual activity sometimes depicted in relationships. Stories that portray the struggle of young people coming to terms with a homosexual or lesbian sexual orientation are seen more frequently than they were in the past; other stories show the cruelty of society toward young homosexuals or lesbians. See *Deliver Us from Evie* by M. E. Kerr and *Geography Club* by Brent Hartinger.

Rites of Passage

From birth to age 10, most children's lives revolve around family, friends, and classmates, but during the preteen and teen years a shift toward self-discovery and independence occurs. Sometimes books that deal with the trials and tribulations encountered during growth from childhood to adulthood are called *rite of passage* books. A *rite of passage* refers to an event in one's life that marks a change in one's status. Examples of rite of passage books are *A Fine White Dust* by Cynthia Rylant and *Olive's Ocean* by Kevin Henkes.

Adventure and Survival

Facing physical danger, an external force, also contributes to the maturing process. Stories of *survival and adventure* are ones in which the young protagonist must rely on will and ingenuity to survive a life-threatening situation. Although most survival stories are set in isolated places, a growing number are being set in cities where gangs, drug wars, and abandonment are life threatening. Adventure stories may be set in any environment where the protagonist has freedom of action. *Hatchet* by Gary Paulsen and *The Several Lives of Orphan Jack* by Sarah Ellis are examples of this type of book.

Stories in the realistic fiction genre present familiar situations with which children can readily identify, often reflect contemporary life, and portray settings not so different from the homes, schools, towns, and cities known to today's children. The protagonists of these stories are frequently testing themselves as they grow toward adulthood; young readers can therefore empathize and gain insight into their own predicaments. Your challenge will be to stay abreast of good realistic stories in order to provide a wide range of books that will entertain, encourage, and inspire your students.

REFERENCES

Marshall, M. R. (1988). *An introduction to the world of children's books* (2nd ed.). Brookfield, VT: Gower.

Whitman, R. (1968). Listening to grownups quarreling. In R. Whitman (Ed.), *The marriage wig and other stories.* Orlando, FL: Harcourt.

RECOMMENDED REALISTIC FICTION BOOKS

Ages refer to approximate interest levels.
YA = young adult readers.

Families

Banks, Kate. *Dillon Dillon.* Farrar, 2002. Ages 10–13.

———. *Walk Softly, Rachel.* Farrar, 2003. Ages 12–YA.

Baskin, Nora Raleigh. *What Every Girl (Except Me) Knows.* Little, Brown, 2001. Ages 10–13.

Bauer, Marion Dane. *A Question of Trust.* Scholastic, 1994. Ages 10–13.

Byars, Betsy C. *After the Goat Man.* Illustrated by Ronald Himler. Viking, 1974. Ages 9–12.

———. *The Pinballs.* Harper, 1977. Ages 10–13.

Cameron. Ann. *The Stories Julian Tells.* Illustrated by Ann Strugnell. Random, 1989 (1981). Ages 8–11.

Choldenko, Gennifer. *Notes from a Liar and Her Dog.* Putnam, 2001. Ages 10–13.

Cleary, Beverly. *Dear Mr. Henshaw.* Illustrated by Paul Zelinsky. Morrow, 1983. Ages 9–12.

———. *Ramona and Her Father.* Illustrated by Alan Tiegreen. Morrow, 1977. Ages 7–10. Humorous.

———. *Ramona Quimby, Age 8.* Illustrated by Alan Tiegreen. Morrow, 1981. Ages 7–10. Humorous.

———. *Ramona the Pest.* Illustrated by Louis Darling. Morrow, 1968. Ages 5–8. Humorous.

Cleaver, Vera and Bill Cleaver. *Where the Lilies Bloom.* Illustrated by Jim Spanfeller. Lippincott, 1969. Ages 11–YA.

Cohn, Rachel. *The Steps.* Simon & Schuster, 2003. Ages 10–YA.

Coman, Carolyn. *Many Stones.* Front Street, 2000. Ages 11–YA.

Conly, Jane Leslie. *While No One Was Watching.* Holt, 1998. Ages 11–YA.

Creech, Sharon. *Chasing Redbird.* HarperCollins, 1997. Ages 10–13.

———. *Ruby Holler.* HarperCollins, 2002. Ages 8–11.

———. *Walk Two Moons.* HarperCollins, 1994. Ages 10–13.

Danziger, Paula. *Amber Brown Goes Fourth.* HarperCollins, 1995. Ages 7–10.

———. *Forever Amber Brown.* Illustrated by Tony Ross. Putnam, 1996. Ages 7–10.

Doherty, Berlie. *The Snake-Stone.* Orchard, 1996. Ages 12–YA.

Doyle, Eugene. *Stray Voltage.* Front Street, 2002. Ages 9–12.

Fine, Anne. *Step by Wicked Step.* Little, Brown, 1996. Ages 9–12.

Fogelin, Adrian. *Anna Casey's Place in the World.* Peachtree, 2001. Ages 10–13.

———. *Sister Spider Knows All.* Peachtree, 2003. Ages 11–YA.

Fox, Paula. *One-Eyed Cat.* Bradbury, 1984. Ages 9–12.

———. *The Village by the Sea.* Watts, 1988. Ages 10–13.

Gantos, Jack. *What Would Joey Do?* Farrar, 2002. Ages 9–12.

Giff, Patricia Reilly. *Pictures of Hollis Woods.* Wendy Lamb, 2002. Ages 10–12.

Griffin, Adele. *The Other Shepards.* Hyperion, 1998. Ages 11–YA.

Henkes, Kevin. *Sun and Spoon.* Greenwillow, 1997. Ages 8–11.

Holt, Kimberly Willis. *Keeper of the Night.* Holt, 2003. Ages 10–YA.

Horvath, Polly. *The Canning Season.* Farrar, 2003. Ages 12–YA.

———. *Everything on a Waffle.* Farrar, 2001. Ages 9–12.

———. *Trolls.* Farrar, 1999. Ages 8–12. Humorous.

Johnson, Angela. *Toning the Sweep.* Orchard, 1993. Ages 11–YA.

Konigsburg, E. L. *From the Mixed-Up Files of Mrs. Basil E. Frankweiler.* Atheneum, 1967. Ages 9–12.

Koss, Amy Goldman. *The Ashwater Experiment.* Dial, 1999. Ages 9–13.

Little, Jean. *Mama's Going to Buy You a Mockingbird.* Viking, 1985. Ages 10–13.

Lowry, Lois. *Anastasia Krupnik.* Houghton, 1985. Ages 8–11. Humorous.

McKay, Hilary. *The Exiles in Love.* Simon & Schuster, 1998. Ages 9–12.

———. *Saffy's Angel.* Simon & Schuster, 2002. Ages 9–12.

Morgenstern, Susie. *Secret Letters from 0–10.* Translated from French by Gill Rosner. Viking, 1998. Ages 10–13.

Naylor, Phyllis Reynolds. *Alice in April.* Atheneum, 1993. Ages 9–13. Humorous.

Nelson, Theresa. *Ruby Electric.* Simon & Schuster, 2003. Ages 10–13.

Nolan, Han. *Dancing on the Edge.* Harcourt, 1997. Ages 12–YA.

O'Connor, Barbara. *Moonpie and Ivy.* Farrar, 2001. Ages 10–13.

Park, Barbara. *Mick Harte Was Here.* Knopf, 1995. Ages 9–12.

Paterson, Katherine. *The Great Gilly Hopkins.* Crowell, 1978. Ages 9–12.

———. *The Same Stuff as Stars.* Clarion, 2002. Ages 10–13.

Powell, Randy. *Run If You Dare.* Farrar, 2001. Ages 10–YA.

Rylant, Cynthia. *Missing May.* Orchard, 1992. Ages 10–YA.

Stolz, Mary. *The Bully of Barkham Street.* Illustrated by Leonard Shortall. Harper, 1963. Ages 8–11.

———. *A Dog on Barkham Street.* Harper, 1960. Ages 8–11.

Testa, Maria. *Becoming Joe DiMaggio.* Illustrated by Scott Hunt. Candlewick, 2002. Ages 10–13. Story told in 24 poems.

Tolan, Stephanie S. *Surviving the Applewhites.* HarperCollins, 2002. Ages 10–14.

Voigt, Cynthia. *Homecoming.* Atheneum, 1981. Ages 9–12.

White, Ruth. *Belle Prater's Boy.* Farrar, 1996. Ages 10–13.

Williams, Vera B. *Amber Was Brave, Essie Was Smart: The Story of Amber and Essie Told Here in Poems and Pictures.* Greenwillow, 2001. Ages 6–10.

Peers

Blume, Judy. *Blubber.* Bradbury, 1974. Ages 9–12.

———. *Tales of a Fourth Grade Nothing.* Illustrated by Roy Doty. Dutton, 1972. Ages 8–12. Humorous.

Clements, Andrew. *Frindle.* Illustrated by Brian Selznick. Simon & Schuster, 1996. Ages 8–12. Humorous.

Cole, Brock. *The Goats.* Farrar, 1987. Ages 11–YA.

Creech, Sharon. *Granny Torrelli Makes Soup.* Illustrated by Chris Raschka. HarperCollins, 2003. Ages 9–13.

———. *Love That Dog.* HarperCollins, 2001. Ages 9–14.

Estes, Eleanor. *The Hundred Dresses.* Illustrated by Louis Slobodkin. Harcourt, 1944. Ages 8–11.

Fine, Anne. *The Tulip Touch.* Little, Brown, 1997. Ages 10–YA.

———. *Up on Cloud Nine.* Delacorte, 2002. Ages 10–13.

Fitzhugh, Louise. *Harriet the Spy.* Harper, 1964. Ages 9–12.

Gantos, Jack. *Heads or Tails: Stories from the Sixth Grade.* Farrar, 1994. Ages 10–14.

Grove, Vicki. *Reaching Dustin.* Putnam, 1998. Ages 10–13.

Hesse, Karen. *Phoenix Rising.* Holt, 1994. Ages 12–YA.

Howe, James. *The Misfits.* Simon & Schuster, 2001. Ages 10–13.

Lisle, Janet Taylor. *Afternoon of the Elves.* Watts, 1989. Ages 9–12.

Marsden, John. *Letters from the Inside.* Houghton, 1994. Ages 12–YA.

———. *So Much to Tell You.* Joy Street, 1989. Ages 12–YA.

O'Connor, Barbara. *Fame and Glory in Freedom, Georgia.* Farrar, 2003. Ages 11–14.

Park, Barbara. *Skinnybones.* Knopf, 1982. Ages 9–12. Humorous.

Paterson, Katherine. *Bridge to Terabithia.* Illustrated by Donna Diamond. Crowell, 1977. Ages 9–13.

Perkins, Lynne Rae. *All Alone in the Universe.* Greenwillow, 1999. Ages 10–14.

Rapp, Adam. *The Buffalo Tree.* Front Street, 1997. Ages 12–YA.

Smith, Doris Buchanan. *A Taste of Blackberries.* Illustrated by Charles Robinson. Crowell, 1973. Ages 9–12.

Spinelli, Jerry. *Wringer.* HarperCollins, 1997. Ages 9–12.

Stauffacher, Sue. *Donuthead.* Knopf, 2003. Ages 9–12.

Voigt, Cynthia. *Bad Girls.* Scholastic, 1996. Ages 8–12. See also sequel: *Bad, Badder, Baddest.* 1997.

Special Challenges

Anderson, Rachel. *The Bus People.* Holt, 1992. Ages 10–14. Character portrayals, different disabilities.

Byars, Betsy. *The Summer of the Swans.* Illustrated by Ted CoConis. Viking, 1970. Ages 10–14. Mental retardation.

Conly, Jane Leslie. *Crazy Lady!* HarperCollins, 1993. Ages 10–YA. Mental retardation.

Cowen-Fletcher, Jane. *Mama Zooms.* Scholastic, 1993. Ages 5–8. Physical disability. Picture book.

Fleming, Virginia. *Be Good to Eddie Lee.* Illustrated by Floyd Cooper. Philomel, 1993. Ages 6–8. Down syndrome. Picture book.

Gantos, Jack. *Joey Pigza Loses Control.* Farrar, 2000. Ages 9–12. Attention deficit/hyperactivity.

———. *Joey Pigza Swallowed the Key.* Farrar, 1998. Ages 9–13. AD/HD.

Hines, Anna Grossnickle. *Gramma's Walk.* Greenwillow, 1993. Ages 5–8. Physical disability. Picture book.

Konigsburg, E. L. *Silent to the Bone.* Simon & Schuster, 2000. Ages 11–YA. Mutism.

Levin, Betty. *Fire in the Wind.* Greenwillow, 1995. Ages 11–YA. Mental disability.

Little, Jean. *Take Wing.* Little, Brown, 1968. Ages 9–12. Mental retardation.

Madsen, Jane M., and Bockoras, Diane. *Please Don't Tease Me. . . .* Illustrated by Kathleen T. Brinko. Judson, 1983. Ages 11–14. Physical disability.

Mazer, Harry. *The Wild Kid.* Simon & Schuster, 1998. Ages 9–13. Down syndrome.

McCormick, Patricia. *Cut.* Front Street, 2000. Ages 13–YA. Mental health.

Mikaelsen, Ben. *Petey.* Hyperion, 1998. Ages 12–YA. Cerebral palsy.

Oneal, Zibby. *The Language of Goldfish.* Viking, 1980. Ages 12–YA. Emotional disability.

Philbrick, Rodman. *Freak the Mighty.* Blue Sky, 1993. Ages 12–YA. Learning disability.

Slepian, Jan. *Risk n' Roses.* Putnam, 1990. Ages 11–YA. Mental retardation.

Trueman, Terry. *Stuck in Neutral.* HarperCollins, 2000. Ages 11–YA. Cerebral palsy.

Voigt, Cynthia. *Dicey's Song.* Atheneum, 1983. Ages 10–YA. Mental illness.

Wilson, Nancy Hope. *The Reason for Janey.* Macmillan, 1994. Ages 10–13. Mental retardation.

Wolff, Virginia Euwer. *Probably Still Nick Swansen.* Holt, 1988. Ages 12–YA. Learning disability.

Wood, June Rae. *About Face.* Putnam, 1999. Ages 9–12. Birthmark.

———. *The Man Who Loved Clowns.* Putnam, 1992. Ages 9–12. Down syndrome.

Cultural Diversity

See also Chapter 10, "Multicultural and International Literature."

Abelove, Joan. *Go and Come Back.* DK Ink, 1998. Ages 12–YA.

Berry, James. *The Future-Telling Lady and Other Stories.* HarperCollins, 1993. Ages 10–YA.

Cameron, Ann. *Colibrí.* Farrar, 2003. Ages 10–YA. Set in Guatemala.

Casey, Maude. *Over the Water.* Holt, 1994. Ages 12–YA.

Creech, Sharon. *Bloomability.* HarperCollins, 1998. Ages 10–13.

Danticat, Edwidge. *Behind the Mountains.* Orchard, 2002. Ages 11–14. Set in Haiti and Brooklyn, NY.

Dorris, Michael. *The Window.* Hyperion, 1997. Ages 11–14.

Fogelin, Adrian. *Crossing Jordan.* Peachtree, 2000. Ages 11–14.

Johnston, Tony. *Any Small Goodness: A Novel of the Barrio.* Illustrated by Raoúl Colón. Scholastic, 2001. Ages 9–12. A Mexican family in Los Angeles.

Kurtz, Jane. *The Storyteller's Beads.* Harcourt, 1998. Ages 10–13.

Mah, Adeline Yen. *Chinese Cinderella: The True Story of an Unwanted Daughter.* Delacorte, 1999. Ages 12–YA. Set in China in latter part of twentieth century.

Martinez, Victor. *Parrot in the Oven: Mi Vida.* HarperCollins, 1996. Ages 12–YA.

McDonald, Janet. *Spellbound.* Farrar, 2001. Ages 12–YA. Set in New York City housing projects.

Naidoo, Beverley. *Journey to Jo'burg: A South African Story.* Illustrated by Eric Velasquez. Lippincott, 1986. Ages 8–12.

———. *No Turning Back: A Novel of South Africa.* HarperCollins, 1997. Ages 10–13.

———. *The Other Side of Truth.* HarperCollins, 2001. Ages 11–YA. Set in Nigeria, then in London.

———. *Out of Bounds: Seven Stories of Conflict and Hope.* HarperCollins, 2003. Ages 10–YA. Set in South Africa in the period 1940–2000.

Nye, Naomi Shihab. *Habibi.* Simon & Schuster, 1997. Ages 12–YA.

Saldaña, René. *The Jumping Tree: A Novel.* Delacorte, 2001. Ages 11–14. Set in a Texas town near the Mexican border.

Smith, Hope Anita. *The Way a Door Closes.* Illustrated by Shane W. Evans. Holt, 2003. Ages 10–13. Narrative about an African-American family in poetic verse.

Staples, Suzanne Fisher. *Haveli: A Young Woman's Courageous Struggle for Freedom in Present-day Pakistan.* Knopf, 1993. Ages 12–YA.

———. *Shabanu: Daughter of the Wind.* Knopf, 1989. Ages 12–YA.

———. *Shiva's Fire.* Farrar, 2000. Ages 12–YA.

Temple, Frances. *Grab Hands and Run.* Orchard, 1993. Ages 12–YA.

———. *Taste of Salt: A Story of Modern Haiti.* Watts, 1992. Ages 12–YA.

———. *Tonight, by Sea.* Orchard, 1995. Ages 12–YA.

Whelan, Gloria. *Homeless Bird.* HarperCollins, 2000. Ages 10–13.

Williams-Garcia, Rita. *No Laughter Here.* Harper-Collins, 2004. Ages 10–YA. Female circumcision.

Woodson, Jacqueline. *I Hadn't Meant to Tell You This.* Delacorte, 1994. Ages 12–YA.

————. *Locomotion.* Putnam, 2003. Ages 9–12. Free verse. Emotional survival, African-American family.

Yep, Laurence. *Thief of Hearts.* HarperCollins, 1995. Ages 10–13.

Yumoto, Kazumi. *The Friends.* Translated by Cathy Hirano. Farrar, 1996. Ages 8–12.

Animals

Burnford, Sheila. *The Incredible Journey.* Illustrated by Carl Burger. Little, 1961. Ages 8–11.

DiCamillo, Kate. *Because of Winn-Dixie.* Candlewick, 2000. Ages 8–11.

————. *The Tiger Rising.* Candlewick, 2001. Ages 8–11.

Eckert, Allan W. *Incident at Hawk's Hill.* Illustrated by John Schoenherr. Little, Brown, 1971. Ages 10–YA.

Farley, Steven. *The Black Stallion's Shadow.* Random, 1996. Ages 9–12.

Gardiner, John Reynolds. *Stone Fox.* Illustrated by Marcia Sewall. Crowell, 1980. Ages 7–11.

Gipson, Fred. *Old Yeller.* Illustrated by Carl Burger. Harper, 1956. Ages 10–YA.

Haas, Jessie. *A Blue for Beware.* Illustrated by Joseph A. Smith. Greenwillow, 1995. Ages 8–11.

Henry, Marguerite. *King of the Wind.* Illustrated by Wesley Dennis. Rand, 1948. Ages 7–11.

————. *Misty of Chincoteague.* Illustrated by Wesley Dennis. Rand, 1947. Ages 7–11.

Hiaasen, Carl. *Hoot!* Knopf, 2003. Ages 10–14. Environment, humorous.

McKay, Hilary. *Dog Friday.* Simon & Schuster, 1995. Ages 9–11.

Mowat, Farley. *Owls in the Family.* Illustrated by Robert Frankenberg. Little, 1962. Ages 9–12.

Naylor, Phyllis Reynolds. *Shiloh.* Atheneum, 1991. Ages 8–11. A dog story with sequels.

Rawls, Wilson. *Summer of the Monkeys.* Doubleday, 1976. Ages 9–11. Humorous.

————. *Where the Red Fern Grows.* Doubleday, 1961. Ages 9–11.

Rylant, Cynthia. *Every Living Thing.* Illustrated by S. D. Schindler. Bradbury, 1985. Ages 11–YA.

Savage, Deborah. *Under a Different Sky.* Houghton, 1997. Ages 12–YA.

Sewell, Anna. *Black Beauty.* Illustrated by John Speirs. Simon & Schuster, 1982 (1877). Ages 9–11.

Sports

Christopher, Matt. *Undercover Tailback.* Illustrated by Paul Casale. Little, 1992. Ages 8–11.

Crutcher, Chris. *Athletic Shorts: Six Short Stories.* Greenwillow, 1991. Ages 13–YA.

————. *Ironman.* Greenwillow, 1995. Ages 12–YA.

Deans, Sis. *Racing the Past.* Holt, 2001. Ages 10–13.

Hughes, Dean. *Team Picture.* Simon & Schuster, 1996. Ages 11–14.

Koertge, Ron. *Shakespeare Bats Cleanup.* Candlewick, 2003. Ages 11–14.

Myers, Walter Dean. *Slam!* Scholastic, 1996. Ages 12–YA.

Ritter, John H. *The Boy Who Saved Baseball.* Philomel, 2003. Ages 10–13.

————. *Choosing Up Sides.* Philomel, 1998. Ages 10–14.

Slote, Alfred. *Hang Tough, Paul Mather.* Lippincott, 1973. Ages 9–12.

Mysteries

Crew, Gary. *Angel's Gate.* Simon & Schuster, 1995. Ages 11–YA.

DeFelice, Cynthia. *Death at Devil's Track.* Farrar, 2000. Ages 10–13. Also, moral issue and adventure.

Fitzgerald, John D. *The Great Brain Is Back.* Dial, 1995. Ages 8–11.

Jennings, Richard W. *Mystery in Mt. Mole.* Houghton, 2003. Ages 9–12.

Nixon, Joan Lowery. *The Name of the Game Was Murder.* Delacorte, 1993. Ages 11–14.

Raskin, Ellen. *The Westing Game.* Dutton, 1978. Ages 9–12.

Sachar, Louis. *Holes.* Farrar, 1998. Ages 10–14.

Sobol, Donald J. *Encyclopedia Brown.* Lodestar/Dutton, 1963. Ages 8–10.

————. *Encyclopedia Brown and the Case of Pablo's Nose.* Illustrated by Eric Velasquez. Delacorte, 1996. Ages 8–11.

Van Draanen, Wendelin. *Sammy Keyes and the Hotel Thief.* Knopf, 1998. Another in this series with a female protagonist is *Sammy Keyes and the Sisters of Mercy.* Knopf, 1999. Ages 9–12. Also *Sammy Keyes and the Search for Snake Eyes.* Knopf, 2002. Ages 10–13.

Werlin, Nancy. *Black Mirror.* Dial, 2001. Ages 12–YA.

Moral Choices

Avi. *Nothing but the Truth.* Orchard, 1991. Ages 11–YA.

Bauer, Marion Dane. *On My Honor.* Clarion, 1986. Ages 8–12.

Cole, Brock. *The Goats.* Farrar, 1987. Ages 11–YA.

Flake, Sharon. G. *Money Hungry.* Hyperion, 2001. Ages 12–YA.

Fleischman, Paul. *Whirligig.* Holt, 1998. Ages 12–YA.

Hinton, S. E. *The Outsiders.* Viking, 1967. Ages 13–YA.

Lynch, Chris. *Slot Machine.* HarperCollins, 1995. Ages 12–YA.

Myers, Walter Dean. *Monster.* HarperCollins, 1999. Ages 13–YA.

————. *Somewhere in the Darkness.* Scholastic, 1992. Ages 12–YA.

Naylor, Phyllis Reynolds. *Shiloh.* Atheneum, 1991. Ages 8–11.

Soto, Gary. *Baseball in April and Other Stories.* Harcourt, 1991. Ages 10–YA.

Spinelli, Jerry. *Maniac Magee.* HarperCollins, 1990. Ages 9–12.

Woodson, Jacqueline. *Hush.* Putnam, 2002. Ages 11–YA.

Yolen, Jane, and Bruce Coville. *Armageddon Summer.* Harcourt, 1998. Ages 11–13. Chapters alternate between boy and girl protagonists.

Romance and Sexuality

Bauer, Marion Dane, Editor. *Am I Blue? Coming Out from the Silence.* HarperCollins, 1994. Ages 14–YA.

Blume, Judy. *Then Again, Maybe I Won't.* Bradbury, 1971. Ages 10–YA.

Doherty, Berlie. *Dear Nobody.* Orchard, 1992. Ages 12–YA.

Fox, Paula. *The Eagle Kite.* Orchard, 1995. Ages 12–YA.

Hartinger, Brent. *Geography Club.* HarperTempest, 2003. Ages 13–YA.

Kerr, M. E. *Deliver Us from Evie.* HarperCollins, 1994. Ages 13–YA.

Lawrence, Iain. *Ghost Boy.* Delacorte, 2000. Ages 12–YA.

Naylor, Phyllis Reynolds. *The Grooming of Alice.* Simon & Schuster, 2000. Ages 11–13.

Nelson, Theresa. *Earthshine.* Watts, 1994. Ages 11–YA.

Van Draanen, Wendelin. *Flipped.* Knopf, 2001. Ages 11–YA.

Williams-Garcia, Rita. *Like Sisters on the Homefront.* Lodestar, 1995. Ages 12–YA.

Winick, Judd. *Pedro and Me: Friendship, Loss, and What I Learned.* Holt, 2000. Ages YA. (Graphic novel)

Wolff, Virginia Euwer. *Make Lemonade.* Holt, 1993. Ages 12–YA.

————. *True Believer.* Atheneum, 2001. Ages 11–YA. Free verse.

Woodson, Jacqueline. *From the Notebooks of Melanin Sun.* Scholastic, 1995. Ages 12–YA.

————. *The House You Pass on the Way.* Delacorte, 1997. Ages 12–YA.

Rites of Passage

Bedard, Michael. *Stained Glass.* Tundra, 2001. Ages 12–YA.

Blume, Judy. *Are You There, God? It's Me, Margaret.* Bradbury, 1970. Ages 10–YA.

Fine, Anne. *Flour Babies.* Little, Brown, 1994. Ages 10–14.

French, Simon. *Where in the World.* Peachtree, 2003. Ages 10–13.

Henkes, Kevin. *Olive's Ocean.* Greenwillow, 2003. Ages 10–YA.

Lawrence, Iain. *Ghost Boy.* Delacorte, 2000. Ages 12–YA.

Rylant, Cynthia. *A Fine White Dust.* Bradbury, 1986. Ages 9–12.

Saldaña, René. *Finding Our Way.* Wendy Lamb, 2003. Ages 13–YA. Collection of 12 short stories about Latino experiences.

Adventure and Survival

Carter, Alden R. *Between a Rock and a Hard Place.* Scholastic, 1995. Ages 11–YA.

Coleman, Michael. *Weirdo's War.* Orchard, 1998. Ages 9–13.

Creech, Sharon. *The Wanderer.* HarperCollins, 2000. Ages 11–YA.

Ellis, Sarah. *The Several Lives of Orphan Jack.* Illustrated by Bruno St.-Aubin. Groundwood, 2003. Ages 7–11.

Farmer, Nancy. *A Girl Named Disaster.* Orchard, 1996. Ages 11–YA.

Fleischman, Sid. *Bo and Mzzz Mad.* Greenwillow, 2001. Ages 10–13.

George, Jean Craighead. *Julie.* HarperCollins, 1994. Ages 11–YA.

———. *Julie of the Wolves.* Illustrated by John Schoenherr. Harper, 1972. Ages 11–YA.

———. *My Side of the Mountain.* Dutton, 1959. Ages 9–12.

Jennings, Richard W. *The Great Whale of Kansas.* Houghton, 2001. Ages 10–13.

Mikaelson, Ben. *Stranded.* Hyperion, 1995. Ages 11–YA.

Myers, Walter Dean. *Scorpions.* Harper, 1988. Ages 10–YA.

Paulsen, Gary. *Hatchet.* Bradbury, 1987. Ages 9–12.

———. *The River.* Delacorte, 1991. Ages 11–YA.

NOTABLE *AUTHORS OF REALISTIC FICTION*

Betsy Byars, author of stories about children who face and overcome family and personal problems. *The Pinballs; The Summer of the Swans.*

Ann Cameron, U.S. author who lives in Guatemala and is known for *The Stories Julian Tells* and its sequels. Also has written the novel *Colibrí*, set in Guatemala.

Beverly Cleary, author of humorous family stories about everyday happenings. *Ramona Quimby, Age 8; Dear Mr. Henshaw.*

Sharon Creech, author of novels about girls seeking their families to find themselves. *Walk Two Moons; Ruby Holler.*

Anne Fine, British author of realistic peer stories and Carnegie Medal–winning author. *Flour Babies; The Tulip Touch.*

Jack Gantos, author of Joey Pigza novels about a boy with attention deficit disorder and autobiographical books. *Heads or Tails: Stories from the Sixth Grade; Joey Pigza Swallowed the Key.*

Jean Craighead George, author of ecological fiction and survival in nature stories. *Julie of the Wolves; My Side of the Mountain.*

Walter Dean Myers, author of novels about African-American adolescents in city settings. *Scorpions; Monster.*

Phyllis Reynolds Naylor, author of eight books about Alice and her family, including *Alice in April*. Also noted for Newbery Medal winner *Shiloh* and its sequels.

Katherine Paterson, author of stories featuring relationships with peers and family. *The Great Gilly Hopkins; Bridge to Terabithia.*

Gary Paulsen, author of nature survival adventures often set in northern United States or Canada. *Hatchet; The River.*

Cynthia Rylant, author of introspective realistic stories often set in Appalachia. *Every Living Thing; Missing May.*

Louis Sachar, author of *Holes*, a warm and humorous novel that intertwines past and present events to solve a mystery. (Also, *Wayside School Is Falling Down*, a light, humorous modern fantasy series.)

Jerry Spinelli, author of realistic novels of peers and their escapades, including Newbery Medal winner *Maniac Magee* and Newbery Honor book *Wringer.*

Suzanne Fisher Staples, author of the Newbery Honor books *Shabanu* and its sequel *Haveli*, set in the Cholistan Desert of Pakistan. Her stories present conflicts within and between diverse cultures.

Virginia Euwer Wolff, author of novels about unique teen characters, including *True Believer*, winner of the National Book Award for Young People. *Make Lemonade; Bat 6.*

Jacqueline Woodson, African-American author whose novels often treat sensitive issues of sexuality, abuse, and race. *Locomotion; From the Notebooks of Melanin Sun.*

8

HISTORICAL FICTION

ANCESTORS

On the wind-beaten plains
once lived my ancestors.
In the days of peaceful moods,
they wandered and hunted.
In days of need or greed,
they warred and loafed.
Beneath the lazy sun, kind winds above,
they laughed and feasted.
Through the starlit night, under the moon,
they dreamed and loved.
Now, from the wind-beaten plains,
only their dust rises.

— GREY COHOE

Historical fiction brings history to life by placing appealing child characters in accurately described historical settings. By telling the stories of these characters' everyday lives as well as presenting their triumphs and failures, authors of historical fiction provide young readers with the human side of history, making it more real and more memorable.

DEFINITION AND DESCRIPTION

Historical fiction is realistic fiction set in a time remote enough from the present to be considered history. Stories about events that occurred at least one generation (defined as 20 years or more) prior to the date of the original publication have been included in this chapter and categorized as historical fiction.

Although historical fiction stories are imaginary, it is within the realm of possibility that such events could have occurred. In these stories, historical facts blend with imaginary characters and plot. The facts are actual historical events, authentic period settings, and real historical figures. An imaginary story is constructed around these facts. In the *Reference Guide to Historical Fiction for Children and Young Adults,* Adamson (1987) states:

> Historical fiction recreates a particular historical period with or without historical figures as incidental characters. It is generally written about a time period in which the author has not lived or no more recently than one generation before its composition. For example, fiction written in 1987 must be set, at the latest, in 1967, to be considered historical. Fiction written in 1930 but set in 1925 does not fulfill this criterion for legitimate historical fiction. (p. ix)

In the most common form of historical fiction, the main characters of the story are imaginary, but some secondary characters may be actual historical figures. An example of this type of historical fiction is the 1944 Newbery Medal winner, *Johnny Tremain* by Esther Forbes. Set in the U.S. Revolutionary War period, this story tells of Johnny, a fictitious character, who is apprenticed to a silversmith. In the course of the story, Samuel Adams, John Hancock, and Paul Revere are introduced as minor characters.

In another form of historical fiction, the past is described complete with the social traditions, customs, morals, and values of the period but with no mention of an actual historical event nor actual historical figures as characters. The physical location is also accurately reconstructed for the readers. An example of this story type is *The Witch of Blackbird Pond* by Elizabeth George Speare. The Puritan way of life in Connecticut in the 1600s is depicted in this story about young Kit from Barbados who becomes involved in a witchcraft trial.

A third type of historical story is one in which elements of fantasy are found, and therefore the story does *not* qualify as historical fiction. For example, time warps and other supernatural features may be found in Thea Beckman's *Crusade in Jeans* and in Jane Yolen's *The Devil's Arithmetic.* These stories are *historical fantasy* and are included in Chapter 6, "Modern Fantasy."

EVALUATION AND SELECTION OF HISTORICAL FICTION

Historical fiction must first tell an engaging story, have rounded, complex characters with whom children can identify, and impart a universal theme that is worthy and thought provoking without being didactic. In addition, historical fiction must present historical facts with as much accuracy and objectivity as books of history. This means that a setting must be described in sufficient detail as to provide an authentic sense of that time and that place without overwhelming the story. Details such as hair and clothing styles, home architecture and furnishings, foods and food preparation, and modes of transportation must

---

Excellent *HISTORICAL FICTION* to Read Aloud

Bunting, Eve. *Train to Somewhere.* Illustrated by Ronald Himler. Ages 5–8.
Curtis, Christopher Paul. *Bud, Not Buddy.* Ages 9–13.
Lowry, Lois. *Number the Stars.* Ages 8–12.
Park, Linda Sue. *A Single Shard.* Ages 9–13.
Peck, Richard. *The River Between Us.* Ages 12–YA.
Polacco, Patricia. *Pink and Say.* Ages 8–11.
Ray, Delia. *Ghost Girl: A Blue Ridge Mountain Story.* Ages 10–13.
Reeder, Carolyn. *Shades of Gray.* Ages 8–11.
Speare, Elizabeth George. *The Sign of the Beaver.* Ages 8–12.
Turner, Ann. *Mississippi Mud: Three Prairie Journals.* Illustrated by Robert J. Clark. Ages 5–8.
White, Ruth. *Tadpole.* Ages 9–YA.
Wolff, Virginia Euwer. *Bat 6.* Ages 10–YA.

---

be subtly woven into the story to provide a convincing, authentic period setting. The characters must act within the traditions and norms of their times.

Expressing the language or dialect of the period presents a particular challenge to the author of historical stories. Dialogue that occurs within the text often becomes problematic for the writer. If the speech of the period is greatly different from that of today, then the author faces a decision: Remain true to the language of the time but cause readers difficulties in comprehending, or present the language in today's dialect but lose the flavor and authenticity of the language of the period. In any case, it seems important that the language not jar the reader by its obvious inappropriateness or lose the reader by its extreme difficulty. Most children's authors strive to attain the middle ground—some flavor of a language difference but modified to be understandable to the child reader.

Many educators are convinced of the benefits students gain through integrating history and literature as part of the social studies curriculum. Smith, Monson, and Dobson (1992) found that the students in fifth-grade classrooms in which historical novels were used along with standard instructional materials recalled more historical facts and indicated greater enjoyment in their social studies classes than the students in classrooms that had a similar curriculum without the addition of historical novels.

Many adults today are unaware that the history they learned as children may have been biased or one-sided. Some authors attempt to include more modern interpretations of historical events in historical fiction by setting the record straight or adding a minority presence to the story. However, as was previously mentioned, care must be taken that the characters behave in a historically accurate fashion.

The Scott O'Dell Award, established in 1982 by the author Scott O'Dell, honors what is judged to be the most outstanding work of children's historical fiction published in the previous year. The work must be written by a U.S. citizen and be set in the New World. The Scott O'Dell Award winners found in Appendix A can be a source of outstanding historical fiction for use with students. The National Council of Social Studies publishes a list of the most notable trade books in the field of social studies from the preceding year in the April/May issue of its journal, *Social Education.* This list includes many works of historical fiction, as well as nonfiction works, and is a useful source to locate recent books of this genre.

EARLY BOOKS AND TRENDS
IN HISTORICAL FICTION

Although historical stories were written for children as early as the 1800s, few titles remain of interest from those early years. The early books placed an emphasis on exciting events and idealized real-life characters—much in the style of heroic legends.

Between World War I and World War II, a few historical stories appeared in which well-developed characters involved in realistic events were portrayed in authentic period settings. Between 1932 and 1943, the first eight books of the Little House series by Laura Ingalls Wilder were published. These stories have continued to grow in popularity, partially as a result of the long-lasting television series based

MILESTONES

in the Development of HISTORICAL FICTION

DATE	EVENT	SIGNIFICANCE
1888	*Otto of the Silver Hand* by Howard Pyle	Early recognized work of historical fiction
1929	The Newbery Medal given to *The Trumpeter of Krakow* by Eric Kelly	National recognition for an early work of historical fiction
1932–1943	Publication of the first eight books of *Little House* series by Laura Ingalls Wilder	Classic historical fiction
1944	*Johnny Tremain* by Esther Forbes given the Newbery Medal	Classic historical adventure set during the American Revolution era
1949–1960	Many historical novels published, including *The Witch of Blackbird Pond* by Elizabeth George Speare and *The Lantern Bearers* by Rosemary Sutcliff	Dramatic increase in the quality and quantity of historical novels for children
1954	Establishment of the Laura Ingalls Wilder Award, first awarded to Wilder	Recognition of an historical fiction author for the entire body of her work
1961	Scott O'Dell's *Island of the Blue Dolphins* awarded the Newbery Medal	Landmark book of historical fiction with a strong female protagonist from a minority culture
1971	*Journey to Topaz* by Yoshiko Uchida	Early historical work about and by a minority (Japanese American)
1972	Scott O'Dell awarded the Hans Christian Andersen Award	International recognition of a U.S. author of historical novels
1975	*The Song of the Trees* by Mildred Taylor	First in a series of books about an African-American family's struggle starting in the Depression era
1982	Establishment of the Scott O'Dell Award	Award given for outstanding historical novel set in North America brings recognition to the genre
1989	Elizabeth George Speare awarded the Laura Ingalls Wilder Award	Recognition of an author of historical fiction for her substantial contribution to children's literature

on the books. *Johnny Tremain* by Esther Forbes was awarded the Newbery Medal in 1944 and is considered a children's classic.

The period after World War II saw a flowering of historical fiction for children in both English and American literature. Many outstanding books were published in the fifteen years following the war. Examples are *The Door in the Wall* by Marguerite de Angeli, published in 1949; *Calico Captive,* by Elizabeth George Speare, published in 1957; the best-selling Newbery Medal–winning book *The Witch of Blackbird Pond* by Elizabeth George Speare, published in 1958; and *The Cabin Faced West* by Jean Fritz, published in 1958. In 1954, the Laura Ingalls Wilder Award was awarded to (and named for) Laura Ingalls Wilder, an author of historical fiction. This award, the "Hall of Fame" of children's authors and illustrators, honors an author or illustrator whose books, published in the United States, have made a substantial and lasting contribution to children's literature. By 1960, the genre of historical fiction was well established as a fine resource for children's enjoyment and enrichment. Milestones in the development of historical fiction are highlighted on page 149.

Historical fiction continues to flourish today. Some older historical fiction novels have been criticized for portraying some cultural groups in an extremely negative light. For example, two Newbery Medal winners, *Caddie Woodlawn* by Carol Ryrie Brink and *The Matchlock Gun* by Walter D. Edmonds, have been faulted for their negative portrayals of Native Americans. However, minority authors have written a number of excellent works based on the early experiences of their cultural groups in North America; for example, see *Song of the Trees* and its sequels by Mildred Taylor and *Journey to Topaz* and its sequel by Yoshiko Uchida. The establishment in 1982 of the Scott O'Dell Award for Historical Fiction has begun to offer additional recognition for authors of this genre.

T O P I C S   I N   H I S T O R I C A L   F I C T I O N

Two ways of considering the topics treated in historical fiction novels are by the universal themes presented in the books and by the historical periods in which the books are set.

Themes in Historical Fiction

Common themes that extend across time and place in historical stories can be an approach for presenting historical fiction to children. For example, a theme, such as seeking new frontiers, is explored through a small group of books set in different times and places. In the feature "Using Historical Fiction and Nonfiction across the Curriculum: Social Studies," two themes, technological advances and economic challenges, are presented with books that relate to each theme, but are set in different historical eras. Although a few nonfiction books are included, most of these works are historical fiction. Other themes may be discovered when you read historical fiction novels and consider the commonalities to be found among them.

Periods of History in Fiction

The natural relationship of historical fiction stories to the study of history and geography suggests building whole units of study around periods of both world and U.S. history in which good stories for children are set. The following capsule statements about seven historical periods will give you an idea of how these units might be organized. The feature "Using Historical Fiction and Biography across the

Curriculum: Social Studies" lists books about two eras, the Revolutionary War and World War II, suitable for different grade levels. A few biographies from the same era are also included. Historical fiction books for units on other eras can be selected from the lists at the end of this chapter, and biographies can be found in the lists at the end of Chapter 9, "Nonfiction," where you will find books organized by the six historical periods beginning 3000 B.C.

USING HISTORICAL FICTION AND NONFICTION ACROSS THE CURRICULUM: *Social Studies*

THEME	GRADE LEVEL	SUGGESTED BOOKS
Technological advances	6–8	*The Great Wheel* by Robert Lawson *The Clock* by James L. and Christopher Collier *Lyddie* by Katherine Paterson *Fair Weather: A Novel* by Richard Peck *Stop the Train!* by Geraldine McCaughrean *Mack Made Movies* by Don Brown *The Wright Brothers: How They Invented the Airplane* by Russell Freedman *Charles A. Lindbergh: A Human Hero* by James C. Giblin *Skyscrapers: How America Grew Up* by John B. Severance
Economic challenges	3–5	*Bud, Not Buddy* by Christopher Paul Curtis *I Have Heard of a Land* by Joyce Carol Thomas, illustrated by Floyd Cooper *Coolies* by Yin, illustrated by Chris Soentpiet *Working Cotton* by Sherley Anne Williams *How Many Days to America? A Thanksgiving Story* by Eve Bunting, illustrated by Beth Peck *Uncle Jed's Barbershop* by Margaree King Mitchell, illustrated by James Ransome *Vision of Beauty: The Story of Sarah Breedlove Walker* by Kathryn Lasky, illustrated by Nneka Bennett *Kids at Work: Lewis Hine and the Crusade Against Child Labor* by Russell Freedman
Economic challenges	6–8	*Tadpole* by Ruth White *The Traitor* by Lawrence Yep *Esperanza Rising* by Pam Muñoz Ryan *The Ballad of Lucy Whipple* by Karen Cushman *Lyddie* by Katherine Paterson *Molly Bannaky* by Alice McGill, illustrated by Chris K. Soentpiet *Buffalo Gals: Women of the Old West* by Brandon Marie Miller *Kids on Strike!* by Susan Campbell Bartoletti *Voices from the Fields: Children of Migrant Farmworkers Tell Their Stories* by Beth S. Atkin *Across America on an Emigrant Train* by Jim Murphy

BEGINNINGS OF CIVILIZATION UP TO 3000 B.C.   This period represents prehistoric cultures and civilizations. Early peoples (Java, Neanderthals, Cro-Magnons) and early civilizations in the Middle East and Asia are included. Egyptians, Syrians, and Phoenicians developed civilizations; and Hebrews produced a religious faith, Judaism, that resulted in the Old Testament. The subcontinent of India was the site of Aryan civilizations. Chinese dynasties were responsible for excellent works of art and agricultural systems of irrigation. An example of an historical novel set in this time period is A. Linevski's *An Old Tale Carved Out of Stone.*

CIVILIZATIONS OF THE ANCIENT WORLD, 3000 B.C. TO A.D. 600   The era of the Greek city-states was followed by a period of Roman rule in western Europe. Christianity was founded in Jerusalem and spread throughout Europe. Ancient Asia was the site of enduring civilizations that bred two remarkable men born about 560 B.C.: the Indian religious leader Buddha and the Chinese philosopher Confucius. Both have had a lasting influence on their civilizations. Sonia Levitin's *Escape from Egypt,* a novel set in this time period, retells the story of Moses leading his people from Egypt to the promised land.

CIVILIZATIONS OF THE MEDIEVAL WORLD, 600 TO 1500   The eastern part of the Roman Empire maintained its stability and preserved the civilization from the capital of Constantinople. This civilization, the Byzantine Empire, created a distinct culture and branch of the Christian Church— the Orthodox Church—which influenced Russia to adopt both the religion and the culture. Following the fall of the Roman Empire, western Europe dissolved into isolated separate regions without strong governments. Many of the responsibilities of government were carried out by the Christian Church. The Church dominated the economic, political, cultural, and educational life of the Middle Ages in western Europe. These feudal societies eventually gave rise to the separate nations of modern Europe. During this era, early African and American civilizations arose independently. The great civilizations of China and Japan continued to flourish throughout these centuries. As examples, Marguerite de Angeli's *The Door in the Wall* and Karen Cushman's *Catherine, Called Birdy* portray medieval life in England.

THE EMERGENCE OF MODERN NATIONS, 1500 TO 1800   The Renaissance, a literary and artistic movement, swept western Europe. Many important developments of this period included the invention of the printing press, a new emphasis on reason, a reformation of the Christian Church, and advances in science. During this same period, central governments throughout Europe increased their power. Spain, and then France, dominated Europe in the 1500s and 1600s. In the 1700s, Russia, Austria, and Prussia rose to power. This was also a time when Europeans explored and settled in Africa, India, and the Americas. The Portuguese and Spanish took the lead in explorations and acquired many foreign colonies. England, the Netherlands, France, and Russia also colonized and influenced East Asia, India, Africa, and the Americas.

Revolutions created new governments and new nations. The American Revolution (1776–1781) created a new nation; the French Revolution in 1789 affected the direction of governments toward democracy in all of Europe. Napoleon built an empire across Europe, resulting in the uniting of European nations to defeat Napoleon. The nations of Latin America also began to gain their independence. China expanded gradually under the Ming and Ch'ing dynasties. Japan prospered under the Tokugawa shogunate. The United States and Canada were the sites of rapid population increases due to immigration; the settlements in North America were predominantly along the eastern coasts. Some westward expansion was beginning in the United States and Canada. For example, a story relating the challenges of settling the Maine frontier in the 1700s is Elizabeth George Speare's *The Sign of the Beaver.*

THE DEVELOPMENT OF INDUSTRIAL SOCIETY, 1800 TO 1914   The 1800s were marked by a rapid shift from agricultural societies to industrial societies. Great Britain was an early site for this change. The factory system developed and prospered, while working and living conditions deteriorated for the worker. Two stories about life as a millworker in this period are Katherine Paterson's *Lyddie* and James Lincoln Collier and Christopher Collier's *The Clock.* New technology—railroad trains, steamboats, the telegraph and telephone—affected transportation and communications. Advances in science and medicine helped to explain the nature of life and improved the quality of life. Education developed into an important institution in western Europe and North America. Europe underwent revolutions that readjusted boundaries and eventually led to the unification of new nations.

The westward movement was fully realized as pioneers settled across the United States and Canada. The building of railroads hastened the establishment of new settlements. Native Americans struggled for survival in the face of these massive population shifts. Black slavery had existed in the American colonies from earliest days, but in the 1800s, slavery became a social and economic issue resulting in the Civil War (1861–1865). Slavery was abolished and the Union was preserved at the cost of 600,000 lives and a major rift between the North and the South. Carolyn Reeder's *Shades of Gray* portrays a family torn apart by this war.

The United States grew in economic and political strength. An age of imperialism resulted in firm control of large areas of the world by other world powers such as England, France, and Belgium. Great Britain dominated India and parts of Africa and continued its influence over Canada, Australia, and New Zealand, while Japan became a powerful force in east Asia.

WORLD WARS IN THE TWENTIETH CENTURY, 1914 TO 1945   This era includes World War I (1914–1918) in Europe, in which the United States and Canada joined and fought with the Allies (Great Britain, France, Russia, Greece, and Rumania); the between-wars period that included the Great Depression; Hitler's rise to power in 1933; and World War II (1939–1945) in Europe and Asia, in which Canada and the United States joined forces with England, France, and Russia to battle Germany, Italy, and Japan. In 1917, the Bolshevik Revolution established a Communist government in Russia. In 1931, Great Britain recognized Canada, Australia, New Zealand, and South Africa as completely independent. However, each nation declared its loyalty to the British monarch and continued its cultural ties with Great Britain. The Holocaust during World War II—the persecution and killing of Jewish and other people by the Nazi regime—stands out as one of the most atrocious periods in modern history. Hans Peter Richter's *Friedrich* tells of the horrors of the Holocaust as it affected a Jewish boy's life. World War II ended shortly after the United States dropped nuclear devices on Hiroshima and Nagasaki, Japan.

POST–WORLD WAR II ERA, 1945 TO 1980s   During this era, the United States and western European nations were involved in a struggle for world influence against the communist nations, particularly the Soviet Union and China. A massive arms buildup, including nuclear weapons, was undertaken by the major nations of both sides. The Korean War (1950–1953) and the Vietnam War (1965–1973) were major conflicts in which the United States fought to contain Communist expansion. The Korean War, combined with the postwar economic recovery of Japan, drew attention to the growing importance of East Asia in world affairs. A novel for children, *The Purple Heart* by Marc Talbert, describes the Vietnam War era. The Soviet Union launched a series of satellites beginning with Sputnik I on October 4, 1957, inaugurating the space age. An explosion of scientific knowledge occurred as a result of increased spending for weapons development and space exploration. The 1950s, 1960s, and 1970s have been described as the Cold War decades because of the increasing hostility between the Soviet Union and the United States, gradually ending with the defeat of the Soviet regime in the early 1990s. In the 1970s, public pressure mounted in the United States to reduce the nation's external military commitments following the Vietnam War.

During the 1960s a strong civil rights movement, led by Martin Luther King, Jr., and other prominent figures of the era, fought for equal treatment of African Americans. The movement led to desegregation of schools, restaurants, transportation, and housing. Another racial struggle occurred in South Africa against the policies of racial separation in the 1970s and 1980s. The end of apartheid was declared in 1990, followed by free elections in 1994. Equal rights for women were also sought during the feminist movement in the 1970s. An example of a book depicting the civil rights struggle is Christopher Paul Curtis's *The Watsons Go to Birmingham—1963*.

Many fine works of historical fiction for children can now be found. Children have an opportunity to live vicariously the lives of people from long ago—people from different cultures and from different parts of the world.

REFERENCES

Adamson, L. G. (1987). *A reference guide to historical fiction for children and young adults.* Westport, CT: Greenwood Press.

Cohoe, G. (1972). Ancestors. In T. Allen (Ed.), *The whispering wind: Poetry by young American Indians.* New York: Doubleday.

Smith, J. A., Monson, J. A., & Dobson, D. (1992). A case study on integrating history and reading instruction through literature. *Social Education, 56,* 370–375.

NOTABLE   *AUTHORS OF HISTORICAL FICTION*

Avi [Wortis], author noted for the Newbery Award–winning historical fiction novel *Crispin: The Cross of Lead* and two Newbery Honor books including *The True Confessions of Charlotte Doyle*.

Christopher Paul Curtis, African-American author of two historical novels: the Newbery Medal book, *Bud, Not Buddy*, a Depression era novel, and Newbery Honor book, *The Watsons Go to Birmingham—1963*.

Karen Cushman, author of two Newbery acclaimed historical novels set in the Middle Ages. *Catherine, Called Birdy; The Midwife's Apprentice*.

Karen Hesse, author of 1998 Newbery Medal winner, *Out of the Dust*, set in Oklahoma in the 1930s. Also noted for historical novel *Letters from Rifka*.

Kimberly Willis Holt, author of novels about characters with disabilities and set in small towns of the American South. *My Louisiana Sky; When Zachary Beaver Came to Town*.

Lois Lowry, author of the historical fiction novel *Number the Stars*, Newbery Medal winner in 1990. Also noted for realistic fiction and modern fantasy novels.

Linda Sue Park, Newbery Award–winning author whose four novels about historical eras in Korea bring understanding about another culture. *A Single Shard; When My Name Was Keoko*.

Richard Peck, Newbery Award–winning author noted for his young adult novels and his historical novels set in rural Illinois. *A Year Down Yonder; The River Between Us*.

Carolyn Reeder, author of two historical novels set in the U.S. Civil War era. *Across the Lines; Shades of Gray*.

Elizabeth George Speare, winner of Scott O'Dell, Newbery, and Laura Ingalls Wilder Awards for her works of historical fiction. *The Sign of the Beaver*.

Mildred Taylor, author of seven stories of an African-American land-owning family, beginning in the 1930s and set in rural Mississippi. *Roll of Thunder, Hear My Cry*.

Gloria Whelan, winner of the National Book Award for young people's literature for *Homeless Bird*, set in India. Also wrote *Angel on the Square*, set in Russia.

Laurence Yep, author of historical fiction about Chinese Americans and their adjustments to life in the United States. *Dragonwings*.

RECOMMENDED HISTORICAL FICTION BOOKS

Ages refer to approximate interest levels. YA = young adult readers. Locales and dates of settings are noted. Historical biographies are arranged by these same eras and placed at the end of Chapter 9.

Beginnings of Civilization up to 3000 B.C.

Dickinson, Peter. *Po's Story.* Putnam, 1998. Ages 8–12. Prehistoric clans. (Others in The Kin series include *Suth's Story,* Putnam, 1998; *Mana's Story,* Putnam, 1999; and *Noli's Story,* Putnam, 1999.)

Linevski, A. *An Old Tale Carved Out of Stone.* Translated by Maria Polushkin. Crown, 1973. Ages 10–14. Early Siberia.

Osborne, Chester. *The Memory String.* Atheneum, 1984. Ages 8–12. Siberian Peninsula, 25,000 B.C.

Steele, William O. *The Magic Amulet.* Harcourt, 1979. Ages 10–14. North America, 10,000 B.C.

Treece, Henry. *The Dream-Time.* Meredith, 1968. Ages 11–14. British Isles, 11,000 B.C.

Wibberley, Leonard. *Attar of the Ice Valley.* Farrar, 1968. Ages 11–YA. Europe, 50,000 B.C.

Civilizations of the Ancient World, 3000 B.C. to A.D. 600

Lawrence, Caroline. *The Thieves of Ostia: A Roman Mystery.* Millbrook, 2002. Ages 11–14. Roman port city Ostia, A.D. 79.

Levitin, Sonia. *Escape from Egypt.* Little, Brown, 1994. Ages 14–YA. Jews, 1200 B.C.

Speare, Elizabeth George. *The Bronze Bow.* Houghton, 1961. Ages 10–14. Jerusalem, A.D. 30.

Sutcliff, Rosemary. *Song for a Dark Queen.* Crowell, 1978. Ages 10–14. British Isles, A.D. 50.

———. *Sun Horse, Moon Horse.* Dutton, 1978. Ages 10–14. British Isles, 100 B.C.

Civilizations of the Medieval World, 600 to 1500

Alder, Elizabeth. *The King's Shadow.* Farrar, 1995. Ages 12–YA. England, end of Saxon era, pre-1066.

Avi. *Crispin: The Cross of Lead.* Hyperion, 2002. Ages 12–YA. England, fourteenth century.

Branford, Henrietta. *The Fated Sky.* Candlewick, 1999. Ages 12–YA. Norway, Iceland, Viking era.

———. *Fire, Bed, and Bone.* Candlewick, 1998. Ages 10–YA. Fourteenth-century England.

Cadnum, Michael. *Book of the Lion.* Viking, 2000. Ages 12–YA. Twelfth-century England.

———. *Raven of the Waves.* Orchard, 2001. Ages 12–YA. England, Norsemen, AD. 794.

Cushman, Karen. *Catherine, Called Birdy.* Clarion, 1994. Ages 11–YA. England, manor life, 1290s.

———. *Matilda Bone.* Clarion, 2000. Ages 11–YA. Medieval England, medical practitioner.

———. *The Midwife's Apprentice.* Clarion, 1995. Ages 12–YA. England, Middle Ages.

de Angeli, Marguerite. *The Door in the Wall.* Doubleday, 1949. Ages 9–12. England, 1300s.

Dorris, Michael. *Morning Girl.* Hyperion, 1992. Ages 9–12. Taino Indians, 1490s.

Fleischman, Sid. *The Whipping Boy.* Greenwillow, 1986. Ages 9–11. England, Middle Ages.

Love, D. Anne. *The Puppeteer's Apprentice.* Simon & Schuster, 2003. Ages 9–12. England in the Middle Ages.

McCaughrean, Geraldine. *The Kite Rider: A Novel.* HarperCollins, 2002. Ages 12–YA. China, thirteenth century.

Napoli, Donna Jo. *Daughter of Venice.* Random, 2002. Ages 11–15. Venice, Italy in the sixteenth century.

Newth, Mette. *The Transformation.* Translated by Faith Ingwarsen. Farrar, 2000. Ages YA. Greenland, Inuit girl, 1400s.

Park, Linda Sue. *A Single Shard.* Clarion, 2001. Ages 9–13. Korean village in twelfth century.

Sedgwick, Marcus. *The Dark Horse.* Random, 2003. Ages 12–YA. Set in ancient Britain, Viking tribes.

Skurzynski, Gloria. *What Happened in Hamelin.* Four Winds, 1979. Ages 10–14. Germany, 1200s.

Temple, Frances. *The Ramsay Scallop.* Orchard, 1994. Ages 12–YA. England, 1299.

Tingle, Rebecca. *The Edge on the Sword.* Putnam, 2001. Ages 11–YA. Feudal England in the late 800s.

Yolen, Jane, and Robert Harris. *Girl in a Cage.* Putnam, 2002. Ages 11–YA. England in 1306.

The Emergence of Modern Nations, 1500 to 1800

Anderson, Laurie Halse. *Fever 1793.* Simon & Schuster, 2000. Ages 11–YA. Philadelphia, yellow fever epidemic, freed slaves' role, 1793.

Bosse, Malcolm. *The Examination.* Farrar, 1994. Ages 11–YA. China, sixteenth-century Ming Dynasty.

Bruchac, Joseph. *The Arrow over the Door.* Dial, 1998. Ages 9–12. Quaker boy and Abenaki Indian boy in 1777.

———. *The Winter People.* Dial, 2002. Ages 11–YA. French and Indian War, Abenaki village, 1759.

Collier, James Lincoln, and Christopher Collier. *My Brother Sam Is Dead.* Four Winds, 1974. Ages 10–14. U.S. Revolutionary War era, 1770s.

Dorris, Michael. *Guests.* Hyperion, 1994. Ages 8–12. First Thanksgiving feast, Native-American boy.

———. *Sees behind Trees.* Hyperion, 1996. Ages 8–12. Sixteenth century, pre-Colonial America, partially sighted, Native-American boy.

Forbes, Esther. *Johnny Tremain.* Houghton, 1943. Ages 10–13. U.S. Revolutionary War era, 1770s.

Fritz, Jean. *The Cabin Faced West.* Coward, 1958. Ages 7–10. U.S. pioneers, 1700s.

Gauch, Patricia. *This Time, Tempe Wick?* Coward, 1974. Ages 7–10. U.S. Revolutionary War era, 1780s.

Hesse, Karen. *Stowaway.* Simon & Schuster, 2000. Ages 10–YA. British sailing ship, Captain Cook's voyage, 1768.

Lasky, Kathryn. *Beyond the Burning Time.* Scholastic, 1994. Ages 11–YA. U.S. colonial era, Salem witch trials, 1690s.

Lawrence, Iain. *The Wreckers.* Delacorte, 1998. Ages 10–14. Cornwall, England in 1799, a survival mystery.

Lunn, Janet. *The Hollow Tree.* Viking, 2000. Ages 10–14. U.S. Revolutionary War, 1777.

Myers, Laurie. *The Keeping Room.* Walker, 1997. Ages 9–12. U.S. Revolutionary War, South Carolina.

Namioka, Lensey. *The Coming of the Bear.* HarperCollins, 1992. Ages 10–YA. Japan, 1600s.

Rees, Celia. *Pirates!* Bloomsbury, 2003. Ages 12–YA. Swashbuckling adventure in 1725.

Rinaldi, Ann. *A Break with Charity: A Story about the Salem Witch Trials.* Harcourt, 1992. Ages 12–YA. Salem witch trials, 1692.

———. *The Fifth of March: A Story of the Boston Massacre.* Harcourt, 1993. Ages 11–YA. Boston, indentured servant, 1770s.

———. *A Stitch in Time.* Scholastic, 1994. Ages 12–YA. Salem, Massachusetts, family saga, 1788–1791.

Rockwell. Anne. *They Called Her Molly Pitcher.* Illustrated by Cynthia Von Buhler. Knopf, 2002. Ages 8–11. U.S. Revolutionary War, 1778. Picture book.

Speare, Elizabeth George. *The Sign of the Beaver.* Houghton, 1983. Ages 8–12. Maine frontier, 1700s.

———. *The Witch of Blackbird Pond.* Houghton, 1958. Ages 10–14. U.S. colonial era, 1680s.

Turner, Ann. *Katie's Trunk.* Illustrated by Ron Himler. Simon & Schuster, 1992. Ages 7–10. U.S. Revolutionary War, Tory supporters.

Van Leeuwen, Jean. *Going West.* Illustrated by Thomas B. Allen. Doubleday/Dial, 1992. Ages 5–8. Wagon train, picture book.

———. *Hannah's Helping Hands.* Phyllis Fogelman, 1999. Ages 7–10. U.S. Revolutionary War, Connecticut, 1779.

The Development of Industrial Society, 1800 to 1914

Anderson, Rachel. *Black Water.* Holt, 1995. Ages 9–12. Late nineteenth-century England, boy with epilepsy.

Armstrong, Jennifer. *Black-Eyed Susan.* Illustrated by Emily Martindale. Crown, 1995. Ages 8–12. Dakota Territory, pioneer life.

Avi. *Beyond the Western Sea: The Escape from Home.* Orchard, 1996. Ages 11–14. Ireland, 1851.

———. *The True Confessions of Charlotte Doyle.* Orchard, 1990. Ages 8–12. England, United States, 1830s.

Beatty, Patricia. *Charley Skedaddle.* Morrow, 1987. Ages 11–14. U.S. Civil War, 1860s.

———. *Jayhawker.* Morrow, 1991. Ages 10–14. Kansas, slavery, underground railroad, 1800s.

———. *Turn Homeward, Hannalee.* Morrow, 1984. Ages 10–14. U.S. Civil War, 1860s.

Belpré, Pura. *Firefly Summer.* Piñata, 1996. Ages 10–13. Puerto Rico, about 1900.

Berry, James. *Ajeemah and His Son.* HarperCollins, 1992. Ages 12–YA. Slavery, United States, 1807.

Blos, Joan. *A Gathering of Days: A New England Girl's Journal, 1830–32.* Scribner's, 1979. Ages 8–11. New England, 1830s.

Bunting, Eve. *Train to Somewhere.* Illustrated by Ronald Himler. Clarion, 1996. Ages 5–8. Orphan train from New York to the Midwest in 1878. Picture book.

Byars, Betsy. *Keeper of the Doves.* Viking, 2002. Ages 9–13. Kentucky in 1899.

Clark, Clara Gillow. *Nellie Bishop.* Boyds Mills, 1996. Ages 12–YA. Pennsylvania canal town, 1880s.

Collier, James Lincoln, and Christopher Collier. *The Clock.* Delacorte, 1992. Ages 9–12. Connecticut mill life, early 1800s.

———. *With Every Drop of Blood.* Delacorte, 1994. Ages 10–14. Virginia, race relations, slavery, Civil War era.

Conlon-McKenna, Marita. *Fields of Home.* Illustrated by Donald Teskey. Holiday, 1997. Ages 9–12. Ireland, mid-1800s.

———. *Under the Hawthorn Tree.* Illustrated by Donald Teskey. Holiday, 1990. Ages 10–12. Ireland, mid-1800s.

Crew, Gary. *Bright Star.* Illustrated by Anne Spudvillas. Kane/Miller, 1997. Ages 9–12. Australia, 1861, dairy farm. Picture book.

Cushman, Karen. *The Ballad of Lucy Whipple.* Clarion, 1996. Ages 10–13. Massachusetts to California, Gold Rush.

———. *Rodzina.* Clarion, 2003. Ages 9–YA. Trip from Chicago to California, orphan train, 1881.

De Felice, Cynthia. *Weasel.* Macmillan, 1990. Ages 9–12. Ohio frontier, 1830s.

DeVries, David. *Home at Last.* Dell, 1992. Ages 10–13. Orphan train, New York to Nebraska, 1800s.

Donnelly, Jennifer. *A Northern Light.* Harcourt, 2003. Ages 11–YA. Mystery and suspense in Adirondacks in 1906.

Fleischman, Paul. *Bull Run.* HarperCollins, 1993. Ages 10–YA. U.S. Civil War era, 1860s.

Fleischman, Sid. *Bandit's Moon.* Illustrated by Joseph A. Smith. Greenwillow, 1998. Ages 8–12. California Gold Rush era, Mexican bandit Joaquin Murieta.

Giff, Patricia Reilly. *Maggie's Door.* Random, 2003. Ages 9–13. Ireland, potato famine, immigration, 1840s.

———. *Nory Ryan's Song.* Delacorte, 2000. Ages 9–13. Ireland, potato famine, 1845.

Hansen, Joyce. *The Captive.* Scholastic, 1994. Ages 11–YA. U.S. slave trade, Civil War era.

———. *Which Way Freedom?* Walker, 1986. Ages 11–YA. United States, slavery, Civil War era.

Harvey, Brett. *Cassie's Journey: Going West in the 1860s.* Illustrated by Deborah Kogan Ray. Holiday, 1988. Ages 7–9. U.S. frontier, 1860s.

Hill, Kirkpatrick. *Minuk: Ashes in the Pathway.* Illustrated by Patrick Faricy. Pleasant, 2002. Ages 10–14. Eskimo village in Alaska, 1890.

Holland, Isabelle. *Behind the Lines.* Scholastic, 1994. Ages 11–YA. U.S. Civil War.

Hunt, Irene. *Across Five Aprils.* Follett, 1964. Ages 10–YA. U.S. Civil War era, 1860s.

Hurst, Carol Otis. *Through the Lock.* Houghton, 2001. Ages 10–13. Farm community, nineteenth-century Connecticut.

Ibbotson, Eva. *Journey to the River Sea.* Dutton, 2002. Ages 11–14. Brazil, 1910.

Irwin, Hadley. *Jim-Dandy.* Macmillan, 1994. Ages 11–YA. General Custer, horse story, 1870s.

Kudlinsky, Kathleen V. *Night Bird: A Story of the Seminole Indians.* Viking, 1993. Ages 8–11. Florida, Seminole Indians, 1850s.

Lasky, Kathryn. *Beyond the Divide.* Macmillan, 1983. Ages 12–YA. Westward expansion, 1849.

———. *The Bone Wars.* Morrow, 1988. Ages 11–YA. U.S. frontier, mid-1800s.

Lawlor, Laurie. *George on His Own.* Whitman, 1993. Ages 9–12. Frontier life, homesteading in South Dakota, early 1900s.

Lawson, Robert. *The Great Wheel.* Viking, 1957. Ages 10–14. United States, 1890s.

Lowry, Lois. *The Silent Boy.* Houghton, 2003. Ages 9–YA. Small New England town during 1908–1911, character with developmental disability, autism.

Lyons, Mary E. *Dear Ellen Bee: A Civil War Scrapbook of Two Union Spies.* Simon & Schuster, 2000. Ages 10–13. Richmond, Virginia, Civil War era.

————. *Letters from a Slave Girl: The Story of Harriet Jacobs.* Scribner's, 1992. Ages 10–YA. North Carolina, slavery, early 1800s.

MacLachlan, Patricia. *Sarah, Plain and Tall.* Harper, 1985. Ages 7–10. U.S. frontier, 1850s.

————. *Skylark.* HarperCollins, 1994. Ages 8–11. Sequel to *Sarah, Plain and Tall.*

McCaughrean, Geraldine. *Stop the Train!* HarperCollins, 2003. Ages 10–13. Homesteading in Enid, Oklahoma, in 1893.

Morrow, Honoré. *On to Oregon!* Morrow, 1954. Ages 9–12. U.S. frontier, 1840s.

Nixon, Joan Lowery. *A Family Apart.* Bantam, 1987. Ages 10–13. New York City, Orphan Train, 1860s.

O'Dell, Scott. *Island of the Blue Dolphins.* Houghton, 1960. Ages 10–14. Pacific island, Native Americans, mid-1800s.

————. *Sing Down the Moon.* Houghton, 1970. Ages 12–YA. United States, Navajo Indians, 1860s.

Paterson, Katherine. *Jip, His Story.* Dutton, 1996. Ages 10–14. Vermont poor farm, 1850s.

————. *Lyddie.* Dutton, 1991. Ages 12–YA. Massachusetts, mill life, mid-1800s.

————. *Preacher's Boy.* Clarion. 1999. Ages 10–13. Vermont, turn of the century.

Paulsen, Gary. *Nightjohn.* Delacorte, 1993. Ages 11–YA. U.S. slavery.

————. *Sarny: A Life Remembered.* Delacorte, 1997. Ages 11–YA. New Orleans, freed slaves, 1860s.

————. *Soldier's Heart.* Delacorte, 1998. Ages 10–13. Minnesota, Civil War.

Pearsall, Shelley. *Trouble Don't Last.* Knopf, 2002. Ages 11–YA. Northern Kentucky, slavery, 1859.

Peck, Richard. *Fair Weather.* Dial, 2001. Ages 9–12. Rural Illinois in 1893.

————. *The River Between Us.* Dial, 2003. Ages 12–YA. 1861, early Civil War era, Southern Illinois town.

Polacco, Patricia. *Pink and Say.* Philomel, 1994. Ages 8–11. U.S. Civil War, race relations. Picture book.

Reeder, Carolyn. *Across the Lines.* Simon & Schuster, 1997. Ages 8–11. Race relations, 1864–1965.

————. *Shades of Gray.* Macmillan, 1989. Ages 9–12. U.S. Civil War era, 1860s.

Rinaldi, Ann. *An Acquaintance with Darkness.* Harcourt, 1997. Ages 12–YA. Washington, D.C., Lincoln assassination.

————. *In My Father's House.* Scholastic, 1993. Ages 12–YA. U.S. Civil War era, 1860s.

Robinet, Harriette Gillem. *Forty Acres and Maybe a Mule.* Atheneum, 1998. Ages 8–12. Reconstruction era treatment of former slave families in 1865; set in South Carolina and Georgia.

Savage, Deborah. *To Race a Dream.* Houghton, 1994. Small Minnesota town, horse story, early 1900s.

Snyder, Zilpha Keatley. *Gib Rides Home.* Delacorte, 1998. Ages 9–12. Taken from an orphanage to work on a farm, early 1900s. Also, *Gib and the Gray Ghost.* Delacorte, 2000.

Taylor, Mildred D. *The Well.* Dial, 1995. Ages 9–11. Mississippi, 1910 drought, Logan family.

Thomas, Joyce Carol. *I Have Heard of a Land.* Illustrated by Floyd Cooper. HarperCollins, 1998. Ages 8–12. Picture book. Homesteading, African-American woman, Oklahoma territory, 1800s.

Turner, Ann. *Mississippi Mud: Three Prairie Journals.* Illustrated by Robert J. Clark. HarperCollins, 1997. Ages 5–8. Kentucky to Oregon, pioneers, in verse. Picture book.

Whelan, Gloria. *Angel on the Square.* HarperCollins, 2001. Ages 11–YA. St. Petersburg, Russia, fall of the Russian Empire, 1913.

Wilder, Laura Ingalls. *Little House in the Big Woods.* Harper, 1932. Ages 7–10. Wisconsin frontier, 1800s.

Yee, Paul. *Tales from Gold Mountain: Stories of the Chinese in the New World.* Illustrated by Simon Ng. Macmillan, 1990. Ages 10–14. United States and Canada, 1800s.

Yep, Lawrence. *Dragon's Gate.* HarperCollins, 1993. Ages 9–12. Sierra Nevada, transcontinental railroad, 1867.

————. *Dragonwings.* Harper, 1979. Ages 9–12. California, early 1900s.

————. *The Traitor.* Farrar, 2003. Ages 10–14. Chinese and Western coal miners in the Wyoming Territory in 1885.

Yin. *Coolies.* Illustrated by Chris Soentpiet. Philomel, 2001. Ages 8–12. Picture book. Transcontinental railroad in 1860s.

World Wars in the Twentieth Century, 1914 to 1945

Anderson, Rachel. *Paper Faces.* Holt, 1993. Ages 12–YA. England, World War II.

Avi. *Who Was That Masked Man, Anyway?* Orchard, 1992. Ages 9–12. United States, World War II.

Bat-Ami, Miriam. *Two Suns in the Sky.* Front Street, 1999. Ages 13–YA. World War II in New York state, relations among European refugees and U.S. citizens.

Booth, Martin. *War Dog: A Novel.* Margaret K. McElderry, 1997. Ages 10–14. A spy dog sent to France in World War II.

Chang, Margaret, and Raymond Chang. *In the Eye of the War.* Macmillan, 1990. Ages 10–12. China, World War II.

Cormier, Robert. *Frenchtown Summer.* Delacorte, 1999. Monument, Massachusetts, post–World War I. Ages 11–14.

Curtis, Christopher Paul. *Bud, Not Buddy.* Delacorte, 1999. Ages 9–13. Michigan, Depression era.

Doucet, Sharon Arms. *Fiddle Fever.* Clarion, 2000. Ages 9–13. Cajun life in southern Louisiana, World War I.

Dowell, Frances O'Roark. *Dovey Coe.* Atheneum, 2000. Ages 9–13. North Carolina, 1928 murder trial.

Gee, Maurice. *The Fat Man.* Simon & Schuster, 1997. Ages 13–YA. Depression, New Zealand, haunting psychological thriller.

Giff, Patricia Reilly. *Lily's Crossing.* Delacorte, 1997. Ages 9–12. United States, World War II.

Greene, Bette. *Summer of My German Soldier.* Dial, 1973. Ages 9–12. United States, World War II.

Hahn, Mary Downing. *Following My Footsteps.* Clarion, 1996. Ages 10–13. North Carolina, physical disability, polio, World War II.

Hall, Donald. *The Farm Summer 1942.* Illustrated by Barry Moser. Dial, 1994. Ages 7–11. Set in the United States during World War II. Picture book.

Hartnett, Sonya. *Thursday's Child.* Candlewick, 2002. Ages 12–YA. Australia in the Great Depression.

Hautzig, Esther. *The Endless Steppe.* Harper, 1968. Ages 10–14. Russia, Jews, World War II.

Hesse, Karen. *Letters from Rifka.* Holt, 1992. Ages 9–12. Russian immigration to the United States, 1919.

———. *Out of the Dust.* Scholastic, 1997. Ages 11–YA. Oklahoma, 1930s.

———. *Witness.* Scholastic, 2001. Ages 10–YA. Ku Klux Klan, Vermont, 1924. Told in a series of poems in five acts.

Hoestlandt, Jo. *Star of Fear, Star of Hope.* Illustrated by Johanna Kang. Translated by Mark Polizzotti. Walker, 1995. Ages 9–12. Northern France, 1942, German occupation, persecution of Jews. Picture book.

Hughes, Dean. *Soldier Boys.* Atheneum, 2001. Ages 11–YA. An American and a German boy in World War II.

Lawrence, Iain. *Land of the Nutcracker Men.* Delacorte, 2001. Ages 11–YA. England and France, World War I.

Levitin, Sonia. *Anne's Promise.* Atheneum, 1993. Ages 10–14. German immigration to United States, World War II era.

Lisle, Janet Taylor. *The Art of Keeping Cool.* Simon & Schuster, 2000. Ages 10–13. United States and Canada, World War II.

Lowry, Lois. *Number the Stars.* Houghton, 1989. Ages 8–12. Denmark, World War II.

Lyon, George Ella. *Borrowed Children.* Watts, 1988. Ages 10–14. Kentucky, Depression era, 1930s.

Maguire, Gregory. *The Good Liar.* Clarion, 1999. Ages 9–12. World War II, occupied France.

Mitchell, Margaree King. *Uncle Jed's Barbershop.* Illustrated by James Ransome. Simon & Schuster, 1993. Ages 7–10. Picture book. African American, rural south in 1920s.

Myers, Anna. *Fire in the Hills.* Walker, 1996. Ages 11–YA. Rural Oklahoma, World War I, German immigrant family, conscientious objector.

Napoli, Donna Jo. *Stones in Water.* Dutton, 1997. Ages 9–13. Italy, work camps, World War II.

Orlev, Uri. *The Island on Bird Street.* Translated from the Hebrew by Hillel Halkin. Houghton, 1983. Ages 9–13. Poland, Jews, World War II.

Park, Linda Sue. *When My Name Was Keoko: A Novel of Korea in World War II.* Clarion, 2002. Ages 10–14. Japanese occupation of Korea, 1940s.

Peck, Richard. *A Long Way from Chicago.* Dial, 1998. Ages 9–12. Southern Illinois, 1930s. Humorous.

Peck, Robert Newton. *A Year Down Yonder.* Dial, 2000. Ages 10–YA. Southern Illinois, Recession era, 1937. Humorous.

———. *Horse Thief.* HarperCollins, 2002. Ages 12–YA. Depression-era Florida.

Polacco, Patricia. *The Butterfly.* Philomel, 2000. Ages 10–YA. Picture book. French Resistance, Jewish persecution, World War II.

Ray, Delia. *Ghost Girl: A Blue Ridge Mountain Story.* Clarion, 2003. Ages 10–13. Depression era 1929–1932, Virginia.

Reiss, Johanna. *The Upstairs Room.* Crowell, 1972. Ages 10–14. Holland, Jews, World War II.

Richter, Hans Peter. *Friedrich.* Translated from the German by Edite Kroll. Holt, 1970. Ages 10–14. Germany, Jews, World War II.

Ryan, Pam Muñoz. *Esperanza Rising.* Scholastic, 2000. Ages 9–13. Mexico and United States, Depression era.

Salisbury, Graham. *Under the Blood-Red Sun.* Delacorte, 1994. Ages 10–YA. Japanese residents of Hawaii, World War II era.

Siegal, Aranka. *Upon the Head of the Goat: A Childhood in Hungary 1939–44.* Farrar, 1981. Ages 12–YA. Hungary, World War II.

Snyder, Zilpha Keatley. *Cat Running.* Delacorte, 1994. Ages 9–12. California, U.S. Depression, 1933.

Spinelli, Jerry. *Milkweed.* Random, 2003. Ages 11–YA. Warsaw, persecution of Jews, 1940s.

Taylor, Mildred. *Let the Circle Be Unbroken.* Dial, 1981. Ages 10–14. U.S. South, African Americans, 1930s.

———. *The Road to Memphis.* Dial, 1990. Ages 12–YA. U.S. South, African Americans, 1941.

———. *Roll of Thunder, Hear My Cry.* Dial, 1976. Ages 10–14. U.S. South, African Americans, 1930s.

Taylor, Theodore. *The Bomb.* Harcourt, 1995. Ages 12–YA. Hiroshima, 1944–1945.

———. *The Cay.* Doubleday, 1969. Ages 8–12. Caribbean, World War II era.

Uchida, Yoshiko. *Journey to Topaz.* Illustrated by Donald Carrick. Scribner's, 1971. Ages 10–14. United States, internment of Japanese Americans, World War II.

Van Dijk, Lutz. *Damned Strong Love: The True Story of Willi G. and Stefan K.* Translated by Elizabeth D. Crawford. Holt, 1995. Ages 13–YA. Occupied Poland, homosexuality, World War II.

Walters, Eric. *Caged Eagles.* Orca, 2000. Ages 11–YA. Canada, World War II, internment of Japanese Canadians.

———. *War of the Eagles.* Orca, 1998. Ages 11–YA. Canada, World War II, internment of Japanese Canadians.

Wells, Rosemary. *Wingwalker.* Illustrated by Brian Selznick. Hyperion, 2002. Ages 8–11. Oklahoma in the Depression era, 1930s.

Westall, Robert. *The Kingdom by the Sea.* Farrar, 1991. Ages 10–13. England, World War II.

Post–World War II Era, 1945 to 1980s

Brooks, Martha. *Two Moons in August.* Little, 1992. Ages 12–YA. Canada, August 1959.

Bunting, Eve. *How Many Days to America? A Thanksgiving Story.* Illustrated by Beth Peck. Clarion, 1988. Ages 7–11. Picture book. Caribbean refugees to the United States.

Clinton, Catherine. *A Stone in My Hand.* Candlewick, 2002. Ages 11–YA. Palestine, 1980s.

Conrad, Pam. *Our House: The Stories of Levittown.* Illustrated by Brian Selznick. Scholastic, 1995. Ages 9–12. Six family stories set on Long Island, each decade from 1940.

Curtis, Christopher Paul. *The Watsons Go to Birmingham—1963.* Delacorte, 1995. Ages 8–12. Flint, Michigan, to Birmingham, Alabama, Civil Rights Movement.

de Jenkins, Lyll Becerra. *The Honorable Prison.* Lodestar, 1988. Ages 12–YA. South America, 1950s.

Grimes, Nikki. *Jazmin's Notebook.* Dial, 1998. Ages 11–YA. Harlem, 1960s.

Holt, Kimberly Willis. *My Louisiana Sky.* Holt, 1998. Ages 10–13. Small town in Louisiana in 1957.

———. *When Zachary Beaver Came to Town.* Holt, 1999. Ages 10–14. Small town in Texas in 1971, Vietnam War era.

Jiang, Ji-li. *Red Scarf Girl: A Memoir of the Cultural Revolution.* HarperCollins, 1997. Ages 12–14. China, Mao's Cultural Revolution, 1960s.

Kim, Helen. *The Long Season of Rain.* Holt, 1996. Ages 12–YA. Seoul, Korea in 1960s.

Krisher, Trudy. *Spite Fences.* Delacorte, 1994. Ages 13–YA. Georgia, race relations, 1960s.

Martin, Ann M. *Belle Teal.* Scholastic, 2001. Ages 9–12. Rural South, 1962.

———. *A Corner of the Universe.* Scholastic, 2002. Ages 9–13. Small town, 1960.

Park, Frances, and Ginger Park. *My Freedom Trip: A Child's Escape from North Korea.* Illustrated by Debra Reid Jenkins. Boyds Mills, 1998. Ages 7–10. Picture book. Crossing the 38th parallel prior to the Korean War.

Perera, Hilda. *Kiki: A Cuban Boy's Adventures in America.* Translated from Spanish by Warren Hampton and Hilda Gonzales. Pickering, 1992. Ages 9–12. Miami, Cuba, Florida's Seminole and Miccosukee tribes, 1960s.

Sacks, Margaret. *Beyond Safe Boundaries.* Lodestar, 1989. Ages 12–YA. South Africa, Jews, 1960s.

Talbert, Marc. *The Purple Heart.* HarperCollins, 1992. Ages 10–13. United States, Vietnam War era.

Veciana-Suarez, Ana. *The Flight to Freedom.* Orchard, 2002. Ages 11–YA. Cuban immigrant to Miami, 1967.

White, Ruth. *Memories of Summer.* Farrar, 2000. Ages 12–YA. Hills of Virginia, Michigan, 1950s.

———. *Tadpole.* Farrar, 2003. Ages 9–YA. Appalachian mountains, 1950s.

Wolff, Virginia Euwer. *Bat 6.* Scholastic, 1998. Ages 10–YA. California, 1948, Japanese Americans, post-war adjustments.

NONFICTION: BIOGRAPHY *and* INFORMATIONAL BOOKS

Why
Is the sky?

What starts the thunder overhead?
Who makes the crashing noise?
Are the angels falling out of bed?
Are they breaking all their toys?

Why does the sun go down so soon?
Why do the night-clouds crawl
Hungrily up to the new-laid moon
And swallow it, shell and all?

If there's a bear among the stars,
As all the people say,
Won't he jump over those pasture-bars
And drink up the Milky Way?

Does every star that happens to fall
Turn into a firefly?
Can't it ever get back to Heaven at all?
And why
Is the sky?

— LOUIS UNTERMEYER

Children are naturally curious. Their interest in the world around them is boundless. Teachers, librarians, and parents want to nourish that curiosity with lively, intelligent answers, provocative questions, and stimulating books that provide answers and a thirst for further knowledge. Today's constantly innovative and improving works of nonfiction are an excellent source of information for children and the adults who guide their learning.

DEFINITION AND DESCRIPTION

Nonfiction can best be defined in terms of emphasis: the content emphasis of children's nonfiction is documented fact about the natural or social world. Its primary purpose is to inform. In contrast, the content of fictional literature is largely, if not wholly, a product of the imagination, and its purpose is to entertain. Nonfiction writing is often referred to as *expository* writing, or writing that explains, whereas fiction writing is called *narrative* writing, or writing that tells a story.

Some countries now recognize a type of literature that has elements of both fiction and nonfiction and call it *faction*. Mogens Jansen of the Danish National Association of Reading Teachers describes *faction* as " 'nonfiction' the presentation of which is mainly sustained by 'fiction elements': the well-told nonfiction which has fictional overtones, but *is* nonfictional—and absolutely correct" (Jansen, 1987, p. 16). Although North America has not designated faction as an independent genre, but considers it a part of nonfiction, adults who deal with books and children are well aware of this type of literature and its appeal to 8- to 12-year-old boys, in particular. Today a great number of books present factual information on a ribbon of narrative. Examples are *Mosque* by David Macaulay and *My Place in Space* by Robin and Sally Hirst, illustrated by Roland Harvey with Joe Levine.

Nonfiction is usually classified as either biography or informational literature. *Biography* gives factual information about the lives of actual people, including their experiences, influences, accomplishments, and legacies. An *autobiography* is similar in every respect to biography, except that the author tells about his or her own life. *Informational books* can be written on any aspect of the biological, social, or physical world, including what is known of outer space.

ELEMENTS OF NONFICTION

Understanding the parts, or elements, of nonfiction and how they work together can help you to become more analytical about this kind of literature. This knowledge can also improve your judgment of nonfiction. Note that biography, which is more narrative than expository in nature, more closely resembles fiction than nonfiction in its elements.

Structure

Structure has to do with how the author organizes the information to be presented. Most informational literature is structured in one or more of the following ways:

- *Description.* The author gives the characteristics of the topic (e.g., *Spiders* by Gail Gibbons).
- *Sequence.* The author lists items in order, usually chronologically or numerically (e.g., *How to Make a Chemical Volcano and Other Mysterious Experiments* by Alan Kramer).
- *Comparison.* The author juxtaposes two or more entities and lists their similarities and differencess (e.g., *Do You Know the Difference?* by Andrea and Michael Bischhoff-Miersch).
- *Cause and effect.* The author states an action and then shows the effect, or result, of this action (e.g., *Blizzard: The Storm That Changed America* by Jim Murphy).
- *Problem and solution* (also referred to as *question and answer*). The author states a problem and its solution or solutions (e.g., *What Do You Do with a Tail Like This?* by Steve Jenkins and Robin Page).

Some works of nonfiction will employ a single text structure; others, particularly longer works, will employ several.

Theme

Theme in nonfiction is the main point made in the work. Though a work of nonfiction may communicate hundreds of facts about a topic, the theme of the work will answer the question "What's the point?" (Colman, 1999, p. 221). Sometimes the theme will be a cognitive concept, such as the way viruses multiply; in other cases it will be an emotional insight, such as a new or deepened awareness of the strength of the human spirit to endure social injustice, as in Schoschana Rabinovici's biography, *Thanks to My Mother.*

Style

Style is how authors and illustrators, with their readers in mind, express themselves in their respective media. Sentence length and complexity, word choice, and formal versus conversational tone are part of the expository style, as are use of technical vocabulary, captions, and graphic elements such as tables, charts, illustrations, photographs, diagrams, maps, and indices. James Cross Giblin's conversational tone and use of period photographs and political cartoons, quotes, and source notes in *The Life and Death of Adolf Hitler* demonstrate how style can make nonfiction more interesting.

R E A D I N G   N O N F I C T I O N

An interesting contradiction concerning nonfiction exists in today's schools. While school and public library records indicate that nonfiction makes up 50–85 percent of the circulation of children's libraries, research studies indicate that children in the United States have trouble reading and writing expository texts, partly because of a lack of classroom experience with nonfiction in the early grades. See Table 9.1 for research evidence supporting the reading of nonfiction in the elementary grades.

TABLE 9.1   Important Studies on Reading and Nonfiction

Researcher(s)	Subjects	Findings
Duke (2000)	20 first-grade classrooms, 10 each from very high and very low SES groups	Presence of nonfiction texts and use of nonfiction in class were rare to nonexistent. Consequently, students were unable to read and write informational texts successfully. Findings applied particularly to low-SES students.
Mullis, Martin, Gonzalez, & Kennedy (2003)	150,000 fourth-graders from 35 countries	U.S. students scored significantly lower in reading nonfiction than in reading fiction.
Campbell, Kapinus, & Beatty (1995)	National sample of fourth-graders	Students with experience reading magazines and nonfiction had higher average reading proficiencies than those who never read these types of materials.

Studies such as the ones reported in Table 9.1 reveal several critical points about children and reading nonfiction. First, it is only through repeated experience with a specific genre that one learns how to read or write that genre. Second, all children, even primary-graders, benefit from learning how to read and enjoy nonfiction, since from middle grades through adulthood, most day-to-day reading demands (textbooks, news reports, instructions, recipes, etc.) are expository. Third, a key factor in comprehending expository text is that readers learn to relate new information found in the text to their own *schemata,* or prior knowledge on the topic stored in their minds.

Particularly in the early grades, teachers and librarians may have to take the lead in introducing nonfiction to their students, since parents and caregivers traditionally select only fiction as read-aloud material. Selecting excellent works of nonfiction for reading aloud and suggesting similar works to par-

USING NONFICTION ACROSS THE CURRICULUM: *Science*

USE	GRADE LEVEL	SUGGESTED BOOKS
Teaching science concepts		
Evolution	4–8	*Evolution* by Joanna Cole *Eyewitness Science: Evolution* by Linda Samlin *Life on Earth: The Story of Evolution* by Steve Jenkins
Solar system	3–5	*My Place in Space* by Robin and Sally Hirst *Our Solar System* by Seymour Simon *The Planets in Our Solar System* by Franklyn Branley
Magnets	2–6	*What Makes a Magnet?* by Franklyn Branley *Batteries, Bulbs, and Wires* by David Glover *The Magnet Book* by Shar Levine and Leslie Johnstone
Introducing science units with nonfiction picture books		
Water cycle	1–3	*Down Comes the Rain* by Franklyn Branley
Earthquakes and volcanoes	4–7	*The Buried City of Pompeii* by Shelley Tanaka
Conservation of natural resources	1–6	*A River Ran Wild: An Environmental History* by Lynne Cherry
Fossils	3–8	*A Dinosaur Named Sue: The Story of the Colossal Fossil: The World's Most Complete T. Rex* by Pat Relf
Human body	3–8	*The Amazing Pull-Out, Pop-Up Body in a Book* by David Hawcock

ents for at-home reading is a good way to begin. Calling attention to students' prior knowledge on a subject and noting the various text structures while reading will help students learn to read and appreciate this genre. In addition, nonfiction can be included and promoted as options in students' self-choice reading, can be added to classroom library collections (Moss & Hendershot, 2002), and can be used across the curriculum in various ways, as suggested in the chart on page 166.

FORMATS OF NONFICTION BOOKS

Some comment on the formats of nonfiction books is in order. Book format has to do with how information is presented on the book page, rather than with the information itself. The most common distinct formats in which informational books for children are currently being produced are as follows:

- *Nonfiction chapter book.* This format features a large amount of text that is organized into chapters. Graphics and illustrations are common in the more recent nonfiction chapter books but are still less important than the text. Almost all biographies, with the exception of picture book biographies, appear in this format. Examples include *Blizzard! The Storm That Changed America* by Jim Murphy and *Columbus and the World Around Him* by Milton Meltzer.
- *Nonfiction picture book.* This format features large, uncomplicated illustrations and brief text. The illustrations help to convey the information as discussed in Chapter 4. Examples include *What Do You Do with a Tail Like This?* by Steve Jenkins and Robin Page and *Leonardo da Vinci* by Diane Stanley.
- *Science and social science concept picture book.* Originally conceived for 4- to 8-year-olds, this book presents one or two scientific or social concepts via brief, uncomplicated text accompanied by numerous, large illustrations. It also encourages participation by including an experiment or hands-on activity. These books are now available for older children as well. *Evolution* by Joanna Cole, illustrated by Aliki, and the *Science Book* series by Neil Ardley are good examples of this type of book.
- *Photo essay.* Presentation of information in the photo essay is equally balanced between text and illustration. Excellent, information-bearing photographs, and crisp, condensed writing style are hallmarks of this nonfictional format. Photo essays are generally written for children in the intermediate grades and up. Examples include *Lincoln: A Photobiography* by Russell Freedman and *Barrio: José's Neighborhood* by George Ancona.
- *Fact books.* Presentation of information in these books is mainly through lists, charts, and tables. Examples include almanacs, books of world records, and sports trivia and statistics books. For example, see *The Guinness Book of World Records.*

EVALUATION AND SELECTION OF NONFICTION

The criteria listed below will help you to distinguish the worthier books of nonfiction from the not so worthy. However, it is important to remember that not every work of nonfiction needs to meet every criterion to be worthy and that no one book can cover a topic completely. By offering children a variety of satisfactory books on the same topic to be read and compared, you more than compensate for the shortcomings of a good-but-not-great book.

- Children's nonfiction must be written in a clear, direct, easily understandable style. In recent years, a tight, compressed, but conversational, writing style has come to be favored in nonfictional text.

- Captions and labels must be clearly written and informative. Though brief, these pieces of text serve the vital function of explaining the significance of illustrations or of drawing the reader's attention to important or interesting details pictured.

- Facts must be accurate and current. A reliable check is to compare the information with that found in other recently published sources on the topic.

- Nonfiction must distinguish between fact, theory, and opinion. When not clearly stated as such, theories or opinions are flagged in good nonfiction by carefully placed phrases such as "maybe," "is believed to be," or "perhaps."

- *Personification*—attributing human qualities to animals, material objects, or natural forces—is part of the charm of works of traditional and modern fantasy. In nonfiction, however, this same device is to be avoided, because the implication is factually inaccurate. Saying in a work of nonfiction that a horse "feels proud to carry his master" is an example of this device. *Teleology*—giving humanlike purpose to natural phenomena—is another rhetorical device to be avoided in nonfiction. People sometimes say that nature has "donned its finery" when they are admiring springtime blossoms, and this is perfectly acceptable in our daily conversation. But to explain the forces of nature in such human terms in a work of nonfiction is unscientific.

- Works of nonfiction must be attractive to the child. An intriguing cover, impressive illustrations, and balance of text and illustrations make books look interesting to a child.

- Presentation of information should be from known to unknown, general to specific, or simple to more complex to aid conceptual understanding and encourage analytical thinking. Subheadings can make text much easier to read and comprehend. Reference aids such as tables of contents, indexes, pronunciation guides, glossaries, maps, charts, and tables make information in books easier to find and retrieve, more comprehensible, and more complete.

- Stereotyping must be avoided. The best nonfiction goes beyond mere avoidance of sexist or racist language and stereotyped images in text and illustrations. It also shows positive images of cultural diversity.

Excellent N O N F I C T I O N to Read Aloud

Bartoletti, Susan Campbell. *Black Potatoes: The Story of the Great Irish Famine, 1845–1850.* Ages 12–YA.
Borden, Louise. *A. Lincoln and Me.* Illustrated by Ted Lewin. Ages 5–8.
Bridges, Ruby, and Margo Lundell. *Through My Eyes.* Ages 9–YA. Memoir.
Chandra, Deborah, and Madeline Comora. *George Washington's Teeth.* Illustrated by Brock Cole. Ages 5–8.
    Story in verse.
Cowley, Joy. *Red-Eyed Tree Frog.* Photographs by Nic Bishop. Ages 6–9.
Giblin, James Cross. *The Amazing Life of Benjamin Franklin.* Illustrated by Michael Dooling. Ages 8–11.
Hamilton, Virginia. *Many Thousand Gone: African Americans from Slavery to Freedom.* Illustrated by Leo
    and Diane Dillon. Ages 10–14. Collected biography.
Hoose, Phillip. *We Were There, Too! Young People in U.S. History.* Ages 10–13. Collected biography.
Martin, Jacqueline Briggs. *Snowflake Bentley.* Illustrated by Mary Azarian. Ages 6–9. Biography.
Perl, Lila. *The Great Ancestor Hunt: The Fun of Finding Out Who You Are.* Ages 8–10.
Stanley, Diane. *Leonardo da Vinci.* Ages 9–13.

- Format and artistic medium should be appropriate to the content. For example, a drawing is preferable to a photograph when an illustrator wishes to highlight a specific feature by omitting irrelevant details. Engineered paper or pop-up illustrations are appropriate when three dimensions are required to give an accurate sense of placement of the parts of a whole, as in human anatomy.
- Depth and complexity of subject treatment must be appropriate for the intended audience. If an explanation must be simplified to the extent that facts must be altered before a child can begin to understand, perhaps the concept or topic should be taken up when the child is older.

Selecting the best of nonfiction for children can be a challenge. Many teachers and librarians find the following professional review sources helpful in identifying outstanding biographies and informational books:

"Outstanding Science Trade Books for Students K–12": An annual annotated list of notable books in the field of science coproduced by the National Science Teachers Association and the Children's Book Council (This list can be found in the March issue of *Science and Children* and at www.cbcbooks.org.)

"Notable Social Studies Trade Books for Young People": An annual annotated list of notable books in the field of social studies coproduced by the National Council for the Social Studies and the Children's Book Council (This list can be found in the April/May issue of *Social Education* and at www.cbcbooks.org.)

For further information on these sources, see "Bibliographies: Annual Lists" in Appendix B.

Two award programs offer additional sources of good nonfiction titles. The NCTE's Orbis Pictus Award for Outstanding Nonfiction for Children and the ALA's Robert F. Sibert Informational Book Medal spotlight what are considered to be the best works of nonfiction published in the preceding year.

For a complete listing of the Orbis Pictus and Sibert Award winners, see Appendix A.

HISTORICAL OVERVIEW OF NONFICTION

The history of children's nonfiction begins in 1657 with the publication of John Amos Comenius's *Orbis Pictus (The World in Pictures)*. Not only was this the first children's picture book, but it was also a work of nonfiction. This auspicious beginning for nonfiction was cut short, however, by the Puritan Movement. For nearly 200 years the vast majority of books published for and read by children were intended more for moralistic instruction than for information.

Although books of nonfiction continued to be written in the eighteenth and nineteenth centuries, much of the growth and development of this genre occurred in the latter half of the twentieth century.

Rapid development of nonfiction as a genre began in the 1950s and 1960s in response to the launching of *Sputnik,* the first artificial space satellite, by the former Soviet Union. Competing in the race for space exploration and new technology, the U.S. Congress funneled money into science education, and publishers responded with new and improved science trade books. (See Milestones in the Development of Nonfiction for Children.) Particularly noteworthy are the introduction of nonfiction picture books for primary grades and the trend toward more illustrations and less text in nonfiction for all levels.

As the stature of nonfiction rose and more top-flight authors and illustrators were engaged in its production, the quality of research, writing, and art in these books improved. A lighter, yet factual, tone

M I L E S T O N E S

in the Development of NONFICTION for CHILDREN

DATE	BOOK	SIGNIFICANCE
1657	*Orbis Pictus* by John Amos Comenius	First known work of nonfiction for children
1683	*New England Primer*	First concept book for American children; reflected didacticism of the Puritan era
1922	*The Story of Mankind* by Hendrik Van Loon	Won the first Newbery Medal; greatly influenced children's books with its lively style and creative approach
1939	*Abraham Lincoln* by Ingri and Edgar Parin d'Aulaire	One of the first picture book biographies for younger children. First biography to win the Caldecott Medal
1940	*Daniel Boone* by James H. Daugherty	First biography to win the Newbery Medal
1948	*The Story of the Negro* by Arna Bontemps	The first important history of the Negro
1952	*Diary of a Young Girl* by Anne Frank	Classic autobiography; helped many to understand the tragedy of the Jewish Holocaust
1960	Let's-Read-and-Find-Out series by Franklyn Branley and Roma Gans	Introduced the science concept picture book for young children
1969	*To Be a Slave* by Julius Lester	African-American nonfiction chosen as Newbery Honor Book
1988	*Lincoln: A Photobiography* by Russell Freedman	First nonfictional photo essay to win a Newbery Medal
1990	First Orbis Pictus Award for Nonfiction (*The Great Little Madison* by Jean Fritz)	Nonfiction as a genre is recognized
2001	First Robert F. Sibert Informational Book Medal (*Sir Walter Ralegh and the Quest for El Dorado* by Marc Aronson)	Nonfiction placed on an equal footing with fiction

balanced with high-quality, informative illustrations and graphics emerged as the preferred nonfiction style (Elleman, 1987).

Children's biographies were greatly affected by the more liberal attitudes and relaxed topic restrictions that revolutionized children's fiction in the 1960s. Before this time, certain subjects (ethnic minorities, women, infamous people) and topics (the subjects' personal weaknesses, mistakes, and tragedies) were not often found in children's biographies. It was thought that subjects who were worthy of being commemorated should be placed on a pedestal. By the mid-1960s, this attitude had changed, as Russell Freedman (1988) pointed out in his Newbery Medal acceptance speech: "The hero worship of the past has given way to a more realistic approach, which recognizes the warts and weaknesses that humanize the great" (p. 447).

Long in the literary shadow of fiction, nonfiction finally achieved equal stature in the 1980s. In the past 25 years, approximately 12 percent of all Newbery and Caldecott Medal winners or Honor Books have been works of nonfiction.

In 1990 the National Council of Teachers of English established the Orbis Pictus Award for Outstanding Nonfiction for Children. Named in honor of Comenius's book written some 300 years earlier, this award program signaled how far children's nonfiction had come. In 2001 the Robert F. Sibert Informational Book Medal, sponsored by the American Library Association, was established, further documenting the acceptance of nonfiction as an equal player in the field of children's literature. Recent multimedia publication (book and CD-ROM versions) of nonfictional books such as David Macaulay's *The Way Things Work* suggests an exciting future for this genre. Milestones in the development of nonfiction for children are highlighted on page 170.

T Y P E S   O F   B I O G R A P H I E S

In adult nonfiction, biographies must be completely documented to be acceptable. In biographies for children, more latitude is allowed, and biographers use varying degrees of invention. This invention ranges from choosing what aspect of the subject the biographer wants to emphasize as the theme of the book (e.g., great energy or love of freedom) to actually inventing fictional characters and conversation.

Biographies, then, can be classified by degree of documentation, as follows:

Authentic Biography

In this type of biography, all factual information is documented through eyewitness accounts, written documents, letters, diaries, and, more recently, audio and videotape recordings. Details in the lives of people who lived long ago, such as conversations, are often difficult to document, however. So, for the sake of art, biographers must use such devices as interior monologue (telling what someone probably thought or said to himself or herself based on known actions), indirect discourse (reporting the gist of what someone said without using quotation marks), attribution (interpretation of known actions to determine probable motives), and inference to make their stories lively and appealing and worth the children's time to read. It is advisable to read and compare several biographies of a subject, if possible, to counteract any bias an author might have. *The Great Little Madison* by Jean Fritz is an example of an authentic biography.

Fictionalized Biography

This type of biography is also based on careful research, but the author creates dramatic episodes from known facts by using imagined conversation. The conversation is, of course, carefully structured around the pertinent facts that are known, but the actual words are invented by the author. An example of this type of biography is *Carry On, Mr. Bowditch* by Jean Lee Latham.

Biographical Fiction

This type of biography allows much artistic license, including invented dialogue, fictional secondary characters, and some reconstructed action. The known achievements of the biographical subjects are reported accurately, but in other respects these works are as much fiction as fact. Due to a trend toward greater authenticity in children's nonfiction, biographical fiction is relatively rare today. A recent example is *If a Bus Could Talk: The Story of Rosa Parks* by Faith Ringgold.

Biographies can also be classified by coverage of the subject's life. In evaluating the following types of biographies, you will want to look for a balance between the need for adequate coverage and the tolerance that the target child audience has for detail.

- The *complete biography* covers the entire life of the subject from birth to death. An example is *Columbus and the World around Him* by Milton Meltzer.
- The *partial biography* covers only part of the life of the subject. Biographies for very young children will often be of this type, as will, of course, the biographies of living persons. An example is *Teammates* by Peter Golenbock, illustrated by Paul Bacon.
- The *collected biography* includes the life stories of several people in one book, organized into chapters. An example is *Lives of the Writers: Comedies, Tragedies (and What the Neighbors Thought)* by Kathleen Krull, illustrated by Kathryn Hewitt.
- The *biography series* is a multivolume set of books with each book containing one separate biography. Most series of this type feature subjects with some common attribute, accomplishment, or skill, such as leadership or legendary sports ability. For example, the First Biographies series by David A. Adler, published by Holiday House, written for beginning independent readers in grades 2 through 4, includes biographies on such subjects as Thomas Jefferson, Martin Luther King, and Jackie Robinson.

TOPICS OF INFORMATIONAL BOOKS

Although nonfiction is confined to just one chapter in this book, it is by far the largest single genre in children's literature in that everything known to humankind is a conceivable topic. Organization of such an enormous variety of topics could, of course, be done in a variety of ways, one of which is the scientific approach used here. The world of information is divided into the biological, the physical, the social, and the applied sciences; the humanities are dealt with separately.

Biological Science

Biological science deals with living organisms and the laws and phenomena that relate to any organism or group of organisms. A topic within this field that is particularly interesting to primary-graders is dinosaurs. Equally interesting to children are information books about pets and their care, breeding, and training, as well as the habits, habitats, life cycles, and migrations of wild animals. Ecology and the environment will be of interest and concern to more and more children who recognize the fragility of our global ecology and their responsibility to help protect it from destruction. *A Dinosaur Named Sue: The Story of the Colossal Fossil: The World's Most Complete T. Rex* by Pat Relf is a good example.

A subtopic of biological science that deserves special attention is human anatomy and sexuality. Young children are naturally interested in their bodies, and as they grow into puberty, they become interested in sex. Experts in the field of sex education suggest that honest, straightforward answers to children's questions about their bodies, bodily functions, sex, and sexual orientation are best. Numerous books provide accurate, well-illustrated information on these topics in terms that children and young people can understand. Robie Harris's two books, *It's So Amazing! A Book about Eggs, Sperm, Birth, Babies and Families* and *It's Perfectly Normal: A Book about Changing Bodies, Growing Up, Sex, and Sexual Health,* both illustrated by Michael Emberley, are good examples.

Physical Science

Physical science, sometimes referred to as natural science, deals primarily with nonliving materials. Rocks, landforms, oceans, the stars, and the atmosphere and its weather and seasons are all likely topics that children could learn about within the fields of geology, geography, oceanography, astronomy, and meteorology that comprise the physical sciences. Not only will children be able to satisfy their curiosity about such topics in this category as volcanoes and earthquakes, but teachers will also find the many books about the planets and our solar system helpful in presenting these topics in class. Examples include *Sand,* written by Ellen J. Prager and illustrated by Nancy Woodman, and *Blizzard! The Storm That Changed America* by Jim Murphy.

Social Science

Social science deals with the institutions and functioning of human society and the interpersonal relationships of individuals as members of society. Through books in this field children can learn about various forms of government, religions, different countries and their cultures, money, and transportation. Most children have a natural interest in books about careers, family relationships, and leisure activities and will appreciate finding answers to their questions without always having to ask an adult. An example is *Kids on Strike* by Susan Bartoletti.

Applied Science

Applied science deals with the practical applications of pure science that people have devised. All machines, for example—from simple levers to supercomputers, from bicycles to space rockets—are part of this field, and many children are naturally interested in finding out how they work. Interest in the applied sciences can be developed in children by pointing out how their lives are affected by these applications. For example, children get sick, and medicine helps to cure them. How? Children get hungry, and food appears. What are the processes by which the food is produced, prepared, packaged, and marketed? Children like toys and buy them in stores. Who designs the toys and how are they manufactured? The answers to questions like these can be found in today's nonfictional literature. For example, see *The Way Things Work* by David Macaulay and *The Longitude Prize* by Joan Dash, illustrated by Dušan Petricic.

A specific type of book within the applied sciences—the experiment or how-to book—capitalizes on children's natural curiosity and fondness for hands-on activities. Its contents range from directions for conducting various scientific experiments to cookbooks, guides to hobbies, and directions for small construction projects, like clubhouses. For example, see *How to Make a Chemical Volcano and Other Mysterious Experiments* by Alan Kramer.

Humanities

The humanities deal with the branches of learning that primarily have a cultural or artistic character. Of greatest interest to children and their teachers are books about the fine arts of drawing, painting, and sculpture; the performing arts of singing, dancing, making instrumental music, and acting; and handicrafts of all sorts. Since many children are artistically creative and often study dance, music, and drawing, they can be led to read about the arts and artists to learn new techniques or to draw inspiration from the experiences of others. Some might read these books to decide whether they are interested in trying to develop their artistic talents. Some books make the arts more accessible or real to children by explaining what to look for in paintings or an opera, for example, or by revealing the hard work required of an artist to achieve a spectacular performance or an intriguing work of art. Examples include *What Do Illustrators Do?* by Eileen Christelow and *i see the rhythm* by Toyomi Igus, illustrated by Michele Wood.

Today's nonfictional literature for children is able to meet the needs and interests of young readers in quality, variety, and reader appeal. With these books, children's appetites for learning can be fed while their curiosity for more information is piqued.

NOTABLE *AUTHORS OF NONFICTION*

Franklyn Branley, originator of the science concept picture book.

Joanna Cole, author of a variety of informational books for beginning independent readers. Magic School Bus series.

Russell Freedman, author of biographies of famous Americans and of informational books about U.S. history. *Lincoln: A Photobiography; Children of the Wild West.*

Jean Fritz, biographer of political leaders during the U.S. Revolutionary War era. *Can't You Make Them Behave, King George?; And Then What Happened, Paul Revere?*

Gail Gibbons, author/illustrator of numerous informational books for the 5- to 7-year-old that explain how everyday things work or get done. *The Post Office Book; Recycle: A Handbook for Kids.*

James Cross Giblin, author of informational books about the social implications of cultural developments and inventions. *From Hand to Mouth: Or, How We Invented Knives, Forks, and Spoons and the Tablemanners to Go with Them; When Plague Strikes: The Black Death, Smallpox, AIDS.*

Jan Greenberg and Sandra Jordan, coauthors of several biographies about renowned artists and their works. *Vincent Van Gogh: Portrait of an Artist; Chuck Close, Up Close; Action Jackson.*

David Macaulay, author/illustrator of several books of faction about construction of monumental buildings and informational picture books for older readers. *Cathedral; Building Big.*

Jim Murphy, author of informational chapter books about events in United States history. *Across America on an Emigrant Train; The Great Fire.*

Laurence Pringle, author of many informational books that express concern for the environment. *Vanishing Ozone: Protecting Earth from Ultraviolet Radiation.*

Seymour Simon, author of over 100 science-related books that often contain practical activities. The Planets series; *The Brain: Our Nervous System.*

Diane Stanley, author/illustrator of picture book biographies for older readers. *Leonardo da Vinci; Joan of Arc.*

REFERENCES

Campbell, J. R., Kapinus, B., & Beatty, A. S. (1995). Interviewing children about their literacy experiences. Data from NAEP's integrated reading performance record at grade 4. Washington, D.C.: U.S. Department of Education.

Colman, P. (1999). Nonfiction is literature, too. *The New Advocate, 12*(3), 215–223.

Duke, N. K. (2000). 3.6 minutes a day: The scarcity of informational texts in first grade. *Reading Research Quarterly, 35*(2), 202–225.

Elleman, Barbara. (1987). Current trends in literature for children. *Library Trends, 35*(3), 413–426.

Freedman, Russell. (1988). Newbery Medal acceptance. *The Horn Book, 64*(4), 444–451.

Jansen, Mogens. (1987). *A little about language, words, and concepts—Or what may happen when children learn to read.* Translated by Lotte Rosbak Juhl. Dragör, Denmark: Landsforeningen af Læsepædagoger.

Moss, B., & Hendershot, J. (2002). Exploring sixth graders' selection of nonfiction trade books. *The Reading Teacher, 56*(1), 6–17.

Mullis, I. V. S., Martin, M. O., Gonzalez, E. J., & Kennedy, A. M. (2003). *PIRLS 2001 international report: IEA's study of reading literacy achievement in primary schools.* Chesnut Hill, MA: Boston College.

Untermeyer, Louis. (1985). Questions at night. In L. Untermeyer (Selector), *Rainbow in the Sky.* San Diego: Harcourt.

RECOMMENDED NONFICTION BOOKS

Ages refer to approximate reading levels. YA = young adult readers. Biography is organized by historical era as in Chapter 8.

BIOGRAPHY

Civilizations of the Ancient World, 3000 B.C. to A.D. 600

Demi. *Muhammed.* Simon & Schuster, 2003. Ages 8–13. (picture book)

Lasker, Joe. *The Great Alexander the Great.* Viking, 1983. Ages 7–9.

Lasky, Kathryn. *The Librarian Who Measured the Earth.* Illustrated by Kevin Hawkes. Little, Brown, 1994. Ages 7–10.

Civilizations of the Medieval World, 600 to 1500

Meltzer, Milton. *Columbus and the World around Him.* Watts. 1990. Ages 12–YA.

Poole, Josephine. *Joan of Arc.* Illustrated by Angela Barrett. Knopf, 1998. Ages 7–11.

Sís, Peter. *Starry Messenger.* Farrar, 1996. Ages 9–14.

Stanley, Diane. *Joan of Arc.* Morrow, 1998. Ages 11–14.

———. *Leonardo da Vinci.* Morrow, 1996. Ages 9–13.

The Emergence of Modern Nations, 1500 to 1800

Adler, David A. *B. Franklin, Printer.* Holiday, 2001. Ages 9–13.

Aliki. *The King's Day: King Louis XIV of France.* Crowell, 1989. Ages 7–9.

Anderson, M. T. *Handel, Who Knew What He Liked.* Illustrated by Kevin Hawkes. Candlewick, 2001. Ages 8–12. (picture book)

Aronson, Marc. *Sir Walter Ralegh and the Quest for El Dorado.* Clarion, 2000. Ages 12–YA.

Bober, Natalie S. *Abigail Adams: Witness to a Revolution.* Atheneum, 1995. Ages 11–YA.

Fleming, Candace. *Ben Franklin's Almanac: Being a True Account of the Good Gentleman's Life.* Atheneum, 2003. Ages 11–14.

Freedman, Russell. *Confucius: The Golden Rule.* Illustrated by Frédéric Clément. Scholastic, 2002. Ages 9–14. (picture book for older readers)

Fritz, Jean. *And Then What Happened, Paul Revere?* Illustrated by Tomie dePaola. Coward/McCann, 1973. Ages 8–10.

———. *Can't You Make Them Behave, King George?* Illustrated by Tomie dePaola. Coward/McCann, 1976. Ages 8–10.

————. *The Double Life of Pocahontas.* Illustrated by Ed Young. Putnam, 1983. Ages 8–10.

————. *The Great Little Madison.* Putnam, 1989. Ages 9–12.

————. *Traitor: The Case of Benedict Arnold.* Putnam, 1981. Ages 9–12.

————. *What's the Big Idea, Ben Franklin?* Illustrated by Margot Tomes. Coward/McCann,1978. Ages 8–10.

————. *Where Do You Think You're Going, Christopher Columbus?* Illustrated by Margot Tomes. Putnam, 1980. Ages 8–10.

————. *Where Was Patrick Henry on the 29th of May?* Illustrated by Margot Tomes. Coward/McCann, 1975. Ages 8–10.

————. *Why Don't You Get a Horse, Sam Adams?* Illustrated by Trina Schart Hyman. Coward/McCann, 1974. Ages 8–10.

————. *Will You Sign Here, John Hancock?* Illustrated by Trina Schart Hyman. Coward/McCann, 1976. Ages 8–10.

Giblin, James Cross. *The Amazing Life of Benjamin Franklin.* Illustrated by Michael Dooling. Scholastic, 2000. Ages 8–11.

————. *George Washington: A Picture Book Biography.* Illustrated by Michael Dooling. Scholastic, 1992. Ages 7–10.

————. *Thomas Jefferson: A Picture Book Biography.* Illustrated by Michael Dooling. Scholastic, 1994. Ages 8–10.

Lasky, Kathryn. *The Man Who Made Time Travel.* Illustrated by Kevin Hawkes. Farrar, 2003. Ages 8–12. (picture book for older readers)

Lyons, Mary E. *Letters from a Slave Girl: The Story of Harriet Jacobs.* Scribner's, 1992. Ages 10–14.

Marrin, Albert. *George Washington and the Founding of a Nation.* Dutton, 2001. Ages 11–YA.

————. *The Sea King: Sir Francis Drake and His Times.* Atheneum, 1995. Ages 11–YA.

Meltzer, Milton. *Thomas Jefferson: The Revolutionary Aristocrat.* Watts, 1991. Ages 12–YA.

Rosen, Michael. *Shakespeare: His Work and His World.* Candlewick, 2001. Ages 10–14.

Stanley, Diane. *Michelangelo.* HarperCollins, 2000. Ages 9–14. (picture book for older readers)

————. *Saladin: Noble Prince of Islam.* HarperCollins, 2002. Ages 9–14. (picture book for older readers)

Stanley, Diane, and Peter Vennema. *Bard of Avon: The Story of William Shakespeare.* Illustrated by Diane Stanley. Morrow, 1992. Ages 8–13.

————. *Good Queen Bess: The Story of Elizabeth I of England.* Four Winds, 1990. Ages 8–10.

The Development of Industrial Society, 1800 to 1914

Adler, David A. *America's Champion Swimmer: Gertrude Ederle.* Illustrated by Terry Widener. Harcourt, 2000. Ages 6–10.

Blumberg, Rhoda. *Commodore Perry in the Land of the Shogun.* Lothrop, 1985. Ages 9–12.

————. *The Incredible Journey of Lewis and Clark.* Lothrop, 1987. Ages 9–12.

————. *Shipwrecked! The True Adventures of a Japanese Boy.* HarperCollins, 2001. Ages 10–14.

Borden, Louise. *A. Lincoln and Me.* Illustrated by Ted Lewin. Scholastic, 1999. Ages 5–8.

Brown, Don. *Uncommon Traveler: Mary Kingsley in Africa.* Houghton, 2000. Ages 7–10.

Cohn, Amy L., and Suzy Schmidt. *Abraham Lincoln.* Illustrated by David A. Johnson. Scholastic, 2002. Ages 7–11. (picture book)

d'Aulaire, Ingri, and Edgar Parin d'Aulaire. *Abraham Lincoln.* Doubleday, 1939, 1957. Ages 7–9.

Fradin, Dennis B., and Judith B. Fradin. *Ida B. Wells: Mother of the Civil Rights Movement.* Clarion, 2000. Ages 10–YA.

Freedman, Russell. *Indian Chiefs.* Holiday, 1987. Ages 9–12.

————. *The Life and Death of Crazy Horse.* Holiday, 1996. Ages 9–12.

————. *Lincoln: A Photobiography.* Clarion, 1987. Ages 9–12.

————. *Out of Darkness: The Story of Louis Braille.* Illustrated by Kate Kiesler. Clarion, 1997. Ages 8–10.

————. *The Wright Brothers: How They Invented the Airplane.* Holiday, 1991. Ages 9–12.

Fritz, Jean. *You Want Women to Vote, Lizzie Stanton?* Illustrated by DyAnne DiSalvo-Ryan. Putnam, 1995. Ages 8–11.

Greenberg, Jan, and Sandra Jordan. *Vincent Van Gogh: Portrait of an Artist.* Delacorte, 2001. Ages 10–YA.

Hamilton, Virginia. *Many Thousand Gone: African Americans from Slavery to Freedom.* Illustrated by Leo and Diane Dillon. Random, 1993. Ages 10–14.

Hopkinson, Deborah. *Fannie in the Kitchen: The Whole Story from Soup to Nuts of How Fannie Farmer Invented Recipes with Precise Measurements.* Illustrated by Nancy Carpenter. Atheneum, 2001. Ages 6–8. (picture book)

Kraft, Betsy H. *Theodore Roosevelt: Champion of the American Spirit.* Clarion, 2003. Ages 10–14.

Krull, Kathleen. *Lives of the Musicians: Good Times, Bad Times (and What the Neighbors Thought).* Harcourt, 1993. Ages 8–10.

———. *Lives of the Writers: Comedies, Tragedies (and What the Neighbors Thought).* Illustrated by Kathryn Hewitt. Harcourt, 1994. Ages 8–10.

Lasky, Kathryn. *Vision of Beauty: The Story of Virginia Breedlove Walker.* Illustrated by Nneka Bennett. Candlewick, 2000. Ages 8–11.

Marrin, Albert. *Sitting Bull and His World.* Dutton, 2000. Ages 11–YA.

Meltzer, Milton, editor. *Frederick Douglass: In His Own Words.* Illustrated by Stephen Alcorn. Harcourt, 1995. Ages 12–14.

———. *Lincoln: In His Own Words.* Illustrated by Stephen Alcorn. Harcourt, 1993. Ages 10–14.

Provensen, Alice, and Martin Provensen. *The Glorious Flight: Across the Channel with Louis Blériot.* Viking, 1983. Ages 5–8.

Old, Wendie C. *To Fly: The Story of the Wright Brothers.* Illustrated by Robert Andrew Parker. Clarion, 2002. Ages 8–11. (picture book)

Reef, Catherine. *Walt Whitman.* Clarion, 1995. Ages 11–14.

Reich, Susanna. *Clara Schumann: Piano Virtuoso.* Clarion, 1999. Ages 10–YA.

Sís, Peter. *The Tree of Life.* Farrar, 2003. Ages 12–YA. (Charles Darwin) (picture book for older readers)

Stanley, Diane, and Peter Vennema. *Charles Dickens: The Man Who Had Great Expectations.* Illustrated by Diane Stanley. Morrow, 1993. Ages 9–12.

Wilson, Janet. *The Ingenious Mr. Peale: Painter, Patriot, and Man of Science.* Atheneum, 1996. Ages 11–14.

World Wars of the Twentieth Century, 1914 to 1945

Adler, David A. *Lou Gehrig: The Luckiest Man.* Illustrated by Terry Widener. Harcourt, 1997. Ages 8–11.

———. *A Picture Book of Eleanor Roosevelt.* Holiday, 1991. Ages 6–8. (See others in the First Biographies series.)

Anderson, M. T. *Strange Mr. Satie.* Illustrated by Petra Mathers. Viking, 2003. Ages 8–12. (picture book)

Bausum, Ana. *Dragon Bones and Dinosaur Eggs: A Photobiography of Explorer Roy Chapman Andrews.* National Geographic, 2000. Ages 9–YA.

Britton-Jackson, Livia. *I Have Lived a Thousand Years: Growing Up in the Holocaust.* Simon & Schuster, 1997. Ages 12–YA.

Brown, Don. *Mack Made Movies.* Millbrook, 2003. Ages 6–10. (picture book)

Burleigh, Robert. *Home Run: The Story of Babe Ruth.* Illustrated by Mike Wimmer. Silver Whistle/ Harcourt, 1998. Ages 7–11.

Christensen, Bonnie. *Woody Guthrie: Poet of the People.* Knopf, 2001. Ages 6–8. (picture book)

Cline-Ransome, Lesa. *Satchel Paige.* Illustrated by James Ransome. Simon & Schuster, 2000. Ages 7–10.

dePaola, Tomie. *26 Fairmount Avenue.* Putnam, 1999. Ages 7–9.

Freedman, Russell. *Eleanor Roosevelt: A Life of Discovery.* Clarion, 1993. Ages 9–12.

———. *Franklin Delano Roosevelt.* Clarion, 1990. Ages 9–12.

Giblin, James C. *Charles A. Lindbergh: A Human Hero.* Clarion, 1997. Ages 9–14.

———. *The Life and Death of Adolf Hitler.* Clarion, 2002. Ages 13–YA.

Grimes, Nikki. *Talkin' about Bessie: The Story of Aviator Elizabeth Coleman.* Illustrated by E. B. Lewis. Scholastic/Orchard, 2002. Ages 7–10.

Jiménez, Francisco. *Breaking Through.* Houghton, 2001. Ages 11–14. (autobiography)

Kraft, Betsy H. *Mother Jones: One Woman's Fight for Labor.* Clarion, 1995. Ages 10–14.

Lyons, Mary E. *Sorrow's Kitchen: The Life and Folklore of Zora Neale Hurston.* Scribner's, 1990. Ages 12–YA.

Martin, Jacqueline Briggs. *Snowflake Bentley.* Illustrated by Mary Azarian. Houghton, 1998. Ages 6–9.

Maurer, Richard. *The Wright Sister.* Millbrook, 2003. Ages 12–YA.

Nelson, Marilyn. *Carver: A Life in Poems.* Front Street, 2000. Ages 12–YA.

Partridge, Elizabeth. *Restless Spirit: The Life and Work of Dorothea Lange.* Viking, 1998. Ages 11–YA.

———. *This Land Was Made for You and Me: The Life and Songs of Woody Guthrie.* Viking, 2002. Ages 11–YA.

Rabinovici, Schoschana. *Thanks to My Mother.* Translated from German by James Skofield. Dial, 1998. Ages 10–14.

Ryan, Pam Muñoz. *When Marian Sang: The True Recital of Marian Anderson.* Illustrated by Brian Selznick. Scholastic, 2002. Ages 6–10. (picture book)

Severance, John B. *Winston Churchill: Soldier, Statesman, Artist.* Clarion, 1996. Ages 10–14.

van der Rol, Ruud, and Rian Verhoeven. *Anne Frank: Beyond the Diary: A Photographic Remembrance.* Translated by Tony Langham and Plym Peters. Viking, 1993. Ages 10–YA.

Wells, Rosemary. *Mary on Horseback: Three Mountain Stories.* Illustrated by Peter McCarty. Dial, 1998. ages 7–11.

Post–World War II Era, 1945 to 2000

Adler, David. A. *A Picture Book of Dwight David Eisenhower.* Holiday, 2002. Ages 7–9.

Andryszewski, Tricia. *The Amazing Life of Moe Berg.* Millbrook, 1996. Ages 11–14.

Besson, Jean-Louis. *October '45: Childhood Memories of the War.* Translated by Carol Volk. Creative Editions, 1995. Ages 9–12. (Autobiography)

Bray, Rosemary L. *Martin Luther King.* Illustrated by Malcah Zeldis. Greenwillow, 1995. Ages 7–11.

Bridges, Ruby, and Margo Lundell. *Through My Eyes.* Scholastic, 1999. Ages 9–YA.

Cleary, Beverly. *My Own Two Feet.* Morrow, 1995. Ages 8–11.

Coerr, Eleanor. *Sadako.* Illustrated by Ed Young. Putnam, 1993. Ages 8–12.

Freedman, Russell. *Babe Didrikson Zaharias: The Making of a Champion.* Clarion, 1999. Ages 10–YA.

———. *Martha Graham: A Dancer's Life.* Clarion, 1998. Ages 10–YA.

Gantos, Jack. *Hole in My Life.* Farrar, 2002. YA (Autobiography)

Golenbock, Peter. *Teammates.* Illustrated by Paul Bacon. Harcourt, 1990. Ages 7–9.

Govenar, Alan B. *Osceola: Memories of a Sharecropper's Daughter.* Illustrated by Shane W. Evans. Jump at the Sun, 2000. Ages 8–12.

Greenberg, Jan, and Sandra Jordan. *Action Jackson.* Illustrated by Robert Andrew Parker. Millbrook, 2002. Ages 7–10. (Picture book)

———. *Chuck Close, Up Close.* DK Ink, 1998. Ages 10–14.

———. *Frank O. Gehry: Outside In.* DK Ink, 2000. Ages 9–YA.

———. *Runaway Girl: The Artist Louise Bourgeois.* Abrams, 2003. Ages 12–YA.

Hearne, Betsy. *Seven Brave Women.* Illustrated by Bethanne Andersen. Greenwillow, 1997. Ages 5–9.

Lobel, Anita. *No Pretty Pictures: A Child of War.* Greenwillow, 1998. Ages 12–YA. (Autobiography)

Niven, Penelope. *Carl Sandburg: Adventures of a Poet.* Illustrated by Marc Nadel. Harcourt, 2003. Ages 7–11. (Picture book)

Pinkney, Andrea Davis. *Duke Ellington: The Piano Prince and His Orchestra.* Ilustrated by Brian Pinkney. Hyperion, 1998. Ages 8–11.

Rappaport, Doreen. *Martin's Big Words: The Life of Dr. Martin Luther King, Jr.* Illustrated by Bryan Collier. Hyperion, 2001. Ages 8–10. (Picture book)

Raschka, Chris. *Mysterious Thelonious.* Orchard, 1997. Ages 5–8.

Rembert, Winfred. *Don't Hold Me Back: My Life and Art.* Cricket, 2003. Ages 9–13. (Autobiographical picture book)

Ringgold, Faith. *If a Bus Could Talk: The Story of Rosa Parks.* Simon & Schuster, 1999. Ages 5–9.

Winter, Jeanette. *My Name Is Georgia: A Portrait.* Harcourt, 1998. Ages 5–8.

INFORMATIONAL BOOKS

Biological Science

Aliki. *Wild and Woolly Mammoths.* HarperCollins, 1996. Ages 5–8.

Arnold, Caroline. *On the Brink of Extinction: The California Condor.* Photos by Michael Wallace. Harcourt, 1993. Ages 9–11.

Arnosky, Jim. *All about Owls.* Scholastic, 1995. Ages 7–9.

Bischhoff-Miersch, Andrea and Michael. *Do You Know the Difference?* Illustrated by Christine Faltermayr. North-South, 1995. Ages 7–10.

Bishop Nic. *Digging for Bird Dinosaurs: An Expedition to Madagascar.* Houghton, 2000. Ages 9–YA.

———. *The Secrets of Animal Flight.* Photography by the author. Illustrated by Amy B. Wright. Houghton, 1997. Ages 8–11.

Brandenburg, Jim. Edited by Joann Bren Guernsey. *To the Top of the World: Adventures with Arctic Wolves.* Walker, 1993. Ages 9–YA.

Brenner, Barbara, and Julia Takaya. *Chibi: A True Story from Japan.* Illustrated by June Otani. Clarion, 1996. Ages 7–9.

Cerullo, Mary M. *The Octopus: Phantom of the Sea.* Photography by Jeffrey L. Rotman. Cobblehill, 1997. Ages 10–14.

Cole, Henry. *Jack's Garden.* Morrow, 1995. Ages 5–9.

Cole, Joanna. *Evolution.* Illustrated by Aliki. Crowell, 1990. Ages 6–8.

———. *How You Were Born.* (rev. ed.). Photos by Margaret Miller. Morrow, 1993. Ages 5–8.

———. *The Magic Schoolbus: Inside the Human Body.* Illustrated by Bruce Degen. Scholastic, 1989. Ages 7–9.

Cowley, Joy. *Red-Eyed Tree Frog.* Photographs by Nic Bishop. Scholastic, 1999. Ages 6–9.

Deem, James M. *Bodies from the Bog.* Houghton, 1998. Ages 9–YA.

Fleischman, John. *Phineas Gage: A Gruesome but True Story about Brain Science.* Houghton, 2002. Ages 12–14.

Gamlin, Linda. *Eyewitness Science: Evolution.* DK Publishing, 2000. Ages 8–12.

George, Jean C. *Everglades.* Illustrated by Wendell Minor. HarperCollins, 1995. Ages 7–11.

Gibbons, Gail. *Spiders.* Holiday, 1993.

Gomi, Taro. *Everyone Poops.* Translated by Amanda M. Stinchecum. Kane/Miller, 1993. (See others in the *My Body Science* series: *The Gas We Pass: The Story of Farts; The Holes in Your Nose; Contemplating Your Bellybutton; All About Scabs; The Soles of Your Feet*). Ages 2–5.

Goodman, Susan E. *Bats, Bugs, and Biodiversity: Adventures in the Amazonian Rain Forest.* Photography by Michael J. Doolittle. Atheneum, 1995. Ages 9–12.

Harris, Robie H. *It's Perfectly Normal: A Book about Changing Bodies, Growing Up, Sex, and Sexual Health.* Illustrated by Michael Emberley. Candlewick, 1994. Ages 11–14.

———. *It's So Amazing! A Book about Eggs, Sperm, Birth, Babies and Families.* Illustrated by Michael Emberley. Candlewick, 1999. Ages 7–12.

Hawcock, David. *The Amazing Pull-Out Pop-Up Body in a Book.* DK Publishing, 1997. Ages 6–12.

Hoyt-Goldsmith, Diane. *Buffalo Days.* Illustrated by Lawrence Migdale. Holiday, 1997. Ages 7–10.

Jenkins, Steve. *Life on Earth: The Story of Evolution.* Houghton, 2002. Ages 8–11. (picture book)

Jenkins, Steve, and Robin Page. *What Do You Do with a Tail Like This?* Houghton, 2003. Ages 4–7. (picture book)

Kitzinger, Sheila. *Being Born.* Photographs by Lennart Nilsson. Grosset, 1986. Ages 6–YA.

Kurlansky, Mark. *The Cod's Tale.* Illustrated by S. D. Schindler. Penguin, 2001. Ages 8–12. (picture book for older readers)

Lasky, Kathryn. *The Most Beautiful Roof in the World: Exploring the Rainforest Canopy.* Illustrated by Christopher G. Knight. Harcourt, 1997. Ages 8–10.

Lauber, Patricia. *Fur, Feathers, and Flippers: How Animals Live Where They Do.* Scholastic, 1994. Ages 8–12.

Lewin, Ted, and Betsy Lewin. *Gorilla Walk.* Lothrop, 1999. Ages 9–YA.

Markle, Sandra. *Outside and Inside Snakes.* Macmillan, 1995. Ages 9–11.

Martin, James. *Hiding Out: Camouflage in the Wild.* Illustrated by Art Wolfe. Crown, 1993. Ages 8–10.

Micucci, Charles. *The Life and Times of the Honeybee.* Ticknor & Fields, 1995. Ages 7–9.

Morrison, Gordon. *Oak Tree.* Houghton, 2000.

Pringle, Laurence. *Vanishing Ozone: Protecting Earth from Ultraviolet Radiation.* Morrow, 1995. Ages 9–12.

Relf, Pat. *A Dinosaur Named Sue: The Story of the Colossal Fossil: The World's Most Complete T. Rex.* Scholastic, 2000. Ages 12–14.

Walker, Sally M. *Fossil Fish Found Alive: Discovering the Coelacanth.* Carolrhoda, 2002. Ages 10–13.

Physical Science

Ardley, Neil. *The Science Book of Sound.* Harcourt, 1991. Ages 4–8.

Arnosky, Jim. *Wild and Swampy.* HarperCollins, 2000. Ages 7–10. (Picture book)

Branley, Franklyn M. *Down Comes the Rain.* Illustrated by James G. Hale. HarperCollins, 1997. Ages 6–8. (picture book)

————. *Eclipse: Darkness in Daytime.* (rev. ed.). Illustrated by Donald Crews. Crowell, 1988. Ages 6–8.

————. *The Planets in Our Solar System.* Illustrated by Kevin O'Malley. HarperCollins, 1998. Ages 6–8. (picture book)

Cole, Joanna. *The Magic Schoolbus: Inside the Earth.* Illustrated by Bruce Degen. Scholastic, 1987. Ages 7–9.

————. *The Magic Schoolbus: Lost in the Solar System.* Illustrated by Bruce Degen. Scholastic, 1990. Ages 7–9.

Dunphy, Madeleine. *Here Is the Arctic Winter.* Illustrated by Alan J. Robinson. Hyperion, 1993. Ages 6–8.

Elkington, John, Julia Hailes, Douglas Hill, and Joel Makower. *Going Green: A Kid's Handbook to Saving the Planet.* Illustrated by Tony Ross. Puffin, 1990. Ages 8–12.

Fraser, Mary Ann. *In Search of the Grand Canyon: Down the Colorado with John Wesley Powell.* Holt, 1995. Ages 8–11.

Gibbons, Gail. *Weather Words and What They Mean.* Holiday, 1990. Ages 6–8.

Hirst, Robin, and Sally Hirst. *My Place in Space.* Illustrated by Roland Harvey with Joe Levine. Orchard, 1988. Ages 9–13.

Krupp, E. C. *The Rainbow and You.* Illustrated by R. Krupp. HarperCollins, 2000. Ages 5–7.

Murphy, Jim. *Blizzard!: The Storm That Changed America.* Scholastic, 2000. Ages 10–14.

Prager, Ellen J. *Sand.* Illustrated by Nancy Woodman. National Geographic, 2000. Ages 4–8.

Pringle, Laurence. *Global Warming: Assessing the Greenhouse Threat.* Arcade, 1990. Ages 7–9.

Simon, Seymour. *The Brain: Our Nervous System.* Morrow, 1997. Ages 9–12.

————. *Jupiter.* Morrow, 1985. Ages 8–10. (Others in The Planets series: *Mars,* 1987; *Saturn,* 1985; *Uranus,* 1987.)

————. *Our Solar System.* Morrow, 1992. Ages 8–11.

————. *The Stars.* Morrow, 1986. Ages 8–10.

————. *Storms.* Morrow, 1989. Ages 8–10.

————. *The Sun.* Morrow, 1986. Ages 8–10.

————. *Volcanoes.* Morrow, 1988. Ages 8–10.

Skurzynski, Gloria. *Waves: The Electromagnetic Universe.* National Geographic, 1996. Ages 8–12.

Tanaka, Shelley. *The Buried City of Pompeii.* Illustrated by Greg Ruhl. Disney, 1997. Ages 10–13. (picture book for older readers)

Tripp, Nathaniel. *Thunderstorm!* Illustrated by Juan Wijngaard. Dial, 1994. Ages 8–10.

Walker, Sally M. *Earthquakes.* Carolrhoda, 1996. Ages 9–12.

————. *Volcanoes: Earth's Inner Fire.* Carolrhoda, 1994. Ages 9–12.

Wick, Walter. *A Drop of Water: A Book of Science and Wonder.* Scholastic, 1997. Ages 8–11.

Zoehfeld, Kathleen, W. *How Mountains Are Made.* Illustrated by James G. Hale. HarperCollins, 1995. Ages 7–9.

Social Science

Aliki. *Communication.* Greenwillow, 1993. Ages 7–9.

————. *A Medieval Feast.* Crowell, 1983. Ages 8–10.

Ambrose, Stephen E. *The Good Fight: How World War II Was Won.* Atheneum, 2001. Ages 11–14.

Ancona, George. *Barrio: José's Neighborhood.* Harcourt, 1998. Ages 8–10.

————. *Charro: The Mexican Cowboy.* Harcourt, 1999. Ages 8–10.

Armstrong, Jennifer. *Shipwreck at the Bottom of the World: The Extraordinary True Story of Shackleton and the Endurance.* Crown, 1998. Ages 10–YA.

Atkin, S. Beth. *Voices from the Fields: Children of Migrant Farmworkers Tell Their Stories.* Little, Brown, 1993. Ages 8–12.

Baer, Edith. *This Is the Way We Go to School: A Book about Children around the World.* Illustrated by Steve Bjorkman. Scholastic, 1990. Ages 6–10.

Bartoletti, Susan Campbell. *Black Potatoes: The Story of the Great Irish Famine, 1845–1850.* Houghton, 2001. Ages 12–YA.

————. *Growing Up in Coal Country.* Houghton, 1996. Ages 9–11.

————. *Kids on Strike.* Houghton, 1999. Ages 11–16.

Bash, Barbara. *In the Heart of the Village: The World of the Indian Banyan Tree.* Sierra Club, 1996. Ages 8–11.

Bial, Raymond. *Tenement: Immigrant Life on the Lower East Side.* Houghton, 2002. Ages 9–14.

Blumberg, Rhoda. *Full Steam Ahead: The Race to Build a Transcontinental Railroad.* National Geographic, 1996. Ages 9–12.

————. *The Great American Gold Rush.* Bradbury, 1989. Ages 9–12.

————. *The Incredible Journey of Lewis and Clark.* Lothrop, 1987. Ages 9–12.

Bober, Natalie S. *Countdown to Independence: A Revolution of Ideas in England and Her American Colonies: 1760–1776.* Atheneum, 2001. Ages 12–YA.

Burns, Khephra, and William Miles. *Black Stars in Orbit: NASA's African American Astronauts.* Harcourt, 1995. Ages 12–14.

Chandra, Deborah, and Madeline Comora. *George Washington's Teeth.* Illustrated by Brock Cole. Farrar, 2003. Ages 5–8. (picture book)

Cherry, Lynn. *A River Ran Wild: An Environmental History.* Gulliver, 1992. Ages 6–10. (picture book)

Coleman, Penny. *Rosie the Riveter: Women Working on the Home Front in World War II.* Crown, 1995. Ages 12–14.

Franklin, Kristine L., and Nancy McGirr, editors. *Out of the Dump: Writings and Photographs by Children from Guatemala.* Translated by Kristine L. Franklin. Lothrop, 1996. Ages 8–13.

Freedman, Russell. *Children of the Wild West.* Illustrated by George Buctel. Clarion, 1982. Ages 8–11.

————. *In Defense of Liberty: The Story of America's Bill of Rights.* Holiday, 2003. Ages 10–14.

————. *An Indian Winter.* Illustrated by Karl Bodmer. Holiday, 1992. Ages 11–14.

————. *Kids at Work: Lewis Hine and the Crusade against Child Labor.* Photos by Lewis Hine. Clarion, 1994. Ages 9–12.

Gaskins, Pearl Fuyo. *What Are You? Voices of Mixed-Race Young People.* Holt, 1999. Ages 13–YA.

Gerstein, Mordicai. *The Wild Boy.* Foster/Farrar, 1998. Ages 7–9.

Gibbons, Gail. *My Baseball Book.* HarperCollins, 2000. Ages 4–8.

————. *The Post Office Book: Mail and How It Moves.* HarperCollins, 1987. Ages 4–8.

————. *Recycle: A Handbook for Kids.* Little, Brown, 1996. Ages 4–8.

Giblin, James Cross. *From Hand to Mouth: Or, How We Invented Knives, Fork, and Spoons and the Tablemanners to Go with Them.* Harper, 1987. Agest 6–10.

————. *When Plague Strikes: The Black Death, Smallpox, AIDS.* Illustrated by David Frampton. HarperCollins, 1995. Ages 12–YA.

Goodman, Joan Elizabeth. *A Long and Uncertain Journey: The 27,000-Mile Voyage of Vasco da Gama.* Illustrated by Tom McNeely. Mikaya/Firefly, 2001. Ages 11–14. (picture book)

Greenfield, Howard. *After the Holocaust.* Greenwillow, 2001. Ages 12–YA. (oral histories)

The Guinness Book of World Records. Guinness Media, Inc. Published annually. Ages 7–13.

Handler, Andrew, and Susan Meschel. *Young People Speak: Surviving the Holocaust in Hungary.* Watts, 1993. Ages 10–14.

Haskins, Jim. *Get on Board: The Story of the Underground Railroad.* Scholastic, 1993. Ages 10–14.

Hinds, Kathryn. *The City.* Cavendish, 2000. (See others in Life in the Middle Ages series.) Ages 11–14.

Hinojosa, Maria. *Crews: Gang Members Talk to Maria Hinojosa.* Photography by German Perez. Harcourt, 1995. Ages 14–YA.

Hoose, Phillip. *We Were There, Too! Young People in U.S. History.* Farrar, 2001. Ages 10–13.

Hopkinson, Deborah. *Shutting Out the Sky: Life in the Tenements of New York 1880–1924.* Scholastic, 2003. Ages 11–14.

Jenkins, Steve. *Biggest, Strongest, Fastest.* Ticknor & Fields, 1995. Ages 5–7.

———. *The Top of the World: Climbing Mount Everest.* Houghton, 1999. Ages 9–12.

———. *What Do You Do When Something Wants to Eat You?* Houghton, 1997. Ages 4–8.

Jukes, Mavis. *It's a Girl Thing: How to Stay Healthy, Safe, and in Charge.* Illustrated by Debbie Tilley. Knopf, 1996. Ages 10–14.

Kalman, Maira. *Fireboat: The Heroic Adventures of the John J. Harvey.* Putnam, 2002. Ages 6–8. (picture book)

Kenna, Kathleen. *A People Apart.* Houghton, 1995. Ages 9–11.

Kimmel, Eric. *Bar Mitzvah: A Jewish Boy's Coming of Age.* Illustrated by Erika Weihs. Viking, 1995. Ages 11–14.

Knight, Amelia Stewart. Adapted by Lillian Schlissel. *The Way West: Journal of a Pioneer Woman.* Illustrated by Michael McCurdy. Simon & Schuster, 1993. Ages 7–12.

Kroll, Steven. *Pony Express!* Illustrated by Dan Andreason. Scholastic, 1996. Ages 6–9.

Lauber, Patricia. *Who Came First? New Clues to Prehistoric Americans.* National Geographic, 2003. Ages 10–14.

Lester, Julius. *To Be a Slave.* Dial, 1968. Ages 12–YA.

Martin, Bill, Jr., and Michael Sampson. *I Pledge Allegiance: The Pledge of Allegiance.* Illustrated by Chris Raschka. Candlewick, 2002. Ages 6–9. (picture book)

Marzollo, Jean. *In 1776.* Illustrated by Steve Björkman. Scholastic, 1994. Ages 7–10.

McKee, Tim. *No More Strangers Now: Young Voices from a New South Africa.* Photographs by Anne Blackshaw. DK Ink, 1998. Ages 12–YA.

McKissack, Patricia, and Fredrick McKissack. *The Civil Rights Movement in America from 1865 to the Present.* Childrens Press, 1987. Ages 9–YA.

Meltzer, Milton. *The Amazing Potato: A Story in Which the Incas, Conquistadors, Marie Antoinette, Thomas Jefferson, Wars, Famines, Immigrants, and French Fries All Play a Part.* HarperCollins, 1992. Ages 10–13.

———. *The American Revolutionaries: A History in Their Own Words 1750–1800.* Crowell, 1988. Ages 12–YA.

Miller, Brandon M. *Buffalo Gals: Women of the Old West.* Lerner, 1995. Ages 9–13.

Murphy, Jim. *Across America on an Emigrant Train.* Clarion, 1993. Ages 11–14.

———. *An American Plague: The True and Terrifying Story of the Yellow Fever Epidemic of 1793.* Clarion, 2003. Ages 9–14.

———. *The Boy's War: Confederate and Union Soldiers Talk about the Civil War.* Clarion, 1990. Ages 12–YA.

———. *Gone A-Whaling: The Lure of the Sea and the Hunt for the Great Whale.* Clarion, 1998. Ages 11–YA.

———. *The Great Fire.* Scholastic, 1995. Ages 10–14.

———. *Inside the Alamo.* Delacorte, 2003. Ages 9–14.

———. *A Young Patriot: The American Revolution as Experienced by One Boy.* Clarion, 1996. Ages 10–13.

Onyefulu, Ifeoma. *Ogbu: Sharing Life in an African Village.* Harcourt, 1996. Ages 6–10.

Perl, Lila. *The Great Ancestor Hunt: The Fun of Finding Out Who You Are.* Clarion, 1989. Ages 8–10.

Philbrick, Nathaniel. *Revenge of the Whale: The True Story of the Whaleship Essex.* Putnam, 2002. Ages 12–14.

Priceman, Marjorie. *How to Make an Apple Pie and See the World.* Knopf, 1994. Ages 5–8.

Rhoades, Diane. *Garden Crafts for Kids: 50 Great Reasons to Get Your Hands Dirty.* Sterling, 1995. Ages 8–11.

Rogasky, Barbara. *Smoke and Ashes: The Story of the Holocaust.* Holiday, 1988. Ages 12–YA.

Rogers, Fred. *Let's Talk about It: Adoption.* Illustrated by Jim Judkis. Putnam, 1995. Ages 5–8.

Rounds, Glen. *Sod Houses on the Great Plains.* Holiday, 1995. Ages 5–8.

Scott, Elaine. *Adventure in Space: The Flight to Fix the Hubble.* Photography by Margaret Miller. Hyperion, 1995. Ages 10–14.

Sloan, Christopher. *Bury the Dead: Tombs, Corpses, Mummies, Skeletons and Rituals.* National Geographic, 2002. Ages 10–14.

Stanley, Jerry. *Children of the Dust Bowl: The True Story of the School at Weedpatch.* Crown, 1992. Ages 9–13.

Wilson, Lori Lee. *The Salem Witch Trials.* Lerner, 1997. Ages 11–YA.

Wolf, Bernard. *HIV Positive.* Dutton, 1997. Ages 9–12.

Yue, Charlotte, and David Yue. *The Wigwam and the Longhouse.* Houghton, 2000. Ages 9–YA.

Applied Science

Ardley, Neil. *The Science Book of Machines.* Harcourt, 1992. Ages 9–12.

Branley, Franklyn M. *What Makes a Magnet?* Illustrated by True Kelley. HarperCollins, 1996. Ages 5–8. (picture book)

Curlee, Lynn. *Capital.* Atheneum, 2003. Ages 7–11. (picture book)

Dash Joan. *The Longitude Prize.* Illustrated by Dušan Petricic. Farrar. Ages 6–YA.

Glover, David. *Batteries, Bulbs, and Wires.* Kingfisher, 1993. Ages 8–11. (picture book)

Kramer, Alan. *How to Make a Chemical Volcano and Other Mysterious Experiments.* Franklin Watts, 1989. Ages 8–10.

Levine, Shar, and Leslie Johnstone. *The Magnet Book.* Sterling, 1997. Ages 9–12.

Macaulay, David. *Building Big.* Houghton, 2000. Ages 12–YA.

———. *Castle.* Houghton, 1977. Ages 10–YA.

———. *Cathedral: The Story of Its Construction.* Houghton, 1973. Ages 10–YA.

———. *Mosque.* Houghton, 2003. Ages 12–YA. (picture book for older readers)

———. *The Way Things Work.* Houghton, 1988. Ages 10–YA. [CD-ROM version: Dorling Kindersley, 1995.]

Markle, Sandra. *Measuring Up!: Experiments, Puzzles, and Games Exploring Measurement.* Atheneum, 1995. Ages 9–12.

Maurer, Richard. *Rocket! How a Toy Launched the Space Age.* Crown, 1995. Ages 9–12.

Ross, Val. *The Road to There: Mapmakers and Their Stories.* Tundra, 2003. Ages 12–YA.

Rubin, Susan Goldman. *There Goes the Neighborhood: Ten Buildings People Loved to Hate.* Holiday House, 2001. Ages 12–YA.

Severance, John. *Skyscrapers: How America Grew Up.* Holiday, 2000.

Humanities

Aliki. *Ah, Music!* HarperCollins, 2003. Ages 6–9. (picture book)

———. *William Shakespeare and the Globe.* HarperCollins, 1999. Ages 8–12.

Christelow, Eileen. *What Do Illustrators Do?* Clarion, 1999. Ages 6–10.

Cummings, Pat, compiler-editor. *Talking with Artists,* Vol. 1. Illustrated by various artists. Bradbury, 1992. Ages 8–12. Vol. 2, 1995; Vol. 3, 1999.

Davidson, Rosemary. *Take a Look: An Introduction to the Experience of Art.* Viking, 1994. Ages 8–12.

Fritz, Jean. *Leonardo's Horse.* Illustrated by Hudson Talbot. Putnam, 2001. Ages 9–13.

Hamanaka, Sheila, and Ayano Ohmi. *In Search of the Spirit: The Living National Treasures of Japan.* Morrow, 1999. Ages 10–14.

Igus, Toyomi. *i see the rhythm.* Illustrated by Michele Wood. Children's, 1998. Ages 9–14.

Kehoe, Michael. *A Book Takes Root: The Making of a Picture Book.* Carolrhoda, 1993. Ages 7–9.

Marcus, Leonard S. *A Caldecott Celebration: Six Artists Share Their Paths to the Caldecott Medal.* Walker, 1998. Ages 8–YA.

Monroe, Jean G., and Ray Williamson. *First Houses: Native American Homes and Sacred Structures.* Illustrated by Susan Carlson. Houghton, 1993. Ages 9–12.

Mühlberger, Richard. *What Makes a Van Gogh a Van Gogh?* The Metropolitan Museum of Art/Viking, 1993. (Others in this series: Bruegal, Degas, Monet, Raphael, Rembrandt.) Ages 8–12.

Nichol, Barbara. *Beethoven Lives Upstairs.* Illustrated by Scott Cameron. Orchard, 1994. Ages 8–10.

O'Connor, Jane. *The Emperor's Silent Army: Terracotta Warriors of Ancient China.* Viking, 2002. Ages 9–12.

Swain, Gwenyth. *Bookworks: Making Books by Hand.* Illustrated by Jennifer Hagerman. Photography by Andy King. Carolrhoda, 1995. Ages 8–12.

Thomson, Peggy, and Barbara Moore. *The Nine-Ton Cat: Behind the Scenes at an Art Museum.* Houghton, 1997. Ages 9–14.

Warhola, James. *Uncle Andy's: A Faabbulous Visit with Andy Warhol.* Putnam, 2003. Ages 5–8. (picture book)

MULTICULTURAL *and* INTERNATIONAL LITERATURE

TABLEAU

Locked arm in arm they cross the way,
The black boy and the white,
The golden splendor of the day,
The sable pride of night.

From lowered blinds the dark folk stare,
And here the fair folk talk,
Indignant that these two should dare
In unison to walk.

Oblivious to look and word
They pass, and see no wonder
That lightning brilliant as a sword
Should blaze the path of thunder.

— COUNTEE CULLEN

This chapter is presented in two parts. The first part focuses on literature written about the major racial, religious, and language cultural groups in the United States other than the Euro-American group. The second part focuses on literature written originally for children living in other lands but also read and enjoyed by children in the United States.

According to Banks and Banks (1993), each modern nation-state has a shared core culture—a *macroculture*—and a number of *microcultures* that are part of or integrated into the macroculture to greater or lesser degrees. It must be noted that the western European culture, although traditionally the prevailing culture in the United States, is itself a microculture and not the macroculture. Because the Bankses' schema and nomenclature are inclusive in their emphasis on the contributions of *all* citizens of a country to that country's overarching culture, we have chosen to use their terms in this chapter. We will refer to the western European group as Euro-American.

You will have noted many references to multicultural and international books and authors throughout the previous genre chapters in discussions of trends and issues, notable author and illustrator lists, and end-of-chapter recommended booklists. In an ideal, culturally integrated world, such inclusion would be sufficient. But the groups represented in multicultural literature have, until recently, been totally absent from or misrepresented in books for children. Furthermore, neither multicultural nor international literature is well known or recognized by the educational mainstream. We have chosen to include this special focus chapter to draw attention to these two important bodies of literature.

SECTION ONE: *Multicultural Literature*

DEFINITION AND DESCRIPTION

Multicultural literature refers to trade books, regardless of genre, that have as the main character a person who is a member of a racial, religious, or language microculture other than the Euro-American one. This section of the chapter will focus on the five most populous microcultures in the United States, each of which has an established and growing body of children's literature that describes its experience. These groups are African American; Asian American (including people of Chinese, Japanese, Korean, and Vietnamese descent); Latinos (including Cuban Americans, Mexican Americans, Puerto Ricans, and others of Spanish descent); Jewish; and Native American (a general term referring to the many tribes of American Indians).

VALUES OF MULTICULTURAL LITERATURE FOR CHILDREN

Multicultural literature has value for all children for the following reasons:

- Children who see people like themselves represented positively in excellent multicultural literature derive self-esteem and pride in their own heritage.
- Reading multicultural literature is a way for Euro-American children (and their parents, teachers, and librarians) to learn about or to become aware of other peoples and their cultures.
- Multicultural literature shows Euro-American children not only that other groups are worthy, but also that they have something to teach others.
- Emotional involvement and vicarious experience with multicultural characters through works of literature reduce students' prejudices toward the microculture.

- Reading about issues and problems peculiar to children of a specific microculture from the perspective of story characters who are members of the group may help children of that microculture to cope with the same problems.

EVALUATION AND SELECTION OF MULTICULTURAL LITERATURE

With respect to multicultural literature, your first concern as a teacher, librarian, or parent should be that well-written books of this kind are available to the children under your care. This task is often not as simple as it may at first seem. Some cultural groups in the United States are not yet well represented in children's books. Also, a wide variety of the most current and best multicultural books are not readily available everywhere. Someone, perhaps you, has to take the time and the effort to learn about, read, evaluate, and then introduce the best of this literature into a school or community. The following criteria should be considered in evaluating multicultural books:

- Multicultural literature should exhibit high literary and artistic quality, worthy themes, and appropriate reading levels for the intended audience.
- Racial and cultural *stereotyping* should be avoided; instead, multifaceted, well-rounded characters of the featured microculture should be found in these stories. The nature of stereotyping is that it unfairly assigns a fixed image or fixed characteristics to everyone within a group, thereby denying everyone within the group the right to any individuality or choice.
- Positive images of characters should be evident.
- Cultural details must be accurate. These details must be accurate when they describe subgroups *within* a microculture.
- Not only should there be books about the microcultures represented in a classroom, but there also should be books about the many other microcultures living in this country.

Variety also extends to authorship. Multicultural books written by both non-Euro-Americans and Euro-Americans should be readily available to children. In her landmark book *Shadow and Substance*, Rudine Sims (1982) established a classification system for books about African Americans that can be applied to any multicultural literature and can be helpful in evaluation and selection of these books. In the following categories we have broadened her labels and definitions to include all multicultural literature.

Social conscience books: These books about microcultural groups other than Euro-American are written to help all readers know the condition of their fellow humans. Examples are *Nightjohn* and its sequel, *Sarny,* by Gary Paulsen.

Melting pot books: These books, which feature multicultural characters, are written for all young readers on the assumption that everyone needs to be informed that children of all microcultures are exactly alike, except for the color of their skins, their language, or their religious preference. *Bloomability* by Sharon Creech is an example.

Culturally conscious books: These books are written primarily (though not exclusively) by microcultural authors other than Euro-American for readers belonging to that microculture. An attempt is made to reveal the true, unique character of that microculture. *Miracle's Boys* by Jacqueline Woodson is a good example.

Having examples of all three types of multicultural books in your classroom will ensure that your students will be able to read from the perspective of both the Euro-American author and the authors of other microcultures. Students of less integrated microcultures in particular should have the experience of reading stories written about children like themselves from the perspective of someone within their microculture.

Several book selection aids focus on multicultural books. *Kaleidoscope: A Multicultural Booklist for Grades K–8,* fourth edition (Hansen-Krening, Aoki, and Mizokawa, 2003) provides hundreds of annotated fiction and nonfiction titles published by and about people of color. Sponsored by the National Council of Teachers of English, this bibliography is updated every three years. *Through Indian Eyes: The Native Experience in Books for Children,* fourth edition (Slapin and Seale, 1998), through its frank reviews, guides readers toward greater discrimination in their choices of books by and about Native Americans. *Recommended Books in Spanish for Children and Young Adults* (Schon, 2000), a guide for choosing Spanish-language books for Hispanic children, is organized by country of origin, including a large section on the United States. These books are of all genres, and some are bilingual.

Book awards for special content also can guide teachers and librarians toward high-quality multicultural books. The best known of these is the Coretta Scott King Award, founded in 1969 and, since 1979, sponsored by the American Library Association. This annual award is given to the African-American author and (since 1974) illustrator whose books published in the preceding year are judged to be the most outstanding inspirational and educational literature for children. The Américas Award, founded in 1993, and the Pura Belpré Award, founded in 1996, by honoring outstanding Latino authors and illustrators of children's books, have done much to encourage the publication of high-quality books for this rapidly growing segment of the population. The first Asian Pacific American Award for Literature, honoring outstanding work of Asian-American authors and illustrators, was given in 2001. Awards such as these encourage the publication of more and better-quality multicultural literature.

In recent years, small presses have given teachers and librarians a source of multicultural books that are particularly valuable for their distinctly multicultural (versus Euro-American) point of view. For an extensive, up-to-date list of small presses that publish multicultural books for children, go to www.soemadison.wisc.edu/ccbc/pclist.htm. The following publishers have focused on multicultural literature, and so their catalogs are a treasure trove for those looking for such literature:

Asian American Curriculum Project. In addition to its own publications, this company distributes Asian-American books from other small and large presses. E-mail: aacpinc@best.com

Black Butterfly/Writers and Readers, Box 461, Village Station, New York, NY 10014. This company produces children's books with an Afrocentric perspective and written by African-American writers and artists.

Children's Book Press. This company publishes folktales and contemporary stories, often bilingual, in picture book format for Native American, Asian-American, and Latino-American children. Web page: www.cbookpress.org

Piñata Books/Arte Público, University of Houston, 4800 Calhoun, Houston, TX 77204. This alternative press publishes children's books with a Latino perspective.

Just Us Books. This company produces Afrocentric books that enhance the self-esteem of African-American children. Web page: www.justusbooks.com

Lee & Low Books. This Asian-American-owned company stresses authenticity in its contemporary stories for Asian-American, Latino-American, and African-American children. Its Latino titles are also offered in Spanish. Web page: www.leeandlow.com

Northland Publishing, P.O. Box 1389, Flagstaff, AZ 86002. This company produces high-quality books by Native American authors and illustrators from the Southwest. Web page: www.northland.pub.com

Pemmican Publications. This Canadian company publishes excellent realistic stories about contemporary Native American children and educational books for the Métis people about Métis history and culture. Web page: www.pemmican.mb.ca

Evaluating, selecting, and then bringing multicultural literature to your classroom, though essential, are not enough to ensure that your students will actually read the books. Without adult guidance, children tend to choose books about children like themselves (Rudman, 1984), so you must also purposefully expose mainstream children to multicultural books through reading aloud, booktalking, and selecting particular titles for small group reading.

HISTORICAL OVERVIEW OF MULTICULTURAL LITERATURE

Members of many microcultures living in the United States were long ignored as subjects for children's books. On the few occasions that representatives of these groups did appear, they did so as crudely stereotyped characters, objects of ridicule, or shadowy secondary characters. Helen Bannerman's *The Story of Little Black Sambo* (1900), Claire Bishop's *The Five Chinese Brothers* (1938), Sara Cone Bryant's *Epaminondas and His Auntie* (1907), and Hugh Lofting's *The Voyages of Dr. Dolittle* (1922) come under this category. Today, books such as these either have been rewritten to eliminate the racism or have disappeared from children's library shelves.

Although many of the Newbery Medal winners and honor books of the 1920s and 1930s were set in foreign countries, almost none had to do with multicultural groups in the United States. Laura Adams Armer's novel about Native Americans, *Waterless Mountain,* the Newbery Medal winner in 1932, was the only exception.

The 1940s offered little improvement. Although Florence Crannell Means wrote sympathetic and informative novels such as *The Moved-Outers* (1945) about American ethnic microcultures during the 1930s and 1940s, negative stereotypes, such as those of Native Americans as savages projected in Newbery Medal winners *Daniel Boone* by James Daugherty (1939) and *The Matchlock Gun* by Walter D. Edmonds (1941), were more prevalent by far.

The first harbinger of change came in 1949 when an African-American author, Arna Bontemps, won a Newbery Honor Award for his *Story of the Negro* and became the first member of a minority group to receive this honor. A more sympathetic attitude toward American microcultures, at least in literature, emerged in the 1950s, as evidenced by the positive, yet somewhat patronizing, treatment of multicultural characters in such Newbery Medal winners as *Amos Fortune, Free Man* by Elizabeth Yates (1950) and . . . *And Now Miguel* by Joseph Krumgold (1953).

The Civil Rights movement of the 1960s focused attention on the social inequities and racial injustices that prevailed in the United States. The spirit of the times resulted in two landmark publications. The first of these was *The Snowy Day* by Ezra Jack Keats (1962), the first Caldecott Medal–winning book to have an African American as the protagonist. The great popularity of this book no doubt encouraged other authors to produce books with multicultural protagonists. The second publication was a powerful article by Nancy Larrick entitled "The All-White World of Children's Books." In this article, which appeared in the September 11, 1965, issue of *Saturday Review,* Larrick reported that in nearly all U.S. children's books the African American either was omitted entirely or was scarcely mentioned (p. 63). American trade book publishers, the education system, and the public library system were called upon to fill this void.

For a time the spirit of social consciousness born in the 1960s had good results. In 1966, the Council on Interracial Books for Children was founded and helped to promote young African-American authors. In 1969 the Coretta Scott King Award was established to recognize distinguished writing in children's books by African-American authors. Also, several books with multicultural protagonists or themes were chosen as Newbery winners in the early 1970s: *Sounder* by William H. Armstrong won in 1970; *Julie of the Wolves* by Jean Craighead George won in 1973; and *The Slave Dancer* by Paula Fox won in 1974. Judging from this record, the establishment had accepted multicultural protagonists in award-winning books; but it was not until 1975 that an author of color, Virginia Hamilton, author of *M. C. Higgins, the Great,* won a Newbery Medal.

In quick succession, other African-American and Asian-American authors were recognized for their outstanding literary and artistic efforts. In 1976, Leo Dillon (in collaboration with his wife, Diane Dillon) won a Caldecott Medal for *Why Mosquitoes Buzz in People's Ears* (Aardema, 1975), and Sharon Bell Mathis and Laurence Yep received Newbery Honor Awards for *The Hundred Penny Box* and *Dragonwings,* respectively. The following year, 1977, Mildred D. Taylor, author of *Roll of Thunder, Hear My Cry,* became the second African American to win the Newbery Medal. After 1975, the prevailing opinion among U.S. children's book publishers and professional reviewers seemed to be that members of a microcultural group were the ones most able to write authoritatively about their own particular cultures and experiences. Euro-American authors were no longer as likely to win major awards for writing about minorities as they were in the early 1970s.

During the 1980s and 1990s the number of multicultural books published by large, corporate publishers increased only slightly. In response to the continuing dearth of good multicultural literature for children, a number of small, alternative presses devoted exclusively to multicultural literature have been founded. Interest in multicultural literature continues, although the number of multicultural authors and illustrators entering the field is still very small. The late 1990s saw some much-needed development in Latino-American literature. Bilingual books published in response to the demands of ESOL (English for Speakers of Other Languages) programs and the founding of the Américas Award and the Pura Belpré Awards contributed to this growth. The fledgling Asian Pacific American Award for Literature, given jointly by the Asian/Pacific American Librarians Association and the Chinese American Librarians Association for the first time in 2001, promises to encourage a greater output of high-quality Asian-American literature for children.

Although the last several decades have seen positive changes in the status of multicultural literature in the United States, there is still a marked shortage of books of this kind. Multicultural authors and illustrators of children's books are also in short supply. In 2002, for instance, only 69 (1%), of the approximately 5,000 children's books published in the United States were written or illustrated by

African Americans (Horning, Lindgren, & Schliesman, 2003), a group that represents 12.3 percent of the U.S. population. A broader indication of this shortage is that in 2002 only 415 (8%) of the approximately 5,000 children's books published in the United States were by or about all people of color (principally African Americans, Asian Americans, Latinos, and Native Americans), even though these groups represent approximately 30 percent of the population (U.S. Census Bureau, 2000).

A new-found public interest in family heritage that began in the 1980s in the United States began to be reflected in multicultural literature by the end of the decade. Interest in books about ethnic heritage has helped multicultural authors and illustrators to regain some of the publishing momentum of the 1970s. Awakening to the meaning and importance of one's heritage is a recurring theme in all genres of multicultural literature.

As microcultural groups intermingle, more children of mixed heritage will be born. Already this group is growing rapidly. Perhaps the experience of growing up with a mixed heritage will be a topic featured in the multicultural literature of the future, as in Lawrence Yep's *Thief of Hearts* and Pearl F. Gaskins' *What Are You? Voices of Mixed-Race Young People.* Milestones in the development of multicultural literature are highlighted on page 191.

T Y P E S   O F   M U L T I C U L T U R A L   L I T E R A T U R E

Before discussing the literature of each microculture, a general caution is in order. Each of these groups contains subgroups that differ remarkably from one another in country of origin, language, race, traditions, and present location. Teachers must be especially conscious of and sensitive to these differences and guard against presenting these groups as completely uniform or of selecting literature that does so. Gross overgeneralization is not only inaccurate but also a form of stereotyping.

Each of the following types of multicultural literature can include bilingual books, that is, books having text in two languages. Bilingual books are appearing in the United States with greater frequency each year, particularly English/Spanish books. These books, if well done, are particularly helpful to children in ESOL programs and to their teachers. Not all bilingual books have artful, or even accurate, translations, so selection should be limited to the best of those published. See the bilingual section in the Recommended Multicultural Books list at the end of this chapter.

African-American Literature

Of all multicultural groups living in the United States, African Americans have produced the largest and most rapidly growing body of children's literature. Every genre is well represented in African-American literature, but none better than poetry. Because it is so personal, poetry portrays a culture well, as is evident in the sensitive yet powerful work of poets Arnold Adoff, Gwendolyn Brooks, Nikki Giovanni, Eloise Greenfield, and Langston Hughes. For example, see *In Daddy's Arms I Am Tall: African Americans Celebrating Fathers* by Javaka Steptoe.

Tapping into their rich oral tradition, African Americans have contributed Anansi the Spider, Brer Rabbit, High John the Conqueror, and John Henry the Steel Drivin' Man to the list of favorite U.S. folklore characters. Even today, authors are bringing folktales to the United States from Africa. Examples

M I L E S T O N E S

in the Development of MULTICULTURAL   LITERATURE

DATE	EVENT	SIGNIFICANCE
1932	*Waterless Mountain* by Laura Armer wins Newbery Medal	One of the few children's books about minorities in the first half of the twentieth century
1946	*The Moved-Outers* by Florence C. Means wins Newbery Honor	A departure from stereotyped depiction of minorities begins
1949	*Story of the Negro* by Arna Bontemps wins Newbery Honor	First minority author to win a Newbery Honor
1950	*Song of the Swallows* by Leo Politi wins Caldecott Medal	First picture book with a Hispanic-American protagonist to win the Caldecott Medal
1963	*The Snowy Day* by Ezra Jack Keats wins Caldecott Medal	First picture book with an African-American protagonist to win the Caldecott Medal
1965	"The All-White World of Children's Books" by Nancy Larrick published in *Saturday Review*	Called the nation's attention to the lack of multicultural literature
1969	Coretta Scott King Award founded	African-American literature and authors begin to be promoted and supported
1975	*M. C. Higgins, the Great* by Virginia Hamilton wins Newbery Medal	First book by a minority author to win the Newbery Medal
1976	*Why Mosquitoes Buzz in People's Ears* illustrated by Leo and Diane Dillon wins Caldecott Medal	First picture book illustrated by an African American to win the Caldecott Medal
1990	*Lon Po Po: A Red-Riding Hood Story from China* translated and illustrated by Ed Young wins Caldecott Medal	First picture book illustrated by a Chinese American to win the Caldecott Medal
1993	Américas Award founded	Encouraged authors and illustrators to publish excellent books portraying Latin America, the Caribbean, and Latinos in the United States
1994	*Grandfather's Journey* written and illustrated by Allen Say wins Caldecott Medal	First picture book illustrated by a Japanese American to win the Caldecott Medal
1996	Pura Belpré Award founded	Latino literature, authors, and illustrators promoted
2001	*The Trip Back Home* by Janet S. Wong, illustrated by Bo Jia, wins first Asian Pacific American Award for Literature	Asian-American literature, authors, and illustrators promoted

include *Ananse and the Lizard: A West African Tale* by Pat Cummings and *The Girl Who Spun Gold* by Virginia Hamilton, illustrated by Leo and Diane Dillon.

In some cases, African Americans have reclaimed their tales by retelling (without racist elements) stories that were first written down in this country by Euro-American authors, as Julius Lester has done in his retelling of Joel Chandler Harris's *The Tales of Uncle Remus: The Adventures of Brer Rabbit.* More recent memories and family stories have begun to be written by African-American authors as modern folktales. For example, see *Mirandy and Brother Wind* by Patricia McKissack.

African Americans have told the stories of their lives in the United States through both historical and realistic fiction. The stories for older readers often include painfully harsh but accurate accounts of racial oppression, as in James Berry's slavery story *Ajeemah and His Son* or Mildred Taylor's historical fiction saga of the close-knit Logan family (*The Song of the Trees; Roll of Thunder, Hear My Cry; Let the Circle Be Unbroken; The Road to Memphis;* and *The Land*). The characters, settings, and incidents created by these authors will be recognized by many African Americans who have lived through similar experiences; others will appreciate these stories as windows onto an understanding of today's racial situation. Teachers can see to it that such stories are balanced, however, with more positive, encouraging contemporary stories such as Jacqueline Woodson's contemporary realistic novel, *Locomotion.*

Recently, African-American faces have begun to appear more frequently in picture books. While these books tend to address universal topics rather than those dealing specifically with race, they can still be culturally conscious. The works of illustrators Floyd Cooper, Pat Cummings, Leo and Diane Dillon, Tom Feelings, Jerry Pinkney, Brian Pinkney, and James Ransome deserve special notice. Examples include *Quinnie Blue* by Dinah Johnson, illustrated by James Ransome, and *The Middle Passage: White Ships/Black Cargo* by Tom Feelings.

African-American nonfiction is mainly biography. In the 1960s and 1970s a large percentage of these biographical subjects were sports heroes, but more recent subjects have come from a broader spectrum of achievement. For example, see *Through My Eyes* by Ruby Bridges and edited by Margo Lundell.

Asian-American Literature

Asian-American children's literature is mainly represented in the United States by stories about Chinese Americans, Japanese Americans, and Korean Americans possibly because these groups have lived as microcultures in this country longer than others such as Vietnamese Americans. A major theme in much of the fiction and nonfiction for older readers is the oppression that drove the people out of their homelands and the prejudice that they faced as newcomers in this country. A more positive theme is that of learning to appreciate one's cultural heritage while adjusting to life in the United States. A good example is An Na's *A Step from Heaven.*

Traditional stories from Asia retold in English have contributed many interesting folktales and folktale variants to children's libraries. Characters who are generally thought of as European, such as Little Red Riding Hood and Cinderella, have their Asian counterparts. Examples are *Lon Po Po: A Red-Riding Hood Story from China* translated and illustrated by Ed Young, and *Yeh Shen: A Cinderella Story from China* by Ai-Ling Louie, illustrated by Ed Young.

Asian-American artists have brought the sophisticated style and technical artistry of the Orient to U.S. children's book illustration. Ed Young's use of screenlike panels and exotic, textured paper and Allen Say's precision are especially noteworthy. Examples are *Tea with Milk* by Allen Say and *Monkey King* by Ed Young.

The body of Asian-American children's literature is small. Nonfiction, poetry, and fantasy are almost unrepresented, with the notable exception of Rhoda Blumberg's works of nonfiction, such as

Shipwrecked! The True Adventures of a Japanese Boy. The recently established Asian Pacific American Award for Literature, as well as small presses, such as Lee & Low Books, will help to improve this situation.

Jewish Literature

The terrible experience of the Jewish Holocaust in Europe during the 1930s and 1940s has had a tremendous influence on Jewish children's literature. The prejudice and cruelty that led to the Holocaust and the nightmare of the death camps themselves are recurring themes in both fiction and nonfiction for older readers. Since many Jewish people immigrated to the United States as the Nazi threat grew in Europe, much Holocaust literature has been written by eyewitnesses or by those whose relatives were victims. Examples are *Thanks to My Mother* by Schoschana Rabinovici and *Smoke and Ashes: The Story of the Holocaust* by Barbara Rogasky.

Jewish emigration from Europe during the war years brought to the United States many outstanding artists whose work has greatly influenced children's book illustration. Two subjects often presented in Jewish picture books are Jewish holidays and folktales. Illustrated Jewish folktale collections, particularly those by Isaac Bashevis Singer, offer excellent, witty stories and high literary quality. Examples include *Gershon's Monster: A Story for the Jewish New Year,* retold by Eric Kimmel and illustrated by Jon J. Muth, and Adèle Geras's *My Grandmother's Stories: A Collection of Jewish Folktales,* illustrated by Anita Lobel.

The Jewish-American community has produced a number of excellent authors and illustrators of children's books. Literary creativity is promoted through two book award programs: the National Jewish Book Awards and the Association of Jewish Libraries' Sydney Taylor Awards for children's and young adult literature.

Latino Literature

Few Latino children's books are published in the United States, despite the fact that Latinos represent an estimated 13 percent of the population and are considered the fastest-growing segment of the population (U.S. Census Bureau, 2000). Recent developments hold promise for improvement in the amount and quality of Latino literature. The books that are available are mainly about Puerto Ricans and Mexican Americans; the works of Alma Flor Ada, George Ancona, Lulu Delacre, and Gary Soto are outstanding examples. Good examples are *Chato and the Party Animals* by Gary Soto, illustrated by Susan Guevara, and *The Circuit: Stories from the Life of a Migrant Child* by Francisco Jiménez.

The rise of small press publishers, such as Children's Book Press, that focus on Latino literature, has already resulted in more literature being written for and about this group. The trend toward marketing more Spanish-English bilingual texts in the United States also will improve the availability of Latino books, particularly to younger children who are learning to read. For example, see *Gathering the Sun: An Alphabet in Spanish and English* by Alma Flor Ada, illustrated by Simon Silva. The establishment in 1993 of the Américas Award for a U.S. work that authentically presents the experience of individuals in Latin America or the Caribbean or of Latinos in the United States and, in 1996, of the Pura Belpré Award honoring outstanding Latino children's authors and illustrators will undoubtedly promote the creation of more high-quality Latino literature for children.

Native American Literature

Almost from the moment that European explorers landed on this continent some 500 years ago, Native Americans have suffered at the hands of Euro-Americans. Consequently, in books written from the Native American perspective, oppression by the white population is a pervasive theme. Appreciation, celebration, and protection of nature—central tenets of Native American cultures—are other recurrent themes in this body of literature. Examples are *Crazy Horse's Vision* by Joseph Bruchac, illustrated by S. D. Nelson, and *The Birchbark House* by Louise Erdrich.

Although much has been written *about* Native Americans, relatively little has been written *by* members of this microculture. Small press publishers specializing in literature by Native Americans may help to change this situation. Northland Press, for example, features the work of Native Americans of the southwestern United States. Native Americans who are known for their children's books include Cynthia Leitich Smith for her novels, Joseph Bruchac for his retold stories, and Michael Lacapa and Shonto Begay for their illustrations. Examples are *Rain Is Not My Indian Name* by Cynthia Leitich Smith and *The First Strawberries* retold by Joseph Bruchac, illustrated by Anna Vojtech.

Numerous other writers and illustrators have told and retold the folktales and history of Native Americans in picture books, historical fiction, and informational books. Paul Goble is particularly well known for his impressively illustrated retellings of the legends of the Plains Indians, as are Scott O'Dell and Canadian Jan Hudson for their award-winning works of historical fiction featuring young Native American women. The body of nonfictional works about Native Americans is particularly rich, the works of Ann Nolan Clark, Russell Freedman, Milton Meltzer, John Bierhorst, Brent Ashabranner, and Alex Bealer being outstanding. Examples include *The Girl Who Loved Wild Horses* by Paul Goble, *Island of the Blue Dolphins* by Scott O'Dell, and *Only the Names Remain: The Cherokees and the Trail of Tears* by Alex Bealer.

SECTION TWO: *International Literature*

DEFINITION AND DESCRIPTION

International literature in the United States is defined as literary selections that were originally published for the children in a country other than the United States in a language of that country and later published in the United States. The key elements of this definition are the book's country of origin and the determination of the primary audience for the book. If a book was written and published in France for French children and then translated and published for U.S. children, it is considered an international book in the United States. Books that are classified as international literature by this definition include the following:

1. English language books that were originally written and published in English in another country, such as Canada or Australia, then published or distributed in the United States.
2. Translated books that were written and published in a foreign language and then translated into English and published in the United States.
3. Foreign language books that were written and published in a foreign language in another country for children of that country and later published or distributed in the United States in the foreign language.

If a book about Australian life is written and published in the United States, then the primary audience is U.S. children, and the book is not considered international. Such books about other countries written and published in the United States are included in the lists of recommended books in the genre chapters.

Sometimes it is difficult to ascertain a book's country of origin. The publishing history page is the most reliable source of this information. (Note that in some foreign books, this publishing history is placed at the end of the book.) In any case, a careful reading will inform you of the book's original date and place of publication.

VALUE OF INTERNATIONAL LITERATURE FOR CHILDREN

The value of international children's literature in developing an understanding of and appreciation for other cultures is undeniable. The understanding of people of other countries must be fostered early and allowed to grow throughout life.

*   Through this literature, the history, traditions, and people of other countries are brought to life.
*   By interpreting events in the everyday lives of their characters and by depicting long-term changes in the characters' lives, authors present a truer and more understandable picture of life in other countries than does the crisis-prone, single-event coverage of television and newspapers.
*   Compelling stories build students' interest in the people and places they are reading about and pave the way to a deeper understanding and appreciation of the geographical and historical content encountered in textbooks.

- Literature written by natives of the country or region under study gives authenticity and an international perspective to classroom materials.

- Today, many students in the United States speak a foreign language and have a foreign heritage. International literature reflects the cultural and language diversity often found in classrooms today. By reading international books, students can learn to respect the heritage of others and take pride in their own.

- Through international literature, children are given an opportunity to enjoy the best-loved stories of their peers around the world. This, in turn, can help students to develop a bond of shared experience with children of other nations and can enable them to acquire cultural literacy with a global perspective.

In a study by Monson, Howe, and Greenlee (1989), 200 U.S. children, ages 9 to 11, were asked what they would like to know about their counterparts in other countries. Their responses, categorized into nine questions, then formed the basis for a comparison of eight social studies textbooks and fifteen works of fiction appropriate for the age group about one country, Australia. It was found that both textbooks and trade books gave information about the country. The novels answered more of the children's questions, however, and were richer in detail of daily life and human emotion than the textbooks. The social studies texts gave many facts about the country, while the novels showed the implications of the facts for children's lives and helped the readers "live in" the country for a time.

EVALUATION AND SELECTION OF INTERNATIONAL LITERATURE

International books, both chapter books and picture books, should first be judged by the standards for all good literature.

- Translated works should exhibit a good, fluent writing style that is not stilted or awkward. Some flavor of the country of origin should remain. For example, place and character names should usually remain true to the original text to foster in children a tolerance for and an appreciation of other languages and customs. Some translated books include a glossary of foreign words, meanings, and pronunciations. This permits readers to risk new and different words and sounds with no loss of confidence.

- Teachers and librarians may note in some international books differences in writing and illustrating styles. International chapter books for intermediate- and upper-grade readers lean toward introspection by the main character. An example is the Dutch book *Bare Hands* by Bart Moeyaert. Students could be alerted to the differences and could be asked to reflect on why the author may have chosen that manner of telling the story. In some cases, illustrations in international books are more surreal than is usual for U.S. picture books. Aspects of plot and theme in these books are heavily embedded in the pictorial details. For example, many layers of meaning can be unraveled with repeated readings of the book *Collector of Moments* by Quint Buchholz.

With the increase of internationalism in all domains of our social and cultural life, more international children's books are becoming available in the United States. A number of selection sources will prove useful and necessary in locating international children's book titles. *Bookbird: Journal of International Children's Literature,* the International Board on Books for Young People (IBBY) journal, announces recent international award-winning books and national award winners from many nations and is, therefore, an important source for current information on international books. It also features articles on international children's literature. The *USBBY Newsletter* from the United States section of IBBY highlights events of interest in the United States and other countries related to this field and also devotes a column to translated books recently published in the United States.

The lists of past winners of the Hans Christian Andersen Award; the Mildred L. Batchelder Award; and the British, Australian, New Zealand, and Canadian awards for children's books are excellent sources of international titles and authors. (See Appendix A.) The major children's book review sources include reviews of notable international books in their monthly review columns. (See Appendix B for lists of these journals.)

Four professional books that are invaluable in selecting international children's books and in learning about international children's literature have recently been published or updated:

- *Children's Books: Awards & Prizes* from the Children's Book Council (2003) is a complete listing of major book awards in other countries with an explanation of each of the awards. It is now also available online at www.cbcbooks.com.
- *International Companion Encyclopedia of Children's Literature,* Vol. 1, edited by Peter Hunt and Sheila G. Ray (1996), is a 923-page book featuring 28 essays on children's literature in different countries around the world.
- *Children's Books from Other Countries,* edited by Carl M. Tomlinson (1998), is a 304-page book with strategies for sharing books with children, activities for promoting international understanding, and an annotated bibliography of 724 international books published in the United States in English. Volume 2, *The World through Children's Books,* edited by Susan Stan (2002), has updated books and references.
- *Global Perspectives in Children's Literature,* by Evelyn Freeman and Barbara Lehman (2001), is a 136-page book discussing the values of international literature for children, with chapters on current status, issues, and trends in the field. Also included is a chapter on sharing international books across the curriculum.

A few publishers have specialized in international children's books and deserve special mention here:

Creative Editions (Creative Company, 123 South Broad Street, P.O. Box 227, Mankato, MN 56002) publishes a number of translated books annually.

Farrar, Straus, and Giroux (www.fsgbooks.com) publishes a number of translated Swedish books every year as a result of a translation and distribution agreement with the largest Swedish publisher of children's books, Rabén and Sjögren.

Front Street (www.frontstreetbooks.com) is an independent publisher specializing in young adult literature and European children's books in translation.

Kane/Miller Book Publishers (www.kanemiller.com) is a small press that specializes in translated foreign children's picture books from around the world.

North-South Books (www.northsouth.com) publishes high-quality multinational copublications and the English language editions of Michael Neugebauer Books, a Swiss publisher.

Tundra Books (www.tundrabooks.com) specializes in Canadian and French/English bilingual books for children.

HISTORICAL OVERVIEW OF INTERNATIONAL LITERATURE

Much of the children's literature that was available in the United States during the seventeenth, eighteenth, nineteenth, and early twentieth centuries came from Europe. These early children's books are an important part of our cultural heritage, but we seldom think of the fact that they were originally published in other countries and many in other languages. They are so familiar to us in the United States that we consider them our children's classics, and indeed they have become so. Page 199 lists a sampling of international children's classics published from the end of the seventeenth century up to World War II.

With the rapid growth in the U.S. children's book field in the twentieth century, the flow of books from other countries became overshadowed by large numbers of U.S. publications. In addition, during World War II, little cultural exchange occurred across international borders. The end of World War II saw a change in the international mood, and two developments occurred that had far-reaching effects on the children's book field: (1) children's books in translation began to be published in unprecedented numbers (Carus, 1980), and (2) the international children's book field was established and fostered by an international organization, awards, and publishers' bookfairs of children's books.

The establishment of an international children's book field was advanced by Jella Lepman, who described these early developments in *A Bridge of Children's Books* (2002). Lepman, a German-born Jew who left Germany during World War II for England, returned to Germany after the war to work in the field of children's books as a way to promote international understanding and world peace. Lepman began a traveling exhibit of children's books for German children, which in 1949 was established as the International Youth Library (IYL) in Munich. The IYL is the largest collection of children's books from around the world and currently holds well over 500,000 books. In reflecting on these accomplishments, Lepman concludes in her book that "in many parts of the world children were holding books in their hands and meeting over a bridge of children's books" (p. 154).

Lepman also worked with others from many countries in establishing the IBBY in 1953. IBBY is organized by sections from member countries. The members of national sections are children's book editors, agents, librarians, publishers, educators, translators, authors, and illustrators—anyone who works in the children's book field. In 1956, IBBY founded the Hans Christian Andersen Award, an international award program that honors outstanding authors of children's literature. The award is given every two years, and in 1966 an award to outstanding illustrators was added. (See Appendix A for Hans Christian Andersen Award winners.) IBBY holds a biennial world congress in September (www.ibby.org).

In 1963, IBBY founded *Bookbird,* an international quarterly periodical on literature for children and young people. The journal is now named *Bookbird: Journal of International Children's Literature.* In the United States the chapter of IBBY is the United States Board on Books for Young People (USBBY), an organization that welcomes teachers, editors, librarians, and all who are interested in the interna-

Early MILESTONES in INTERNATIONAL CHILDREN'S LITERATURE

DATE	EVENT	SIGNIFICANCE
1657	*Orbis Pictus* by John Amos Comenius	Earliest nonfiction picture book
1697	*Tales of Mother Goose* by Charles Perrault	Earliest folktales from France
1719	*Robinson Crusoe* by Daniel Defoe	Two early adult adventure books from England,
1726	*Gulliver's Travels* by Jonathan Swift	adopted by children
1812	*Nursery and Household Tales* by Jakob and Wilhelm Grimm	Traditional folktales from Germany
1836	*Fairy Tales* by Hans Christian Andersen	Early modern folktales from Denmark
1846	*Book of Nonsense* by Edward Lear	Early humorous poetry from England
1865	*Alice's Adventures in Wonderland* by Lewis Carroll	Classic English modern fantasy
1880	*Heidi* by Johanna Spyri	Early realistic story from Switzerland
1881	*The Adventures of Pinocchio* by Carlo Collodi	Modern fantasy from Italy
1883	*Treasure Island* by Robert Louis Stevenson	Adventure tale from England by a Scottish author
1885	*A Child's Garden of Verses* by Robert Louis Stevenson	Classic collection of Golden Age poems from England
1894	*The Jungle Book* by Rudyard Kipling	Animal stories set in India by an English author
1901	*The Tale of Peter Rabbit* by Beatrix Potter	Classic English picture book
1906	*The Wonderful Adventures of Nils* by Selma Lagerlöf	A fantasy trip around Sweden
1908	*The Wind in the Willows* by Kenneth Grahame	Animal fantasy from England
1908	*Anne of Green Gables* by Lucy M. Montgomery	Realistic family story from Canada
1926	*Winnie-the-Pooh* by A. A. Milne	Personified toy story from England
1928	*Bambi* by Felix Salten	Personified deer story from Germany
1931	*The Story of Babar* by Jean de Brunhoff	Personified elephant story from France
1945	*Pippi Longstocking* by Astrid Lindgren	Classic fantasy from Sweden

tional exchange of children's literature. For information on membership, publications, and conferences, contact Secretariat, USBBY, P. O. Box 8139, Newark, DE 19714-8139, or go to USBBY's web site at www.usbby.org.

In 1967, the Biennale of Illustrations Bratislava (BIB), an international exposition of children's book illustrations, was established and takes place every other year in Bratislava, Slovakia. An international jury selects prize-winning children's book illustrations for a Grand Prix, the highest award, and recognizes honor books.

In 1968, the first Mildred L. Batchelder Award was announced by the American Library Association in honor of a U.S. publisher of the most distinguished translated children's book published in the preceding year. This award is given annually to encourage the translation and publication of international books in the United States. (See Appendix A for the award list.)

An international children's bookfair is convened in Bologna, Italy, every April for children's book publishers. This forum has proved to be an important one for the international exchange of children's books—a time when publishers display their best in the interests of attracting publishers from other nations to publish the new books in their own countries.

The future of international children's literature depends upon our success in several arenas. First, we must encourage the development of stronger national literatures from developing nations where most literature remains at the stage of the oral tradition. We must also promote more literary exchange with nations whose literature is now growing rapidly to bring more of the world's best literature to our children's attention. Finally, we must support those organizations that can assist in these endeavors.

INTERNATIONAL BOOKS BY WORLD REGIONS

Quite logically, the international books that are most often available in the United States have been and continue to be books from other English-speaking countries. These English language books originate in many different countries, but the largest numbers of them come from Great Britain, Australia, and Canada. Although the books do not require translation, they are often published in the United States with other changes: spelling, characters' names, place names, and, sometimes titles and cover illustrations. These changes are made ostensibly to increase the marketability of the books in this country and may indeed accomplish that end in some cases. Because of the shared primary language and some cultural commonalities among these nations, the literary exchange has been relatively easy. Teachers are often surprised to discover that one of their favorite authors is British, Canadian, or Australian. An example is *The Jolly Postman* by Janet and Allan Ahlberg, a book that was first published in England. However, many English language books do feature cultural attitudes and customs not typically found in the United States that warrant comparison and discussion by students. The major awards and award winners from English-speaking countries are listed in Appendix A.

Translated books come to the United States from around the world, but the largest numbers come from Europe. Today, many books come from Sweden, Norway, Denmark, Switzerland, the Netherlands, Germany, France, and Belgium. A few books come from Italy and Spain. An example from Sweden is *In Ned's Head* by Anders Jacobsson and Sören Olsson.

Translated children's literature from Asia originates mostly in Japan, but books from Korea, China, and Thailand can occasionally be found. Japan has an extremely sophisticated field of book illustrating, and many beautifully illustrated picture books are now making their way into the U.S. market. An example from South Korea is *While We Were Out* by Ho Baek Lee.

African nations have produced little children's literature that has been exported to the United States. The reasons for this are many, but the most influential one is probably that of economics. Publishing books is expensive, especially in full color; therefore, the publishing industry is not firmly established in developing countries. An example from Ghana is *Sosu's Call* by Meshack Asare. Central and South American countries suffer from similar economic problems. Traditional literature is usually the first genre of children's literature to be published in a developing nation and, therefore, is often the only literature available to our students from those countries. Books of realistic fiction in which contemporary life in another country is portrayed are rare but worth locating. Beverley Naidoo's *The Other Side of Truth,* for example, is set in Nigeria, then London, and addresses political persecution.

The difficulties of locating and translating good books from non-English-speaking countries contribute to the dearth of available titles. Certain publishing companies have been attempting to overcome this dearth of foreign literature in our country by focusing solely on foreign children's literature, whereas other publishers have made a concerted effort to increase the percentage of foreign books among their titles. These efforts are encouraging. As more librarians, teachers, and parents become interested in purchasing this body of literature, more publishers will become willing to meet the market need.

There is reason to hope that the current unrest between cultures will not always be the case. Ethnic prejudice and bias are not natural behaviors; they are learned. One of the most intriguing challenges to those who work with children is to combat the ignorance that is at the root of racial, cultural, and religious prejudice and intolerance. Children's literature, particularly the rich multicultural and international selections that are currently available, is a powerful tool in this effort, for it shows that the similarities between all people are much more fundamental than the differences.

REFERENCES

Banks, J. A., & Banks, C. A. (1993). *Multicultural education: Issues and perspectives.* Boston: Allyn and Bacon.

Carus, M. (1980). Translation and internationalism in children's literature. *Children's Literature in Education, 11*(4), 171–179.

Children's Book Council (Ed.). (2003). *Children's books: Awards & prizes.* New York: Children's Book Council.

Cullen, C. (1998). Tableau. In *I, too, sing America.* New York: Houghton.

Freeman, E., & Lehman, B. (2001). *Global perspectives in children's literature.* Needham Heights: Allyn and Bacon.

Hansen-Krening, N., Aoki, E. M., & Mizokawa, D. T. (Eds.). (2003). *Kaleidoscope: A multicultural booklist for grades K–8* (4th ed.). Urbana, IL: NCTE.

Horning, K. T., Lindgren, M. V., & Schliesman, M. (2003). *CCBC Choices, 2003.* Madison: University Publications, University of Wisconsin–Madison.

Hunt, P., & Ray, S. G. (Eds.). (1996). *International companion encyclopedia of children's literature.* London: Routledge.

Larrick, N. (1965). The all-white world of children's books. *Saturday Review* (September 11), 63–65, 84–85.

Lepman, J. (2002/1969). *A bridge of children's books.* Dublin: O'Brien Press.

Monson, D. L., Howe, K., & Greenlee, A. (1989). Helping children develop cross-cultural understanding with children's books. *Early Child Development and Care, 48*(special issue), 3–8.

Rudman, M. (1984). *Children's literature: An issues approach* (2nd ed.). New York: Longman.

Schon, I. (2000). *Recommended books in Spanish for children and young adults 1996 through 1999.* Lanham, MD: Scarecrow.

Sims, R. (1982). *Shadow and substance: Afro-American experience in contemporary children's fiction.* Urbana, IL: NCTE.

Slapin, B., & Seale, D. (Eds.). (1998). *Through Indian eyes: The native experience in books for children* (4th ed.). Los Angeles: American Indian Studies Center, UGLA.

Stan, S. (Ed.). (2002). *The world through children's books.* Lanham, MD: Scarecrow.

Tomlinson, C. M. (Ed.). (1998). *Children's books from other countries.* Lanham, MD: Scarecrow.

U.S. Census Bureau. www.census.gov.

NOTABLE   *AUTHORS AND ILLUSTRATORS OF MULTICULTURAL LITERATURE*

African-American

Leo and Diane Dillon, illustrators of two Caldecott Medal–winning books. Leo Dillon is the first African American to win a Caldecott Medal. *Why Mosquitoes Buzz in People's Ears; Ashanti to Zulu.*

Patricia McKissack, author of modern African-American folktales and informational books. *Mirandy and Brother Wind.*

Walter Dean Myers, author of sometimes gritty contemporary realistic fiction about African Americans growing up. *Scorpions; Monster.*

Brian Pinkney, illustrator whose swirling lines and black backgrounds in intricate scratchboard renderings create a sense of intrigue and mystery. *Cendrillon: A Caribbean Cinderella; The Faithful Friend.*

Jerry Pinkney, illustrator whose light-filled watercolors capture the beauty of African Americans. *Goin' Someplace Special.*

James Ransome, illustrator noted for his use of bold colors and representational style. *How Animals Saved the People: Animal Tales from the South.*

Mildred Taylor, author whose award-winning books of historical fiction chronicle the experience of growing up black in southern United States in the 1940s and 1950s. *Roll of Thunder, Hear My Cry; The Land.*

Jacqueline Woodson, author of introspective novels dealing with overcoming adversity and loss. *Miracle's Boys; Hush; Locomotion.*

Asian-American

Laurence Yep, author of historical and contemporary realistic fiction about growing up as an Asian American. *Dragonwings; Traitor: Golden Mountain Chronicles, 1885.*

Ed Young, first Asian-American illustrator to win the Caldecott Award. *Lon Po Po: A Red-Riding Hood Story from China.*

Jewish

Adèle Geras, anthologist of folktales and other stories celebrating the Jewish tradition. *My Grandmother's Stories: A Collection of Jewish Folktales; A Treasury of Jewish Stories.*

Eric Kimmel, reteller of tales, many of which are from the Jewish culture. *Gershon's Monster: A Story for the Jewish New Year.*

Latino

George Ancona, Mexican-American photographer who writes about and photographs the life and culture of Mexico and Mexican Americans. *Carnaval; Fiesta U.S.A.*

Pat Mora, author of picture storybooks, biographies, and poems about the Mexican-American experience. *Tomás and the Library Lady; Confetti: Poems for Children.*

Gary Soto, author of contemporary stories about the Mexican-American experience. *Trading Places; Snapshots from the Wedding.*

Native American

Joseph Bruchac, reteller of Native American folktales and legends and biographer of famous Native Americans. *The First Strawberries; Crazy Horse's Vision.*

Paul Goble, reteller and illustrator of the folktales and legends of the Native Americans of the Great Plains. *The Girl Who Loved Wild Horses; Storm Maker's Tipi.*

Scott O'Dell, author of several works of award-winning historical fiction featuring strong female Native American heroines. *Island of the Blue Dolphins.*

Cross-Cultural

Milton Meltzer, author of nonfictional works about several U.S. microcultures. *Remember the Days: A Short History of the Jewish American; The Black Americans: A History in Their Own Words; The Hispanic Americans.*

Maomi Shihab Nye, Palestinian-American author whose poetry and novels celebrate the value of different cultures. *19 Varieties of Gazelle: Poems of the Middle East; The Tree Is Older Than You Are: Bilingual Poems and Stories from Mexico; Habibi.*

NOTABLE *AUTHORS AND ILLUSTRATORS OF INTERNATIONAL LITERATURE*

David Almond, British Carnegie Medal–winning author of novels often described as magical realism. *Skellig; Kit's Wilderness.*

Meshak Asare, Ghanaian author/illustrator whose works draw on traditional tales from Ghana. *Sosu's Call; Cat in Search of a Friend.*

Jeannie Baker, Australian artist who uses relief collages in her illustrations. *Where the Forest Meets the Sea; Window.*

Anthony Browne, British author/illustrator whose stark surrealism reveals modern social ills. *Willy the Wizard; Gorilla.*

Roald Dahl, British author of extremely popular and wildly humorous modern fantasies. *James and the Giant Peach; Charlie and the Chocolate Factory.*

Mem Fox, Australian author of picture storybooks often employing Australian animals. *Wilfrid Gordon McDonald Partridge.*

Taro Gomi, Prolific Japanese author/illustrator of many books for children including picture books that present a frank view of the body and its functions. *Everyone Poops; I Lost My Dad!*

Bob Graham, Australian author and illustrator of whimsical picture books. *Jethro Byrd, Fairy Child.*

Jean Little, Canadian author of realistic chapter books featuring children with emotional and physical disabilities. *Mama's Going to Buy You a Mockingbird.*

Bart Moeyaert, Dutch author of works of contemporary realism about youth struggling with growing up and dealing with families. *Bare Hands; It's Love We Don't Understand.*

Susie Morgenstern, Resident of Nice, France, who writes children's books in French about the lives of French children. Known for *A Book of Coupons; Secret Letters from 0 to 10,* both of which were recognized as Batchelder Honor Books.

Beverley Naidoo, South African author and Carnegie Medalist whose novels deal with the effects of political injustice on children. *The Other Side of Truth; No Turning Back.*

Philip Pullman, British creator of *His Dark Materials* fantasies, a trilogy comprised of *The Golden Compass, The Subtle Knife,* and *The Amber Spyglass.*

Emily Rodda, Australian writer of popular fantasy adventures for intermediate-grade readers. *Rowan of Rin* and its sequels.

J. K. Rowling, British author of the popular, best-selling series about Harry Potter, a child wizard. *Harry Potter and the Sorcerer's Stone* and its sequels.

Julie Vivas, Australian illustrator of picture books. *Wilfrid Gordon McDonald Partridge.*

Margaret Wild, Australian author of picture books about friendship and its power to heal. *Fox; The Pocket Dogs; The Very Best of Friends.*

Paul Yee, Canadian author who writes about the Chinese Canadian experience. *Tales from the Gold Mountain; Dead Man's Gold and Other Stories.*

RECOMMENDED MULTICULTURAL BOOKS

Ages refer to approximate interest levels.
YA = young adult readers.

African-American Literature

Aardema, Verna. **Why Mosquitoes Buzz in People's Ears.** Illustrated by Leo and Diane Dillon. Dial, 1975. Ages 5–7. (picture book)

Armstrong, William H. **Sounder.** Harper, 1969. Ages 9–12. (chapter book)

Berry, James. **Ajeemah and His Son.** HarperCollins, 1992. Ages 9–12. (chapter book)

Binch, Caroline. **Gregory Cool.** Dial, 1994. Ages 6–9. (picture book)

Bridges, Ruby and Margo Lundell (ed.). *Through My Eyes.* Scholastic, 1999. Ages 9–YA.

Cline-Ransome, Lesa. *Satchel Paige.* Illustrated by James Ransome. Simon & Schuster, 2000. Ages 7–10. (biography)

Feelings, Tom. *The Middle Passage: White Ships/ Black Cargo.* Dial, 1995. Ages 9–14. (wordless picture book)

Fox, Paula. *The Slave Dancer.* Bradbury, 1973. Ages 9–12. (chapter book)

Fradin, Dennis Brindell, and Judith Bloom Fradin. *Ida B. Wells: Mother of the Civil Rights Movement.* Clarion, 2000. Ages 10–YA. (biography)

Greenfield, Eloise. *Honey, I Love You and Other Love Poems.* Viking, 1978. Ages 6–10. (poetry)

Grimes, Nikki. *Bronx Masquerade.* Dial, 2002. (picture book)

———. *Talkin' about Bessie: The Story of Aviator Elizabeth Coleman.* Illustrated by E. B. Lewis. Orchard/ Scholastic, 2002. (picture book biography)

Hamilton, Virginia. *Many Thousand Gone: African Americans from Slavery to Freedom.* Illustrated by Leo and Diane Dillon. Random, 1992. Ages 10–14. (chapter book)

Hansen, Joyce. *I Thought My Soul Would Rise and Fly: The Diary of Patsy, a Freed Girl.* Scholastic, 1997. Ages 10–13. (chapter book)

Hopkinson, Deborah. *A Band of Angels: A Story Inspired by the Jubilee Singers.* Illustrated by Raúl Colón. Atheneum, 1999. Ages 8–10. (picture book)

Howard, Elizabeth Fitzgerald. *Virgie Goes to School with Us Boys.* Illustrated by E. B. Lewis. Simon & Schuster, 2000. Ages 6–9. (picture book)

Hudson, Wade, and Cheryl W. Hudson, compilers. *In Praise of Our Fathers and Our Mothers: A Black Family Treasury of Outstanding Authors and Artists.* Just Us Books, 1997. Ages 9–YA. (collected biography)

Johnson, Angela. *The First Part Last.* Simon & Schuster, 2003. Ages 12–YA. (chapter book)

———. *Heaven.* Simon & Schuster,1998. Ages 12–YA. (chapter book)

Johnson, Dinah. *Quinnie Blue.* Illustrated by James Ransome. Holt, 2000. Ages 6–8. (picture book)

Johnson, Dolores. *The Children's Book of Kwanzaa: A Guide to Celebrating the Holiday.* Atheneum, 1996. Ages 8–14. (nonfiction chapter book)

Keats, Ezra Jack. *Goggles.* Macmillan, 1969, Ages 5–7. (picture book)

———. *The Snowy Day.* Viking, 1962. Ages 4–6. (picture book)

Lester, Julius. *From Slave Ship to Freedom Road.* Illustrated by Rod Brown. Dial, 1998. Ages 11–15. (informational)

———. *John Henry.* Illustrated by Jerry Pinkney. Dial, 1994. Ages 7–10. (picture book)

———, reteller. *The Tales of Uncle Remus: The Adventures of Brer Rabbit.* Illustrated by Jerry Pinkney. Dial, 1987. Ages 7–9. (collected stories) (See also *More Tales of Uncle Remus: Further Adventures of Brer Rabbit, His Friends, Enemies, and Others,* 1988; *The Last Tales of Uncle Remus,* 1994.)

McGill, Alice. *Molly Bannaky.* Illustrated by Chris K. Soentpiet. Houghton, 1999. Ages 7–11. (picture book)

McKissack, Patricia. *Goin' Someplace Special.* Illustrated by Jerry Pinkney. Scholastic, 2001. Ages 6–9. (picture book)

———. *Mirandy and Brother Wind.* Illustrated by Jerry Pinkney. Knopf, 1988. Ages 7–9. (picture book)

———. *Rebels against Slavery: American Slave Revolts.* Scholastic, 1996. Ages 11–YA. (nonfiction chapter book)

McKissack, Patricia, and Fredrick McKissack. *Christmas in the Big House, Christmas in the Quarters.* Illustrated by John Thompson. Scholastic, 1994. Ages 8–11. (chapter book)

Mollel, Tololwa M. *My Rows and Piles of Coins.* Illustrated by E. B. Lewis. Clarion, 1999. Ages 4–8. (picture book)

Musgrove, Margaret. *Ashanti to Zulu: African Traditions.* Illustrated by Leo and Diane Dillon. Dial, 1976. Ages 8–10. (picture book)

Myers, Walter Dean. *Glorious Angels: A Celebration of Children.* HarperCollins, 1995. Ages 3–14. (poetry)

———. *Malcolm X: A Fire Burning Brightly.* Illustrated by Leonard Jenkins. HarperCollins, 2000. Ages 7–11. (picture book biography)

———. *Scorpions.* Harper, 1988. Ages 9–12. (chapter book)

Nelson, Marilyn. *Carver: A Life in Poems.* Front Street, 2000. Ages 12–YA. (biography)

O'Connor, Barbara. *Me and Rupert Goody.* Farrar/ Frances Foster, 1999. Ages 9–12. (chapter book)

Pinkney, Andrea D. *Bill Pickett: Rodeo-Ridin' Cowboy.* Illustrated by Brian Pinkney. Harcourt, 1996. Ages 7–10. (picture book)

Schroeder, Alan. *Minty: The Story of Young Harriet Tubman.* Illustrated by Jerry Pinkney. Dial, 1996. Ages 7–10. (picture book)

Taylor, Mildred. *The Land.* Putnam, 2001. Ages 12–YA. (chapter book)

————. *Roll of Thunder, Hear My Cry.* Dial, 1976. (See others in the Logan family saga: *The Song of the Trees,* 1975; *Let the Circle Be Unbroken,* 1981; *The Road to Memphis,* 1990; *The Land,* 2001) Ages 9–12. (chapter book)

Tillage, Leon W. *Leon's Story.* Illustrated by Susan L. Roth. Farrar, 1997. Ages 9–13. (nonfiction picture book)

Williams-Garcia, Rita. *Every Time a Rainbow Dies.* HarperCollins, 2001. Ages 14–YA. (chapter book)

Woodson, Jacqueline. *Hush.* Putnam, 2002. Ages 11–14. (chapter book)

————. *Locomotion.* Putnam, 2003. Ages 9–12. (chapter book)

————. *Miracle's Boys.* Putnam, 2000. Ages 10–YA. (chapter book)

————. *The Other Side.* Illustrated by E. B. Lewis. Putnam, 2001. Ages 5–8. (picture book)

Asian-American Literature

Balgassi, Haemi. *Peacebound Trains.* Illustrated by Chris K. Soentpiet. Clarion, 1996. Ages 8–12. (picture book)

Bercaw, Edna Coe. *Halmoni's Day.* Illustrated by Robert Hunt. Dial, 2000. Ages 5–8. (picture book)

Blumberg, Rhoda. *Full Steam Ahead: The Race to Build a Transcontinental Railroad.* National Geographic, 1996. Ages 9–12. (nonfiction chapter book)

Cha, Dia. *Dia's Story Cloth: The Hmong People's Journey to Freedom.* Stitchery by Chue and Nhia Thao Cha. Lee & Low, 1996. Ages 8–11. (picture book)

Falwell, Cathryn. *Butterflies for Kiri.* Lee & Low, 2003. Ages 5–7. (picture book)

Gilmore, Rachna. *A Gift for Gita.* Illustrated by Alice Priestley. Tilbury, 2002. Ages 6–9. (See others in the series: *Lights for Gita; Roses for Gita*) (picture book)

Krishnaswami, Uma. *Chachaji's Cap.* Illustrated by Sumeya Sitaraman. Children's Book Press, 2003. Ages 5–9. (picture book)

Kuklin, Susan. *Kodomo: Children of Japan.* Putnam, 1995. Ages 5–11. (photoessay)

Lasky, Kathryn. *Jahanara, Princess of Princesses.* Scholastic, 2002. Ages 12–14 (Part of the Royal Diaries series.) (chapter book)

Lee, Milly. *Nim and the War Effort.* Illustrated by Yangsook Choi. Farrar, 1997. Ages 7–10. (picture book)

Levine, Ellen. *A Fence Away from Freedom: Japanese Americans and World War II.* Putnam, 1995. Ages 12–YA. (nonfiction chapter book)

Look, Lenore. *Henry's First-Moon Birthday.* Illustrated by Yumi Heo. Atheneum, 2001. Ages 4–8. (picture book)

McKay, Lawrence, Jr. *Journey Home.* Illustrated by Dom and Keunhee Lee. Lee & Low, 1998. Ages 8–12. (picture book)

Mochizuki, Ken. *Baseball Saved Us.* Illustrated by Dom Lee. Lee and Low, 1993. Ages 7–10. (picture book)

————. *Passage to Freedom: The Sugihara Story.* Illustrated by Dom Lee. Lee & Low, 1997. Ages 7–11. (picture book, biography)

Na, An. *A Step from Heaven.* Front Street, 2001. Ages 13–YA. (chapter book)

Salisbury, Graham. *Lord of the Deep.* Delacorte, 2001. Ages 10–14. (chapter book)

Say, Allen. *Grandfather's Journey.* Houghton, 1993. Ages 7–9. (picture book)

————. *Tea with Milk.* Lorraine/Houghton, 1999. Ages 6–9. (picture book)

Schmidt, Jeremy, and Ted Wood. *Two Lands, One Heart: An American Boy's Journey to His Mother's Vietnam.* Photography by Ted Wood. Walker, 1995. Ages 7–10. (photoessay)

Shea, Pegi Deitz. *The Whispering Cloth.* Illustrated by Anita Riggio. Stitchery by You Yang. Boyds Mills, 1995. Ages 7–11. (picture book)

Staples, Suzanne Fisher. *Shiva's Fire.* Farrar, 2000. Ages 12–YA. (chapter book)

Strom, Yale. *Quilted Landscape: Conversations with Young Immigrants.* Simon & Schuster, 1996. Ages 11–14. (varied cultures)

Tunnell, Michael O., and George W. Chilcoat. *The Children of Topaz: The Story of a Japanese-American Internment Camp, Based on a Classroom Diary.* Holiday, 1996. Ages 8–14. (nonfiction chapter book)

Uchida, Yoshiko. *Journey to Topaz.* Scribner's, 1971. Ages 9–12. (chapter book) (See sequel: *Journey Home,* Atheneum, 1978.)

Whelan, Gloria. *Homeless Bird.* HarperCollins, 2000. Ages 12–14. (chapter book)

Wong, Janet S. *Apple Pie 4th of July.* Illustrated by Margaret Chodos-Irvine. Harcourt, 2002. Ages 4–7. (picture book)

————. *The Trip Back Home.* Illustrated by Bo Jia. Harcourt, 2000. Ages 7–9. (picture book)

Yee, Paul. *Dead Man's Gold and Other Stories.* Illustrated by Harvey Chan. Groundwood, 2002. Ages 12–YA. (collected stories)

Yep, Laurence. *Dragon's Gate.* HarperCollins, 1993. Ages 12–YA. (chapter book)

————. *Dragonwings.* Harper, 1975. Ages 9–12. (chapter book)

————. *Sea Glass. Golden Mountain Chronicles, 1970.* HarperCollins, 2002 (1979). Ages 9–12. (chapter book)

————. *Thief of Hearts.* HarperCollins,1995. Ages 10–14. (chapter book)

————. *The Tiger's Apprentice.* HarperCollins, 2003. Ages 9–14. (chapter book)

————. *Traitor. Golden Mountain Chronicles, 1885.* HarperCollins, 2003. Ages 12–14. (chapter book)

Young, Ed. *Monkey King.* HarperCollins, 2001. Ages 5–8. (picture book)

Jewish Literature

Bunting, Eve. *One Candle.* Illustrated by Wendy Popp. HarperCollins, 2002. Ages 6–9. (picture book)

Fagan, Cary, adapter. *The Market Wedding.* Illustrated by Regolo Ricci. Tundra, 2000. Ages 6–8. (picture book)

Feder, Paula K. *The Feather-Bed Journey.* Illustrated by Stacey Schuett. Albert Whitman, 1995. Ages 5–8. (picture book)

Geras, Adèle. *My Grandmother's Stories: A Collection of Jewish Folk Tales.* Illustrated by Anita Lobel. Knopf, 2003 (1990). Ages 8–10. (picture book)

Hautzig, Esther. *The Endless Steppe: A Girl in Exile.* Crowell, 1968. Ages 9–12. (chapter book)

————. *A Picture of Grandmother.* Illustrated by Beth Peck. Farrar, 2002. Ages 7–10. (transitional)

Hershenhorn, Esther. *Chicken Soup by Heart.* Illustrated by Rosanne Litzinger. Simon & Schuster, 2002. Ages 4–7. (picture book)

Hesse, Karen. *The Stone Lamp: Eight Stories of Hanukkah through History.* Illustrated by Brian Pinkney. Hyperion, 2003. Ages 9–13. (collected stories)

Hest, Amy. *Love You, Soldier.* Illustrated by Sonja Lamut. Candlewick, 2000 (1991). Ages 8–11. (transitional)

Kimmel, Eric, reteller. *A Cloak for the Moon.* Illustrated by Katya Krenina. Holiday, 2001. Ages 4–8. (modern folktale)

————, reteller. *Gershon's Monster: A Story for the Jewish New Year.* Illustrated by Jon J. Muth. Scholastic, 2000. Ages 6–11. (legend)

Levine, Karen. *Hana's Suitcase: A True Story.* Second Story Press, 2002. Ages 11–14. (chapter book)

Levitin, Sonia. *Journey to America.* Atheneum, 1970. Ages 12–YA. (chapter book) (See sequel: *Silver Days,* 1989.)

Lowry, Lois. *Number the Stars.* Houghton, 1989. Ages 7–9. (chapter book)

Newman, Lesléa. *Remember That.* Illustrated by Karen Ritz. Clarion, 1996. Ages 4–8. (picture book)

Oberman, Sheldon. *The Wisdom Bird. A Tale of Solomon and Sheba.* Illustrated by Neil Waldman. Boyds Mills, 2000. Ages 5–9. (picture book)

Rabinovici, Schoschana. *Thanks to My Mother.* Translated from the German by James Skofield. Dial, 1998. Ages 12–YA. (autobiography)

Rael, Elsa O. *What Zeesie Saw on Delancy Street.* Illustrated by Marjorie Priceman. Simon & Schuster, 1996. Ages 5–8. (picture book)

Reef, Catherine. *Sigmund Freud: Pioneer of the Mind.* Clarion, 2001. Ages 11–YA. (biography)

Reiss, Johanna. *The Upstairs Room.* Crowell, 1972. Ages 9–12. (chapter book)

Rocklin, Joanne. *Strudel Stories.* Delacorte, 1999. Ages 7–12. (chapter book)

Rogasky, Barbara. *Smoke and Ashes: The Story of the Holocaust.* Holiday, 1988; revised and expanded, 2002. Ages 12–YA. (chapter book)

Rubin, Susan Goldman. *Fireflies in the Dark: The Story of Friedl Dicker-Brandeis and the Children of Terezin.* Holiday, 2000. Ages 11–14. (picture book for older readers; biography)

Schmidt, Gary. *Mara's Stories: Glimmers in the Darkness.* Holt, 2001. Ages 11–YA. (traditional and modern folktales)

Schur, Maxine Rose. *The Peddler's Gift.* Illustrated by Kimberly Bulken Root. Dial, 1999. Ages 5–8. (modern folktale)

Siegal, Aranka. *Upon the Head of the Goat: A Childhood in Hungary 1939–1944.* Farrar, 1981. (See sequel: *Grace in the Wilderness: After the Liberation, 1945–1948,* 1985.) Ages 9–12. (chapter book)

Vos, Ida. *The Key Is Lost.* Translated by Terese Edelstein. HarperCollins, 2000. Ages 10–13. (chapter book)

Wisniewski, David. *Golem.* Clarion, 1996. Ages 6–12. (picture book)

Yolen, Jane. *The Devil's Arithmetic.* Penguin, 1988. Ages 10–13. (chapter book)

Latino Literature

Ada, Alma Flor. *I Love Saturdays y Domingos.* Illustrated by Elivia Savadier. Atheneum, 2002. Ages 4–8. (picture book)

Alvarez, Julia. *Before We Were Free.* Knopf, 2002. Ages 11–14. (chapter book)

Ancona, George. *Barrio: José's Neighborhood.* Harcourt,1998. Ages 6–9. (photoessay)

———. *Carnaval.* Harcourt, 1999. Ages 7–11. (photoessay)

———. *Fiesta U.S.A.* Lodestar, 1995. Ages 8–10.

Carling, Amelia Lau. *Mama and Papa Have a Store.* Dial, 1998. Ages 6–8. (picture book; Spanish, Mayan, and Chinese cultures)

Cofer, Judith O. *An Island Like You.* Orchard, 1995. Ages 12–YA. (short stories)

Delacre, Lulu, reteller. *Golden Tales: Myths, Legends and Folktales from Latin America.* Scholastic, 1996. Ages 8–12. (anthology)

Freedman, Russell. *In the Days of the Vaqueros: America's First True Cowboys.* Clarion, 2001. Ages 10–14. (nonfiction chapter book)

Hanson, Regina. *The Face at the Window.* Illustrated by Linda Saport. Clarion, 1997. Ages 6–9. (picture book)

Herrera, Juan Felipe. *Crashboomlove. A Novel in Verse.* University of New Mexico Press, 1999. Ages 14–YA. (chapter book).

Jiménez, Francisco. *Breaking Through.* Houghton, 2001. Ages 12–14. (chapter book)

———. *The Circuit: Stories from the Life of a Migrant Child.* Houghton, 1999 (1996). (new ed.) Ages 10–14. (short stories)

———. *La Mariposa.* Illustrated by Simón Silva. Houghton, 1998. Ages 8–11. (picture book)

Joseph, Lynn. *The Color of My Words.* HarperCollins, 2000. Ages 10–14. (chapter book)

Kroll, Virginia. *Butterfly Boy.* Illustrated by Gerardo Suzán. Boyds Mills, 1997. Ages 5–8. (picture book)

Lee, Hector V. *I Had a Hippopotamus.* Lee & Low, 1996. Ages 2–5. (picture book)

Mora, Pat. *Confetti: Poems for Children.* Illustrated by Enrique O. Sanchez. Lee & Low, 1996. Ages 6–9.

———. *A Library for Juana: The World of Sor Juana Ines.* Illustrated by Beatriz Vidal. Knopf, 2002. Ages 7–9. (picture book biography)

———. *Tomás and the Library Lady.* Illustrated by Raul Colón. Knopf, 1997. Ages 6–8. (picture book biography)

Ryan, Pam Muñoz. *Esperanza Rising.* Scholastic, 2001. Ages 11–14. (chapter book)

Skármeta, Antonio. *The Composition.* Illustrated by Alfonso Ruano. Translated from the Spanish by Elisa Amado. Groundwood, 2000. Ages 8–12. (picture book)

Soto, Gary. *Chato and the Party Animals.* Illustrated by Susan Guevara. Putnam, 2000. Ages 5–8. (picture book)

———. *Chato's Kitchen.* Illustrated by Susan Guevara. Putnam, 1995. Ages 5–8. (picture book)

———. *Snapshots from the Wedding.* Illustrated by Stephanie Garcia. Putnam, 1997. Ages 5–8. (picture book)

———. *Trading Places.* Harcourt, 1993. Ages 10–13. (chapter book)

Temple, Frances. *Tonight, by Sea.* Orchard, 1995. Ages 12–YA. (docu-novel)

Veciana-Suarez, Ana. *Flight to Freedom.* Orchard, 2002. Ages 12–14. (chapter book)

Winter, Jonah. *Frida.* Illustrated by Ana Juan. Scholastic, 2002. Ages 6–9. (picture book biography)

Bilingual Literature

Ada, Alma Flor. *Gathering the Sun: An Alphabet in Spanish and English.* English translation by Rosa Zubizarreta. Illustrated by Simón Silva. Lothrop, 1997. (poetry) English/Spanish

———. *The Lizard and the Sun/La Lagartija y el Sol.* Illustrated by Felipe Davalos. Doubleday, 1997. Ages 5–7. (picture book) English/Spanish

Afanasév, A. *Skazki: Russian Fairy Tales.* Illustrated by I. V. Bilibin. Translated by D. Martin and L. Lisitskya. Terra, 1996. (picture book) English/Russian

Alarcon, Francisco X. *Angels Ride Bikes and Other Fall Poems/Los Ángeles Andan en Bicicleta y otros poemas de otoño.* Illustrated by Christina González. Children's Book Press, 1999. Ages 6–12. (poetry) English/Spanish

———. *From the Bellybutton of the Moon and Other Summer Poems/Del Ombligo de la Luna y otros poemas de verano.* Illustrated by Christina González. Children's Book Press, 1998. Ages 6–12. (poetry) English/Spanish

———. *Iguanas in the Snow and Other Winter Poems.* Illustrated by Maya Christina González. Children's Book Press, 2001. Ages 6–12. (picture book/poetry)

———. *Laughing Tomatoes and Other Spring Poems/Jitomates Risuenos y otros poemas de primavera.* Illustrated by Christina González. Children's Book Press, 1997. Ages 6–12. (poetry) English/Spanish

Andaldúa, Gloria. *Prietita and the Ghost Woman/Prietita y la Llorona.* Illustrated by Christina González. Children's Book Press, 1996. Ages 7–10. (picture book). English/Spanish

Argueta, Jorge. *A Movie in My Pillow/Una película en mi almohada: Poems.* Illustrated by Elizabeth Gómez. Children's Book Press, 2001. Ages 8–12. (picture book/poetry) English/Spanish

Bateson-Hill, Margaret. *Lao-ao of Dragon Mountain.* Illustrated by Francesca Pelizzoli. Paper cuts by Sha-liu Qu. Stewart, Tabori & Chang, 1996. Ages 4–8. (picture book) English/Chinese

Bertrand, Diane Gonzales. *Family.* Spanish translation by Julia Mercedes Castilla. Illustrated by Pauline Rodriguez Howard. Piñata Books, 1999. Ages 4–8. (picture book). English/Spanish

Brusca, Christina Maria, and Tona Wilson. *Three Friends: A Counting Book/Tres Amigos: un cuento para cuntar.* Holt, 1995. Ages 2–5. (picture book). English/Spanish

Carlson, Lori, selector. *You're On! Seven Plays in English and Spanish.* Morrow, 1999. Ages 9–15.

Cohn, Diana. *¡Sí, se puede!/Yes, We Can!: Janitor Strike in L.A.* Translated by Sharon Franco. Illustrated by Francisco Delgado. Cinco Puntos, 2002. Ages 6–8. (picture book) English/Spanish

Corpi, Lucha. *Where Fireflies Dance/Ahi, Donde Bailan las Luciernagas.* Illustrated by Mira Reisberg. Children's Book Press, 1997. Ages 7–12. (picture book) English/Spanish

Cowcher, Helen. *Tigress.* Translated by Mei-Ling Christine Lee. Millet, 1997. Ages 5–9. (picture book). English/Vietnamese

Delgado, Maria Isabel. *Chaves's Memories/Los Recuerdos de Chave.* Illustrated by Yvonne Symank. Piñata Books, 1996. Ages 4–7. (picture book) English/Spanish

Despain, Pleasant, reteller. *The Emerald Lizard: Fifteen Latin American Tales to Tell.* Illustrated by Don Bell. Translated by Mario Lamo-Jiménez. August House, 1999. Ages 7–12. (folklore collection) English/Spanish

Ehlert, Lois. *Cuckoo: A Mexican Folktale/Cucu: Un Cuento Folklorico Mexicano.* Translated by de Aragon Andujar. Harcourt, 1997. Ages 3–8. (picture book) English/Spanish

Galindo, Mary Sue. *Icy Watermelon/Sandía fría.* Illustrated by Pauline Rodriguez Howard. Arte Público, 2000. Ages 3–8. (picture book) English/Spanish

Garza, Carmen L., with Harriet Rohmer. *In My Family/En Mi Familia.* Edited by David Schecter. Translated by Francisco X. Alarcón. Children's Book Press, 1996. Ages 5–12. (picture book) English/Spanish

———, as told to Harriet Rohmer. *Magic Windows: Cut-paper Art and Stories/Ventanas Magicas.* Children's Book Press, 1999. Ages 5–12. (picture book) English/Spanish

Gonzalez, Ralfka, and Ana Ruiz. *My First Book of Proverbs/Mi primer libro de dichos.* Children's Book Press, 1995. Ages 4–8. (proverbs) English/Spanish

Han, Suzanne Crowder. *The Rabbit's Escape/Kusa Il-saenghan Tooki.* Illustrated by Yumi Heo. Holt, 1995. Ages 5–8. (picture book). English/Korean

Herrera, Juan Felipe. *Calling the Doves/El canto de las palomas.* Illustrated by Elly Simmons. Children's Book Press, 1995. Ages 4–8. (picture book) English/ Spanish

————. *Grandma and Me at the Flea/Los meros meros remateros.* Illustrated by Anita DeLucio-Brock. Children's Book Press, 2002. Ages 4–8. (picture book) English/Spanish

Ho, Minfong. *Maples in the Mist: Children's Poems from the Tang Dynasty.* Illustrated by Jean and Mou-sien Tseng. Translated by Minfong Ho. Lothrop, 1996. (poetry) English/Chinese

Holt, Daniel D. (Ed.). *Tigers, Frogs, and Rice Cakes: A Book of Korean Proverbs.* Illustrated by Lu Han Stickler. Shen's Books, 1998. (picture book) English/Korean

Jiménez, Francisco. *The Christmas Gift/El regalo de Navidad.* Illustrated by Claire B. Cotts. Houghton, 2000. Ages 6–8. (picture book) English/Spanish

Keister, Douglas. *Fernando's Gift/El regalo de Fernando.* Sierra Club, 1995. Ages 5–8. (picture book) English/Spanish

Kitsao, Jay. *McHeshi Goes to the Market* (see others in the McHeshi series). Illustrated by Wanjiku Mathenge et al. Jacaranda Designs, 1995. Ages 3–5. (picture book) English/Swahili

Lee, Jeanne. *Song of Mu Lan.* Front Street, 1995. Ages 5–8. (picture book) English/Chinese

Loya, Olga. *Magic Moments: Tales from Latin America/Momentos mágicos.* Translated by Carmen Lizardo-Rivera. August House, 1998. Ages 10–YA. (short stories) English/Spanish

Luenn, Nancy. *A Gift for Abuelita: Celebrating the Day of the Dead/Un regalo para Abuelita: En celebración del Día de los Muertos.* Illustrated by Robert Chapman. Rising Moon, 1998. Ages 4–8. (picture book) English/Spanish

MacDonald, Margaret Read. *The Girl Who Wore Too Much: A Folktale from Thailand.* Thai text by Supaporn Vathanaprida. Illustrated by Yvonne Le-Brun Davis. August House, 1998. Ages 4–8. (picture book) English/Thai

Mado, Michio. *The Magic Pocket.* Illustrated by Mitsumasa Anno. Translated by the Empress Michiko of Japan. McElderry Books, 1998. Ages 3–5. (poetry) English/Japanese

Masurel, Claire. *Un gato y un perro/A Cat and a Dog.* Illustrated by Bob Kolar. Translated by Andrés Antreasyan. Ediciones Norte-Sur, 2003. Ages 4–7. (picture book) Spanish-English.

Nye, Naomi Shihab, editor. *The Tree Is Older Than You Are: A Bilingual Gathering of Poems and Stories from Mexico with Paintings by Mexican Artists.* Simon & Schuster, 1995. Ages 8–YA. (literature anthology) English/Spanish

Orozco, J. *Diez deditos/Ten Little Fingers and Other Play Rhymes and Action Songs from Latin America.* Illustrated by Elisa Kleven. Dutton, 1997. Ages 4–7. Spanish/English

Pérez, Amada Irma. *My Diary from Here to There/Mi diario de aquí hasta allá.* Illustrated by Maya Christina González. Children's Book Press, 2002. Ages 8–10. (picture book) English/Spanish

————. *My Very Own Room/Mi propio cuartito.* Illustrated by Maya Christina González. Children's Book Press, 2000. Ages 7–10. (picture book) English/Spanish

Rodríguez, Luis J. *It Doesn't Have to Be This Way: A Barrio Story/No tiene que ser así: Una historia del barrio.* Illustrated by Daniel Galvez. Children's Book Press, 1999. Ages 10–14. (picture book) English/Spanish

Saenz, Benjamin Alira. *A Gift from Papa Diego/Un regalo de Papa Diego.* Illustrated by Geronimo Garcia. Cinco puntas Press, 1998. Ages 5–8. (picture book) English/Spanish

Stewart, Mark, and Mike Kennedy. *Latino Baseball's Finest Fielders/Los más destacados guantes del béisbol latino.* Translated by Manuel Kalmanovitz. Millbrook, 2002. Ages 9–13. (collected biographies) English-Spanish. See companion volume, *Latino Baseball's Hottest Hitters* (2002).

Wyndham, Robert. *Chinese Mother Goose Rhymes.* Illustrated by Ed Young. PaperStar, 1998 (originally published by World Publishing Company, 1968). English/Chinese

Zhang, Sonng Nan, reteller/illustrator. *The Ballad of Mulan/Bai Ca Moc Lau.* Translated by Nguyen

Ngoc Ngan. Pan Asian Publications, 1998. Ages 5–7. (picture book) English/Vietnamese

Native American Literature

Ancona, George. *Mayeros: A Yucatec Maya Family.* Lothrop, 1997. Ages 7–11. (photoessay)

Baker, Olaf. *Where the Buffaloes Begin.* Illustrated by Stephen Gammell. Warne, 1981. Ages 7–9. (picture book)

Bealer, Alex. *Only the Names Remain: The Cherokees and the Trail of Tears.* Little, Brown, 1972. Ages 9–12. (chapter book)

Begay, Shonto. *Navajo: Visions and Voices across the Mesa.* Scholastic, 1995. Ages 12–YA. (poetry)

Boyden, Linda. *The Blue Roses.* Illustrated by Amy Córdova. Lee & Low, 2002. Ages 5–8. (picture book)

Bruchac, Joseph. *The Boy Who Lived with the Bears: And Other Iroquois Stories.* HarperCollins, 1995. Ages 6–9. (collection)

———. *Crazy Horse's Vision.* Illustrated by S. D. Nelson. Lee & Low, 2000. Ages 6–10. (picture book; biography)

———. *Eagle Song.* Illustrated by Dan Andreasen. Dial, 1997. Ages 9–11. (chapter book)

———. *The First Strawberries.* Illustrated by Anna Vojtech. Dial, 1993. Ages 7–10. (picture book)

———. *Pushing Up the Sky: Seven Native American Plays for Children.* Illustrated by Teresa Flavin. Dial, 2000. Ages 7–11. (plays)

———. *Seeing the Circle.* Photographs by John Christopher Fine. Richard K. Owen, 1999. Ages 7–10. (autobiography)

———. *Skeleton Man.* HarperCollins, 2001. Ages 10–14. (chapter book)

———. *The Winter People.* Dial, 2002. Ages 12–YA. (chapter book)

Curry, Jane Louise. *Hold Up the Sky and Other Indian Tales from Texas and the Southern Plains.* Illustrated by James Watts. McElderry, 2003. Ages 8–12. (folktales)

Erdrich, Louise. *The Birchbark House.* Hyperion, 1999. Ages 8–12. (historical fiction)

George, Jean Craighead. *Julie.* HarperCollins, 1994. Ages 10–14. (chapter book)

———. *Julie of the Wolves.* Harper, 1972. Ages 9–12. (chapter book)

Goble, Paul. *The Girl Who Loved Wild Horses.* Bradbury, 1978. Ages 6–8. (picture book)

———. reteller. *The Return of the Buffaloes: A Plains Indian Story about Famine and Renewal of the Earth.* National Geographic, 1996. Ages 8–12. (picture book)

Hudson, Jan. *Sweetgrass.* Philomel, 1989. Ages 12–YA. (chapter book)

Hunter, Sally M. *Four Seasons of Corn: A Winnebago Tradition.* Photography by Joe Allen. Lerner, 1996. Ages 7–11. (photoessay)

McKissack, Patricia C. *Run Away Home.* Scholastic, 1997. Ages 10–12. (chapter book; also African American)

Mikaelsen, Ben. *Touching Spirit Bear.* HarperCollins, 2001. Ages 12–14. (chapter book)

Miles, Miska. *Annie and the Old One.* Illustrated by Peter Parnall. Little, Brown, 1971. Ages 7–9. (picture book)

O'Dell, Scott. *Island of the Blue Dolphins.* Houghton, 1960. Ages 9–12. (chapter book)

———. *Sing Down the Moon.* Houghton, 1970. Ages 12–YA. (chapter book)

Rappaport, Doreen. *The Flight of Red Bird: The Life of Zilkala-Sa.* Dial, 1997. Ages 11–YA. (chapter book; biography)

Rendon, Marcie R. *Powwow Summer: A Family Celebrates the Circle of Life.* Photography by Cheryl W. Bellville. Carolrhoda, 1996. Ages 7–11. (photoessay)

Ross, Gayle. *How Turtle's Back Was Cracked: A Traditional Cherokee Tale.* Illustrated by Murv Jacob. Dial, 1995. Ages 7–9. (picture book)

Smith, Cynthia Leitich. *Rain Is Not My Indian Name.* HarperCollins, 2001. Ages 10–14. (chapter book)

Sneve, Virginia Driving Hawk. *The Sioux.* Illustrated by Ronald Himler. Holiday House, 1993. Ages 7–10. (picture book) (See others in the First Americans Book series)

Steltzer, Ulli. *Building an Igloo.* Holt, 1995. Ages 7–11. (picture book)

Viola, Herman J. *It Is a Good Day to Die: Indian Eyewitnesses Tell the Story of the Battle of the Little Bighorn.* Crown, 1998. Ages 11–YA. (informational)

R E C O M M E N D E D   I N T E R N A T I O N A L   B O O K S

Ages refer to approximate interest levels.
YA = young adult readers. Country
of original publication is noted.

English Language Books

Ahlberg, Janet, and Allan Ahlberg. *Each Peach Pear Plum.* Viking, 1979. Ages 3–6. U.K.

———. *The Jolly Postman.* Little, Brown, 1986. Ages 5–8. U.K.

———. *The Jolly Christmas Postman.* Heinemann, 1991. Ages 5–8. U.K.

Alborough, Jez. *Fix-It Duck.* HarperCollins, 2002. Ages 2–5. U.K.

Almond, David. *Heaven Eyes.* Delacorte, 2001. Ages 10–YA. U.K.

———. *Kit's Wilderness.* Delacorte, 2000. Ages 12–YA. U.K.

———. *Skellig.* Delacorte, 1999. Ages 10–YA. U.K.

Anderson, Rachel. *Black Water.* Holt, 1995. Ages 10–14. U.K.

Ardagh, Philip. *A House Called Awful End.* Illustrated by David Roberts. Holt, 2002. Ages 9–12. U.K. (Also in the trilogy, *Dreadful Acts,* 2002, and *Terrible Times,* 2003.)

Armstrong, Carole. *Lives and Legends of the Saints.* Simon & Schuster, 1995. Ages 9–12. U.K.

Asare, Meshack. *Cat in Search of a Friend.* Kane/Miller, 1986. Ages 4–10. Ghana.

———. *Sosu's Call.* Kane/Miller, 2002. Ages 6–9. Ghana.

Baker, Jeannie. *The Hidden Forest.* Greenwillow, 2000. Ages 6–10. Australia.

———. *Where the Forest Meets the Sea.* Greenwillow, 1987. Ages 7–12. Australia.

———. *Window.* Julia McRae, 1991. Ages 8–11. Australia.

Base, Graeme. *The Water Hole.* Abrams, 2001. Ages 4–8. Australia.

Breslin, Theresa. *Whispers in the Graveyard.* Heinemann, 1994. Ages 12–14. U.K.

Briggs, Raymond. *The Man.* Random House, 1995. Ages 9–14. U.K.

Brooks, Martha. *Traveling on into the Light: And Other Stories.* Orchard, 1994. Ages 12–YA. Canada.

Browne, Anthony. *Gorilla.* Knopf, 1985. Ages 6–8. U.K.

———. *Willy the Champ.* Knopf, 1986. Ages 4–8. U.K.

———. *Willy the Wizard.* Knopf, 1996. Ages 4–7. U.K.

———. *Zoo.* Julia McRae, 1992. Ages 6–10. U.K.

Burgess, Melvin. *Kite.* Farrar, 2000. Ages 12–YA. U.K.

Child, Lauren. *I Will Never Not Ever Eat a Tomato.* Candlewick, 2000. Ages 3–8. U.K.

———. *What Planet Are You from, Clarice Bean?* Candlewick, 2002. Ages 6–8. U.K.

Colfer, Eoin. *Artemis Fowl.* Hyperion, 2001. Ages 10–12. Ireland.

Crew, Gary. *Angel's Gate.* Simon & Schuster, 1995. Ages 12–YA. Australia.

Crossley-Holland, Kevin. *The Seeing Stone.* Scholastic, 2001. Ages 10–YA. U.K.

Dahl, Roald. *Matilda.* Illustrated by Quentin Blake. Viking, 1988. Ages 9–12. U.K.

Daly, Niki. *The Boy on the Beach.* Simon & Schuster, 1999. Ages 3–7. South Africa.

———. *Jamela's Dress.* Farrar, 1999. Ages 4–7. South Africa.

———. *Once Upon a Time.* Farrar, 2003. Ages 4–8. South Africa.

Doyle, Brian. *Mary Ann Alice.* Douglas & McIntyre, 2002. Ages 9–13. Canada.

Doyle, Malachy. *Who Is Jesse Flood?* Bloomsbury, 2002. Ages 11–YA. Northern Ireland.

Ellis, Sarah. *Out of the Blue.* McElderry, 1995. Ages 9–12. Canada.

Fine, Anne. *The Jamie and Angus Stories.* Illustrated by Penny Dale. Candlewick, 2002. Ages 7–9. U.K.

Foreman, Michael. *Saving Sinbad.* Kane/Miller, 2002. Ages 4–8. U.K.

Fox, Mem. *Wilfrid Gordon McDonald Partridge.* Illustrated by Julie Vivas. Kane/Miller, 1985. Ages 5–10. Australia.

French, Jackie. *Hitler's Daughter.* HarperCollins, 2003. Ages 9–12. Australia.

Gavin, Jamila. *Coram Boy.* Farrar, 2001. Ages 11–YA. U.K.

Gilmore, Rachna. *A Group of One.* Holt, 2001. Ages 11–YA. Canada.

Graham, Bob. *Jethro Byrd, Fairy Child.* Candlewick, 2002. Ages 4–7. Australia.

———. *Let's Get a Pup! Said Kate.* Candlewick, 2003. Ages 3–8. Australia.

Greenwood, Kerry. *A Different Sort of Real: The Diary of Charlotte McKenzie, Melbourne 1918–1919.* Scholastic, 2001. Ages 10–13. Australia.

Hartnett, Sonya. *Thursday's Child.* Candlewick, 2002. Ages 13–YA. Australia.

Heaney, Marie. *The Names upon the Harp: Irish Myth and Legend.* Illustrated by P. J. Lynch. Scholastic, 2000. Ages 10–13. Ireland.

Hendry, Diana. *Harvey Angell.* Aladdin, 2001. Ages 9–12. U.K.

Heneghan, James. *Flood.* Farrar, 2002. Ages 10–14. Canada.

Hoffman, Mary. *Amazing Grace.* Illustrated by Caroline Binch. Dial, 1991. Ages 4–9. U.K. (See also sequel: *Boundless Grace,* Dial, 1995.)

Honey, Elizabeth. *Fiddleback.* Knopf, 2001. Ages 9–12. Australia.

———. *Remote Man.* Knopf, 2002. Ages 11–YA. Australia.

Hughes, Monica. *The Keeper of the Isis Light.* Nelson, 1980. Ages 11–YA. Canada.

Hughes, Shirley. *Tales of Trotter Street.* Candlewick, 1997. Ages 4–10. U.K.

Ibbotson, Eva. *Journey to the River Sea.* Illustrated by Kevin Hawkes. Dutton, 2001. Ages 9–12. U.K.

———. *The Secret of Platform 13.* Dutton, 1998. Ages 9–13. U.K.

———. *Which Witch?* Dutton, 1999. Ages 10–14. U.K.

Ihimaera, Witi. *Whale Rider.* Harcourt, 2003. Ages 12–YA. New Zealand.

Jacques, Brian. *Redwall.* Philomel, 1986. Ages 11–YA. U.K. (First of many books in this series.)

Jennings, Paul. *Unreal: Eight Surprising Stories.* Viking, 1991. Ages 11–14. Australia.

Johnston, Julie. *In Spite of Killer Bees.* Tundra, 2001. Ages 12–YA. Canada.

Kindersley, Barnabas, and Anabel Kindersley. *Children Just Like Me.* Dorling Kindersley, 1995. Ages 7–12. U.K.

King-Smith, Dick. *The Nine Lives of Aristotle.* Illustrated by Bob Graham. Candlewick, 2003. Ages 7–9. U.K.

Lewis, C. S. *The Lion, the Witch, and the Wardrobe.* Macmillan, 1950. Ages 10–YA. U.K.

Little, Jean. *Mama's Going to Buy You a Mockingbird.* Viking, 1985. Ages 10–YA. Canada.

———. *Willow and Twig.* Viking, 2003. Ages 11–14. Canada.

Loyie, Larry, with Constance Brissenden. *As Long as the Rivers Flow.* Illustrated by Heather D. Holmlund. Douglas & McIntyre, 2002. Ages 8–12. Canada.

Lunn, Janet. *Laura Secord: A Story of Courage.* Illustrated by Maxwell Newhouse. Tundra, 2001. Ages 9–12. Canada.

———. *The Root Cellar.* Scribner's, 1983. Ages 11–YA. Canada.

Mahy, Margaret. *The Good Fortunes Gang.* Illustrated by Marion Young. Delacorte, 1993. Ages 8–11. New Zealand.

Marsden, John. *Letters from the Inside.* Houghton, 1994. Ages 12–YA. Australia.

———. *So Much to Tell You.* Joy Street, 1989. Ages 12–YA. Australia.

Matas, Carol. *Sparks Fly Upward.* Clarion, 2002. Ages 9–13. Canada.

McCaughrean, Geraldine. *The Kite Rider: A Novel.* HarperCollins, 2002. Ages 10–14. U.K.

McKay, Hilary. *The Exiles.* Macmillan, 1992. Ages 9–12. U.K.

———. *Saffy's Angel.* McElderry, 2002. Ages 9–12. U.K.

Montgomery, Lucy M. *Anne of Green Gables.* Bantam, 1908. Ages 9–13. Canada.

Morpurgo, Michael. *The Wreck of the Zanzibar.* Illustrated by François Place. Viking, 1995. Ages 12–14. U.K.

Mowat, Farley. *Owls in the Family.* Little, Brown, 1962. Ages 8–11. Canada.

Murray, Martine. *The Slightly True Story of Cedar B. Hartley (Who Planned to Live an Unusual Life).* Scholastic, 2003. Ages 9–13. Australia.

Naidoo, Beverley. *Chain of Fire.* Lippincott, 1990. Ages 11–YA. South Africa.

———. *Journey to Jo'burg.* Lippincott, 1986. Ages 10–YA. South Africa.

———. *No Turning Back: A Novel of South Africa.* HarperCollins, 1997. Ages 10–14. South Africa.

———. *The Other Side of Truth.* HarperCollins, 2001. Ages 10–YA. South Africa.

———. *Out of Bounds: Seven Stories of Conflict and Hope.* HarperCollins, 2003. Ages 10–14. South Africa.

Nicholson, William. *The Wind Singer.* Hyperion, 2000. Ages 10–13. U.K. First of trilogy, Wind on Fire, that includes *Slaves of the Master* (2001) and *Firesong* (2002).

Norling, Beth. *Little School.* Kane/Miller, 2003. Ages 3–5. Australia.

Orr, Wendy. *Peeling the Onion.* Holiday, 1997. Ages 11–YA. Australia.

Overend, Jenni. *Welcome with Love.* Illustrated by Julie Vivas. Kane/Miller, 2000. Ages 5–8. Australia.

Pearce, Philippa. *Tom's Midnight Garden.* Lippincott, 1959. Ages 9–12. U.K.

Pratchett, Terry. *The Amazing Maurice and His Educated Rodents.* HarperCollins, 2001. Ages 11–YA. U.K.

Pullman, Philip. *Clockwork.* Illustrated by Leonid Gore. Scholastic, 1998. Ages 9–13. U.K.

———. *The Golden Compass.* Knopf, 1996. Ages 12–YA. First of His Dark Materials trilogy. Also, *The Subtle Knife,* Knopf, 1997, and *The Amber Spyglass,* Knopf, 1999. U.K.

———. *I Was a Rat!* Illustrated by Kevin Hawkes. Knopf, 2000. Ages 8–12. U.K.

Rees, Celia. *Pirates!* Bloomsbury, 2003. Ages 12–YA. U.K.

———. *Witch Child.* Candlewick, 2001. Ages 11–YA. U.K. The sequel is *Sorceress,* 2002.

Riddle, Toby. *The Singing Hat.* Farrar, 2001. Ages 5–8.

Rodda, Emily. *The Charm Bracelet.* Illustrated by Raoul Vitale. HarperCollins, 2003. Ages 7–11. Australia.

———. *Power and Glory.* Illustrated by Geoff Kelly. Greenwillow, 1996. Ages 5–7. Australia.

———. *Rowan of Rin.* Greenwillow, 2001. Ages 8–12. Australia. (Also in this series, *Rowan and the Travelers,* 2001; *Rowan and the Keeper of the Crystal,* 2002; *Rowan and the Zebak,* 2002; and *Rowan and the Ice-Creepers,* 2003.)

Rowling, J. K. *Harry Potter and the Sorcerer's Stone.* Scholastic, 1998. The first in a series of quest fantasies, including *Harry Potter and the Chamber of Secrets,* 1999; *Harry Potter and the Prisoner of Azkaban,* 1999; *Harry Potter and the Goblet of Fire,* 2000; and *Harry Potter and the Order of the Phoenix,* 2003. Ages 9–13. U.K.

Rubinstein, Gillian. *Foxspell.* Simon & Schuster, 1996. Ages 12–14. Australia.

———. *Galax-Arena.* Simon & Schuster, 1995. Ages 12–YA. Australia.

Scrimger, Richard. *The Nose from Jupiter.* Tundra, 1998. Ages 10–13. Canada.

Slade, Arthur. *Dust.* Wendy Lamb, 2003. Ages 11–YA. Canada.

Stanley, Elizabeth. *The Deliverance of Dancing Bears.* Kane/Miller, 2002. Ages 5–9. Australia.

Thompson, Kate. *Wild Blood.* Hyperion, 2000. Ages 11–YA. Ireland. Last in the trilogy that began with *Switchers,* 1998, and was followed by *Midnight's Choice,* 1999.

Tomlinson, Theresa. *The Forestwife.* Orchard, 1995. Ages 10–14. U.K.

Trottier, Maxine. *The Tiny Kite of Eddie Wing.* Illustrated by Al Van Mil. Kane/Miller, 1996. Ages 4–9. Canada.

Valgardson, W. D. *Sarah and the People of Sand River.* Illustrated by Ian Wallace. Groundwood, 1996. Ages 8–11. Canada.

———. *Winter Rescue.* Illustrated by Ange Zhang. McElderry Books, 1995. Ages 7–9. Canada.

Waddell, Martin. *Farmer Duck.* Illustrated by Helen Oxenbury. Candlewick, 1992. Ages 4–6. U.K.

Wallace, Ian. *Boy of the Deeps.* DK Ink, 1999. Ages 8–11. Canada.

———. *The Naked Lady.* Roaring Brook, 2002. Ages 6–12. Canada.

———. *The True Story of Trapper Jack's Left Big Toe.* Roaring Brook, 2002. Ages 5–9. Canada.

Walsh, Alice. *Heroes of Isles aux Morts.* Illustrated by Geoff Butler. Tundra, 2001. Ages 4–8. Canada.

Waugh, Sylvia. *Space Race.* Delacorte, 2000. Ages 9–12. U.K.

Wild, Margaret. *Fox.* Illustrated by Ron Brooks. Kane/Miller, 2001. Ages 6–8. Australia.

————. *The Pocket Dogs.* Illustrated by Stephen Michael King. Scholastic, 2001. Ages 3–7. Australia.

————. *The Very Best of Friends.* Illustrated by Julie Vivas. Harcourt, 1990. Ages 4–9. Australia.

Wilson, Budge. *A Fiddle for Angus.* Illustrated by Susan Tooke. Tundra, 2001. Ages 5–9. Canada.

————. *The Leaving and Other Stories.* Philomel, 1992. Ages 12–14. Canada.

Wilson, Jacqueline. *The Story of Tracy Beaker.* Illustrated by Nick Sharratt. Delacorte, 2001. Ages 9–12. U.K.

Wojciechowski, Susan. *The Christmas Miracle of Jonathan Toomey.* Illustrated by P. J. Lynch. Walker, 1995. Ages 4–9. U.K. Copublication with an American author and Irish illustrator.

Wynne-Jones, Tim. *The Boy in the Burning House.* Farrar, 2001. Ages 12–YA. Canada.

Yee, Paul. *Dead Man's Gold and Other Stories.* Illustrated by Harvey Chan. Douglas & McIntyre, 2002. Ages 11–14. Canada.

————. *Tales from Gold Mountain: Stories of the Chinese in the New World.* Macmillan, 1990. Ages 7–12. Canada.

Translated Books

Arcellana, Francisco. *The Mats.* Illustrated by Hermès Allègre. Kane/Miller, 1999. Ages 5–9. Philippines.

Ashbé, Jeanne. *What's Inside.* Kane/Miller, 2000. Ages 2–5. Belgium.

Björk, Christina. *Linnea in Monet's Garden.* Illustrated by Lena Anderson. Translated from the Swedish by Joan Sandin. Farrar (R & S), 1987. Ages 7–11. Sweden.

————. *Vendela in Venice.* Illustrated by Inga-Karin Eriksson. Translated from the Swedish by Patricia Crampton. R & S, 1999. Ages 9–12. Sweden.

Bluitgen, Kåre. *A Boot Fell from Heaven.* Illustrated by Chiara Carrer. Kane/Miller, 2003. Ages 5–9. Denmark.

Brunhoff, Jean de. *The Story of Babar.* Translated from the French by Merle Haas. Random, 1933. Ages 5–7. France.

Buchholz, Quint. *The Collector of Moments.* Translated from the German by Peter F. Niemeyer. Farrar, 1999. Ages 9–12. Germany.

Carmi, Daniella. *Samir and Yonatan.* Translated from the Hebrew by Yael Lotan. Scholastic, 2000. Ages 9–12. Israel.

Collodi, Carlo. *The Adventures of Pinocchio.* Translated from the Italian by Marianna Mayer. Macmillan, 1981 (1881). Ages 6–9. Italy.

Duquennoy, Jacques. *The Ghost's Trip to Loch Ness.* Translated by Kathryn Nanovic. Harcourt, 1996. Ages 5–7. France.

Dumas, Felipe. *A Farm.* Creative Company, 1999. Ages 7–14. France.

Fournier le Ray, Anne-Laure. *Grandparents!* Illustrated by Roser Capdevila. Kane/Miller, 2003. Ages 4–7. France.

Frank, Anne. *Anne Frank: The Diary of a Young Girl.* Translated from the Dutch by B. M. Mooyaart. Doubleday, 1967. Netherlands.

Friedrich, Joachim. *4½ Friends and the Secret Cave.* Translated from the German by Elizabeth D. Crawford. Hyperion, 2001. Ages 8–11. Germany.

Funke, Cornelia. *The Thief Lord.* Translated by Oliver Latsch. Scholastic, 2002. Ages 10–14. Germany.

Gaarder, Jostein. *The Solitaire Mystery.* Illustrated by Hilde Kramer. Translated by Sarah Jane Hails. Farrar, 1996. Ages 12–YA. Norway.

Gallaz, Christophe, and Roberto Innocenti. *Rose Blanche.* Translated from the French by Martha Coventry and Richard Graglia. Creative Education, 1985. Ages 9–YA. France.

Gomi, Taro. *Everyone Poops.* Translated from the Japanese by Amanda Mayer Stinchecum. Kane/Miller, 1993. Ages 2–5. Japan.

————. *I Lost My Dad!* Kane/Miller, 2001. Ages 4–7. Japan.

Gündisch, Karin. *How I Became an American.* Translated from the German by James Skofield. Cricket, 2001. Ages 9–12. Germany.

Harel, Nira. *The Key to My Heart.* Illustrated by Yossi Abulafia. Kane/Miller, 2002. Ages 4–7. Israel.

Highet, Alistair. *The Yellow Train.* Based on a story by Fred Bernard. Illustrated by François Roca. Creative, 2000. Ages 4–7. Canada.

Ho, Minfong, compiler. *Maples in the Mist: Children's Poems from the Tang Dynasty.* Illustrated by Jean and Mou-sien Tseng. Translated from the Chinese by Minfong Ho. Lothrop, 1996. Ages 7–12. China.

Hoestlandt, Jo. *Star of Fear, Star of Hope.* Illustrated by Johanna Kang. Translated from the French by Mark Polizzotti. Walker, 1995. Ages 7–12. France.

Hogeweg, Margriet. *The God of Grandma Forever.* Translated from the Dutch by Nancy Forest-Flier. Front Street, 2001. Ages 9–13. Netherlands.

Holtwijz, Ineke. *Asphalt Angels.* Front Street, 1999. Translated from the Dutch by Wanda Boeke. Ages 12–YA. The Netherlands. Story set in Rio de Janeiro.

Jacobsson, Anders, and Sören Olsson. *In Ned's Head.* Translated by Kevin Read. Atheneum, 2001. Ages 9–12. Sweden.

Jung, Reinhard. *Dreaming in Black and White.* Translated from the German by Anthea Bell. Phyllis Fogelman Books, 2003. Ages 10–14. Germany.

Kaldhol, Marit. *Goodbye Rune.* Illustrated by Wenche Öyen. Translated from the Norwegian. Kane/Miller, 1987. Ages 5–10. Norway.

Karvoskaia, Natacha (story told by Zidrou). *Dounia.* Translated from the French. Kane/Miller, 1995. Ages 4–7. Belgium.

Kerner, Charlotte. *Blueprint.* Translated from the German by Elizabeth D. Crawford. Lerner, 2000. Ages YA. Germany.

Kodama, Tatsuharu. *Shin's Tricycle.* Illustrated by Ando. Translated by Kazuko Hokumen-Jones. Walker, 1995. Ages 10–13. Japan.

Kurusa. *The Streets Are Free.* Illustrated by Monica Doppert. Translated from the Spanish by Karen Englander. Annick Press, 1995 (1985). Ages 7–9. Venezuela.

Lee, Ho Baek. *While We Were Out.* Kane/Miller, 2003. Ages 3–6. South Korea.

Léonard, Marie. *Tibili, the Little Boy Who Didn't Want to Go to School.* Translated from the French. Illustrated by Andrée Prigent. Kane/Miller, 2001. Set in Africa. Ages 5–8. France.

Lindgren, Astrid. *Pippi Longstocking.* Illustrated by Louis S. Glanzman. Translated by Florence Lamborn. Viking, 1950. Ages 8–11. Sweden.

Liu, Jae Soo. *Yellow Umbrella.* Kane/Miller, 2002. Ages 2–6. (Includes a companion CD with music composed by Sheen Dong Il.) South Korea.

Lucht, Irmgard. *The Red Poppy.* Translated from the German by Frank-Jacoby Nelson. Hyperion, 1995. Ages 5–9. Germany.

Maruki, Toshi. *Hiroshima No Pika.* Translated from the Japanese. Lothrop, 1982. Ages 9–YA. Japan.

Moeyaert, Bart. *Bare Hands.* Translated by David Colmer. Front Street, 1998. Ages 10–YA. Netherlands.

———. *It's Love We Don't Understand.* Translated from the Dutch by Wanda Boeke. Front Street, 2001. Ages 13–YA. Netherlands.

Morgenstern, Susie. *A Book of Coupons.* Translated from the French by Gil Rosner. Illustrated by Serge Bloch. Viking, 2001. Ages 9–12. France.

———. *Princesses Are People, Too: Two Modern Fairy Tales.* Translated from the French by Bill May. Illustrated by Serge Bloch. Viking, 2002. Ages 7–10. France.

———. *Secret Letters from 0 to 10.* Translated from the French by Gil Rosner. Viking, 1998. Ages 9–13. France.

Nomura, Takaaki. *Grandpa's Town.* Translated from the Japanese by Amanda Mayer Stinchecum. Kane/Miller, 1991. Ages 4–8. Japan.

Orlev, Uri. *The Island on Bird Street.* Translated from the Hebrew by Hillel Halkin. Houghton, 1984. Ages 9–12. Israel.

———. *Run, Boy, Run.* Translated by Hillel Halkin. Houghton, 2003. Ages 10–13. Israel.

Place, François. *The Last Giants.* Translated from the French by William Rodarmor. David R. Godine, 1993. Ages 9–12. Belgium.

Popov, Nikolai. *Why?* Translated from the German. North-South, 1996. Ages 7–14. Switzerland.

Pressler, Mirjam. *Halinka.* Translated from the German by Elizabeth D. Crawford. Holt, 1998. Ages 10–YA. Germany.

———. *Malka.* Translated from the German by Brian Murdoch. Philomel, 2003. Ages 12–YA. Germany.

Richter, Hans Peter. *Friedrich.* Translated from the German by Edite Kroll. Holt, 1970. Ages 11–YA. Germany.

Schami, Rafik. *Fatima and the Dream Thief.* Illustrated by Els Cools and Oliver Streich. Translated from the German by Anthea Bell. North-South, 1996. Ages 7–9. Germany.

Sellier, Marie. *Cézanne from A to Z.* Translated from the French by Claudia Zoe Bedrick. Peter Bedrick Books, 1996. Ages 9–YA. France.

Spyri, Johanna. *Heidi.* Crown, 1880. Ages 9–12. Switzerland.

Stark, Ulf. *Can You Whistle, Johanna?: A Boy's Search for a Grandfather.* Illustrated by Anna Hoglund. Translated from the Swedish by Ebba Segerberg. RDR Books, 1999. Ages 6–8. Sweden.

van der Rol, Ruud, and Rian Verhoeven. *Anne Frank, Beyond the Diary: A Photographic Remembrance.* Translated from the Dutch by Tony Longham and Plym Peters. Viking, 1993. Ages 11–YA. Netherlands.

Weninger, Brigitte. *Special Delivery.* Translated by J. Alison James. Illustrated by Alexander Reichstein. North-South, 2000. Ages 3–5. Austria.

Yumoto, Kazumi. *The Friends.* Translated by Cathy Hirano. Farrar, 1996. Ages 10–14. Japan.

———. *The Letters.* Translated from the Japanese by Cathy Hirano. Farrar, 2002. Ages 13–YA. Japan.

Zullo, Germano. *Marta and the Bicycle.* Translated from the French. Illustrated by Albertine. Kane/Miller, 2002. Ages 4–8. Switzerland.

III

LITERATURE
IN THE
SCHOOL

Chapters 11 and 12 focus on curriculum and teaching strategies. Planning for and evaluating a literature curriculum as it pertains to a specific lesson, a unit of instruction, a yearlong classroom plan, or a schoolwide literature program is explained in Chapter 11. Two planning webs, one on the literary element, *character,* and one on *immigration,* demonstrate how teachers can organize and plan for literature across the curriculum. We have included information on national directives on the teaching of reading, and we explain how literature can help you meet these expectations. Chapter 11 concludes with a discussion of censorship, selection, and First Amendment rights.

Strategies for sharing literature successfully with children and encouraging them to respond in a variety of ways to these literary experiences are presented in Chapter 12. The value of using literature across the curriculum, highlighted in Chapters 5, 8, and 9 in the "Using Literature across the Curriculum" features, is fully treated in Chapter 12. A discussion of reading in the content areas underscores the importance of helping students learn to read both fiction and nonfiction, and a table showing how books can be used as writing models demonstrates another important and practical value of reading good books.

P LANNING *the* CURRICULUM

READING

. . . We get no good
By being ungenerous even to a book,
And calculating profits . . . so much help
By so much reading. It is rather when
We gloriously forget ourselves and plunge
Soul-forward, headlong, into a book's profound,
Impassioned for its beauty and salt of truth—
'Tis then we get the right good from a book.

—ELIZABETH BROWNING

Literature is not a regularly mandated part of the elementary school curriculum as are reading, mathematics, and social studies. Yet knowing how literature works can be valuable. Knowledge of the elements and devices of writing and illustration enriches our appreciation of an interesting story, just as knowing something of music or architecture enhances our appreciation of a beautiful song or a handsome building.

This chapter deals with long-range planning for literature instruction (short-range planning is dealt with in Chapter 12). First, the literature curriculum is defined, and ways to organize such a curriculum are presented. Ways to develop the literature curriculum are explained, followed by a discussion of how literature can be integrated into a school's reading program. The latter part of the chapter includes sections on evaluating a literature program; implementing a schoolwide literature program; and censorship, selection, and First Amendment rights.

DEFINING THE LITERATURE CURRICULUM

Literature is more than a collection of well-written stories and poems. Literature also has its own body of knowledge. A term that is sometimes used to label this treatment of literature is *discipline-based literature instruction.* The object of such a course of study is to teach children the mechanics of literature: the terms used to define it, its components or elements, its genres, and the craft of creating it. The terms and elements of fiction are presented in Chapter 2; the terms and elements of nonfiction are presented in Chapter 9; the genres and their characteristics are presented in Chapters 3–10.

ORGANIZING THE LITERATURE CURRICULUM

Some teachers plan for a yearlong strand of literature instruction organized variously by genre, by author or illustrator, by literary element or device, by notable books, by topic or theme, or by some combination of these. In each case, there should be goals for the course of study, specific children's trade books to be read or listened to by each child, guidelines for selection of materials, a schedule, and criteria for evaluating the course of study.

Genre

By organizing a literature curriculum around literary genres, teachers provide a context for students to learn about the various types of literature and the characteristics of each. In the beginning, the teacher will have to direct students' attention to similarities in books of like genre—for example, the students will learn that works of historical fiction are always set in the past or that characters in folktales are two-dimensional. Soon, however, students will begin to read with more genre awareness and will enjoy finding common elements within and differences between genres.

One advantage of this plan is that students over the school year can be exposed to a wide variety of literature. Knowledge of different genres gives students useful *schemata*—frameworks for understanding borne of prior knowledge and experience—for story types. A genre approach can work in all grade levels, given thoughtful selection of titles and delivery of literary concepts. Planning involves choosing the genres to be studied, selecting the representative children's books for each, and determining the order in which the genres will be studied.

Author or Illustrator

The goal of a curriculum in literature organized by author or illustrator is to make students more familiar with the works and styles of selected children's book authors and illustrators. An additional goal may be knowledge of the authors' or illustrators' lives insofar as these life experiences influenced the subjects' works. The choice of authors and illustrators will naturally be guided both by students' reading interests and the teacher's desire to introduce students to important authors and illustrators and their works. The number of works chosen to represent an author or illustrator will vary, but even when an author's books are lengthy, more than one work is recommended.

As a class experiences a sampling of the chosen author's or illustrator's work, attention will be focused on trademark stylistic elements such as unusual use of words or color or media, as well as themes, characters, character types, or settings common to these works. Later, information about the person's life can be introduced through reports, audiotaped and videotaped interviews, and even guest appearances by the author or illustrator. Web sites, biographies, and biographical reference volumes, such as *Something about the Author* (Hedblad, 2001), provide information about children's book authors and illustrators. (For more information about this resource, see Appendix B.)

Success of author and illustrator studies is not necessarily defined by wholesale student approval of the featured artists. Students must be allowed to decide whether they like a person's work or not and should be encouraged to discover why they have these feelings. Wholesale *disapproval* by students of the works of a featured author or illustrator, however, is an important form of *teacher* evaluation that should not be ignored. In such a case, the teacher's choice of author or books to be studied was not appropriate for this purpose and should be reconsidered. Students are evaluated informally through observation of their recognition of featured authors' or illustrators' works and their ability to compare literary and artistic styles of various authors and illustrators.

Literary Element and Device

When teachers say that their teaching of literature is organized by literary element, they are usually referring to the elements of fiction and nonfiction, as presented in Chapters 2 and 9, respectively. Other elements, such as artistic styles, media, and book format, could be addressed as well. A *literary device* is "any literary technique deliberately employed to achieve a special effect" (Baldick, 1990, p. 55). Irony, symbolism, parody, and foreshadowing are examples of devices that add richness to stories.

The goal of a literature curriculum organized by literary elements and devices is to give students a better understanding of the craft of writing so that they can read more perceptively and appreciatively and possibly apply this knowledge to their own writing. Since this approach is analytical and somewhat abstract, it is more appropriate for students in the fourth grade or above.

Careful selection of children's books to accompany the investigation of each literary element or device is crucial to the success of this approach. The featured element must be prominent and must have been used by the author with extraordinary skill. In addition, the story itself must captivate young readers. Note that in this approach, books of various genres can be grouped to demonstrate the same literary element. Note also that picture books are particularly good at presenting literary elements and devices clearly and in relatively simple contexts so that they can be understood more easily. An excellent resource for selecting picture books for this use is Hall's *Using Picture Books to Teach Literary Devices,* Vols. 1 and 2 (1990, 1994).

Students' acquaintance with the literary elements and devices can go far beyond mere definition. Close reading of key passages reveals the author's craft at developing character, establishing mood, authenticating setting, or using such devices as inference, symbolism, or foreshadowing. Re-creation of these elements and devices in their own art, drama, and writing not only gives students a personal and more complete understanding of these concepts, but also gives teachers a way to evaluate their students' grasp of these concepts.

Notable Book

In the primary grades, teachers will most likely read the notable books aloud to students. Reading aloud by teachers works for intermediate and middle grades as well, but an alternative at these levels is independent reading of the selected books by students. In this approach, the teacher or students read one or more chapters of the selected book each day and then discuss what they have read. Students can compare their understandings of the story with one another, clarify word meanings and any confusing parts of the story, make predictions about where the story is heading, or analyze any of the story's literary elements. Traditionally, these discussions are lead by the teacher, but some instructors have found that student-led discussions in small groups, if well managed, are just as effective and have the added advantage of giving students practice in leading serious discussions.

Teachers who organize their literature curriculum by notable books must be careful to remain flexible in book selections from year to year so that the list of notable books reflects students' current interests and reading preferences. A list of notable books that never varies can result in student disinterest and stale teaching.

Theme or Topic

Teachers who choose to organize a study of literature by theme or topic want their students generally to become aware of the power of literature to explain the human condition. Themes and topics will vary according to ages and circumstances of students. For example, primary-grade children will be interested in themes and topics having to do with school and family life. Those in the middle grades, on the other hand, will be more intrigued by themes and topics dealing with the discovery and use of inner resources to become more independent or even to survive.

Possible themes that a seventh- or eighth-grade class might explore through a year include the following:

Surviving in the Modern World
Alienation
Coping with Parents and Younger Siblings
Teenagers through History: The Same Old Problems?
Dependence and Independence
The Future World
Beneath the Skin: What Is the True Nature of Difference?

Possible themes and topics for a younger group might include these:

Families Come in All Shapes and Sizes
School Now and in the Past

Use Your Wits

The Importance of Having Good Friends

Stories from Other Countries

Old Ones and Young Ones Together

Famous People Were Children, Too

In this approach, each child reads or listens to the book or books chosen by the teacher to accompany each theme. After the reading, students explore the theme through discussion, writing, drama, art, and further reading on the theme or topic.

Themes and topics are chosen by the teacher on the basis of students' needs and interests, current events, and prior successes with previously developed thematic units. The length of time spent on any one theme or topic can vary from a school year to a day, but several weeks' duration is the norm.

Two pitfalls of thematic learning curriculum models must be avoided. The first is choosing a unit theme or topic just because a few related books are at hand. Remember: The unit theme or topic drives literature selection, not vice versa. The second pitfall is choosing literature just because it relates to the theme or topic but with no regard to its quality or appropriateness for the students. Boring books make boring thematic instructional units.

DEVELOPING THE LITERATURE CURRICULUM

P lanning for a literature curriculum involves many important practical considerations in addition to choosing the approach one takes to teaching literature. The classroom environment must be constructed, the materials collected, and the plans written.

Designing the Classroom Environment

Much can be learned about a teacher's philosophy of learning and teaching simply by taking a look around the classroom.

The traditional classroom arrangement, with students' desks arranged in straight rows facing the teacher's desk, implies a more teacher-centered environment: The teacher is the center of attention and the main source of information. The preponderant type of discourse in this classroom is most likely a whole-class lecture, and its direction is from teacher to student. The interactive classroom arrangement, with students' desks arranged in groups so that the occupants face one another, implies a more student-centered environment. Various types of discourse seem to be encouraged here: student-to-student discussions, small-group activities, and teacher-student conferences. The direction of this discourse is as much from student to student and student to teacher as it is teacher to student.

In addition to room arrangement, other aspects of a classroom reveal the nature of what goes on from day to day. What materials and resources are most apparent? What is the nature of displays and bulletin boards? What level of thinking and inquiry is indicated by the student work on display? Teachers who recognize the importance of good literature will design an attractive and comfortable classroom environment in which books are featured.

Many teachers promote literature and literature-related activities by designating a specific area of the classroom as the *library corner*. The library corner is made conducive to reading by being located as far as possible from noisy activities and by being outfitted with comfortable seating (carpeting, pillows, soft chairs) and lots of conveniently placed and easy-to-find books. The library corner houses the classroom library and can be the setting for independent silent reading, paired and small-group reading, and whole-class read-aloud sessions during the day. Low shelving can serve many purposes: It provides boundaries for the corner; sound buffers; and storage for books, book circulation records, book club order forms, and audiotapes and videotapes relating to books.

The library corner is a logical place to display students' book-related writing and artwork, such as student-produced books, students' book reviews, charts showing the class's favorite books and authors, and letters to and from authors and illustrators. Walls and bulletin boards in this way become an integral part of the library corner.

Teachers with self-contained classrooms might have several centers, each devoted to a specific activity, such as acting out plays, or curricular subject, such as science or health, mathematics, and writing. By outfitting each center with appropriate books and displaying student writing and art related to their work in these areas, teachers naturally integrate the subject areas and show students the relationships between them. Another noticeable feature of the interactive classroom is the proximity and availability of books. Providing students with a rich supply of trade literature is also the result of planning.

Building a Classroom Library Collection

Most, if not all, of the responsibility for acquiring a sufficiently large and varied collection of books in your classroom will be yours. With perseverance, it can be done. Most good classroom libraries have a permanent collection as well as a collection that comes from the school or public library and changes regularly. Beginning teachers who are willing to plan ahead with their school and public librarians can borrow enough books for adequate temporary classroom libraries while they build their own collections. Even after a large permanent collection is established, a rotating selection from the school and public library can be coordinated with specific units of study, providing depth and breadth to the unit content and to the students' learning experience.

Careful selection of titles for the classroom library makes the most of limited resources. Children's librarians can provide invaluable advice in selecting titles for a classroom library and should be consulted. If this is not an option, browsing in a well-stocked children's bookstore and consulting publishers' catalogs are alternative ways of finding out what is available. Publishers of children's books issue one or two catalogs annually in which they describe their new publications and list their previous publications that are currently available (the backlist). If your school or public librarian does not have these catalogs, publishers will supply them on request. Some teachers use catalogs to get an overview of what is available before going to a bookstore.

Your own permanent trade book collection can be built inexpensively by using several proven approaches. These include the following:

- Requesting an allocation from your principal or PTO for purchase of books
- Submitting a small grant proposal ($250–$1,000) to your school district or professional organization for purchase of trade books
- Taking advantage of bonus books offered by student paperback book clubs
- Informing students' parents that you are building a collection and would like to have first refusal of any children's books that they plan to discard

- Establishing a "give a book to the classroom" policy for parents who want to celebrate their child's birthday or a holiday at school in some way
- Frequenting garage sales and library book sales, where good books can often be purchased for pennies

Most bookstores offer a 20 percent discount to teachers who use their own money to buy books to add to their classroom collections. An alternative to the bookstore is the book jobber, or wholesale dealer for many publishers. Jobbers offer even greater discounts to teachers, sometimes up to 40 percent, but it is important to remember that most jobbers do not carry small-press publications. Your school librarian probably uses a jobber and can assist you in setting up a staff account with the same firm. Some of the larger firms include Baker & Taylor, Brodart, and Ingram Book Company.

With these methods and sources, classroom collections grow quickly. From the beginning, you will need to devise a coding system for your permanent collection to streamline shelving and record keeping. Many teachers find that color coding their books by genre with colored tape on the spines works well. If at all possible, students should be trained and given the responsibility for color coding, checking in and out, repairing, and reshelving books.

Remember that the whole point of building a classroom library is to promote reading, not to provide a handsome display. Inevitably, if children use their classroom library, books will be lost and damaged. Severe reprimands for losing or damaging a book may work against your ultimate goal.

Outlining a Yearlong Literature Curriculum

Planning for the school year permits the teacher to have resources available when they are needed. In outlining for a yearlong literature curriculum, several steps must be taken.

DETERMINING THE APPROACH   A teacher must first determine which literature curriculum to teach: genre, author/illustrator, literary element or device, notable book, or topic/theme. Another alternative is to create a hybrid literature curriculum by including aspects of several of these approaches in the plan.

ESTABLISHING GOALS   Goals in a literature curriculum are those aims one expects to accomplish by the end of the course of study. The term *objectives* refers to short-range aims to be accomplished day by day or week by week. Central to this part of the planning process is deciding on the literary concepts to be taught. Since goals largely determine the parameters of the course of study, they must be established early in the planning process.

Goals for a literature curriculum are established by individual teachers and sometimes by schools or school districts. Likely goals for a fifth-grade teacher who has determined to use a mixed genre/author organization to teaching literature would be these:

- Students will enjoy reading a variety of genres of literature.
- Students will be familiar with the characteristics of traditional literature, modern fantasy, historical fiction, contemporary realistic fiction, mystery, and science fiction and will be able to classify a book as belonging to one of the featured genres when reading it.
- Students will become familiar with several leading authors of each of the above genres and will be able to identify characteristics of the writing of each author.

DETERMINING UNITS OF STUDY   After goals have been identified and set, the next step in outlining a literature curriculum is to determine the units of study through which the literature content will be delivered. In this way, a tentative schedule can be set in order to foresee needs in terms of time and materials.

SELECTING FOCUS BOOKS   Each unit will require certain trade books for reading aloud by the teacher and trade books for class or small-group study or independent reading. Early selection of these titles is important for several reasons. Balance in the overall book selection, for instance, is achieved much more easily in the planning stages. *Balance in book selection,* as presented in Chapter 2, means that the books selected present a diversity of characters (type, sex, age, ethnicity, place of origin), settings (urban, rural, familiar, foreign), and themes. Another advantage of early selection is being able to estimate the time necessary for each unit. Some units will take longer than others, depending on such variables as the extent of content to be covered, the length and difficulty of books to be read, and the type and complexity of planned book extension activities. A sample list of units, books, and featured authors for a fifth-grade teacher who is implementing a combined genre/author organization for teaching literature would be as follows:

UNIT 1: TRADITIONAL LITERATURE

MYTHOLOGY

The Gods and Goddesses of Olympus retold and illustrated by Aliki
Theseus and the Minotaur adapted by Leonard Everett Fisher

LEGENDS

The Legend of King Arthur retold by Robin Lister. Illustrated by Alan Baker
Sir Gawain and the Loathly Lady by Selina Hastings. Illustrated by Juan Wijngaard
Dragonslayer: The Story of Beowulf by Rosemary Sutcliff

FOLKTALES

Snow White and the Seven Dwarfs translated by Randall Jarrell. Illustrated by Nancy Ekholm Burkert
Snow White in New York by Fiona French (modern folktale)

READ-ALOUD

Not One Damsel in Distress: World Folktales for Strong Girls by Jane Yolen. Illustrated by Susan Guevara

UNIT 2: MODERN FANTASY

Tuck Everlasting by Natalie Babbitt
Orwell's Luck by Richard Jennings
The Doll People by Ann Martin and Laura Godwin

READ-ALOUD

The Lion, the Witch, and the Wardrobe by C. S. Lewis
Featured Author: C. S. Lewis

U N I T   3 :   H I S T O R I C A L   F I C T I O N   (W O R L D   W A R   I I)

The Island on Bird Street by Uri Orlev
Milkweed by Jerry Spinelli
Summer of My German Soldier by Bette Greene
Under the Blood-Red Sun by Graham Salisbury

R E A D - A L O U D

Journey to Topaz by Yoshiko Uchida
Featured Author: Yoshiko Uchida

U N I T   4 :   C O N T E M P O R A R Y   R E A L I S T I C   F I C T I O N

The Bridge to Terabithia by Katherine Paterson
The Friends by Kazumi Yumoto
Trading Places by Gary Soto
Everything on a Waffle by Polly Horvath

R E A D - A L O U D

Ruby Holler by Sharon Creech
Featured Author: Sharon Creech

U N I T   5 :   M Y S T E R Y

Peppermints in the Parlor by Barbara Brooks Wallace
Dovey Coe by Frances O. Dowell
The Man Who Was Poe by Avi
The Dollhouse Murders by Betty Ren Wright

R E A D - A L O U D

Midnight Is a Place by Joan Aiken
Featured Author: Joan Aiken

U N I T   6 :   S C I E N C E   F I C T I O N

The Green Book by Jill Paton Walsh
The White Mountains by John Christopher
The House of the Scorpion by Nancy Farmer
The Giver by Lois Lowry

R E A D - A L O U D

A Wrinkle in Time by Madeleine L'Engle
Featured Author: Madeleine L'Engle

An issue often discussed among children's literature instructors is the efficacy of a *literary canon* of children's literature, an official list of children's books judged by experts to be worthy of inclusion in a literature curriculum. Elementary teachers and librarians have largely rejected the idea of a literary canon mainly because its sole criterion for selection is literary excellence, with no consideration for a book's appeal or relevance to children. Moreover, teachers know that they are in the best position to select books that match their students' interests and their own planned curricula. A literary canon is rarely revised and quickly becomes dated. Being so rigid and select, it cannot reflect the varied and changing interests of a particular group of children. Although the term *literary canon* most often refers to a nationally recognized booklist, teachers should be aware that when they stick rigidly to the same set of books year after year, they are, in effect, proclaiming that their own personal literary canon of children's literature is more important than the needs and interests of the children they teach.

SCHEDULING   With an overview of the plan established, the teacher can begin to set dates and time allotments for each unit and for activities within units. With each year of experience, the teacher's time estimates become more accurate. At this point, it is still easy to adjust the yearlong plan if it becomes obvious that too much or too little has been planned.

Fleshing Out the Units of Study

Thinking through, organizing, and writing down the details of daily lessons and activities are the final steps in planning for a literature curriculum. Two methods of organizing the details of units of study are to create webs and literature units.

WEBS   Webbing is a way of creating a visual overview of a unit of study complete with its focus, related book titles, and activities. Ideas for a web are generated through brainstorming. The main advantage of webbing is that the process clarifies and even suggests ties or associations between concepts, books, and activities. Webs can be organized around a theme or topic, a single book, a book genre, an author or illustrator, or a literary concept. Activities can be drawn from all skill areas—writing, reading, listening, thinking, speaking, art, crafts, drama, and music.

The web in Figure 11.1 demonstrates planning to teach a literary element, in this case, character. The web in Figure 11.2 demonstrates planning for the use of literature across the curriculum, in this case, history or social studies.

Teachers who use webbing as a way to plan literature units will appreciate the many topics, themes, and resources suggested in *Book Links,* a journal published by the American Library Association. (For further information on this resource, see Appendix B.) A disadvantage of webbing is that it gives no indication of the chronology of events or time allotments. Eventually, the web must be transferred to a more linear format, which is similar to the literature unit.

LITERATURE UNITS   The literature unit resembles an outline organized by day or by week. As with webs, units can be organized around a theme or topic, a single book, a book genre, an author or illustrator, or a literary concept or device. Specificity will vary according to the needs and experience of the teacher, but each day's plan usually includes the following components:

- *Objectives.* These are short-term aims that can conceivably be met by the end of the day or week. For example, a teacher conducting a literature unit around the literary element, *character,* as is found in Figure 11.1, may state as an objective for the second week of his unit that he will read aloud Chapters 5–7 of *Rowan of Rin* and focus on physical description and the character's actions as ways that an author helps a reader get to know a character. During that same week, a likely objective for his students would be that they will be able to correctly define "protagonist" and "antagonist" and identify these character types in the books that they are reading independently.

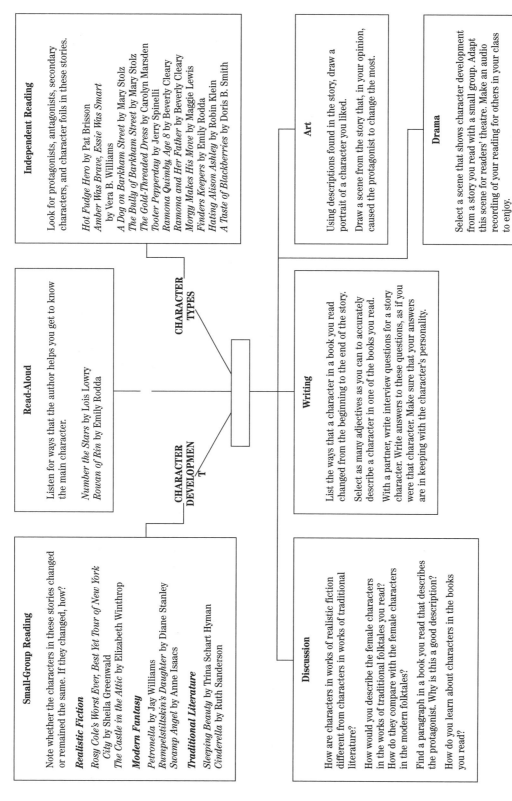

Independent Reading

Look for protagonists, antagonists, secondary characters, and character foils in these stories.

Hot Fudge Hero by Pat Brisson
Amber Was Brave, Essie Was Smart by Vera B. Williams
A Dog on Barkham Street by Mary Stolz
The Bully of Barkham Street by Mary Stolz
The Gold-Threaded Dress by Carolyn Marsden
Tooter Pepperday by Jerry Spinelli
Ramona Quimby, Age 8 by Beverly Cleary
Ramona and Her Father by Beverly Cleary
Morgy Makes His Move by Maggie Lewis
Finders Keepers by Emily Rodda
Hating Alison Ashley by Robin Klein
A Taste of Blackberries by Doris B. Smith

Read-Aloud

Listen for ways that the author helps you get to know the main character.

Number the Stars by Lois Lowry
Rowan of Rin by Emily Rodda

CHARACTER TYPES

CHARACTER DEVELOPMENT

Small-Group Reading

Note whether the characters in these stories changed or remained the same. If they changed, how?

Realistic Fiction

Rosy Cole's Worst Ever, Best Yet Tour of New York City by Sheila Greenwald
The Castle in the Attic by Elizabeth Winthrop

Modern Fantasy

Petronella by Jay Williams
Rumpelstiltskin's Daughter by Diane Stanley
Swamp Angel by Anne Isaacs

Traditional Literature

Sleeping Beauty by Trina Schart Hyman
Cinderella by Ruth Sanderson

Art

Using descriptions found in the story, draw a portrait of a character you liked.

Draw a scene from the story that, in your opinion, caused the protagonist to change the most.

Drama

Select a scene that shows character development from a story you read with a small group. Adapt this scene for readers' theatre. Make an audio recording of your reading for others in your class to enjoy.

Writing

List the ways that a character in a book you read changed from the beginning to the end of the story.

Select as many adjectives as you can to accurately describe a character in one of the books you read.

With a partner, write interview questions for a story character. Write answers to these questions, as if you were that character. Make sure that your answers are in keeping with the character's personality.

Discussion

How are characters in works of realistic fiction different from characters in works of traditional literature?

How would you describe the female characters in the works of traditional folktales you read?
How do they compare with the female characters in the modern folktales?

Find a paragraph in a book you read that describes the protagonist. Why is this a good description?

How do you learn about characters in the books you read?

FIGURE 11.1   Web Demonstrating Investigation of a Literary Element, Grades 2–4

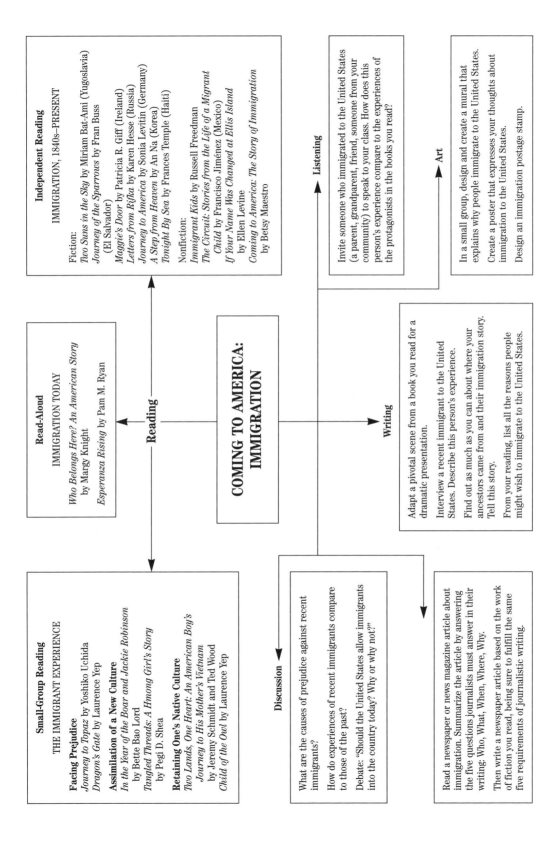

Independent Reading

IMMIGRATION, 1840s–PRESENT

Fiction:
Two Suns in the Sky by Miriam Bat-Ami (Yugoslavia)
Journey of the Sparrows by Fran Buss (El Salvador)
Maggie's Door by Patricia R. Giff (Ireland)
Letters from Rifka by Karen Hesse (Russia)
Journey to America by Sonia Levitin (Germany)
A Step from Heaven by An Na (Korea)
Tonight By Sea by Frances Temple (Haiti)

Nonfiction:
Immigrant Kids by Russell Freedman
The Circuit: Stories from the Life of a Migrant Child by Francisco Jiménez (Mexico)
If Your Name Was Changed at Ellis Island by Ellen Levine
Coming to America: The Story of Immigration by Betsy Maestro

Read-Aloud

IMMIGRATION TODAY

Who Belongs Here? An American Story by Margy Knight
Esperanza Rising by Pam M. Ryan

Reading

COMING TO AMERICA: IMMIGRATION

Small-Group Reading

THE IMMIGRANT EXPERIENCE

Facing Prejudice
Journey to Topaz by Yoshiko Uchida
Dragon's Gate by Laurence Yep

Assimilation of a New Culture
In the Year of the Boar and Jackie Robinson by Bette Bao Lord
Tangled Threads: A Hmong Girl's Story by Pegi D. Shea

Retaining One's Native Culture
Two Lands, One Heart: An American Boy's Journey to His Mother's Vietnam by Jeremy Schmidt and Ted Wood
Child of the Owl by Laurence Yep

Listening

Invite someone who immigrated to the United States (a parent, grandparent, friend, someone from your community) to speak to your class. How does this person's experience compare to the experiences of the protagonists in the books you read?

Art

In a small group, design and create a mural that explains why people immigrate to the United States.

Create a poster that expresses your thoughts about immigration to the United States.

Design an immigration postage stamp.

Writing

Adapt a pivotal scene from a book you read for a dramatic presentation.

Interview a recent immigrant to the United States. Describe this person's experience.

Find out as much as you can about where your ancestors came from and their immigration story. Tell this story.

From your reading, list all the reasons people might wish to immigrate to the United States.

Discussion

What are the causes of prejudice against recent immigrants?

How do experiences of recent immigrants compare to those of the past?

Debate: "Should the United States allow immigrants into the country today? Why or why not?"

Read a newspaper or news magazine article about immigration. Summarize the article by answering the five questions journalists must answer in their writing: Who, What, When, Where, Why.

Then write a newspaper article based on the work of fiction you read, being sure to fulfill the same five requirements of journalistic writing.

FIGURE 11.2   Web Demonstrating Use of Literature across the Curriculum, Grades 5–8

- *Procedures and methods.* This part of the unit tells what the teacher does, in what order, and with what materials. The procedures of the teacher conducting the *immigration* unit in Figure 11.2 may call for her to conduct a whole-class discussion in which students compare the immigration experiences of the protagonists in the books they are reading independently and in small groups and listening to the teacher read aloud. Then, in small groups, students could list the reasons why people leave their native lands and immigrate to the United States. The lists could be integrated and a poster made to use as a reference during the remainder of the unit. Such planning allows teachers to project the materials that are likely to be needed so as to have them at hand.
- *Evaluation.* Teachers must consider how they intend to evaluate each day's activities in terms of both how well they worked (a form of self-evaluation) and how well the students met the objectives.

Because units of study are several weeks long, they usually include a culminating activity that gives students an opportunity to reflect on what they have learned, review major points, and sometimes celebrate the focus of the unit in some way. Culminating activities for the *Journey to Topaz* unit might include table and bulletin board displays of books and other resources the students have read, artwork, poems, plays, letters, and stories written in response to these literary experiences, and a debate about the World War II internment issue.

An overall unit evaluation is valuable to a teacher, particularly if he or she intends to use the unit with another group of students. Revisions can make the unit even more successful in succeeding years. The unit plan should indicate how the unit will be evaluated.

Commercially developed literature units can be found. Beginning teachers may find good ideas in such resources but should avoid considering these units as complete or unalterable. Rather, you should tailor these prepared units to reflect your students' prior experiences, interests, and abilities, and your goals and objectives. Many of these commercially published units consist of little more than basal-like worksheets.

LITERATURE IN THE READING PROGRAM

Teaching literature and teaching reading are similar in some respects: Both use similar materials—narrative and expository writing; both have the purpose of making meaning from texts; and both have the ultimate goal of a greater or deeper understanding of and response to the written text. Because of these similarities, literature and reading can be taught simultaneously.

A critical goal of teachers in grades K through 8 is to help students become literate—that is, to be able to read and write. Inservice and preservice teachers at the beginning of the twenty-first century will encounter two different approaches to literacy subscribed to in schools and teacher training institutions: the basal reader approach and the literature-based reading approach. Underlying the differences in these two approaches are the different learning theories upon which they are based. Your approach to literacy development will depend on your own philosophy of teaching and learning, that is, the ideas you believe in strongly enough to act on.

The philosophy you accept will affect many aspects of your teaching: the materials you choose and how you present them to your students, how you arrange your classroom furniture, the activities you engage your students in, how you behave in class, and how you encourage your students to behave. In the following discussion it is important to note the theoretical differences underlying each curriculum model in literature. You should begin to form your own philosophy of learning and literacy development.

Basal Reading Program Supplemented by Children's Literature

Just as children bring a variety of learning styles and needs to the task of learning, so do teachers bring a variety of teaching styles and needs to teaching. A single approach to teaching reading cannot suit all teachers or all students. The most common approach to the teaching of reading is the *basal reading approach supplemented by children's literature.*

The basal reading program has been the traditional approach to teaching reading in U.S. elementary schools for decades. According to Durkin (1987), it is "composed of a series of readers said to be written at successively more difficult levels" (p. 417). The core materials include a student reader, a teacher's manual, student workbooks, ditto masters, and tests. The strength of the basal program is that it provides teachers with an organized instructional framework upon which to build (Lapp, Flood, & Farnan, 1992). In other words, the teacher using this approach does not develop a reading program by selecting materials and planning the related activities. Basal reading programs offer teachers considerable guidance and help with the decisions and challenges involved in teaching children to read.

The learning theory upon which basal reading materials have been based for the last century is that learning complex skills begins with mastering the simplest components of that skill before attempting the next larger components and so on until the whole skill is learned. In terms of learning to read, this means that the letters of the alphabet are learned first, followed by letter-sound patterns, words, and then sentences. Finally, when the components of reading are learned, whole works of literature, such as stories, plays, and poems, are read. As late as the beginning of the 1980s, the embodiment of this philosophy was the basal reader—with its emphasis on progressive skill and subskill mastery and its use of short and simple sentences and a controlled vocabulary. The concern with basals of the 1950s, 1960s, and 1970s was with the limitations of the story selections—specifically, the controlled vocabulary, the uninteresting plots, and the poor writing styles.

In the 1980s, U.S. publishers of basal readers made an effort to improve the quality of stories written specifically for the basal readers. Multicultural characters began to appear in basal stories with more frequency than in the past. Most important, excerpts from high-quality trade books and some whole, albeit brief, literary works were integrated into basal readers. These changes were incorporated while retaining the skill-based instruction (particularly phonics instruction for beginning readers) that researchers regard as important to well-rounded reading programs (Anderson, Hiebert, Scott, and Wilkinson, 1985).

Even with these changes, basal readers are not designed to be a complete substitute for trade books. Even though some basal stories are good literature, not excerpted or adapted, the brevity of these selections is a problem for intermediate grades. Most students in these grades are capable of reading novel-length chapter books and should be doing so regularly in their school reading program. Students in classes where anthologies and basal readers are used exclusively are denied the all-important self-selection of reading material from a wide variety of books.

Ideally, each teacher should be allowed to choose the approach to teaching reading that best suits his or her philosophy of learning and teaching style. In many school districts across the United States, however, the use of a basal approach to teach reading is mandated. Even more restrictive is mandated Direct Instruction (DI), a lockstep method of teaching reading relying on highly scripted, prescribed teacher plans that must be followed to the letter, accommodating no teacher or student variation. School administrators would be wise to note Ryder, Sekulski, and Silberg's (2003) three-year study of methods of teaching reading that showed that DI has limited applicability, should not be used as the main method of reading instruction, and is not as effective as traditional teaching methods that allow teachers a more flexible approach.

Many teachers, despite mandates, have begun to move away from a slavish, "read-every-page-or-bust" attitude toward these programs. They have found ways to improve their teaching of reading by using their basal programs in innovative ways that eliminate some of the skills exercises of this approach and allow time for literature as well. Some guidelines drawn from the example of these teachers are as follows:

- Use only the best literary selections the basal offers. Substitute good trade literature for the rest.
- Let students read some of the better-written basal selections simply for enjoyment. It is the joy and wonder of reading marvelous tales or interesting information that motivate children to learn to read, not the tests on their comprehension of these stories. Use the time saved from skill, drill, and comprehension questions for silent reading.
- Eliminate the stigma of ability grouping by forming one whole-class, heterogeneous reading group. Use the time saved from planning and conducting three or four different reading lessons to hold individual reading conferences.
- Use basal readers' phonics lessons and drills only when, in the teacher's opinion, an individual student or group of students will benefit from them. (This need is exhibited by students in their individual reading conferences and in their writing.) Children do not learn according to an imposed schedule, but only when they are ready to learn. Use the time saved from ineffective exercises to read aloud from good books or for silent reading from self-choice books.
- Avoid comprehension questions at the end of basal reading lessons that trivialize the stories or demean the students. Use the time saved to allow children to share their personal reactions to the story, to offer literary criticisms of the selection, or to respond to the story in writing, drama, or art.
- Make phonics instruction a regular but brief (10–15 minutes) part of primary-grade reading instruction. Avoid letting phonics instruction become the main attraction of reading. That role should be reserved for good stories.

Basal readers are most effective when used in concert with a wide variety of trade books that reflect students' interests and reading abilities. In this arrangement, the basal reader provides guidance and structure to both teaching and learning, while the trade books provide the variety, opportunity for self-selection, and interest that motivates children to want to read.

Literature-Based Reading

Literature-based reading is an approach to teaching reading through the exclusive use of trade books. The learning theory in which literature-based reading is grounded is that children learn by searching for meaning in the world around them, constantly forming hypotheses, testing them to determine whether they work, and subsequently accepting or rejecting them.

Teachers using the literature-based approach to reading will structure a classroom environment in which children are immersed in good literature. In these classrooms, children hear literature read aloud several times a day, they see good readers reading voluntarily, they discover that good books can entertain them and tell them things they want to know, and they constantly practice reading books that they themselves have chosen because they are interested in the topics. Frequent student-teacher conferences allow teachers to check students' comprehension, discover skills weaknesses, and prescribe remediation.

As in basal reading programs, explicit reading instruction is an important feature of literature-based reading, particularly in the primary grades. Phonics, concepts of print, and vocabulary are taught in literature-based reading, *but within the context of interesting literature.* Unlike basal reading programs, these skills are never taught in isolation, where they have no real meaning, are never the focus of the entire reading period, and are taught only when needed.

As noted in Chapter 1, literature-based reading instruction addresses the components of instruction considered essential to the teaching of reading by the National Reading Panel: phonemic awareness, phonics, vocabulary, and comprehension. By including daily teacher read-aloud and self-choice independent reading components, this method of teaching reading is more likely to engender some valuable intrinsic behaviors in students that cannot be taught: a positive attitude toward reading, self-motivation to read, and a lifelong reading habit.

Key elements of the literature-based reading classroom include the following:

- Daily reading aloud of good literature by the teacher
- Reading skills taught when needed and then within meaningful contexts, never in isolation
- Quantities of good trade books in the classroom (five or more books per child) selected to match specific interests and approximate reading abilities of the students in the class
- Daily silent reading by students of books that they choose
- Daily opportunities for students to share their reactions to books orally
- Daily opportunities for students to respond to literature in a variety of ways, including writing, drama, and art
- Frequent individual student–teacher reading conferences (See the discussion of individual conferences in Chapter 12.)

Decisions about what to teach, when to teach it, and what materials to use are made by the teacher in the literature-based reading classroom. These decisions and the responsibility for materials selection and acquisition may make literature-based reading more demanding of teachers' professional judgment than other reading instruction methods; however, when it is managed well, this approach has proven to be very effective, not only in teaching students to read but also in creating a positive attitude toward reading. Moreover, the stimulus of new and exciting materials and students' unique personal responses to them can make teaching more exciting and enjoyable.

The absence of a prescribed, lockstep program is one of the greatest strengths of literature-based reading, but it also makes this approach vulnerable to many abuses. The following practices have no place in the literature-based reading classroom:

- Using quantities of mediocre literature in the reading program solely on the basis of having them at hand and with no regard to their interest to students or their suitability to curricular goals
- Regularly using class sets of single trade books with a predetermined reading schedule and fill-in-the-blank worksheets (This practice is referred to as the "basalization of literature.")
- Reading works of literature by round-robin reading
- Selecting and assigning every title read by students
- Assigning book reports regularly under the guise of book response to check comprehension
- Excluding multicultural and international titles, poetry, and a balance of genres and character types from the classroom selection

There is no one right way to teach literature-based reading. The method cannot be packaged. Your best protection against bogus claims, materials, and practices is to have a complete understanding of the theory behind the practice. *Transitions* and *Invitations* by Routman (1988, 1991); *Literature-Based Reading Programs at Work,* edited by Hancock and Hill (1987); and *How to Teach Reading with Children's Books* by Veatch (1968) are a few of the excellent, practical resources available to provide this information.

EVALUATING THE LITERATURE PROGRAM

Ongoing evaluation is part of responsible teaching, since it reveals students' strengths and weaknesses in learning and teachers' strengths and weaknesses in instruction and indicates where intervention or revision is needed. In today's schools, reading and mathematics skills are given the lion's share of attention in standardized evaluation programs, and all too often, no attention is paid to children's growth in literary understanding. This section focuses on how to evaluate a literature program from both students' and teachers' perspectives.

Well-known student assessment methods include traditional paper-and-pencil testing, portfolio assessment, conferencing, and observing. Teachers have found the latter three most informative in assessing how well a literature program is meeting children's needs. Portfolio assessment and conferencing can leave information gaps, however, and do not necessarily assess the teacher's performance or the program itself. We find that observation, when carefully directed, provides a full description of the students' progress, the teacher's strengths and weaknesses, and the literature program. It is also the most efficient method of assessment, since it can be done while one is engaged in other tasks.

Observation and Assessment of Student Learning

Evaluation of students in relation to a literature curriculum will focus mainly on the curriculum's effect on student behaviors rather than on the students' grasp of concepts. Consequently, the evaluation will be accomplished primarily by observing students rather than by testing them. An important principle to remember in planning for evaluation of teaching and learning is that evaluation must parallel the goals and objectives of the instructional plan. To look for conceptual understandings or behaviors in students when those concepts or behaviors have not been taught or encouraged is to invite failure and disappointment.

Experienced teachers often develop checklists to use in observation and assessment of various aspects of their literature programs. Also, generic checklists can be developed by teams of teachers and librarians at each grade level in a school and then may be tailored by individual teachers to fit their own specific plans.

CHECKLIST FOR STUDENT INVOLVEMENT WITH BOOKS   Some of the behaviors that teachers look for in their students' interaction with literature will vary by grade level and the students' development. Other behaviors will show up on checklists for all grade levels. For example, preschool or first-grade teachers would be likely to look for evidence that their students know the terms *author* and *illustrator,* use the terms correctly in their discussions of books, and recognize the work of specific authors and illustrators. Middle-grade teachers, on the other hand, would be more likely to look for evidence that students are choosing and reading novel-length stories independently. Teachers at all grade levels will be looking for evidence that their students are enjoying reading and voluntarily choosing to read. The following generic checklist gives an idea of what such an evaluation instrument might look like.

Checklist for Student Involvement with Literature

Evaluator: _____   Date: _____

Behavior	Yes	No	Comment
Reading			
Student reads voluntarily and willingly	___	___	_____
Student enjoys reading	___	___	_____
Student reads during silent reading time	___	___	_____
Student reads for entertainment	___	___	_____
Student reads for information	___	___	_____
Student reads a variety of fiction, nonfiction, and poems	___	___	_____
Response to Literature			
Student talks intelligently about books read or heard	___	___	_____
Student shares responses to books with peers	___	___	_____
Student is attentive during read-aloud sessions	___	___	_____
Student is able to discuss a work of fiction in terms of			
character	___	___	_____
plot	___	___	_____
setting	___	___	_____
theme	___	___	_____
style	___	___	_____
Student is able to discuss a work of nonfiction in terms of			
structure	___	___	_____
theme	___	___	_____
style	___	___	_____
Student is able to accept that different people may have different responses to the same story	___	___	_____
Student is able to relate stories to personal experience, where applicable	___	___	_____
Student is able to compare and contrast stories, authors' writing styles, and illustrators' artistic styles	___	___	_____
Selection of Literature			
Student knows how to select appropriate books for independent reading	___	___	_____
Student keeps a log of books read independently	___	___	_____
Student is developing personal preferences in literature	___	___	_____
Student tries new book genres	___	___	_____

Observation and Assessment of Teacher Effectiveness

Regular self-assessment is an important part of a teacher's professional development. The following two checklists may be used for this purpose as well as for assessment by one's peers.

CHECKLIST FOR CLASSROOM ENVIRONMENT   The environment of a classroom is determined mainly by what the resident teacher values in learning and teaching. These values, in turn, determine how the classroom is arranged, which materials are available, and what sorts of events and activities are regularly scheduled. The following checklist incorporates all of these features.

Checklist for Promoting Literature through Classroom Environment

Evaluator: _____   Date: _____

Behavior	Yes	No	Comment
Physical Plant			
Desks are arranged to promote student-to-student discussion	___	___	_____
Room arrangement provides quiet areas for reading and thinking	___	___	_____
Reading area is well lighted	___	___	_____
Reading area has comfortable seating	___	___	_____
Reading area has adequate and convenient shelving for books	___	___	_____
Reading area is well organized and orderly	___	___	_____
Student response projects are displayed	___	___	_____
Materials			
Classroom has a trade book library	___	___	_____
Classroom library is adequate in			
scope (variety of genres, both fiction and nonfiction)	___	___	_____
depth (variety of books within a genre)	___	___	_____

Checklist for Promoting Literature through Classroom Environment *(Continued)*			
Behavior	*Yes*	*No*	*Comment*
quality (light reading for entertainment to excellent quality for study)	——	——	———————
providing for varying reading abilities	——	——	———————
recent books	——	——	———————
multicultural and international books	——	——	———————
poetry collections	——	——	———————
Classroom has a temporary collection	——	——	———————
Temporary collection			
addresses gaps in permanent collection	——	——	———————
is exchanged regularly	——	——	———————
provides for varying student interests	——	——	———————
is coordinated with topics of study	——	——	———————
Classroom library materials are			
easy for students to reach and reshelve	——	——	———————
coded and organized logically	——	——	———————
Scheduling			
Time is provided for self-choice reading every day	——	——	———————
Time is provided for browsing and selection of books regularly	——	——	———————
Time is provided for response to literature	——	——	———————

CHECKLIST FOR TEACHING ACTIVITIES   Success in making children lovers of books and reading certainly does not depend upon generous supplies of equipment or a certain physical layout, although these can facilitate the job. In the end, it is what the teacher does with literature that makes the biggest impression on children. Activities that make the learning experience positive and nonthreatening are generally the most successful with children. This point of view is evident in the following checklist of teaching activities.

Checklist for Promoting Literature through Teaching Activities

Evaluator: _____   Date: _____

Behavior	Yes	No	Comment

Making Literature Enjoyable

Read aloud daily (high-quality literature)   ____ ____   _____

Select books for read-aloud that
   reflect students' interests   ____ ____   _____

    represent a wide variety of genres   ____ ____   _____

    represent outstanding examples of each genre   ____ ____   _____

Share poetry orally on a regular basis   ____ ____   _____

    Popular poets   ____ ____   _____

    NCTE Award–winning poets   ____ ____   _____

    Golden Age poets   ____ ____   _____

Share stories through storytelling   ____ ____   _____

Motivating Students to Read

Introduce books regularly through booktalks   ____ ____   _____

Encourage student response to literature

    by asking open-ended or divergent questions   ____ ____   _____

    by encouraging varied responses   ____ ____   _____

      oral response   ____ ____   _____

      written response   ____ ____   _____

      graphic response   ____ ____   _____

Allow students to choose books for
   independent reading   ____ ____   _____

Make both fiction and nonfiction options
   for independent reading   ____ ____   _____

Take class to school library weekly or more
   frequently for book browsing or selection   ____ ____   _____

Take class to public library for a field trip   ____ ____   _____

Invite a librarian to your class to booktalk
   and tell stories   ____ ____   _____

Checklist for Promoting Literature through Teaching Activities *(Continued)*

Behavior	Yes	No	Comment
Modeling Reading Behaviors			
Read during silent reading time	——	——	_____
Talk enthusiastically about books read	——	——	_____
Show students how to select books	——	——	_____
Showing the Relevance of Literature			
Integrate literature across the curriculum	——	——	_____
health/science	——	——	_____
social studies/history	——	——	_____
language arts/reading	——	——	_____
mathematics	——	——	_____
Encouraging Literature Appreciation			
Present a yearlong literature curriculum	——	——	_____
Reaching beyond the Classroom			
Send read-aloud suggestions to parents	——	——	_____
Encourage parents to visit library with their children	——	——	_____
Invite parents and community leaders to be guest readers for read-aloud	——	——	_____
Evaluation			
Record student growth			
in understanding literary concepts	——	——	_____
in choices of books to read	——	——	_____
in attitude toward reading	——	——	_____
in quality of responses (verbal, written, artistic)	——	——	_____

IMPLEMENTING A SCHOOLWIDE CURRICULUM IN LITERATURE

Having a schoolwide curriculum in literature benefits teachers and students and is worth pursuing. The main benefit to students is that their teachers' efforts will be coordinated from year to year. Repetition of content and titles will be avoided, and continuity will be improved. The main benefits to teachers are that ideas, expertise, and materials will be shared and planning will be facilitated by knowing what experiences with literature incoming students have had or should have. The task of developing a schoolwide literature curriculum should be shared by a committee that has a representative from each grade level and the library media specialist.

A literature curriculum committee's function is to determine what literature content will be presented at each grade level. A set of trade books appropriate for delivering the literature curriculum at each grade level can also be suggested by the committee, although the ultimate choice of books to be used in a classroom will be the individual teacher's decision. Literature curriculum committees often select and update their schoolwide read-aloud list. Such a list helps to prevent duplication of teachers' read-aloud choices at different grade levels and to assure that students hear a well-balanced selection of books over the years. Having such a list may also convince some teachers to begin a read-aloud program.

The Library Media Center

The well-stocked, efficiently run library media center is the heart of a school, and the knowledgeable media center director has his or her finger on the pulse of each classroom. As literature-based reading and literature across the curriculum have gained acceptance, library media specialists and teachers have been moving toward a shared responsibility for teaching. Teachers tell librarians their resource needs, and librarians help teachers by identifying and locating appropriate resources, keeping teachers updated with the newest literature and suggesting ways to present books to students. For these reasons, the librarian should be encouraged to play a key role in planning and developing a schoolwide curriculum in literature.

Book Clubs

A marketing phenomenon of our times is the publisher-owned book club. These clubs send monthly catalogs to teachers who then distribute them to students, collect and process student book orders, and receive bonus points for each item ordered. Paperback books representing a full range of quality from award-winning books to joke books, posters, and stickers are offered at prices far below bookstore cost. Children and teachers who lack access to well-stocked libraries are especially dependent on these clubs. Another advantage of book clubs is that the selection, ownership, and reading of these books involves parents.

Being knowledgeable about children's literature enables you to help your students select the best book club titles. You can gently redirect children's choices from the "junk" offerings to the better books by going over the catalog with students and giving booktalks about the titles you recommend. Care should be given to verify topic and age appropriateness of any selections with which you are unfamiliar.

Teachers who participate in these clubs often use their bonus points to build their classroom book collections. With this in mind, you may want to subscribe to more than one club to have a wider choice of titles.

Bookfairs

A bookfair is a book sale that is organized by a book vendor, such as a bookstore owner, and held in the school building for one or more days. Books are displayed so that children and their parents can browse and select items for purchase. Bookfairs always call attention to literature and reading and can even be considered a reading motivator. They are especially appropriate in areas where there are no children's bookstores or well-stocked libraries.

Bookfairs send strong messages to children and their parents about a school's stance on reading and about what sorts of reading materials teachers and librarians in the school endorse. Bookfairs in which joke collections, scented stickers, stamps, commercialized series books, coloring books, and posters are prominent send the wrong message to children and their parents about reading. Bookfairs in which a wide variety of good literature is prominent send an entirely different (and more defensible) message about reading. Excellent bookfairs are the result of careful planning and active involvement in selection of books by teachers and school librarians. Book selection should not be left solely to the book vendor.

Parent Involvement

Parental involvement in literature begins with getting support for the school reading program at home. Parents are almost always willing to promote their children's academic efforts at home if they are told how to do it. Many teachers give parents lists of activities that support reading, including brief, carefully worded explanations where necessary. Some typical suggestions include the following:

- Read to your child at night, especially if he or she is a reluctant reader. (Lists of good read-alouds can be sent home regularly.)
- Listen to your child read aloud.
- Take your child to the library to select books.
- Give books to your child as gifts. (Lists of good gift book suggestions can be sent home prior to birthdays and holidays.)

Some parents are willing to help in classrooms on a regular basis. Ways in which parents can help teachers include the following:

- Listen to children read orally.
- Read aloud to small groups or individual students.
- Type, assemble, and bind the storybooks that children write.
- Read stories and poems on audiotapes for listening.
- Make book bags for carrying books back and forth from home.

Guest Authors and Illustrators

Professional children's authors and illustrators often visit schools to speak to children about their careers and their books. Teachers are usually instrumental in selecting, inviting, and organizing these visits. Guest authors and illustrators may be chosen on the basis of availability, but more often they are chosen because of the students' interest in their books or the relevance of their work to a topic that students are studying. Such visits are powerful reading motivators.

The standard procedure is to contact the marketing director or editor of the author's or artist's publishing house to determine availability and terms. Since most established children's authors and illustrators charge an honorarium and travel expenses, schools within a system often share the author and the costs. Many state reading associations have developed lists of children's authors and illustrators who live in state. These lists can usually be found in public libraries.

Local Public Library

The community has no more valuable resource than its public library. Each time students, teachers, and parents seek the educational resources they need in their public libraries, the natural link between schools and public libraries is reaffirmed. Public libraries provide many services in addition to loaning books. Consider the impact of the following list of services:

- The interlibrary loan system, which gives patrons access to library holdings throughout the state, region, or nation
- Summertime reading programs for children
- Summertime bookmobile programs
- Special observances, such as National Book Week, Banned Book Week, and Hans Christian Andersen Day, which help to bring important literacy issues to the public's attention
- Story hour for young children
- Audiovisual versions of many books
- Guest appearances of authors and illustrators

Teachers can help to make the public library more effective by making students and their parents aware of the library and its programs and services.

CENSORSHIP, SELECTION, AND FIRST AMENDMENT RIGHTS

Censorship is the actual removal, suppression, or restricted circulation of literary, artistic, or educational materials (images, ideas, and information) on the grounds that they are morally or otherwise objectionable (Reichman, 2001). Censors want to make moral decisions for all others, and, in so doing, they deny intellectual freedom not only to children, but also to those who often select books for children, such as teachers, librarians, and parents.

Selection is the right to object to books on the bases of literary quality and knowledge of child development and child psychology without insisting upon removing them from the shelves for everyone else. An important part of teacher and librarian training is learning how to select books that are of good quality and appropriate for children. The following discussion assumes that children should have broad reading options from books selected by professionally trained adults for their excellent quality and age and topic appropriateness for children.

The First Amendment to the Constitution of the United States guarantees to its citizens the freedoms of religion, of speech, and of the press—collectively called "intellectual freedom." As adults, we cherish our right to choose our reading material and use it nearly every day of our lives. Elementary and middle-school social studies and civics textbooks proudly proclaim the freedom of choice that citizens of the United States have in their daily lives. But do we, as parents, teachers, and librarians, actually extend these rights to our children? Specifically,

- Do we allow ourselves to be bullied by outspoken special-interest groups into taking good, but controversial, books off the library shelves, or do we stand by our convictions and book selections?

- Do we self-censor by only selecting books on "safe" topics, or do we select books on the bases of quality and age appropriateness?
- Do we listen to young readers' ideas about the books that they have read, or do we only ask them "comprehension" questions?
- Do we allow children to reject books that they do not like, or do we force them to read what we have chosen for them to read?

In other words, do we actually teach students, by our actions as well as by our words, about their First Amendment rights?

A study by Wollman-Bonilla (1998) of pre- and inservice teachers' ideas about acceptable and unacceptable children's books reveals a tendency toward teacher bias in book selection for children. The researcher found that teachers "commonly objected to texts that reflect gender, ethnic, race, or class experiences that differed from their own" (p. 289). This subtle form of censorship is made worse by the fact that most teachers are unaware of their own biases in text selection (Jipson & Paley, 1991; Luke, Cooke, & Luke, 1986). Wollman-Bonilla makes a strong point in favor of First Amendment rights for children when she concludes, "If we are to know how books actually affect children, we need to hear *children's* voices and understand *their* experiences before, during, and after reading" (p. 293).

Dealing with Censorship Attempts

According to the American Library Association, "A *challenge* is an attempt to remove or restrict materials, based upon the objections of a person or group. A *banning* is the removal of those materials. Challenges do not simply involve a person expressing a point of view; rather, they are an attempt to remove material from the curriculum or library, thereby restricting the access of others" (www.ala.org/ala/oif). Most book challenges occur locally, and most fail.

The American Library Association's Office of Intellectual Freedom monitors the challenges made against children's books in the United States. Most adults and children who have read the highly regarded books that often appear on these "most challenged books" lists find the reasons given for the challenges perplexing, if not incredible. For example, the following titles appeared on the ALA's list of Most Frequently Challenged Children's Books for 2002:

The *Harry Potter* series by J. K. Rowling for its focus on wizardry and magic
The *Alice* series by Phyllis Reynolds Naylor for being sexually explicit, using offensive
    language, and being unsuited to the age group
Captain Underpants by Dav Pilkey for insensitivity, being unsuited to the age group, and
    encouraging children to disobey authority
Bridge to Terabithia by Katerine Paterson for offensive language, sexual content,
    and occult/satanism

Often, individuals challenge books on the basis of a single word or phrase, or on hearsay, and have not read the book at all. Teachers and library media specialists have found that a written procedure is helpful for bringing order and reason into discussions with parents who want to censor school materials. Most procedures call for teachers and librarians to give would-be censors a complaint form and ask them to specify their concerns in writing. There are advantages to such a system: Both teachers and parents are given time to reflect on the issue and to control their emotions; and the would-be censor is given time to read the book in its entirety, if he or she has not done so already. Developing written procedures and complaint forms for dealing with a would-be censor are important tasks for the literature curriculum committee. Figure 11.3 presents a model form produced by the National Council of Teachers of English (NCTE) for reconsideration of a work of literature.

The American Library Association's Office for Intellectual Freedom has several publications about censorship such as Reichman's *Censorship and Selection: Issues and Answers for Schools* (2001) that provide important and helpful information to schools on this topic. (For a catalog of all ALA publications, write to ALA Publishing, 50 East Huron Street, Chicago, IL 60611 or visit the web site given earlier in this section). People for the American Way, an organization that provides advice and assistance in combatting school censorship, can be contacted at 2000 M St. NW, Suite 400, Washington, DC 20036.

The National Council of Teachers of English also offers a valuable document about censorship, *The Students' Right to Read* (Committee on the Right to Read, 1982), which explains the nature of censorship, the stand of those opposed to it, and ways to combat it. This document and the *Citizen's Request for Reconsideration of a Work* are available free of charge from NCTE Order Department, 1111 W. Kenyon Road, Urbana, IL 61801, or from the Internet at http://www.ncte.org/position/right.html.

In dealing with censorship attempts, teachers should let their actions be guided by two precepts: (1) A parent has the right to object to his or her child's reading or listening to a specific book, and that right should be respected; and (2) a parent does not have the right to deny everyone else the right to read or hear a book. Teachers often find that censorship problems can be solved by being flexible. For example, if a parent objects to a book that is being read aloud to his or her child, the teacher can allow that child to visit another classroom or the media center when the book is being read.

Teaching the First Amendment

Teaching children about First Amendment rights is important today, because there are those who would take these rights away. Individuals, but more often organized groups from the political left and right as well as conservative religious groups, want to assume power over what all children read and learn. Their goal is to suppress anything that conflicts with their own beliefs. According to media specialist Pat Scales (1995), "The problem is obvious. Censors want to control the minds of the young. They are fearful of the educational system because students who read learn to think. Thinkers learn to see. Those who see often question. And young people who question threaten the 'blind' and the 'nonthinkers'" (p. 20).

Teaching students about their First Amendment rights might begin by posting a copy of the First Amendment, having students read it, and then discussing what this amendment means to them and what its loss might mean to them. Lists of children's books that some have declared "objectionable," such as those listed previously, could be posted. Children who have read the books could discuss why they might have been found objectionable and why banning these books would violate their First Amendment rights. Children's and young adults' fiction about censorship could be read and discussed. Good examples are *The Rebellious Alphabet* by Jorge Diaz, *The Last Safe Place on Earth* by Richard Peck, *The Trials of Molly Sheldon* by Julian Thompson, and *Save Halloween!* by Stephanie Tolan. As teachers and librarians, we should do everything possible to promote the kinds of books that encourage critical thinking, inquiry, and self-expression, while maintaining respect for the views of others.

FIGURE 11.3   Citizen's Request for Reconsideration of a Work

Author _____ Paperback _____ Hardcover _____

Title _____

Publisher (if known) _____

Request initiated by _____

Telephone _____

Address _____ City _____ Zip Code _____

Complainant represents:

____ Himself/Herself

____ (Name Organization) _____

____ (Identify other group) _____

1. Have you been able to discuss this work with the teacher or librarian who ordered it or used it? ____ Yes ____ No

2. What do you understand to be the general purpose for using this work?

    a. Provide support for a unit in the curriculum? ____ Yes ____ No

    b. Provide a learning experience for the reader in one kind of literature? ____ Yes ____ No

    c. Other _____
                     _____

3. Did the general purpose for the use of the work, as described by the teacher or librarian, seem a suitable one to you? ____ Yes ____ No
    If not, please explain. _____
    _____

4. What do you think is the general purpose of the author in this book? _____

5. In what ways do you think a work of this nature is not suitable for the use the teacher or librarian wishes to carry out? _____
    _____

6. Have you been able to learn what is the students' response to this work? ____ Yes ____ No

7. What response did the students make? _____
    _____

8. Have you been able to learn from your school library what book reviewers or other students of literature have written about this work? ____ Yes ____ No

9. Would you like the teacher or librarian to give you a written summary of what book reviewers and other students have written about this book or film? ____ Yes ____ No

10. Do you have negative reviews of the book? ____ Yes ____ No

11. Where were they published? _____

12. Would you be willing to provide summaries of the reviews you have collected? ____ Yes ____ No

13. What would you like your library/school to do about this work?
    ____ Do not assign/lend it to my child.
    ____ Return it to the staff selection committee/department for reevaluation.
    ____ Other–Please explain
    _____

14. In its place, what work would you recommend that would convey as valuable a picture and perspective of the subject treated? _____

Signature _____ Date _____

Source: Committee on the Right to Read. (1982). *The students' right to read.* Urbana, IL: National Council of Teachers of English.

REFERENCES

Aiken, J. (1974/2002). *Midnight is a place.* Boston: Houghton.

Aliki. (1994). *The gods and goddesses of Olympus.* New York: HarperCollins.

Anderson, R. C., Hiebert, E. H., Scott, J. A., & Wilkinson, I. A. (1985). *Becoming a nation of readers: The report of the commission on reading.* Champaign, IL: Center for the Study of Reading.

Avi. (1989). *The man who was Poe.* New York: Orchard.

Babbitt, N. (1975). *Tuck everlasting.* New York: Farrar.

Baldick, C. (1990). *The concise Oxford dictionary of literary terms.* New York: Oxford University Press.

Bat-Ami, M. (2000). *Two suns in the sky.* Chicago: Front Street/Cricket.

Brisson, P. (1997). *Hot fudge hero.* Illustrated by D. K. Blumenthal. New York: Holt.

Browning, E. B. (1902). Reading. In K. D. Wiggins & N. A. Smith (Eds.), *Golden numbers.* New York: Doubleday.

Buss, F. L., & Cubias, D. (1991). *Journey of the sparrows.* New York: Lodestar.

Christopher, J. (1967). *The white mountains.* New York: Macmillan.

Cleary, B. (1977). *Ramona and her father.* Illustrated by A. Tiegreen. New York: Morrow.

———. (1981). *Ramona Quimby, age 8.* Illustrated by A. Tiegreen. New York: Morrow.

Committee on the Right to Read (1982). *The students' right to read.* Urbana, IL: National Council of Teachers of English.

Creech, S. (2002). *Ruby Holler.* New York: HarperCollins.

Dowell, F. O. (2000). *Dovey Coe.* New York: Atheneum.

Durkin, D. (1987). *Teaching young children to read* (4th ed.). Boston: Allyn and Bacon.

Farmer, N. (2002). *The house of the scorpion.* New York: Simon & Schuster.

Fisher, L. E., adapter. (1988). *Theseus and the Minotaur.* New York: Holiday.

Freedman, R. (1980). *Immigrant kids.* New York: Dutton.

French, F. (1986). *Snow White in New York.* New York: Oxford.

Giff, P. R. (2003). *Maggie's door.* New York: Delacorte.

Green, Bette. (1973). *Summer of my German soldier.* New York: Dial.

Greenwald, S. (2003). *Rosy Cole's worst ever, best yet tour of New York City.* New York: Holt.

Hall, S. (1990). *Using picture storybooks to teach literary devices: Recommended books for children and young adults.* Phoenix: Oryx.

———. (1994). *Using picture storybooks to teach literary devices: Recommended books for children and young adults* (Vol. 2). Phoenix: Oryx.

Hancock, J., & Hill, S. (1987). *Literature-based reading programs at work.* Portsmouth, NH: Heinemann.

Hastings, S. (1985). *Sir Gawain and the loathly lady.* Illustrated by Juan Wijngaard. New York: Lothrop.

Hedblad, A. (Ed.). (2001). *Something about the author* (Vol. 118). Detroit: Gale Research.

Hesse, K. (1992). *Letters from Rifka.* New York: Holt.

Horvath, P. (2001). *Everything on a waffle.* New York: Farrar.

Hyman, T. S. (1977/2001). *The sleeping beauty.* New York: Little, Brown.

Isaacs, A. (1994). *Swamp angel.* Illustrated by P. O. Zelinsky. New York: Dutton.

Jarrell, R., translator. (1972). *Snow White and the seven dwarfs.* Illustrated by N. E. Burkert. New York: Farrar.

Jennings, R. W. (2000). *Orwell's luck.* Boston: Houghton.

Jiménez, F. (1999). *The circuit: Stories from the life of a migrant child.* Boston: Houghton.

Jipson, J., & Paley, N. (1991) The selective tradition in children's literature: Does it exist in the elementary classroom? *English Education, 23,* 148–159.

Klein, R. (1987). *Hating Alison Ashley.* New York: Viking.

Knight, M. B. (1993/2003). *Who belongs here: An American story.* Illustrated by A. S. O'Brien. Gardiner, ME: Tilbury House.

Lapp, D., Flood, J., & Farnan, N. (1992). Basal readers and literature: A tight fit or a mismatch? In K. D. Wood & A. Moss (Eds.), *Exploring literature in the classroom: Content and methods* (pp. 33–57). Norwood, MA: Christopher-Gordon.

L'Engle, M. (1962). *A wrinkle in time.* New York: Farrar.

Levine, E. (1993). *If your name was changed at Ellis Island.* Illustrated by W. Parmenter. New York: Scholastic.

Levitin, S. (1970). *Journey to America.* New York: Atheneum.

Lewis, C. S. (1950). *The lion, the witch, and the wardrobe.* New York: Macmillan.

Lewis, M. (1999). *Morgy makes his move.* Boston: Houghton.

Lister, R., reteller. (1990). *The legend of King Arthur.* Illustrated by Alan Baker. New York: Doubleday.

Lord, B. B. (1984). *In the year of the boar and Jackie Robinson.* Illustrated by M. Simont. New York: Harper.

Lowry, L. (1993). *The giver.* Boston: Houghton.

———. (1989). *Number the stars.* Boston: Houghton.

Luke, A., Cooke, J., & Luke, C. (1986). The selective tradition in action: Gender bias in student teachers' selections of children's literature. *English Education, 18,* 209–218.

Maestro, B. (1996). *Coming to America: The story of immigration.* Illustrated by S. Ryan. New York: Scholastic.

Marsden, C. (2002). *The gold-threaded dress.* Cambridge, MA: Candlewick.

Martin, A. M., & Godwin, L. (2000). *The doll people.* New York: Hyperion.

Na, A. (2001). *A step from heaven.* Asheville, NC: Front Street.

Orlev, U. (1983). *The island on Bird Street.* Translated from the Hebrew by H. Halkin. Boston: Houghton.

Paterson, K. (1977). *Bridge to Terabithia.* New York: Crowell.

Reichman, H. (2001). *Censorship and selection: Issues and answers for schools.* Chicago: American Library Association Editions.

Rodda, E. (1991). *Finders keepers.* New York: Greenwillow.

———. (2001). *Rowan of Rin.* New York: Greenwillow.

Routman, R. (1988). *Transitions: From literature to literacy.* Portsmouth: Heinemann.

———. (1991). *Invitations: Changing as teachers and learners K–12.* Portsmouth: Heinemann.

Ryan, P. M. (2000). *Esperanza rising.* New York: Scholastic.

Ryder, R. J., Sekulski, J. L., & Silberg, A. (2003). "Results of direct instruction reading program evaluation longitudinal results: First through third grade, 2000–2003." Madison: Wisconsin Department of Public Instruction.

Salisbury, G. (1994). *Under the blood-red sun.* New York: Delacorte.

Sanderson, R. (2002). *Cinderella.* New York: Little, Brown.

Scales, P. (1995). Studying the First Amendment. *Book Links, 5*(1), 20–24.

Schmidt, J., & Wood, T. (1995). *Two lands, one heart: An American boy's journey to his mother's Vietnam.* New York: Walker.

Shea, P. D. (2003). *Tangled threads: A Hmong girl's story.* New York: Clarion.

Smith, D. B. (1973). *A taste of blackberries.* New York: HarperCollins.

Soto, G. (1993). *Trading places.* New York: Harcourt

Spinelli, J. (2003). *Milkweed.* New York: Random.

———. (1995). *Tooter Pepperday.* Illustrated by D. Nelson. New York: Random.

Stanley, D. (1997). *Rumpelstiltskin's daughter.* New York: Morrow.

Stolz, M. (1963). *The bully of Barkham Street.* Illustrated by Leonard Shortall. New York: Harper.

———. (1960). *A dog on Barkham Street.* Illustrated by Leonard Shortall. New York: Harper.

Sutcliff, R. (1986). *Dragonslayer: The story of Beowulf.* New York: Puffin.

Temple, F. (1995). *Tonight by sea.* New York: Orchard.

Uchida, Y. (1971). *Journey to Topaz.* New York: Scribner's.

Veatch, J. (1968). *How to teach reading with children's books* (2nd ed.). New York: Richard C. Owen.

Wallace, B. B. (1980). *Peppermints in the parlor.* New York: Atheneum.

Walsh, J. P. (1982). *The green book.* Illustrated by L. Bloom. New York: Farrar.

Williams, J. (1973/2000). *Petronella.* Illustrated by M. Organ-Kean. North Kingstown, RI: Moon Mountain.

Williams, V. B. (2001). *Amber was brave, Essie was smart: The story of Amber and Essie told here in poems and pictures.* New York: Greenwillow.

Winthrop, E. (1985). *The castle in the attic.* New York: Holiday.

Wollman-Bonilla, J. E. (1998). Outrageous viewpoints: Teachers' criteria for rejecting works of children's literature. *Language Arts, 75*(4), 287–295.

Wright B. R. (1983). *The dollhouse murders.* New York: Holiday.

Yep, L. (1977). *Child of the owl.* New York: Harper.

———. (1993). *Dragon's gate.* New York: Harper-Collins.

Yolen, J. (2000). *Not one damsel in distress: World folktales for strong girls.* Illustrated by S. Guevara. New York: Silver Whistle.

Yumoto, K. (1996). *The friends.* Translated by C. Hirano. New York: Farrar.

12

DEVELOPING TEACHING STRATEGIES

The teacher is the key to a well-planned, effective literature program. In the previous chapter, we addressed the long-term aspects of planning and preparing for the literature program. This chapter will focus on the strategies teachers need to carry out such a program. Having students experience and respond to literature are two major responsibilities that a teacher must assume to ensure a good literature program.

EXPERIENCING   LITERATURE

Many teaching strategies can be used to provide students with opportunities to experience enjoyable, exciting, and thought-provoking literature. Students experience prose, poetry, fiction, and nonfiction (1) by having it read aloud to them by a skillful oral reader; (2) by reading it silently to themselves; (3) through shared reading activities with a parent, librarian, teacher, or peer; (4) through stories told to them; and (5) through other media such as audiotapes and videotapes.

Reading Aloud by Teachers

Reading aloud to students is a powerful way to provide them with literary experiences; it is the centerpiece of a curriculum in literature. Beginning in their infancy and throughout their elementary school years and beyond, children should hear books read aloud. Although some teachers at the intermediate-grade level do not read aloud, this teaching strategy is just as important in the development of readers at this stage as it is in kindergarten.

Some of the more important reasons that teachers read aloud are as follows:

- To share with students exciting and stimulating reading material that is beyond their reading ability, but well within their listening ability
- To provide a model of good fluent reading by sharing emotional, funny, exciting, and stimulating literature with students
- To build background and interest in subject matter that will soon be taught in an upcoming content area unit of instruction
- To assist students in developing their meaning vocabularies, their ability to comprehend connected discourse, and their ability to think critically

Three distinct aspects of the read-aloud experience need to be examined to make it as effective a teaching strategy as possible. Those aspects are (1) selecting the literature to read, (2) preparing the students for read-aloud time, and (3) reading the book aloud. Each aspect needs to be taken into consideration for a successful read-aloud experience.

BOOK SELECTION   No matter which book you choose to read aloud, it is essential that you first read the book to yourself. When you preread a book, you can determine whether you find the story enjoyable and worthy of children's time and whether you believe it is of an appropriate level of difficulty for your students. You also can begin to note ways in which the story lends itself to student response.

Over the course of a school year you will want to read aloud a variety of literature: poems, short stories, picture books, and chapter books of different genres and moods. You will also want to ensure that there is a balance of males and females as main characters in the books and that the main characters come from different backgrounds and settings, including multicultural and international ones.

The most recognized works in children's literature, though sometimes complex, deserve to be shared with students over the course of their elementary school years. When a book or poem is challenging for students, you need to be prepared to guide the students' understanding. Without this help, many children would never experience and enjoy some of the more difficult but worthy pieces of literature. Conversely, you will want to avoid choosing books for reading aloud that students can and will consume eagerly on their own, reserving those books for students' independent reading.

When first reading aloud to a new class, however, you will want to start with shorter and easier works, known to be popular with students, and gradually build up to longer and more challenging works as you become better acquainted with your students, their interests, and their abilities. For more discussion of students' preferences in literature, refer to Chapter 1, "Learning about Children and Their Literature," and Chapter 3, "Poetry and Plays."

PREPARATION   Once a selection is made, the next step is to prepare the class for read-aloud time. For students to profit from read-aloud experiences, they need to be attentive. You can prepare students for reading aloud by having them remove distractions, such as pencils and other objects, from their immediate vicinity; by having them sit quietly in the designated place for read-aloud time; and by asking them to be ready to listen. If the book has concepts that you believe will baffle your students, you may want to clarify their meaning before beginning to read.

Introduce the book by stating the title, author, and illustrator of the book, even with the smallest children. This will teach children that books are written by real people called authors and that the illustrations are made by people called illustrators. Sometimes you may want to ask the students to predict what they believe the story will be about from looking at the cover and the title; other times you may want to explain briefly why you chose this book to read to them. For example, you may say that you are going to read this book because "it's another story by one of our favorite authors, William Steig" or that "the book will tell us more about what it was like to live on the prairie in the nineteenth century." Introductions should be kept short. They serve the purpose of preparing students to be attentive to and interested in the story.

READING PICTURE BOOKS ALOUD EFFECTIVELY   Consider the following steps:

- Position yourself close to the class so that all students can see the pictures.
- Show the pictures as you read the book. Remember that in a good picture book the text and pictures are carefully integrated to convey the story as a whole. Hearing and seeing picture books should be simultaneous.
- After the introduction, begin reading the book aloud, placing emphasis on the meaning of the story. Think of reading aloud as a type of dramatic performance.
- Your body movements and facial expressions can also be used to enhance the drama of the read-aloud experience. Leaning forward during a scary, suspenseful part of a story and smiling or chuckling during a funny part can convey to the students your involvement in the story.
- Maintain eye contact with your students. Be sure you are aware of their nonverbal responses to this reading experience. Good eye contact with the students helps you observe when a word of explanation may be needed.
- Read the book from beginning to end without interruptions except on an as-needed basis. Some books, such as concept books and interactive books, do call for interruptions in the read-aloud process. This is particularly true for informational books.

READING CHAPTER BOOKS ALOUD EFFECTIVELY   Many of the same considerations discussed in reading aloud picture books also hold true with chapter book read-alouds. Of course, chapter books have few, if any, illustrations, so holding the book for students to see the pictures is not necessary. In addition, chapter books are usually read aloud over a relatively long period of time, from a few days to many weeks. Often, teachers find reading novel-length chapter books aloud challenging, and sometimes not successful.

Following are some practices that teachers have used successfully during chapter book read-alouds to help hook the students on the book and to keep them tuned in and involved.

- Keep a chart of the characters—their names, relationships, and roles in the story—as the characters appear. This strategy is especially helpful if the story has a large number of characters. For example, in *The Westing Game* (1978) by Ellen Raskin, the many characters of this mystery must be remembered for the plot to make sense.
- Design and display a map of the story setting to track the events of the story in sequence. In most quest fantasies this visual aid can assist students in following the characters' journey for the quest.
- Develop a time line, somewhat like a horizontal mural, on which the dates are set at intervals above the line and the story events placed below the line at the appropriate date. For historical fiction and biographies, a time line can serve as a mnemonic device for the storyline as well as for the historic events of the era. For this purpose, the dates and historic events would be noted on a third tier of the time line.

Silent Reading by Students

Another way for students to experience good literature is to read it to themselves. Indeed, the ultimate goal of a literature program is to turn students into readers who, of their own free will, read self-selected good literature with enjoyment, understanding, and appreciation. To assist students in becoming independent, lifelong readers, teachers in grades K–8 need to set aside time each day for students to read silently in these formative years of reading development. The amount of time for silent reading must be tailored to the reading attention spans of students. Kindergarten and first-grade students may spend only five to ten minutes reading independently, but fourth- and fifth-grade students will often read silently for up to an hour.

Many schools have instituted sustained silent reading (SSR) programs on a schoolwide basis in order to promote the reading habit in students. In these SSR programs a certain time each day is set aside for all students, teachers, librarians, coaches, principals, custodians, and office and kitchen staff to take a "reading break." The philosophy behind SSR programs is that students need to see adults who read and who place a high priority on reading. In SSR programs, students read materials of their own choosing and are not required to write book reports or give oral reports on these materials.

Whether or not you are in a school that has an SSR program, you will want to provide your students with silent reading time each day. Many schools have purchased *computerized reading incentive programs* to motivate and encourage students to read more widely. Programs such as Accelerated Reading (AR) pretest students to determine their reading levels, then assign each student to a level of books with predetermined numbers of points according to difficulty. After students finish reading a book silently, they complete multiple-choice tests to assess literal comprehension of the book to earn points based on the score. Students can then earn prizes according to their performance. Reports on the success of such programs are mixed. Many teachers and schools report disappointment in the programs. Teachers need to be cautious about whether such programs are having a positive impact on their students' interest in reading. Concerns include the following:

- Students' free choices of books for reading are limited.
- Only books on the program's database are considered worthy by students.
- Extrinsic rewards can diminish the desire of students to read for the pleasure of reading.
- Testing students' literal comprehension can undermine the importance of reading books for vicarious experiences.
- Commercially produced literal comprehension tests often emphasize inconsequential information, thus demeaning both the story and the reading act.
- Many students find ways to gain the rewards without reading the books by, for example, asking other students for the answers, skimming the books for facts, and seeing the movie.
- Personal enjoyment of literature is often deemphasized.

Teachers can design their own *reading incentive programs* that avoid these drawbacks and still help students get started as independent readers. In these programs students usually keep a record of their own free-choice silent reading, have opportunities to respond to books in a variety of ways, and work to achieve individual silent reading goals set by the student and teacher together. The rewards, such as a special celebration party, are provided for the whole class for reading, as a group, more total pages or books than were read during the last grading period. Such group rewards avoid the negative consequences of highly competitive programs.

Here are some tips for having successful silent reading periods:

- Have a well-stocked classroom collection of books—poetry books, plays, picture books, novels, and information books. See Chapter 11 for more information on this topic.
- Conduct booktalks regularly so that students become aware of books they may wish to read. These booktalks can be given by teachers and librarians, who will often serve as resource persons.
- Display new books attractively in the classroom and show videos of notable authors talking about their books and craft. These techniques are effective in "selling" books to children.
- Schedule the same time each day for silent reading and adhere to it. Allow enough time for students to get well into their books and to achieve some level of satisfaction from the reading.
- Insist on attentiveness to books during this time. With primary-grade students, quiet talking in pairs about books or individual lipreading aloud may be on-task behavior, but children in intermediate grades can read silently and should be expected to do so.
- Spend the silent reading period engrossed in books, setting yourself as an example of a reader. Be knowledgeable of and interested in the books the students are reading.

Booktalks

A booktalk is an oral presentation by a teacher, a librarian, or a student who tells about a book to stimulate the students' interest and motivate them to read it. Booktalks are not book reports, analyses of the author's style, or the old-fashioned book report that discusses characters, setting, theme, and plot (Bodart, 1980). Booktalks have been used effectively for years by librarians who have developed this strategy into an art for the purpose of encouraging students to check out books from the library. Teachers can give booktalks on five to ten books each week from their classroom and school library collections; in this way, they can entice students to read and experience good literature.

Some teachers who give frequent booktalks also advocate having students give booktalks to induce other students to read the suggested books. A regular feature of *Reading Rainbow,* the public television program about children's books, is children giving booktalks. One teacher taped two or three of these *Reading Rainbow* booktalks and showed them in class to help her students learn how to give good booktalks. The following are recommendations for giving a good booktalk:

- Read the book before trying to do a booktalk on it.
- Choose books that you have liked, wholly or in part, or that you think your students will enjoy. Sincere enthusiasm for a book is stimulating and infectious.
- Have the book available to show to the students as you give the booktalk. Format aspects—such as cover illustrations, length, size, and shape of the books—which also influence book choices, can be weighed by students only if they can see the book.
- Keep the booktalk brief, generally no more than two or three minutes. Do not tell too much about the book or the students will see no reason to read it. For most books, four to six sentences will suffice.
- Tell the topic and something about the action in the story, but *do not tell the plot.* Feature a scene or character that the story revolves around, but do not discuss the scene that gives away the ending.
- Booktalk a group of books that share the same theme; in this case you will want to talk briefly about each book and how it fits with the others.

The following is an example of a booktalk on *The House of the Scorpion* (2002) by Nancy Farmer:

If you ever think about what life will be like in the future, 100 years from now, you will enjoy reading *The House of the Scorpion,* a novel about young Matt, who has spent his life locked away in a hut because he is a clone and clones are outcasts hated by human society. As Matt comes of age he discovers that he is the clone of El Patrón, the cruel ruler of Opium, a drug kingdom farmed by "eejits," brain-dead clones. Opium is located between the United States and Aztlán, once called Mexico. In El Patrón's household, Matt finds support from a cook and a bodyguard, and eventually Maria, who begins to care about Matt. When Matt realizes that his life is at risk, he makes a break for freedom and escapes to Aztlán only to face more hardships and adventures. Matt wonders who he is, why he exists, and whether, as a clone, he has free will. *The House of the Scorpion* by Nancy Farmer has received many honors, including winning the National Book Award for young people's literature.

After you have given the booktalk, place the book back on the reading table for students to peruse and to consider for reading. Over time, you should give booktalks on a variety of books at different levels of reading difficulty, on different topics, and with male and female protagonists from many cultures. In this way, you will appeal to the wide range of interests and abilities that exist among students in a classroom.

Storytelling

Storytelling is the oldest medium for sharing literature. Oral literature flourished for thousands of years before writing was invented and books became commonly available. When a teacher tells stories, another delightful means for children to experience literature becomes available to the class. Teachers who tell stories in their classrooms report that their students are appreciative listeners and soon begin telling stories themselves.

By bringing stories to life through personal expression and interpretation, a storyteller establishes a close communication with the audience. A storyteller begins by selecting a good story. Next, she practices it until she is able to tell it with ease and then tells it to different audiences again and again.

SELECTION OF A STORY   To find stories for telling, begin with collections of folktales and short stories. Read some of these until you find a few you especially like. Then consider these two points:

- Good stories for telling usually have few characters (from two to five), high conflict, action that builds to a climax, and a quick conclusion that ties together all the threads of the story. Humorous elements are also worth seeking.
- The first stories you tell should take no longer than ten minutes. As you develop your storytelling gifts, you may want to tell longer stories.

A good resource for teachers and students in grades 4 and above who want to tell stories more formally is Pellowski's *The Storytelling Handbook: A Young People's Collection of Unusual Tales and Helpful Hints on How to Tell Them* (1995).

PREPARATION FOR TELLING   Once you have selected a story to tell, outline the story content in terms of the plot. Many storytellers note on 3" × 5" cards the title and source of the tale, the characters' names and story events, and any other information that may be helpful. These cards can then be consulted quickly just before one tells a story. A story file can be a nice resource to keep as more stories are prepared for telling. One storyteller tapes her stories and then uses them to refresh her memory for later retellings.

PRACTICE   Tell the story aloud to yourself again and again. Do not memorize the story, but keep in mind the characters and sequence of main story events. Each time you tell the story, it will change a bit, becoming more and more your own story as you include personal touches. Some storytellers find props useful. They can be simple (a hat, a stick-on mustache, or a stuffed toy) or more elaborate (a mask, a puppet, or a costume).

When puppets are used, a separate puppet is made for each character and is held by the storyteller while the character speaks. Puppets can be purchased or made by the storyteller. Another more elaborate use of props is the feltboard story—a storytelling aid some teachers especially enjoy. Pictures or objects are attached to a feltboard or display board and are moved around during the story. Cumulative stories, especially, lend themselves to feltboard presentations.

Shared Reading

Shared reading is a term we use to describe a number of teaching strategies that attempt to draw on the natural literacy learning that has long occurred in book-loving homes around the world. These various strategies—*shared-book experience, assisted reading,* and *paired reading*—provide children with opportunities to experience good literature as they are learning to read. The strategies have in common a semistructured modification of the parent-child interaction with repeated readings of favorite books as the child gradually acquires an understanding of print and its relationship to our sound system or to the words we speak. A list of pattern books suitable for use in shared reading activities can be found at the end of Chapter 4, "Picture Books."

The *shared-book experience* is an adaptation of a natural home-learning strategy used with groups of beginning readers in school settings. Enlarged-text books of 24" × 30" or larger, called *Big Books,* usually well-loved children's picture books, are presented to groups of beginning readers in a sequence proposed by Holdaway in 1982. First, favorite, well-known poems and songs are repeated in unison by the students and the teacher while the teacher points to the text of the Big Book. A review story is then used to teach skills in context. Following this activity, the teacher involves the students in language play, such as alphabet games, rhymes, and songs that use letter names. Then a new story in Big Book format is presented by the teacher. Students participate by repeating the story, line by line, after the teacher. Later, students read independently from a wide selection of favorite books and compose original stories, often modeled after the new story.

Assisted reading (Hoskisson, Sherman, and Smith, 1974) is a one-to-one strategy for use with impaired readers. In assisted reading, the child and the adult sit side by side with a book. The child reads aloud until she or he has difficulty, at which point the adult supplies the word.

Paired reading is guided practice with an adult who reads in a soft voice and invites the child to fill in words when the adult pauses and the child knows the word. Paired reading can also be enjoyed by two children of compatible personalities who read back and forth to one another.

In all of these strategies, well-chosen literature is important; the nature of the experience is companionable, not authoritative; and the child reader must see the text and hear the words simultaneously. Sometimes, the adult places a finger under each word as it is being read to draw the child's attention to the print. Selecting favorite, loved stories is essential because the success of these strategies is contingent on frequent rereadings of the same book.

The primary purpose of these three shared-reading strategies is to provide learning situations in which children can learn to read using books and activities familiar to them in home and preschool settings. The effect of these strategies can also be the promotion of a love of literature.

Literature across the Curriculum

Students may also experience good literature in content-area classes when teachers supplement or replace textbooks with trade books for instruction. *Literature across the curriculum* refers to using works of literature in the content areas of social studies, science, health, and mathematics. Many advantages accrue to teachers who incorporate trade books into their teaching. Students will also gain from this practice.

Students who lack motivation and struggle in reading can benefit from reading attractively illustrated trade books on the topic under study. Selection of trade books of both greater and lesser difficulty can meet the needs of students of different reading levels, unlike textbooks written on a single readability level, usually at a higher level than the grade at which they are used.

Trade books make social studies content more memorable because the stories are presented from a child's point of view. Children see the world through a narrative framework. In learning about their world, stories and narrative are more real to children than informational texts. Children are more likely to understand and remember history if it is presented as a story with characters, settings, and events. Later, they move from an interest in the narrative to an interest in the history itself.

Trade books also permit students to read multiple perspectives on topics, which helps them develop critical thinking. Comparing historical information from various sources is a valued practice that helps students encounter differing perspectives on any particular era of history. Students may start with the textbook, then research the facts from other books, or read a work of fiction and then seek to verify to what extent the facts within the story are accurate. In addition, trade books couch political and social events in terms of the moral events related to them. Children can see how these events affected the lives of real people and can better understand the morality underlying their choices. Unlike textbook authors who must write to please all viewpoints, authors of children's literature are more likely to face controversial issues head-on. For ideas on planning social studies units incorporating trade books, fiction and nonfiction, see the web on immigration, Figure 11.2, page 229, and the features titled "Using Traditional Literature across the Curriculum: Social Studies" in Chapter 5, page 106; "Using Historical Fiction and Nonfiction across the Curriculum: Social Studies"; and "Using Historical Fiction and Biography across the Curriculum: Social Studies," the last two in Chapter 8, pages 151 and 152.

Trade books in science and health offer the advantage of presenting different sources as a means to verify facts. Students can compare the facts presented in the textbook with those found in various trade books on the same topic. Global warming, a topic of general discussion in the news, is addressed in science textbooks, and a number of trade books are concerned with this topic. For example, Laurence Pringle's *Global Warning: The Threat of Earth's Changing Climate* (2001) and Alvin Silverstein, Virginia Silverstein, and Laura Silverstein Nunn's *Global Warning* (2002) are two fairly short, well-written informational books, while Marcus Sedgwick's science fiction novel *Floodland* (2001) features a girl who searches for her parents after the sea, as a result of global warming, has risen causing cities to become islands. Another work of science fiction, *The House of the Scorpion* (2002) by Nancy Farmer, can become the basis for investigations into cloning and its ramifications. The feature "Using Nonfiction across the Curriculum: Science" offers suggestions of trade books on three science concepts and on nonfiction picture books suitable for unit introductions in Chapter 9, "Nonfiction," page 166.

Trade books can benefit all subjects. For example, many trade books on health and science present information in interesting ways through graphs, tables, figures, authentic photographs, and other visual presentations, coupled with a lively style of writing in the text. Comparison of information from different sources can be readily provided when students are not limited to a single source for their information. Teachers who draw on materials of various types for their instruction have discovered that literature has the power to educate the mind, while enlightening the spirit and warming the heart.

Content-area reading is the ability to read to acquire, understand, and connect to new content in a particular discipline. When students enter schools with departmentalized organizations, the teaching of reading is often neglected. Content-area teachers feel more responsibility to impart knowledge about the particular subject matter in which they specialize and may ignore the need to assist students in their literacy development. For example, technical vocabulary in a subject needs to be explained, practiced, and developed over time before students "own" it. Most students require substantial exposure to new vocabulary.

In content-area classes students are often assigned textbooks, a type of expository text. Mullis, Martin, Gonzalez, and Kennedy's (2003) report of findings from an international study suggests that children in the United States read expository texts with more difficulty than narrative texts. Teachers can make the reading of textbooks easier if they teach students how such texts are structured and explain other specialized features of them. In Chapter 9, "Nonfiction," the elements of nonfiction are explained with examples provided. Robb (2003) also provides practical ideas for teaching social studies, science, and mathematics.

Today schools and society as a whole are more concerned than ever with the need to continue to develop the reading skills of students in middle and high schools. Reading development is a continuum and must be addressed at all educational levels. Older students need to be encouraged to read widely from a variety of material, including trade books, magazines, newspapers, and textbooks. Wide reading results in growth in vocabulary and reading comprehension, yet the 1996 National Assessment of Educational Progress (NAEP) findings demonstrate that as U.S. students grow older the amount of time they read for enjoyment diminishes dramatically from fourth grade to high school years (Campbell, Voelkl, & Donahue, 1998). Time spent reading is closely related to reading success.

Students deserve access to an ample variety of excellent books that they can read and want to read. They are entitled to sufficient time to visit the school media center and time to read as part of their weekly routines. Teachers can support independent reading by assigning some homework time as reading time. Some individual teachers and teams of content teachers have made this request explicit by requiring 100–150 minutes a week to be logged onto a form with date, author, book title, number of minutes read, and parent signature. This form is turned in once a week for credit. If teachers in schools with departmentalized organizations agree that spending time reading is important, then the time set aside becomes part of the homework expectations. Teachers help make this type of effort successful by showing and talking about books, by reading aloud books or excerpts from books, by inviting the media specialist to talk about new books, and by sharing their personal enthusiasm for books. Each content-area teacher can focus on books that relate to the current focus of study in class. Trade books can enhance the teaching of other subjects while providing students with rich literary experiences.

Audiotapes, Videotapes, and CD-ROM Storybooks

Many tapes are available today to bring literature to students. Recently, some well-known actors have made excellent audio recordings of favorite children's stories. Animated and iconographic videos are also readily available. *Animated videos* are cartoons or images that move; *iconographic videos* are films in which the camera moves over static illustrations. A few videos are movies based on children's books, performed by actors. Predictably, these selections vary widely in quality.

Some audiovisual media re-creations are artistically well done and deserve to be considered as another means for students to experience literature. It is generally preferable to have students read the book first and form their own images of the story. Then, after viewing the tape, students can make comparisons between the book and the tape.

Audiotapes and videotapes are usually available in school libraries, through school districts' media repositories, or from nearby public libraries. Book clubs sometimes offer audiotapes to teachers with the purchase of a certain number of books by the class.

CD-ROM multimedia storybooks, also referred to as electronic storybooks, are becoming more widely available. An advantage of electronic storybooks is that they appeal to most children and permit their independent reading to become more interactive. An electronic story can provide scaffolding for a child when no adult is available to guide reading. One disadvantage is that electronic storybooks may interfere with the child's development of print concepts; another is that the interactive options of CD-ROM storybooks may distract students from the meaning of the story (Labbo & Reinking, 2000). When one selects electronic storybooks for classroom use, one should take into consideration the quality and appropriateness of the literature itself. The best CD-ROM storybooks can add variety and interest to a classroom literature collection.

For assistance in selecting excellent-quality audiotapes, videotapes, and CD-ROM storybooks, the *School Library Journal* provides a multimedia review section in each month's issue. In addition, the American Library Association selects and publishes on their web site an annual list, ALSC's Notable Videos, Recordings, and Software for Children; this list can also be found in the April issue of the *School Library Journal.* Since 1991 the American Library Association has awarded on an annual basis the Andrew Carnegie Medal for Excellence in Children's Video, awarded to the producer of the video.

Bibliotherapy

Bibliotherapy is the use of books by professionally trained therapists in treating emotionally disturbed individuals. Most teachers and librarians are not trained as psychologists, and misguided bibliotherapy may damage students. On the other hand, we know that our students benefit psychologically from reading and talking about powerful stories and the thoughts, feelings, and actions of characters in these stories. Children all face difficult situations at times; discovering that other children have faced similar problems is reassuring. Learning how others have coped successfully with problems gives children confidence that they too will be able to solve problems that may arise later in their lives. Books shared by sensitive and caring teachers and librarians may help students to develop understanding and empathy for others and come to a realization of their own unkind behaviors. Bibliotherapy as a professional treatment should, however, be left to trained therapists.

RESPONDING TO LITERATURE

When students experience a story by listening to it, by reading it, or by viewing it, they may naturally wish to respond or express their reactions to the experience in some way. In sharing their responses with others, students profit by recapturing the experience through translating it to a new form or medium; they develop a better understanding of what they experienced by organizing and deepening their feelings and thoughts on the experience; they discover that other readers' experiences with the same book may not have been the same as theirs; and they bring closure to the experience. Although it is important to give students opportunities to respond to books, not every book needs or merits a lengthy response. Rosenblatt (1978) reminds us that no two people have the same prior experiences and that it is the transaction that occurs between the text, the reader, and the present context that provokes a particular response. Teachers may generate opportunities for students to share their individual insights to literary experiences in many different ways.

Book Discussions

Whole-class discussion usually accompanies the reading aloud of a book to the class. In these discussions, comprehension is assumed and the discussion centers on the different ways students feel and think about the book, its characters, its events, and its outcome. Thus, to stimulate a good class discussion, a teacher will encourage students to share their individual responses to open-ended questions; the teacher will not seek supposedly right answers in order to check comprehension or recall. In a class discussion, the teacher has the pivotal role as discussion leader. The discussion tends to be a teacher-to-students, students-to-teacher format. And with a large class, only some of the students will have an opportunity to express their viewpoints.

Another format for students to discuss their responses to literature is the *literature response group.* In literature response groups, students share their responses with peers about a book they have read as a group or a book read aloud by the teacher to the whole class. One of the goals of literature response groups is to have all children learn to work with one another and to value the opinions and views of others. The following features are typically found in the literature response group format:

- Groups can be established by the desire to read the same book, by friendship, by heterogeneous assignment by the teacher, or by random assignments.
- Small groups are usually set up with two to six students for optimal functioning. Students who have less skill working in groups often function better in dyads or triads.
- The small-group discussion is a student-to-student form of communication that permits students more control over the discussion and more roles to perform as group members. For example, students may assume the role of leader, recorder, arbiter, listener, or devil's advocate.
- The advantages of small-group discussions are that students are in control, have more opportunities to express their opinions, and can become more actively involved. Unless students have been taught to work together, however, groups do not function well.
- Small-group discussions with the teacher as a participating member and joint planning by teacher and class before groups begin working can enable the group to set rules, goals, and time lines.

Individual conferences between a teacher and a student are another means of discovering students' responses to literature. Although a teacher may choose to set up conferences daily, occasional conferences in which the student comes prepared to talk about a book she has recently finished can be instructive for the teacher and motivating for the student. The conference is focused on what the student thought and felt about the book. Some teachers ask the student to read aloud a favorite part of the story and tell why it was selected. Individual conferences are from five to ten minutes long and usually end with considering the next book the student will read or the response activity the student has planned (Veatch, 1968).

Eliciting a good discussion with substantial student participation is not an easy art. Certain strategies for promoting discussions need to be considered for use in leading class discussions, in guiding literature response groups, and in interacting with students in individual conferences. Whether you, as the teacher, will be leading the discussion or guiding your students in the art of discussion leader, the questions to be posed are very important. The purpose of discussions of fiction, then, is to elicit students' responses to the work, in other words, to find out what the students think about the story and feel about the story.

A question that can be answered by "yes," "no," or a single word or phrase will not lead to an interactive discussion. The question, "Did you like the story?" may result in a simple "yes." "Which part of the story did you like best and what did you like about it?" is likely to elicit a more detailed response. *Di-*

vergent questions have no one right answer but a number of possible answers. They naturally provoke more discussion than convergent questions, for which only one answer is correct.

The best ideas for questions to stimulate book discussions flow directly from your response to the particular book and why you want the students to experience the book. Usually, you will have students read works of fiction for the aesthetic experience they will have with it—enjoyment, appreciation, emotional involvement, deeper understanding of life, and so on. In this case, your questions need to permit students to talk about their experiences. *Divergent* questions are best suited to this goal. Your questions will tell your students what you believe is important in reading. If your questions are *convergent* ones about the details of the plot, characters, and setting, then you are telling your students that reading fiction is a type of egg hunt for the particular eggs laid by this author and previously located by you. On the other hand, if you ask *divergent* questions that permit them to explore their individual experiences with a work of fiction, students will soon discover that you really want to understand their feelings and thoughts about books.

The purpose of reading informational books, though perhaps partially aesthetic, is usually efferent; that is, the reader's attention is centered on what should be retained after the actual reading event. Locating specific pieces of information to support an argument and comparing information from two or more sources are examples of reasons for efferent reading of literature. *Convergent* questions in this case would reflect that purpose. The following questions can be adapted to different books and may help you in designing good questions for specific books:

- What important ideas did you find in this story?
- How do you think the story should have ended, and why do you think so?
- How would you have acted if you had been (*book character*)?
- What do you think the author's main message (theme) was in this story? Why do you think so?
- Which part of the story did you like best or least? Why?
- Which character did you like best or least? Why?
- Which character do you identify with? Tell why and how you identify with him or her.
- What has happened in your life that you are reminded of by this story (character, situation)?
- What would (*character*) have done if . . . ?

Creative Drama

Creative drama is informal drama that lends itself readily to the reenactment of story experiences. In discussing the features of creative drama, McCaslin (1990) urges teachers and librarians to keep the following in mind:

- The drama is based on a piece of literature.
- Dialogue is created by the actors; lines are not written or memorized.
- Improvisation is an essential element.
- Movement on "stage" by actors is an integral part of creative drama.
- Scenery and costumes are not used, although an occasional prop may assist the children's imaginations.
- Drama is a process rather than a product. It is performed not for an audience, but for the benefit of the participants. Several different dramas or different dramatic interpretations of the same piece of literature can occur simultaneously in the classroom.

Creative drama can be used with students at all grade levels, from kindergarten to high school. A single scene from a chapter book may be enacted, or a picture book or short story may be dramatized in its entirety. The most suitable stories to start with are relatively simple, involving two to six characters and high action. Many folktales fit this description and lend themselves to being enacted.

These are the steps to follow in guiding creative drama in the classroom:

- Once a story is selected, the students listen to it being read to them or they read it independently.
- Next, they decide whether they like the story enough to want to act it out. If so, they listen to it again or read it, paying particular attention to the characters and the story scenes in sequence.
- The students then list the characters and the scenes on the chalkboard or on chart paper.
- They assign parts to actors. If enough students are interested in dramatizing the same story, you may want to assign two or more casts of actors immediately. In this way, each cast of characters can observe the performances of the others and learn from them.
- Next, each cast uses the list of scenes to review the plot, ensuring that all actors recall the events. Discuss the characters at this time, too, having students describe the actions, talk, and appearance for each.
- Give the cast of characters a few minutes to decide how to handle the performance. Then run through it. The first attempt may be a bit bumpy, but by the second time, it usually goes quite smoothly.
- After completing the drama, the class or the group of students then evaluates its success. McCaslin (1990) suggests these questions:

  1. Did they tell the story?
  2. What did you like about the opening scene?
  3. Did the characters show that they were excited (angry, unhappy, etc.)?
  4. When we play it again, can you think of anything that would improve it?
  5. Was anything important left out? (p. 174)

A useful resource book, *Making Make-Believe: Fun Props, Costumes, and Creative Play Ideas* (Kohl, 1999), offers many ideas for engaging prekindergarten to fourth grade students in dramatic play. One chapter presents numerous open-ended dramatic activities related to popular children's books.

Because of its improvisational nature and simplicity of costumes and scenery, creative drama appropriately places importance on the learning and experiencing process, not on performance, and it permits drama to become a frequent means of responding to literature in the classroom. Informal performances for the principal, the class next door, and so on, give students additional opportunities for practice and provide them with an opportunity to feel proud of their efforts.

Readers' Theatre

Readers' theatre is the oral presentation of literature by two or more actors, and usually a narrator, reading from a script. Children's literary response is made evident through expressive oral reading and group interpretation. This form of response is especially enjoyable for children who are able to read aloud with some fluency. Features typically associated with readers' theatre include the following:

- The readers and narrator typically remain on the "stage" throughout the production.
- Readers use little movement; instead, they suggest action with simple gestures and facial expressions.

- Chairs or stools are used for readers and narrator to sit on, and performers usually remain seated throughout the performance. Sometimes, certain readers sit with their backs to the audience to suggest that they are not in a particular scene.
- No costumes or stage settings are necessary and, at most, should be suggestive, rather than complete or literal, to permit the imaginations of the audience to have full rein. The use of sound effects may enhance the performance and give the impression of a radio play.

Scripts can be developed for readers' theatre by the teacher or by older students adapting a work of literature enjoyed by the class. Picture books readily lend themselves to adaptation, as do short stories. Some teachers have successfully adapted well-selected scenes from a favorite chapter book. (See Figure 12.1.) The qualities to seek in a promising story are natural-sounding dialogue, strong characterization, drama or humor, and a satisfactory ending. If the original work has extensive dialogue, the script writing is a very easy activity. The script begins with the title of the book being adapted, the name of the author, a list of characters, and usually an opening statement by the narrator. Following the introduction, the dialogue is written into script form, with the narrator scripted for the remaining nondialogue, narrative parts.

Scripts can also be purchased, but finding scripts that are both well written and adapted from the literature you are using in your classroom may prove difficult. In Chapter 3, "Poetry and Plays," is a list of recommended plays; some are adaptations of well-known literature and may suit your purpose. If you decide to develop readers' theatre scripts from the literature you are using, remember that developing the first script is the most difficult. Once you have created the first one, you will find out how easy the process is. Intermediate-grade students take readily to script development once they have a model to imitate. Readers' theatre can become a frequently selected response option of literature response groups.

Choice of literature to use can include virtually any literary genre—picture storybooks, novels, biographies, long poems, letters, diaries, and journals. See the two lists (in boxes on page 265) for books suitable for script development. Another example, Paul Fleischman's *Bull Run* (1993), a historical novel set during the Civil War, is written as a series of episodes told by different characters at different stages of the war. At the end of the book, the author provides a list of each character's entries for the use of those who wish to produce readers' theatre performances. Variations on readers' theatre can be accomplished through the addition of background music, choral poems, and brief scenes from different stories tied together by a common theme, among other options to enliven this dramatic enactment of literature.

Preparation for a readers' theatre presentation gives students a good opportunity to strengthen their oral reading abilities and to try out their expressive skills. The group typically reads through the script once or twice and then works on refining the interpretive aspects of each performer. Decisions need to be made on the arrangement of chairs and speakers for greatest visual effect. Following each presentation, an evaluation is made by the group with the goal of improving future performances.

McCaslin (1990) states that "the simplicity of production and effectiveness of result make it [readers' theatre] singularly desirable in schools with inadequate stage facilities and where rehearsal time is at a premium" (p. 263). For these same reasons, readers' theatre is extremely well suited to classroom reenactments of literary experiences. In readers' theatre, students have the opportunity to translate their experiences with a literary work to a new medium—the medium of drama—with considerable ease and pleasure.

<u>Scorpions</u> (adapted from Chapter 3, pp. 15-16)
by Walter Dean Myers
Harper, 1988

CHARACTERS NEEDED: 7

Narrator
Mama
Jamal
Sassy
Mr. Davidson, principal
Mrs. Rich, teacher
Christine, a student

Mama: Jamal, wait for Sassy so you can walk to school with her.

Jamal: I'm going to be late waiting for her.

Mama: Sassy put some vaseline on your face before you leave.

Narrator: Sassy went into the bathroom. Jamal saw her standing in front of the sink and went to the bathroom door to watch her. She took some Vaseline from the jar, rubbed it between her palms, and then put it on her face. She made a tight face as she smoothed it on her cheeks. and squinted her eyes as she put it on the top of her nose. Then she turned toward Jamal and smiled.

Jamal: You think you cute or something?

Sassy: All I know is what I see in the mirror.

Narrator: Sassy walked past her brother.

Jamal: Mama, she think she cute.

Mama: She is cute.

Jamal: No she ain't.

Sassy: Tito think I'm cute.

Jamal: Tito told me you were ugly.

Sassy: No, he didn't, 'cause he told Mary I was the cutest girl in third grade.

Jamal: They must got some ugly girls in the third grade, then.

Mama: Y'all get on to school. And don't fool around on the way.

Etc....

FIGURE 12.1   Sample Opening of a Script for Readers' Theatre

PICTURE BOOKS ADAPTABLE FOR READERS' THEATRE SCRIPTS

Albert and the Angels by Leslie Norris

Amazing Grace by Mary Hoffman

Buttons by Brock Cole

Chrysanthemum by Kevin Henkes

Duck on a Bike by David Shannon

Frog and Toad Are Friends by Arnold Lobel (easy to read book)

The Great Kapok Tree: A Tale of the Amazon Rainforest by Lynne Cherry

Little Brown Bear Won't Go to School by Jane Dyer

Nice Work, Little Wolf! by Hilda Offen

Three Little Pigs and the Big Bad Wolf by Glen Rounds

The Three Little Wolves and the Big Bad Pig by Eugene Trivizas

Tommy at the Grocery Store by Bill Grossman

Two Old Potatoes and Me by John Coy

NOVELS ADAPTABLE FOR READERS' THEATRE SCRIPTS

Bud, Not Buddy by Christopher Paul Curtis

Dave at Night by Gail Levine

Ella Enchanted by Gail Levine

Ghost Girl: A Blue Ridge Mountain Story by Delia Ray

The Giver by Lois Lowry

Number the Stars by Lois Lowry

Rowan and the Zebak by Emily Rodda

The View from Saturday by E. L. Konigsburg

Story Tellings and Retellings

Children who hear good stories read aloud by teachers, librarians, and parents often recapture those happy experiences by making the stories their own through retellings. In addition, in their natural play activities during preschool years, children enjoy role-playing and making up their own stories to tell to a playmate, real or imagined. The foundation for children's storytelling comes from the children's language environment—the talk they have heard and the stories that have been read to them. As young students learn to tell and retell stories, they reinforce their concept of story and are provided with opportunities for oral language development and expansion. Children who can tell a story with a beginning, a middle, and an end have the groundwork laid for later writing activities. You will note that story tellings and retellings by children are different in purpose than storytelling by teachers, as discussed in an earlier section of this chapter. Teachers tell stories as one of many ways of sharing literature with their students.

Teachers can foster the telling and retelling of stories by structuring a classroom environment that is conducive to this activity. Setting off an area of the classroom where children can gather for quiet talk and equipping it with some props such as story puppets, feltboards with cut-out story figures, toy story characters (stuffed animals, dolls, plastic and metal figures), wordless books, and children's favorite storybooks can entice children into telling and retelling their favorite stories. Some children take the book shared by the teacher during storytime and page through it, retelling the story from the pictures; others take story puppets and re-create the story or make up an entirely new adventure with the same characters.

Tape recorders also inspire younger students to record and listen to their favorite stories, while older students find a tape recorder an incentive for developing radio shows based on favorite books. Their favorite readers' theatre performances are well suited to radio show productions.

Written Expression

The simplest and most direct way for teachers to elicit written responses to stories is to ask students to write their ideas and feelings about a book listened to or read. *Divergent,* open-ended questions, rather than *convergent* questions, will elicit students' feelings and ideas about a scene, a character, or the story as a whole, and will help students explore their personal involvement with the story. Each student's writing ability must be considered in selecting an appropriate writing activity. Emergent writers may find it possible to write the name of their favorite character and draw a picture of that character; more able writers may be able to write a detailed character description. A notable children's author, Marion Dane Bauer, has published a book useful to young writers, *What's Your Story? A Young Person's Guide to Writing Fiction* (1992).

Some teachers have found a literature journal—in which students make frequent written responses to books read—a motivating tool for students. Teachers read and comment on the entries periodically, and students gain a sense of pride in their reading accomplishments.

In some cases, reactions to books by one student can be enjoyed by the rest of the class. One teacher clipped blank response sheets with columns for responses (Author, Title, Reaction) inside the front cover of books in the classroom collection. After reading the book, a student enters his or her name and writes views on the book. Other students enjoy reading the book to see whether their reaction will be the same. Some teachers have had students write 4" × 6" notecards about each book as it is read. These cards are kept on file in the library corner so that each new reader can add his or her impressions to the card.

Literary Works as Writing Models

When children read and listen to stories, they accumulate vocabulary, sentence structures, stylistic devices, and story ideas and structures. Well-written stories and poems serve as models for children in their own writing. When an 8-year-old boy who wrote extremely well-developed, interesting stories was asked how he learned to make up such good stories, he replied, "It's really a secret, but I'll tell you if you won't tell my teacher. I don't really make up the stories. When I was little, my mother read lots of

USING LITERARY WORKS AS WRITING MODELS IN GRADES 2–4

Literary Device or Element	Suggested Books
Characterization	*Olivia* by Ian Falconer *Sheila Rae the Brave* by Kevin Henkes *Farmer Duck* by Martin Waddell *Albert and the Angels* by Leslie Norris *Duck on a Bike* by David Shannon
Dialogue	*Albert and the Angels* by Leslie Norris *Little Brown Bear Won't Go to School* by Jane Dyer *Two Old Potatoes and Me* by John Coy *Owen Foote, Super Spy* by Stephanie Greene
Episodic Plot	*Starring Grace* by Mary Hoffman *Double Fudge* by Judy Blume *When Mules Flew on Magnolia Street* by Angela Johnson
Journal Writing	*The Journey* by Sarah Stewart *Good-bye for Today: The Diary of a Young Girl at Sea* by Peter and Connie Roop
Setting	*The 18 Penny Goose* by Sally M. Walker *The Snowy Day* by Ezra Jack Keats *Miss Rumphius* by Barbara Cooney

books to me; then in school my teachers read a lot more. So what I do is take a beginning from one of the stories, a middle from another, and the end from another. And then I make up a title." Children who have a rich literary background have a well-stocked storehouse of beginnings, middles, and endings to put to use in their storytelling and writing.

Modeling after different literary forms can be used as a means of response to a literary work. Writing a story modeled after another story can be an enjoyable re-creation of the experience. In modeling, the student adapts a story form or idea into a new creation. Examples include the following:

- Students create another episode using the same characters.
- Students write a different ending to the story read.
- Students take the perspective of another character in the story and recast the story with a shift in point of view. Two examples of a change in point of view can be found in Jon Scieszka's *The True Story of the 3 Little Pigs by A. Wolf* (1989), which gives the Big Bad Wolf's version, and Scieszka's *The Frog Prince Continued* (1991), which tells the shocking truth about "happily ever after."
- Students write a prequel to a story.
- Students take a story set in the past and rewrite it with a modern-day setting. Alternatively, a character from the historical narrative can become a visitor to modern times.

USING LITERARY WORKS AS WRITING MODELS IN GRADES 5–8

Literary Device or Element	Suggested Books
Characterization	*Goose Girl* by Shannon Hale
	The Seeing Stone by Kevin Crossley-Holland
Dialogue	*Ruby Holler* by Sharon Creech
	Don't You Know There's a War On? by Avi
Metaphor	*Uptown* by Bryan Collier
	Dovey Coe by Frances O'Roark Dowell
	Green Angel by Alice Hoffman
Mood	*Dawn* by Uri Shulevitz
	Don't Let the Pigeon Drive the Bus by Mo Willems
	The Wolves in the Walls by Neil Gaiman
	Star of Fear, Star of Hope by Jo Hoestlandt
Journal Writing	*Tibet: Through the Red Box* by Peter Sís
	Catherine, Called Birdy by Karen Cushman
	Stowaway by Karen Hesse
	Witch Child by Celia Rees
	Maata's Journal: A Novel by Paul Sullivan
Point of View	*Faith and the Electric Dogs* by Patrick Jennings
	Lewis and Clark and Me: A Dog's Tale by Laurie Myers
	Flipped by Wendelin Van Draanen
	The Misfits by James Howe
Flashbacks	*Who Is Jesse Flood?* by Malachy Doyle
	Racing the Past by Sis Deans
	Hush by Jacqueline Woodson
	Pictures of Hollis Woods by Patricia Reilly Giff
	A Northern Light by Jennifer Donnelly

Traditional Book Reports

Requiring students to list author, title, date, genre, setting, main characters, and a summary of the plot seldom causes students to delve more deeply into their experiences with literature. Students usually view traditional book reports as tedious busywork. Although teachers assign book reports to get students to read, students often report that they never read the books they report on, but rather read the bookflap, read a page or two at the beginning and end, and write the report.

Recently, some so-called literature response forms or worksheets have been published for use by teachers who adopt literature-based reading approaches. Be cautious in your use of these worksheets. They need to be examined carefully; some of them are little more than disguised book report forms asking for plot, setting, characters, and theme. Such comprehension assessment may be justified occasionally in the reading class, but if your interest is to elicit students' responses to literature, you should stay away from worksheets.

Following are some alternatives to traditional book reports. Some of the suggestions are suited to individuals, others to groups of students.

A L T E R N A T I V E S T O T R A D I T I O N A L B O O K R E P O R T S

I N D I V I D U A L

1. List ten facts learned from this work of nonfiction.
2. Draw a picture of the main character in a major scene from this book. Then write a sentence below the picture that describes the scene.
3. Write a newspaper article summarizing this book. Be sure to include a title and to answer "who, what, when, where, and why."
4. Collect at least eight interesting words or phrases from your book. Tell what each means and why you think it is interesting.
5. Choose one of the main characters from this story. Tell the class the name of the character and five things that happened to him or her in the order that they happened. Use complete sentences.
6. Design and keep a word book in which you record interesting words, phrases, and sentences in each book you read for use in your own writing.
7. Select a character from each of two different stories you have read. Write or tell a story that might result from the interactions between these two characters.
8. Select a character from this story. Write interview questions for this character, based on what happened in the story and on what might have happened to the character after the story ended. Then, with a friend, tape the interview, with your friend being the interviewer and you being the character.
9. Select new vocabulary words from this book. Write each word on one card and the meaning of each word on another card. The cards may be designed to look like a feature symbolizing the story. For example, after reading *Donuthead* (2003) by Sue Stauffacher, design each word card to look like a donut and each meaning card to look like a filled doughnut. Then have your classmates try to match them.
10. Find out as much as you can about the topics that the author of this book writes about. Make a poster about this author to get others interested in his or her books. Use the author's web site, if he or she has one.
11. Describe the author or book character you would like to meet in person. Explain why you want to meet this person or character.
12. Make a book cover for this book. Include an illustration, the book title, and author's name on the front. Design the illustration so that it is faithful to the story and will interest others in reading the book. On the front inside flap, write a story blurb, making sure not to give the story away. On the back inside flap, put your name and a description of your favorite part of the book. Display the book cover in the classroom reading center.
13. Plan a booktalk for this book. Broadcast your booktalk on the school sound system, or videotape or audiotape it for the school media center or class use.
14. Write a letter to another classmate to recommend this book. Tell why you liked the book, but don't tell the ending! Alternatively, write the letter to your classmates and post it on the bulletin board.
15. Select a favorite author and look up information about the author either online or in the library. Then write a brief biography of the person and list two or three of the author's best-known books. Tell why you believe this author's books will be remembered.

I N D I V I D U A L   *(continued)*

16. Write the story's problem or conflict on 4″ × 6″ index cards. Tell how the author might have handled the problem differently. Finally, tell how the author did handle the problem.

17. Find objects that were part of this story. Place these objects in a bag. Then booktalk your story, and take out each object to show when appropriate.

18. Write a comparison of the movie and book versions of this story. Tell the similarities and differences and which version you preferred and why.

19. Contribute a card to the class book review file in which you write the title of this book, author, illustrator, and your review of the book. Tell what you liked and didn't like. Finally, give the book a 1–5-star rating.

20. Select a character from this work of historical fiction. Divide a page into two columns, and compare your life with the life of that character. Include as many similarities and differences as you can.

21. What was the main problem in this story? State the problem, how the main character dealt with it, and how you would have dealt with it differently.

22. After reading this biography, list the subject's good and not-so-good qualities.

23. Write a letter to the main character of this book giving him or her advice about dealing with future problems.

24. Pretend that you are the main character of this book. Think about how the events in the story changed you. In two paragraphs, describe yourself at the beginning and at the end of this story.

25. Look carefully at the cover illustration of this book. List the ways that you would change the illustration and why. If you wish, draw an improved cover illustration.

26. Go online or ask a librarian to help you find five other books for someone your age about the same topic as this book. Write the topic at the top of a page and list these titles. Display the list for others who might be interested in reading about this topic.

S M A L L   G R O U P

1. Have a panel discussion for the class by 4–6 students who have read this book. Likely topics are why others would enjoy the book, why others would relate to the characters or theme, or what readers would gain from the book.

2. Select a brief, but important, scene from this book. Rewrite the scene as a readers' theatre script, and audiotape the group reading. Place the tape in the classroom listening center as a way to encourage others to read the book.

W H O L E   C L A S S

1. As a class, write news stories, personal ads, want ads, for sale ads, advice columns, editorials, comic strips, and sports stories based on the books you have read. Write the headline and a brief news article about the events leading up to the publication of this newspaper. Collate all contributions into a class newspaper.

2. (For near the end of a school year) Nominate your favorite books read this year. Booktalk any books that are not well known, then vote on the five class favorites. Advertise the winning books to other classes for summer reading.

Pictures and Collages

Students can make pictures and collages—artistic compositions made by pasting onto a background such items as fabric, string, fragments of paper, newspapers, and photographs—to illustrate a favorite story or poem. Having a variety of materials available to choose from in designing their re-creations of literature increases students' enthusiasm and creativity. Paints, colored pencils, chalk, crayons, collage materials (cloth, yarn, lace, tissue paper), colored construction paper, and magazines with pictures and printed words for cutting up and shaping into pictures can be kept readily available for use in the classroom. Teachers foster good design by asking students to think about the purpose and desired effects and by pointing out interesting visual elements in other media, especially in picture books. For example, when students observe the different ways in which illustrators frame their pictures, outline figures, and use blank space and perspective for highlighting an object, they often can replicate and adapt these techniques for their own classroom design projects.

Teachers have often overused the activity of "draw a picture of the story" by assigning it too frequently, by not planning the activity adequately, and by permitting students little or no choice of media and project. An activity that is repeated to the point of monotony becomes little more than busywork to students. Remember that it may be unnecessary to have a response activity of any kind after reading a book or that a worthy response to a book would be finding another book by the same author and reading it next.

When more active response seems warranted, however, it is important to plan worthwhile ways for students to express those responses. Providing students with a choice of projects and media and then planning collaboratively with the students on the execution of the project are the roles the teacher needs to assume. Your art specialists and school and public librarians can be of great assistance in helping you plan response activities.

Murals

Murals are made from a long roll of paper mounted horizontally. The entire length of paper is usually divided into sections and often presents a chronology of the story events. Murals may feature a particular theme, such as animals from stories around the world, different kinds of homes the characters live in, personified dolls and toys from a unit on stories with personification, or various ways young story characters have overcome obstacles as they grow and mature. Groups of children decide on the theme or topic, design the segments, and allocate tasks to group members. Sometimes, students work directly on the mounted mural; other times they cut it into sections and work at tables then tape it back together for mounting. This device is well suited for literature response groups whose members collaborate in selecting, planning, and implementing the mural. The product is often dramatic and showy, offering the group members a feeling of real accomplishment.

Roller Movies

This technique produces a simulated movie or filmstrip of a story. The pictures are designed, frame by frame, on a long roll of paper. Once completed, each end of the paper is taped to a dowel rod or broom handle; then the paper is rolled onto the feeder rod so that the beginning frame is viewed first when the paper is unrolled. The ends of each rod are inserted into holes on the sides of a cardboard box so that the paper can be stretched from one roller to the other across the box opening and then rolled to the receiver rod to move the frames along. The box is turned on its side, television style, to face the audience, and the story unfolds as the frames are rolled onto the receiver rod. The group writes a script to go along with each frame. The need for group collaboration makes this an ideal project for literature response groups. Roller movies are useful to help students decide on the major events and their sequence in the story. Then the finished movie lends itself to story retellings.

Dioramas and Displays

A diorama is a three-dimensional display in which objects and figures are placed into a background or setting to create a scene. Dioramas are often made in classrooms by using shoeboxes set on the side, providing a framework on which to construct a setting, such as a floor, ceiling, and three walls of a room. Many materials may be used to make the figures, their background, furniture, and clothes, including modeling clay, collage materials, matchboxes, dried leaves, pine straw, and tiny dolls. Dioramas are especially well suited to individuals and pairs of students who may work alone or cooperatively in selecting and recreating in miniature an important scene from a story.

Displays are three-dimensional re-creations of a setting—a town or a battle scene, for instance—placed on a large flat surface, such as a table or piece of plywood. The use of clay and cardboard for figures, papier-mâché for hills, colored construction paper for lakes and land surfaces, and so on permits students to design impressive displays from story settings. More artistically talented students can be given opportunities to excel in these design activities.

Books and Big Books

Children can make their own stories and poems into books for a more finished presentation of their writing efforts. There are many different ways to make books in the classroom, ranging from the simple process of stapling together students' separate pictures on a topic with an illustrated cover to the more complex task of developing books with hard covers made of cardboard covered in clear or patterned adhesive paper or fabric, and then sewn together and bound for a "real book" look.

Big Books are often modeled after a favorite picture book that the class enjoyed, with the pictures drawn by students and the text printed by the teacher on 24" × 30" heavy paper or posterboard, which is then laminated, bound on metal rings, and hung on an easel. Many schools have laminators for use in these projects. Lamination is also done at many commercial copy and print shops at a moderate cost.

Making books is an activity that is most suited for individuals or pairs of students. However, a collaborative book organized around a theme or pattern can be made by a larger group in which each member contributes a story or poem. In this type of book, a table of contents with the names of each contributor offers recognition of all students while also calling students' attention to this useful part of a book. When students are first learning the steps of making books, considerable guidance from an adult is required. Parent volunteers and teacher aides can be shown how to provide this assistance. The step-by-step processes of making different types of books can be found in these sources:

- Bohning, Phillips, and Bryant's *Literature on the Move: Making and Using Pop-Up and Lift-Flap Books* (1993) is a 115-page book for teachers and students, with instructions for planning, writing, drawing, and assembling pop-up books.
- Guthrie, Bentley, and Arnsteen's *The Young Author's Do-It-Yourself Book: How to Write, Illustrate, and Produce Your Own Books* (1994) is a 64-page illustrated book for beginning writers with step-by-step instructions on how to write a fiction or nonfiction story, illustrate it, assemble it, and hand bind it.
- Johnson's *Making Books* (2000), a 64-page illustrated book, offers 30 well-planned book projects, including some for every grade level.

- Stevens's *From Pictures to Words: A Book about Making a Book* (1995) is a picture book about how a book is made for students, ages 5–8.
- Stowell's *Step-by-Step Making Books* (1994) is an easy, helpful guide for making books, appropriate for students, ages 8–12.

Completed books need to be displayed for admiration and made available for reading by others. A special place in the reading corner can be reserved to exhibit student-made books.

Newspapers and Newsletters

A collaborative endeavor in which students write about the books they have been reading and tell about their book-related projects can result in class newspapers and newsletters. Each issue of the paper can focus on a different topic, such as favorite authors, illustrators, story characters, and poetic forms. In some intermediate-grade classrooms, a different literature response group accepts editing responsibilities for the newsletter each month, selecting the focus, soliciting manuscripts, designing pages, and making editorial decisions. The newsletters are sent home to parents with suggestions of good books to read and new authors to check out. Since computers are generally available in schools, individuals with word processing skills can usually be found, often among the students, to produce interesting newspapers and newsletters.

Time Lines, Maps, Diagrams, and Charts

A type of visual figure that details a period of time covered in a story is a time line. The figure is made by drawing a line on a long strip of mural paper, then placing the dates below the line at scaled intervals. The story events are logged in above the line. This graphic aid organizes the events of the story and can permit the students to compare events from a novel of historical fiction or from a biography with actual dates from history.

Time lines can be excellent visual aids when used in conjunction with reading aloud a progressive plot chapter book. The time line is set up with the dates, then the story events are recorded after each day's reading. The time line can also serve as a reminder of what has happened thus far as a review before beginning the next chapter.

Time lines can also be useful when students are reading a variety of material on a single period of history: biographies, historical fiction novels, and photo essays on World War II, for instance. Historical events from different sources can be compared for authenticity by using parallel time lines or by adding more tiers to the same time line. Individual students may develop time lines to follow the events of an entire series of books, such as science fiction novels and quest adventure stories.

Maps are especially suitable for charting the settings in chapter books of many genres. They can be designed by individuals or groups of students and make interesting and helpful visual aids for telling others about books. Some chapter books in which maps are included as part of the book can be used by students as models to imitate for drawing storymaps on other books. Some books with maps that can be used as models are *The Thief Lord* (2002) by Cornelia Funke, *Lewis and Clark and Me: A Dog's Tale* (2002) by Laurie Myers, *The Kite Rider: A Novel* (2001) by Geraldine McCaughrean, and *Stowaway* (2000) by Karen Hesse. Maps are also suitable for laying out the events in picture books and books with a circular journey motif in which the protagonist leaves home, encounters adversity, overcomes it, and returns home.

A *diagram* presents textual material in visual form and can be used to illustrate arrangements and relations within a story. For example, in Björk's *Linnea in Monet's Garden* (1987) a family tree of Monet's family is displayed. Many information books use diagrams, and students can develop ideas for presenting information through diagrams by perusing these books. Another Linnea story, *Linnea's Windowsill Garden* (1988), has a diagram of plants and their seeds. Diagrams can also be developed to show relationships found in book series and long works, such as the Arthurian legends. Teachers and students can use diagrams to display the progression of a story, which is especially useful to help students understand unusual plot twists.

Charts give information in table form to show relationships, summarize information, and present facts in a capsule form. For example, on page 8 of Björk's *Linnea's Almanac* (1989) a chart showing species of birds and their feeding habits assists readers in the art of feeding winter birds. When students use nonfiction books for studying content areas, they can be encouraged to consider visual means for presenting and summarizing the information gained.

Jackdaws

Jackdaws are collections of artifacts or copies of realia from a particular historical period or event; jackdaws are often available in museums for study of a period of history, and some museums lend them to teachers for use in schools. The term *jackdaw* refers to a common European bird that is related to the crow and known to collect colorful objects for its nest. Educators have borrowed the term to refer to a teaching tool that can be used to connect historical books with the real events of the times depicted through concrete objects (Devitt, 1970). For example, a teacher may put together a jackdaw based on homesteaders in Oklahoma in the 1800s, then use the jackdaw to build background knowledge to introduce the study of the historical fiction novel *Stop the Train!* (2001) by Geraldine McCaughrean.

Jackdaws are made by collecting a wide array of related materials in their original form or in reproductions. Materials that are often collected are regional maps, photographs or models of homes, farms, machines, household furnishings, toys and dolls, kitchen tools, recipes for foods commonly eaten, newspapers and books of the era, clothing, modes of transportation, government of the time (president, congress, political parties, statehood), educational institutions, cultural artifacts such as songs, paintings, and architectural landmarks. After collection the realia are placed in a decorated box with labels and explanations attached, if desired. The jackdaw can be used as an extension activity for a book read in class as well as for building background. Many teachers enlist students in the development of jackdaws and share jackdaws with other teachers who are studying the same historical book.

Bulletin Boards

Designing and making bulletin boards provide groups of students with opportunities to demonstrate their book experiences in innovative ways. Planning bulletin boards and displays requires students to select an interesting and worthy focus or message to call attention to the display and to get the message across effectively. Students will appreciate seeing bulletin boards displaying their own book-related projects more than having sophisticated commercial displays about books.

Giving students choices of books to read and choices in the ways in which they respond to them is an essential component of a good curriculum in literature. This chapter presented a smorgasbord of ideas for having students experience literature and respond to those literary experiences.

REFERENCES

Avi. (2001). *Don't you know there's a war on?* New York: HarperCollins.

Bauer, M. D. (1992). *What's your story? A young person's guide to writing fiction.* Boston: Houghton.

Björk, C. (1989). *Linnea's almanac.* Illustrated by L. Anderson. Translated by J. Sandin. Stockholm: Rabén & Sjögren.

———. (1987). *Linnea in Monet's garden.* Illustrated by L. Anderson. Translated by J. Sandin. Stockholm: Rabén & Sjögren.

———. (1988). *Linnea's windowsill garden.* Illustrated by L. Anderson. Translated by J. Sandin. Stockholm: Rabén & Sjögren.

Blume, J. (2002). *Double Fudge.* New York: Dutton.

Bodart, J. (1980). *Booktalk!* New York: H. W. Wilson.

Bohning, G., Phillips, A. & Bryant, S. (1993). *Literature on the move: Making and using pop-up and lift-flap books.* Illustrated by S. Bryant. Englewood, CO: Libraries Unlimited.

Campbell, J. R., Voelkl, K. E., & Donahue, P. L. (1998). *Report in brief: NAEP 1996 trends in academic progress* (Pub. No. 98-530). Washington, DC: National Center for Educational Statistics.

Cherry, L. (1990). *The great kapok tree: A tale of the Amazon rainforest.* San Diego: Harcourt.

Cole, B. (2000). *Buttons.* New York: Farrar.

Collier, B. (2000). *Uptown.* New York: Holt.

Cooney, B. (1982). *Miss Rumphius.* New York: Viking.

Coy, J. (2002). *Two old potatoes and me.* Illustrated by C. Fisher. New York: Knopf.

Creech, S. (2002). *Ruby Holler.* New York: HarperCollins.

Crossley-Holland, K. (2001). *The seeing stone.* New York: Arthur A. Levine.

Curtis, C. P. (1999). *Bud, not Buddy.* New York: Delacorte.

Cushman, K. (1994). *Catherine, called Birdy.* New York: Clarion.

Deans, S. (2001). *Racing the past.* New York: Holt.

Devitt, M. (Ed.). (1970). *Learning with jackdaws.* London: St. Paul's Press.

Donnelly, J. (2003). *A northern light.* San Diego: Harcourt.

Dowell, F. O. (2000). *Dovey Coe.* New York: Atheneum.

Doyle, M. (2002). *Who is Jesse Flood?* New York: Bloomsbury.

Dyer, J. (2002). *Little Brown Bear won't go to school.* Boston: Little, Brown.

Falconer, I. (2000). *Olivia.* New York: Atheneum.

Farmer, N. (2002). *The house of the scorpion.* New York: Atheneum.

Fatchen, M. (1988). Tailpiece. In M. Harrison and C. Stuart-Clark (Eds.), *The Oxford Teasury of Children's Poems.* Oxford: Oxford University Press.

Fleischman, P. (1993). *Bull Run.* New York: HarperCollins.

Funke, C. (2002). *The thief lord.* Translated by O. Latsch. New York: Scholastic.

Gaiman, N. (2003). *The wolves in the walls.* New York: HarperCollins.

Giff, P. R. (2002). *Pictures of Hollis Woods.* New York: Wendy Lamb.

Greene, S. (2001). *Owen Foote, super spy.* Illustrated by M. Weston. New York: Clarion.

Grossman, B. (1989). *Tommy at the grocery store.* Illustrated by V. Chess. New York: Harper.

Guthrie, D., Bentley, N., & Arnsteen, K. K. (1994). *The young author's do-it-yourself book: How to write, illustrate, and produce your own books.* Brookfield, CT: Millbrook.

Hale, S. (2003). *Goose girl.* New York: Bloomsbury.

Henkes, K. (1991). *Chrysanthemum.* New York: Greenwillow.

———. (1987). *Sheila Rae the Brave.* New York: Greenwillow.

Hesse, K. (2000). *Stowaway.* New York: McElderry.

Hoestlandt, J. (1995). *Star of fear, star of hope.* Illustrated by J. Kang. Translated by M. Polizzotti. New York: Walker.

Hoffman, A. (2003). *Green angel.* New York: Scholastic.

Hoffman, M. (1991). *Amazing Grace.* Illustrated by C. Binch. New York: Dial.

———. (2000). *Starring Grace.* Illustrated by C. Binch. New York: Fogelman.

Holdaway, D. (1982). Shared book experience: Teaching reading using favorite books. *Theory into practice, 21,* 293–300.

Hoskisson, K., Sherman, T. M., & Smith, L. L. (1974). Assisted reading and parent involvement. *The Reading Teacher, 27,* 710–714.

Howe, J. (2001). *The misfits.* New York: Atheneum.

Jennings, P. (1996). *Faith and the electric dogs.* New York: Scholastic.

Johnson, A. (2000). *When mules flew on Magnolia Street.* Illustrated by J. Ward. New York: Knopf.

Johnson, P. (2000). *Making books.* Markham, Ontario: Pembroke.

Keats, E. J. (1962). *The snowy day.* New York: Viking.

Kohl, M. F. (1999). *Making make-believe: Fun props, costumes, and creative play ideas.* Beltsville, MD: Gryphon House.

Konigsburg, E. L. (1996). *The view from Saturday.* New York: Atheneum.

Labbo, L. D., & Reinking, D. (2000). Once upon an electronic story time. *The New Advocate, 13*(1), 25–32.

Levine, G. (1999). *Dave at night.* New York: Harper-Collins.

———. (1997). *Ella enchanted.* New York: Harper-Collins.

Lobel, A. (1970). *Frog and Toad are friends.* New York: Harper.

Lowry, L. (1993). *The giver.* New York: Houghton.

———. (1989). *Number the stars.* New York: Houghton.

McCaslin, N. (1990). *Creative drama in the classroom* (5th ed.). New York: Longman.

McCaughrean, G. (2001). *The kite rider.* New York: HarperCollins.

———. (2001). *Stop the train!* New York: Harper-Collins.

Mullis, I. V. S., Martin, M. O., Gonzalez, E. J., & Kennedy, A. M. (2003). *PIRLS 2001 international report: IEA's study of reading literacy achievement in primary schools.* Chestnut Hill, MA: Boston College.

Myers, L. (2002). *Lewis and Clark and me: A dog's tale.* Illustrated by M. Dooling. New York: Holt.

Myers, W. D. (1988). *Scorpions.* New York: Harper.

Norris, L. (2000). *Albert and the angels.* Illustrated by M. Gerstein. New York: Farrar.

Offen, H. (1992). *Nice work, Little Wolf!* New York: Dutton.

Pellowski, A. (1995). *The storytelling handbook: A young people's collection of unusual tales and helpful hints on how to tell them.* Illustrated by M. Stoberock. New York: Simon & Schuster.

Pringle, L. (2001). *Global warming: The threat of earth's changing climate.* New York: SeaStar.

Raskin, E. (1978). *The westing game.* New York: Dutton.

Ray, D. (2003). *Ghost girl: A Blue Ridge Mountain story.* New York: Clarion.

Rees, C. (2001). *Witch child.* Cambridge, MA: Candlewick.

Robb, L. (2003). *Teaching reading in social studies, science, and math.* New York: Scholastic.

Rodda, E. (2002). *Rowan and the Zebak.* New York: Greenwillow.

Roop, P., & Roop, C. (2000). *Good-bye for today: The diary of a young girl at sea.* Illustrated by T. B. Allen. New York: Atheneum.

Rosenblatt, L. M. (1978). *The reader, the text, the poem: The transactional theory of the literary work.* Carbondale: Southern Illinois University Press.

Rounds, G. (1992). *Three little pigs and the big bad wolf.* New York: Holiday.

Scieszka, J. (1991). *The frog prince continued.* Illustrated by S. Johnson. New York: Viking.

———. (1989). *The true story of the 3 little pigs by A. Wolf.* Illustrated by L. Smith. New York: Viking.

Sedgwick, M. (2001). *Floodland.* New York: Delacorte.

Shannon, D. (2002). *Duck on a bike.* New York: Blue Sky.

Shulevitz, U. (1974). *Dawn.* New York: Farrar.

Silverstein, A., Silverstein, V., & Nunn, L. S. (2002). *Global warming.* Brookfield, CT: Twenty-First Century.

Sís, P. (1998). *Tibet: Through the red box.* New York: Farrar.

Stauffacher, S. (2003). *Donuthead.* New York: Knopf.

Stevens, J. (1995). *From pictures to words: A book about making a book.* New York: Holiday.

Stewart, S. (2001). *The journey.* Illustrated by D. Small. New York: Atheneum.

Stowell, C. (1994). *Step-by-step making books.* New York: Kingfisher.

Sullivan, P. (2001). *Maata's journal: A novel.* New York: Atheneum.

Trivizas, E. (1993). *The three little wolves and the big bad pig.* Illustrated by H. Oxenbury. New York: Macmillan.

Van Draanen, W. (2001). *Flipped.* New York: Knopf.

Veatch, J. (1968). *How to teach reading with children's books* (2nd ed). New York: Richard C. Owen.

Waddell, M. (1992). *Farmer Duck.* Illustrated by H. Oxenbury. Cambridge, MA: Candlewick.

Walker, S. M. (1998). *The 18 penny goose.* Illustrated by E. Beier. New York: HarperCollins.

Willems, M. (2003). *Don't let the pigeon drive the bus.* New York: Hyperion.

Woodson, J. (2002). *Hush.* New York: Putnam.

CHILDREN'S BOOK AWARDS

THE UNITED STATES

Caldecott Medal

This award, sponsored by the Association for Library Service to Children division of the American Library Association, is given to the illustrator of the most distinguished picture book for children published in the United States during the preceding year. Only U.S. residents or citizens are eligible for this award.

1938   *Animals of the Bible, A Picture Book.* Text selected from the King James Bible by Helen Dean Fish. Illustrated by Dorothy P. Lathrop. Lippincott (Bible, ages 3–8).

HONOR BOOKS:

Seven Simeons: A Russian Tale by Boris Artzybasheff. Viking (Traditional, ages 6–8).

Four and Twenty Blackbirds compiled by Helen Dean Fish. Illustrated by Robert Lawson/Stokes. Lippincott (Traditional, ages 3–6).

1939   *Mei Li* by Thomas Handforth. Doubleday (Realism, ages 6–7).

HONOR BOOKS:

The Forest Pool by Laura Adams Armer. McKay/Longmans (Realism, ages 6–7).

Wee Gillis by Munro Leaf. Illustrated by Robert Lawson. Viking (Realism, ages 5–7).

Snow White and the Seven Dwarfs. Translated and illustrated by Wanda Gág. Coward-McCann (Traditional, ages 3–6).

Barkis by Clare Turlay Newberry. Harper (Realism, ages 3–7).

Andy and the Lion by James Daugherty. Viking (Fantasy, ages 3–7).

1940   *Abraham Lincoln* by Ingri d'Aulaire and Edgar Parin d'Aulaire. Doubleday (Biography, ages 6–8).

HONOR BOOKS:

Cock-a-Doodle-Doo by Berta and Elmer Hader. Macmillan (Animal realism, ages 3–7).

Madeline by Ludwig Bemelmans. Viking (Realism, ages 5–7).

The Ageless Story by Lauren Ford. Dodd (Bible, ages 5–8).

1941   *They Were Strong and Good* by Robert Lawson. Viking (Biography, ages 6–7).

HONOR BOOK:

April's Kittens by Clare Turlay Newberry. Harper (Realism, ages 3–6).

1942   *Make Way for Ducklings* by Robert McCloskey. Viking (Animal fantasy, ages 3–6).

HONOR BOOKS:

An American ABC by Maud and Miska Petersham. Macmillan (Alphabet, ages 3–6).

In My Mother's House by Ann Nolan Clark. Illustrated by Velino Herrera. Viking (Informational, ages 6–8).

Paddle-to-the-Sea by Holling Clancy Holling. Houghton (Informational, ages 6–8).

Nothing at All by Wanda Gág. Coward-McCann (Animal fantasy, ages 3–6).

1943   *The Little House* by Virginia Lee Burton. Houghton (Fantasy, ages 3–6).

HONOR BOOKS:

Dash and Dart by Mary and Conrad Buff. Viking (Realism, ages 3–6).

Marshmallow by Clare Turlay Newberry. Harper (Realism, ages 3–6).

1944   *Many Moons* by James Thurber. Illustrated by Louis Slobodkin. Harcourt (Modern folktale, ages 5–7).

HONOR BOOKS:

Small Rain: Verses from the Bible. Text arranged from the Bible by Jessie Orton Jones. Illustrated by Elizabeth Orton Jones. Viking (Bible, ages 3–7).

Pierre Pigeon by Lee Kingman. Illustrated by Arnold Edwin Bare. Houghton (Realism, ages 6–7).

The Mighty Hunter by Berta and Elmer Hader. Macmillan (Fantasy, ages 3–6).

A Child's Good Night Book by Margaret Wise Brown. Illustrated by Jean Charlot. Scott (Realism, ages 3–6).

Good Luck Horse by Chih-Yi Chan. Illustrated by Plato Chan. Whittlesey (Traditional, ages 6–7).

1945   *Prayer for a Child* by Rachel Field. Illustrated by Elizabeth Orton Jones. Macmillan (Realism, ages 3–6).

HONOR BOOKS:

Mother Goose: Seventy-Seven Verses with Pictures. Illustrated by Tasha Tudor. Walck (Traditional, ages 3–6).

In the Forest by Marie Hall Ets. Viking (Fantasy, ages 3–6).

Yonie Wondernose by Marguerite de Angeli. Doubleday (Realism, ages 6–7).

The Christmas Anna Angel by Ruth Sawyer. Illustrated by Kate Seredy. Viking (Modern folktale, ages 6–7).

1946   *The Rooster Crows* selected and illustrated by Maud and Miska Petersham. Macmillan (Mother Goose/Nursery rhymes, ages 3–6).

HONOR BOOKS:

Little Lost Lamb by Golden MacDonald. Illustrated by Leonard Weisgard. Doubleday (Realism, ages 3–6).

Sing Mother Goose by Opal Wheeler. Illustrated by Marjorie Torrey. Dutton (Nursery songs, ages 3–6).

My Mother Is the Most Beautiful Woman in the World retold by Becky Reyher. Illustrated by Ruth Gannett. Lothrop (Traditional, ages 5–7).

You Can Write Chinese by Kurt Wiese. Viking (Informational, ages 6–8).

1947   *The Little Island* by Golden MacDonald. Illustrated by Leonard Weisgard. Doubleday (Fantasy, ages 3–6).

HONOR BOOKS:

Rain Drop Splash by Alvin Tresselt. Illustrated by Leonard Weisgard. Lothrop (Informational, ages 5–7).

Boats on the River by Marjorie Flack. Illustrated by Jay Hyde Barnum. Viking (Informational, ages 6–7).

Timothy Turtle by Al Graham. Illustrated by Tony Palazzo. Viking (Animal fantasy, ages 3–6).

Pedro, the Angel of Olvera Street by Leo Politi. Scribner's (Realism, ages 3–6).

Sing in Praise: A Collection of the Best Loved Hymns by Opal Wheeler. Illustrated by Marjorie Torrey. Dutton (Informational, ages 3–8).

1948   *White Snow, Bright Snow* by Alvin Tresselt. Illustrated by Roger Duvoisin. Lothrop (Realism, ages 3–6).

HONOR BOOKS:

Stone Soup: An Old Tale by Marcia Brown. Scribner's (Traditional, ages 6–8).

McElligot's Pool by Dr. Seuss (pseudonym of Theodor Geisel). Random (Fantasy, ages 3–6).

Bambino the Clown by George Schreiber. Viking (Realism, ages 5–7).

Roger and the Fox by Lavinia Davis. Illustrated by Hildegard Woodward. Doubleday (Realism, ages 5–7).

Song of Robin Hood edited by Anne Malcolmson. Illustrated by Virginia Lee Burton. Houghton (Traditional, ages 9–YA).

1949   *The Big Snow* by Berta and Elmer Hader. Macmillan (Animal realism, ages 3–6).

HONOR BOOKS:

Blueberries for Sal by Robert McCloskey. Viking (Realism, ages 3–6).

All Around Town by Phyllis McGinley. Illustrated by Helen Stone. Lippincott (Alphabet, ages 3–6).

Juanita by Leo Politi. Scribner's (Realism, ages 3–6).

Fish in the Air by Kurt Wiese. Viking (Fantasy, ages 5–7).

1950 *Song of the Swallows* by Leo Politi. Scribner's (Realism, ages 3–6).

HONOR BOOKS:

America's Ethan Allen by Stewart Holbrook. Illustrated by Lynd Ward. Houghton (Biography, ages 6–8).

The Wild Birthday Cake by Lavinia R. Davis. Illustrated by Hildegard Woodward. Doubleday (Realism, ages 5–6).

The Happy Day by Ruth Krauss. Illustrated by Marc Simont. Harper (Animal fantasy, ages 3–6).

Henry-Fisherman by Marcia Brown. Scribner's (Realism, ages 5–7).

Bartholomew and the Oobleck by Dr. Seuss (pseudonym of Theodor Geisel). Random (Modern folktale, ages 5–7).

1951 *The Egg Tree* by Katherine Milhous. Scribner's (Realism, ages 3–6).

HONOR BOOKS:

Dick Whittington and His Cat. Translated and illustrated by Marcia Brown. Scribner's (Traditional, ages 6–8).

The Two Reds by Will (pseudonym of William Lipkind). Illustrated by Nicolas (pseudonym of Nicolas Mordvinoff). Harcourt (Fantasy, ages 3–6).

If I Ran the Zoo by Dr. Seuss (pseudonym of Theodor Geisel). Random (Fantasy, ages 3–6).

T-Bone, the Baby-Sitter by Clare Turlay Newberry. Harper (Realism, ages 3–6).

The Most Wonderful Doll in the World by Phyllis McGinley. Illustrated by Helen Stone. Lippincott (Realism, ages 6–7).

1952 *Finders Keepers* by Will (pseudonym of William Lipkind). Illustrated by Nicolas (pseudonym of Nicolas Mordvinoff). Harcourt (Modern folktale, ages 3–6).

HONOR BOOKS:

Mr. T. W. Anthony Woo by Marie Hall Ets. Viking (Modern folktale, ages 3–6).

Skipper John's Cook by Marcia Brown. Scribner's (Realism, ages 5–7).

All Falling Down by Gene Zion. Illustrated by Margaret Bloy Graham. Harper (Informational, ages 3–6).

Bear Party by William Pène du Bois. Viking (Animal fantasy, ages 3–7).

Feather Mountain by Elizabeth Olds. Houghton (Modern folktale, ages 5–7).

1953 *The Biggest Bear* by Lynd Ward. Houghton (Realism, ages 3–7).

HONOR BOOKS:

Puss in Boots. Translated and illustrated by Marcia Brown. Scribner's (Traditional, ages 5–7).

One Morning in Maine by Robert McCloskey. Viking (Realism, ages 5–7).

Ape in a Cape: An Alphabet of Odd Animals by Fritz Eichenberg. Harcourt (Alphabet, ages 3–6).

The Storm Book by Charlotte Zolotow. Illustrated by Margaret Bloy Graham. Harper (Informational, ages 3–6).

Five Little Monkeys by Juliet Kepes. Houghton (Animal fantasy, ages 3–6).

1954 *Madeline's Rescue* by Ludwig Bemelmans. Viking (Realism, ages 3–6).

HONOR BOOKS:

Journey Cake, Ho! by Ruth Sawyer. Illustrated by Robert McCloskey. Viking (Traditional, ages 5–7).

When Will the World Be Mine? by Miriam Schlein. Illustrated by Jean Charlot. Scott (Animal fantasy, ages 3–6).

The Steadfast Tin Soldier by Hans Christian Andersen. Translated by M. R. James. Illustrated by Marcia Brown. Scribner's (Modern folktale, ages 5–7).

A Very Special House by Ruth Krauss. Illustrated by Maurice Sendak. Harper (Fantasy, ages 3–6).

Green Eyes by Abe Birnbaum. Capitol (Animal fantasy, ages 3–6).

1955 *Cinderella, or the Little Glass Slipper* by Charles Perrault. Translated and illustrated by Marcia Brown. Scribner's (Traditional, ages 3–7).

HONOR BOOKS:

Book of Nursery and Mother Goose Rhymes compiled and illustrated by Marguerite de Angeli. Doubleday (Nursery rhymes, ages 3–6).

Wheel on the Chimney by Margaret Wise Brown. Illustrated by Tibor Gergely. Lippincott (Realism, ages 6–7).

The Thanksgiving Story by Alice Dalgliesh. Illustrated by Helen Sewell. Scribner's (Historical fiction [United States, 1700s], ages 5–7).

1956 *Frog Went A-Courtin'* retold by John Langstaff. Illustrated by Feodor Rojankovsky. Harcourt (Traditional, ages 3–7).

HONOR BOOKS:

Play with Me by Marie Hall Ets. Viking (Realism, ages 3–6).

Crow Boy by Taro Yashima. Viking (Realism, ages 5–7).

1957 *A Tree Is Nice* by Janice May Udry. Illustrated by Marc Simont. Harper (Informational, ages 3–7).

HONOR BOOKS:

Mr. Penny's Race Horse by Marie Hall Ets. Viking (Animal fantasy, ages 5–7).

1 Is One by Tasha Tudor. Walck. (Counting, ages 3–6).

Anatole by Eve Titus. Illustrated by Paul Galdone. McGraw (Animal fantasy, ages 5–7).

Gillespie and the Guards by Benjamin Elkin. Illustrated by James Daugherty. Viking (Realism, ages 5–7).

Lion by William Pène du Bois. Viking (Animal fantasy, ages 5–7).

1958 *Time of Wonder* by Robert McCloskey. Viking (Realism, ages 6–8).

HONOR BOOKS:

Fly High, Fly Low by Don Freeman. Viking (Animal fantasy, ages 3–6).

Anatole and the Cat by Eve Titus. Illustrated by Paul Galdone. McGraw (Animal fantasy, ages 3–6).

1959 *Chanticleer and the Fox* by Chaucer. Adapted and illustrated by Barbara Cooney. Crowell (Traditional, ages 5–7).

HONOR BOOKS:

The House That Jack Built ("La Maison Que Jacques a Bâtie"): A Picture Book in Two Languages by Antonio Frasconi. Harcourt (Informational, ages 5–8).

What Do You Say, Dear? A Book of Manners for All Occasions by Sesyle Joslin. Illustrated by Maurice Sendak. Scott (Fantasy, ages 3–6).

Umbrella by Taro Yashima. Viking (Realism, ages 3–6).

1960 *Nine Days to Christmas* by Marie Hall Ets and Aurora Labastida. Illustrated by Marie Hall Ets. Viking (Realism, ages 3–7).

HONOR BOOKS:

Houses from the Sea by Alice E. Goudey. Illustrated by Adrienne Adams. Scribner's (Informational, ages 5–7).

The Moon Jumpers by Janice May Udry. Illustrated by Maurice Sendak. Harper (Realism, ages 3–6).

1961 *Baboushka and the Three Kings* by Ruth Robbins. Illustrated by Nicolas Sidjakov. Parnassus (Traditional, ages 5–7).

HONOR BOOK:

Inch by Inch by Leo Lionni. Obolensky (Animal fantasy, ages 3–6).

1962 *Once a Mouse* retold by Marcia Brown. Scribner's (Traditional, ages 5–7).

HONOR BOOKS:

The Fox Went Out on a Chilly Night: An Old Song by Peter Spier. Doubleday (Traditional, ages 3–6).

Little Bear's Visit by Else Minarik. Illustrated by Maurice Sendak. Harper (Animal fantasy, ages 3–7).

The Day We Saw the Sun Come Up by Alice Goudey. Illustrated by Adrienne Adams. Scribner's (Informational, ages 5–7).

1963 *The Snowy Day* by Ezra Jack Keats. Viking (Realism, ages 3–6).

HONOR BOOKS:

The Sun Is a Golden Earring by Natalia Belting. Illustrated by Bernarda Bryson. Holt (Modern folktale, ages 7–10).

Mr. Rabbit and the Lovely Present by Charlotte Zolotow. Illustrated by Maurice Sendak. Harper (Animal fantasy, ages 3–6).

1964 *Where the Wild Things Are* by Maurice Sendak. Harper (Fantasy, ages 3–7).

HONOR BOOKS:

Swimmy by Leo Lionni. Pantheon (Animal fantasy, ages 5–7).

All in the Morning Early by Sorche Nic Leodhas (pseudonym of Leclaire Alger). Illustrated by Evaline Ness. Holt (Traditional, ages 3–6).

Mother Goose and Nursery Rhymes by Philip Reed. Atheneum (Traditional, ages 3–6).

1965 *May I Bring a Friend?* by Beatrice Schenk de Regniers. Illustrated by Beni Montresor. Atheneum (Fantasy, ages 5–7).

HONOR BOOKS:

Rain Makes Applesauce by Julian Scheer. Illustrated by Marvin Bileck. Holiday (Fantasy, ages 5–7).

The Wave by Margaret Hodges. Illustrated by Blair Lent. Houghton (Traditional, ages 6–9).

A Pocketful of Cricket by Rebecca Caudill. Illustrated by Evaline Ness. Holt (Realism, ages 5–7).

1966 *Always Room for One More* by Sorche Nic Leodhas (pseudonym of Leclaire Alger). Illustrated by Nonny Hogrogian. Holt (Traditional, ages 3–6).

HONOR BOOKS:

Hide and Seek Fog by Alvin Tresselt. Illustrated by Roger Duvoisin. Lothrop (Realism, ages 5–7).

Just Me by Marie Hall Ets. Viking (Realism, ages 3–5).

Tom Tit Tot adapted by Joseph Jacobs. Illustrated by Evaline Ness. Scribner's (Traditional, ages 5–7).

1967 *Sam, Bangs and Moonshine* by Evaline Ness. Holt (Realism, ages 6–8).

HONOR BOOK:

One Wide River to Cross adapted by Barbara Emberley. Illustrated by Ed Emberley. Prentice Hall (Bible, ages 3–6).

1968 *Drummer Hoff* adapted by Barbara Emberley. Illustrated by Ed Emberley. Prentice Hall (Traditional, ages 3–6).

HONOR BOOKS:

Frederick by Leo Lionni. Pantheon (Animal fantasy, ages 5–7).

Seashore Story by Taro Yashima. Viking (Realism, ages 6–8).

The Emperor and the Kite by Jane Yolen. Illustrated by Ed Young. World (Modern folktale, ages 5–7).

1969 *The Fool of the World and the Flying Ship: A Russian Tale* by Authur Ransome. Illustrated by Uri Shulevitz. Farrar (Traditional, ages 6–8).

HONOR BOOK:

Why the Sun and the Moon Live in the Sky: An African Folktale by Elphinstone Dayrell. Illustrated by Blair Lent. Houghton (Traditional, ages 6–8).

1970 *Sylvester and the Magic Pebble* by William Steig. Windmill (Animal fantasy, ages 5–7).

HONOR BOOKS:

Goggles! by Ezra Jack Keats. Macmillan (Realism, ages 3–6).

Alexander and the Wind-Up Mouse by Leo Lionni. Pantheon (Animal fantasy, ages 3–6).

Pop Corn and Ma Goodness by Edna Mitchell Preston. Illustrated by Robert Andrew Parker. Viking (Modern folktale, ages 5–7).

Thy Friend, Obadiah by Brinton Turkle. Viking (Historical fiction [New England, 1700s], ages 3–7).

The Judge: An Untrue Tale by Harve Zemach. Illustrated by Margot Zemach. Farrar (Modern folktale, ages 5–7).

1971 *A Story, A Story: An African Tale* by Gail E. Haley. Atheneum (Traditional, ages 5–7).

HONOR BOOKS:

The Angry Moon retold by William Sleator. Illustrated by Blair Lent. Atlantic/Little, Brown (Traditional, ages 6–8).

Frog and Toad Are Friends by Arnold Lobel. Harper (Animal fantasy, ages 3–7).

In the Night Kitchen by Maurice Sendak. Harper (Fantasy, ages 5–7).

1972 *One Fine Day* by Nonny Hogrogian. Macmillan (Traditional, ages 5–7).

HONOR BOOKS:

If All the Seas Were One Sea by Janina Domanska. Macmillan (Traditional, ages 3–6).

Moja Means One: Swahili Counting Book by Muriel Feelings. Illustrated by Tom Feelings. Dial (Counting, ages 5–8).

Hildilid's Night by Cheli Duran Ryan. Illustrated by Arnold Lobel. Macmillan (Modern folktale, ages 3–6).

1973 *The Funny Little Woman* retold by Arlene Mosel. Illustrated by Blair Lent. Dutton (Traditional, ages 5–7).

HONOR BOOKS:

Hosie's Alphabet by Hosea Baskin, Tobias Baskin, and Lisa Baskin. Illustrated by Leonard Baskin. Viking (Alphabet, ages 6–9).

When Clay Sings by Byrd Baylor. Illustrated by Tom Bahti. Scribner's (Informational, ages 6–8).

Snow-White and the Seven Dwarfs by the Brothers Grimm. Translated by Randall Jarrell. Illustrated by Nancy Ekholm Burkert. Farrar (Traditional, ages 3–7).

Anansi the Spider: A Tale from the Ashanti adapted and illustrated by Gerald McDermott. Holt (Traditional, ages 6–8).

1974 *Duffy and the Devil* retold by Harve Zemach. Illustrated by Margot Zemach. Farrar (Traditional, ages 6–8).

HONOR BOOKS:

Three Jovial Huntsmen adapted and illustrated by Susan Jeffers. Bradbury (Traditional, ages 3–6).

Cathedral: The Story of Its Construction by David Macaulay. Houghton (Informational, ages 8–YA).

1975 *Arrow to the Sun* adapted and illustrated by Gerald McDermott. Viking (Traditional, ages 7–9).

HONOR BOOK:

Jambo Means Hello: Swahili Alphabet Book by Muriel Feelings. Illustrated by Tom Feelings. Dial (Alphabet, ages 6–8).

1976 *Why Mosquitoes Buzz in People's Ears* retold by Verna Aardema. Illustrated by Leo and Diane Dillon. Dial (Traditional, ages 6–8).

HONOR BOOKS:

The Desert Is Theirs by Byrd Baylor. Illustrated by Peter Parnall. Scribner's (Informational, ages 6–8).

Strega Nona retold and illustrated by Tomie de Paola. Prentice Hall (Traditional, ages 5–8).

1977 *Ashanti to Zulu: African Traditions* by Margaret Musgrove. Illustrated by Leo and Diane Dillon. Dial (Informational, ages 7–11).

HONOR BOOKS:

The Amazing Bone by William Steig. Farrar (Fantasy, ages 6–8).

The Contest by Nonny Hogrogian. Greenwillow (Traditional, ages 6–8).

Fish for Supper by M. B. Goffstein. Dial (Realism, ages 3–6).

The Golem: A Jewish Legend retold and illustrated by Beverly Brodsky McDermott. Lippincott (Traditional, ages 6–9).

Hawk, I'm Your Brother by Byrd Baylor. Illustrated by Peter Parnall. Scribner's (Realism, ages 7–9).

1978 *Noah's Ark* by Peter Spier. Doubleday (Bible/Wordless, ages 3–7).

HONOR BOOKS:

Castle by David Macaulay. Houghton (Informational, ages 8–YA).

It Could Always Be Worse retold by Margot Zemach. Farrar (Traditional, ages 5–7).

1979 *The Girl Who Loved Wild Horses* by Paul Goble. Bradbury (Traditional, ages 6–8).

HONOR BOOKS:

Freight Train by Donald Crews. Greenwillow (Concept, ages 3–6).

The Way to Start a Day by Byrd Baylor. Illustrated by Peter Parnall. Scribner's (Informational, ages 6–9).

1980 *Ox-Cart Man* by Donald Hall. Illustrated by Barbara Cooney. Viking (Historical fiction [New England, 1800s], ages 5–8).

HONOR BOOKS:

Ben's Trumpet by Rachel Isadora. Greenwillow (Realism, ages 5–7).

The Treasure by Uri Shulevitz. Farrar (Traditional, ages 6–8).

The Garden of Abdul Gasazi by Chris Van Allsburg. Houghton (Fantasy, ages 6–8).

1981 *Fables* by Arnold Lobel. Harper (Modern folktales, ages 3–6).

HONOR BOOKS:

The Bremen-Town Musicians retold and illustrated by Ilse Plume. Doubleday (Traditional, ages 5–7).

The Grey Lady and the Strawberry Snatcher by Molly Bang. Four Winds (Fantasy/Wordless, ages 6–8).

Mice Twice by Joseph Low. Atheneum (Animal fantasy, ages 3–6).

Truck by Donald Crews. Greenwillow (Concept, ages 3–6).

1982 *Jumanji* by Chris Van Allsburg. Houghton (Fantasy, ages 6–8).

HONOR BOOKS:

A Visit to William Blake's Inn: Poems for Innocent and Experienced Travelers by Nancy Willard. Illustrated by Alice and Martin Provensen. Harcourt (Biography/Poetry, ages 7–10).

Where the Buffaloes Begin by Olaf Baker. Illustrated by Stephen Gammell. Warne (Traditional, ages 7–10).

On Market Street by Arnold Lobel. Illustrated by Anita Lobel. Greenwillow (Alphabet, ages 4–6).

Outside Over There by Maurice Sendak. Harper (Fantasy, ages 7–10).

1983 *Shadow* by Blaise Cendrars. Translated and illustrated by Marcia Brown. Scribner's (Traditional, ages 8–11).

HONOR BOOKS:

When I Was Young in the Mountains by Cynthia Rylant. Illustrated by Diane Goode. Dutton (Realism, ages 7–9).

A Chair for My Mother by Vera B. Williams. Greenwillow (Realism, ages 6–8).

1984 *The Glorious Flight: Across the Channel with Louis Blériot* by Alice and Martin Provensen. Viking (Historical fiction [France, 1909], ages 7–10).

HONOR BOOKS:

Ten, Nine, Eight by Molly Bang. Greenwillow (Counting, ages 3–6).

Little Red Riding Hood by the Brothers Grimm. Retold and illustrated by Trina Schart Hyman. Holiday (Traditional, ages 5–8).

1985 *Saint George and the Dragon* adapted by Margaret Hodges. Illustrated by Trina Schart Hyman. Little, Brown (Traditional, ages 9–12).

HONOR BOOKS:

Hansel and Gretel adapted by Rika Lesser. Illustrated by Paul O. Zelinsky. Dodd (Traditional, ages 6–8).

The Story of Jumping Mouse retold and illustrated by John Steptoe. Lothrop (Traditional, ages 7–10).

Have You Seen My Duckling? by Nancy Tafuri. Greenwillow (Animal fantasy, ages 4–6).

1986 *The Polar Express* by Chris Van Allsburg. Houghton (Fantasy, ages 5–9).

HONOR BOOKS:

The Relatives Came by Cynthia Rylant. Illustrated by Stephen Gammell. Bradbury (Realism, ages 6–9).

King Bidgood's in the Bathtub by Audrey Wood. Illustrated by Don Wood. Harcourt (Fantasy, ages 5–8).

1987 *Hey, Al* by Arthur Yorinks. Illustrated by Richard Egielski. Farrar (Fantasy, ages 7–10).

HONOR BOOKS:

The Village of Round and Square Houses by Ann Grifalconi. Little, Brown (Traditional, ages 7–9).

Alphabatics by Suse MacDonald. Bradbury (Alphabet, ages 4–6).

Rumpelstiltskin by the Brothers Grimm. Retold and illustrated by Paul O. Zelinsky. Dutton (Traditional, ages 6–9).

1988 *Owl Moon* by Jane Yolen. Illustrated by John Schoenherr. Philomel (Realism, ages 5–8).

HONOR BOOK:

Mufaro's Beautiful Daughters retold by John Steptoe. Lothrop (Traditional, ages 6–9).

1989 *Song and Dance Man* by Karen Ackerman. Illustrated by Stephen Gammell. Knopf (Realism, ages 7–10).

HONOR BOOKS:

Free Fall by David Wiesner. Lothrop (Fantasy/Wordless, ages 7–10).

Goldilocks and the Three Bears retold and illustrated by James Marshall. Dial (Modern folktale, ages 5–8).

Mirandy and Brother Wind by Patricia McKissack. Illustrated by Jerry Pinkney. Knopf (Traditional, ages 7–9).

The Boy of the Three-Year Nap by Diane Snyder. Illustrated by Allen Say. Houghton (Traditional, ages 7–10).

1990 *Lon Po Po: A Red-Riding Hood Story from China* translated and illustrated by Ed Young. Philomel (Traditional, ages 5–8).

HONOR BOOKS:

Hershel and the Hanukkah Goblins by Eric Kimmel. Illustrated by Trina Schart Hyman. Holiday (Modern folktale, ages 7–10).

The Talking Eggs adapted by Robert D. San Souci. Illustrated by Jerry Pinkney. Dial (Traditional, ages 6–9).

Bill Peet: An Autobiography by Bill Peet. Houghton (Biography, ages 7–10).

Color Zoo by Lois Ehlert. Lippincott (Concept, ages 3–6).

1991 *Black and White* by David Macaulay. Houghton (Mystery, ages 8–12).

HONOR BOOKS:

Puss in Boots by Charles Perrault. Illustrated by Fred Marcellino. Farrar (Traditional, ages 5–7).

"More, More, More." Said the Baby: 3 Love Stories by Vera Williams. Greenwillow (Realism, ages 3–5).

1992 *Tuesday* by David Wiesner. Clarion (Fantasy/Wordless, ages 7–10).

HONOR BOOK:

Tar Beach by Faith Ringgold. Crown (Multicultural [African-American], ages 6–9).

1993 *Mirette on the High Wire* by Emily Arnold McCully. Putnam (Realism, ages 7–9).

HONOR BOOKS:

Seven Blind Mice by Ed Young. Philomel (Modern folktale, ages 6–10).

The Stinky Cheese Man and Other Fairly Stupid Tales by Jon Scieszka and Lane Smith. Illustrated by Lane Smith. Viking (Modern folktales, ages 7–11).

Working Cotton by Sherley Anne Williams. Illustrated by Carole Byard. Harcourt (Realism [African-American], ages 7–9).

1994 *Grandfather's Journey* by Allen Say. Houghton (Biography, ages 7–9).

HONOR BOOKS:

Peppe the Lamplighter by Elisa Bartone. Illustrated by Ted Lewin. Lothrop (Realism, ages 7–9).

In the Small, Small Pond by Denise Fleming. Holt (Pattern, ages 5–7).

Owen by Kevin Henkes. Greenwillow (Animal fantasy, ages 5–7).

Raven: A Trickster Tale from the Pacific Northwest by Gerald McDermott. Harcourt (Traditional [Native American], ages 7–9).

Yo! Yes? by Chris Raschka. Orchard (Realism/Multicultural, ages 5–7).

1995 *Smoky Night* by Eve Bunting. Illustrated by David Diaz. Harcourt (Realism/Multicultural, ages 6–8).

HONOR BOOKS:

Swamp Angel by Anne Isaacs. Illustrated by Paul O. Zelinsky. Dutton (Modern folktale, ages 6–9).

John Henry by Julius Lester. Illustrated by Jerry Pinkney. Dial (Traditional, ages 6–9).

Time Flies by Eric Rohmann. Crown (Wordless, ages 6–9).

1996 *Officer Buckle and Gloria* by Peggy Rathmann. Putnam (Animal fantasy, ages 5–7).

HONOR BOOKS:

Alphabet City by Stephen T. Johnson. Viking (Concept, ages 7–9).

The Faithful Friend by Robert D. San Souci. Illustrated by Brian Pinkney. Simon & Schuster (Traditional, ages 10–14).

Tops & Bottoms by Janet Stevens. Harcourt (Traditional, ages 6–8).

Zin! Zin! Zin! A Violin by Lloyd Moss. Illustrated by Marjorie Priceman. Simon & Schuster (Concept, ages 5–7).

1997 *Golem* by David Wisniewski. Clarion (Traditional, ages 6–12).

HONOR BOOKS:

Hush! A Thai Lullaby by Minfong Ho. Illustrated by Holly Meade. Orchard (Poetry, ages 2–6).

The Graphic Alphabet by David Pelletier. Orchard (ABC/Art, ages 7–10).

The Paperboy by Dav Pilkey. Orchard (Realism, ages 8–10).

Starry Messenger by Peter Sís. Farrar (Biography, ages 9–14).

1998 *Rapunzel* by Paul O. Zelinsky. Dutton (Traditional, ages 7–10).

HONOR BOOKS:

The Gardener by Sarah Stewart. Illustrated by David Small. Farrar (Realism, ages 7–10).

Harlem by Walter Dean Myers. Illustrated by Christopher Myers. Scholastic (Poetry, ages 10–14).

There Was an Old Lady Who Swallowed a Fly by Simms Taback. Viking (Folk poem/Engineered, ages 5–7).

1999 *Snowflake Bentley* by Jacqueline Briggs Martin. Illustrated by Mary Azarian. Houghton (Biography, ages 8–12).

HONOR BOOKS:

Duke Ellington: The Piano Prince and His Orchestra by Andrea Davis Pinkney. Illustrated by Brian Pinkney. Hyperion (Biography, ages 8–10).

No, David! by David Shannon. Scholastic. (Realism/Pattern, ages 3–5).

Snow by Uri Shulevitz. Farrar (Realism, ages 4–6).

Tibet through the Red Box by Peter Sís. Farrar (Biography/Magic realism, ages 7 and Up).

2000 *Joseph Had a Little Overcoat* by Simms Taback. Viking (Traditional/Pattern, ages 4–7).

HONOR BOOKS:

When Sophie Gets Angry—Really, Really Angry by Molly Bang. Scholastic (Realism, ages 4–6).

A Child's Calendar by John Updike. Illustrated by Trina Schart Hyman. Holiday (Poetry, ages 5–9).

The Ugly Duckling adapted and illustrated by Jerry Pinkney. Morrow (Modern folktale, ages 4–7).

Sector 7 by David Weisner. Clarion (Modern fantasy/Wordless, ages 5–9).

2001 *So You Want to Be President?* by Judith St. George. Illustrated by David Small. Philomel (Informational/Biography, ages 7–10).

HONOR BOOKS:

Casey at the Bat: A Ballad of the Republic Sung in the Year 1888 by Ernest L. Thayer. Illustrated by Christopher Bing. Handprint (Poetry, ages 7–12).

Click, Clack, Moo: Cows That Type by Doreen Cronin. Illustrated by Betsy Lewin. Simon & Schuster (Animal fantasy, ages 6–9).

Olivia by Ian Falconer. Atheneum (Animal fantasy, ages 4–8).

2002 *The Three Pigs* by David Wiesner. Clarion/Houghton Mifflin (Traditional, ages 5–7).

HONOR BOOKS:

The Dinosaurs of Waterhouse Hawkins by Barbara Kerley. Illustrated by Brian Selznick. Scholastic (Informational, ages 7–10).

Martin's Big Words: The Life of Dr. Martin Luther King, Jr. by Doreen Rappaport. Illustrated by Bryan Collier. Hyperion (Biography, ages 5–9).

The Stray Dog by Marc Simont. HarperCollins (Realism, ages 4–7).

2003 *My Friend Rabbit* by Eric Rohmann. Roaring Brook/Millbrook (Animal fantasy, ages 4–8).

HONOR BOOKS:

The Spider and the Fly by Mary Howitt. Illustrated by Tony DiTerlizzi. Simon & Schuster (Poetry, ages 6–12).

Hondo and Fabian by Peter McCarty. Holt (Realism, ages 3–6)

Noah's Ark by Jerry Pinkney. SeaStar/North-South (Traditional, ages 6–10).

2004 *The Man Who Walked Between the Towers* by Mordecai Gerstein. Roaring Brook/Millbrook (Realism, ages 5–9).

HONOR BOOKS:

Ella Sarah Gets Dressed by Margaret Chodos-Irvine. Harcourt. (Realism, ages 3–5).

What Do You Do With a Tail Like This? by Steve Jenkins and Robin Page. Houghton Mifflin (Informational, ages 4–7).

Don't Let the Pigeon Drive the Bus by Mo Willems. Hyperion (Fantasy, ages 4–7).

Newbery Medal

This award, sponsored by the Association for Library Service to Children division of the American Library Association, is given to the author of the most distinguished contribution to children's literature published during the preceding year. Only U.S. citizens or residents are eligible for this award.

1922 *The Story of Mankind* by Hendrik Willem Van Loon. Liveright (Informational, ages 12–YA).

HONOR BOOKS:

The Great Quest by Charles Boardman Hawes. Little, Brown (Historical fiction [New England, 1826], ages 11–YA).

Cedric the Forester by Bernard G. Marshall. Appleton (Historical fiction [England, 1200s], ages 11–YA).

The Old Tobacco Shop by William Bowen. Macmillan (Fantasy, ages 9–12).

The Golden Fleece and the Heroes Who Lived before Achilles by Padraic Colum. Macmillan (Traditional, ages 9–13).

Windy Hill by Cornelia Meigs. Macmillan (Realism, ages 9–12).

1923 *The Voyages of Doctor Dolittle* by Hugh Lofting. Lippincott (Modern fantasy, ages 8–12).

(No record of the runners-up.)

1924 *The Dark Frigate* by Charles Boardman Hawes. Little, Brown (Historical fiction [England, 1600s], ages 10–YA).

(No record of the runners-up.)

1925 *Tales from Silver Lands* by Charles J. Finger. Illustrated by Paul Honoré. Doubleday (Traditional, ages 9–YA).

HONOR BOOKS:

Nicholas by Anne Carroll Moore. Putnam (Modern fantasy [Little people], ages 8–11).

Dream Coach by Anne and Dillwyn Parrish. Macmillan (Modern fantasy, ages 7–11).

1926 *Shen of the Sea* by Arthur Bowie Chrisman. Illustrated by Else Hasselriis. Dutton (Modern fantasy [Literary tales], ages 9–12).

HONOR BOOK:

The Voyagers by Padraic Colum. Macmillan (Traditional/Informational, ages 10–12).

1927 *Smoky, the Cowhorse* by Will James. Scribner's (Animal realism, ages 9–12).

(No record of the runners-up.)

1928 *Gay-Neck, The Story of a Pigeon* by Dhan Gopal Mukerji. Illustrated by Boris Artzybasheff. Dutton (Animal realism, ages 9–YA).

HONOR BOOKS:

The Wonder Smith and His Son by Ella Young. McKay/Longmans (Traditional [Ireland], ages 10–YA).

Downright Dencey by Caroline Dale Snedeker. Doubleday (Historical fiction [New England, 1812], ages 9–13).

1929 *The Trumpeter of Krakow* by Eric P. Kelly. Illustrated by Angela Pruszynska. Macmillan (Historical fiction [Poland, 1400s], ages 11–YA).

HONOR BOOKS:

The Pigtail of Ah Lee Ben Loo by John Bennett. McKay/Longmans (Fantasy/Poetry, ages 8–13).

Millions of Cats by Wanda Gág. Coward-McCann (Picture book; Fantasy, ages 5–7).

The Boy Who Was by Grace T. Hallock. Dutton (Historical fiction [Italy through 3,000 years], ages 10–YA).

Clearing Weather by Cornelia Meigs. Little, Brown (Historical fiction [USA, 1787], ages 11–YA).

The Runaway Papoose by Grace P. Moon. Doubleday (Realism/Multicultural, ages 8–11).

Tod of the Fens by Eleanor Whitney. Macmillan (Historical fiction [England 1400s], ages 11–YA).

1930 *Hitty: Her First Hundred Years* by Rachel Field. Illustrated by Dorothy P. Lathrop. Macmillan (Historical fantasy, ages 9–13).

HONOR BOOKS:

The Tangle-Coated Horse and Other Tales: Episodes from the Fionn Saga by Ella Young. Illustrated by Vera Brock. Longmans (Traditional, ages 10–13).

Vaino: A Boy of New Finland by Julia Davis Adams. Illustrated by Lempi Ostman. Dutton (Historical fiction [Finland, 1920s], ages 11–YA).

Pran of Albania by Elizabeth C. Miller. Doubleday (Realism, ages 11–YA).

The Jumping-Off Place by Marian Hurd McNeely. McKay/Longmans (Realism, ages 10–YA).

A Daughter of the Seine by Jeanette Eaton. Harper (Biography, ages 12–YA).

Little Blacknose by Hildegarde Hoyt Swift. Illustrated by Lynd Ward. Harcourt (Modern fantasy, ages 8–11).

1931 *The Cat Who Went to Heaven* by Elizabeth Coatsworth. Illustrated by Lynd Ward. Macmillan (Modern fantasy, ages 10–13).

HONOR BOOKS:

Floating Island by Anne Parrish. Harper (Modern fantasy, ages 8–11).

The Dark Star of Itza by Alida Malkus. Harcourt (Historical fiction [Mayan Empire], ages 11–YA).

Queer Person by Ralph Hubbard. Doubleday (Historical fiction/Multicultural [Native American], ages 9–13).

Mountains Are Free by Julia Davis Adams. Dutton (Historical fiction [Switzerland], ages 11–YA).

Spice and the Devil's Cave by Agnes D. Hewes. Knopf (Historical fiction [Portugal, 1400s], ages 11–YA).

Meggy McIntosh by Elizabeth Janet Gray. Doubleday (Historical fiction [Scotland, USA, 1775], ages 10–YA).

Garram the Hunter: A Boy of the Hill Tribes by Herbert Best. Illustrated by Allena Best (Erick Berry). Doubleday (Realism [Africa], ages 9–13).

Ood-Le-Uk, the Wanderer by Alice Lide and Margaret Johansen. Illustrated by Raymond Lufkin. Little, Brown (Realism [Alaska], ages 11–14).

1932 *Waterless Mountain* by Laura Adams Armer. Illustrated by Sidney Armer and Laura Adams Armer. McKay/Longmans (Realism/Multicultural [Native American], ages 9–13).

HONOR BOOKS:

The Fairy Circus by Dorothy Lathrop. Macmillan (Modern fantasy, ages 6–9).

Calico Bush by Rachel Field. Macmillan (Historical fiction, [USA, 1743], ages 9–13).

Boy of the South Seas by Eunice Tietjens. Coward-McCann (Realism, ages 9–12).

Out of the Flame by Eloise Lownsbery. McKay/Longmans (Historical fiction [France, 1500s], ages 10–YA).

Jane's Island by Marjorie Hill Alee. Houghton (Realism, ages 9–13).

The Truce of the Wolf and Other Tales of Old Italy by Mary Gould Davis. Harcourt (Traditional fantasy, ages 8–13).

1933 *Young Fu of the Upper Yangtze* by Elizabeth Foreman Lewis. Illustrated by Kurt Wiese. Holt (Realism, ages 10–YA).

HONOR BOOKS:

Swift Rivers by Cornelia Meigs. Little, Brown (Historical fiction [USA, 1835], ages 10–13).

The Railroad to Freedom by Hildegarde Swift. Harcourt (Biography, ages 10–YA).

Children of the Soil by Nora Burglon. Doubleday (Realism, ages 9–12).

1934 *Invincible Louisa: The Story of the Author of "Little Women"* by Cornelia Meigs. Little, Brown (Biography, ages 10–12).

HONOR BOOKS:

The Forgotten Daughter by Caroline Dale Snedeker. Doubleday (Historical fiction [Italy, second century B.C.], ages 11–YA).

Swords of Steel by Elsie Singmaster. Houghton (Historical fiction [USA, 1859], ages 11–YA).

ABC Bunny by Wanda Gág. Coward-McCann (Picture book. Modern fantasy/Alphabet, ages 3–7).

Winged Girl of Knossos by Erik Berry. Appleton (Historical fiction [Ancient Greece], ages 10–YA).

New Land by Sarah L. Schmidt. McBride (Realism, ages 10–YA).

The Apprentice of Florence by Anne Kyle. Houghton (Historical fiction [Italy, 1400s], ages 11–YA).

The Big Tree of Bunlahy: Stories of My Own Countryside by Padraic Colum. Illustrated by Jack Yeats. Macmillan (Modern fantasy, ages 8–YA).

Glory of the Seas by Agnes D. Hewes. Illustrated by N. C. Wyeth. Knopf (Historical fiction [USA, 1850s], ages 11–YA).

1935 *Dobry* by Monica Shannon. Illustrated by Atanas Katchamakoff. Viking (Realism, ages 9–11).

HONOR BOOKS:

The Pageant of Chinese History by Elizabeth Seeger. McKay/Longmans (Informational, ages 11–YA).

Davy Crockett by Constance Rourke. Harcourt (Biography, ages 12–YA).

A Day on Skates: The Story of a Dutch Picnic by Hilda Van Stockum. Harper (Realism, ages 6–8).

1936 *Caddie Woodlawn* by Carol Ryrie Brink. Illustrated by Kate Seredy. Macmillan (Historical fiction [USA, 1860s], ages 9–12).

HONOR BOOKS:

Honk: The Moose by Phil Strong. Illustrated by Kurt Wiese. Dodd (Realism, ages 7–11).

The Good Master by Kate Seredy. Viking (Realism, ages 9–11).

Young Walter Scott by Elizabeth Janet Gray. Viking (Biography, ages 11–YA).

All Sail Set by Armstrong Sperry. Winston (Historical fiction [United States, 1851], ages 10–13).

1937 *Roller Skates* by Ruth Sawyer. Illustrated by Valenti Angelo. Viking (Realism, ages 8–10).

HONOR BOOKS:

Phoebe Fairchild: Her Book by Lois Lenski. Lippincott (Historical fiction [New England, 1830s], ages 9–12).

Whistler's Van by Idwal Jones. Viking (Realism, ages 9–13).

The Golden Basket by Ludwig Bemelmans. Viking (Realism, ages 6–9).

Winterbound by Margery Bianco. Viking (Realism, ages 11–YA).

Audubon by Constance Rourke. Harcourt (Biography, ages 11–YA).

The Codfish Musket by Agnes D. Hewes. Doubleday (Historical fiction [USA, 1780s], ages 11–YA).

1938 *The White Stag* by Kate Seredy. Viking (Traditional, ages 10–YA).

HONOR BOOKS:

Bright Island by Mabel L. Robinson. Random (Realism, ages 11–YA).

Pecos Bill by James Cloyd Bowman. Little, Brown (Traditional, ages 9–YA).

On the Banks of Plum Creek by Laura Ingalls Wilder. Harper (Historical fiction [USA, 1870s], ages 8–11).

1939 *Thimble Summer* by Elizabeth Enright. Holt (Realism, ages 8–11).

HONOR BOOKS:

Leader by Destiny: George Washington, Man and Patriot by Jeanette Eaton. Harcourt (Biography, ages 11–YA).

Penn by Elizabeth Janet Gray. Viking (Biography, ages 11–YA).

Nino by Valenti Angelo. Viking (Realism, ages 9–11).

"Hello, the Boat!" by Phyllis Crawford. Holt (Historical fiction [USA, 1817], ages 9–13).

Mr. Popper's Penguins by Richard and Florence Atwater. Little, Brown (Animal fantasy, ages 7–11).

1940 *Daniel Boone* by James H. Daugherty. Viking (Biography, ages 10–YA).

HONOR BOOKS:

The Singing Tree by Kate Seredy. Viking (Historical fiction [Eastern Europe, 1910s], ages 9–12).

Runner of the Mountain Tops by Mabel L. Robinson. Random (Biography, ages 11–YA).

By the Shores of Silver Lake by Laura Ingalls Wilder. Harper (Historical fiction [USA, 1880s], ages 8–10).

Boy with a Pack by Stephen W. Meader. Harcourt (Historical fiction [USA, 1837], ages 9–13).

1941 *Call It Courage* by Armstrong Sperry. Macmillan (Realism, ages 9–12).

HONOR BOOKS:

Blue Willow by Doris Gates. Viking (Historical fiction [USA, 1930s], ages 8–11).

Young Mac of Fort Vancouver by Mary Jane Carr. Crowell (Historical fiction [Canada, early 1800s], ages 10–YA).

The Long Winter by Laura Ingalls Wilder. Harper (Historical fiction [USA, 1880s], ages 9–13).

Nansen by Anna Gertrude Hall. Viking (Biography, ages 11–YA).

1942 *The Matchlock Gun* by Walter D. Edmonds. Illustrated by Paul Lantz. Dodd (Historical fiction [Colonial America, 1757], ages 8–11).

HONOR BOOKS:

Little Town on the Prairie by Laura Ingalls Wilder. Harper (Historical fiction [USA, 1881], ages 8–10).

George Washington's World by Genevieve Foster. Scribner's (Informational/Biography, ages 10–YA).

Indian Captive: The Story of Mary Jemison by Lois Lenski. Lippincott (Historical fiction [USA, 1750s], ages 9–11).

Down Ryton Water by Eva Roe Gaggin. Illustrated by Elmer Hader. Viking (Historical fiction [England, Netherlands, 1600s], ages 12–YA).

1943 *Adam of the Road* by Elizabeth Janet Gray. Illustrated by Robert Lawson. Viking (Historical fiction [England, 1290s], ages 9–12).

HONOR BOOKS:

The Middle Moffat by Eleanor Estes. Harcourt (Realism, ages 8–10).

"Have You Seen Tom Thumb?" by Mabel Leigh Hunt. Lippincott (Biography, ages 10–YA).

1944 *Johnny Tremain* by Esther Forbes. Illustrated by Lynd Ward. Houghton (Historical fiction [Boston, 1770s], ages 12–YA).

HONOR BOOKS:

These Happy Golden Years by Laura Ingalls Wilder. Harper (Historical fiction [USA, 1880s], ages 8–10).

Fog Magic by Julia L. Sauer. Viking (Modern fantasy, ages 9–12).

Rufus M. by Eleanor Estes. Harcourt (Realism, ages 8–10).

Mountain Born by Elizabeth Yates. Coward-McCann (Animal realism, ages 9–11).

1945 *Rabbit Hill* by Robert Lawson. Viking (Animal fantasy, ages 7–9).

HONOR BOOKS:

The Hundred Dresses by Eleanor Estes. Harcourt (Realism, ages 7–9).

The Silver Pencil by Alice Dalgliesh. Scribner's (Realism, ages 10–YA).

Abraham Lincoln's World by Genevieve Foster. Scribner's (Informational/Biography, ages 10–YA).

Lone Journey: The Life of Roger Williams by Jeanette Eaton. Illustrated by Woodi Ishmael. Harcourt (Biography, ages 13–YA).

1946 *Strawberry Girl* by Lois Lenski. Lippincott (Historical fiction [Florida, early 1900s], ages 8–10).

HONOR BOOKS:

Justin Morgan Had a Horse by Marguerite Henry. Follett (Animal Realism, ages 8–10).

The Moved-Outers by Florence Crannell Means. Houghton (Multicultural, ages 10–12).

Bhimsa, the Dancing Bear by Christine Weston. Scribner's (Realism, ages 8–10).

New Found World by Katherine B. Shippen. Viking (Informational, ages 10–YA).

1947 *Miss Hickory* by Carolyn Sherwin Bailey. Illustrated by Ruth Gannett. Viking (Modern fantasy/Toys and dolls, ages 7–9).

HONOR BOOKS:

The Wonderful Year by Nancy Barnes. Messner (Realism, ages 9–12).

The Big Tree by Mary and Conrad Buff. Viking (Informational, ages 9–13).

The Heavenly Tenants by William Maxwell. Harper (Modern fantasy, ages 10–YA).

The Avion My Uncle Flew by Cyrus Fisher. Appleton (Realism, ages 10–13).

The Hidden Treasure of Glaston by Eleanore M. Jewett. Viking (Historical fiction [England, 1172], ages 10–13).

1948 *The Twenty-One Balloons* by William Pène du Bois. Lothrop (Modern fantasy, ages 9–11).

HONOR BOOKS:

Pancakes-Paris by Claire Huchet Bishop. Viking (Realism, ages 8–11).

Li Lun, Lad of Courage by Carolyn Treffinger. Abingdon (Realism, ages 9–12).

The Quaint and Curious Quest of Johnny Longfoot, The Shoe-King's Son by Catherine Besterman. Bobbs-Merrill (Traditional, ages 8–10).

The Cow-Tail Switch, And Other West African Stories by Harold Courlander and George Herzog. Holt (Traditional, ages 8–13).

Misty of Chincoteague by Marguerite Henry. Illustrated by Wesley Dennis. Rand (Animal realism [horse], ages 9–12).

1949 *King of the Wind* by Marguerite Henry. Illustrated by Wesley Dennis. Rand (Historical fiction [Morocco, Europe, 1700s], ages 9–12).

HONOR BOOKS:

Seabird by Holling Clancy Holling. Houghton (Informational, ages 9–12).

Daughter of the Mountains by Louise Rankin. Viking (Realism, ages 9–11).

My Father's Dragon by Ruth S. Gannett. Random (Modern fantasy, ages 6–9).

Story of the Negro by Arna Bontemps. Knopf (Informational, ages 10–YA).

1950 *The Door in the Wall* by Marguerite de Angeli. Doubleday (Historical fiction [England, 1300s], ages 9–11).

HONOR BOOKS:

Tree of Freedom by Rebecca Caudill. Viking (Historical fiction [USA, 1780s], ages 10–12).

The Blue Cat of Castle Town by Catherine Coblentz. McKay/Longmans (Traditional, ages 9–YA).

Kildee House by Rutherford Montgomery. Doubleday (Realism, ages 8–12).

George Washington by Genevieve Foster. Scribner's (Biography, ages 8–11).

Song of the Pines by Walter and Marion Havighurst. Holt (Historical fiction [USA, 1850s], age YA).

1951 *Amos Fortune, Free Man* by Elizabeth Yates. Illustrated by Nora Unwin. Dutton (Biography, ages 9–11).

HONOR BOOKS:

Better Known as Johnny Appleseed by Mabel Leigh Hunt. Lippincott (Biography, ages 11–YA).

Gandhi, Fighter without a Sword by Jeanette Eaton. Morrow (Biography, ages 11–YA).

Abraham Lincoln, Friend of the People by Clara I. Judson. Follett (Biography, ages 9–13).

The Story of Appleby Capple by Anne Parrish. Harper (Modern fantasy, ages 6–8).

1952 *Ginger Pye* by Eleanor Estes. Harcourt (Realism, ages 8–10).

HONOR BOOKS:

Americans before Columbus by Elizabeth Chesley Baity. Viking (Informational, ages 10–YA).

Minn of the Mississippi by Holling Clancy Holling. Houghton (Informational, ages 7–9).

The Defender by Nicholas Kalashnikoff. Scribner's (Realism, ages 9–13).

The Light at Tern Rock by Julia L. Sauer. Viking (Realism, ages 7–9).

The Apple and the Arrow by Mary and Conrad Buff. Houghton (Biography, ages 8–10).

1953 *Secret of the Andes* by Ann Nolan Clark. Illustrated by Jean Charlot. Viking (Realism/Multicultural [Native American], ages 11–13).

HONOR BOOKS:

Charlotte's Web by E. B. White. Harper (Animal fantasy, ages 7–9).

Moccasin Trail by Eloise J. McGraw. Coward-McCann (Historical fiction [USA, 1830s], ages 11–YA).

Red Sails to Capri by Ann Weil. Viking (Historical fiction [Italy, 1826], ages 9–11).

The Bears on Hemlock Mountain by Alice Dalgliesh. Scribner's (Historical fiction [USA, 1800s], ages 6–9).

Birthdays of Freedom (Vol. 1), by Genevieve Foster. Scribner's (Informational/Biography, ages 10–13).

1954 *And Now Miguel* by Joseph Krumgold. Illustrated by Jean Charlot. Crowell (Historical fiction [New Mexico, 1940s], ages 9–12).

HONOR BOOKS:

All Alone by Claire Huchet Bishop. Viking (Realism, ages 8–11).

Shadrach by Meindert DeJong. Harper (Animal realism, ages 8–10).

Hurry Home, Candy by Meindert DeJong. Harper (Animal realism, ages 8–10).

Theodore Roosevelt, Fighting Patriot by Clara I. Judson. Follett (Biography, ages 9–11).

Magic Maize by Mary and Conrad Buff. Houghton (Realism, ages 8–11).

1955 *The Wheel on the School* by Meindert DeJong. Illustrated by Maurice Sendak. Harper (Realism, ages 8–11).

HONOR BOOKS:

The Courage of Sarah Noble by Alice Dalgliesh. Scribner's (Historical fiction [USA, 1707], ages 8–10).

Banner in the Sky by James Ramsey Ullman. Lippincott (Historical fiction [Europe, 1860s], ages 10–YA).

1956 *Carry On, Mr. Bowditch* by Jean Lee Latham. Houghton (Biography, ages 10–13).

HONOR BOOKS:

The Golden Name Day by Jennie D. Lindquist. Harper (Realism, ages 8–11).

The Secret River by Marjorie Kinnan Rawlings. Scribner's (Fantasy, ages 6–9).

Men, Microscopes and Living Things by Katherine B. Shippen. Viking (Informational, ages 10–YA).

1957 *Miracles on Maple Hill* by Virginia Sorensen. Illustrated by Beth and Joe Krush. Harcourt (Realism, ages 8–10).

HONOR BOOKS:

Old Yeller by Fred Gipson. Harper (Animal realism, ages 9–12).

The House of Sixty Fathers by Meindert DeJong. Harper (Historical fiction [China, 1940s], ages 9–13).

Mr. Justice Holmes by Clara I. Judson. Follett (Biography, ages 9–13).

The Corn Grows Ripe by Dorothy Rhoads. Viking (Realism, ages 9–11).

The Black Fox of Lorne by Marguerite de Angeli. Doubleday (Historical fiction [Scotland, tenth century], ages 9–12).

1958 *Rifles for Watie* by Harold Keith. Illustrated by Peter Burchard. Crowell (Historical fiction, [USA, 1860s], ages 10–YA).

HONOR BOOKS:

The Horsecatcher by Mari Sandoz. Westminster (Realism, ages 11–YA).

Gone-Away Lake by Elizabeth Enright. Harcourt (Realism, ages 8–11).

The Great Wheel by Robert Lawson. Viking (Historical fiction [USA, 1890s], ages 9–12).

Tom Paine, Freedom's Apostle by Leo Gurko. Crowell (Biography, ages 11–YA).

1959 *The Witch of Blackbird Pond* by Elizabeth George Speare. Houghton (Historical fiction [USA, 1680s], ages 12–YA).

HONOR BOOKS:

The Family under the Bridge by Natalie S. Carlson. Harper (Realism, ages 8–10).

Along Came a Dog by Meindert DeJong. Harper (Animal realism, ages 9–YA).

Chucaro: Wild Pony of the Pampa by Francis Kalnay. Harcourt (Animal realism, ages 9–13).

The Perilous Road by William O. Steele. Harcourt (Historical fiction [USA, 1860s], ages 9–13).

1960 *Onion John* by Joseph Krumgold. Illustrated by Symeon Shimin. Crowell (Realism, ages 9–12).

HONOR BOOKS:

My Side of the Mountain by Jean George. Dutton (Realism, ages 10–12).

America Is Born by Gerald Johnson. Morrow (Informational, ages 9–13).

The Gammage Cup by Carol Kendall. Harcourt (Modern fantasy, [little people], ages 9–12).

1961 *Island of the Blue Dolphins* by Scott O'Dell. Houghton (Historical fiction [USA, 1800s]/ Multicultural [Native American], ages 9–13).

HONOR BOOKS:

America Moves Forward by Gerald Johnson. Morrow (Informational, ages 9–13).

Old Ramon by Jack Schaefer. Houghton (Realism, ages 10–YA).

The Cricket in Times Square by George Selden. Farrar (Animal fantasy, ages 7–9).

1962 *The Bronze Bow* by Elizabeth George Speare. Houghton (Historical fiction [Jerusalem, 1st century A.D.], ages 12–YA).

HONOR BOOKS:

Frontier Living by Edwin Tunis. World (Informational, ages 10–YA).

The Golden Goblet by Eloise J. McGraw. Coward (Historical fiction [Ancient Egypt], ages 10–YA).

Belling the Tiger by Mary Stolz. Harper (Modern fantasy, ages 7–9).

1963   *A Wrinkle in Time* by Madeleine L'Engle. Farrar (Fantasy [science fiction], ages 9–12).

HONOR BOOKS:

Thistle and Thyme by Sorche Nic Leodhas (pseudonym of Leclaire Alger). Holt (Traditional fantasy, ages 7–11).

Men of Athens by Olivia Coolidge. Houghton (Biography, ages 11–YA).

1964   *It's Like This, Cat* by Emily Cheney Neville. Harper (Realism, ages 10–YA).

HONOR BOOKS:

Rascal by Sterling North. Dutton (Animal realism, ages 9–11).

The Loner by Esther Wier. McKay/Longmans (Realism, ages 9–13).

1965   *Shadow of a Bull* by Maia Wojciechowska. Atheneum (Realism, ages 10–12).

HONOR BOOK:

Across Five Aprils by Irene Hunt. Follett (Historical fiction [USA, 1860s], ages 10–13).

1966   *I, Juan de Pareja* by Elizabeth Borten de Treviño. Farrar (Biography, ages 10–12).

HONOR BOOKS:

The Black Cauldron by Lloyd Alexander. Holt (Modern fantasy, [quest], ages 10–12).

The Animal Family by Randall Jarrell. Pantheon (Modern fantasy, ages 10–13).

The Noonday Friends by Mary Stolz. Harper (Realism, ages 9–11).

1967   *Up a Road Slowly* by Irene Hunt. Follett (Realism, ages 10–YA).

HONOR BOOKS:

The King's Fifth by Scott O'Dell. Houghton (Historical fiction [Spain, 1500s], ages 10–12).

Zlateh the Goat and Other Stories by Isaac Bashevis Singer. Harper (Modern fantasy, ages 8–11).

The Jazz Man by Mary H. Weik. Atheneum (Realism, ages 9–12).

1968   *From the Mixed-up Files of Mrs. Basil E. Frankweiler* by E. L. Konigsburg. Atheneum (Realism, ages 10–12).

HONOR BOOKS:

Jennifer, Hecate, Macbeth, William McKinley, and Me, Elizabeth by E. L. Konigsburg. Atheneum (Realism, ages 9–11).

The Black Pearl by Scott O'Dell. Houghton (Realism, ages 9–11).

The Fearsome Inn by Isaac Bashevis Singer. Scribner's (Modern fantasy, ages 10–YA).

The Egypt Game by Zilpha Keatley Snyder. Atheneum (Realism, ages 9–11).

1969   *The High King* by Lloyd Alexander. Holt (Modern fantasy [quest], ages 10–12).

HONOR BOOKS:

To Be a Slave by Julius Lester. Dial (Informational, ages 11–YA).

When Shlemiel Went to Warsaw and Other Stories by Isaac Bashevis Singer. Farrar (Modern fantasy, ages 9–YA).

1970   *Sounder* by William H. Armstrong. Harper (Historical fiction [Southern USA, early twentieth century], ages 10–13).

HONOR BOOKS:

Our Eddie by Sulamith Ish-Kishor. Pantheon (Realism, ages 11–YA).

The Many Ways of Seeing: An Introduction to the Pleasure of Art by Janet Gaylord Moore. World (Informational, ages 10–YA).

Journey Outside by Mary Q. Steele. Viking (Modern fantasy, ages 10–13).

1971   *The Summer of the Swans* by Betsy Byars. Viking (Realism, ages 10–13).

HONOR BOOKS:

Kneeknock Rise by Natalie Babbitt. Farrar (Modern fantasy, ages 9–13).

Enchantress from the Stars by Sylvia Louise Engdahl. Atheneum (Modern fantasy, [science fiction], ages 11–YA).

Sing Down the Moon by Scott O'Dell. Houghton (Historical fiction [USA, 1860s], ages 12–YA).

1972   *Mrs. Frisby and the Rats of NIMH* by Robert C. O'Brien. Atheneum (Animal fantasy, ages 10–12).

HONOR BOOKS:

Incident at Hawk's Hill by Allan W. Eckert. Little, Brown (Historical fiction [Canada, 1870]/Animal realism, ages 10–12).

The Planet of Junior Brown by Virginia Hamilton. Macmillan (Realism, ages 11–YA).

The Tombs of Atuan by Ursula K. LeGuin. Atheneum (Modern fantasy [quest], ages 10–YA).

Annie and the Old One by Miska Miles. Little, Brown. (Picture book; Realism/Multicultural [Native American], ages 8–10).

The Headless Cupid by Zilpha Keatley Snyder. Atheneum (Realism [mystery], ages 10–12).

1973 *Julie of the Wolves* by Jean Craighead George. Harper (Realism/Multicultural [Native American], ages 10–13).

HONOR BOOKS:

Frog and Toad Together by Arnold Lobel. Harper (Picture book; Animal fantasy, ages 3–7).

The Upstairs Room by Johanna Reiss. Crowell (Historical fiction [Holland, 1940s], ages 9–13).

The Witches of Worm by Zilpha Keatley Snyder. Atheneum (Realism, ages 10–12).

1974 *The Slave Dancer* by Paula Fox. Bradbury (Historical fiction [USA, Africa, 1840s], ages 10–13).

HONOR BOOK:

The Dark Is Rising by Susan Cooper. Atheneum/ McElderry (Modern fantasy [quest], ages 11–YA).

1975 *M. C. Higgins, the Great* by Virginia Hamilton. Macmillan (Realism/Multicultural [African-American], ages 10–13).

HONOR BOOKS:

Figgs & Phantoms by Ellen Raskin. Dutton (Realism, ages 10–13).

My Brother Sam Is Dead by James Lincoln Collier and Christopher Collier. Four Winds (Historical fiction [Colonial America, 1700s], ages 10–YA).

The Perilous Gard by Elizabeth Marie Pope. Houghton (Historical fiction [England, 1558], ages 12–YA).

Philip Hall Likes Me. I Reckon Maybe by Bette Greene. Dial (Realism/Multicultural [African-American], ages 9–11).

1976 *The Grey King* by Susan Cooper. Atheneum/ McElderry (Modern fantasy [quest], ages 11–YA).

HONOR BOOKS:

The Hundred Penny Box by Sharon Bell Mathis. Viking (Realism/Multicultural [African-American], ages 8–11).

Dragonwings by Laurence Yep. Harper (Historical fiction [San Francisco, 1903–1909]/Multicultural [Chinese-American], ages 10–13).

1977 *Roll of Thunder, Hear My Cry* by Mildred D. Taylor. Dial (Historical fiction [Mississippi, 1934]/ Multicultural [African-American], ages 9–13).

HONOR BOOKS:

Abel's Island by William Steig. Farrar (Animal fantasy, ages 8–10).

A String in the Harp by Nancy Bond. Atheneum/ McElderry (Modern fantasy, ages 11–13).

1978 *The Bridge to Terabithia* by Katherine Paterson. Crowell (Realism, ages 9–11).

HONOR BOOKS:

Anpao: An American Indian Odyssey by Jamake Highwater. Lippincott (Traditional/Multicultural [Native American], ages 10–12).

Ramona and Her Father by Beverly Cleary. Morrow (Realism, ages 7–9).

1979 *The Westing Game* by Ellen Raskin. Dutton (Realism [mystery], ages 10–12).

HONOR BOOK:

The Great Gilly Hopkins by Katherine Paterson. Crowell (Realism, ages 9–12).

1980 *A Gathering of Days: A New England Girl's Journal, 1830–32* by Joan Blos. Scribner's (Historical fiction [New England, 1830s], ages 11–YA).

HONOR BOOK:

The Road from Home: The Story of an Armenian Girl by David Kherdian. Greenwillow (Historical fiction [Turkey, Greece, 1907–24], ages 11–YA).

1981 *Jacob Have I Loved* by Katherine Paterson. Crowell (Historical fiction [USA, 1940s], ages 12–YA).

HONOR BOOKS:

The Fledgling by Jane Langton. Harper (Modern fantasy, ages 9–11).

A Ring of Endless Light by Madeleine L'Engle. Farrar (Modern fantasy [science fiction], ages 10–12).

1982 *A Visit to William Blake's Inn: Poems for Innocent and Experienced Travelers* by Nancy Willard. Illustrated by Alice and Martin Provensen. Harcourt (Picture book biography/ Poetry, ages 7–10).

HONOR BOOKS:

Ramona Quimby, Age 8 by Beverly Cleary. Morrow (Realism, ages 7–9).

Upon the Head of the Goat: A Childhood in Hungary, 1939–1944 by Aranka Siegal. Farrar (Historical fiction, ages 10–13).

1983 *Dicey's Song* by Cynthia Voigt. Atheneum (Realism, ages 9–12).

HONOR BOOKS:

The Blue Sword by Robin McKinley. Greenwillow (Modern fantasy [quest], ages 12–YA).

Doctor De Soto by William Steig. Farrar (Picture book/Animal fantasy, ages 5–8).

Graven Images by Paul Fleischman. Harper (Modern fantasy, ages 10–12).

Homesick: My Own Story by Jean Fritz. Putnam (Biography, ages 9–11).

Sweet Whispers, Brother Rush by Virginia Hamilton. Philomel (Modern fantasy/Multicultural [African-American], ages 12–YA).

1984 *Dear Mr. Henshaw* by Beverly Cleary. Morrow (Realism, ages 8–10).

HONOR BOOKS:

The Sign of the Beaver by Elizabeth George Speare. Houghton (Historical fiction [Colonial America], ages 9–11).

A Solitary Blue by Cynthia Voigt. Atheneum (Realism, ages 11–13).

Sugaring Time by Kathryn Lasky. Photographs by Christopher Knight. Macmillan (Informational, ages 9–13).

The Wish Giver by Bill Brittain. Harper (Modern fantasy, ages 9–12).

1985 *The Hero and the Crown* by Robin McKinley. Greenwillow (Modern fantasy [quest], ages 12–YA).

HONOR BOOKS:

Like Jake and Me by Mavis Jukes. Illustrated by Lloyd Bloom. Knopf (Picture book; Realism, ages 7–9).

The Moves Make the Man by Bruce Brooks. Harper (Realism/Multicultural [African-American], ages 11–YA).

One-Eyed Cat by Paula Fox. Bradbury (Realism, ages 9–12).

1986 *Sarah, Plain and Tall* by Patricia MacLachlan. Harper (Historical fiction [U.S. western frontier, 1800s], ages 8–10).

HONOR BOOKS:

Commodore Perry in the Land of the Shogun by Rhoda Blumberg. Lothrop (Informational, ages 9–13).

Dogsong by Gary Paulsen. Bradbury (Realism/Multicultural [Native American], ages 10–13).

1987 *The Whipping Boy* by Sid Fleischman. Greenwillow (Historical fiction [Medieval England], ages 9–11).

HONOR BOOKS:

On My Honor by Marion Dane Bauer. Clarion (Realism, ages 8–11).

Volcano: The Eruption and Healing of Mount St. Helens by Patricia Lauber. Bradbury (Informational, ages 8–13).

A Fine White Dust by Cynthia Rylant. Bradbury (Realism, ages 10–12).

1988 *Lincoln: A Photobiography* by Russell Freedman. Clarion (Biography, ages 8–12).

HONOR BOOKS:

After the Rain by Norma Fox Mazer. Morrow (Realism, ages 12–YA).

Hatchet by Gary Paulsen. Bradbury (Realism, ages 9–13).

1989 *Joyful Noise: Poems for Two Voices* by Paul Fleischman. Harper (Poetry, ages 9–YA).

HONOR BOOKS:

In the Beginning: Creation Stories from around the World by Virginia Hamilton. Harcourt (Traditional, ages 9–YA).

Scorpions by Walter Dean Myers. Harper (Realism/Multicultural [African-American, Hispanic-American], ages 10–13).

1990 *Number the Stars* by Lois Lowry. Houghton (Historical fiction [Denmark, 1940s], ages 8–10).

HONOR BOOKS:

Afternoon of the Elves by Janet Taylor Lisle. Orchard (Realism, ages 10–13).

Shabanu, Daughter of the Wind by Suzanne Fisher Staples. Knopf (Realism, ages 12–YA).

The Winter Room by Gary Paulsen. Orchard (Realism, ages 10–13).

1991 *Maniac Magee* by Jerry Spinelli. Little, Brown (Realism, ages 9–13).

HONOR BOOK:

The True Confessions of Charlotte Doyle by Avi. Orchard (Historical fiction [England, USA, 1830], ages 10–13).

1992 *Shiloh* by Phyllis Reynolds Naylor. Atheneum (Animal realism, ages 8–10).

HONOR BOOKS:

Nothing but the Truth by Avi. Orchard (Realism, ages 10–14).

The Wright Brothers: How They Invented the Airplane by Russell Freedman. Holiday (Informational/Biography, ages 9–12).

1993 *Missing May* by Cynthia Rylant. Orchard (Realism, ages 10–13).

HONOR BOOKS:

The Dark-Thirty: Southern Tales of the Supernatural by Patricia McKissack. Knopf (Modern fantasy/Ghost stories [African-American], ages 8–12).

Somewhere in the Darkness by Walter Dean Myers. Scholastic (Realism [African-American], ages 11–14).

What Hearts by Bruce Brooks. HarperCollins (Realism, ages 11–14).

1994 *The Giver* by Lois Lowry. Houghton (Modern fantasy, ages 10–12).

HONOR BOOKS:

Crazy Lady by Jane Leslie Conly. HarperCollins (Realism, ages 10–12).

Dragon's Gate by Laurence Yep. HarperCollins (Historical fiction [China, USA West, 1860s], ages 12–14).

Eleanor Roosevelt: A Life of Discovery by Russell Freedman. Clarion (Biography, ages 10–14).

1995 *Walk Two Moons* by Sharon Creech. HarperCollins (Realism [Native-American], ages 11–14).

HONOR BOOKS:

Catherine, Called Birdy by Karen Cushman. Clarion (Historical fiction, [England, 1200s] ages 10–14).

The Ear, the Eye, and the Arm by Nancy Farmer. Orchard (Modern fantasy, ages 10–13).

1996 *The Midwife's Apprentice* by Karen Cushman. Clarion (Historical fiction [England, 1200s], ages 10–14).

HONOR BOOKS:

The Great Fire by Jim Murphy. Scholastic (Informational, ages 9–13).

The Watsons Go to Birmingham—1963 by Christopher Paul Curtis. Delacorte (Historical fiction [U.S. South, 1960s; African-American], ages 10–14).

What Jamie Saw by Carolyn Coman. Front Street (Realism, ages 10–14).

Yolanda's Genius by Carol Fenner. McElderry (Realism/Multicultural [African-American], ages 10–14).

1997 *The View from Saturday* by E. L. Konigsburg. Atheneum (Realism, ages 9–12).

HONOR BOOKS:

A Girl Named Disaster by Nancy Farmer. Orchard (Realism/Multicultural [Black African], ages 12–14).

The Moorchild by Eloise McGraw. McElderry/Simon & Schuster (Modern fantasy, ages 9–12).

The Thief by Megan Whalen Turner. Greenwillow (Modern fantasy, ages 12–YA).

Belle Prater's Boy by Ruth White. Farrar (Realism, ages 10–12).

1998 *Out of the Dust* by Karen Hesse. Scholastic (Historical fiction [USA, 1920–1934], ages 14–YA).

HONOR BOOKS:

Lily's Crossing by Patricia Reilly Giff. Delacorte (Historical fiction [United States, 1944], ages 9–11).

Ella Enchanted by Gail Carson Levine. HarperCollins (Modern fantasy, ages 9–12).

Wringer by Jerry Spinelli. HarperCollins (Realism, ages 9–12).

1999 *Holes* by Louis Sachar. Farrar (Realism, ages 10–13).

HONOR BOOK:

A Long Way from Chicago by Richard Peck. Dial (Historical fiction [United States, 1930s], ages 9–12).

2000 *Bud, Not Buddy* by Christopher Paul Curtis. Delacorte (Multicultural [African-American], ages 9–12).

HONOR BOOKS:

Getting Near to Baby by Audrey Couloumbis. Putnam (Realism, ages 10–12).

26 Fairmount Avenue by Tomie dePaola. Putnam (Biography, ages 7–9).

Our Only May Amelia by Jennifer L. Holm. HarperCollins (Historical fiction [United States, 1899], ages 10–14).

2001 *A Year Down Yonder* by Richard Peck. Dial (Historical fiction [United States, 1930s], ages 10–14).

HONOR BOOKS:

Because of Winn Dixie by Kate DiCamillo. Candlewick (Animal realism, ages 8–12).

Hope Was Here by Joan Bauer. Putnam (Realism, ages 12–14).

Joey Pigza Loses Control by Jack Gantos. Farrar (Realism, ages 9–12).

The Wanderer by Sharon Creech. HarperCollins (Realism, ages 12–14).

2002 *A Single Shard* by Linda Sue Park. Clarion/Houghton (Realism, ages 10–14).

HONOR BOOKS:

Everything on a Waffle by Polly Horvath. Farrar (Realism, ages 12–14).

Carver: A Life In Poems by Marilyn Nelson. Front Street (Poetry/Biography, ages 12–14).

2003 *Crispin: The Cross of Lead* by Avi. Hyperion (Modern fantasy, ages 8–12).

HONOR BOOKS:

The House of the Scorpion by Nancy Farmer. Atheneum (Modern fantasy, ages 11–14).

Pictures of Hollis Woods by Patricia Reilly Giff. Random House (Realism, ages 10–13).

Hoot by Carl Hiaasen. Knopf (Realism, ages 9–12).

A Corner of the Universe by Ann M. Martin. Scholastic (Realism, ages 11–14).

Surviving the Applewhites by Stephanie S. Tolan. HarperCollins (Realism, ages 12–YA).

2004 *The Tale of Despereaux: Being the Story of a Mouse, a Princess, Some Soup, and a Spool of Thread* by Kate DiCamillo. Illustrated by Timothy Basil Ering. Candlewick (Modern fantasy, ages 5–8).

HONOR BOOKS:
Olive's Ocean by Kevin Henkes. Greenwillow (Realism, ages 9–12).
An American Plague: The True and Terrifying Story of the Yellow Fever Epidemic of 1793 by Jim Murphy. Clarion (Informational, ages 9–14).

Boston Globe—Horn Book Awards

*These awards, sponsored by **The Boston Globe** and **The Horn Book Magazine**, are given to an author for outstanding fiction or poetry for children, to an illustrator for outstanding illustration in a children's book, and, since 1976, to an author for outstanding nonfiction for children.*

1967   TEXT: *The Little Fishes* by Erik Christian Haugaard. Houghton.

ILLUSTRATION: *London Bridge Is Falling Down* by Peter Spier. Doubleday.

1968   TEXT: *The Spring Rider* by John Lawson. Crowell.

ILLUSTRATION: *Tikki Tikki Tembo* by Arlene Mosel. Illustrated by Blair Lent. Holt.

1969   TEXT: *A Wizard of Earthsea* by Ursula K. Le Guin. Houghton.

ILLUSTRATION: *The Adventures of Paddy Pork* by John S. Goodall. Harcourt.

1970   TEXT: *The Intruder* by John Rowe Townsend. Lippincott.

ILLUSTRATION: *Hi, Cat!* by Ezra Jack Keats. Macmillan.

1971   TEXT: *A Room Made of Windows* by Eleanor Cameron. Atlantic/Little.

ILLUSTRATION: *If I Built a Village* by Kazue Mizumura. Crowell.

1972   TEXT: *Tristan and Iseult* by Rosemary Sutcliff. Dutton.

ILLUSTRATION: *Mr. Gumpy's Outing* by John Burningham. Holt.

1973   TEXT: *The Dark Is Rising* by Susan Cooper. Atheneum/McElderry.

ILLUSTRATION: *King Stork* by Trina Schart Hyman. Little, Brown.

1974   TEXT: *M. C. Higgins, the Great* by Virginia Hamilton. Macmillan.

ILLUSTRATION: *Jambo Means Hello* by Muriel Feelings. Illustrated by Tom Feelings. Dial.

1975   TEXT: *Transport 7–41-R* by T. Degens. Viking.

ILLUSTRATION: *Anno's Alphabet* by Mitsumasa Anno. Crowell.

1976   FICTION: *Unleaving* by Jill Paton Walsh, Farrar.

NONFICTION: *Voyaging to Cathay: Americans in the China Trade* by Alfred Tamarin and Shirley Glubok. Viking.

ILLUSTRATION: *Thirteen* by Remy Charlip and Jerry Joyner. Parents.

1977   FICTION: *Child of the Owl* by Laurence Yep. Harper.

NONFICTION: *Chance, Luck and Destiny* by Peter Dickinson. Atlantic/Little, Brown.

ILLUSTRATION: *Granfa' Grig Had a Pig and Other Rhymes* by Wallace Tripp. Little, Brown.

1978   FICTION: *The Westing Game* by Ellen Raskin. Dutton.

NONFICTION: *Mischling, Second Degree: My Childhood in Nazi Germany* by Ilse Koehn. Greenwillow.

ILLUSTRATION: *Anno's Journey* by Mitsumasa Anno. Philomel.

1979   FICTION: *Humbug Mountain* by Sid Fleischman. Atlantic/Little, Brown.

NONFICTION: *The Road from Home: The Story of an Armenian Girl* by David Kherdian. Greenwillow.

ILLUSTRATION: *The Snowman* by Raymond Briggs. Random.

1980   FICTION: *Conrad's War* by Andrew Davies. Crown.

NONFICTION: *Building: The Fight against Gravity* by Mario Salvadori. Atheneum/McElderry.

ILLUSTRATION: *The Garden of Abdul Gasazi* by Chris Van Allsburg. Houghton.

1981   FICTION: *The Leaving* by Lynn Hall. Scribner's.

NONFICTION: *The Weaver's Gift* by Kathryn Lasky. Warne.

ILLUSTRATION: *Outside over There* by Maurice Sendak. Harper.

1982 FICTION: *Playing Beatie Bow* by Ruth Park. Atheneum.

NONFICTION: *Upon the Head of the Goat: A Childhood in Hungary, 1939–1944* by Aranka Siegal. Farrar.

ILLUSTRATION: *A Visit to William Blake's Inn: Poems for Innocent and Experienced Travelers* by Nancy Willard. Illustrated by Alice and Martin Provensen. Harcourt.

1983 FICTION: *Sweet Whispers, Brother Rush* by Virginia Hamilton. Philomel.

NONFICTION: *Behind Barbed Wire: The Imprisonment of Japanese Americans during World War II.* by Daniel S. Davis. Dutton.

ILLUSTRATION: *A Chair for My Mother* by Vera B. Williams. Greenwillow.

1984 FICTION: *A Little Fear* by Patricia Wrightson. McElderry/Atheneum.

NONFICTION: *The Double Life of Pocahontas* by Jean Fritz. Putnam.

ILLUSTRATION: *Jonah and the Great Fish* retold and illustrated by Warwick Hutton. McElderry/Atheneum.

1985 FICTION: *The Moves Make the Man* by Bruce Brooks. Harper.

NONFICTION: *Commodore Perry in the Land of the Shogun* by Rhoda Blumberg. Lothrop.

ILLUSTRATION: *Mama Don't Allow* by Thatcher Hurd. Harper.

1986 FICTION: *In Summer Light* by Zibby Oneal. Viking Kestrel.

NONFICTION: *Auks, Rocks, and the Odd Dinosaur* by Peggy Thomson. Crowell.

ILLUSTRATION: *The Paper Crane* by Molly Bang. Greenwillow.

1987 FICTION: *Rabble Starkey* by Lois Lowry. Houghton.

NONFICTION: *Pilgrims of Plimoth* by Marcia Sewall. Atheneum.

ILLUSTRATION: *Mufaro's Beautiful Daughters* by John Steptoe. Lothrop.

1988 FICTION: *The Friendship* by Mildred Taylor. Dial.

NONFICTION: *Anthony Burns: The Defeat and Triumph of a Fugitive Slave* by Virginia Hamilton. Knopf.

ILLUSTRATION: *The Boy of the Three-Year Nap* by Diane Snyder. Illustrated by Allen Say. Houghton.

1989 FICTION: *The Village by the Sea* by Paula Fox. Orchard.

NONFICTION: *The Way Things Work* by David Macaulay. Houghton.

ILLUSTRATION: *Shy Charles* by Rosemary Wells. Dial.

1990 FICTION: *Maniac Magee* by Jerry Spinelli. Little, Brown.

NONFICTION: *The Great Little Madison* by Jean Fritz. Putnam.

ILLUSTRATION: *Lon Po Po: A Red-Riding Hood Story from China* retold and illustrated by Ed Young. Philomel.

1991 FICTION: *The True Confessions of Charlotte Doyle* by Avi. Orchard.

NONFICTION: *Appalachia: The Voices of Sleeping Birds* by Cynthia Rylant. Illustrated by Barry Moser. Harcourt.

ILLUSTRATION: *The Tale of the Mandarin Ducks* retold by Katherine Paterson. Illustrated by Leo and Diane Dillon. Lodestar.

1992 FICTION: *Missing May* by Cynthia Rylant, Orchard.

NONFICTION: *Talking with Artists* by Pat Cummings, Bradbury.

ILLUSTRATION: *Seven Blind Mice* by Ed Young, Philomel.

1993 FICTION: *Ajeemah and His Son* by James Berry, Harper.

NONFICTION: *Sojourner Truth: Ain't I a Woman?* by Patricia and Fredrick McKissack, Scholastic.

ILLUSTRATION: *The Fortune-Tellers* by Lloyd Alexander. Illustrated by Trina Schart Hyman, Dutton.

1994 FICTION: *Scooter* by Vera B. Williams, Greenwillow.

NONFICTION: *Eleanor Roosevelt: A Life of Discovery* by Russell Freedman, Clarion.

ILLUSTRATION: *Grandfather's Journey* by Allen Say, Houghton.

1995 FICTION: *Some of the Kinder Planets* by Tim Wynne-Jones, Orchard.

NONFICTION: *Abigail Adams: Witness to a Revolution* by Natalie S. Bober. Atheneum.

ILLUSTRATION: *John Henry* retold by Julius Lester. Illustrated by Jerry Pinkney. Dial.

1996 FICTION: *Poppy* by Avi. Illustrated by Brian Floca. Orchard.

NONFICTION: *Orphan Train Rider: One Boy's True Story* by Andrea Warren. Houghton.

ILLUSTRATION: *In the Rain with Baby Duck* by Amy Hest. Illustrated by Jill Barton. Candlewick.

1997 FICTION: *The Friends* by Kazumi Yumoto. Farrar.

NONFICTION: *A Drop of Water: A Book of Science and Wonder* by Walter Wick. Scholastic.

ILLUSTRATION: *The Adventures of Sparrow Boy* by Brian Pinkney. Simon & Schuster.

1998 FICTION: *The Circuit: Stories from the Life of a Migrant Child* by Francisco Jiménez. University of New Mexico Press.

NONFICTION: *Leon's Story* by Leon Walter Tillage. Illustrated by Susan L. Roth. Farrar.

ILLUSTRATION: *And If the Moon Could Talk* by Kate Banks. Illustrated by Georg Hallensleben. Farrar.

1999 FICTION: *Holes* by Louis Sachar. Farrar.

NONFICTION: *The Top of the World: Climbing Mount Everest* by Steve Jenkins. Houghton.

ILLUSTRATION: *Red-Eyed Tree Frog* by Joy Cowley. Illustrated with photographs by Nic Bishop. Scholastic.

2000 FICTION: *The Folk Keeper* by Franny Billingsley. Atheneum.

NONFICTION: *Sir Walter Ralegh and the Quest for El Dorado* by Marc Aronson. Clarion.

ILLUSTRATION: *Henry Hikes to Fitchburg* by D. B. Johnson. Houghton.

2001 FICTION: *Carver: A Life In Poems* by Marilyn Nelson. Front Street.

NONFICTION: *The Longitude Prize* by Joan Dash. Illustrated by Dušan Petricic. Farrar.

ILLUSTRATION: *Cold Feet* by Cynthia DeFelice. Illustrated by Robert Andrew Parker. DK Ink.

2002 FICTION: *Lord of the Deep* by Graham Salisbury. Delacorte.

NONFICTION: *This Land was Made for You and Me: The Life and Songs of Woody Guthrie* by Elizabeth Partridge. Viking.

ILLUSTRATION: *"Let's Get a Pup!" Said Kate* by Bob Graham. Candlewick.

2003 FICTION: *The Jamie and Angus Stories* by Anne Fine. Illustrated by Penny Dale. Candlewick.

NONFICTION: *Fireboat: The Heroic Adventures of the John J. Harvey* by Maira Kalman. Putnam.

ILLUSTRATION: *Big Momma Makes the World* by Phyllis Root. Illustrated by Helen Oxenbury. Candlewick.

National Book Award for Young People's Literature

This award, sponsored by the National Book Foundation, is presented annually to recognize what is judged to be the outstanding contribution to children's literature, in terms of literary merit, published during the previous year. The award committee considers books of all genres written for children and young adults by U.S. writers. The award, which was added to the U.S. National Book Awards in 1996, carries a $10,000 cash prize.

1996 *Parrot in the Oven: Mi Vida* by Victor Martinez. HarperCollins.

1997 *Dancing on the Edge* by Han Nolan. Harcourt.

1998 *Holes* by Louis Sachar. Farrar.

1999 *When Zachary Beaver Came to Town* by Kimberley Willis Holt. Holt.

2000 *Homeless Bird* by Gloria Whelan. HarperCollins.

2001 *True Believer* by Virginia Euwer Wolff. Atheneum.

2002 *The House of the Scorpion* by Nancy Farmer. Atheneum.

2003 *The Canning Season* by Polly Horvath. Farrar.

GREAT BRITAIN

Kate Greenaway Medal

This award, sponsored by the Chartered Institute of Library and Information Professionals, is given to the illustrator of the most distinguished work in illustration in a children's book first published in the United Kingdom during the preceding year.

1957 *Tim All Alone* by Edward Ardizzone. Oxford.

1958 *Mrs. Easter and the Storks* by V. H. Drummond. Faber.

1959 No award

1960 *Kashtanka and a Bundle of Ballads* by William Stobbs. Oxford.

1961 *Old Winkle and the Seagulls* by Elizabeth Rose. Illustrated by Gerald Rose. Faber.

1962 *Mrs. Cockle's Cat* by Philippa Pearce. Illustrated by Anthony Maitland. Kestrel.

1963 *Brian Wildsmith's ABC* by Brian Wildsmith. Oxford.

1964 *Borka* by John Burningham. Jonathan Cape.

1965 *Shakespeare's Theatre* by C. W. Hodges. Oxford.

1966 *Three Poor Tailors* by Victor Ambrus. Hamilton.

1967 *Mother Goose Treasury* by Raymond Briggs. Hamilton.

1968 *Charlie, Charlotte & the Golden Canary* by Charles Keeping. Oxford.

1969 *Dictionary of Chivalry* by Grant Uden. Illustrated by Pauline Baynes. Kestrel.

1970 *The Quangle-Wangle's Hat* by Edward Lear. Illustrated by Helen Oxenbury. Heinemann.
Dragon of an Ordinary Family by Margaret Mahy. Illustrated by Helen Oxenbury. Heinemann.

1971 *Mr. Gumpy's Outing* by John Burningham. Jonathan Cape.

1972 *The Kingdom under the Sea* by Jan Piénkowski. Jonathan Cape.

1973 *The Woodcutter's Duck* by Krystyna Turska. Hamilton.

1974 *Father Christmas* by Raymond Briggs. Hamilton.

1975 *The Wind Blew* by Pat Hutchins. Bodley Head.

1976 *Horses in Battle* by Victor Ambrus. Oxford.
Mishka by Victor Ambrus. Oxford.

1977 *The Post Office Cat* by Gail E. Haley. Bodley Head.

1978 *Dogger* by Shirley Hughes. Bodley Head.

1979 *Each Peach Pear Plum* by Janet and Allan Ahlberg. Kestrel.

1980 *The Haunted House* by Jan Piénkowski. Heinemann.

1981 *Mr. Magnolia* by Quentin Blake. Jonathan Cape.

1982 *The Highwayman* by Alfred Noyes. Illustrated by Charles Keeping. Oxford.

1983 *Long Neck and Thunder Foot.* Kestrel; and *Sleeping Beauty and Other Favorite Fairy Tales.* Gollancz. Both illustrated by Michael Foreman.

1984 *Gorilla* by Anthony Browne. Julia MacRae Books.

1985 *Hiawatha's Childhood* by Errol LeCain. Faber.

1986 *Sir Gawain and the Loathly Lady* by Selina Hastings. Illustrated by Juan Wijngaard. Walker.

1987 *Snow White in New York* by Fiona French. Oxford.

1988 *Crafty Chameleon* by Mwenye Hadithi. Illustrated by Adrienne Kennaway. Hodder & Stoughton.

1989 *Can't You Sleep, Little Bear?* by Martin Waddell. Illustrated by Barbara Firth. Walker.

1990 *War Boy: A Country Childhood* by Michael Foreman. Arcade.

1991 *The Whale's Song* by Dyan Sheldon. Illustrated by Gary Blythe. Dial.

1992 *The Jolly Christmas Postman* by Janet and Allan Ahlberg. Heinemann.

1993 *Zoo* by Anthony Browne. Julia MacRae.

1994 *Black Ships before Troy* retold by Rosemary Sutcliff. Illustrated by Alan Lee. Frances Lincoln.

1995 *Way Home* by Libby Hathorn. Illustrated by Gregory Rogers. Random House.

1996 *The Christmas Miracle of Jonathon Toomey* by Susan Wojciechowski. Illustrated by P. J. Lynch. Walker.

1997 *The Baby Who Wouldn't Go to Bed* by Helen Cooper. Doubleday.

1998 *When Jessie Came Across the Sea* by Amy Hest. Illustrated by P. J. Lynch. Candlewick.

1999 *Pumpkin Soup* by Helen Cooper. Farrar.

2000 *Alice's Adventures in Wonderland* by Lewis Carroll. Illustrated by Helen Oxenbury. Walker.

2001 *I Will Never Not Ever Eat a Tomato* by Lauren Child. Orchard.

2002 *Pirate Diary* by Chris Riddell. Walker.

2003 *Jethro Byrd—Fairy Child* by Bob Graham. Walker.

Carnegie Medal

This award, sponsored by the Chartered Institute of Library and Information Professionals, is given to the author of the most outstanding children's book first published in English in the United Kingdom during the preceding year.

1937 *Pigeon Post* by Arthur Ransome. Cape.

1938 *The Family from One End Street* by Eve Garnett. Muller.

1939 *The Circus Is Coming* by Noel Streatfield. Dent.

1940 *Radium Woman* by Eleanor Doorly. Heinemann.

1941 *Visitors from London* by Kitty Barne. Dent.

1942 *We Couldn't Leave Dinah* by Mary Treadgold. Penguin.

1943 *The Little Grey Men* by B. B. Eyre & Spottiswoode.

1944 No award

1945 *The Wind on the Moon* by Eric Linklater. Macmillan.

1946 No award

1947 *The Little White Horse* by Elizabeth Goudge. Brockhampton Press.

1948 *Collected Stories for Children* by Walter de la Mare. Faber.

1949 *Sea Change* by Richard Armstrong. Dent.

1950 *The Story of Your Home* by Agnes Allen. Transatlantic.

1951 *The Lark on the Wing* by Elfrida Vipont Foulds. Oxford.

1952 *The Wool-Pack* by Cynthia Harnett. Methuen.

1953 *The Borrowers* by Mary Norton. Dent.

1954 *A Valley Grows Up* by Edward Osmond. Oxford.

1955 *Knight Crusader* by Ronald Welch. Oxford.

1956 *The Little Bookroom* by Eleanor Farjeon. Oxford.

1957 *The Last Battle* by C. S. Lewis. Bodley Head.

1958 *A Grass Rope* by William Mayne. Oxford.

1959 *Tom's Midnight Garden* by Philippa Pearce. Oxford.

1960 *The Lantern Bearers* by Rosemary Sutcliff. Oxford.

1961 *The Making of Man* by I. W. Cornwall. Phoenix.

1962 *A Stranger at Green Knowe* by Lucy Boston. Faber.

1963 *The Twelve and the Genii* by Pauline Clarke. Faber.

1964 *Time of Trial* by Hester Burton. Oxford.

1965 *Nordy Banks* by Sheena Porter. Oxford.

1966 *The Grange at High Force* by Philip Turner. Oxford.

1967 No award

1968 *The Owl Service* by Alan Garner. Collins.

1969 *The Moon in the Cloud* by Rosemary Harris. Faber.

1970 *The Edge of the Cloud* by K. M. Peyton. Oxford.

1971 *The God beneath the Sea* by Leon Garfield and Edward Blishen. Kestrel.

1972 *Josh* by Ivan Southall. Angus and Robertson.

1973 *Watership Down* by Richard Adams. Rex Collings.

1974 *The Ghost of Thomas Kempe* by Penelope Lively. Heinemann.

1975 *The Stronghold* by Mollie Hunter. Hamilton.

1976 *The Machine-Gunners* by Robert Westall. Macmillan.

1977 *Thunder and Lightnings* by Jan Mark. Kestrel.

1978 *The Turbulent Term of Tyke Tiler* by Gene Kemp. Faber.

1979 *The Exeter Blitz* by David Rees. Hamish Hamilton.

1980 *Tulku* by Peter Dickinson. Dutton.

1981 *City of Gold* by Peter Dickinson. Gollancz.

1982 *The Scarecrows* by Robert Westall. Chatto and Windus.

1983 *The Haunting* by Margaret Mahy. Dent.

1984 *Handles* by Jan Mark. Kestrel.

1985 *The Changeover* by Margaret Mahy. Dent.

1986 *Storm* by Kevin Crossley-Holland. Heinemann.

1987 *Granny Was a Buffer Girl* by Berlie Doherty. Methuen.

1988 *The Ghost Drum* by Susan Price. Faber.

1989 *Pack of Lies* by Geraldine McCaughrean. Oxford.

1990 *My War with Goggle-Eyes* by Anne Fine. Joy Street.

1991 *Wolf* by Gillian Cross. Oxford.

1992 *Dear Nobody* by Berlie Doherty. Hamish Hamilton.

1993 *Flour Babies* by Anne Fine. Hamish Hamilton.

1994 *Stone Cold* by Robert Swindells. Hamish Hamilton.

1995 *Whispers in the Graveyard* by Theresa Bresling. Methuen.

1996 *Dark Materials: Book 1, Northern Lights* by Philip Pullman. Scholastic.

1997 *Junk* by Melvin Burgess. Andersen.

1998 *River Boy* by Tim Bowler. Oxford.

1999 *Skellig* by David Almond. Delacorte.

2000 *Postcards from No Man's Land* by Aidan Chambers. Bodley Head.

2001 *The Other Side of Truth* by Beverly Naidoo. Puffin/HarperCollins.

2002 *The Amazing Maurice and His Educated Rodents* by Terry Pratchett. Doubleday/HarperCollins.

2003 *Ruby Holler* by Sharon Creech. Bloomsbury/HarperCollins.

CANADA

The Governor General's Literary Awards

The Governor General's Literary Awards were inaugurated in 1937, with separate prizes for children's literature (text and illustration) being *added in 1987. The Canada Council for the Arts assumed responsibility for funding, administering, and adjudicating the awards in 1959, and added prizes for works written in French. Monetary prizes were introduced in 1951. The current prize to winners in each category—$15,000—dates from 2000. In addition, publishers of the winning books receive $3,000 to assist with promotion.*

1987 ILLUSTRATION: *Rainy Day Magic* by Marie-Louise Gay. Stoddart.

TEXT: *Galahad Schwartz and the Cockroach Army* by Morgan Nyberg. Douglas & McIntyre.

1988 ILLUSTRATION: *Amos's Sweater* by Janet Lunn. Illustrated by Kim LeFave. Douglas & McIntyre.

TEXT: *The Third Magic* by Welwyn Wilton Katz. Douglas & McIntyre.

1989 ILLUSTRATION: *The Magic Paintbrush* by Robin Muller. Doubleday Canada.

TEXT: *Bad Boy* by Diana Wieler. Douglas & McIntyre.

1990 ILLUSTRATION: *The Orphan Boy* by Tololwa Mollel. Illustrated by Paul Morin. Oxford.

TEXT: *Redwork* by Michael Bedard. Lester & Orpen Dennys.

1991 ILLUSTRATION: *Doctor Kiss Says Yes* by Teddy Jam. Illustrated by Joanne Fitzgerald. Groundwood.

TEXT: *Pick-Up Sticks* by Sarah Ellis. Groundwood.

1992 ILLUSTRATION: *Waiting for the Whales* by Sheryl McFarlane. Illustrated by Ron Lightburn. Orca.

TEXT: *Hero of Lesser Causes* by Julie Johnson. Lester.

1993 ILLUSTRATION: *Sleep Tight, Mrs. Ming* by Sharon Jennings. Illustrated by Mireille Levert. Annick.

TEXT: *Some of the Kinder Planets* by Tim Wynne-Jones. Groundwood.

1994 ILLUSTRATION: *Josepha: A Prairie Boy's Story* by Jim McGugen. Illustrated by Murray Kimber. Red Deer College Press.

TEXT: *Adam and Eve and Pinch-Me* by Julie Johnson. Lester.

1995 ILLUSTRATION: *The Last Quest of Gilgamesh* by Ludmila Zeman, reteller. Tundra.

TEXT: *The Maestro* by Tim Wynne-Jones. Groundwood.

1996 ILLUSTRATION: *The Rooster's Gift* by Pam Conrad. Illustrated by Eric Beddows. Groundwood.

TEXT: *Ghost Train* by Paul Yee. Groundwood.

1997 ILLUSTRATION: *The Party* by Barbara Reid. Scholastic Canada.

TEXT: *Awake and Dreaming* by Kit Pearson. Viking.

1998 ILLUSTRATION: *A Child's Treasury of Nursery Rhymes* by Kady MacDonald Denton. Kids Can.

TEXT: *The Hollow Tree* by Janet Lunn. Knopf Canada.

1999 ILLUSTRATION: *The Great Poochini* by Gary Clement. Groundwood.

TEXT: *A Screaming Kind of Day* by Rachna Gilmore. Fitzhenry & Whiteside.

2000 ILLUSTRATION: *Yuck, a Love Story* by Don Gillmore. Illustrated by Marie-Louise Gay. Stoddart Kids.

TEXT: *Looking for X* by Deborah Ellis. Groundwood.

2001 ILLUSTRATION: *An Island in the Soup* by Mireille Levert. Groundwood.

TEXT: *Dust* by Arthur Slade. HarperCollins Canada.

2002 ILLUSTRATION: *Alphabeasts* by Wallace Edwards. Kids Can.

TEXT: *True Confessions of a Heartless Girl* by Martha Brooks. Groundwood.

2003 ILLUSTRATION: *The Song within My Heart* by Dave Bouchard. Illustrated by Allen Sapp. Raincoast.

TEXT: *Stitches* by Glen Huser. Groundwood.

AUSTRALIA

Australian Children's Books of the Year Awards

The Children's Book Council of Australia sponsors five awards for excellence in children's books: the Picture Book of the Year Award; the Book of the Year for Early Childhood (since 2001); The Australian Younger Reader Award; the Australian Older Reader Award; and the Eve Pownall Award for Information Books (not listed here).

Australian Picture Book of the Year Award

(May be for mature readers.)

1956 *Wish and the Magic Nut* by Peggy Barnard. Illustrated by Shelia Hawkins. Sands.

1957 No award

1958 *Piccaninny Walkabout* by Axel Poignant. Angus & Robertson.

1959–1964 No awards

1965 *Hugo's Zoo* by Elizabeth MacIntyre. Angus & Robertson.

1966–1968 No awards

1969 *Sly Old Wardrobe* by Ivan Southall. Illustrated by Ted Greenwood. Cheshire.

1970 No award

1971 *Waltzing Matilda* by A. B. Paterson. Illustrated by Desmond Digby.

1972–1973 No awards

1974 *The Bunyip of Berkeley's Creek* by Jenny Wagner. Illustrated by Ron Brooks. Kestrel.

1975 *The Man from Ironbark* by A. B. Paterson. Illustrated by Quentin Hole. Collins.

1976 *The Rainbow Serpent* by Dick Roughsey. Collins.

1977 *ABC of Monsters* by Deborah Niland. Hodder & Stoughton.

1978 *John Brown, Rose and the Midnight Cat* by Jenny Wagner. Illustrated by Ron Brooks. Kestrel.

1979 *The Quinkins* written and illustrated by Percy Trezise and Dick Roughsey. Collins.

1980 *One Dragon's Dream* by Peter Pavey. Nelson.

1981 No award

1982 *Sunshine* by Jan Ormerod. Kestrel.

1983 *Who Sank the Boat?* by Pamela Allen. Nelson.

1984 *Bertie and the Bear* by Pamela Allen, Nelson.

1985 No award

Highly commended: *The Inch Boy* by Junko Morimoto. Collins.

1986 *Felix and Alexander* written and illustrated by Terry Denton. Oxford.

1987 *Kojuro and the Bears* adapted by Helen Smith. Illustrated by Junko Morimoto. Collins.

1988 *Crusher Is Coming!* by Bob Graham. Lothian.

1989 *Drac and the Gremlins* by Allan Baillie. Illustrated by Jane Tanner. Viking/Kestrel.

The Eleventh Hour by Graeme Base. Viking/Kestrel.

1990 *The Very Best of Friends* by Margaret Wild. Illustrated by Julie Vivas. Margaret Hamilton.

1991 *Greetings from Sandy Beach* by Bob Graham. Lothian.

1992 *Window* by Jeannie Baker. Julia MacRae.

1993 *Rose Meets Mr Wintergarden* by Bob Graham. Viking/Penguin.

1994 *First Light* by Gary Crew. Illustrated by Peter Gouldthorpe. Lothian.

1995 *The Watertower* by Gary Crew. Illustrated by Steven Woolman. Era.

1996 *The Hunt* by Narelle Oliver. Lothian.

1997 *Not a Nibble* by Elizabeth Honey. Allen & Unwin.

1998 *The Two Bullies* by Junko Morimoto. Translated by Isao Morimoto. Crown.

1999 *The Rabbits* by John Marsden. Illustrated by Shaun Tan. Lothian.

2000 *Jenny Angel* by Margaret Wild. Illustrated by Anne Spudvilas. Penguin.

2001 *Fox* by Margaret Wild. Illustrated by Ron Brooks. Allen & Unwin.

2002 *An Ordinary Day* by Libby Gleeson. Illustrated by Armin Greder. Scholastic.

2003 *In Flanders Fields* by Norman Jorgensen. Illustrated by Brian Harrison-Lever. Sandcastle.

Australian Book of the Year for Early Childhood Award

2001 *You'll Wake the Baby!* by Catherine Jinks. Illustrated by Andrew McLean. Penguin.

2002 *Let's Get a Pup!* by Bob Graham. Walker/Candlewick.

2003 *A Year on Our Farm* by Penny Matthews. Omnibus/Scholastic Australia.

Australian Children's Book of the Year for Younger Readers Award

1982 *Rummage* by Cristobel Mattingley. Illustrated by Patricia Mullins. Angus & Robertson.

1983 *Thing* by Robin Klein. Illustrated by Allison Lester. Oxford.

1984 *Bernice Knows Best* by Max Dann. Illustrated by Ann James. Oxford.

1985 *Something Special* by Emily Rodda. Illustrated by Noela Young. Angus & Robertson.

1986 *Arkwright* by Mary Steele. Hyland House.

1987 *Pigs Might Fly* by Emily Rodda. Illustrated by Noela Young. Angus & Robertson.

1988 *My Place* by Nadia Wheatley and Donna Rawlins. Collins Dove.

1989 *The Best-Kept Secret* by Emily Rodda. Angus & Robertson.

1990 *Pigs and Honey* by Jeanie Adams. Omnibus.

1991 *Finders Keepers* by Emily Rodda. Omnibus.

1992 *The Magnificent Nose and Other Marvels* by Anna Fienberg. Illustrated by Kim Gamble. Allen and Unwin.

1993 *The Bamboo Flute* by Garry Disher. Collins/Angus & Robertson.

1994 *Rowan of Rin* by Emily Rodda. Omnibus.

1995 *Ark in the Park* by Wendy Orr. HarperCollins.

1996 *Swashbuckler* by James Moloney. University of Queensland Press.

1997 *Hannah Plus One* by Libby Gleeson. Illustrated by Ann James. Penguin.

1998 *Someone Like Me* by Elaine Forrestal. Penguin.

1999 *My Girragundji* by Meme McDonald and Boori Pryor. Illustrated by Meme McDonald. Allen & Unwin

2000 *Hitler's Daughter* by Jackie French. HarperCollins.

2001 *Two Hands Together* by Diana Kidd. Penguin.

2002 *My Dog* by John Heffernan. Illustrated by Andrew McLean. Scholastic Australia.

2003 *Rain May and Captain Daniel* by Catherine Bateson. University of Queensland Press.

Australian Children's Book of the Year for Older Readers Award

(For mature readers)

1946 *Karrawingi, the Emu* by Leslie Rees. Sands.

1947 No award

1948 *Shackleton's Argonauts* by Frank Hurley. Angus & Robertson.

1949 *Whalers of the Midnight Sun* by Alan Villiers. Angus & Robertson.

1950 No award

1951 *Verity of Sydney Town* by Ruth Williams. Angus & Robertson.

1952 *The Australia Book* by Eve Pownall. Sands.

1953 *Aircraft of Today and Tomorrow* by J. H. Martin and W. D. Martin. Angus & Robertson.
Good Luck to the Rider by Joan Phipson. Angus & Robertson.

1954 *Australian Legendary* by K. L. Parker. Angus & Robertson.

1955 *The First Walkabout* by H. A. Lindsay and N. B. Tindale. Kestrel.

1956 *The Crooked Snake* by Patricia Wrightson. Angus & Robertson.

1957 *The Boomerang Book of Legendary Tales* by Enid Moodie-Heddle. Kestrel.

1958 *Tiger in the Bush* by Nan Chauncy. Oxford.

1959 *Devil's Hill* by Nan Chauncy. Oxford.
Sea Menace by John Gunn. Constable.

1960 *All the Proud Tribesmen* by Kylie Tennant. Macmillan.

1961 *Tangara* by Nan Chauncy. Oxford.

1962 *The Racketty Street Gang* by H. L. Evers. Hodder & Stoughton.
Rafferty Rides a Winner by Joan Woodbery. Parrish.

1963 *The Family Conspiracy* by Joan Phipson. Angus & Robertson.

1964 *The Green Laurel* by Eleanor Spence. Oxford.

1965 *Pastures of the Blue Crane* by Hesba F. Brinsmead. Oxford.

1966 *Ash Road* by Ivan Southall. Angus & Robertson.

1967 *The Min Min* by Mavis Thorpe Clark. Landsdowne.

1968 *To the Wild Sky* by Ivan Southall. Angus & Robertson.

1969 *When Jays Fly to Barbmo* by Margaret Balderson. Oxford.

1970 *Uhu* by Annette Macarther-Onslow. Ure Smith.

1971 *Bread and Honey* by Ivan Southall. Angus & Robertson.

1972 *Longtime Passing* by Hesba F. Brinsmead. Angus & Robertson.

1973 *Family at the Lookout* by Noreen Shelly. Oxford.

1974 *The Nargun and the Stars* by Patricia Wrightson. Hutchinson.

1975 No award

1976 *Fly West* by Ivan Southall. Angus & Robertson.

1977 *The October Child* by Eleanor Spence. Oxford.

1978 *The Ice Is Coming* by Patricia Wrightson. Hutchinson.

1979 *The Plum-Rain Scroll* by Ruth Manley. Hodder & Stoughton.

1980 *Displaced Person* by Lee Harding. Hyland House.

1981 *Playing Beatie Bow* by Ruth Park. Nelson.

1982 *The Valley Between* by Colin Thiele. Rigby.

1983 *Master of the Grove* by Victor Kelleher. Penguin.

1984 *A Little Fear* by Patricia Wrightson. Hutchinson.

1985 *The True Story of Lilli Stubeck* by James Aldridge. Hyland House.

1986 *The Green Wind* by Thurley Fowler. Rigby.

1987 *All We Know* by Simon French. Angus & Robertson.

1988 *So Much to Tell You* by John Marsden. Walter McVitty Books.

1989 *Beyond the Labyrinth* by Gillian Rubinstein. Hyland House.

1990 *Came Back to Show You I Could Fly* by Robin Klein. Viking/Kestrel.

1991 *Strange Objects* by Gary Crew. Heinemann Australia.

1992 *The House Guest* by Eleanor Nilsson. Viking.

1993 *Looking for Alibrandi* by Melina Marchetta. Penguin.

1994 *The Gathering* by Isobelle Carmody. Penguin. *Angel's Gate* by Gary Crew. Heinemann.

1995 *Foxspell* by Gillian Rubinstein. Hyland House.

1996 *Pagan's Vows* by Catherine Jinks. Omnibus.

1997 *A Bridge to Wiseman's Cove* by James Moloney. University of Queensland Press.

1998 *Eye to Eye* by Catherine Jinks. Penguin.

1999 *Deadly, Unna?* by Phillip Gwynne. Penguin.

2000 *48 Shades of Brown* by Nick Earls. Penguin.

2001 *Wolf on the Fold* by Judith Clarke. Allen & Unwin.

2002 *Forest* by Sonya Hartnett. Viking.

2003 *The Messenger* by Markus Zusak. Pan Macmillan Australia.

AWARDS FOR A BODY OF WORK

Hans Christian Andersen Award

This international award, sponsored by the International Board on Books for Young People, is given every two years to a living author and, since 1966, to a living illustrator whose complete works have made important international contributions to children's literature.

1956 Eleanor Farjeon (Great Britain)

1958 Astrid Lindgren (Sweden)

1960 Erich Kästner (Germany)

1962 Meindert DeJong (USA)

1964 René Guillot (France)

1966 AUTHOR: Tove Jansson (Finland)
ILLUSTRATOR: Alois Carigiet (Switzerland)

1968 AUTHORS: James Krüss (Germany) and José Maria Sanchez-Silva (Spain)
ILLUSTRATOR: Jirí Trnka (Czechoslovakia)

1970 AUTHOR: Gianni Rodari (Italy)
ILLUSTRATOR: Maurice Sendak (USA)

1972 AUTHOR: Scott O'Dell (USA)
ILLUSTRATOR: Ib Spang Olsen (Denmark)

1974 AUTHOR: Maria Gripe (Sweden)
ILLUSTRATOR: Farshid Mesghali (Iran)

1976 AUTHOR: Cecil Bödker (Denmark)
ILLUSTRATOR: Tatjana Mawrina (USSR)

1978 AUTHOR: Paula Fox (USA)
ILLUSTRATOR: Otto S. Svend (Denmark)

1980 AUTHOR: Bohumil Riha (Czechoslovakia)
ILLUSTRATOR: Suekichi Akaba (Japan)

1982 AUTHOR: Lygia Bojunga Nunes (Brazil)
ILLUSTRATOR: Zbigniew Rychlicki (Poland)

1984 AUTHOR: Christine Nöstlinger (Austria)
ILLUSTRATOR: Mitsumasa Anno (Japan)

1986 AUTHOR: Patricia Wrightson (Australia)
ILLUSTRATOR: Robert Ingpen (Australia)

1988 AUTHOR: Annie M. G. Schmidt (Netherlands)
ILLUSTRATOR: Dušan Kállay (Czechoslovakia)

1990 AUTHOR: Tormod Haugen (Norway)
ILLUSTRATOR: Lisbeth Zwerger (Austria)

1992 AUTHOR: Virginia Hamilton (USA)
ILLUSTRATOR: Kveta Pacovská (Czechoslovakia)

1994 AUTHOR: Michio Mado (Japan)
ILLUSTRATOR: Jörg Müller (Switzerland)

1996 AUTHOR: Uri Orlev (Israel)
ILLUSTRATOR: Klaus Ensikat (Germany)

1998 AUTHOR: Katherine Paterson (USA)
ILLUSTRATOR: Tomi Ungerer (France)

2000 AUTHOR: Ana Maria Machado (Brazil)
ILLUSTRATOR: Anthony Browne (United Kingdom)

2002 AUTHOR: Aidan Chambers (United Kingdom)
ILLUSTRATOR: Quentin Blake (United Kingdom)

2004 AUTHOR: Martin Waddell (Ireland)
ILLUSTRATOR: Max Velthuijs (The Netherlands)

Laura Ingalls Wilder Award

This award, sponsored by the Association for Library Service to Children of the American Library Association, is given to a U.S. author or illustrator whose body of work has made a lasting contribution to children's literature. Between 1960 and 1980, the Wilder Award was given every five years. From 1980 to 2001, it was given every three years. Beginning in 2001, it has been given every two years.

1954 Laura Ingalls Wilder

1960 Clara Ingram Judson

1965 Ruth Sawyer

1970 E. B. White

1975 Beverly Cleary

1980 Theodore S. Geisel (Dr. Seuss)

1983 Maurice Sendak

1986 Jean Fritz

1989 Elizabeth George Speare

1992 Marcia Brown

1995 Virginia Hamilton

1998 Russell Freedman

2001 Milton Meltzer

2003 Eric Carle

NCTE Excellence in Poetry for Children Award

For the list of award winners, see Chapter 3, page 49.

AWARDS FOR SPECIFIC GENRES OR GROUPS

Mildred L. Batchelder Award

This award, sponsored by the ALA's Association for Library Service to Children, is given to the American publisher of a children's book considered to be the most outstanding of those books originally published in a country other than the United States in a language other than English and subsequently translated and published in the United States during the previous year.

1968 *The Little Man* by Erich Kästner. Translated from German by James Kirkup. Illustrated by Rick Schreiter. Knopf.

1969 *Don't Take Teddy* by Babbis Friis-Baastad. Translated from Norwegian by Lise Sömme McKinnon. Scribner's.

1970 *Wildcat under Glass* by Alki Zei. Translated from Greek by Edward Fenton. Holt.

1971 *In the Land of Ur: The Discovery of Ancient Mesopotamia* by Hans Baumann. Translated from German by Stella Humphries. Illustrated by Hans Peter Renner. Pantheon.

1972 *Friedrich* by Hans Peter Richter. Translated from German by Edite Kroll. Holt.

1973 *Pulga* by Siny Rose Van Iterson. Translated from Dutch by Alexander and Alison Gode. Morrow.

1974 *Petros' War* by Alki Zei. Translated from Greek by Edward Fenton, Dutton.

1975 *An Old Tale Carved Out of Stone* by Aleksandr M. Linevski. Translated from Russian by Maria Polushkin. Crown.

1976 *The Cat and Mouse Who Shared a House* written and illustrated by Ruth Hürlimann. Translated from German by Anthea Bell. Walck.

1977 *The Leopard* by Cecil Bödker. Translated from Danish by Gunnar Poulsen. Atheneum.

1978 No award

1979 *Konrad* by Christine Nöstlinger. Translated from German (Austrian) by Anthea Bell. Illustrated by Carol Nicklaus. Watts.

Rabbit Island by Jörg Steiner. Translated from German (Swiss) by Ann Conrad Lammers. Illustrated by Jörg Müller. Harcourt.

1980 *The Sound of Dragon's Feet* by Alki Zei. Translated from Greek by Edward Fenton. Dutton.

1981 *The Winter When Time Was Frozen* by Els Pelgrom. Translated from Dutch by Raphael and Maryka Rudnik. Morrow.

1982 *The Battle Horse* by Harry Kullman. Translated from Swedish by George Blecher and Lone Thygesen-Blecher. Bradbury.

1983 *Hiroshima No Pika* written and illustrated by Toshi Maruki. Translated from Japanese through Kurita-Bando Literary Agency. Lothrop.

1984 *Ronia, the Robber's Daughter* by Astrid Lindgren. Translated from Swedish by Patricia Crampton. Viking.

1985 *The Island on Bird Street* by Uri Orlev. Translated from Hebrew by Hillel Halkin. Houghton.

1986 *Rose Blanche* by Christophe Gallaz and Roberto Innocenti. Translated from French by Martha Coventry and Richard Graglia. Illustrated by Roberto Innocenti. Creative Education.

1987 *No Hero for the Kaiser* by Rudolf Frank. Translated from German by Patricia Crampton. Illustrated by Klaus Steffens. Lothrop.

1988 *If You Didn't Have Me* by Ulf Nilsson. Translated from Swedish by Lone Thygesen-Blecher and George Blecher. Illustrated by Eva Eriksson. McElderry.

1989 *Crutches* by Peter Härtling. Translated from German by Elizabeth D. Crawford. Lothrop.

1990 *Buster's World* by Bjarne Reuter. Translated from Danish by Anthea Bell. Dutton.

1991 *A Hand Full of Stars* by Rafik Schami. Translated from German by Rika Lesser. Dutton.
HONOR BOOK:
Two Short and One Long by Nina Ring Aamundsen. Translated from Norwegian by the author. Houghton.

1992 *The Man from the Other Side* by Uri Orlev. Translated from Hebrew by Hillel Halkin. Houghton.

1993 No award

1994 *The Apprentice* by Pilar Molina Llorente. Illustrated by Juan Ramón Alonso. Translated from Spanish by Robin Longshaw. Farrar.
HONOR BOOKS:
Anne Frank, Beyond the Diary: A Photographic Remembrance by Ruud van der Rol and Rian Verhoeven. Translated from Dutch by Tony Langham and Plym Peters. Viking.
The Princess in the Kitchen Garden by Annemie and Margriet Heymans. Translated from Dutch by Johanna H. Prins and Johanna W. Prins. Farrar.

1995 *The Boys from St. Petri* by Bjarne Reuter. Translated from Danish by Anthea Bell. Dutton.

1996 *The Lady with the Hat* by Uri Orlev. Translated from Hebrew by Hillel Halkin. Houghton.

1997 *The Friends* by Kazumi Yumoto. Translated from Japanese by Cathy Hirano. Farrar.

1998 *The Robber and Me* by Joseph Holub. Translated from German by Elizabeth D. Crawford. Holt.

1999 *Thanks to My Mother* by Schoschana Rabinovici. Translated from German by James Skofield. Dial.

2000 *The Baboon King* by Anton Quintana. Translated from Dutch by John Nieuwenhuizen. Walker.

2001 *Samir and Yonatan* by Daniella Carmi. Translated from Hebrew by Yael Lotan. Levine/Scholastic.

2002 *How I Became an American* by Karin Gündisch. Translated from German by James Skofield. Cricket.

2003 *The Thief Lord* by Cornelia Funke. Translated from German by Oliver Latsch. Scholastic.

2004 *Run, Boy, Run* by Uri Orlev. Translated from Hebrew by Hillel Halkin. Houghton Mifflin.

Coretta Scott King Awards

These awards, founded to commemorate the late Dr. Martin Luther King, Jr., and his wife, Coretta Scott King, for their work in promoting peace and world brotherhood, are given to an African-American author and, since 1974, an African-American illustrator whose children's books, published during the preceding year, made outstanding inspirational and educational contributions to literature for children and young people. The awards are sponsored by the Social Responsibilities Round Table of the American Library Association.

1970 *Martin Luther King, Jr.: Man of Peace* by Lillie Patterson. Garrard.

1971 *Black Troubador: Langston Hughes* by Charlemae Rollins. Rand.

1972 *17 Black Artists* by Elton C. Fax. Dodd.

1973 *I Never Had It Made* by Jackie Robinson as told to Alfred Duckett. Putnam.

1974 AUTHOR: *Ray Charles* by Sharon Bell Mathis. Crowell.

ILLUSTRATOR: The same title, illustrated by George Ford.

1975 AUTHOR: *The Legend of Africana* by Dorothy Robinson. Johnson.

ILLUSTRATOR: The same title, illustrated by Herbert Temple.

1976 AUTHOR: *Duey's Tale* by Pearl Bailey. Harcourt.

ILLUSTRATOR: No award

1977 AUTHOR: *The Story of Stevie Wonder* by James Haskins. Lothrop.

ILLUSTRATOR: No award

1978 AUTHOR: *Africa Dream* by Eloise Greenfield. Day/Crowell.

ILLUSTRATOR: The same title, illustrated by Carole Bayard.

1979 AUTHOR: *Escape to Freedom* by Ossie Davis. Viking.

ILLUSTRATOR: *Something on My Mind* by Nikki Grimes. Illustrated by Tom Feelings. Dial.

1980 AUTHOR: *The Young Landlords* by Walter Dean Myers. Viking.

ILLUSTRATOR: *Cornrows* by Camille Yarbrough. Illustrated by Carole Bayard. Coward.

1981 AUTHOR: *This Life* by Sidney Poitier. Knopf.

ILLUSTRATOR: *Beat the Story-Drum, Pum-Pum* by Ashley Bryan. Atheneum.

1982 AUTHOR: *Let the Circle Be Unbroken* by Mildred D. Taylor. Dial.

ILLUSTRATOR: *Mother Crocodile: An Uncle Amadou Tale from Senegal* adapted by Rosa Guy. Illustrated by John Steptoe. Delacorte.

1983 AUTHOR: *Sweet Whispers, Brother Rush* by Virginia Hamilton. Philomel.

ILLUSTRATOR: *Black Child* by Peter Mugabane. Knopf.

1984 AUTHOR: *Everett Anderson's Good-Bye* by Lucille Clifton. Holt.

ILLUSTRATOR: *My Mama Needs Me* by Mildred Pitts Walter. Illustrated by Pat Cummings. Lothrop.

1985 AUTHOR: *Motown and Didi* by Walter Dean Myers. Viking.

ILLUSTRATOR: No award

1986 AUTHOR: *The People Could Fly: American Black Folktales* by Virginia Hamilton. Knopf.

ILLUSTRATOR: *Patchwork Quilt* by Valerie Flournoy. Illustrated by Jerry Pinkney.

1987 AUTHOR: *Justin and the Best Biscuits in the World* by Mildred Pitts Walter. Lothrop.

ILLUSTRATOR: *Half Moon and One Whole Star* by Crescent Dragonwagon. Illustrated by Jerry Pinkney. Macmillan.

1988 AUTHOR: *The Friendship* by Mildred D. Taylor. Illustrated by Max Ginsburg. Dial.

ILLUSTRATOR: *Mufaro's Beautiful Daughters: An African Tale* retold and illustrated by John Steptoe. Lothrop.

1989 AUTHOR: *Fallen Angels* by Walter Dean Myers. Scholastic.

ILLUSTRATOR: *Mirandy and Brother Wind* by Patricia McKissack. Illustrated by Jerry Pinkney. Knopf.

1990   AUTHOR: *A Long Hard Journey* by Patricia C. and Fredrick L. McKissack. Walker.

ILLUSTRATOR: *Nathaniel Talking* by Eloise Greenfield. Illustrated by Jan Spivey Gilchrist. Black Butterfly Press.

1991   AUTHOR: *The Road to Memphis* by Mildred D. Taylor. Dial.

ILLUSTRATOR: *Aïda* retold by Leontyne Price. Illustrated by Leo and Diane Dillon. Harcourt.

1992   AUTHOR: *Now Is Your Time! The African-American Struggle for Freedom* by Walter Dean Myers. HarperCollins.

ILLUSTRATOR: *Tar Beach* by Faith Ringgold. Crown.

1993   AUTHOR: *The Dark-Thirty: Southern Tales of the Supernatural* by Patricia McKissack. Knopf.

ILLUSTRATOR: *Origins of Life on Earth: An African Creation Myth* by David A. Anderson. Illustrated by Kathleen Atkins Smith. Sight Productions.

1994   AUTHOR: *Toning the Sweep* by Angela Johnson. Orchard.

ILLUSTRATOR: *Soul Looks Back in Wonder* compiled and illustrated by Tom Feelings. Dial.

1995   AUTHOR: *Christmas in the Big House, Christmas in the Quarters* by Patricia C. McKissack and Fredrick L. McKissack. Illustrated by John Thompson. Scholastic.

ILLUSTRATOR: *The Creation* by James Weldon Johnson. Illustrated by James E. Ransome. Holiday.

1996   AUTHOR: *Her Stories: African American Folktales, Fairy Tales, and True Tales* by Virginia Hamilton. Illustrated by Leo and Diane Dillon. Blue Sky.

ILLUSTRATOR: *The Middle Passage: White Ships Black Cargo* by Tom Feelings. Dial.

1997   AUTHOR: *Slam!* by Walter Dean Myers. Scholastic.

ILLUSTRATOR: *Minty: A Story of Young Harriet Tubman* by Alan Schroeder. Illustrated by Jerry Pinkney. Dial.

1998   AUTHOR: *Forged by Fire* by Sharon M. Draper. Atheneum.

ILLUSTRATOR: *In Daddy's Arms I Am Tall: African Americans Celebrating Fathers* by Javaka Steptoe. Lee & Low.

1999   AUTHOR: *Heaven* by Angela Johnson. Simon & Schuster.

ILLUSTRATOR: *i see the rhythm* by Toyomi Igus. Illustrated by Michele Wood. Children's Book Press.

2000   AUTHOR: *Bud, Not Buddy* by Christopher Paul Curtis. Delacorte.

ILLUSTRATOR: *In the Time of the Drums* retold by Kim L. Siegelson. Illustrated by Brian Pinkney. Hyperion.

2001   AUTHOR: *Miracle's Boys* by Jacqueline Woodson. Putnam.

ILLUSTRATOR: *Uptown* by Bryan Collier. Holt.

2002   AUTHOR: *The Land* by Mildred D. Taylor. Fogelman/Penguin Putnam.

ILLUSTRATOR: *Goin' Someplace Special* by Patricia McKissack. Illustrated by Jerry Pinkney. Atheneum.

2003   AUTHOR: *Bronx Masquerade* by Nikki Grimes. Dial.

ILLUSTRATOR: *Talkin' about Bessie: The Story of Aviator Elizabeth Coleman* by Nikki Grimes. Illustrated by E. B. Lewis. Orchard/Scholastic.

2004   AUTHOR: *The First Part Last* by Angela Johnson. Simon & Schuster.

ILLUSTRATOR: *Beautiful Blackbird* by Ashley Bryan. Atheneum.

Pura Belpré Award

The Pura Belpré Award honors Latino writers and illustrators whose work best portrays, affirms, and celebrates the Latino cultural experience in a work of literature for youth. This biennial award is sponsored by the Association for Library Service to Children and the National Association to Promote Library Service to the Spanish Speaking.

1996 AUTHOR: *An Island Like You: Stories of the Barrio* by Judith Ortiz Cofer. Orchard.

ILLUSTRATOR: *Chato's Kitchen* by Gary Soto. Illustrated by Susan Guevara. Putnam.

1998 AUTHOR: *Parrot in the Oven: Mi Vida* by Victor Martinez. HarperCollins.

ILLUSTRATOR: *Snapshots from the Wedding* by Gary Soto. Illustrated by Stephanie Garcia. Putnam.

2000 AUTHOR: *Under the Royal Palms: A Childhood in Cuba* by Alma Flor Ada. Atheneum.

ILLUSTRATOR: *Magic Windows: Cut-Paper Art and Stories* by Carmen Lomas Garza. Children's Book Press.

2002 AUTHOR: *Esperanza Rising* by Pam Muñoz Ryan. Scholastic.

ILLUSTRATOR: *Chato and the Party Animals* by Gary Soto. Illustrated by Susan Guevara. Putnam.

2004 AUTHOR: *Before We Were Free* by Julia Alvarez. Knopf.

ILLUSTRATOR: *Just a Minute: A Trickster Tale and Counting Book* by Yuyi Morales. Chronicle.

Distinguished Play Award

This award, sponsored by the American Alliance for Theatre and Education, honors the playwright(s) and the publisher of the work voted as the best play for young people published during the past calendar year (January to December). Starting in 1989, two categories were instituted: Category A— Plays primarily for upper and secondary school–age audiences; Category B—Plays primarily for elementary and middle school–age audiences. Beginning in 1998 Category C was established for adaptations.

1983 *My Days as a Youngling, John Jacob Niles: The Early Years,* a musical adapted for the stage and scripted by Nancy Niles Sexton, Vaughn McBride, Martha Harrison Jones; songs by John Niles; published by Anchorage Press.

1984 *Nightingale* by John Urquhart and Rita Grossberg, published by Anchorage Press.

1985 *A Play Called Noah's Flood* by Suzan Zeder, published by Anchorage Press.

1986 *Doors* by Suzan Zeder, published by Anchorage Press.

1987 *Mother Hicks* by Suzan Zeder, published by Anchorage Press.

1988 *Babies Having Babies* by Kathryn Montgomery and Jeffrey Auerbach, published by Baker's Plays.

1989 Category A: *A Separate Peace* by Nancy Pahl Gilsenan, published by Dramatic Publishing Company.

Category B: *Becca* by Wendy Kesselman, published by Anchorage Press.

1990 Category A: *The Man-Child* by Arnold Rabin, published by Baker's Plays.

Category B: *The Chicago Gypsies* by Virginia Glasgow Koste, published by Dramatic Publishing Company.

Category B: *Aalmauria: The Voyage of the Dragonfly* by Max Bush, published by Anchorage Press.

1991 Category A: *In the Middle of Grand Central Station* by Nancy Pahl Gilsenan, published by Dramatic Publishing Company.

Category A: *Jungalbook* by Edward Mast, published by Anchorage Press.

Category B: *Monkey Magic: Chinese Story Theatre* by Aurand Harris, published by Anchorage Press.

1992 Category A: *The Secret Garden* by Pamela Sterling, published by Dramatic Publishing Company.

Category B: *Amber Waves* by James Still, published by Samuel French, Inc.

1993   Category A: ***This Is Not a Pipe Dream*** by Barry Kornhauser, published by Anchorage Press.

Category B: ***The Pinballs*** by Aurand Harris, published by Anchorage Press.

1994   Category A: ***Song for the Navigator*** by Michael Cowell, published by Dramatic Publishing Company.

Category B: ***A Woman Called Truth*** by Sandra Fenichel Asher, published by Dramatic Publishing Company.

1995   Category A: ***T-Money & Wolf*** by Kevin Willmott and Ric Averill, published by Dramatic Publishing Company.

Category A: ***Scars and Stripes*** by Thomas Cadwaleder Jones, published by Encore Publishing Company.

Category B: ***Ramona Quimby*** by Len Jenkins, published by Dramatic Publishing Company.

1996   Category A: ***Angel in the Night*** by Joanna Halpert Kraus, published by Dramatic Publishing Company.

Category B: ***The Prince and the Pauper*** adapted for the stage by Aurand Harris, published by Anchorage Press.

1997   Category A: ***The Less than Human Club*** by Timothy Mason, published by Smith Kraus, Inc.

Category B: No award

1998   Category A: ***Selkie*** by Laurie Brooks, published by Anchorage Press.

Category B: ***The Yellow Boat*** by David Saar, published by Anchorage Press.

Category C: ***Bambi: A Life in the Woods*** by James DeVita, published by Anchorage Press.

1999   Category A: ***North Star*** by Gloria Bond Clunie, published by Dramatic Publishing Company.

Category B: ***Still Life with Iris*** by Steve Dietz, published by Dramatic Publishing Company.

Category C: ***Journey of the Sparrows*** by Meryl Friedman, published by Dramatic Publishing Company.

2000   Category A: ***And Then They Came for Me: Remembering the World of Anne Frank*** by James Still, published by Dramatic Publishing Company.

Category A: ***The Taste of Sunrise*** by Suzan Zeder, published by Anchorage Press.

Category B: ***The Wolf Child*** by Edward Mast, published by Anchorage Press.

Category C: No award

2001   Category A: ***The Wrestling Season,*** by Laurie Brooks, published by Dramatic Publishing.

Category B: No award

Category C: ***Afternoon of the Elves,*** by Y York, published by Dramatic Publishing.

2002   Category A: ***Belongings,*** by Daniel Fenton, published by Dramatic Publishing.

Category B: No award

Category C: ***Ezigbo, the Spirit Child,*** dramatized by Max Bush, published by Anchorage Press Plays.

Category C: ***A Village Fable,*** by James Still, music by Michael Keck, published by Dramatic Publishing.

2003   Category A: ***Paper Lanterns, Paper Cranes,*** by Brian Kral, published by Anchorage Press Plays.

Category B: ***Salt and Pepper,*** by Jose Cruz Gonzalez, published by Dramatic Publishing.

Category C: ***Spot's Birthday Party,*** adapted for the stage by David Wood, based on the book by Eric Hill, published by Samuel French.

Edgar Allan Poe Award (Mystery)— Best Juvenile Novel Category

This award, sponsored by the Mystery Writers of America, is given to the author of the best mystery of the year written for young readers.

1961   ***The Mystery of the Haunted Pool*** by Phyllis A. Whitney. Westminster.

1962 *The Phantom of Walkaway Hill* by Edward Fenton. Doubleday.

1963 *Cutlass Island* by Scott Corbett. Atlantic/Little.

1964 *The Mystery of the Hidden Hand* by Phyllis A. Whitney. Westminster.

1965 *The Mystery at Crane's Landing* by Marcella Thum. Dodd.

1966 *The Mystery of 22 East* by Leon Ware. Westminster.

1967 *Sinbad and Me* by Kin Platt. Chilton.

1968 *Signpost to Terror* by Gretchen Sprague. Dodd.

1969 *The House of Dies Drear* by Virginia Hamilton. Macmillan.

1970 *Danger at Black Dyke* by Winifred Finlay. Phillips.

1971 *The Intruder* by John Rowe Townsend. Lippincott.

1972 *Night Fall* by Joan Aiken. Holt.

1973 *Deathwatch* by Robb White. Doubleday.

1974 *The Long Black Coat* by Jay Bennett. Delacorte.

1975 *The Dangling Witness* by Jay Bennett. Delacorte.

1976 *Z for Zachariah* by Robert C. O'Brien. Atheneum.

1977 *Are You in the House Alone?* by Richard Peck. Viking.

1978 *A Really Weird Summer* by Eloise Jarvis McGraw. Atheneum.

1979 *Alone in Wolf Hollow* by Dana Brookins. Clarion.

1980 *The Kidnapping of Christina Lattimore* by Joan Lowery Nixon. Harcourt.

1981 *The Seance* by Joan Lowery Nixon. Harcourt.

1982 *Taking Terri Mueller* by Norma Fox Mazer. Avon.

1983 *The Murder of Hound Dog Bates* by Robbie Branscum. Viking.

1984 *The Callender Papers* by Cynthia Voigt. Atheneum.

1985 *Night Cry* by Phyllis Reynolds Naylor. Atheneum.

1986 *The Sandman's Eyes* by Patricia Windsor. Delacorte.

1987 *The Other Side of Dark* by Joan Lowery Nixon. Delacorte.

1988 *Lucy Forever and Miss Rosetree, Shrinks* by Susan Shreve. Holt.

1989 *Megan's Island* by Willo Davis Roberts. Atheneum.

1990 No award

1991 *Stonewords* by Pam Conrad. Harper.

1992 *Wanted . . . Mud Blossom* by Betsy Byars. Delacorte.

1993 *Coffin on a Case* by Eve Bunting. HarperCollins.

1994 *The Twin in the Tavern* by Barbara Brooks Wallace. Atheneum.

1995 *The Absolutely True Story . . . How I Visited Yellowstone Park with the Terrible Rupes* by Willo Davis Roberts. Atheneum.

1996 *Looking for Jamie Bridger* by Nancy Springer. Dial.

1997 *The Clearing* by Dorothy R. Miller. Atheneum.

1998 *Sparrows in the Scullery* by Barbara Brooks Wallace. Atheneum.

1999 *Sammy Keyes and the Hotel Thief* by Wendelin Van Draanen. Knopf.

2000 *The Night Flyers* by Elizabeth McDavid Jones. Pleasant Company.

2001 *Dovey Coe* by Frances O'Roark Dowell. Simon & Schuster.

2002 *Dangling* by Lillian Eige. Atheneum.

2003 *Harriet Spies Again* by Helen Ericson. Random House/Delacorte.

Scott O'Dell Award for Historical Fiction

This award, donated by the author Scott O'Dell, is given to the author of a distinguished work of historical fiction for children or young adults set in the New World and published in English by a U.S. publisher. The author must be a citizen of the United States.

1984 *The Sign of the Beaver* by Elizabeth George Speare. Houghton.

1985 *The Fighting Ground* by Avi (Wortis). Harper.

1986 *Sarah, Plain and Tall* by Patricia MacLachlan. Harper.

1987 *Streams to the River, River to the Sea: A Novel of Sacagawea* by Scott O'Dell. Houghton.

1988 *Charley Skedaddle* by Patricia Beatty. Morrow.

1989 *The Honorable Prison* by Lyll Becerra de Jenkins. Lodestar.

1990 *Shades of Gray* by Carolyn Reeder. Macmillan.

1991 *A Time of Troubles* by Pieter van Raven. Scribner's.

1992 *Stepping on the Cracks* by Mary Downing Hahn. Clarion.

1993 *Morning Girl* by Michael Dorris. Hyperion.

1994 *Bull Run* by Paul Fleischman. HarperCollins.

1995 *Under the Blood-Red Sun* by Graham Salisbury. Delacorte

1996 *The Bomb* by Theodore Taylor. Harcourt Brace.

1997 *Jip: His Story* by Katherine Paterson. Dutton.

1998 *Out of the Dust* by Karen Hesse. Scholastic.

1999 *Forty Acres and Maybe a Mule* by Harriette Gillem Robinet. Atheneum.

2000 *Two Suns in the Sky* by Miriam Bat-Ami. Front Street/Cricket.

2001 *The Art of Keeping Cool* by Janet Taylor Lisle. Atheneum.

2002 *The Land* by Mildred D. Taylor. Fogelman/Penguin Putnam.

2003 *Trouble Don't Last* by Shelley Pearsall. Knopf.

2004 *The River between Us* by Richard Peck. Dial.

Orbis Pictus Award

This award, sponsored by NCTE's Committee on Using Nonfiction in the Elementary Language Arts Classroom, is given to an author in recognition of excellence in writing of nonfiction for children published in the United States in the preceding year.

1990 *The Great Little Madison* by Jean Fritz. Putnam.

1991 *Franklin Delano Roosevelt* by Russell Freedman. Clarion.

1992 *Flight: The Journey of Charles Lindbergh* by Robert Burleigh. Illustrated by Mike Wimmer. Philomel.

1993 *Children of the Dustbowl: The True Story of the School at Weedpatch Camp* by Jerry Stanley. Random.

1994 *Across America on an Emigrant Train* by Jim Murphy. Clarion.

1995 *Safari beneath the Sea* by Diane Swanson. Photographs by the Royal British Columbia Museum. Sierra Club.

1996 *The Great Fire* by Jim Murphy. Scholastic.

1997 *Leonardo da Vinci* by Diane Stanley. Morrow.

1998 *An Extraordinary Life: The Story of a Monarch Butterfly* by Laurence Pringle. Illustrated by Bob Marstall. Orchard.

1999 *Shipwreck at the Bottom of the World: The Extraordinary True Story of Schackleton and the Endurance* by Jennifer Armstrong. Crown.

2000 *Through My Eyes* by Ruby Bridges and Margo Lundell. Scholastic.

2001 *Hurry Freedom: African Americans in Gold Rush California* by Jerry Stanley. Crown.

2002 *Black Potatoes: The Story of the Great Irish Famine, 1845–1850.* Susan Campbell Bartoletti. Houghton.

2003 *When Marian Sang* by Pam Muñoz Ryan. Illustrated by Brian Selznick. Scholastic.

2004 *An American Plague: The True and Terrifying Story of the Yellow Fever Epidemic of 1793* by Jim Murphy. Clarion, 2003.

Robert F. Sibert Informational Book Medal

The Robert F. Sibert Informational Book Medal, established by the Association for Library Service to Children division of the American Library Association in 2001, is awarded annually to the author of the most distinguished informational book published during the preceding year.

2001 *Sir Walter Ralegh and the Quest for El Dorado* by Marc Aronson. Clarion.

2002 *Black Potatoes: The Story of the Great Irish Famine, 1845–1850* by Susan Campbell Bartoletti. Houghton.

2003 *The Life and Death of Adolf Hitler* by James Cross Giblin. Clarion.

2004 *An American Plague: The True and Terrifying Story of the Yellow Fever Epidemic of 1793* by Jim Murphy. Clarion.

Phoenix Award

This award, sponsored by the Children's Literature Association, is given to the author of a book first published 20 years earlier. The book must have been originally published in English and cannot have been the recipient of a major children's book award.

1985 *Mark of the Horse Lord* by Rosemary Sutcliff. Walck.

1986 *Queenie Peavy* by Robert Burch. Viking.

1987 *Smith* by Leon Garfield. Constable.

1988 *The Rider and His Horse* by Eric Christian Haugaard. Houghton.

1989 *The Night Watchmen* by Helen Cresswell. Macmillan.

1990 *Enchantress from the Stars* by Sylvia Louise Engdahl. Atheneum.

1991 *A Long Way from Verona* by Jane Gardam. Macmillan.

1992 *A Sound of Chariots* by Mollie Hunter. Harper.

1993 *Carrie's War* by Nina Bawden. Lippincott.

1994 *Of Nightingales That Weep* by Katherine Paterson. Crowell.

1995 *Dragonwings* by Laurence Yep. HarperCollins.

1996 *The Stone Book* by Alan Garner. Philomel. (Others in The Stone Quartet: *Granny Reardun* [1978], *The Aimer Gate* [1979], *Tom Fobble's Day* [1979])

1997 *I Am the Cheese* by Robert Cormier. Pantheon.

1998 *A Chance Child* by Jill Paton Walsh. Farrar.

1999 *Throwing Shadows* by E. L. Konigsburg. Atheneum.

2000 *The Keeper of the Isis Light* by Monica Hughes. Atheneum.

2001 *Seventh Raven* by Peter Dickinson. Gollancz/Dutton.

2002 *A Formal Feeling* by Zibby Oneal. Orion.

2003 *The Long Night Watch* by Ivan Southall. Methuen.

2004 *White Peak Farm* by Berlie Doherty. Orchard.

OTHER NOTABLE BOOK EXHIBITIONS AND AWARDS

Biennale of Illustrations Bratislava

This biannual international exposition of books was begun in 1967 and is held in Bratislava, Slovak Republic. A Grand Prix and five honor book awards are given to children's books for excellence in illustration.

American Institute of Graphic Arts Book Show

This annual book show features approximately 100 books, both children's and adult, selected for excellence in design and manufacture. Lists of books selected each year can be found in AIGA Graphic Design USA (Watson-Guptil).

New York Times *Best Illustrated Children's Books of the Year*

Sponsored by **The New York Times,** *this list of 10 books appears annually in the* **Times.** *A three-member panel of experts chooses the books.*

International Reading Association Children's Book Award

Sponsored by the Institute for Reading Research and administered by the International Reading Association, this international award is given annually to an author for a first or second book that shows unusual promise in the children's book field.

International Board on Books for Young People Honor List

Sponsored by the International Board on Books for Young People (IBBY), this biennial list is composed of three books (one for text, one for illustration, and one for translation) from each IBBY National Section to represent the best in children's literature published in that country in the past two years.

The books selected are recommended as suitable for publication worldwide.

State Children's Choice Award Programs

Nearly all states have a children's choice book award program. Usually, a ballot of about twenty-five titles is generated from children's or teachers' nominations. Children from all over the state then vote for their favorite title. For information about your state children's choice award program, contact your state library association.

PROFESSIONAL RESOURCES

PROFESSIONAL READINGS

Books

Bamford, R. A., & Kristo, J. V. (Eds.). (2003). *Making facts come alive: Choosing quality nonfiction literature K–8* (2nd ed.). Norwood, MA: Christopher-Gordon.

This practical guide helps users to find and integrate nonfiction titles across the curriculum.

Bany-Winters, L. (2003). *On stage: Theater games and activities for kids.* Chicago: Chicago Review Press.

An assortment of theater games are divided among improvisations, creating characters, puppetry, costumes, suggestions for monologues, scenes, and plays for grades 1–6.

Barchers, S. I. (2000). *Multicultural folktales: Readers' theatre for elementary students.* Englewood, NJ: Libraries Unlimited, 2000.

Barchers provides practical advice on how to get kids reading and performing stories. The book includes 40 scripts with reading level indicated.

Bauer, C. F. (1997). *Leading kids to books through puppets.* Chicago: American Library Association.

Bauer links readers to a wide variety of literature through puppets. She also explains how to make and use different types of puppets.

Bohning, G., Phillips, A., & Bryant, S. H. (1993). *Literature on the move: Making and using pop-up and lift-flap books.* Englewood, CO: Libraries Unlimited.

Directions are provided for making eight basic types of engineered (movable) pages with variations for each.

Buss, K., & Karnowski, L. (2000). *Reading and writing literary genres.* Newark, DE: International Reading Association.

Offers readers and writers suggestions on how to understand and model a variety of different genres of literature and their elements.

Cart, M. (1995). *What's so funny? Wit and humor in American children's literature.* New York: HarperCollins.

An enjoyable study of selected children's books, characters, and authors, and their humor.

Chatton, B. (1993). *Using poetry across the curriculum: A whole language approach.* Phoenix, AZ: Oryx Press.

Ways to integrate poetry into all subject areas.

Cullinan, B. E. (1995). *Three voices: An invitation to poetry across the curriculum.* York, ME: Stenhouse.

Teaching strategies with sample vignettes for integrating poetry into the curriculum.

Day, F. A. (1997). *Latina and Latino voices in literature for children and teenagers.* Portsmouth, NH: Heinemann.

Day explains bias and how to recognize it in books for young people. She also highlights authors and illustrators and describes their works.

Egoff, S., Stubbs, G., Ashley, R., & Sutton, W. (Eds.). (1996). *Only connect: Readings on children's literature* (3rd ed.). New York: Oxford Press.

Essays.

Freeman, E., & Lehman, B. (2001). *Global perspectives in children's literature.* Needham Heights, MA: Allyn and Bacon.

This book reviews the status, value, historical context, and contemporary trends in international children's literature.

Glover, M. K. (1999). *A garden of poets: Poetry writing in the elementary classroom.* Urbana, IL: National Council of Teachers of English.

Glover offers ideas on creating an atmosphere conducive to poetry writing. Includes bibliographies on music for inspiring writing and on bilingual poetry books.

Greene, E., & Baker, A. (1996). *Storytelling: Art and technique.* New Providence, NJ: R. R. Bowker.

An update of this successful guide on storytelling includes a chapter on telling stories to young adults.

Hall, S. (1990, 1994, 2002). *Using picture storybooks to teach literary devices: Recommended books for children and young adults* (Vol. 1, 2, & 3). Phoenix, AZ: Oryx Press.

How picture books can be used to teach complex literary devices.

Hansen, J. (2001). (2nd ed.) *When writers read.* Portsmouth, NH: Heinemann.

Teachers and researchers working together in an elementary school discovered the principles to encourage children to develop helpful reading strategies.

Harris, V. J. (Ed.). (1997). *Using multiethnic literature in the K–8 classroom.* Norwood, MA: Christopher-Gordon.

Essays on important issues concerning the field of multiethnic children's literature and bibliographies of books about different ethnic groups.

Hopkins, L. B. (1998). *Pass the poetry, please!* New York: HarperCollins.

This revised classic introduces favorite works by contemporary poets and is a must for teachers who wish to encourage students to appreciate poetry.

Horning, K. T. (1997). *From cover to cover: Evaluating and reviewing children's books.* New York: HarperCollins.

A handbook on evaluating children's books with recommendations for specific genres.

Janeczko, P. B. (1999). *How to write poetry.* New York: Scholastic.

Poet Janeczko guides would-be poets through the writing process.

Johnson, N. J., Schlick, K. L., & Hill, B. B. (Eds.). (1995). *Literature circles and response.* Norwood, MA: Christopher-Gordon.

The editors advise on how to establish literature circles and how to elicit responses to literature from students.

Koch, K. (1999). *Wishes, lies, and dreams: Teaching children to write poetry.* New York: Harper-Perennial.

Koch describes working with inner-city children who had never done much writing of any kind and encouraging them to express themselves by writing down their feelings.

Marantz, S. S., & Marantz, K. A. (1995). *The art of children's picture books: A selective reference guide.* (2nd ed.). New York: Garland.

A work of history and criticism of children's picture books presents an indepth study of the art within picture books.

Moss, B. (2003). *Exploring the literature of fact: Children's nonfiction trade books in the elementary classroom.* New York: Guilford.

How to address children's literacy needs using children's nonfiction trade books.

Pellowski, A. (1990). *The world of storytelling: A practical guide to the origins, development, and applications of storytelling* (expanded and revised edition). New York: H. W. Wilson.

Comprehensive information about the oral tradition and the history of storytelling as well as a list of storytelling festivals held around the world.

————. (1995). *The storytelling handbook.* New York: Simon & Schuster.

This indispensable guide to the art of storytelling discusses how to tell stories and includes stories from around the world to use for successful storytelling.

Raphael, T. E., & Au, K. H. (Eds.). (1998). *Literature-based instruction: Reshaping the curriculum.* Norwood, MA: Christopher-Gordon.

Theories of literature-based instruction and where and how it fits into the curriculum are discussed by various noted teacher-researchers and teacher educators.

Ray, K. W. (1999). *Wondrous words: Writers and writing in the elementary classroom.* Urbana, IL: National Council of Teachers of English.

Ray uses examples of student writing to show how students learn to write from reading such authors as Gary Paulsen and Cynthia Rylant.

Robb, L. (2003). *Teaching reading in social studies, science, and math.* New York: Scholastic.

Provides practical ways to weave comprehension strategies into content area teaching.

Trelease, J. (2001). *The read-aloud handbook* (4th ed.). New York: Putnam Penguin.

Trelease annotates three hundred of his favorite read-alouds, giving the listening level of each. Many of the annotations include suggestions of other books by the same author.

Zipes, J. D. (2000). *Sticks and stones: The troublesome success of children's literature from Slovenly Peter to Harry Potter.* New York: Routledge.

In this series of essays Zipes comments on the field of children's literature and its too frequent homogeneity.

Books about the History of Children's Literature

Bingham, J., & Scholt, G. (1980). *Fifteen centuries of children's literature: An annotated chronology of British and American works in historical context.* Westport, CT: Greenwood.

Davis, D. (1981). *Theatre for young people.* New York: Beaufort.

Gillespie, M. C. (1970). *History and trends: Literature for children.* Dubuque, IA: Brown.

Hunt, P. (1995). *Children's literature: An illustrated history.* Oxford: Oxford University Press.

Hunt, P., & Ray, S. G. (1996). *International companion encyclopedia of children's literature.* London: Routledge.

Marshall, M. R. (1988). *An introduction to the world of children's books: Books about the history of children's literature* (2nd ed.). Aldershot, England: Gower.

McCaslin, N. (1971). *Theatre for children in the United States.* Norman: University of Oklahoma Press.

Murray, G. S. (1998). *American children's literature and the construction of childhood.* New York: Twayne.

Smith, E. S. (1980). In M. Hodges & S. Steinfirst (Eds.). *The history of children's literature* (rev. ed.). Chicago: ALA.

Journals and Periodicals

Bookbird: Journal of International Children's Literature. Published quarterly by IBBY, the International Board on Books for Young People, Nonnenweg 12 Postfach, CH-4003 Basel, Switzerland. For subscriptions write to Bookbird, c/o University of Toronto Press, 5201 Dufferin Street, North York, ON, Canada M3H 5T8.

This journal includes articles, authors' and illustrators' portraits, reports and announcements, and reviews of children's books and professional literature of international interest.

Book Links: Connecting Books, Libraries, and Classrooms. A bimonthly magazine published by Booklist Publications, an imprint of the American Library Association, 50 E. Huron St., Chicago, IL 60611.

This magazine publishes articles with suggestions for exploring a particular theme through literature. Descriptions of books, strategies for stimulating classroom discussion about them, and activities for student involvement are among the offerings.

Children & Libraries. Journal published three times a year by the Association for Library Service to Children, a division of the American Library Association, 50 E. Huron St., Chicago, IL 60611.

This journal informs librarians who work with children and young adults about current practices. Teachers as well as librarians will find the thorough reviews of professional resources helpful.

Children's Literature in Education: An International Quarterly. Published by Human Sciences Press, Inc., 233 Spring Street, New York, NY 10013-1578.

This journal includes interviews with authors and illustrators, accounts of classroom practice involving literature or the reading process, and commentary on social issues as reflected in books.

The Dragon Lode. The Journal of the Children's Literature and Reading Special Interest Group of the International Reading Association is published three times a year for members. IRA members may join this interest group by obtaining the name and address of its current Membership Chair from IRA, 800 Barksdale Road, P. O. Box 8139, Newark, DE 19714-8139.

This journal publishes articles about children's literature and the teaching of it, classroom ideas, and book reviews of books published internationally as well as in the United States.

Journal of Children's Literature. Journal of the Children's Literature Assembly of the National Council of Teachers of English, published and sent to CLA members twice a year. NCTE members may join the Children's Literature Assembly by obtaining the name and address of the cur-

rent Membership Chair of CLA. Write to NCTE, 111 Kenyon Road, Urbana, IL 61801.

This journal solicits and publishes manuscripts regarding any aspect of children's literature, as well as reviews of children's books and professional resources.

Language Arts. Published monthly, September through April, by the National Council of Teachers of English, for its members. For membership information, write NCTE, 1111 Kenyon Road, Urbana, IL 61801-1096.

This journal publishes themed issues on topics relating to the content and teaching of language arts. Regular features include author profiles, annotations of children's books, and commentaries on trends in the field.

The New Advocate for Those Involved with Young People and Their Literature. Published quarterly since 1988 by Christopher-Gordon Publishers, 480 Washington Street, Norwood, MA 02062.

This journal contains articles on using children's literature in the classroom. Reviews of children's books and literature resources for teachers appear in each issue.

The Reading Teacher. A journal of the International Reading Association, published monthly eight times during the school year. For information on joining the IRA and subscribing to its journals, write to IRA, 800 Barksdale Road, P.O. Box 8139, Newark, DE 19714-8139.

This journal contains articles that reflect current theory, research, and practice regarding the teaching of reading. Regular columns deal with evaluation of children's trade books and professional resources.

The United States Board on Books for Young People, Inc. (USBBY) Newsletter. Published twice a year by the U.S. section of the International Board on Books for Young People (IBBY). To join USBBY and receive the newsletter, write to USBBY Secretariat, c/o International Reading Association, P.O. Box 8139, Newark, DE 19714-8139.

This newsletter includes news and articles concerning national and international activities related to children's literature. It also includes reviews of international children's books.

Information on Authors and Illustrators

Children's literature review: Excerpts from reviews, criticism, and commentary on books for children and young people, 1–50 (1976–2004). Detroit: Gale Research.

This semiannual reference provides information about authors and illustrators, often in their own words, as well as excerpts from reviews of their work. Each volume contains a cumulative index to authors and titles.

Junior Book of Authors (1951). *More junior authors* (1963), and the *Third, fourth, fifth, sixth, seventh, and eighth book of junior authors and illustrators.* (1972–2000). New York: H. W. Wilson.

This reference includes biographical sketches of authors and illustrators written for young people.

Silvey, A. (Ed.). (2002). *The essential guide to children's books and their creators.* Boston: Houghton.

This volume focuses on 475 of the best children's books and includes biographical sketches of authors and illustrators.

Something about the author: Facts and pictures about authors and illustrators of books for young people, 1–122 (1971–2004). Detroit: Gale Research.

This series includes comprehensive information about authors and illustrators, written for young people.

Bibliographies: Annual Lists

"CCBC Choices."

An annual spring annotated booklist, published by and for the members of the Friends of the CCBC, Inc. (Cooperative Children's Book Center). For information about CCBC publications and/or membership in the Friends, send a self-addressed stamped envelope to Friends of the CCBC, P. O. Box 5288, Madison, WI 53705-0288.

"Children's Choices."

This yearly list of newly published books, chosen by young readers themselves, appears each October in The Reading Teacher *as a project of the International Reading Association/Children's Book Council Joint Committee.*

"Notable Children's Books."

This annual American Library Association list appears in the March issue of School Library Journal *and also in the March 15th issue of* Booklist.

"Notable Children's Books in the Language Arts (K–8)."

This annual list of outstanding trade books for enhancing language awareness among students in grades K–8 appears in each October issue of Language Arts.

"Notable Social Studies Trade Books for Young People."

This list appears in the April/May issue of Social Education *and at* www.cbcbooks.org.

"Outstanding Science Trade Books for Students K–12."

This list appears in the March issue of Science and Children *and at* www.cbcbooks.org.

"Teachers' Choices."

This yearly list includes books recommended by teachers. It appears each November in The Reading Teacher *and at* www.reading.org.

"Young Adults' Choices."

The books on this annual list were selected by readers in middle, junior high, and senior high schools. It appears in the November issue of Journal of Adolescent and Adult Literacy *and at* www.reading.org.

Bibliographies

Adamson, L. G. (1998). *Literature connections to American history, K–6: Resources to enhance and entice.* Englewood, NJ: Libraries Unlimited.

An annotated bibliography of materials divided by format includes age ranges, descriptive synopses, and awards received. It also includes an excellent subject index and author, illustrator, and title indices.

———. (1999). *American historical fiction: An annotated guide to novels for adults and young adults published since 1985.* Phoenix, AZ: Oryx.

Adamson provides readers with plot summaries of well-written historical fiction.

Awards & prizes online. (2003 with frequent updates). Children's Book Council, 12 W. 37th St., 2nd floor, New York, NY 10018-7480. www.cbcbooks.org

This online publication replaces the print version and constantly updates awards. Awards include nearly 300 domestic and international English-language children's book awards.

The black experience in children's books. (1999). New York: New York Public Library.

This periodically revised pamphlet briefly annotates folklore, fiction, and nonfiction written for children from preschool to age 12 that portrays African-American life.

Cerullo, M. M. (1997). *Reading the environment: Children's literature in the science curriculum.* Portsmouth, NH: Heinemann.

Cerullo provides criteria for selecting science books and then provides a bibliography of recommended fiction and nonfiction about earth science, oceans, weather, seasons, and movement of water.

Children's book review index. (1975–2003). Detroit: Gale Research.

This annual work indexes the reviews appearing in two hundred periodicals. This work compiles citations appearing in Book Review Index, *which locates reviews of books written for children and young adults.*

Children's books in print. (Published annually). New Providence, NJ: R. R. Bowker.

This is an index of juvenile titles that are listed in publishers' catalogs as "in print," but it does not always include books from smaller publishing companies. This work includes a separate listing of addresses of publishers.

The children's catalog (20th ed, supplement). (2003). A. Price & J. Yaakov (Eds.). New York: H. W. Wilson.

Part 1 lists books and magazines recommended for preschool children through sixth-graders, as well as useful professional resources. Part 2 helps the user locate entries through one alphabetical, comprehensive key that includes author, title, subject, and analytical listings.

Day, F. A. (2000). *Lesbian and gay voices: An annotated guide to literature for children and young adults.* Westport, CT: Greenwood.

This thorough guide provides detailed, critical annotations for more than 275 recommended books.

Fredericks, A. D. (1998). *Science adventures with children's literature: A thematic approach.* Illustrated by A. A. Stoner. Englewood, NJ: Libraries Unlimited.

This idea book features thematic resource lists of more than 400 trade books with activities.

Friedler, A. B. (1997). *Guide to the 400 best children's and adults' multicultural books about lesbian and gay people.* Newton Centre, MA: Lift Every Voice.

An annotated list of books for children and adults about gays and lesbians.

Gunning, T. G. (1998). *Best books for beginning readers.* Needham Heights, MA: Allyn and Bacon.

———. (2000). *Best books for building literacy for elementary school children.* Needham Heights, MA: Allyn and Bacon.

Gunning provides explanations of reading levels and useful lists of recommended books by reading levels for beginning and transitional readers.

International children's digital library. (2004, with frequent updates). University of Maryland and the Internet Archive www.icdlbooks.org.

This online publication is creating a digital library of international children's books in many different languages. The White Raven Annotated Bibliography of children's books throughout the world selected by the specialists at the International Youth Library in Munich, Germany is included on this web site.

Krey, D. (1998). *Children's literature in the social studies: Teaching to the standards.* Washington, DC: National Council for the Social Studies.

Krey identifies excellent children's books published between 1990 and 1997 that can be used for teaching each of 10 social studies themes at different levels.

Lima, C. W., & Lima, J. A. (2001). *A to zoo: Subject access to children's picture books* (6th ed.). Westport, CT: Greenwood.

This index indicates the subject matter of 14,000 picture books for children with access through author, illustrator, and title, as well as 800 subjects.

Muse, D. (Ed.). (1998). *The New Press guide to multicultural resources for young readers.* New York: New Press.

Features more than 1,000 reviews of books that deal with diverse ethnic and racial groups as well as disabled persons and gay and lesbian communities.

NCTE bibliography series (National Council of Teachers of English):

Adventuring with books: A booklist for pre-K–grade 6 (13th ed.). (2002). Urbana, IL: NCTE.

Kaleidoscope: A multicultural booklist for grades K–8. (4th ed.) (2003). Urbana, IL: NCTE.

Your reading: An annotated booklist for junior high and middle-school students (10th ed.). (1995). Urbana, IL: NCTE.

All of these books include annotated listings of fiction and nonfiction books recommended for children and young people in the grades specified in each title.

The Newbery and Caldecott Awards: A guide to the medal and honor books. (1999). Chicago: American Library Association.

This annual guide includes annotations on each of the award winners and honor books, as well as information concerning the criteria on which the awards are based.

Oaks, H. (Ed.). (1996). *Outstanding plays for young audiences: International bibliography,* vol. 5. Seattle, WA: United States Center for the International Association of Theatre for Children and Young People.

Phelan, C. (1996). *Science books for young people.* Chicago: American Library Association.

An annotated bibliography of 500 of the best science books published from 1990 to 1995.

Roberts, P. L. (1997). *Taking humor seriously in children's literature: Literature-based mini-units and humorous books for children.* Lanham, MD: Scarecrow.

Roberts outlines types of humor and describes curriculum units based on popular children's books. A good annotated bibliography that includes more than 500 titles.

Schon, I. (2000). *Recommended books in Spanish for children and young adults, 1996 through 1999.* Lanham, MD: Scarecrow.

Periodic volumes each cover a three-year period. These are selection guides for books in Spanish written by Hispanic authors for children, preschool through high school. The list is comprehensive and includes some negative reviews because not all of the included books are recommended.

Slaight, C., & Esty, J. (Eds.). (1997). *The Smith and Kraus play index for young actors.* North Stratford, NH: Smith and Kraus.

A play index of over 500 plays for elementary, middle, and high school students includes ordering information. Each play is described in detail with the number of cast members, and time and place of setting.

Slapin, B., & Seale, D. (Eds.). (1998). *Through Indian eyes: The native experience in books for children* (4th ed.). Los Angeles: American Indian Studies Center, UCLA.

An annotated bibliography with critical reviews of children's books about Native Americans.

Stan, S., (Ed.). (2002). *The world through children's books.* Lanham, MD: Scarecrow.

A guide to international children's books published in the United States from 1996 to 2000 that includes a selection of children's books written by U.S. authors but set in other countries. An annotated bibliography is included.

Stoll, D. R. (Ed.). (1997). *Magazines for kids and teens.* Newark, DE: International Reading Association.

Describes 249 magazines geared toward children from ages 2 to 17. Information concerning circulation, cost, and frequency of publication is included, as well as indexes of age levels, subjects, and whether the magazine publishes readers' writing.

Susag, D. M. (1998). *Roots and branches: A resource of Native American literature—Themes, lessons, and bibliographies.* Urbana, IL: National Council of Teachers of English.

Susag examines the historical and literary contexts of Native American literature. Also provides lessons, activities, and detailed, annotated bibliographies.

Tomlinson, C. M. (Ed.). (1998). *Children's books from other countries.* Lanham, MD: Scarecrow.

This complete guide to international children's literature with an annotated bibliography of 724 children's books also provides suggestions on sharing international books with children.

Van Orden, P. (2000). *Selecting books for the elementary school library media center: A complete guide.* New York: Neal-Schuman.

An essential tool for new school libraries and useful for most libraries in balancing collections.

Review Journals

Booklist. Published twice monthly September through June and monthly in July and August by American Library Association, 50 E. Huron St., Chicago, IL 60611.

This journal reviews current print and nonprint materials for children and adults that are worthy of consideration for purchase by small and medium-sized public libraries and school media centers.

The Bulletin of the Center for Children's Books. Published monthly except August by the University of Illinois Press, 1325 S. Oak, Champaign, IL 61820.

This publication reviews current children's books, with adverse as well as favorable reviews,

assigning a recommendation code to each. An age or grade level is given to each book, and annotations include information on curricular use, developmental values, and literary merit.

Children's Book and Play Review. Published five times a year by Brigham Young University, Marsha D. Broadway, Managing Editor, Children's Book and Play Review, Harold B. Lee Library, Brigham Young University, Provo, UT 84602.

This journal reviews children's books and plays and includes three or four feature articles about plays in each volume.

The Horn Book Guide to Children's and Young Adult Books. Published twice a year in March and September by the Horn Book, Inc., 11 Beacon Street, Suite 1000, Boston, MA 02108.

The Horn Book Guide contains brief reviews of all hardcover children's trade books published in the United States during the previous six months.

The Horn Book Magazine. Published six times a year by the Horn Book, Inc., 11 Beacon Street, Suite 1000, Boston, MA 02108.

This magazine includes detailed reviews of children's books deemed the best in children's literature by the editorial staff. It also contains articles about literature and interviews with authors. The Newbery and Caldecott acceptance speeches are features in the July/August issue.

School Library Journal: The Magazine of Children's, Young Adult, and School Librarians. A Cahners/ R. R. Bowker Publication, published monthly. For subscription information, write to School Library Journal, P.O. Box 1978, Marion, OH 43305-1978.

This journal prints both negative and positive reviews of most children's books published. It also includes articles of interest to school librarians.

PROFESSIONAL ORGANIZATIONS

American Alliance for Theatre and Education. (AATE). 7475 Wisconsin Ave., Suite 300A, Bethesda, MD: 20814.

American Library Association. 50 E. Huron Street, Chicago, IL 60611. Special Divisions: Associa-

tion for Library Service to Children, Young Adult Library Services Association.

Association of Childhood Education International, 11501 Georgia Avenue, Suite 315, Wheaton, MD 20902-2443.

Children's Book Council. 12 W. 37th St., 2nd floor, New York, NY 10018.

Children's Literature Association. 210 Education Department, Purdue University, West Lafayette, IN 47907.

International Reading Association. 800 Barksdale Road, P.O. Box 8139, Newark, DE 19714-8139. Special Interest Group: Children's Literature and Reading.

National Council of Teachers of English. 1111 W. Kenyon Road, Urbana, IL 61801-1096.

Special Interest Group: Children's Literature Assembly.

United States Board on Books for Young People. USBBY Secretariat, International Reading Association, P.O. Box 8139, Newark, DE 19714-8139.

United States Center for the International Association of Theatre for Children and Young People. (ASSITEJ/USA). 742 2nd Avenue S., Nashville, TN 37210-2006.

WEB SITES

Association for Library Service to Children (ALSC) Site: http://www.ala.org/alsc/

Includes the Newbery and Caldecott home pages. New awards are announced on this site.

Carol Hurst's Children's Literature Site: http://www.carolhurst.com/

Provides a collection of book reviews, curriculum ideas, themes, and professional topics for teachers.

The Children's Book Council (CBC) Site: http://www.cbcbooks.org/

This nonprofit association of children's book publishers offers book-related literacy materials for children. Also provides information on Children's Book Week.

Cooperative Children's Book Center Site: http://www.soemadison.wisc.edu/ccbc/

Learn about the University of Wisconsin's CCBC collections, upcoming events, and publications.

Kay E. Vandergrift's Special Interest Page: http://www.scils.rutgers.edu/kvander

A large site with information about children's and young adult literature that includes many links.

The Looking Glass: An Online Children's Literature Journal: http://www.the-looking-glass.net

Founded in 1997, this electronic journal about children's literature is international in terms of topic and approach. Most contributors have a Canadian connection.

CHILDREN'S MAGAZINES

The following list includes some of the most popular children's magazines available to young people today. A more complete list of children's magazines may be found in D. R. Stoll, Ed. (1997), **Magazines for Kids and Teens** *(International Reading Association). The following list is organized by subject of primary emphasis.*

Drama

Plays, the Drama Magazine for Young People. Scripts for plays, skits, puppet shows, and round-the-table readings (a type of readers' theatre). 8–10 scripts per issue. Ages 6–17. 7 issues/year. Order from: Plays Magazine, P.O. Box 600160, Newton, MA 02460, or www.playsmag.com

Geography

World Newsmap. Current global issues. Two two-sided, poster-sized maps (world map and focus-country map) per issue. Teacher guide. 9 issues/year. Ages 10–17. Order from: World Newsmap, P.O. Box 1880, Highland Park, IL 60035, or worldnewsmap@aol.com

Health

Child Life. Articles, fiction, activities with an emphasis on nutrition and safety. Ages 9–11. 8 is-

sues/year. Similar magazines for different age groups by the same publisher include *Humpty Dumpty's Magazine* (ages 4–6), *Children's Playmate Magazine* (ages 6–8), *Jack and Jill* (ages 7–10), and *Children's Digest* (preteen). Order from: Children's Better Health Institute, 1100 Waterway Blvd., Indianapolis, IN 46202, or www.cbhi.org

History

Calliope. Articles, stories, time lines, maps, and authentic photos to generate an interest in world history. Themed issues. Ages 8–15. 9 issues/year. Order from: Cobblestone Publishing, Inc., 30 Grove Street, Suite C, Peterborough, NH 03458, or www.cobblestonepub.com

Cobblestone. Articles about U.S. history. Themed issues. Ages 9–15. 9 issues/year. Order from: Cobblestone Publishing, Inc., 30 Grove Street, Suite C, Peterborough, NH 03458, or www.cobblestonepub.com

Footsteps. Themed issues related to African-American history. Ages 9–14. 5 issues/year. Order from: Cobblestone Publishing, Inc., 30 Grove Street, Suite C, Peterborough, NH 03458, or www.cobblestonepub.com

Language

Bonjour. Topics of interest to 13- to 15-year-olds in French. Information and cultural details of French-speaking countries. 6 issues/year. Order from: Scholastic, Inc., 2931 E. McCarty St., P.O. Box 3710, Jefferson City, MO 65102–3710, or http://teacher.scholastic.com/products/classmags

Das Rad. Topics of interest to 13- to 16-year-olds in German. Information and cultural details of German-speaking countries. 6 issues/year. Order from: Scholastic, Inc., 2931 E. McCarty St., P.O. Box 3710, Jefferson City, MO 65102–3710, or http://teacher.scholastic.com/products/classmags

¿Qué Tal? Topics of interest to 11- to 16-year-olds in Spanish. Information and cultural details of Spanish-speaking countries. 6 issues/year. Order from: Scholastic, Inc., 2931 E. McCarty Street, P. O. Box 3710, Jefferson City, MO 65102–3710, or http://teacher.scholastic.com/products/classmags

Language Arts

Merlyn's Pen: Fiction, Essays, and Poems by America's Teens. Professionally edited fiction, nonfiction, and poetry by students in grades 6–9. Ages 12–15. 4 issues/year. Order from: Merlyn's Pen, Inc. P. O. Box 910, East Greenwich, RI 02818, or www.merlynspen.org

Scholastic Scope. Plays, short stories, reading lists, writing exercises, and skill builders. Ages 12–14. 18 issues/year. Order from: Scholastic, Inc., 2931 E. McCarty Street, P. O. Box 3710, Jefferson City, MO 65102, or http://teacher.scholastic.com/products/classmags

Storyworks. Focuses on development of grammar, writing, vocabulary, test-taking. Includes read-aloud plays. Ages 8–11. 6 issues/year. Order from: Scholastic, Inc., 2931 E. McCarty Street, P. O. Box 3710, Jefferson City, MO 65102, or http://teacher.scholastic.com/products/classmags

Stone Soup: The Magazine by Young Writers and Artists. Stories, poems, book reviews, and art by children 8–13. 6 issues/year. Order from: Stone Soup, Subscription Dept., P. O. Box 83, Santa Cruz, CA 95063, or www.stonesoup.com

Writing! Articles, advice, exercises for writing improvement, interviews with successful authors. Ages 12–17. 6 issues/year. Order from: Writing!, Weekly Reader Corp., 3001 Cindel Drive, Delran, NJ 08075.

Literature

Cricket. Fiction, nonfiction, book reviews, activities. Features international literature. Ages 9–14. 12 issues/year. Order from: P. O. Box 9306, LaSalle, IL 61301, or www.cricketmag.com

Lady Bug. Fiction, poems, songs, and games. Ages 2–6. 12 issues/year. Order from: P. O. Box 9306, LaSalle, IL 61301, or www.cricketmag.com

Spider. Fiction, poems, songs, and games for the beginning reader. Ages 6–9. 12 issues/year. Order from: P. O. Box 9306, LaSalle, IL 61301, or www.cricketmag.com

Math

DynaMath. Humorously formatted word problems, computation, and test preparation. Ages 8–12. 8 issues/year. Order from: Scholastic, Inc., 2931 E. McCarty Street, P. O. Box 3710, Jefferson City, MO 65102–3710, or http://teacher.scholastic.com/products/classmags

Scholastic Math Magazine. Math problems, computation, statistics, consumer math, real-life applications, career math, critical reasoning. Ages 12–14. 14 issues/year. Order from: Scholastic, Inc., 2931 E. McCarty Street, P. O. Box 3710, Jefferson City, MO 65102–3710, or http://teacher.scholastic.com/products/classmags

Nature

National Geographic Kids. Nonfiction articles and nature photography. Promotes geographic awareness. Ages 8–14. 10 issues/year. Order from: National Geographic Kids, P. O. Box 63002, Tampa, FL 33663–3002, or www.nationalgeographic.com/ngkids

Ranger Rick. Fiction and nonfiction, photoessays, jokes, riddles, crafts, plays, and poetry promoting the appreciation of nature. Superlative nature photography. Ages 7–12. 12 issues/year. Order from: Ranger Rick, National Wildlife Federation, P.O. Box 2038, Harlan, IA 51593, or www.nwf.org

Your Big Backyard. Animal and nature stories and photography for the preschooler. Ages 3–6. 12 issues/year. Order from: Your Big Backyard, National Wildlife Federation, P.O. Box 2038, Harlan, IA 51593, or www.nwf.org

Recreation

Boys' Life. News, nature, sports, history, fiction, science, comics, Scouting, colorful graphics, and photos. Published by the Boy Scouts of America. Ages 7–18. 12 issues/year. Order from: Subscription Service, 1325 Walnut Hill Lane, P. O. Box 152079, Irving, TX 75015–2079, or www.boyslife.org

Highlights. General-interest magazine offering fiction and nonfiction, crafts, poetry, and thinking features. Ages 5–12. 12 issues/year. Order from: Highlights, P. O. Box 2182, Marion, OH 43306, or www.highlights.com

New Moon: The Magazine for Girls and Their Dreams. An international magazine by and about girls. Builds healthy resistance to gender inequities. Ages 8–14. 6 issues/year. Order from: New Moon, 34 East Superior St. #200, Duluth, MN 55808, or www.newmoon.org

Science

Click. Stories, concept pieces, photography, and posters featuring science for the very young. Ages 3–7. 9 issues/year. Order from P.O. Box 9306, LaSalle, IL 61301, or www.cricketmag.com

Current Science. News in science, health, and technology; science activities, U.S. national science projects, science mystery photos, and kids in the news. Ages 12–15. 16 issues/year. Order from: Weekly Reader Corp., 3001 Cindel Drive, Delran, NJ 08075.

Odyssey. Articles and illustrations on astronomy, space exploration, and technology. Ages 8–14. 9 is-

sues/year. Order from: Cobblestone Publishing, Inc., 30 Grove Street, Suite C, Peterborough, NH 03458, or www.cobblestonepub.com

Science World. Articles, experiments, and news to supplement the science curriculum. Ages 12–16. 12 issues/year. Order from: Science World, Scholastic, Inc., 2931 E. McCarty Street, P. O. Box 3710, Jefferson City, MO 65102–9957, or http://teacher.scholastic.com/products/classmags

SuperScience. Science concepts, critical thinking, and reasoning through hands-on activities and experiments. Themed issues. Ages 8–11. 8 issues/year. Order from: SuperScience, Scholastic, Inc., 2931 E. McCarty Street, Jefferson City, MO 65101–3710, or http://teacher.scholastic.com/products/classmags

Social Studies

Faces. Articles and activities exploring world cultures. Ages 9–14. 9 issues/year. Order from: Faces, Cobblestone Publishing, Inc., 30 Grove Street, Suite C, Peterborough, NH 03458, or www.cobblestonepub.com

Junior Scholastic. Features U.S. and world history, current events, world cultures, map skills, and geography. Ages 11–14. 18 issues/year. Order from: Scholastic, Inc., 2931 E. McCarty Street, P. O. Box 3710, Jefferson City, MO 6510–9957, or http://teacher.scholastic.com/products/classmags

Muse. Nonfiction articles, photoessays, biographies, experiments, cartoons, and jokes. Ages 8–14. 9 issues/year. Joint publication of Cricket Magazine Group and Smithsonian Magazine. Order from: P.O. Box 9306, LaSalle, IL 61301, or www.cricketmag.com

Skipping Stones: A Multicultural Children's Magazine. Articles by, about, and for children about world cultures and cooperation. Multilingual. Ages 7–17. 5 issues/year. Order from: Skipping Stones, Box 3939, Eugene, OR 97403–0939. Web site: www.efn.org/~skipping

SHORT STORY COLLECTIONS

Ages refer to approximate interest levels.
YA = young adult readers.

Ahlberg, Allan. *The Better Brown Stories.* Illustrated by Fritz Wagner. Viking, 1996. Ages 10–13.

Armstrong, Jennifer, editor. *Shattered: Stories of Children and War.* Knopf, 2002. Ages 10–YA.

Asher, Sandy, editor. *But That's Another Story: Favorite Authors Introduce Popular Genres.* Walker, 1996. Ages 10–13. Each story a specific genre with author explanation.

Atkin, S. Beth. *Voices from the Streets: Young Former Gang Members Tell Their Stories.* Little, Brown, 1996. Ages 13–YA.

Bierhorst, John. *The Deetkatoo: Native American Stories about Little People.* Morrow, 1998. Ages 9–12.

Carlson, Lori M., & Cynthia Ventura, editors. *American Eyes: New Asian-American Short Stories for Young Adults.* Holt, 1994. Ages 13–YA.

Cart, Michael, editor. *Necessary Noise: Stories about Our Families as They Really Are.* Illustrated by Charlotte Noruzi. HarperCollins, 2003. Ages 12–YA.

Cart, Michael, compiler. *Tomorrowland: Ten Stories about the Future.* Scholastic, 1999. Ages 11–YA.

Carus, Marianne, editor. *That's Ghosts for You.* Front Street, 2000. Ages 9–12.

Cofer, Judith Ortiz. *An Island Like You: Short Stories of the Barrio.* Orchard, 1995. Ages 12–YA.

Coville, Bruce. *Older Than Ever.* Harcourt, 1999. Ages 10–14.

Crutcher, Chris. *Athletic Shorts.* Greenwillow, 1991. Ages 12–YA.

Datlow, Ellen, and Terri Windling, editors. *A Wolf at the Door and Other Retold Fairy Tales.* Simon & Schuster, 2000. Ages 10–YA.

Dickinson, Peter. *The Lion Tamer's Daughter: And Other Stories.* Delacorte, 1997. Ages 10–YA.

Doyle, Malachy. *Tales from Old Ireland.* Barefoot Books, 2000. Ages 8–12.

Duncan, Lois, editor. *On the Edge: Stories at the Brink.* Simon & Schuster, 2000. Ages 10–YA.

Fleischman, Paul. *Seedfolks.* HarperCollins, 1997. Thirteen loosely connected vignettes. Ages 9–14.

Gallo, Donald, editor. *Destination Unexpected.* Candlewick, 2003. Ages 12–YA.

———, *Ultimate Sports: Sports Stories by Outstanding Writers for Young Adults.* Delacorte, 1995. Ages 13–YA.

Galloway, Priscilla. *Truly Grim Tales.* Delacorte, 1995. Ages 12–YA. Eight folktales retold from different points of view.

Gantos, Jack. *Jack's New Power: Stories from a Caribbean Year.* Farrar, 1995. Ages 11–YA.

Hearne, Betsy. *The Canine Connection: Stories about Dogs and People.* McElderry, 2003. Ages 11–YA.

Holt, David, and Bill Mooney, editors. *More Ready-to-Tell Tales from Around the World.* August House, 2000. Ages 9–YA.

Howe, James, editor. *13: Thirteen Stories That Capture the Agony and Ecstasy of Being Thirteen.* Simon & Schuster, 2003. Ages 12–YA.

Hurwitz, Johanna, editor. *Birthday Surprises: Ten Great Stories to Unwrap.* Morrow, 1995. Ages 9–12.

Jiménez, Francisco. *The Circuit: Stories from the Life of a Migrant Child.* University of New Mexico, 1996. Ages 12–14.

Johnson, Angela. *Gone from Home: Short Takes.* DK Ink, 1998. Ages 12–YA.

Koertge, Ron. *The Brimstone Journals.* Candlewick, 2001. Ages 12–YA. Poetic monologues suitable for readers' theatre.

Larsen, Jean Russell, reteller. *The Fish Bride and Other Gypsy Tales.* Illustrated by Michael Larson. Linnet, 2000. Ages 9–13.

Leary, Una, reteller. *Irish Fairy Tales and Legends.* Rinehart, 1997. Ages 8–11.

Lunge-Larsen, Lise, reteller. *The Troll with No Heart in His Body: And Other Tales of Trolls from Norway.* Illustrated by Betsy Bowen. Houghton, 1999. Ages 7–9.

Mama, Raouf, reteller. *The Barefoot Book of Tropical Tales.* Illustrated by Deirdre Hyde. Barefoot Books, 2000. Ages 7–11.

Mazer, Harry, editor. *Twelve Shots: Outstanding Short Stories about Guns.* Delacorte, 1997. Ages 13–YA. Impact of guns on the main characters.

McKee, Tim. *No More Strangers Now: Young Voices from a New South Africa.* Illustrated by Anne Blackshaw. DK Ink, 1998. Ages 10–YA.

Miller, Brandon Marie. *Buffalo Gals: Women of the Old West.* Lerner, 1995. Ages 9–13. Stories of women pioneers in the 1830s to 1890s.

Myers, Walter Dean. *145th Street Stories.* Delacorte, 2000. Ages 11–YA.

Nixon, Joan Lowry. *Ghost Town: Seven Ghostly Stories.* Delacorte, 2000. Ages 10–YA.

Rice, David. *Crazy Loco: Stories.* Dial, 2001. Ages 12–YA.

Rochman, Hazel, & Darlene Z. McCampbell, editors. *Leaving Home.* HarperCollins, 1997. Ages 11–YA.

Rocklin, Joanne. *Strudel Stories.* Delacorte, 1999. Ages 8–11.

Rylant, Cynthia. *A Couple of Kooks and Other Stories.* Watts, 1990. Ages 12–YA.

———. *Every Living Thing.* Bradbury, 1985. Ages 10–14. Effect of animals on the lives of the main characters.

Salisbury, Graham. *Island Boyz: Short Stories.* Random, 2002. Ages 13–YA.

San Souci, Robert D., reteller. *A Terrifying Taste of Short and Shivery: Thirty Creepy Tales.* Illustrated by Lenny Wooden. Delacorte, 1998. Ages 10–14.

Silvey, Anita, editor. *Help Wanted: Short Stories about Young People Working.* Little, Brown, 1997. Ages 12–YA.

Soto, Gary. *Petty Crimes.* Harcourt, 1998. Ages 10–YA.

Taylor, Theodore. *Rogue Wave: And Other Red-Blooded Sea Stories.* Harcourt, 1996. Ages 10–YA.

Testa, Maria. *Dancing Pink Flamingos and Other Stories.* Lerner, 1995. Ages 14–YA.

Thomas, Rob. *Doing Time: Notes from the Undergrad.* Simon & Schuster, 1997. Ages 13–YA. Ten vignettes on volunteer work.

Turner, Megan Whelan. *Instead of Three Wishes.* Greenwillow, 1995. Ages 8–12.

Vande Velde, Vivian. *Curses, Inc.: And Other Stories.* Harcourt, 1997. Ages 11–YA.

———. *The Rumplestiltskin Problem.* Houghton, 2000. Ages 10–YA.

———. *Tales from the Brothers Grimm and the Sisters Weird.* Harcourt, 1995. Ages 9–13. Retelling of traditional folktales.

Van Laan, Nancy. *With a Whoop and a Holler: A Bushel of Lore from Way Down South.* Atheneum, 1998. Ages 9–12.

Wilson, Budge. *The Dandelion Garden.* Philomel, 1995. Ages 13–YA.

Wyeth, Sharon D. *Vampire Bugs: Stories Conjured from the Past.* Illustrated by Curtis E. James. Delacorte, 1995. Ages 8–13.

Wynne-Jones, Tim. *The Book of Changes.* Orchard, 1995. Ages 11–14.

———. *Lord of the Fries and Other Stories.* DK Ink, 1999. Ages 10–13.

———. *Some of the Kinder Planets.* Orchard, 1995. Ages 9–13.

Yee, Paul. *Dead Man's Gold and Other Stories.* Illustrated by Harvey Chan. Groundwood, 2002. Ages 12–YA.

———. *Tales from Gold Mountain: Stories of the Chinese in the New World.* Macmillan, 1989. Ages 9–12.

TRANSITIONAL BOOKS

These books are generally suitable for ages 6–9.

Avi. *The Mayor of Central Park.* Illustrated by Brian Floca. HarperCollins, 2003.

Baker, Barbara. *Digby and Kate and the Beautiful Day.* Dutton, 1998.

Banks, Kate. *Howie Bowles, Secret Agent.* Illustrated by Isaac Millman. Farrar, 1999.

Benton, Jim. *Franny K. Stein, Mad Scientist: Lunch Walks Among Us.* Simon & Schuster, 2003.

Brisson, Pat. *Hot Fudge Hero.* Illustrated by Diana Cain Blumenthal. Holt, 1997.

———. *Little Sister, Big Sister.* Illustrated by Diana Cain Blumenthal. Holt, 1999.

Brown, Marc T. (creator), and Stephen Krensky. *Arthur and the Big Blow-up.* Illustrated by Marc Brown. Little Brown, 2000. (Representative of others in the lengthy Arthur Chapter Book series: *Arthur and the Perfect Big Brother; Francine, the Superstar.*)

Buckley, James. *Roberto Clemente.* Dorling Kindersley, 2001.

Calmenson, Stephanie and Joanna Cole. *The Gator Girls.* Illustrated by Lynn Munsinger. Morrow, 1995.

Cameron, Ann. *Stories Julian Tells.* Illustrated by Ann Strugnell. Knopf, 1989 (1984). (Others in this series: *More Stories Julian Tells; Julian's Glorious Summer; Julian, Dream Doctor; Julian, Secret Agent,* all published by Random House.)

Danziger, Paula. *Amber Brown Is Not a Crayon.* Illustrated by Tony Ross. Putnam, 1994.

Delaney, Michael. *Birdbrain Amos.* Putnam, 2002.

dePaola, Tomie. *26 Fairmount Avenue.* Putnam, 1999.

Doherty, Berlie. *The Famous Adventures of Jack.* Illustrated by Sonja Lamut. Greenwillow, 2001.

Dubowski, Kathy. *Shark Attack.* Dorling Kindersley, 1998.

Fenner, Carol. *Snowed in with Grandmother Silk.* Illustrated by Amanda Harvey. Dial, 2003.

Fine, Anne. *The Jamie and Angus Stories.* Illustrated by Penny Dale. Candlewick, 2002.

Florian, Douglas. *bow wow meow meow: it's rhyming cats and dogs.* Harcourt, 2003.

Fowler, Susi Gregg. *Albertina, the Animals, and Me.* Illustrated by Jim Fowler. Greenwillow, 2000.

———. *Albertina the Practically Perfect.* Illustrated by Jim Fowler. Greenwillow, 1998.

Freedman, Russell. *Out of Darkness: The Story of Louis Braille.* Illustrated by Kate Kiesler. Clarion, 1997.

Graeber, Charlotte. *Nobody's Dog.* Illustrated by Barry Root. Disney, 1998.

Graves, Bonnie. *Taking Care of Trouble.* Illustrated by Robin P. Glasser. Dutton, 2002.

Greene, Stephanie. *Owen Foote, Frontiersman.* Illustrated by Martha Weston. Clarion, 1999.

Greenwald, Sheila. *Rosy Cole's Worst Ever, Best Yet Tour of New York City.* Holt, 2003.

Guiberson, Brenda Z. *Mummy Mysteries: Tales from North America.* Holt, 1998.

Haas, Jesse. *Runaway Radish.* Illustrated by Margot Apple. Greenwillow, 2001.

Hest, Amy. *Love You, Soldier.* Illustrated by Sonja Lamut. Candlewick, 2000 (1991).

Howe, James. *Pinky and Rex and the Just-Right Pet.* Illustrated by Melissa Sweet. Atheneum, 2001.

James, Simon, editor. *Days Like This: A Collection of Small Poems.* Candlewick, 2000.

Jennings, Patrick. *The Bird Shadow: An Ike and Mem Story.* Illustrated by Anna Alter. Holiday, 2001. See others in the Ike and Mem series: *The Ears of Corn* (2003); *The Lightning Bugs* (2003); *The Tornado Watches* (2002); *The Weeping Willow* (2002).

Jukes, Mavis. *Blackberries in the Dark.* Illustrated by Thomas B. Allen. Knopf, 1985/2002.

King-Smith, Dick. *The Nine Lives of Aristotle.* Illustrated by Bob Graham. Candlewick, 2003.

Lewis, Maggie. *Morgy Makes His Move.* Illustrated by Michael Chesworth. Houghton, 1999.

Levy, Elizabeth. *Big Trouble in Little Twinsville.* Illustrated by Mark Elliot. HarperCollins, 2001.

————. *Night of the Living Gerbil.* Illustrated by Bill Basso. HarperCollins, 2001.

Marsden, Carolyn. *The Gold-Threaded Dress.* Cambridge, MA: Candlewick, 2002.

McDonough, Yona Zeldis. *The Dollhouse Magic.* Illustrated by Diane Palmisciano. Holt, 2000.

Parish, Peggy. *Amelia Bedelia.* Illustrated by Lynn Sweat. Econo-Clad, 1999 (originally published by Greenwillow, 1985). (Others in this series: *Amelia Bedelia Helps Out; Amelia Bedelia Goes Camping; Amelia Bedelia and the Baby; Amelia Bedelia's Family Album.*)

Peck, Robert Newton. *Soup.* Knopf, 1998 (1974). (Others in this series: *Soup for President; Soup in the Saddle; Soup's Goat; Soup on Ice; Soup's Hoop-Yearling.*)

Porte, Barbara Ann. *If You Ever Get Lost: The Adventures of Julia and Evan.* Illustrated by Nancy Carpenter. Greenwillow, 2000.

Roberts, Ken. *The Thumb in the Box.* Illustrated by Leanne Franson. Groundwood, 2001.

Rodowsky, Colby. *Not My Dog.* Illustrated by Thomas F. Yezerski. Farrar, 1999.

Sachar, Louis. *Marvin Redpost: A Flying Birthday Cake?* Illustrated by Amy Wummer. Random House, 1999. (Another in this series: *Marvin Redpost: A Magic Crystal?*)

Scieszka, Jon. *Knights of the Kitchen Table.* Illustrated by Lane Smith. Viking, 1991. (Also in *The Time Warp Trio* series: *The Not-So-Jolly Roger.*)

Sobol, Donald J. *Encyclopedia Brown: Boy Detective.* Illustrated by Leonard Shortall, Bantam, 1985 (originally published by Scholastic, 1968). (Others in this series: *Encyclopedia Brown Tracks Them Down; Encyclopedia Brown and the Case of the Midnight Visitor; Encyclopedia Brown Solves Them All.*)

Spinelli, Jerry. *Tooter Pepperday.* Illustrated by Donna Nelson. Random House, 1995.

Stevenson, James. *The Mud Flat Mystery.* Greenwillow, 1997.

These pages constitute a continuation of the copyright page.

Page numbers for figures and tables are followed by f and t, respectively.

GUIDE TO ILLUSTRATIONS

	Source of Book Illustration	Artistic Style	Visual Elements	Elements of Fiction
5.	Browne, Anthony. *Changes.* Knopf, 1986.	Surrealistic	Texture	Plot, theme
6.	Garza, Carmen L. *Family Pictures/Cuadros de familia.* Spanish Version by Rosalma Zubizarreta. Children's Book Press, 1990.	Primitive/folk	Composition, mood	Setting, theme
7.	Ho, Minfong. *Hush!: A Thai Lullaby.* Illustrated by Holly Meade. Orchard, 1996.	Primitive/folk	Line, texture	Character, plot, setting
8.	Rathmann, Peggy. *Officer Buckle and Gloria.* Putnam, 1995.	Cartoon	Composition, line	Plot, theme, character